PROGRAMMING IN C

As per the latest AICTE syllabus

Pradip Dey

Ex-Faculty and Dean – Student Affairs and Support Systems
RCC Institute of Information Technology, Kolkata

Manas Ghosh

Assistant Professor
Department of Computer Application
RCC Institute of Information Technology, Kolkata

OXFORD

UNIVERSITY PRESS

OXFORD
UNIVERSITY PRESS

Oxford University Press is a department of the University of Oxford.
It furthers the University's objective of excellence in research, scholarship,
and education by publishing worldwide. Oxford is a registered trade mark of
Oxford University Press in the UK and in certain other countries.

Published in India by
Oxford University Press
22 Workspace, 2nd Floor, 1/22 Asaf Ali Road, New Delhi 110 002

First published in 2018
Third impression 2021

ISBN-13: 978-0-19-949147-6
ISBN-10: 0-19-949147-X

Typeset in Times New Roman
by Ideal Publishing Solutions, Delhi
Printed in India by Rakmo Press, New Delhi 110 020

Cover image: Harper 3D / Shutterstock

For product information and current price, please visit www.india.oup.com

Third-party website addresses mentioned in this book are provided
by Oxford University Press in good faith and for information only.
Oxford University Press disclaims any responsibility for the material contained therein.

Preface

Since the evolution of computers, a variety of programming languages have come into existence. C stands out among general-purpose programming languages for its unrivaled mix of portability, flexibility, and efficiency. It is a versatile language and is commonly used for developing application and system programs. C has block structures, stand-alone functions, a compact set of keywords, and very few restrictions. For all these reasons, learning and using C is a necessity for most programmers.

ABOUT THE BOOK

This book is intended for an introductory course on programming in C. It assumes no prior programming experience in C or any other language. Readers will find the explanations lucid and effective. Every feature of C has been demonstrated with appropriate programs tested and run on a computer. The output obtained after executing these programs have also been included. The explanations have been depicted with suitable diagrams to convey the concepts more effectively. Readers will be proficient at programming after solving the review questions and programming exercises given at the end of each chapter. Though every attempt has been made to avoid and check errors, we will be grateful to readers if they can bring to our notice any errors that may have crept in inadvertently.

CONTENT AND STRUCTURE

Chapter 1 traces the history of development of computers. It begins by identifying the different generations and the various categories of computers. It then briefly describes the basic hardware units and software components of a computer, with particular reference to the personal computer.

Chapter 2 begins by explaining the concept of programming. It discusses the techniques of forming an organized approach to problem solving. It also identifies the different types of programs and the various categories of programming languages available. The prescribed tools that are used in this process are described and explained with sufficient examples and diagrams.

For a beginner, Chapter 3 is undoubtedly the most important chapter that describes the basic elements of C. This chapter introduces the keywords, the basic data types and their modifiers, operators and their precedence, and expressions and data type conversion rules. The basic structure of a C program along with the common commands used in MS-DOS and Unix/Linux for compiling and running the program has been described at length in this chapter.

Accepting data from and conveying the results to a user is one of the most important actions desired from a program. To satisfy these requirements through the console, there are some commonly used input and output functions in C. These have been explained with illustrations in Chapter 4.

Program flow control and looping constructs in C are explained in Chapter 5. The general statement format with flowcharts and examples illustrate their significance in programs.

Arrays and strings are two important data structures for handling a cluster of homogeneous data. How such clusters are declared and handled is explained with ample examples in Chapter 6.

The concept of functions, its form, and its requirement in a program is discussed in Chapter 7 with well-explained examples. Recursive functions are also described with several examples. Analysis of time and space complexity for an algorithm has also been presented in this chapter.

One of the most important features of C is pointers. Starting with an introduction to pointers, Chapter 8 also elaborates how pointers are used with arrays, strings, and functions. The use of pointers is also described in depth with innumerable examples.

User-defined data types such as structures and unions are described in Chapter 9. What these data types comprise and how these are handled and used are illustrated with examples.

Creating, amending, appending, and many other operations on files in C is a necessity for storing and retrieving data and programs. This has been covered in Chapter 10 with sufficient examples.

Linked list, which is a popular data structure, has been covered in Chapter 11. Singly linked lists and the different operations that can be carried out on such lists have been discussed. In this chapter, readers will also get to know how pointers are used in constructing this data structure.

Frequently asked questions are always a source of learning. Some frequently asked questions have been included at end of each chapter, which will help readers to clear any doubts pertaining to programming in C.

Appendix A contains additional examples where the problem is first defined and then the flowcharts and algorithms are developed, based on which the C program is coded. Appendix B provides exhaustive listing of C library functions.

ACKNOWLEDGEMENTS

We thank our students Rakesh Dutta and Niloy Debnath for verifying the programs in this book and Sonia Khedwal, Priyanka Nawalkar, Sayantani Saha, and Debolina Sharangi for their assistance in the preparation of the model questions. We are grateful to the staff of Oxford University Press for their continuous cooperation, interest, and assistance extended to us during the preparation of the book. We are also thankful to our colleague Mr Manash Sinharoy for helping us in preparing the manuscript in time and Mr Tapas Kumar Tunga and Mr P.N. Pathak for their assistance in the preparation of the manuscript.

Special thanks are due to Mr Steve Summit for his articles on C, which have guided us in preparing some of the topics in this book. We also wish to thank Mr Vijay Kumar R Zanvar and Mr Jayasima Ananth for the article on pointers and arrays as also Mr Thomas Jenkins for the article on recursion, both of which have served as a guide during the development of this manuscript. We express our gratitude to Mr Peter Burden, Mr Mike Banahan, Mr Declan Brady, and Mr Mark Doran for their articles on C.

PRADIP DEY
MANAS GHOSH

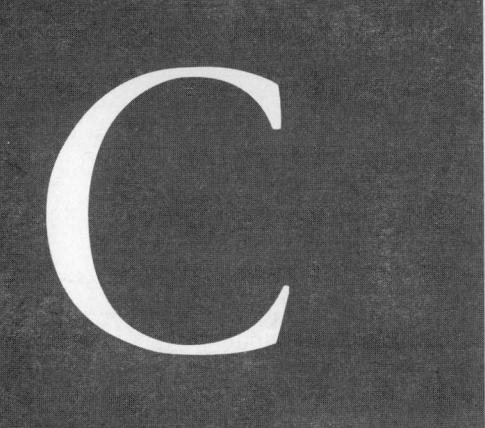

Contents

Computer Fundamentals

Chapter 1

Learning Objectives

After studying this chapter, the readers will be able to

- trace the evolution of computers—generations and classification of computers
- explain the basic units of a computer system
- explain the hardware and software of a personal computer
- load an operating system in a personal computer

1.1 INTRODUCTION—WHAT IS A COMPUTER?

The Oxford Dictionary defines a computer as 'an automatic electronic apparatus for making calculations or controlling operations that are expressible in numerical or logical terms'.

The definition clearly categorizes the computer as an electronic apparatus although the first computers were mechanical and electro-mechanical apparatuses. The definition also points towards the two major areas of computer application: data processing and computer-assisted controls or operations. Another important conclusion of the definition is the fact that the computer can perform only those operations or calculations that can be expressed in logical or numerical terms.

A computer is a data processor. It can accept input, which may be either data or instructions or both. The computer

remembers the input by storing it in memory cells. It then processes the stored input by performing calculations or by making logical comparisons or both. It gives out the result of the arithmetic or logical computations as output information. The computer accepts input and outputs data in an alphanumeric form. Internally it converts the input data to meaningful binary digits, performs the instructed operations on the binary data, and transforms the data from binary digit form to understandable alphanumeric form.

In the present world, a digital computer, which is built with electronic components, can perform operations with great speed and high accuracy. It can store and process a variety of data and instructions, display and print processed data, send and receive data and messages to and from other computers, collect and process data emerging in a real-time working system, perform timely tasks under the control of pre-written instructions and carry out many other tasks which was earlier difficult to do manually. In today's world computers or computer-based techniques are used in almost all areas of human activity. The internet services, weather forecasting services, CT-Scanner and the mobile phone are some, among the many, examples of the application of computer-based techniques.

1.2 EVOLUTION OF COMPUTERS—A BRIEF HISTORY

Computing in the mechanical era

The concept of calculating machines evolved long before the invention of electrical and electronic devices. The first mechanical calculating apparatus was the **abacus**, which was invented in 500 BC in Babylon. It was used extensively without any improvement until 1642 when Blaise Pascal designed a calculator that employed gears and wheels. But it was not until the early 1800s that a practical, geared, mechanical computing calculator became available. This machine could calculate facts but was not able to use a program to compute numerical facts.

In 1823, Charles Babbage, aided by Augusta Ada Byron, the Countess of Lovelace, started an ambitious project of producing a programmable calculating machine for the Royal Navy of Great Britain. Input to this mechanical machine, named the **Analytical Engine**, was given through punched cards. This engine stored 1,000, 20-digit decimal numbers and a modifiable program, which could vary the operation of the machine so that it could execute different computing jobs. But even after several years of effort, the machine that had more than 50,000 mechanical parts could not operate reliably because the parts could not be machined to precision.

Computing in the electrical era

With the availability of electric motors in 1800, a host of motor-operated calculating machines based on Pascal's calculator was developed. A mechanical machine, driven by a single electric motor, was developed in 1889 by Herman Hollerith to count, sort, and collate data stored on punched cards. Hollerith formed the Tabulating Machine Company in 1896. This company soon merged into International Business Machines (IBM) and the mechanical computing machine business thrived.

In 1941, Konrad Zuse developed the first electronic calculating computer, **Z3**. It was used by the Germans in World War II. However, Alan Turing is credited with developing the first electronic computer in 1943. This computer system, named the **Colossus**, was a fixed-program computer; it was not programmable.

J.W. Mauchly and S.P. Eckert of the University of Pennsylvania completed the first general-purpose electronic digital computer in 1946. It was called the **ENIAC**, Electronic Numerical Integrator and Calculator. It used 17,000 vacuum tubes, over 500 miles of wires, weighed 30 tons, and performed around 100,000 operations per second. The **IAS** computer system, under development till 1952 by John von Neumann and others at the Princeton Institute, laid the foundation of the general structure of subsequent general-purpose computers. In the early 1950s, Sperry-Rand Corporation launched the Univac I, Univac II, Univac 1103 series while IBM brought out Mark I and 701 series. All these machines used vacuum tubes.

The transistor was invented at Bell Labs in 1948. In 1958, IBM, International Computers Limited (ICL), Digital Equipment Corporation (DEC), and others brought out general-purpose computers using transistors that were faster, smaller in size, weighed less, needed less power, and were more reliable.

Meanwhile, at Texas Instruments, Jack Kilby invented the integrated circuit in 1958 that led to the development of digital integrated circuits in the 1960s. This led to the development of IBM 360/370, PDP 8/1, and HP 9810 in 1966. These computers used medium- and small-scale integrated circuits (MSI and SSI).

Thereafter, in 1971, Intel Corporation announced the development of the single-chip microprocessor 4004, a very large-scale integrated circuit. In 1972, the 8008 8-bit microprocessor was introduced. Subsequently, the 8080 and MC 6800 appeared in 1973, which were improved 8-bit microprocessors. The last of the 8-bit microprocessor family from Intel, 8085, was introduced as a general-purpose processor in 1974. In 1978, the 8086, and in 1979, the 8088 microprocessors were released.

Though desktop computers were available from 1975 onwards, none could gain as much popularity as the IBM PC. In 1981, IBM used the 8088 microprocessor in the personal computer. The 80286 16-bit microprocessor came in 1983 as an updated version of 8086. The 32-bit microprocessor 80386 arrived in 1986 and the 80486 arrived in 1989. With the introduction of the Pentium in 1993, a highly improved personal computer was available at an affordable price.

From the year 2000 onwards there has been a tremendous effort to increase the speed and computing capability of the processor resulting in the development of multi-core processors by AMD, Intel and others.

The arrival of microprocessors triggered the development of desktop computers, in the form of personal computers and portable computers like the laptops and tablets. Such devices can execute programs, store data and deliver information at much higher speeds with greater reliability than that possible with earlier computers. And with the development of networking technology, in the form of local area network and internet, the whole scenario of computing has undergone a sea change. Furthermore, the available mobile processors have transformed the mobile phone to a phone-cum-micro-computer system that can not only communicate voice and message but also store and process data and access the internet.

Along with the development of computer hardware, programming languages were devised and perfected. In the 1950s, Assembly language was developed for univac computers. In 1957, IBM developed FORTRAN language. And as years went by, programming languages such as ALGOL, COBOL, BASIC, Pascal, C/C++, Ada, Java, Python, PHP, HTML, XML and more followed. This resulted in the development of various software packages like Oracle, Tally, MATLAB, PSpice, AutoCAD and many more that have wide applications in commercial, scientific, and engineering fields.

Further, with the creation of the operating system (OS), a supervisor program for managing computer resources and controlling the CPU to perform various jobs, the computer's operational capability touched a new dimension. There are a variety of operating systems today. Some which gained popularity are Unix for large and mini-computers and MS-DOS and MS-Windows for personal computers. However, with the availability of Linux, a trend to change over to this operating system is on.

As in desktop and laptop computers, operating systems have been developed for mobile devices called smart mobile phones. Some of these OS are the Apple iOS, Google Android, BlackBerry OS, Nokia Symbian, HP webOS, and MS Windows Phone OS.

1.3 GENERATIONS OF COMPUTERS

The generation of a computer is determined by the technology it uses. Table 1.1 shows the technology used in the different generations of computers. With advancement in the generation, the performance of computers improved not only due to the implementation of better hardware technology but also superior operating systems and other software utilities.

Table 1.1 Technology used in different generations of computers

Generation number	Technology	Operating system	Year of introduction	Specific computers
1	Vacuum Tube	None	1945	Mark 1
2	Transistor	None	1956	IBM 1401, ICL 1901, B5000, MINSK-2
3	SSI and MSI	Yes	1964	IBM S/360/370, UNIVAC 1100, HP 2100A, HP 9810
4	LSI and VLSI	Yes	1971	ICL 2900, HP 9845A, VAX 11/780, ALTAIR 8800, IBM PC
5	Artificial Intelligence, Expert Systems and Natural Language	Yes	Present and beyond	—

1.4 CLASSIFICATION OF COMPUTERS

Most designs of computers today are based on concepts developed by John von Neumann and are referred to as the von Neumann architecture. Computers can be classified in variety of ways on the basis of various parameters such as usage, cost, size, processing power, and so on. The classification of computers is presented below based on their power and their use.

Supercomputer

Supercomputer is the most expensive and fastest type of computer that performs at or near the currently highest operational rate for computers. The Cray supercomputer is a typical example. These are employed for specialized applications that require immense amounts of mathematical calculations such as weather forecasting, nuclear energy research, mineral and petroleum exploration etc.

Mainframe

A mainframe computer supports a vast number of users to work simultaneously and remotely. Apart from providing multi-user facility, it can process large amounts of data at very high speeds and support many input, output and auxiliary storage devices. These computers are very large in size and expensive. The main difference between a supercomputer and a mainframe is that a supercomputer can execute a single program faster than a mainframe, whereas a mainframe uses its power to execute many programs concurrently. The IBM 370 and IBM 3090 are examples of mainframe computers.

Minicomputer

A minicomputer is powerful enough to be used by multiple users (between 10 to 100) but is smaller in size and memory capacity and cheaper than mainframes. Two classic examples were the Digital Equipment Corporation VAX and the IBM AS/400.

Microcomputer

The microcomputer has been intended to meet the personal computing needs of an individual. It typically consists of a microprocessor chip, a memory system, interface units and various I/O ports, typically resident in a motherboard. There are many types of microcomputers available.

Desktop computer A micro computer sufficient to fit on a desk.

Laptop computer A portable microcomputer with an integrated screen and keyboard.

Palmtop computer/Digital diary/Notebook/PDAs A hand-sized microcomputer having no keyboard. The screen serves both as an input and output device.

1.5 ANATOMY OF A COMPUTER

A computer can accept input, process or store data, and produce output according to a set of instructions which are fed into it. A computer system can be divided into two components which are responsible for providing the mechanisms to input and output data, to manipulate and process data, and to electronically control the various input, output, and their storage. They are known as hardware and software. The *hardware* is the tangible part of the computer, whereas, the *software* is the intangible set of instructions that control the hardware and make it perform specific tasks. Without software, a computer is effectively useless.

1.5.1 Hardware

Hardware is the physical components of a computer that includes all mechanical, electrical and electronic parts attached to it. A computer consists of the following major hardware components:

- Input and output devices
- Central processing unit (CPU)
- Memory unit and storage devices
- Interface unit

A brief description of the most common hardware found in a personal computer is given in the next few sections.

Input devices

Input devices are electronic or electro-mechanical equipment that provide a means of communicating with the computer system for feeding input data and instructions. The data and instructions are typed, submitted, or transmitted to a computer through input devices. Most common input devices are briefly described below.

Keyboard Keyboard is like a type-writer's key set. A keyboard, normally, consists of 104 keys. These keys are classified into different categories which are briefly described below.

Character keys These keys represent letters, numbers, and punctuation marks. On pressing any character key, the corresponding character is displayed on the screen.

Function keys There are 12 functional keys above the Character keys which are used to perform certain functions depending on the operating system or the software currently being executed. These keys are placed at the top of the key board and can easily be identified with the letter F followed by a number ranging from 1 to 12.

Control keys Alt, Ctrl, Shift, Insert, Delete, Home, End, PgUp, PgDn, Esc and Arrow keys are control keys.

Navigation keys These include four arrows, Page Up and Page Down, Home and End. These keys are normally used to navigate around a document or screen.

Toggle keys Scroll Lock, Num lock, Caps Lock are three toggle keys. The toggle state is indicated by three LEDs at the right-top side of the keyboard. For example, on pressing caps lock, letters typed by the user will appear in upper case. On pressing again, letters are typed on the screen in lower case.

Miscellaneous keys These keys include Insert, Delete, Escape, PrintScreen etc.

The keys on the keyboard are placed in a series of rows and columns called the *key matrix*.

Each key holds a position with respect to a row and column. When a key is pressed, the key switch in that position closes a circuit, sending a signal to the circuit board inside the keyboard. The keyboard controller uses the x and y coordinates of the matrix position to determine which key was pressed, thereby determining the code transmitted to the computer by the keyboard.

Mouse A mouse is the pointing device attached to a computer. It is used to move the cursor around the screen and to point to an object (such as icon, menu, command button) on the computer video screen for the

purpose of selecting or activating objects on graphical interface provided by the operating system or the software currently being executed and executing various tasks. It has two or three buttons for clicking. The mouse tracks the motion of the mouse pointer and senses the clicks and sends them to the computer so it can respond appropriately.

The mouse can be connected to the system either through a USB connector or wirelessly through infrared radiation. A wireless mouse needs to be powered through batteries.

Scanner A scanner is a device that captures pictures or documents so that they can be stored in storage devices, seen on the video screen, modified suitably, transported to other

computers, or printed on a printer. A personal computer with a scanner and printer can function as a photocopier.

Output devices

Output devices mirror the input data, or show the output results of the operations on the input data or print the data. The most common output device is monitor or visual display unit. The printer is used to print the result. A hard copy refers to a printout showing the information. On the other hand soft copy means information stored on a storage device.

Monitor Computer display devices are commonly known as Visual Display Unit (VDU) or monitor. It operates on a principle similar to that of a normal television set. Various technologies have been used for computer monitors. They are also of different sizes. CRT (cathode-ray tube) and LCD (liquid crystal display) monitors are the two common types which are widely used.

The CRT is composed of a vacuum glass tube which is narrower at one end. One electron gun is placed at this end which fires electrons. The electron gun is made up of cathode (negatively charged) and one anode (positively charged). On the other side it has a wide screen, coated with phosphor. The beam of electron strikes on the surface of screen and produces an image by photo luminance process. There is a vertical and a horizontal coil to deflect the electron beam to appropriate position of the screen. An image is formed by constantly scanning the screen. To send an image to the screen, the computer first assembles it in a memory area called a video buffer. The graphics are stored as an array of memory locations that represent the colors of the individual screen dots or pixels. The video card then sends this data through a digital-to-analog converter (DAC), which converts the data to a series of voltage levels that are fed to the monitor.

CRT monitors are too bulky and consume high power. Apart from these, users are very much concerned about potentially damaging non-ionizing radiation from CRT monitor.

Nowadays, LCD monitors are replacing CRTs and becoming the de-facto choice to the users because of their size, display clarity, low radiation emission and power consumption.

An LCD display produces an image by filtering light from a series of cold cathode fluorescent lamps (CCFLs). through a layer of liquid crystal cells. Gradually, CCFL backlighting technology is

being replaced by low-power light-emitting diodes (LEDs). A computer screen that uses this technology is sometimes referred to as an LED display.

Printer A printer is a device that prints any data, report, document, picture, diagrams, etc. Printers are categorized based on the physical contact of the print head with the paper to produce  a text or an image. An *impact printer* is one where the print head will be in physical contact with the paper. In a *non–impact printer*, on the other hand, the print head will have no physical contact with the paper. The dot matrix printer is considered as an impact printer and laser printer is considered as non-impact printer.

In a *dot matrix printer*, the printer head pins physically 'hits' the paper through the ribbon which makes the speed of the printer relatively slow. The printer head consist of a two dimensional array of pins called 'dot matrix'. Every time a character has to be printed, the appropriate pins are selected to strike the paper through the ribbon. The ink in the ribbon falls on the surface of the paper and thus the character gets printed. In *inkjet printer*, instead of a ribbon one ink cartridge holds the ink in it.  They are placed above the inkjet head. The printing head takes some ink from the cartridge and spreads it on the surface of the paper by the jet head. This ink is electrically charged. An electric field is created near the paper surface. Thus the small drops of ink are arranged in the surface according to the character it prints. These printers are fast and  capable of printing good quality graphics. The *laser printer* uses a laser beam to create the image.

Central processing unit (CPU)

Central Processing Unit or CPU can be thought of as the brain of the computer. Most of the processing takes place in CPU. During processing, it locates and executes the program instructions. It also fetches data from memory and input/output devices and sends data back.

Physically, it is an integrated circuit (IC) silicon chip, mounted on a small square plastic slab, surrounded by metal pins. In the world of personal computers, the term microprocessor and CPU are used interchangeably. It is more accurate to describe it as a CPU on a chip because it contains the circuitry that performs processing.

The CPU itself can be divided into different functional units which are described below:

Registers These are high-speed storage devices. In most CPUs, some registers are reserved for special purposes. For example, the Instruction Register (IR) holds the current instruction being executed. The Program Counter (PC) is a register that holds the address of the next instruction to be executed. In addition to such and other special-purpose registers, it also contains a set of general-purpose registers that are used for temporary storage of data values as needed during processing.

Arithmetic logic unit (ALU) It is the part of the CPU that performs arithmetic operations, such as addition and subtraction as well as logical operations, such as comparing two numbers to see if they are equal or greater or less.

Control unit (CU) The control unit coordinates the processing by controlling the transfer of data and instructions between main memory and the registers in the CPU. It also coordinates the execution of the arithmetic logic unit (ALU) to perform operations on data stored in particular registers. It consists of

- an *instruction decoding circuit* that interprets what action should be performed.
- a *control and timing circuit* directs all the other parts of the computer by producing the respective control signals.

Nowadays, a high-speed memory, called *cache memory*, is embedded within the CPU chip. This improves the computer performance by minimizing the processor's need to read data from the slow main memory.

The CPU's processing power is measured in terms of the number of instructions that it can execute per unit time. Every computer comprises of an internal clock, which emits electronic pulses at a constant rate. These pulses are used to control and synchronize the pace of operations. Each pulse is called a *clock cycle* which resembles a rectangular wave with a rising half of the signal and a falling half. In other words, a full clock cycle is the amount of time that elapses between pulses of the oscillating signal. Each instruction takes one or more clock cycles to execute. The higher the clock speed, the more instructions are executed in a given period of time. Hertz (Hz) is the basic unit of computer clock frequency which is equal to one cycle per second. CPU speed has been improved continuously. It is typically measured in megahertz (MHz) or gigahertz (GHz). One megahertz is equal to one million cycles per second, while one gigahertz equals one billion cycles per second.

Nowadays, multiple processors are embedded together on a single integrated-circuit chip, known as multi-core processor e.g. a *dual-core processor* has two CPUs and a *quad core processor* has four CPUs.

> ### Points to Note
>
> - An integrated circuit, or IC, is a matrix of transistors and other electrical components embedded in a small slice of silicon.
> - A microprocessor is a digital electronic component with miniaturized transistors on a single semiconductor integrated circuit (IC). One or more microprocessors typically serve as a central processing unit (CPU) in a computer system or handheld device allocating space to hold the data object.

Memory unit

Components such as the input device, output device, and CPU are not sufficient for the working of a computer. A storage area is needed in a computer to store instructions and data, either temporarily or permanently, so that subsequent retrieval of the instructions and data can be possible on demand. Data are stored in memory as binary digits, called *bits*. Data of various types, such as numbers, characters, are encoded as series of bits and stored in consecutive memory locations. Each memory location comprises of a single byte which is equal to eight bits and has a unique address so that the contents of the desired memory locations can be accessed independently by referring to its address. A single data item is stored in one or more consecutive bytes of memory.

CPU uses registers exclusively to store and manipulate data and instructions during the processing. Apart from registers, there are mainly two types of memory that are used in a computer system. One is called *primary memory* and the other *secondary memory*.

Primary memory   Primary memory is the area where data and programs are stored while the program is being executed along with the data. This memory space, also known as *main memory*, forms the working area of the program. This memory is accessed directly by the processor.

A memory module consists of a large bank of flip-flops arranged together with data traffic control circuitry such that data can be stored on or read out from a set of flip-flops. A flip-flop can store a binary digit. These flip-flops are grouped to form a unit memory of fixed length and each of which is identified by a sequence number known as a memory address. Such a memory is called Random Access Memory, or RAM, where any location can be accessed directly, and its stored contents get destroyed the moment power to this module is switched off. Hence, these are volatile in nature. Primary memory devices are expensive. They are limited in size, consume very low power, and are faster compared to secondary memory devices.

There is another kind of primary memory increasingly being used in modern computers. It is called *cache memory* (pronounced as "cash"). It is a type of high-speed memory that allows the processor to access data more rapidly than from memory located elsewhere on the system. It stores or caches some of the contents of the main memory that is currently in use by the processor. It takes a fraction of the time, compared to main memory, to access cache memory. The management of data stored in the cache memory ensures that for 20 per cent of the total time, during which the cache is searched, the data needed is found to be stored in cache. As a result the performance of the computer improves in terms of speed of processing.

Secondary memory   Secondary memory provides large, non-volatile, and inexpensive storage for programs and data. However, the access time in secondary memory is much larger than in primary memory. Secondary storage permits the storage of computer instructions and data for long periods of time. Moreover, secondary memory, which is also known as *auxiliary memory*, stores a huge number of data bytes at a lesser cost than primary memory devices.

> ### Points to Note
>
> - The memory unit is composed of an ordered sequence of storage cells, each capable of storing one byte of data. Each memory cell has a distinct address which is used to refer while storing data into it or retrieving data from it.
> - Both RAM and cache memory are referred to as primary memory. Primary memory is comparatively expensive, and loses all its data when the power is turned off. Secondary memory provides less expensive storage that is used to store data and instructions on a permanent basis.

Memory operations There are some operations common to both primary and secondary memory devices. These are as follows:

Read During this operation, data is retrieved from memory.

Write In this operation, data is stored in the memory.

Using read and write operations, many other memory-related functions such as copy and delete are carried out.

Unit of memory The memory's interface circuit is designed to logically access a byte or a multiple of a byte of data from the memory during each access. The smallest block of memory is considered to be a byte, which comprises eight bits. The total memory space is measured in terms of bytes. Thus, the unit of memory is a byte. The capacity of memory is the maximum amount of information it is capable of storing. Since the unit of memory is a byte, the memory's capacity is expressed in number of bytes. Some units used to express the memory capacity are as follows:

- Kilobyte (KB) = 1024 bytes
- Megabyte (MB) = 1024 Kilobytes
- Gigabyte (GB) = 1024 Megabytes
- Terabyte (TB) = 1024 Gigabytes
- Petabyte (PB) = 1024 Terabytes
- Exabyte (EB) = 1024 Petabytes
- Zettabyte (ZB) = 1024 Exabytes
- Yottabyte (YB) = 1024 Zettabytes

The size of the register is one of the important considerations in determining the processing capabilities of the CPU. *Word size* refers to the number of bits that a CPU can manipulate at one time. Word size is based on the size of registers in the ALU and the capacity of circuits that lead to those registers. A processor with a 32-bit word size, for example, has 32-bit registers, processes 32 bits at a time, and is referred to as a 32-bit processor. Processor's word size is a factor that leads to increased computer performance. Today's personal computers typically contain 32-bit or 64-bit processors.

Memory hierarchy The various types of memory used in a computer system differ in speed, cost, size, and volatility (permanence of storage). They can be organized in a hierarchy. The memory hierarchy in the computer system is depicted in Fig. 1.1.

Figure 1.1 shows that on moving down the hierarchy, the cost per bit of storage decreases but access times increases (i.e., devices are slow). In other words, from top to bottom, the speed decreases while the capacity increases and the prices become much lower.

Of the various memories specified in the hierarchy, those above the secondary memory are volatile. While designing a computer system, there must always be a balance on all of the above factors, namely speed, cost, volatility, etc. at each level in the hierarchy.

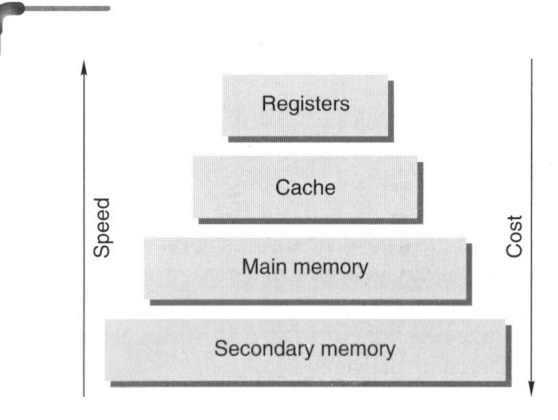

Figure 1.1 Memory hierarchy

The devices in a computer system other than the CPU and main memory are called **peripherals**. Popular peripheral devices include printers, digital cameras, scanners, joysticks, speakers, modems, wi-fi devices and pen drives.

Interface unit

The interface unit interconnects the CPU with memory and also with the various input/output (I/O) devices. The instructions and data move between the CPU and other hardware components through interface unit.

It is a set of parallel wires or lines, logic gates and buffer registers, which connects all the internal computer components to the CPU and main memory. Depending on the type of data transmitted, these lines known as a bus can be classified into the following three types:

Data bus The bus used to carry actual data.

Address bus Lines through which address signals are sent by the CPU to select a memory location or an input/output device.

Control bus This bus carries control information between the CPU and other devices within the computer. The control information entails signals that report the status of various devices, or ask devices to take specific actions.

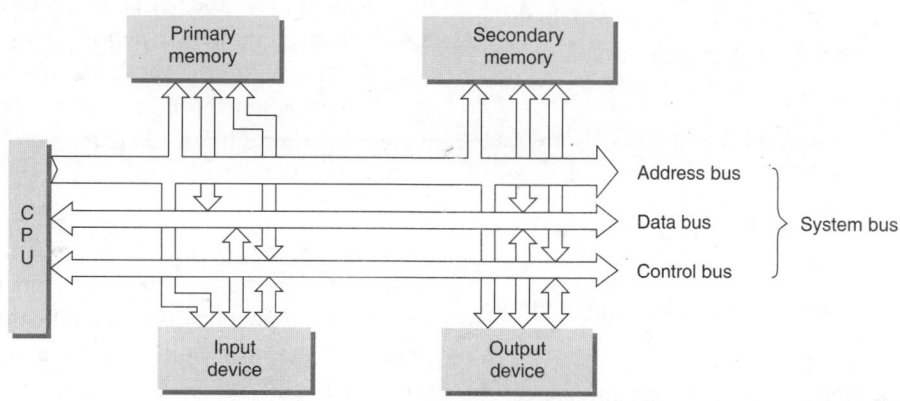

Figure 1.2 Bus-based computer organization

A model of the bus-based computer organization is shown in Fig. 1.2.

Most of the computer devices are not directly connected to the computer's internal bus. Since every device has its own particular way of formatting and communicating data, a device, termed *controller*, coordinates the activities of specific peripherals. The processor reads from the input devices or writes to the output devices with the help of the device controllers. Each input device or output device has a specific address. Using these addresses, the processor selects a particular I/O device through the associated device controller for either transferring data or any control commands.

Motherboard

All the components in the computer system are mounted and connected together on an electronic circuit board called motherboard or main board.

To make all these things work together the motherboard provides suitable electrical connection among them (see Fig. 1.3).

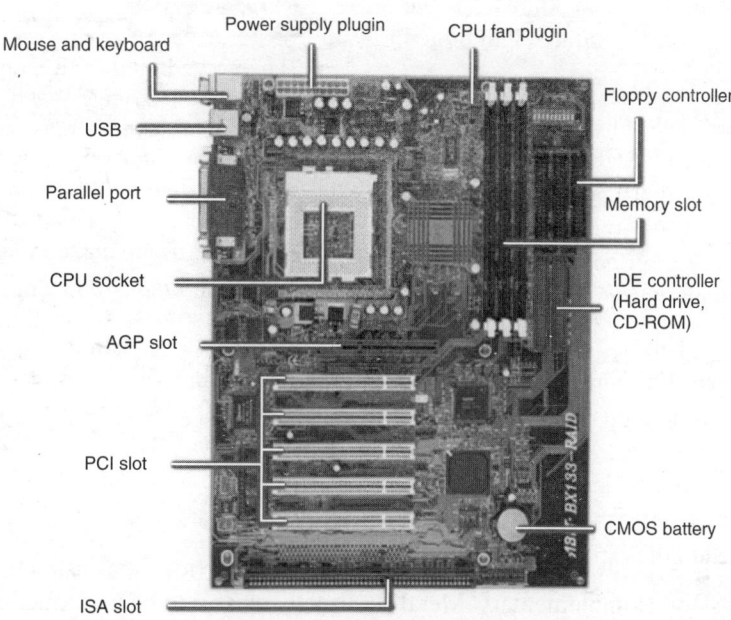

Figure 1.3 Motherboard

In general, a motherboard consists of the following.

CPU socket This holds the central processor which is an integrated chip along with the system clock, cache, cooling fan, etc.

Memory sockets These sockets hold the RAM card that contains RAMs.

Interface module This is for the hard disk, USB drive, and CD-ROM / DVD drives.

ROM integrated chip This is embedded with the basic input/output system software.

Ports and expansion slots Ports are used to connect a device with the system bus. Physical ports include serial and parallel ports, to which peripheral devices such as printers, scanners, and external storage devices can be attached. The slots are used to attach accessories such as graphics (video) cards, disk controllers, and network cards. There are two different standards for expansion slots: ISA (Industry Standard Architecture) and PCI (Peripheral Component Interconnect). Most common types of ports and slots are briefly described below.

ISA slots These are for connecting ISA compatible cards.

PCI slots These are for connecting I/O devices.

Advanced graphics port (AGP) Video card is inserted into this slot.

Parallel port The parallel port is also known as the printer port, or LPT1. It is capable of sending eight bits of information at a time.

Serial ports These are sometimes called communication ports or COM ports. There are two COM ports, COM1 and COM2. Size of COM1 is larger than that of COM2. COM1 has 25 pins and is used for connecting Modems. COM2 is a 9 pin port used for interfacing serial mouse. D-type connectors are used with these ports.

USB (universal serial bus) This is also a serial port but data rate is more than the serial port. USB is used as a general-purpose communication channel in personal computers. Many different devices, such as mouse, keyboards, hard disk drives, portable CD-ROM/DVD drives, pen-drives, scanners, cameras, modems and even printers are usually connected to these ports.

CMOS The CMOS stands for Complementary Metal Oxide Semiconductor memory. It is a type of RAM that stores the necessary attributes of system components, such as the size of the hard disk, the size of RAM, and the resources used by the serial and parallel ports etc. Since RAM loses its content when the power is switched off, a small battery, on the motherboard, powers the CMOS RAM even when the computer power is switched off, thereby retaining its stored data.

System unit

The System Unit holds all the system components in it. It is sometimes also called a cabinet. The main components like motherboard, processor, memory unit, power supply unit, and all the ports to interface computer's peripherals are housed within this cabinet. Inside the unit all the components work together to give the service that the user needs. Based on its use, cabinets are of two types.

   (i) AT cabinets (or mini-tower)

   (ii) ATX cabinets

AT cabinets are smaller and cheaper than ATX cabinets and are popularly called mini-tower cabinets. They are used for older processors and smaller motherboards. ATX cabinets, on the other hand, are marginally larger in size than AT cabinets and are more expensive as they come with more features such as powered sliding front panels and extra disk storage compartments.

Points to Note

- The motherboard is a printed circuit board which contains the circuitry and connections that allow the various components of the computer system to communicate with each other. In most computer systems, the CPU, memory, and other major components are mounted on the motherboard and are connected by the printed wiring on it.

- The input, output, and storage equipment that might be added to a computer system to enhance its functionality are known as peripheral devices. Popular peripheral devices include printers, digital cameras, scanners, joysticks, speakers and modems.

1.5.2 Software

Software provides the instructions that tell the hardware exactly what is to be performed and in what order. This set of instructions is sequenced and organized in a computer program. Therefore, a program is a series of instructions which is intended to direct a computer to perform certain functions and is executed by the processor. In a broader sense, software can be described as a set of related programs. But software is more than a collection of programs. It refers to a set of computer programs, which provide desired functions and performance, the data which the programs use, data structures that facilitate the programs to efficiently manipulate data and documents that describe the operation and use of the programs.

A comparison between computer program and software is listed below (Table 1.2).

Table 1.2 Comparison between computer program and software

Computer program	Software
Programs are developed by individuals. A single developer is involved.	A large number of developers are involved.
Small in size and have limited functionality	Extremely large in size and have enormous functionality.
The user interface may not be very important, because the programmer is the sole user.	For a software product, user interface must be carefully designed and implemented because developers of that product and users of that product are totally different.

Nowadays, most of the software must be installed prior to their use. Installation involves copying several files to computer memory or requires a series of steps and configurations depending on the operating system and the software itself so that it can be run or executed when required.

Software is generally categorized as system software or application software or utility software.

System software

System software is designed to facilitate and coordinate the use of the computer by making hardware operational. It interacts with the computer system at low level. Examples of such software include language translator, operating system, loader, linker, etc. However, the most important system software is the *operating system* which is a set of programs designed to control the input and output operations of the computer, provide communication interface to the user, and manage the resources of the computer system, such as memory, processor, input/output devices, and schedule their operations with minimum manual intervention. Other programs (system and application) rely on facilities provided by the operating system to gain access to computer system resources. The *loader* is the system software which copies an executable program from secondary storage device into main memory and prepares this program for execution and initializes the execution.

Hardware devices, other than the CPU and main memory, have to be registered with the operating system by providing a software, known as *device driver*, for communication between the device and other parts of the computer. This type of system software is used by printers, monitors, graphics cards, sound cards, network cards, modems, storage devices, mouse, scanners, etc. Once installed, a device driver automatically responds when it is needed or may run in the background.

Modern operating systems recognize almost all connected hardware devices and immediately begin the installation process. Such a device, for which the operating system automatically starts the installation process, is called a *plug-and-play* device. However, there are few hardware devices for which the user has to manually initiate the installation process.

Application software

Application software is designed to perform specific tasks for the users. Microsoft Word, Microsoft Excel, Microsoft PowerPoint, Microsoft Access, PageMaker, Corel Draw, Photoshop, Tally, AutoCAD, Acrobat, WinAmp, Micro Media Flash, iLeap, Xing MP3 Player are some of the examples of application software.

There are two categories of application software, *custom software* and *pre-written software packages*. Software that is developed for a specific user or organization in accordance with the user's needs is known as *custom software*.

A *pre-written software package* is bought off the shelf and has predefined generic specifications that may or may not cater to all the requirements of a specific user. The most important categories of software packages available are as follows:

- Database management software, e.g. Oracle, DB2, Microsoft SQL server, etc.
- Spreadsheet software, e.g. Microsoft Excel.
- Word processing, e.g. Microsoft Word, Corel Wordperfect and desktop publishing (DTP), e.g. Pagemaker.
- Graphics software, e.g. Corel Draw.
- Statistical, e.g. SPSS and operation research software, e.g. Tora.

1.6 MEMORY REVISITED

The different types of memories available for a computer are shown in Fig. 1.4.

1.6.1 Primary Memory

All modern computers use semiconductor memory as primary memory. One of the important semiconductor memories used in desktop computers is ***Random Access Memory (RAM)***. Here "random access" means that any storage location can be accessed (both read and write) directly. This memory is faster, cheaper, and provides more storage space in lesser physical area. These very large-scale integrated semiconductor memory chips are mounted on pluggable printed circuit boards (PCBs). Enhancement or replacement of memory with such PCB memory modules is easy. These characteristics have made

semiconductor memory more popular and attractive. The only drawback of semiconductor memory is that it is volatile, i.e., it loses its contents whenever power is switched off. RAM holds the data and instructions waiting to be processed by the processor. In addition to data and program's instructions, RAM also holds operating system instructions that control the basic functions of a computer system. These instructions are loaded into RAM every time the computer is turned on, and they remain there until the computer is turned off. There are two types of RAM used in computer systems– *dynamic* and *static*.

Dynamic RAM (DRAM) is a type of RAM that employs refresh circuits to retain its content in its logic circuits. Each memory cell in DRAM consists of a single transistor. The junction capacitor of the transistor is responsible for holding the electrical charge that designates a single bit as logical 1. The absence of a charge designates a bit as logical 0. Capacitors lose their charge over time and therefore need to be recharged or refreshed at predetermined intervals by a refreshing circuitry.

A more expensive and faster type of RAM, *Static RAM (SRAM)*, does not require such type of refreshing circuitry. It uses between four to six transistors in a special 'flip-flop' circuit that holds a 1 or 0 while the computer system is in

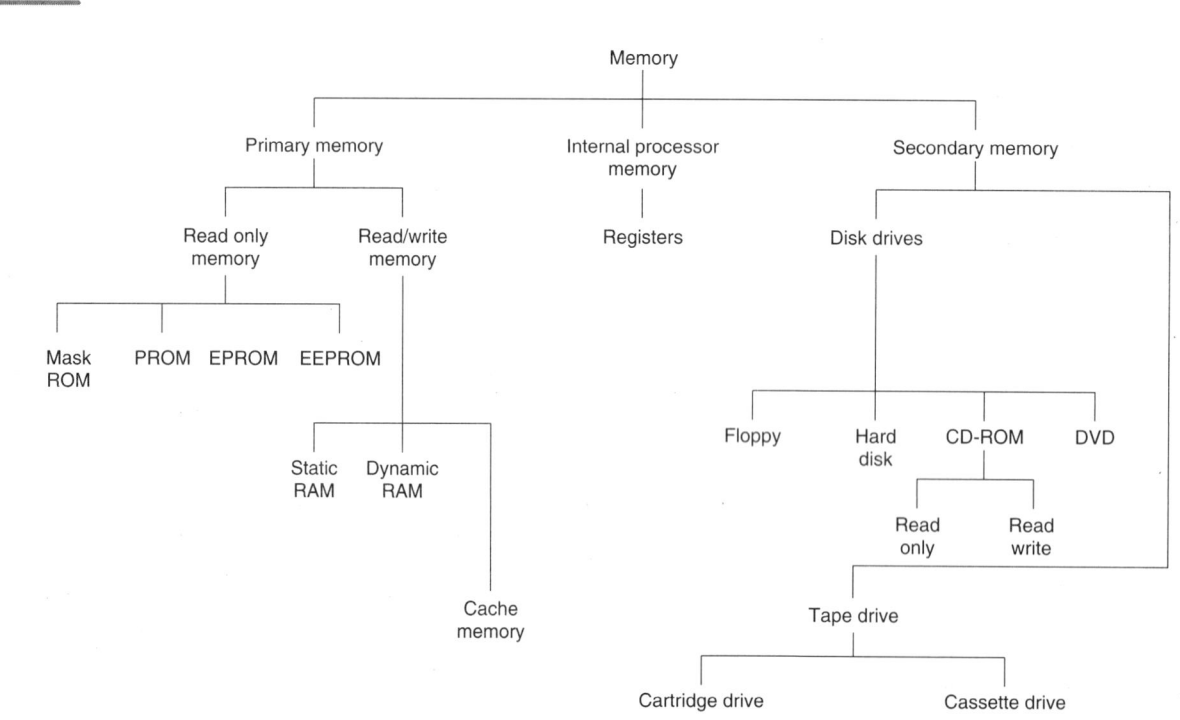

Figure 1.4 Types of memory

operation. SRAM in computer systems is usually used as processor caches and as I/O buffers. Printers and liquid crystal displays (LCDs) often use SRAM to buffer images. SRAM is also widely used in networking devices, such as routers, switches, and cable modems, to buffer transmission information.

Both dynamic and static RAM are volatile in nature and can be read or written to. The basic differences between SRAM and DRAM are listed in Table 1.3.

Table 1.3 Static RAM versus dynamic RAM

Static RAM	Dynamic RAM
• It does not require refreshing.	• It requires extra electronic circuitry that "refreshes" memory periodically; otherwise its content will be lost.
• It is more expensive than dynamic RAM.	• It is less expensive than static RAM.
• It is lower in bit density.	• It holds more bits of storage in a single integrated circuit.
• It is faster than dynamic RAM.	• It is slower than SRAM, due to refreshing.

There are several popular types of dynamic RAM used in computers. They are SDRAM (Synchronous Dynamic RAM), RDRAM (Rambus Dynamic RAM) and DDR RAM (Double Data Rate RAM).

The SDRAM used to be the most common type of RAM for personal computers. It was reasonably fast and inexpensive. It is no more used in the present day personal computers as much improved RAMs are available now.

The RDRAM was developed by Rambus Corporation and is its proprietary technology. It is also the most expensive RAM and is used mostly in video interface cards and high-end computers that require fast computation speed and data transfer. RDRAMs are preferred for high-performance personal computers.

The DDR RAM is a refinement of SDRAM. DDR stands for *Double Data Rate*. It gives faster performance by transmitting data on both the rising and the falling edges of each clock pulse. DDR 2 and DDR3 are other higher-speed versions of DDR RAM.

Another type of RAM, termed Video RAM (VRAM), is used to store image data for the visual display monitor. All types of video RAM are special arrangements of dynamic RAM (DRAM). Its purpose is to act as a data storage buffer between the processor and the visual display unit.

There is a persistent mismatch between processor and main memory speeds. The processor executes an instruction faster than the time it takes to read from or write to memory. In order to improve the average memory access speed or rather to optimize the fetching of instructions or data so that these can be accessed faster when the CPU needs it, cache memory is logically positioned between the internal processor memory (registers) and main memory. The cache memory holds a subset of instructions and data values that were recently accessed by the CPU. Whenever the processer tries to access a location of memory, it first checks with the cache to determine if it is already present in it. If so, the byte or word is delivered to the processor. In such a case, the processor does not need to access the main memory. If the data is not there in the cache, then the processer has to access the main memory. The block of main memory containing the data or instruction is read into the cache and then the byte or word is delivered to the processor.

There are two levels of cache.

Level 1 (Primary) cache This type of cache memory is embedded into the processor chip itself. This cache is very fast and its size varies generally from 8 KB to 64 KB.

Level 2 (Secondary) cache Level 2 cache is slightly slower than L1 cache. It is usually 64 KB to 2 MB in size. Level 2 cache is also sometimes called external cache because it was external to the processor chip when it first appeared.

Read Only Memory (ROM)

It is another type of memory that retains data and instructions stored in it even when the power is turned off. ROM is used in personal computers for storing start-up instructions provided by the manufacturer for carrying out basic operations such as bootstrapping in a PC, and is programmed for specific

purposes during their fabrication. ROMs can be written only at the time of manufacture. Another similar memory, Programmable ROM (PROM), is also non-volatile and can be programmed only once by a special device.

But there are instances where the read operation is performed several times and the write operation is performed more than once though less than the number of read operations and the stored data must be retained even when power is switched off. This led to the development of

EPROMs (Erasable Programmable Read Only Memories). In the EPROM data can be written electrically. The write operation, however, is not simple. It requires the storage cells to be erased by exposing the chip to ultraviolet light, thus bringing each cell to the same initial state. This process of erasing is time consuming. Once all the cells have been brought to the same initial state, the write operation on the EPROM can be performed electrically.

There is another type of Erasable PROM known as Electrically Erasable Programmable Read Only Memory (EEPROM). Like the EPROM, data can be written onto the EEPROM by electrical signals and retained even when power is switched off. The data stored can be erased by electrical signals. However, in EEPROMs the writing time is considerably higher than reading time. The biggest advantage of EEPROM is that it is non-volatile memory and can be updated easily, while the disadvantages are the high cost and the write operation takes considerable time.

Points to Note

- RAM holds raw data waiting to be processed as well as the program instructions for processing that data. It also stores the results of processing until they can be stored more permanently on secondary storage media. Most important point to be noted is that RAM holds operating system instructions which are loaded at start-up and from time to time as and when required.
- Dynamic RAM is less expensive, consumes less electrical power, generates less heat, and can be made smaller, with more bits of storage in a single integrated circuit. Static RAM provides faster access with lower bit density and are more expensive than dynamic RAM.
- ROM contains a small set of instructions that tell the computer how to access the hard disk, find the operating system, and load it into RAM. After the operating system is loaded, the computer can accept input, display output, run software, and access data.
- The programmable read-only memory (PROM) is non-volatile and can be reprogrammed only once by a special write device after fabrication. An erasable programmable ROM (EPROM) can be erased by ultraviolet (UV) light or by high-voltage pulses.

1.6.2 Secondary Memory

There are four main types of secondary storage devices available in a computer system:

- Disk drives
- CD drives (CD-R, CD-RW, and DVD)
- Tape drives
- USB flash drives

Hard disk, floppy disk, compact disc (CD), digital versatile disc (DVD) and magnetic tapes are the most common secondary storage mediums. Hard disks provide much faster performance and have larger capacity, but are normally not removable; that is, a single hard disk is permanently attached to a disk drive. Floppy disks, on the other hand, are removable, but their performance is far slower and their capacity far smaller than those of hard disks. A CD-ROM or DVD-ROM is another portable secondary memory device. CD stands for Compact Disc. It is called ROM because information is stored permanently when the CD is created. Devices for operating storage mediums are known as drives. Most of the drives used for secondary memory are based on electro-mechanical technology. Mechanical components move much more slowly than electrical signals. That's why access to secondary memory is much slower than access to main memory.

The **floppy disk** is a thin, round piece of plastic material, coated with a magnetic medium on which information is magnetically recorded, just as music is recorded on the surface of plastic cassette tapes. The flexible floppy disk is enclosed inside a sturdier, plastic jacket to protect it from damage. The disks used in personal computers are usually 3½ inches in diameter 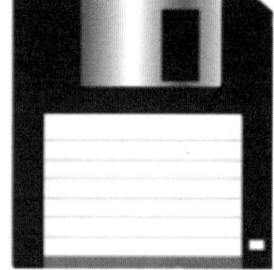 and can store 1.44 MB of data. Earlier PCs sometimes used 5¼ inch disks. The disks store information and can be used to exchange information between computers. The floppy disk drive stores data on and retrieves it from the magnetic material of the disk, which is in the form of a disk. It has two motors one that rotates the disk media and the other that moves two read-write heads, each on either surface of the disk, forward floppy disk drive or backward.

A **hard disk** is a permanent memory device mounted inside the system unit. Physically, a hard disk consists of one or more metal (sometimes aluminum) platters, coated with a metal oxide that can be magnetized. The platters are all mounted on a spindle, which allows them to spin at a constant rate. Read/write heads are attached to metal arms and positioned over each of the platter surfaces. The arms can move the read/write heads radially inwards and outwards over the surfaces of the platters (see Fig. 1.5).

Data and programs are stored on the hard disk by causing the write heads to make magnetic marks on the surfaces of the platters. Read heads  retrieve the data by sensing the magnetic marks on the platters. The surface of each platter is divided into concentric rings called tracks. The tracks form concentric circles on the platter's surface. Each track is divided into a certain number of sectors. A sector is capable of generally 512 bytes or sometimes 1,024 bytes of data. The head is mounted on an arm, which moves or seeks from track to track. The vertical group of tracks at the same position on each surface of each platter is called a cylinder. Cylinders are important because all heads move at the same time. Once the heads arrive at a particular track position, all the sectors on the tracks that form a cylinder can be read without further arm motion. The storage capacity of a hard disk is very large and expressed in terms of gigabytes (GB). The data that is stored on the hard disk remains there until it is erased or deleted by the user.

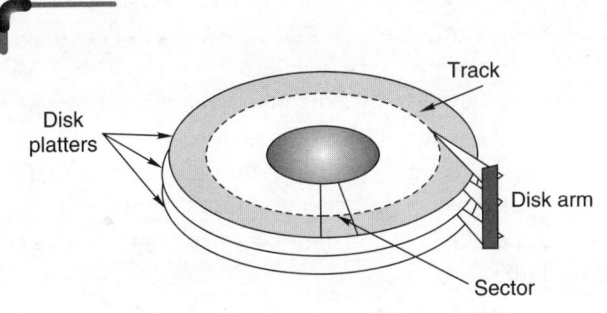

Figure 1.5 Hard disk organization

The hard disk drive provides better performance and become mandatory for computer systems for the following reasons:

- Higher capacity of data storage
- Faster access time of data
- Higher data transfer rates
- Better reliability of operation
- Less data errors or data loss

A CD is a portable secondary storage medium. Various types of CDs are available: CD-R and CD-RW. Once created (i.e. when it has been "burned"), data stored on

CD-R (CD-Recordable) disk can't be changed. On the other hand, a CD-Rewritable (CD-RW) disk can be erased and reused. This disk is made of synthetic resin that is coated with a reflective  material, usually aluminum. When information is written by a CD-writer drive, some microscopic pits are created on the surface of the CD. The information bit on a CD-ROM surface is coded in the form of ups and downs (known as pits and dumps), created by infrared heat. There is one laser diode on the reading head. The bits are read by shining a low-intensity laser beam onto the spinning disc. The laser beam reflects strongly from a smooth area on the disc but weakly from a pitted area. A sensor receiving the reflection determines whether each bit is a 1 or a 0 accordingly. CDs were initially a popular storage media for music; they were later used as general computer storage media. Most personal computers are equipped with a CD-Recordable (CD-R) drive. A CD-Rewritable (CD-RW) disc can be reused because the pits and flat surfaces of a normal CD are simulated on a CD-RW by coating the surface of the disc with a material that, when heated to one temperature, becomes amorphous (and therefore non-reflective) and when heated to a different temperature becomes crystalline (and therefore reflective).

1.7 INTRODUCTION TO OPERATING SYSTEMS

A computer system has many resources such as the processor (CPU), main memory, I/O devices, and files. The operating system acts as the manager of these resources and allocates them to specific programs and uses them as and when necessary for the tasks.

An operating system may be defined as a system software which acts as an intermediary between the user and the hardware, an interface which isolates the user from the details of the hardware implementation. It consists of a set of specialized software modules that makes computing resources (hardware and software) available to users. Thus, the computer system is easier to use with the operating system in place than without it. Some of the operating systems used nowadays are Mac, MS Windows, Linux, Solaris, etc.

The common functions of an operating system includes –

Process(or) management The process abstraction is a fundamental mechanism implemented by the operating system for management of the execution of programs.

A process is basically a program in execution. The operating system decides which process gets to run, for how long and perhaps at what priority or level of importance.

Memory management Operating system is responsible for keeping track of which parts of the memory are currently being used and by whom. It organizes and addresses memory, handles requests to allocate memory, frees up memory no longer being used, and rearranges memory to maximize the useful amount. Often several programs may be in memory at the same time. The operating system selects processes that are to be placed in memory, where they are to be placed, and how much memory is to be given to each.

Device management The operating system allocates the various devices to the processes and initiates the I/O operation. It also controls and schedules accesses to the input/output devices among the processes.

File management A file is just a sequence of bytes. Files are storage areas for programs, source codes, data, documents etc. The operating system keeps track of every file in the system, including data files, program files, compilers, and applications. The file system is an operating system module that allows users and programs to create, delete, modify, open, close, and apply other operations to various types of files. It also allows users to give names to files, to organize the files hierarchically into directories, to protect files, and to access those files using the various file operations.

Apart from these functions, an operating system must provide the facilities for controlling the access of programs, processes, memory segments, and other resources.

The *kernel* is that part of operating system that interacts with the hardware directly. The kernel represents only a small portion of the code of the entire OS but it is intensively used and so remains in primary storage while other portions may be transferred in and out of secondary storage as required. When a computer boots up, it goes through some initialization functions, such as checking the memory. It then loads the kernel and switches control to it. The kernel then starts up all the processes needed to communicate with the user and the rest of the environment.

The user interface is the portion of the operating system that users interact with directly. Operating systems such as MS-DOS and early versions of Unix accepted only typed-in text commands. Now most operating systems provide users a graphical user interface for their interactions with the system. Operating systems such as Microsoft Windows, Solaris and Linux allow the user to interact with the operating system through icons, menus, keyboard and mouse movements. The user interface and way of interactions vary widely from one operating system to another.

1.7.1 Loading an Operating System

In some digital devices like controllers of small appliances, hand-held devices and videogame console, the operating system is relatively simple and small and is stored in ROM. In such a system, it gains immediate control of the processor, the moment it is turned on.

In a personal computer, the operating system is usually stored on hard disk. Because size of the operating system is large enough, it cannot be placed entirely in RAM. The kernel, the core part of the operating system, is loaded into RAM at start-up and is always present in memory. Other parts of the operating system are loaded into RAM as and when required. It is to be noted that there is no operating system resident in a new computer. The operating system is usually sold on a CD or DVD media and has to be permanently transferred from a CD or DVD media to the hard disk by expanding compressed files and initializing the whole system for use.

Booting is the general term for the process that a computer or other digital device follows from the instant it is turned on until the operating system is finally loaded and ready for use.

The Basic Input Output System (BIOS) is a small set of instructions stored on a PROM that is executed when the computer is turned on.

When the computer is switched on, the ROM circuitry receives power and begins the boot process. At first, an address is automatically loaded into the Program Counter (PC) register. This is done by hardware circuitry. The address given is the location of the first executable instruction of the BIOS. The code in the BIOS runs a series of tests called the POST (Power On Self Test) to make sure that system devices such as main memory, monitor, keyboard, the input/output devices are connected and functional. During POST, the BIOS compares the system configuration data obtained from POST with the system information stored on a Complementary Metal-Oxide

Semiconductor (CMOS) memory chip located on the motherboard. The BIOS also sets various parameters such as the organization of the disk drive, using information stored in a CMOS chip. This CMOS chip gets updated whenever new system components are added and contains the latest information about system components.

The BIOS then loads only one block of data, called the *Master Boot Record*, from a specific and fixed place (the very first sector at cylinder 0, head 0, and sector 1) of the bootable device and is placed at a specific and fixed place of main memory. The master boot record is of 512 bytes in size and contains machine code instructions, called a *bootstrap loader*. Then the boot loader program starts the process of loading the OS and transfers control to the OS itself which completes the process.

Points to Note

- *Cold boot* describes the process of starting the computer and loading its operating system by turning the power on. If the computer is running, one can carry out cold boot by first switching it off and then back on.
- *Warm boot* describes the process of restarting the computer and loading its operating system again without switching it off after it has already been running.

1.8 OPERATIONAL OVERVIEW OF A CPU

Any processing executed by central processing unit is directed by an instruction. The processing required for a single instruction is called an *instruction cycle*. The four steps which the CPU carries out for each machine language instruction are *fetch*, *decode*, *execute*, and *store* (Fig. 1.6).

The steps involved in the instruction cycle while executing a program are described below.

The Program Counter (PC) is the register that keeps track of the next instruction to be executed. At the first step, the instruction is *fetched* from main memory and loaded into Instruction Register (IR), whose address is specified by PC register. Immediately the PC is incremented so that it points to the next instruction in the program. Once in IR, the instruction is *decoded* to determine the actions needed for its execution. The control unit then issues the sequence of control signals that enables *execution* of the instruction.

Data needed to be processed by the instructions are either fetched from a register or from RAM through the *memory data register*. The result of the instruction is *stored* (written) to either a register or a memory location. The next instruction of a program will follow the same steps. This will continue until there is no more instruction in the program or the computer is turned off, or some sort of unrecoverable error occurs.

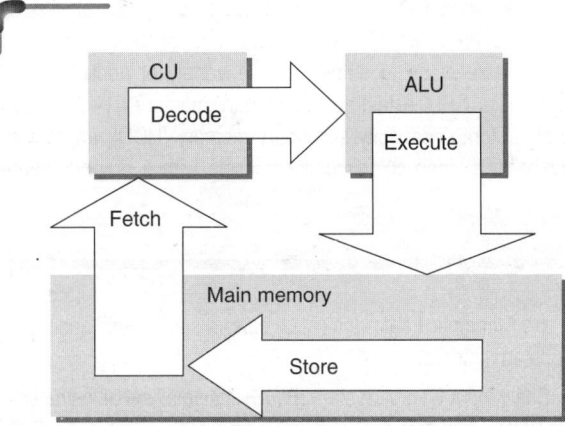

Figure 1.6 A simplified view of an instruction cycle

Points to Note

A register is a single, permanent storage location within the CPU used for a particular, defined purpose. CPU contains several important registers such as

- The *program counter* (PC) register holds the address of the current instruction being executed.
- The *instruction register* (IR) holds the actual instruction being executed currently by the computer.

To access data in memory, CPU makes use of two internal registers:

- The memory address register (MAR) holds the address of a memory location.
- The memory data register (MDR), sometimes known as the memory buffer register, will hold a data value that is being stored to or retrieved from the memory location currently addressed by the memory address register.

SUMMARY

A computer is defined as 'an automatic electronic apparatus for making calculations or controlling operations that are expressible in numerical or logical terms'.

Starting from the days of the abacus, the concept of developing a computing machine has led to the development of the modern electronic computing machine. There are five generations of computers. Today computers are available in various forms such as personal computers, laptop, palmtop, and mainframes. The electronic computer, of all sizes, perfected through years of development, has become a powerful machine capable of being employed in a variety of applications. A computer has a CPU, a fast-access primary memory (RAM), a non-volatile high storage capacity secondary memory (HDD), an easy-to-use keyboard, a video color monitor console with a graphic pointer device such as mouse and a non-impact printer.

Thus, broadly, the basic computer system consists of a CPU, memory, and input and output devices. Memory can be classified into primary, secondary, and internal processor memory. Cache memory is a part of the primary memory and normally resides near the CPU. The rest of the primary memory consists of various types of ROMs and RAMs.

A PC consists of hardware and software. Software can be classified into system software and application software. The most important system software is the operating system that manages all resources of the computer system and acts as an interface between hardware and software. When the personal computer is switched on, a power on self test (POST) is executed and the operating system is loaded.

KEY-TERMS

ALU The Arithmetic Logic Unit (ALU) performs arithmetic and logical operations on the data.

BIOS Basic Input-Output System (BIOS) is a small set of instructions stored in ROM which runs every time the computer is switched on. BIOS is responsible for Power On Self Test to make sure every immediately required device is connected and functional and finally loading the core part of the operating system into RAM.

Cache memory It is a special high-speed memory that allows a microprocessor to access data more rapidly than from memory located elsewhere on the system board.

CMOS The Complementary Metal Oxide Semiconductor (CMOS) chip in the computer stores information about various attributes of the devices connected to the computer.

Control unit It interprets each instruction and determines the appropriate course of action.

Computer It is programmable device that can store, retrieve, and process data.

CPU It is an Integrated circuit chip which is the ultimate controller of the computer, as well as the place where all calculations are performed.

Hardware It refers to the physical components of a computer.

RAM Random Access Memory (RAM) is a volatile memory that is used to store data and instructions temporarily. It holds raw data waiting to be processed as well as the program instructions for processing that data. It also holds operating system instructions, which control the basic functions of a computer system.

ROM Read Only Memory (ROM) is permanent and nonvolatile memory. It is the place to store the "hard-wired" startup instructions of a computer. These instructions are a permanent part of the circuitry and remain in place even when the computer power is turned off.

Software It refers to the set of computer programs and to the data that the programs use.

FREQUENTLY ASKED QUESTIONS

1. What is a microprocessor?

A microprocessor is an integrated circuit chip that contains all of the essential components for the central processing unit (CPU) of a microcomputer system.

2. What is a chip?

A chip is a small, thin piece of silicon onto which the transistors making up the integrated circuits, which forms the microprocessor, are imprinted.

3. What is a chipset?

In personal computers a chipset is a group of integrated circuits that together perform a particular function.

4. What is booting?

The sequence of events that occurs between the time that a computer is turned on and the time it is ready for use is referred to as booting.

5. Where is the operating system stored?

In some digital devices—typically handhelds and videogame consoles—the entire operating system is small enough to be stored in ROM (read-only memory). For most other computers, the operating system program is quite large, so most of it is stored on a hard disk. During the boot process, the operating system kernel is loaded into RAM. The kernel provides essential operating system services. Other parts of the operating system are loaded into RAM as and when they are needed.

6. What is a plug-and-play device?

A device for which the installation process starts automatically by the operating system and which usually does not require any human intervention is called a plug-and-play device.

7. If a computer contains RAM, why does it need ROM too?

Normally, the instructions and data are stored in a secondary storage device permanently. In addition to data and program instructions currently being processed, RAM also holds operating system instructions that control the basic functions of a computer system. These instructions are loaded into RAM every time the computer is booted, and they remain resident until the computer is turned off. But RAM is a volatile memory i.e. its content will be lost when the power is turned off. Now ROM plays the important role. ROM contains a small set of instructions called the BIOS (Basic Input Output System). These instructions access the hard disk, find the operating system, and load it into RAM. After the operating system is loaded, the system is ready to be used.

EXERCISE

1. Write full forms of the following:

   ENIAC, ALU, CU, RAM, ROM, EPROM, EEPROM, BIOS, POST, MIPS, CMOS

2. Briefly describe the functions of the different components of a conventional digital computer with the help of a suitable block diagram.

3. What is a CPU? What is its function? Mention its several components.

4. Explain the different memory units.

5. Discuss the memory hierarchy within a computer system.

6. What is cache memory? Why is it necessary?

7. Give three examples of system software.

8. Briefly state the role of the operating system in a computer system.

9. What is BIOS? Describe its functions.

10. What is meant by POST?

11. What is the boot sector?

12. Describe the bootstrap process.

13. Distinguish between the following:

    (a) Compiler and interpreter

    (b) System software and application software

    (c) RAM and ROM

    (d) Primary memory and secondary memory

    (e) Bit and byte

    (f) Hardware and software

14. Briefly explain the terms *hardware* and *software* of a computer system.

15. What is meant by "loading an operating system"?

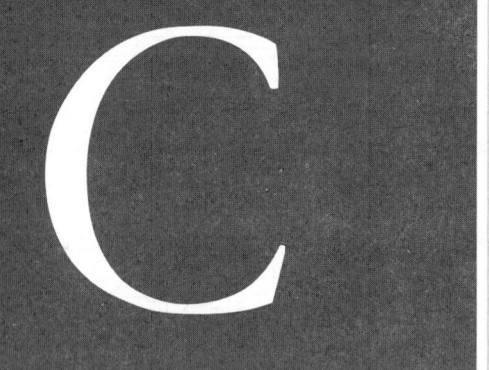

Introduction to Programming, Algorithms and Flowcharts

Chapter 2

Learning Objectives

After reading this chapter, the readers will be able to

- define program and programming
- identify system programs and application programs
- get a basic concept of high-, middle-, and low-level languages
- briefly understand compiler, interpreter, linker, and loader functions
- understand algorithms and the key features of an algorithm—sequence, decision, and repetition
- learn the different ways of stating algorithms—step-form, pseudo-code, flowchart
- define variables, types of variables, and naming conventions for variables
- decide a strategy for designing algorithms

2.1 PROGRAMS AND PROGRAMMING

A computer can neither think nor make a decision on its own. In fact, it is not possible for any computer to independently analyze a given data and find a solution on its own. It needs a program which will convey what is to be done. A program is a set of logically related instructions that is arranged in a sequence that directs the computer to solve a problem.

The process of writing a program is called programming. It is a necessary and critical step in data processing. An incorrect program delivers results that cannot be used. There are two ways by which one can acquire a program—either purchase an existing program, referred to as *packaged software* or create a new program from scratch, in which case it is called *customized software*.

Computer software can be broadly classified into two categories: system software and application software.

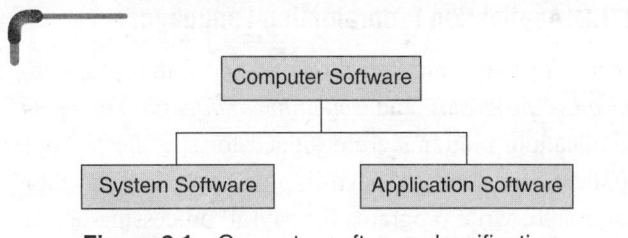

Figure 2.1   Computer software classification

2.1.1 System Software

System software is a collection of programs that interfaces with the hardware. Some common categories of system software are described as follows.

Language translator It is a system software that transforms a computer program written by a user into a form that can be understood by the machine.

Operating system (OS) This is the most important system software that is required to operate a computer system. An operating system manages the computer's resources effectively, takes care of scheduling multiple jobs for execution, and manages the flow of data and instructions between the input/output units and the main memory. Operating systems have become a part of computer software with the advent of the third generation computers. Since then a number of operating systems have been developed and some have undergone several revisions and modifications to achieve better utilization of computer resources. Advances in computer hardware have helped in the development of more efficient operating systems.

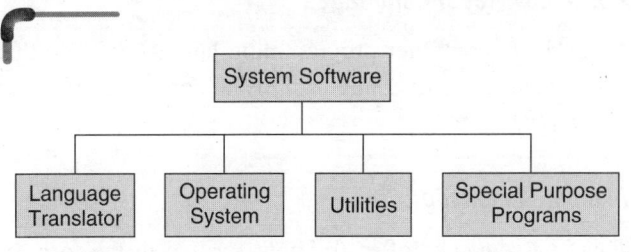

Figure 2.2   Categories of system software

2.1.2 Application Software

Application software is written to enable the computer to solve a specific data processing task. There are two categories of application software: pre-written software packages and user application programs.

A number of powerful application software packages that do not require significant programming knowledge have been developed. These are easy to learn and use compared to programming languages. Although these packages can perform many general and special functions, there are applications where these packages are found to be inadequate. In such cases, user application programs are written to meet the exact requirements. A user application program may be written using one of the pre-written packages or a programming language. The most important categories of software packages available are

- Database management software
- Spreadsheet software
- Word processing, Desktop Publishing (DTP), and presentation software
- Multimedia software
- Data communication software
- Statistical and operational research software

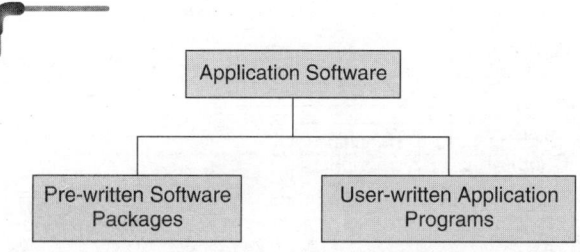

Figure 2.3   Categories of application software

Points to Note

1. A program is a sequence of logically related instructions and the process of writing programs it is programming.
2. A program is a software that is broadly categorized as system software and application software.

2.2 PROGRAMMING LANGUAGES

To write a computer program, a standard programming language is used. A programming language is composed of a set of instructions in a language understandable to the programmer and recognizable by a computer. Programming languages can be classified as high-level, middle-level, and low-level. High-level languages such as BASIC, COBOL (Common Business Oriented Programming Language), and FORTRAN (Formula Translation Language) are used to write application programs. A middle-level language such as C is used for writing application and system programs. A low-level language such as the assembly language is mostly used to write system programs.

Low-level programming languages were the first category of programming languages to evolve. Gradually, high-level and middle-level programming languages were developed and put to use.

Figure 2.4 depicts the growth in computer languages since the 1940s. The figure is meant to give some idea of the times that the different generations appeared, time scales, and relativity of computer languages to each other and the world of problem solving.

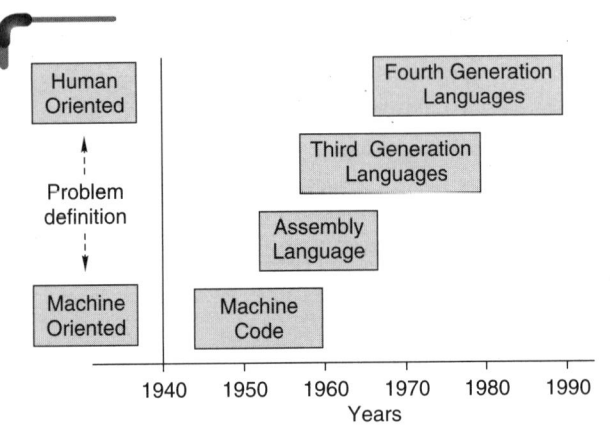

Figure 2.4 Evolution of computer languages

2.2.1 System Programming Languages

System programs or softwares are designed to make the computer easier to use. An example of system software is an operating system consisting of many other programs that control input/output devices, memory, processor, schedule the execution of multiple tasks, etc. To write an operating system program, the programmer needs instructions to control the computer's circuitry as well as manage the resources of the computer. For example, instructions to move data from one location of storage to a register of the processor. Assembly language, which has a one-to-one correspondence with machine code, was the normal choice for writing system programs like operating systems. Nowdays C is widely used to develop system software.

2.2.2 Application Programming Languages

There are two main categories of application programs: *business programs* and *scientific application programs.* Application programs are designed for specific computer applications, such as payroll processing and inventory control. To write programs for payroll processing or other such applications, the programmer does not need to control the basic circuitry of a computer. Instead, the programmer needs instructions that make it easy to input data, produce output, perform calculations, store and retrieve data. Programming languages suitable for such application programs have the appropriate instructions. Most programming languages are designed to be good for one category of applications but not necessarily for the other, although there are some general-purpose languages that support both types. Business applications are characterized by processing of large inputs and high-volume data storage and retrieval but call for simple calculations. Languages which are suitable for business program development must support high-volume input, output, and storage but do not need to support complex calculations. On the other hand, programming languages designed for writing scientific programs contain very powerful instructions for calculations but have poor instructions for input, output, etc. Among the traditionally used programming languages, COBOL is more suitable for business applications whereas FORTRAN is more suitable for scientific applications.

2.2.3 Low-level Languages

A low-level computer programming language is one that is closer to the native language of the computer, which is 1's and 0's.

Machine language

This is a sequence of instructions written in the form of binary numbers consisting of 1's and 0's to which the computer responds directly. The machine language is also referred to as the machine code, although the term is used more broadly to refer to any program text.

A machine language instruction generally has three parts as shown in Fig. 2.5. The first part is the command or operation code that conveys to the computer what function has to be performed by the instruction. All computers have operation codes for functions such as adding, subtracting and moving. The second part of the instruction either specifies that the operand contains data on which the operation has to be performed or it specifies that the operand contains a location, the contents of which have to be subjected to the operation.

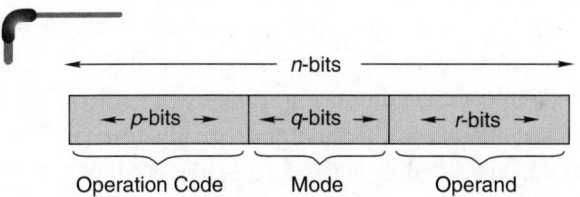

Figure 2.5 General format of a machine language instruction

Just as hardware is classified into generations based on technology, computer languages also have a generation classification based on the level of interaction with the machine. Machine language is considered to be the *first generation language* (1GL).

Advantage of machine language The CPU directly understands machine instructions, and hence no translation is required. Therefore, the computer directly starts executing the machine language instructions, and it takes less execution time.

Disadvantages of machine language

- ***Difficult to use*** It is difficult to understand and develop a program using machine language. For anybody checking such a program, it would be difficult to forecast the output when it is executed. Nevertheless, computer hardware recognizes only this type of instruction code.
- ***Machine dependent*** The programmer has to remember machine characteristics while preparing a program. As the internal design of the computer is different across types, which in turn is determined by the actual design or construction of the ALU, CU, and size of the word length of the memory unit, the machine language also varies from one type of computer to another. Hence, it is important to note that after becoming proficient in the machine code of a particular

computer, the programmer may be required to learn a new machine code and would have to write all the existing programs again in case the computer system is changed.

- ***Error prone*** It is hard to understand and remember the various combinations of 1's and 0's representing data and instructions. This makes it difficult for a programmer to concentrate fully on the logic of the problem, thus frequently causing errors.
- ***Difficult to debug and modify*** Checking machine instructions to locate errors is about as tedious as writing the instructions. Further, modifying such a program is highly problematic.

The following is an example of a machine language program for adding two numbers.

Example

1.	Machine Code		Comments
	0011	1100	Load register *A* with value 7
	0000	0111	
	0000	0110	Load register *B* with 10
	0000	1010	
	1000	0000	A = A + B
	0011	1010	Store the result into the memory location whose address is 100 (decimal)
	0110	0110	
	0111	0110	Halt processing

Assembly language

When symbols such as letters, digits, or special characters are employed for the operation, operand, and other parts of the instruction code, the representation is called an assembly language instruction. Such representations are known as mnemonic codes. A program written with mnemonic codes forms an assembly language program. This is considered to be a *second generation language* (2GL).

Machine and assembly languages are referred to as low-level languages since the coding for a problem is at the individual instruction level. Each computer has its own assembly language that is dependent upon the internal architecture of the processor.

An *assembler* is a translator that takes input in the form of the assembly language program and produces machine language code as its output. An instruction word consists of parts shown in Fig. 2.5 where,

- the Opcode (Operation Code) part indicates the operation to be performed by the instruction and
- the mode and operand parts convey the address of the data to be found or stored.

The following is an example of an assembly language program for adding two numbers and storing the result in some memory location.

Example

2. Mnemonics	Comments	Register/ Location
LD A, 7	Load register A with 7	⟹ A [7]
LD B, 10	Load register B with 10	⟹ B [10]
ADD A, B	A + B: Add contents of A with contents of B and store result in register A	⟹ A [17]
LD (100), A	Save the result in the main memory location 100	⟹ 100 [17]
HALT	Halt process	

From this example program, it is clear that using mnemonics such as LD, ADD, and HALT, the readability of the program has improved significantly.

An assembly language program cannot be executed by a machine directly as it is not in a binary machine language form. An assembler is needed to translate an assembly language program into the object code, which can then be executed by the machine. The object code is the machine language code. This is illustrated in Fig. 2.6.

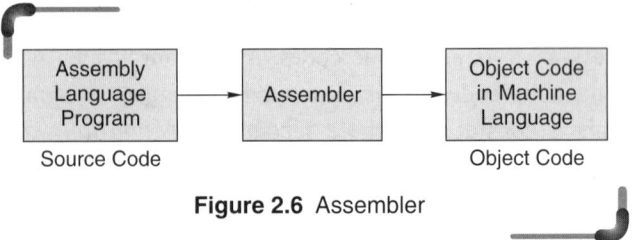

Figure 2.6 Assembler

Advantage of assembly language Writing a program in assembly language is more convenient than writing one in machine language. Instead of binary sequence, as in machine language, a program in assembly language is written in the form of symbolic instructions. This gives the assembly language program improved readability.

Disadvantages of assembly language

- Assembly language is specific to a particular machine architecture, i.e., machine dependent. Assembly languages are designed for a specific make and model of a microprocessor. This means that assembly language programs written for one processor will not work on a different processor if it is architecturally different. That is why an assembly language program is not portable.
- Programming is difficult and time consuming.
- The programmer should know all about the logical structure of the computer.

2.2.4 High-level Languages

High-level programming languages such as COBOL, FORTRAN, and BASIC were mentioned earlier in the chapter. Such languages have instructions that are similar to human languages and have a set grammar that makes it easy for a programmer to write programs and identify and correct errors in them. To illustrate this point, a program written in BASIC, to obtain the sum of two numbers, is shown below.

Example

3. Stmt. No.	Program stmnt	Comments
10	LET X = 7	Put 7 into X
20	LET Y = 10	Put 10 into Y
30	LET SUM = X + Y	Add values in X and Y and put in SUM
40	PRINT SUM	Output the content in SUM
50	END	Stop

The time and cost of creating machine and assembly language programs were quite high. This motivated the development of high-level languages.

Advantages of high-level programming languages

Readability Programs written in these languages are more readable than those written in assembly and machine languages.

Portability High-level programming languages can be run on different machines with little or no change. It is, therefore, possible to exchange software, leading to creation of program libraries.

Easy debugging Errors can be easily detected and removed.

Ease in the development of software Since the commands of these programming languages are closer to the English language, software can be developed with ease.

High-level languages are also called *third generation languages* (3GLs).

Points to Note

1. There are two kinds of programming languages — the low-level and high level.
2. High level programming languages are easy to read, portable, allow swift development of programs and are easy to debug.
3. Low level programming languages are not portable, take more time to develop programs and debugging is difficult.

2.3 COMPILER, INTERPRETER, LOADER, AND LINKER

For executing a program written in a high-level language, it must be first translated into a form the machine can understand. This is done by a software called the *compiler*. The compiler takes the high-level language program as input and produces the machine language code as output for the machine to execute the program. This is illustrated in Fig. 2.7.

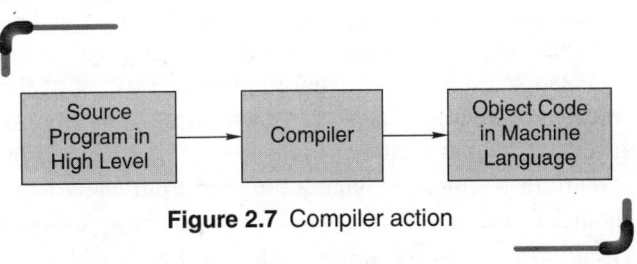

Figure 2.7 Compiler action

During the process of translation, the compiler reads the source program statement-wise and checks for syntax errors. In case of any error, the computer generates a printout of the same. This action is known as *diagnostics*.

There is another type of software that also does translation. This is called an *interpreter*.

The compiler and interpreter have different approaches to translation. Table 2.1 lists the differences between a compiler and an interpreter.

Table 2.1 Differences between a compiler and an Interpreter

Compiler	Interpreter
Scans the entire program before translating it into machine code.	Translates and executes the program line by line.
Converts the entire program to machine code and executes program only when all the syntax errors are removed.	The interpreter executes one line at a time, after checking and correcting its syntax errors and then converts it into machine code.
Slow in debugging or removal of mistakes from a program.	Good for fast debugging.
Program execution time is less.	Program execution time is more.

2.3.1 Compiling and Executing High-level Language Programs

The compiling process consists of two steps: the analysis of the source program and the synthesis of the object program in the machine language of the specified machine.

The analysis phase uses the precise description of the source programming language. A source language is described using *lexical* rules, *syntax* rules, and *semantic* rules.

Lexical rules specify the valid syntactic elements or words of the language. Syntax rules specify the way in which valid syntactic elements are combined to form the statements of the language. Syntax rules are often described using a notation known as BNF (Backus Naur Form) grammar. Semantic rules assign meanings to valid statements of the language.

The steps in the process of translating a source program in a high-level language to executable code are depicted in Fig. 2.8.

The first block is the *lexical analyzer*. It takes successive lines of a program and breaks them into individual lexical items, namely identifier, operator delimiter, and attaches a type tag to each of these. Beside this, it constructs a *symbol table* for each identifier and finds the internal representation of each constant. The symbol table is used later to allocate memory to each variable.

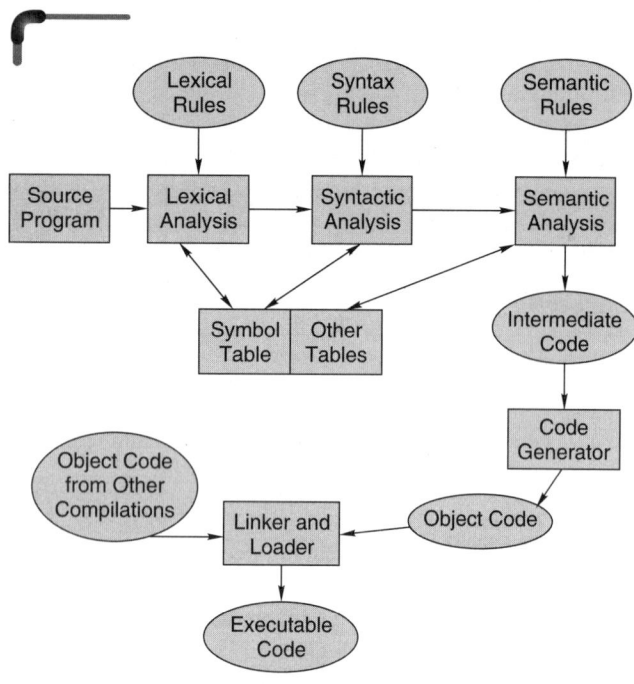

Figure 2.8 Process of compilation

Therefore, the execution of a program written in high-level language involves the following steps:

1. *Translation* of the program resulting in the object program.
2. *Linking* of the translated program with other object programs needed for execution, thereby resulting in a binary program.
3. *Relocation* of the program to execute from the specific memory area allocated to it.
4. *Loading* of the program in the memory for the purpose of execution.

2.3.2 Linker

Linking resolves symbolic references between object programs. It makes object programs known to each other. The features of a programming language influence the linking requirements of a program. In FORTRAN/COBOL, all program units are translated separately. Hence, all subprogram calls and common variable references require linking. Pascal procedures are typically nested inside the main program. Hence, procedure references do not require linking; they can be handled through relocation. References to built-in functions however require linking. In C, files are translated separately. Thus, only function calls that cross file boundaries and references to global data require linking. Linking makes the addresses of programs known to each other so that transfer of control from one subprogram to another or a main program takes place during execution.

Relocation

Relocation means adjustment of all address-dependent locations, such as address constant, to correspond to the allocated space, which means simple modification of the object program so that it can be loaded at an address different from the location originally specified. Relocation is more than simply moving a program from one area to another in the main memory. It refers to the adjustment of address fields. The task of relocation is to add some constant value to each relative address in the memory segment.

2.3.3 Loader

Loading means physically placing the machine instructions and data into main memory, also known as primary storage area.

The second stage of translation is called *syntax analysis* or *parsing*. In this phase, expressions, declarations, and other statements are identified by using the results of lexical analysis. Syntax analysis is done by using techniques based on formal grammar of the programming language.

In the semantic analysis phase, the syntactic units recognized by the syntax analyzer are processed. An intermediate representation of the final machine language code is produced.

The last phase of translation is code generation, when optimization to reduce the length of machine language program is carried out. The output of the code generator is a machine level language program for the specified computer. If a subprogram library is used or if some subroutines are separately translated and compiled, a final linking and loading step is needed to produce the complete machine language program in an executable form.

If subroutines were compiled separately, then the address allocation of the resulting machine language instructions would not be final. When all routines are connected and placed together in the main memory, suitable memory addresses are allocated. The linker's job is to find the correct main memory locations of the final executable program. The loader then places the executable program in memory at its correct address.

A loader is a system program that accepts object programs and prepares them for execution and initiates the execution (see Fig. 2.9). The functions performed by the loader are :

- Assignment of load-time storage area to the program
- Loading of program into assigned area
- Relocation of program to execute properly from its load time storage area
- Linking of programs with one another

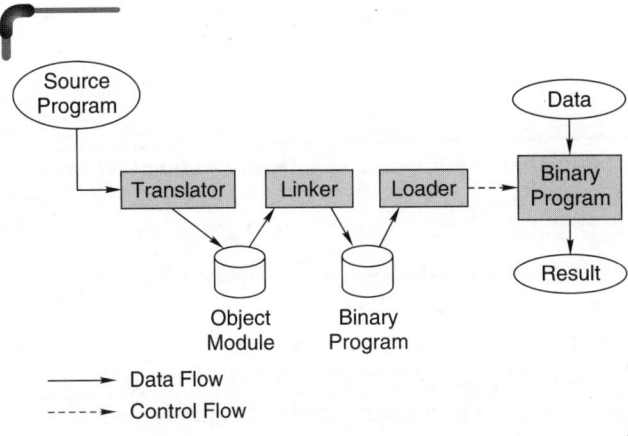

Figure 2.9 A schematic of program execution

Thus, a loader is a program that places a program's instructions and data into primary storage locations. An *absolute loader* places these items into the precise locations indicated in the machine language program. A *relocating loader* may load a program at various places in primary storage depending on the availability of primary storage area at the time of loading. A program may be relocated dynamically with the help of a *relocating register*. The base address of the program in primary storage is placed in the relocating register. The contents of the relocation register are added to each address developed by a running program. The user is able to execute the program as if it begins at location zero. At execution time, as the program runs, all address references involve the relocation register. This allows the program to reside in memory locations other than those for which it was translated to occupy.

2.3.4 Linking Loader and Linkage Editor

User programs often contain only a small portion of the instructions and data needed to solve a given problem. Large subroutine libraries are provided so that a programmer wanting to perform certain common

operations may use system-supplied routines to do so. Input/output, in particular, is normally handled by routines outside the user program. Hence, the machine language program produced by the translator must normally be combined with other machine language programs residing within the library to form a useful execution unit. This process of program combination is called linking and the software that performs this operation is variously known as a *linking loader* or a *linkage editor*. Linking is done after object code generation and prior to program execution time.

At load time, a linking loader combines whatever programs are required and loads them directly into primary storage. A linkage editor also performs the same task, but it creates a load image that it preserves on secondary storage for future reference. Whenever a program is to be executed, the load image produced by the linkage editor may be loaded immediately without the overhead of recombining program segments.

> **Points to Note**
>
> 1. A compiler converts a high-level language program into executable machine instructions after the removal of syntax errors.
> 2. An interpreter executes a high-level language program one line at a time after removing its syntax errors and converting it into machine instructions.
> 3. A linker makes the addresses of programs known to each other so that transfer of control from one subprogram to another or a main program takes place properly during execution.
> 4. A loader is a program that places a program's executable machine instructions and data into primary storage locations.

2.4 PROGRAM EXECUTION

The primary memory of a computer, also called the Random Access Memory, is divided into units known as words.

Depending on the computer, a word of memory may be two, four, or even eight bytes in size. Each word is associated with a unique address, which is a positive integer that helps the CPU to access the word. Addresses increase consecutively from the top of the memory to its bottom. When a program is compiled and linked, each instruction and each item of data is assigned an address. At execution time, the CPU finds instructions and data from these addresses.

The PC, or program counter, is a CPU register that holds the address of the next instruction to be executed in a program. In the beginning, the PC holds the address of the zeroth instruction of the program. The CPU fetches and then executes the instruction found at this address. The PC is meanwhile incremented to the address of the next instruction in the program. Having executed one instruction, the CPU goes back to look up the PC where it finds the address of the next instruction in the program. This instruction may not necessarily be in the next memory location. It could be at quite a different address. For example, the last statement could have been a goto statement, which unconditionally transfers control to a different point in the program; or there may have been a branch to a function subprogram. The CPU fetches the contents of the words addressed by the PC in the same amount of time, whatever their physical locations. The CPU has random access capability to any and all words of the memory, no matter what their addresses. Program execution proceeds in this way until the CPU has processed the last instruction.

Points to Note

1. When a program is compiled and linked, each instruction and each item of data is assigned an address.
2. During program execution, the CPU finds instructions and data from the assigned addresses.

2.5 FOURTH GENERATION LANGUAGES

Fourth Generation Languages are non-procedural languages that allow the user to simply specify what the output should be without describing how data should be processed to produce the result. Fourth generation programming languages are not as clearly defined as are the other earlier generation languages. Most people feel that a fourth generation language, commonly referred to as 4GL, is a high-level language that requires significantly fewer instructions to accomplish a particular task than does a third generation language. Thus, a programmer should be able to write a program faster in 4GL than in a third generation language.

Most third generation languages are procedural languages. That is, the programmer must specify the steps of the procedure the computer has to follow in a program. By contrast, most fourth generation languages are non-procedural languages. The programmer does not have to give the details of the procedure in the program, but specify, instead, what is wanted. For example, assume that a programmer needs to display some data on the screen, such as the address of a particular employee, say MANAS, from the EMP file. In a procedural language, the programmer would have to write a series of instructions using the following steps:

Step 1: Get a record from the EMP file.

Step 2: If this is the record for MANAS, display the address.

Step 3: If this is not the record for MANAS, go to step 1, until end-of-file.

In a non-procedural language (4GL), however, the programmer would write a single instruction that says:

Get the address of MANAS from EMP file.

Major fourth generation languages are used to get information from files and databases, as in the previous example, and to display or print the information. These fourth generation languages contain a query language, which is used to answer queries or questions with data from a database. The following example shows a query in a common query language, SQL.

SELECT ADDRESS FROM EMP WHERE NAME = 'MANAS'

End user-oriented 4GLs are designed for applications that process low data volumes. These 4GLs run on mainframe computers and may be employed either by information users or by the programmers. This type of 4GL may have its own internal database management software that in turn interacts with the organization's DBMS package. People who are not professional programmers use these products to query databases, develop their own custom-made applications, and generate their own reports with minimum amount of training. For example, Oracle offers a number of tools suitable for the end user.

Some fourth generation languages are used to produce complex printed reports. These languages contain certain types of programs called generators. With a report generator, the programmer specifies the headings, detailed data, and totals needed in a report. Thus, the report generator produces the required report using data from a file. Other fourth generation languages are used to design screens for data input and output and for menus. These languages contain certain types of programs called screen painters. The programmer designs the screen to look as desired and, therefore, it can be said that the programmer paints the screen using the screen painter program. Fourth generation languages are mostly machine independent. Usually they can be used on more than one type of computer. They are mostly used for office automation or business applications, and not for scientific programs. Some fourth generation languages are designed to be easily learnt and employed by end users.

Advantages of 4GLs

- Programming productivity is increased. One line of a 4GL code is equivalent to several lines of a 3GL code.
- System development is faster.
- Program maintenance is easier.
- End users can often develop their own applications.
- Programs developed in 4GLs are more portable than those developed in other generation languages.
- Documentation is of improved order because most 4GLs are self-documenting.

The differences between third generation languages and fourth generated languages are shown in Table 2.2.

Table 2.2 3GL vs 4GL

3GL	4GL
Meant for use by professional programmers	May be used by non-professional programmers as well as by professional programmers
Requires specifications of how to perform a task	Requires specifications of what task to perform
All alternatives must be specified	System determines how to perform the task
Execution time is less	Default alternatives are built-in. User need not specify these alternatives
Requires large numbers of procedural instructions. Code may be difficult to read, understand, and maintain by the user	Requires fewer instructions
Typically, file oriented	Difficult to debug

2.6 FIFTH GENERATION LANGUAGES

Natural languages represent the next step in the development of programming languages belonging to fifth generation languages. Natural language is similar to query language, with one difference: it eliminates the need for the user or programmer to learn a specific vocabulary, grammar, or syntax. The text of a natural-language statement resembles human speech closely. In fact, one could word a statement in several ways, perhaps even misspelling some words or changing the order of the words, and get the same result. Natural language takes the user one step further away from having to deal directly and in detail with computer hardware and software. These languages are also designed to make the computer smarter—that is, to simulate the human learning process. Natural languages already available for microcomputers include CLOUT, Q & A, and SAVY RETRIEVER (for use with databases) and HAL (Human Access Language) for use with LOTUS.

Points to Note

1. Third generation programming languages specify how to perform a task using a large number of procedural instructions and are file oriented.
2. Fourth generation programming languages specify what task has to be performed using fewer instructions and are database oriented.
3. Fifth generation programming languages resemble human speech and eliminate the need for the user or programmer to learn a specific vocabulary, grammar, or syntax.

2.7 CLASSIFICATION OF PROGRAMMING LANGUAGES

2.7.1 Procedural Languages

Algorithmic languages These are high-level languages designed for forming convenient expression of procedures, used in the solution of a wide class of problems. In this language, the programmer must specify the steps the computer has to follow while executing a program. Some of languages that fall in the category are C, COBOL, and FORTRAN.

Object-oriented languages The basic philosophy of object-oriented programming is to deal with objects rather than functions or subroutines as in strictly algorithmic languages. Objects are self-contained modules that contain data as well as the functions needed to manipulate the data within the same module. In a conventional programming language, data and subroutines or functions are separate. In object-oriented programming, subroutines as well as data are locally defined in objects. The difference affects the way a programmer goes about writing a program as well as how information is represented and activated in the computer. The most important object-oriented programming features are

- abstraction
- encapsulation and data hiding
- polymorphism
- inheritance
- reusable code

C++, Java, and Smalltalk are examples of object-oriented languages.

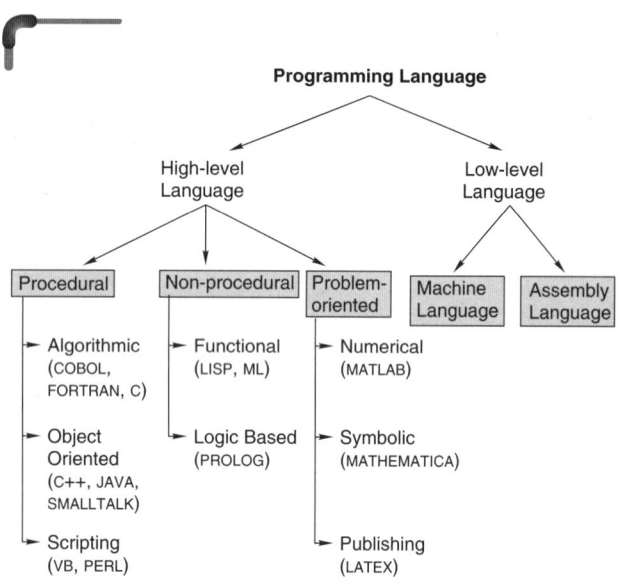

Figure 2.10 Programming language classification

Scripting languages These languages assume that a collection of useful programs, each performing a task, already exists. It has facilities to combine these components to perform a complex task. A scripting language may thus be thought of as a glue language, which sticks a variety of components together. One of the earliest scripting languages is the Unix shell. Now there are several scripting languages such as VBScript and Perl.

2.7.2 Problem-oriented Languages

These are high-level languages designed for developing a convenient expression for a given class of problems.

2.7.3 Non-procedural Languages

Functional (applicative) languages These languages solve a problem by applying a set of functions to the initial variables in specific ways to get the answer. The functional programming style relies on the idea of function application rather than on the notion of variables and assignments. A program written in a functional language consists of function calls together with arguments to functions. LISP and ML are examples of functional languages.

Logic-based programming languages A logic program is expressed as a set of atomic sentences, known as fact, and horn clauses, such as if-then rules. A query is then posed. The execution of the program now begins and the system tries to find out if the answer to the query is true or false for the given facts and rules. Such languages include PROLOG.

Points to Note

1. Programming languages can be categorized as high-level or low-level.
2. High-level languages are classified as procedural, non-procedural and problem-oriented languages. Programs in high-level languages are easy to write and debug. Such languages are not machine oriented.
3. Low-level languages are machine oriented languages.

2.8 STRUCTURED PROGRAMMING CONCEPT

In 1968, computer scientist Edsger Dijkstra of Netherlands published a letter to the editor in the Journal of the Association of Computing Machinery with the title 'Go To statement considered harmful'. goto is a command available in most programming languages to transfer a control to a particular statement. For three decades, Dijkstra had been crusading for a better way of programming—a systematic way to organize programs—called structured programming.

Structured programming has been called a revolution in programming and is considered as one of the most important advancements in software. Both academic and industrial professionals are inclined towards the philosophy and techniques of structured programming. Today, it can be safely said that virtually all software developers acknowledge the merits of the structured programming approach and use it in software development.

There is no standard definition of structured programming available but it is often thought to be programming without the use of a goto statement. Indeed, structured programming does discourage the frequent use of goto but there is more to it than that.

Structured programming is:

- concerned with improving the programming process through better organization of programs and better programming notation to facilitate correct and clear description of data and, control structure.
- concerned with improved programming languages and organized programming techniques which should be understandable and, therefore, more easily modifiable and suitable for documentation.
- more economical to run because good organization and notation make it easier for an optimizing compiler to understand the program logic.
- more correct and therefore more easily debugged, because general correctness theorems dealing with structures can be applied to proving the correctness of programs.

Structured programming can be defined as a

- top–down analysis for program solving
- modularization for program structure and organization
- structured code for individual modules

2.8.1 Top–Down Analysis

A program is a collection of instructions in a particular language that is prepared to solve a specific problem. For larger programs, developing a solution can be very complicated. From where should it start? Where should it terminate? Top-down analysis is a method of problem solving and problem analysis. The essential idea is to subdivide a large problem into several smaller tasks or parts for ease of analysis.

Top-down analysis, therefore, simplifies or reduces the complexity of the process of problem solving. It is not limited by the type of program. Top-down analysis is a general method for attending to any problem. It provides a strategy that has to be followed for solving all problems.

There are two essential ideas in top-down analysis:

- subdivision of a problem
- hierarchy of tasks

Subdivision of a problem means breaking a big problem into two or more smaller problems. Therefore, to solve the big problem, first these smaller problems have to be solved.

Top-down analysis does not simply divide a problem into two or more smaller problems.

It goes further than that. Each of these smaller problems is further subdivided. This process continues downwards, creating a hierarchy of tasks, from one level to the next, until no further break up is possible.

The four basic steps to top-down analysis are as follows:

Step 1: Define the complete scope of the problem to determine the basic requirement for its solution. Three factors must be considered in the definition of a programming problem.

- Input: What data is required to be processed by the program?
- Process: What must be done with the input data? What type of processing is required?
- Output: What information should the program produce? In what form should it be presented?

Step 2: Based on the definition of the problem, divide the problem into two or more separate parts.

Step 3: Carefully define the scope of each of these separate tasks and subdivide them further, if necessary, into two or more smaller tasks.

Step 4: Repeat step 3. Every step at the lowest level describes a simple task, which cannot be broken further.

2.8.2 Modular Programming

Modular programming is a programming approach in which a program is divided into logically independent smaller sections, which can be written separately. These sections, being separate and independent units, are called modules.

- A module consists of a series of program instructions or statements in some programming language.
- A module is clearly terminated by some special markers required by the syntax of the language. For example, a BASIC language subroutine is terminated by the return statement.
- A module as a whole has a unique name.
- A module has only one entry point to which control is transferred from the outside and only one exit point from which control is returned to the calling module.

The following are some advantages of modular programming:

- Complex programs may be divided into simpler and more manageable elements.
- Simultaneous coding of different modules by several programmers is possible.
- A library of modules may be created, and these modules may be used in other programs as and when needed.
- The location of program errors may be traced to a particular module; thus, debugging and maintenance may be simplified.

2.8.3 Structured Code

After the top-down analysis and design of the modular structure, the third and final phase of structured programming involves the use of structured code. Structured programming is a method of coding, i.e., writing a program that produces a well-organized module.

A high-level language supports several control statements, also called structured control statements or structured code, to produce a well-organized structured module. These control statements represent conditional and repetitive type of executions. Each programming language has different syntax for these statements.

In C, the `if` and `case` statements are examples of conditional execution whereas `for`, `while`, and `do...while` statements represent repetitive execution. In BASIC, `for-next` and `while-wend` are examples of repetitive execution. Let us consider the `goto` statement of BASIC, which is a simple but not a structured control statement. The `goto` statement can break the normal flow of the program and transfer control to any arbitrary point in a program. A module that does not have a normal flow control is unorganized and unreadable.

The following example is a demonstration of a program using several `goto` statements. Note that at line numbers 20, 60, and 80, the normal flow control is broken. For example, from line number 60, control goes back to line 40 instead of line 70 in case value of $(R - G)$ is less than 0.001.

```
10 INPUT X
20 IF X < 0 THEN GOTO 90
30 G = X/2
40 R = X/G
50 G = (R + G)/2
60 IF ABS(R - G) < 0.001 THEN GOTO 40
70 PRINT G
```

```
80 GOTO 100
90 PRINT "INVALID INPUT"
100 END
```

The structured version of this program using `while-wend` statement is given below.

```
INPUT X
IF X > 0
   THEN
G = X/2
R = X/G
   WHILE ABS (R - G) < 0.001
      R = X/G
      G = (R + G)/2
   WEND
   PRINT G
ELSE
   PRINT "INVALID INPUT"
END
```

Now if there is no normal break of control flow, `goto`'s are inevitable in unstructured languages but they can be and should always be avoided while using structured programs except in unavoidable situations.

2.8.4 Process of Programming

The job of a programmer is not just writing program instructions. The programmer does several other additional jobs to create a working program. There are some logical and sequential job steps which the programmer has to follow to make the program operational. These are as follows:

1. Understand the problem to be solved
2. Think and design the solution logic
3. Write the program in the chosen programming language
4. Translate the program to machine code
5. Test the program with sample data
6. Put the program into operation

The first job of the programmer is to understand the problem. To do that the requirements of the problem should be clearly defined. And for this, the programmer may have to interact with the user to know the needs of the user. Thus this phase of the job determines the 'what to' of the task.

The next job is to develop the logic of solving the problem. Different solution logics are designed and the order in which these are to be used in the program is defined. Hence, this phase of the job specifies the 'how to' of the task.

Once the logic is developed, the third phase of the job is to write the program using a chosen programming language. The rules of the programming language have to be observed while writing the program instructions.

The computer recognizes and works with 1's and 0's. Hence program instructions have to be converted to 1's and 0's for the computer to execute it. Thus, after the program is written, it is translated to the machine code, which is in 1's and 0's with the help of a translating program.

Now, the program is tested with dummy data. Errors in the programming logic are detected during this phase and are removed by making necessary changes in either the logic or the program instructions.

The last phase is to make the program operational. This means, the program is put to actual use. Errors occurring in this phase are rectified to finally make the program work to the user's satisfaction.

Points to Note

1. Structured programming involves top–down analysis for program solving, modularization of program structure and organizing structured code for individual module.
2. Top-down analysis breaks the whole problem into smaller logical tasks and defines the hierarchical link between the tasks.
3. Modularization of program structure means dividing a program into independent program modules that carries out the desired tasks.
4. Structured coding is structured programming which consists of writing a program that produces a well-organized module.

2.9 ALGORITHMS

2.9.1 What is an Algorithm?

Computer scientist Niklaus Wirth stated that

Program = Algorithms + Data

An algorithm is a part of the plan for the computer program. In fact , an algorithm is 'an effective procedure for solving a problem in a finite number of steps'.

It is effective, which means that an answer is found and it has a finite number of steps. A well-designed algorithm will always provide an answer; it may not be the desired answer but there will be an answer. It may be that the answer is that there is no answer. A well-designed algorithm is also guaranteed to terminate.

2.9.2 Different Ways of Stating Algorithms

Algorithms may be represented in various ways. There are four ways of stating algorithms. These are as follows:

- Step-form
- Pseudo-code
- Flowchart
- Nassi-Shneiderman diagram

In the step form representation, the procedure of solving a problem is stated with written statements. Each statement solves a part of the problem and these together complete the solution. The step-form uses just normal language to define each procedure. Every statement that defines an action is logically related to the preceding statement. This form of algorithm has been discussed in the following section with the help of an example.

The pseudo-code is a written form representation of the algorithm. However it differs from the step-form as it uses a restricted vocabulary to define its action of solving the problem. One problem with human language is that it can seem to be imprecise. But the pseudo-code, which is in human language, tends toward more precision by using a limited vocabulary.

Flowcharts and Nassi-Shneiderman diagrams are graphically oriented representation forms. They use symbols and language to represent sequence, decision, and repetition actions. Only the flowchart method of representing the problem solution has been explained with several examples. The Nassi-Shneiderman technique is beyond the scope of this book.

Points to Note

1. An algorithm is an effective procedure for solving a problem in a finite number of steps.
2. A program is composed of algorithm and data.
3. The four common ways of representing an algorithm are the Step-form, Pseudo-code, Flowchart and Nassi-Shneiderman diagram.

2.9.3 Key Features of an Algorithm and the Step-form

Here is an example of an algorithm, for making a pot of tea.

1. If the kettle does not contain water, then fill the kettle.
2. Plug the kettle into the power point and switch it on.
3. If the teapot is not empty, then empty the teapot.

4. Place tea leaves in the teapot.

5. If the water in the kettle is not boiling, then go to step 5.

6. Switch off the kettle.

7. Pour water from the kettle into the teapot.

It can be seen that the algorithm has a number of steps and that some steps (steps 1, 3, and 5) involve decision making and one step (step 5 in this case) involves repetition, in this case the process of waiting for the kettle to boil.

From this example, it is evident that algorithms show these three features:

- Sequence (also known as process)
- Decision (also known as selection)
- Repetition (also known as iteration or looping)

Therefore, an algorithm can be stated using three basic constructs: sequence, decision, and repetition.

Sequence

Sequence means that each step or process in the algorithm is executed in the specified order. In the above example, each process must be in the proper place otherwise the algorithm will fail.

Decision constructs—if ... then ..., if ... then ... else ...

In algorithms the outcome of a decision is either true or false; there is no state in between.

The outcome of the decision is based on some condition that can only result in a true or false value. For example,

if today is Friday then collect pay

is a decision and the decision takes the general form:

if proposition then process

A proposition, in this sense, is a statement, which can only be true or false. It is either true that 'today is Friday' or it is false that 'today is not Friday'. It can not be both true and false. If the proposition is true, then the process or procedure that follows the then is executed. The decision can also be stated as:

if proposition

then process1
else process2

This is the if ... then ... else ... form of the decision. This means that if the proposition is true then execute process1, else, or otherwise, execute process2.

The first form of the decision—if proposition then process has a null else, that is, there is no else.

Repetition constructs—repeat and while

Repetition can be implemented using constructs like the repeat loop, while loop, and if... then ... goto ... loop.

The repeat loop is used to iterate or repeat a process or sequence of processes until some condition becomes true. It has the general form:

Repeat
        Process1
        Process2
        ....
        ....
        ProcessN
Until proposition

Here is an example.

Repeat
        Fill water in kettle
Until kettle is full

The process is 'Fill water in kettle,' the proposition is 'kettle is full'.

The repeat loop does some processing before testing the state of the proposition.

What happens though if in the above example the kettle is already full? If the kettle is already full at the start of the repeat loop, then filling more water will lead to an overflow.

This is a drawback of the repeat construct.

In such a case the while loop is more appropriate. The above example with the while loop is shown as follows:

while kettle is not full
        fill water in kettle

Since the decision about the kettle being full or not is made before filling water, the possibility of an overflow is eliminated. The while loop finds out whether some condition is true before repeating a process or a sequence of processes.

If the condition is false, the process or the sequence of processes is not executed. The general form of while loop is:

while proposition
begin
Process 1

Process 2

....

....

Process N

end

The `if ... then goto ...` is also used to repeat a process or a sequence of processes until the given proposition is false. In the kettle example, this construct would be implemented as follows:

1. Fill some water in kettle

2. `if` kettle not full `then goto` 1

So long as the proposition 'kettle not full' is true the process, 'fill some water in kettle' is repeated. The general form of `if .. then goto ..` is:

Process1

Process2

....

....

ProcessN

`if` proposition `then goto` Process1

Termination

The definition of algorithm cannot be restricted to procedures that eventually finish. Algorithms might also include procedures that could run forever without stopping. Such a procedure has been called a computational method by Donald Knuth or calculation procedure or algorithm by Kleene. However, Stephen Kleene notes that such a method must eventually exhibit 'some object.' Minsky (1967) makes the observation that if an algorithm has not terminated, then how can the following question be answered: "Will it terminate with the correct answer?" Thus the answer is: undecidable. It can never be known, nor can the designer do an analysis beforehand to find it out. The analysis of algorithms for their likelihood of termination is called termination analysis.

Correctness

An algorithm needs to be verified for its correctness. Correctness means how easily its logic can be argued to meet the algorithm's primary goal. This requires the algorithm to be made in such a way that all the elements in it are traceable to the requirements.

Correctness requires that all the components like the data structures, modules, external interfaces, and module interconnections are completely specified.

In other words, correctness is the degree to which an algorithm performs its specified function. The most common measure of correctness is defects per Kilo Lines of Code (KLOC) that implements the algorithm, where defect is defined as the verified lack of conformance to requirements.

Points to Note

1. The key features of an algorithm are sequence, selection and repetition.
2. The stepwise form has sequence, selection and repetition constructs.
3. Termination means the action of closing. A well-designed algorithm always terminates.
4. Correctness of algorithm means how easily its logic can be argued to meet the algorithm's primary goal.

2.9.4 What are Variables?

So long, the elements of algorithm have been discussed. But a program comprises of algorithm and data. Therefore, it is now necessary to understand the concept of data. It is known that data is a symbolic representation of value and that programs set the context that gives data a proper meaning. In programs, data is transformed into information. The question is, how is data represented in programs?

Almost every algorithm contains data and usually the data is 'contained' in what is called a variable. The variable is a container for a value that may vary during the execution of the program. For example, in the tea-making algorithm, the level of water in the kettle is a variable, the temperature of the water is a variable, and the quantity of tea leaves is also a variable.

Each variable in a program is given a name, for example,

- Water_Level
- Water_Temperature
- Tea_Leaves_Quantity

and at any given time the value, which is represented by Water_Level, for instance, may be different to its value at some other time. The statement

`if` the kettle does not contain water `then` fill the kettle could also be written as

`if` Water_Level is 0 `then` fill the kettle

or

`if` Water_Level = 0 `then` fill the kettle

At some point Water_Level will be the maximum value, whatever that is, and the kettle will be full.

Variables and data types

The data used in algorithms can be of different types. The simplest types of data that an algorithm might use are

- numeric data, e.g., 12, 11.45, 901, etc.
- alphabetic or character data such as 'A', 'Z', or 'This is alphabetic'
- logical data, that is, propositions with true/false values

Naming of variables

One should always try to choose meaningful names for variables in algorithms to improve the readability of the algorithm or program. This is particularly important in large and complex programs.

In the tea-making algorithm, plain English was used. It has been shown how variable names may be used for some of the algorithm variables. In Table 2.3, the right-hand column contains variable names which are shorter than the original and do not hide the meaning of the original phrase. Underscores have been given to indicate that the words belong together and represent a variable.

Table 2.3 Algorithm using variable names

Algorithm in Plain English	Algorithm using Variable Names
1. If the kettle does not contain water, then fill the kettle.	**1.** If kettle_empty then fill the kettle.
2. Plug the kettle into the power point and switch it on.	**2.** Plug the kettle into the power point and switch it on.
3. If the teapot is not empty, then empty the teapot.	**3.** If teapot_not_empty then empty the teapot.
4. Place tea leaves in the teapot.	**4.** Place tea leaves in the teapot.
5. If the water in the kettle is not boiling then go to step 5.	**5.** If water_not_boiling then go to step 5.
6. Switch off the kettle.	**6.** Switch off the kettle.
7. Pour water from the kettle into the teapot.	**7.** Pour water from the kettle into the teapot.

There are no hard and fast rules about how variables should be named but there are many conventions. It is a good idea to adopt a conventional way of naming variables.

The algorithms and programs can benefit from using naming conventions for processes too.

2.9.5 Subroutines

A simple program is a combination of statements that are implemented in a sequential order. A statement block is a group of statements. Such a program is shown in Fig. 2.11(i). There might be a specific block of statements, which is also known as a procedure, that is run several times at different points in the implementation sequence of the larger program. This is shown in Fig. 2.11(ii). Here, this specific block of statement is named "procedure X". In this example program, the "procedure X" is written twice in this example. This enhances the size of the program. Since this particular procedure is required to be run at two specific points in the implementation sequence of the larger program, it may be treated as a separate entity and not included in the main program. In fact, this procedure may be called whenever required as shown in Fig. 2.11(iii). Such a procedure is known as a subroutine.

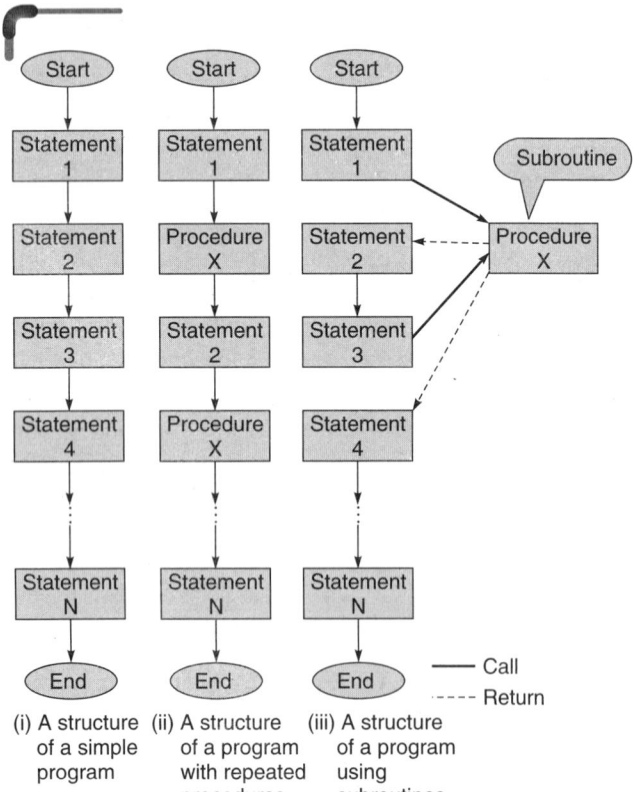

(i) A structure of a simple program
(ii) A structure of a program with repeated procedures
(iii) A structure of a program using subroutines

Figure 2.11 Program structures

Therefore, a subroutine, also known as procedure, method or function, is a portion of instruction that is invoked from within a larger program to perform a specific task. At the same time the subroutine is relatively independent of the remaining statements of the larger program. The subroutine behaves in much the same way as a program that is used as one step in a larger program. A subroutine is often written so that it can be started ("called") several times and/or from several places during a single execution of the program, including from other subroutines, and then branch back (*return*) to the next instruction after the "call", once the subroutine's task is done. Thus, such subroutines are invoked with a CALL statement with or without passing of parameters from the calling program. The subroutine works on the parameters if given to it, otherwise it works out the results and gives out the result by itself and returns to the calling program or passes the results to the calling program before returning to it.

The technique of writing subroutine has some distinct advantages. The subroutine reduces duplication of block of statements within a program, enables reuse of the block of statements that forms the subroutine across multiple programs, decomposes a complex task into simpler steps, divides a large programming task among various programmers or various stages of a project and hides implementation details from users.

However, there are some disadvantages in using subroutines. The starting or invocation of a subroutine requires some computational overhead in the call mechanism itself. The subroutine requires some well-defined housekeeping techniques at its entry and exit from it.

Points to Note

1. A subroutine is a logical collection of instructions that is invoked from within a larger program to perform a specific task.
2. The subroutine is relatively independent of the remaining statements of the program that invokes it.
3. A subroutine can be invoked several times from several places during a single execution of the invoking program.
4. After completing the specific task, a subroutine returns to the point of invocation in the larger program.

2.9.6. Examples on Developing Algorithms using Step-form

For illustrating the step-form the following conventions are assumed:

1. Each algorithm will be logically enclosed by two statements START and STOP.
2. To accept data from user, the INPUT or READ statements are to be used.
3. To display any user message or the content in a variable, PRINT statement will be used. Note that the message will be enclosed within quotes.
4. There are several steps in an algorithm. Each step results in an action. The steps are to be acted upon sequentially in the order they are arranged or directed.
5. The arithmetic operators that will be used in the expressions are

(i) '$\leftarrow$' Assignment (the left-hand side of '$\leftarrow$' should always be a single variable)

Example: The expression $x \leftarrow 6$ means that a value 6 is assigned to the variable x. In terms of memory storage, it means a value of 6 is stored at a location in memory which is allocated to the variable x.

(ii) '+' Addition

Example: The expression $z \leftarrow x + y$ means the value contained in variable x and the value contained in variable y is added and the resulting value obtained is assigned to the variable z.

(iii) '$-$' Subtraction

Example: The expression $z \leftarrow x - y$ means the value contained in variable y is subtracted from the value contained in variable x and the resulting value obtained is assigned to the variable z

(iv) '*' Multiplication

Example: Consider the following expressions written in sequence:

$$x \leftarrow 5$$
$$y \leftarrow 6$$
$$z \leftarrow x * y$$

The result of the multiplication between x and y is 30. This value is assigned to z.

(v) '/' Division

Example: The following expressions written in sequence illustrates the meaning of the division operator :

$$x \leftarrow 10$$
$$y \leftarrow 6$$
$$z \leftarrow x/y$$

The quotient of the division between x and y is 1 and the remainder is 4. When such an operator is used the quotient is taken as the result whereas the remainder is rejected. So here the result obtained from the expression x/y is 1 and this is assigned to z.

6. In propositions, the commonly used relational operators will include

(i) '>' Greater than

Example: The expression x > y means if the value contained in x is larger than that in y then the outcome of the expression is true, which will be taken as 1. Otherwise, if the outcome is false then it would be taken as 0.

(ii) '<=' Less than or equal to

Example: The expression x <= y implies that if the value held in x is either less than or equal to the value held in y then the outcome of the expression is true and so it will be taken as 1.

But if the outcome of the relational expression is false then it is taken as 0.

(iii) '<' Less than

Example: Here the expression x < y implies that if the value held in x is less than that held in y then the relational expression is true, which is taken as 1, otherwise the expression is false and hence will be taken as 0.

(iv) '=' Equality

Example: The expression x = y means that if the value in x and that in y are equal then this relational expression is true and hence the outcome is 1 other wise the outcome is false or 0.

(v) '>=' Greater than or equal to

Example: The expression x >= y implies that if the value in x is larger or equal to that in y then the outcome of the expression is true or 1, otherwise it is false or 0.

(vi) '!=' Non-equality

Example: The expression x != y means that if the value contained in x is not equal to the value contained in y then the outcome of the expression is true or 1, otherwise it is false or 0.

Note: The 'equal to (=)' operator is used both for assignment as well as equality specification. When used in proposition, it specifies equality otherwise assignment. To differentiate 'assignment' from 'equality' left arrow (←) may be used. For example, a ← b is an assignment but a = b is a proposition for checking the equality.

7. The most commonly used logical operators are AND, OR and NOT. These operators are used to specify multiple test conditions forming composite propositions. These are

(i) 'AND' Conjunction

The outcome of an expression is true or 1 when both the propositions AND-ed are true otherwise it is false or 0.

Example: Consider the expressions

x ← 2

y ← 1

x = 2 AND y = 0

In the above expression the proposition 'x = 2' is true because the value in x is 2. Similarly, the proposition 'y = 0' is untrue as y holds 1 and therefore this proposition is false or 0. Thus, the above expression may be represented as 'true' AND 'false' the outcome for which is false or 0.

(ii) 'OR' Disjunction

The outcome of an expression is true or 1 when any one of the propositions OR-ed is true otherwise it is false or 0.

Example: Consider the expressions

x ← 2

y ← 1

x = 2 OR y = 0

Here, the proposition 'x = 2' is true since x holds 2 while the proposition 'y = 0' is untrue or false. Hence the third expression may be represented as 'true' OR 'false' the outcome for which is true or 1.

(iii) 'NOT' Negation

If outcome of a proposition is 'true', it becomes 'false' when negated or NOT-ed.

Example: Consider the expression

x ← 2

NOT x = 2

The proposition 'x = 2' is true as x contains the value 2. But the second expression negates this by the logical operator NOT which gives an outcome false.

Examples

4. Write an algorithm for finding the sum of any two numbers.

Solution Let the two numbers be A and B and let their sum be equal to C. Then, the desired algorithm is given as follows:

1. START
2. PRINT "ENTER TWO NUMBERS"
3. INPUT A, B
4. C ← A + B   *(Add values assigned to A and B and assign this value to C)*
5. PRINT C
6. STOP

Explanation The first step is the starting point of the algorithm. The next step requests the programmer to enter the two numbers that have to be added. Step 3 takes in the two numbers given by the programmer and keeps them in variables A and B. The fourth step adds the two numbers and assigns the resulting value to the variable C. The fifth step prints the result stored in C on the output device. The sixth step terminates the procedure.

5. Write an algorithm for determining the remainder of a division operation where the dividend and divisor are both integers.

Solution Let N and D be the dividend and divisor, respectively. Assume Q to be the quotient, which is an integer, and R to be the remainder. The algorithm for the given problem is as follows.

1. START
2. PRINT "ENTER DIVIDEND"
3. INPUT N
4. PRINT "ENTER DIVISOR"   *(Only integer value is obtained and remainder ignored)*
5. INPUT D
6. Q ← N/D (Integer division)
7. R ← N - Q * D
8. PRINT R
9. STOP

Explanation The first step indicates the starting point of the algorithm. The next step asks the programmer to enter the dividend value. The third step keeps the dividend value in the variable N. Step 4 asks for the divisor value to be entered. This is kept in the variable D. In step 6, the value in N is divided by that in D. Since both the numbers are integers, the result is an integer. This value is assigned to Q. Any remainder in this step is ignored. In step 7, the remainder is computed by subtracting the product of the integer quotient and the integer divisor from integer dividend N. The computed value of the remainder is an integer here and obviously less than the divisor. The remainder

value is assigned to the variable R. This value is printed on an output device in step 8. Step 9 terminates the algorithm.

6. Construct an algorithm for interchanging the numeric values of two variables.

Solution Let the two variables be A and B. Consider C to be a third variable that is used to store the value of one of the variables during the process of interchanging the values.

The algorithm for the given problem is as follows.

1. START
2. PRINT "ENTER THE VALUE OF A & B"
3. INPUT A, B
4. C ← A
5. A ← B
6. B ← C
7. PRINT A, B
8. STOP

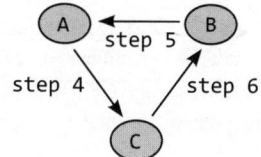

Explanation Like the previous examples, the first step indicates the starting point of the algorithm. The second step is an output message asking for the two values to be entered. Step 3 puts these values into the variables A and B. Now, the value in variable A is copied to variable C in step 4. In fact the value in A is saved in C. In step 5 the value in variable B is assigned to variable A. This means a copy of the value in B is put in A. Next, in step 6 the value in C, saved in the earlier step 4, is copied into B. In step 7 the values in A and B are printed on an output device. Step 8 terminates the procedure.

7. Write an algorithm that compares two numbers and prints either the message identifying the greater number or the message stating that both numbers are equal.

Solution This example demonstrates how the process of selection or decision making is implemented in an algorithm using the step-form. Here, two variables, A and B, are assumed to represent the two numbers that are being compared. The algorithm for this problem is given as follows.

1. START
2. PRINT "ENTER TWO NUMBERS"
3. INPUT A, B
4. IF A > B THEN
        PRINT "A IS GREATER THAN B"
5. IF B > A THEN
        PRINT "B IS GREATER THAN A"
6. IF A = B THEN
        PRINT "BOTH ARE EQUAL"
7. STOP

Explanation The first step indicates the starting point of the algorithm. The next step prints a message asking for the entry of the two numbers. In step 3 the numbers entered are kept in the variables A and B. In steps 4, 5 and 6, the values in A, B and C are compared with the IF ...THEN construct. The relevant message is printed whenever the proposition between IF and THEN is found to agree otherwise the next step is acted upon. But in any case one of the messages would be printed because one of the propositions would be true. Step 7 terminates the procedure.

8. Write an algorithm to check whether a number given by the user is odd or even.

Solution Let the number to be checked be represented by N. The number N is divided by 2 to give an integer quotient, denoted by Q. If the remainder, designated as R, is zero, N is even; otherwise N is odd. This logic has been applied in the following algorithm.

```
1. START
2. PRINT "ENTER THE NUMBER"
3. INPUT N
4. Q ← N/2 (Integer division)
5. R ← N - Q * 2
6. IF R = 0 THEN
        PRINT "N IS EVEN"
7. IF R != 0 THEN
        PRINT "N IS ODD"
8. STOP
```

Explanation The primary aim here is to find out whether the remainder after the division of the number with 2 is zero or not. If the number is even the remainder after the division will be zero. If it is odd, the remainder after the division will not be zero. So by testing the remainder it is possible to determine whether the number is even or odd.

The first step indicates the starting point of the algorithm while the next step prints a message asking for the entry of the number. In step 3, the number is kept in the variable N. N is divided by 2 in step 4. This operation being an integer division, the result is an integer. This result is assigned to Q. Any remainder that occurs is ignored. Now in step 5, the result Q is multiplied by 2 which obviously produces an integer that is either less than the value in N or equal to it. Hence in step 5 the difference between N and Q * 2 gives the remainder. This remainder value is then checked in step 6 and step 7 to either print out that it is either even or odd respectively. Step 8 terminates the procedure.

9. Write an algorithm to print the largest number among three numbers.

Solution Let the three numbers be represented by A, B, and C. There can be three ways of solving the problem. The three algorithms, with some differences, are given below.

```
1. START
2. PRINT "ENTER THREE NUMBERS"
3. INPUT A, B, C
4. IF A >= B AND B >= C
        THEN PRINT A
5. IF B >= C AND C >= A
        THEN PRINT B
   ELSE
        PRINT C
6. STOP
```

Explanation To find the largest among the three numbers A, B and C, A is compared with B to determine whether A is larger than or equal to B. At the same time it is also determined whether B is larger than or equal to C. If both these propositions are true then the number A is the largest otherwise A is not the largest. Step 4 applies this logic and prints A.

If A is not the largest number as found by the logic in step 4, then the logic stated in step 5 is applied. Here again, two propositions are compared. In one, B is compared with C and in the other C is compared with A. If both these propositions are true then B is printed as the largest otherwise C is printed as the largest.

Or

This algorithm uses a variable *MAX* to store the largest number.

```
1. START
2. PRINT "ENTER THREE NUMBERS"
3. INPUT A, B, C
4. MAX ← A
5. IF B > MAX THEN MAX ← B
6. IF C > MAX THEN MAX ← C
7. PRINT MAX
8. STOP
```

Explanation This algorithm differs from the previous one. After the numbers are stored in the variables A, B and C, the value of A is assigned to a variable MAX. This is done in step 4. In step 5, the value assigned to MAX is compared with that assigned to B and if the value in B is larger only then its value is assigned to

MAX otherwise it remains unchanged. In step 6, the proposition " IF C > MAX " is true then the value in C is assigned to MAX. On the other hand, if the proposition is false then the value in MAX remains unchanged. So at the end of step 6, the value in MAX is the largest among the three numbers.

Or

Here, the algorithm uses a **nested if** construct.

```
1. START
2. PRINT "ENTER THREE NUMBERS"
3. INPUT A, B, C
4. IF A > B THEN
     IF A > C THEN
      PRINT A
     ELSE
      PRINT C
     ELSE IF B > C THEN
      PRINT B
     ELSE
      PRINT C
5. STOP
```

Explanation Here, the nested if construct is used. The construct "IF p1 THEN action1 ELSE action2" decides if the proposition " p1" is true then action1 is implemented otherwise if it is false action2 is implemented. Now, action1 and action2 may be either plain statements like PRINT X or INPUT X or another "IF p2 THEN action3 ELSE action4" construct, were p2 is a proposition. This means that a second "IF p1 THEN action1 ELSE action2" construct can be interposed within the first "IF p1 THEN action1 ELSE action2" construct. Such an implementation is known as nested if construct.

Step 4 implements the nested if construct. First the proposition "A > B" is checked to find whether it is true or false. If true, the proposition "A > C " is verified and if this is found to be true, the value in A is printed otherwise C is printed. But if the first proposition "A > B" is found to be false then the next proposition that is checked is "B > C". At this point if this proposition is true then the value in B is printed whereas if it is false C is printed.

10. Take three sides of a triangle as input and check whether the triangle can be drawn or not. If possible, classify the triangle as equilateral, isosceles, or scalene.

    Solution Let the length of three sides of the triangle be represented by A, B, and C. Two alternative algorithms for solving the problem are given, with explanations after each step,

as follows:

```
1. START
```
   Step 1 starts the procedure.
```
2. PRINT "ENTER LENGTH OF THREE SIDES OF A
   TRIANGLE"
```
   Step 2 outputs a message asking for the entry of the length for each side of the triangle.
```
3. INPUT A, B, C
```
   Step 3 reads the values for the lengths that have been entered and assigns them to A, B and C.
```
4. IF A + B > C AND B + C > A AND A + C > B THEN
     PRINT "TRIANGLE CAN BE DRAWN"
   ELSE
     PRINT "TRIANGLE CANNOT BE DRAWN": GO TO 6
```

It is well known that in a triangle, the summation of lengths of any two sides is always greater than the length of the third side. This is checked in step 4. So for a triangle all the propositions "A + B > C ", " B + C > A " and " A + C > B " must be true. In such a case, with the lengths of the three sides, which have been entered, a triangle can be formed. Thus, the message "TRIANGLE CAN BE DRAWN" is printed and the next step 5 is executed. But if any one of the above three propositions is not true then the message "TRIANGLE CANNOT BE DRAWN" is printed and so no classification is required. Thus in such a case the algorithm is terminated in step 6.

```
5. IF A = B AND B = C THEN
     PRINT "EQUILATERAL"
   ELSE
     IF A != B AND B != C AND C !=A THEN
     PRINT "SCALENE"
   ELSE
     PRINT "ISOSCELES"
```

After it has been found in step 4 that a triangle can be drawn, this step is executed. To find whether the triangle is an "EQUILATERAL" triangle the propositions "A = B" and "B = C" are checked. If both of these are true, then the message "EQUILATERAL" is printed which means that the triangle is an equilateral triangle. On the other hand if any or both the propositions "A = B" and "B = C" are found to be untrue then the propositions "A != B" and "B != C" and "C !=A" are checked.

If none of the sides are equal to each other then all these propositions are found to be true and so the message "SCALENE" will be printed. But if these propositions

"A != B" and "B != C" and "C !=A" are false then the triangle is obviously an isosceles triangle and hence the message "ISOSCELES" is printed.

```
6. STOP
```

The procedure terminates here.

Or

This algorithm differs from the previous one and applies an alternate way to test whether a triangle can be drawn with the given sides and also identify its type.

```
1. START
2. PRINT "ENTER THE LENGTH OF 3 SIDES OF A
   TRIANGLE"
3. INPUT A, B, C
4. IF A + B > C AND B + C > A AND C + A > B
   THEN
          PRINT "TRIANGLE CAN BE DRAWN"
   ELSE
          PRINT "TRIANGLE CANNOT BE DRAWN"
            : GO TO 8
5. IF A = B AND B = C THEN
          PRINT "EQUILATERAL TRIANGLE"
            : GO TO 8
6. IF A = B OR B = C OR C = A THEN
          PRINT "ISOSCELES TRIANGLE"
            : GO TO 8
7. PRINT "SCALENE TRIANGLE"
8. STOP
```

Having followed the explanations given with each of the earlier examples, the reader has already understood how the stepwise method represents the algorithms with suitable statements.

In a similar way the following example exhibits the stepwise representation of algorithms for various problems using the stepwise method.

11. In an academic institution, grades have to be printed for students who appeared in the final exam. The criteria for allocating the grades against the percentage of total marks obtained are as follows.

Marks	Grade	Marks	Grade
91–100	O	61–70	B
81–90	E	51–60	C
71–80	A	<= 50	F

The percentage of total marks obtained by each student in the final exam is to be given as input to get a printout of the grade the student is awarded.

Solution The percentage of marks obtained by a student is represented by N. The algorithm for the given problem is as follows.

```
1. START
2. PRINT
     "ENTER THE OBTAINED PERCENTAGE MARKS"
3. INPUT N
4. IF N > 0 AND N <= 50 THEN
     PRINT "F"
5. IF N > 50 AND N <= 60 THEN
     PRINT "C"
6. IF N > 60 AND N <= 70 THEN
     PRINT "B"
7. IF N > 70 AND N <= 80 THEN
     PRINT "A"
8. IF N > 80 AND N <= 90 THEN
     PRINT "E"
9. IF N > 90 AND N <= 100 THEN
     PRINT "O"
10. STOP
```

12. Construct an algorithm which increments the value of a variable that starts with an initial value of 1 and stops when the value becomes 5.

Solution This problem illustrates the use of iteration or loop construct. Let the variable be represented by C. The algorithm for the said problem is given as follows.

```
1. START
2. C ← 1
3. WHILE C <= 5
4. BEGIN
5. PRINT C
6. C ← C + 1
7. END
8. STOP
```

While loop construct for looping till C is less than 5

13. Write an algorithm for the addition of N given numbers.

Solution Let the sum of N given numbers be represented by S. Each time a number is given as input, it is assigned to the variable A. The algorithm using the loop construct 'if … then goto …' is used as follows:

```
1. START
2. PRINT "HOW MANY NUMBERS?"
3. INPUT N
4. S ← 0
5. C ← 1
6. PRINT "ENTER NUMBER"
7. INPUT A
8. S ← S + A
9. C ← C + 1
```

```
10. IF C <= N THEN GOTO 6
11. PRINT S
12. STOP
```

14. Develop an algorithm for finding the sum of the series 1 + 2 + 3 + 4 + ... up to N terms.

Solution Let the sum of the series be represented by S and the number of terms by N. The algorithm for computing the sum is given as follows.

```
1. START
2. PRINT "HOW MANY TERMS?"
3. INPUT N
4. S ← 0
5. C ← 1
6. S ← S + C
7. C ← C + 1
8. IF C <= N THEN GOTO 6
9. PRINT S
10. STOP
```

15. Write an algorithm for determining the sum of the series 2 + 4 + 8 + ... up to N.

Solution Let the sum of the series be represented by S and the number of terms in the series by N. The algorithm for this problem is given as follows.

```
1. START
2. PRINT "ENTER THE VALUE OF N"
3. INPUT N
4. S ← 0
5. C ← 2
6. S ← S + C
7. C ← C * 2
8. IF C <= N THEN GOTO STEP 6
9. PRINT S
10. STOP
```

16. Write an algorithm to find out whether a given number is a prime number or not.

Solution The algorithm for checking whether a given number is a prime number or not is as follows.

```
1. START
2. PRINT "ENTER THE NUMBER"
3. INPUT N
4. IF N = 2 THEN
     PRINT "CO-PRIME" GOTO STEP 12
5. D ← 2
6. Q ← N/D (Integer division)
7. R ← N - Q*D
```

```
8. IF R = 0 THEN GOTO STEP 11
9. D ← D + 1
10. IF D <= N/2 THEN GOTO STEP 6
11. IF R = 0 THEN
     PRINT "NOT PRIME"
    ELSE
     PRINT "PRIME"
12. STOP
```

17. Write an algorithm for calculating the factorial of a given number N.

Solution The algorithm for finding the factorial of number N is as follows.

```
1. START
2. PRINT "ENTER THE NUMBER"
3. INPUT N
4. F ← 1
5. C ← 1
6. WHILE C <= N
7. BEGIN
8. F ← F * C
9. C ← C + 1
10. END
11. PRINT F
12. STOP
```

While loop construct for looping till C is less than N

18. Write an algorithm to print the Fibonacci series up to N terms.

Solution The Fibonacci series consisting of the following terms 1, 1, 2, 3, 5, 8, 13, ... is generated using the following algorithm.

```
1. START
2. PRINT "ENTER THE NUMBER OF TERMS"
3. INPUT N
4. C ← 1
5. T ← 1
6. T1 ← 0
7. T2 ← 1
8. PRINT T
9. T ← T1 + T2
10. C ← C + 1
11. T1 ← T2
12. T2 ← T
13. IF C <= N THEN GOTO 8
14. STOP
```

19. Write an algorithm to find the sum of the series $1 + x + x^2 + x^3 + x^4 + ...$ up to N terms.

Solution
```
1. START
2. PRINT "HOW MANY TERMS?"
3. INPUT N
```

```
 4. PRINT "ENTER VALUE OF X"
 5. INPUT X
 6. T ← 1
 7. C ← 1
 8. S ← 0
 9. S ← S + T
10. C ← C + 1
11. T ← T * X
12. IF C <= N THEN GOTO 9
13. PRINT S
14. STOP
```

20. Write an algorithm for computing the sum of digits in a number.

Solution

```
 1. START
 2. PRINT "ENTER THE NUMBER"
 3. INPUT N
 4. S ← 0
 5. Q ← N/10 (Integer division)
 6. R ← N - Q * 10
 7. S ← S + R
 8. N ← Q
 9. IF N > 0 THEN GOTO 5
10. PRINT S
11. STOP
```

21. Write an algorithm to find the largest number among a list of numbers.

Solution The largest number can be found using the following algorithm.

```
 1. START
 2. PRINT "ENTER,
        TOTAL COUNT OF NUMBERS IN LIST"
 3. INPUT N
 4. C ← 0
 5. PRINT "ENTER FIRST NUMBER"
 6. INPUT A
 7. C ← C + 1
 8. MAX ← A
 9. PRINT "ENTER NEXT NUMBER"
10. INPUT B
11. C ← C + 1
12. IF B > MAX THEN
            MAX ← B
13. IF C <= N THEN GOTO STEP 9
14. PRINT MAX
15. STOP
```

22. Write an algorithm to check whether a given number is an Armstrong number or not. An Armstrong number is one in which the sum of the cube of each of the digits equals that number.

Solution If a number 153 is considered, the required sum is (1^3 + 5^3 + 3^3), i.e., 153. This shows that the number is an Armstrong number. The algorithm to check whether 153 is an Armstrong number or not is given as follows.

```
 1. START
 2. PRINT "ENTER THE NUMBER"
 3. INPUT N
 4. M ← N
 5. S ← 0
 6. Q ← N/10 (Integer division)
 7. R ← N - Q * 10
 8. S ← S + R * R * R
 9. N ← Q
10. IF N > 0 THEN GOTO STEP 6
11. IF S = M THEN
       PRINT "THE NUMBER IS ARMSTRONG"
       ELSE PRINT "THE NUMBER IS NOT ARMSTRONG"
12. STOP
```

23. Write an algorithm for computing the sum of the series $1 + x + x^2/2! + x^3/3! + x^4/4! + \ldots$ up to N terms.

Solution

```
 1. START
 2. PRINT "ENTER NUMBER OF TERMS"
 3. INPUT N
 4. PRINT "ENTER A NUMBER"
 5. INPUT X
 6. T ← 1
 7. S ← 0
 8. C ← 1
 9. S ← S + T
10. T ← T * X/C
11. C ← C + 1
12. IF C <= N THEN GO TO STEP 9
13. PRINT S
14. STOP
```

2.9.7 Pseudo-code

Like step-form, pseudo-code is a written statement of an algorithm using a restricted and well-defined vocabulary. It is similar to a 3GL, and for many programmers and program designers it is the preferred way to state algorithms and program specifications.

Although there is no standard for pseudo-code, it is generally quite easy to read and use. For instance, a sample pseudo-code is written as follows:

```
dowhile kettle_empty
    Add_Water_To_Kettle
end dowhile
```

As can be seen, it is a precise statement of a while loop.

2.9.8 Flowcharts

A flowchart depicts appropriate steps to be followed in order to arrive at the solution to a problem. It is a program design tool which is used before writing the actual program. Flowcharts are generally developed in the early stages of formulating solutions to problems.

A flowchart comprises a set of standard shaped boxes that are interconnected by flow lines. Flow lines have arrows to indicate the direction of the flow of control between the boxes. The activity to be performed is written within the boxes in English. In addition, there are connector symbols that are used to indicate that the flow of control continues elsewhere, for example, the next page.

Flowcharts facilitate communication between programmers, users, and business persons. These flowcharts play a vital role in the programming of a problem and are quite helpful in understanding the logic of complicated and lengthy problems. Once the flowchart is drawn, it becomes easy to write the program in any high-level language. Often flowcharts are helpful in explaining the program to others. Hence, a flowchart is a must for better documentation of a complex program.

Standards for flowcharts

The following standards should be adhered to while drawing flowcharts.

- Flowcharts must be drawn on white, unlined 8½″ × 11″ paper, on one side only.
- Flowcharts start on the top of the page and flow down and to the right.
- Only standard flowcharting symbols should be used.
- A template to draw the final version of flowchart should be used.
- The contents of each symbol should be printed legibly.
- English should be used in flowcharts, not programming language.

- The flowchart for each subroutine, if any, must appear on a separate page. Each subroutine begins with a terminal symbol with the subroutine name and a terminal symbol labeled return at the end.
- Draw arrows between symbols with a straight edge and use arrowheads to indicate the direction of the logic flow.

Guidelines for drawing a flowchart

Flowcharts are usually drawn using standard symbols; however, some special symbols can also be developed when required. Some standard symbols frequently required for flowcharting computer programs are shown in Fig. 2.12.

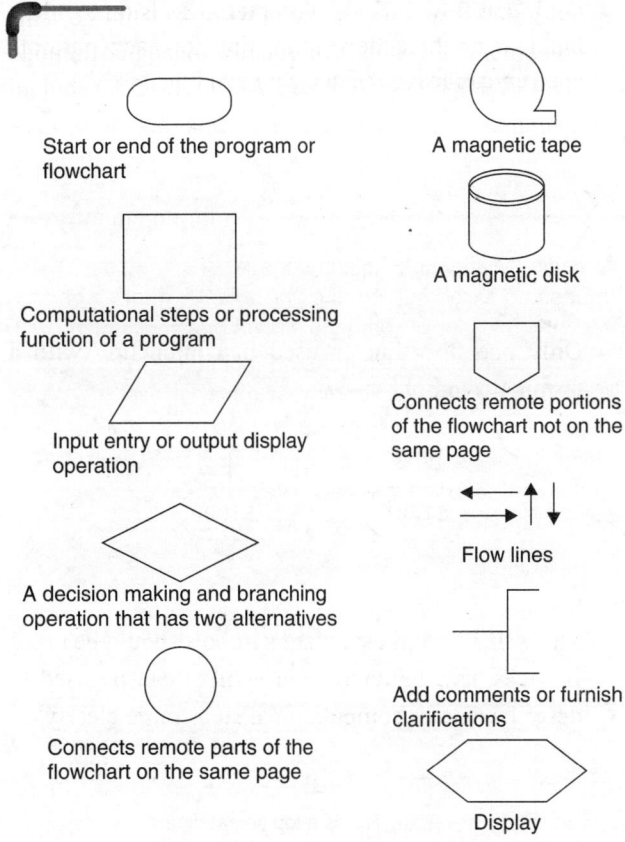

Figure 2.12 Flowchart symbols

The following are some guidelines in flowcharting.

- In drawing a proper flowchart, all necessary requirements should be listed out in a logical order.
- There should be a logical start and stop to the flowchart.

- The flowchart should be clear, neat, and easy to follow. There should be no ambiguity in understanding the flowchart.
- The usual direction of the flow of a procedure or system is from left to right or top to bottom.
- Only one flow line should emerge from a process symbol.

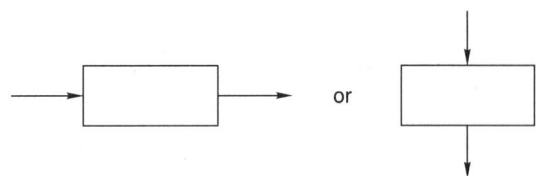

- Only one flow line should enter a decision symbol, but two or three flow lines, one for each possible answer, can leave the decision symbol.

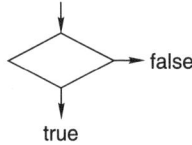

- Only one flow line is used in conjunction with a terminal symbol.

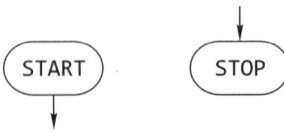

- The writing within standard symbols should be brief. If necessary, the annotation symbol can be used to describe data or computational steps more clearly.

- If the flowchart becomes complex, connector symbols should be used to reduce the number of flow lines. The intersection of flow lines should be avoided to make the flowchart a more effective and better way of communication.

- The validity of the flowchart should be tested by passing simple test data through it.
- A *sequence* of steps or processes that are executed in a particular order is shown using process symbols connected with flow lines. One flow line enters the first process while one flow line emerges from the last process in the sequence.

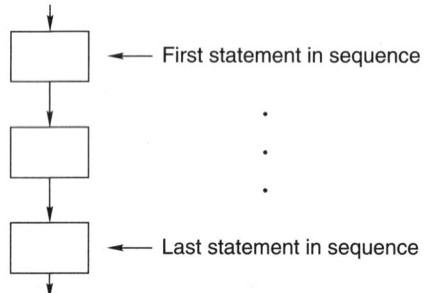

- *Selection* of one or more statement is depicted by the decision making and process symbols. Only one input indicated by one incoming flow line and one or more output flowing out of this structure exists. The decision symbol and the process symbols are connected by flow lines.

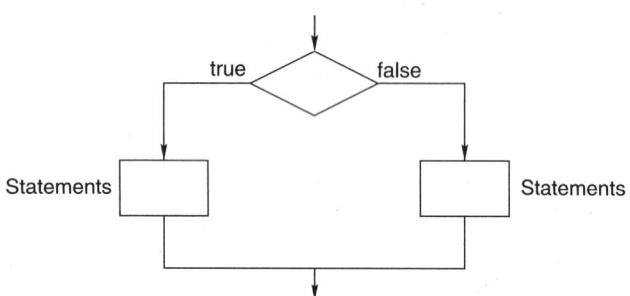

- *Iteration* or *looping* is depicted by a combination of processes and decision symbols placed in proper order. Here flow lines are used to connect the symbols and depict input and output to this structure.

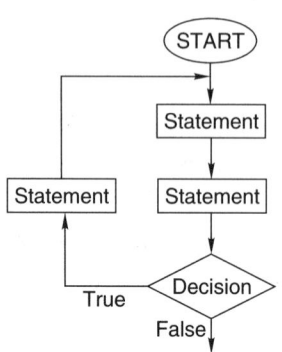

Advantages of using flowcharts

- *Communication*: Flowcharts are a better way of communicating the logic of a system to all concerned.
- *Effective analysis*: With the help of flowcharts, problems can be analyzed more effectively.
- *Proper documentation*: Program flowcharts serve as a good program documentation needed for various purposes.
- *Efficient coding*: Flowcharts act as a guide or blueprint during the systems analysis and program development phase.
- *Proper debugging*: Flowcharts help in the debugging process.
- *Efficient program maintenance*: The maintenance of an operating program becomes easy with the help of a flowchart.

Limitations of using flowcharts

- *Complex logic*: Sometimes, the program logic is quite complicated. In such a case, a flowchart becomes complex and clumsy.
- *Alterations and modifications*: If alterations are required, the flowchart may need to be redrawn completely.
- *Reproduction*: Since the flowchart symbols cannot be typed in, the reproduction of a flowchart becomes a problem.
- *Loss of objective*: The essentials of what has to be done can easily be lost in the technical details of how it is to be done.

Points to Note

1. A flowchart comprises a set of standard shaped boxes that are interconnected by flow lines to represent an algorithm.
2. There should be a logical start and stop to the flowchart.
3. The usual direction of the flow of a procedure or system is from left to right or top to bottom.
4. The intersection of flow lines should be avoided.
5. Flowcharts facilitate communication between programmers and users.

Flowcharting examples

A few examples on flowcharting are presented for a proper understanding of the technique. This will help students in the program development process at a later stage.

Examples

24. Draw a flowchart to find the sum of the first 50 natural numbers.
Solution

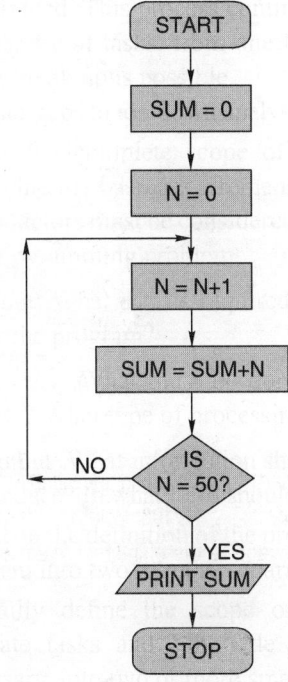

25. Draw a flowchart to find the largest of three numbers A, B, and C.
Solution

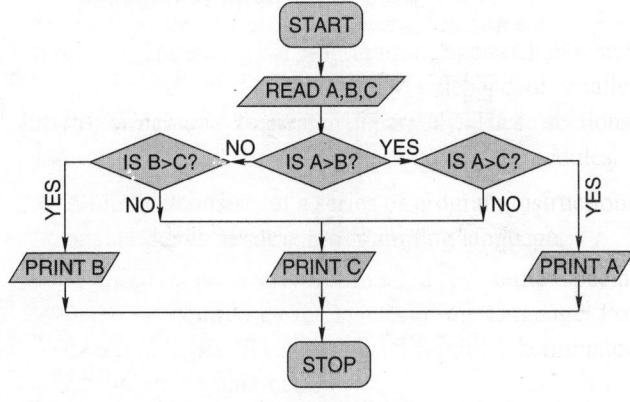

26. Draw a flowchart for computing factorial of N (N!) where N! = 1 × 2 × 3 × ... × N.

Solution

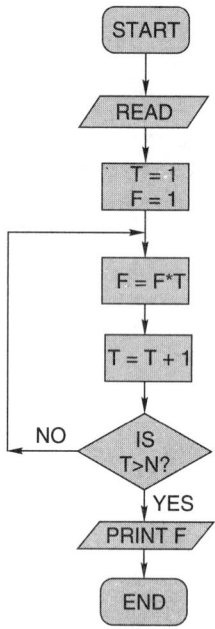

27. Draw a flowchart for calculating the simple interest using the formula SI = (P * T * R)/100, where P denotes the principal amount, T time, and R rate of interest. Also, show the algorithm in step-form.

Solution

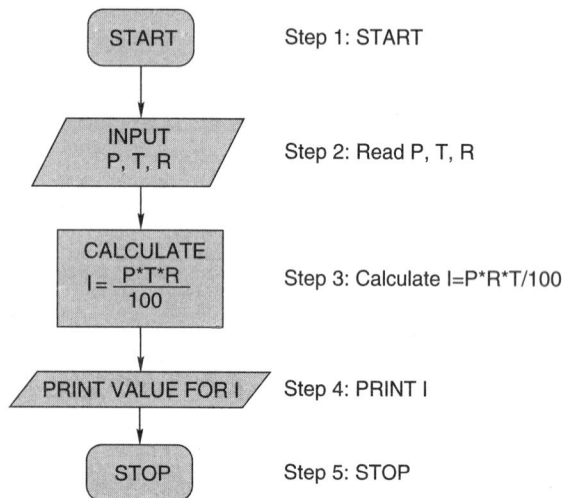

Step 1: START

Step 2: Read P, T, R

Step 3: Calculate I=P*R*T/100

Step 4: PRINT I

Step 5: STOP

28. The XYZ Construction Company plans to give a 5% year-end bonus to each of its employees earning Rs 5,000 or more per year, and a fixed bonus of Rs 250 to all other employees. Draw a flowchart and write the step-form algorithm for printing the bonus of any employee.

Solution

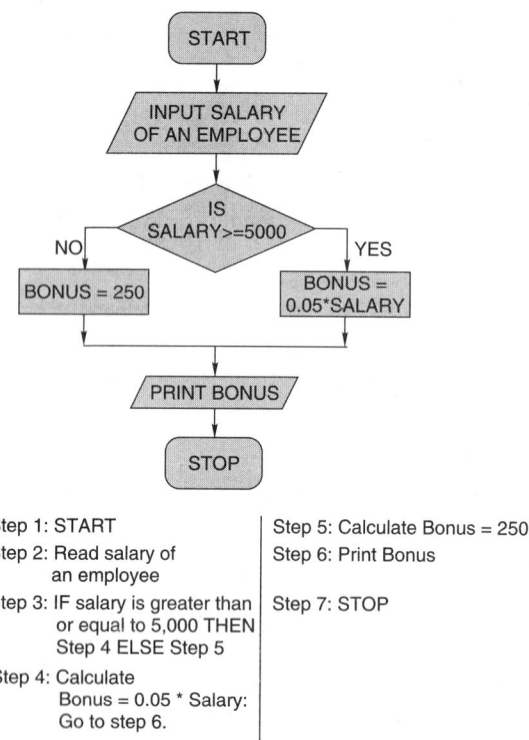

Step 1: START

Step 2: Read salary of an employee

Step 3: IF salary is greater than or equal to 5,000 THEN Step 4 ELSE Step 5

Step 4: Calculate Bonus = 0.05 * Salary; Go to step 6.

Step 5: Calculate Bonus = 250

Step 6: Print Bonus

Step 7: STOP

29. Prepare a flowchart to read the marks of a student and classify them into different grades. If the marks secured are greater than or equal to 90, the student is awarded Grade A; if they are greater than or equal to 80 but less than 90, Grade B is awarded; if they are greater than or equal to 65 but less than 80, Grade C is awarded; otherwise Grade D is awarded.

Solution

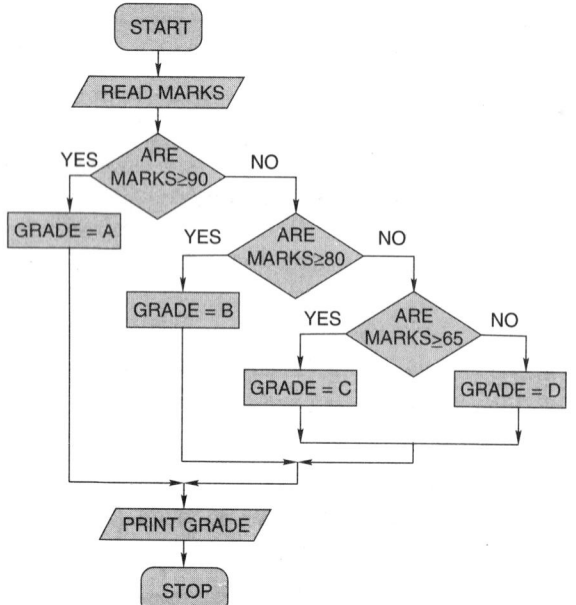

30. Draw a flowchart to find the roots of a quadratic equation.

Solution

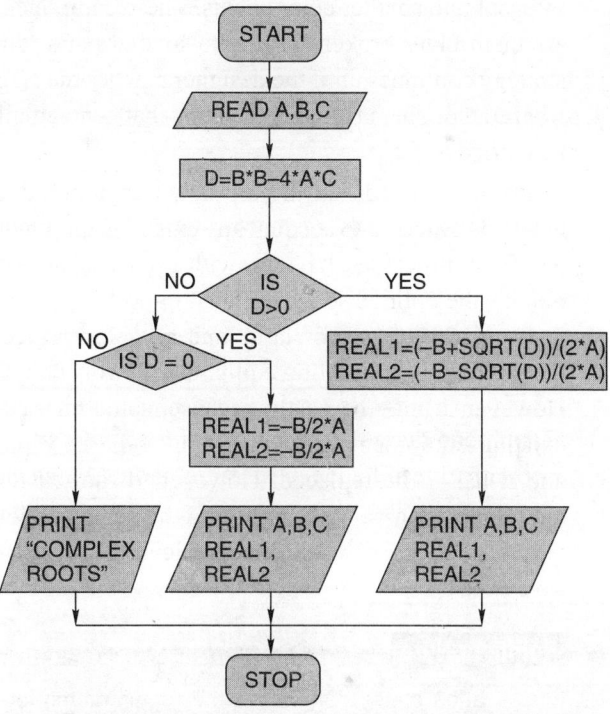

31. Draw a flowchart for printing the sum of even terms contained within the numbers 0 to 20.

Solution

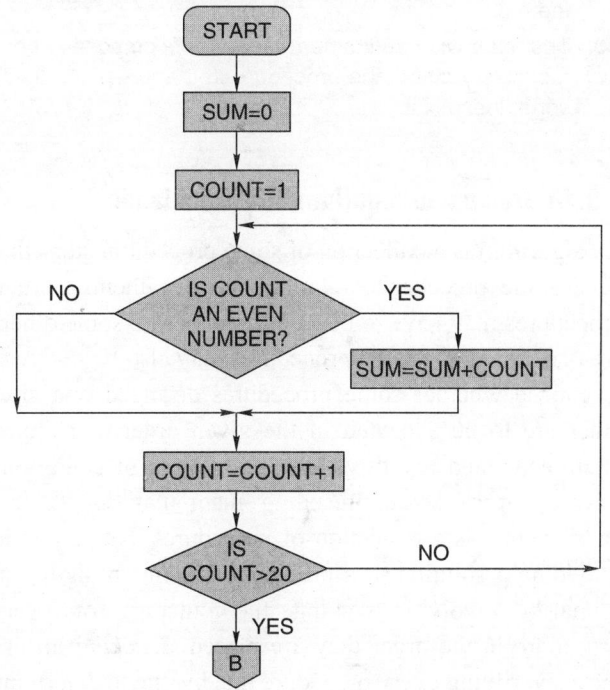

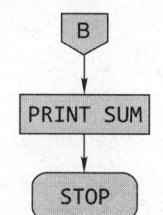

2.9.9 Strategy for Designing Algorithms

Now that the meaning of algorithm and data has been understood, strategies can be devised for designing algorithms. The following is a useful strategy.

Investigation step

1. *Identify the outputs needed.*

   This includes the form in which the outputs have to be presented. At the same time, it has to be determined at what intervals and with what precision the output data needs to be given to the user.

2. *Identify the input variables available.*

   This activity considers the specific inputs available for this problem, the form in which the input variables would be available, the availability of inputs at different intervals, the ways in which the input would be fed to the transforming process.

3. *Identify the major decisions and conditions.*

   This activity looks into the conditions imposed by the need identified and the limitations of the environment in which the algorithm has to be implemented.

4. *Identify the processes required to transform inputs into required outputs.*

   This activity identifies the various types of procedures needed to manipulate the inputs, within the bounding conditions and the limitations mentioned in step 3, to produce the needed outputs.

5. *Identify the environment available.*

   This activity determines the kind of users and the type of computing machines and software available for implementing the solution through the processes considered in steps.

Top-down development step

1. *Devise the overall problem solution by identifying the major components of the system.*

The goal is to divide the problem solution into manageable small pieces that can be solved separately.

2. *Verify the feasibility of breaking up the overall problem solution.*

The basic idea here is to check that though each small piece of solution procedure is independent, they are not entirely independent of each other, as they together form the whole solution to the problem. In fact, the different pieces of solution procedures have to cooperate and communicate in order to solve the larger problem.

Stepwise refinement

1. *Work out each and every detail for each small piece of manageable solution procedure.*

Every input and output dealt with and the transformation algorithms implemented in each small piece of solution procedure, which is also known as process, is detailed. Even the interfacing details between each small procedure are worked out.

2. *Decompose any solution procedure into further smaller pieces and iterate until the desired level of detail is achieved.*

Every small piece of solution procedure detailed in step 1 is checked once again. If necessary any of these may be further broken up into still smaller pieces of solution procedure till it can no more be divided into meaningful procedure.

3. *Group processes together which have some commonality.*

Some small processes may have to interface with a common upper level process. Such processes may be grouped together if required.

4. *Group variables together which have some appropriate commonality.*

Certain variables of same type may be dealt as elements of a group.

5. *Test each small procedure for its detail and correctness and its interfacing with the other small procedures.*

Walk through each of the small procedures to determine whether it satisfies the primary requirements and would deliver the appropriate outputs. Also, suitable tests have to be carried out to verify the interfacing between various procedures. Hence, the top-down approach starts with a big and hazy goal. It breaks the big goal into smaller components. These components are themselves broken down into smaller parts. This strategy continues until the designer reaches the stage where he or she has concrete steps that can actually be carried out.

It has to be noted that the top-down approach does not actually take into account any existing equipment, people, or processes. It begins with a "clean slate" and obtains the optimal solution. The top-down approach is most appropriate for large and complex projects where there is no existing equipment to worry about. However, it may be costly because, sometimes, the existing equipments may not fit into the new plan and it has to be replaced. However, if the existing equipments can be made to fit into the new plan with very less effort, it would be beneficial to use it and save cost.

Points to Note

1. Investigation phase determines the requirements for the problem solution.
2. The top-down development phase plans out the way the problem can be solved by breaking it into smaller modules and establishing a logical connection among them.
3. The step-wise refinement further decomposes the modules, defines the procedure in it and verifies the correctness of it.

2.9.10 Tracing an Algorithm to Depict Logic

An algorithm is a collection of some procedural steps that have some precedence relation between them. Certain procedures may have to be performed before some others are performed. Decision procedures may also be involved to choose whether some procedures arranged one after other are to be executed in the given order or skipped or implemented repetitively on fulfillment of conditions arising out of some preceding manipulations. Hence, an algorithm is a collection of procedures that results in providing a solution to a problem. *Tracing* an algorithm primarily involves tracking the outcome of every procedure in the order they are placed. *Tracking* in turn means verifying every procedure one by one to determine and confirm the corresponding result that is to be obtained. This in turn can be traced to offer an overall output from the implementation of the algorithm as a whole. Consider Example 29 given in this chapter for the purpose of tracing the algorithm to correctly depict the logic of the solution. Here at the start, the "marks obtained by a student in a subject" is accepted as input to the algorithm. This procedure is determined to be essential and alright. In the next step, the marks entered is compared with 90. As given, if the marks is greater than 90, then the marks obtained is categorized as Grade A and printed, otherwise it is further compared. Well, this part of the algorithm matches with the requirement and therefore this part of the logic is correct.

For the case of further comparison, the marks is again compared with 80 and if it is greater, then Grade B is printed. Otherwise, if the marks is less than 80, then further comparison is carried out. This part of the logic satisfies the requirement of the problem. In the next step of comparison, the marks is compared with 65. If the marks is lesser than 65, Grade C is printed, otherwise Grade D is printed. Here also, the flowchart depicts that the correct logic has been implemented.

The above method shows how the logic of an algorithm, planned and represented by a tool like the flowchart, can be verified for its correctness. This technique, also referred to as *deskcheck* or *dry run*, can also be used for algorithms represented by tools other than the flowchart.

2.9.11 Specification for Converting Algorithms into Programs

By now, the method of formulating an algorithm has been understood. Once the algorithm, for solution of a problem, is formed and represented using any of the tools like step-form or flowchart or pseudo-code, it has to be transformed into some programming language code. This means that a program, in a programming language, has to be written to represent the algorithm that provides a solution to a problem.

Hence, the general procedure to convert an algorithm into a program is given as follows:

Code the algorithm into a program—Understand the syntax and control structures used in the language that has been selected and write the equivalent program instructions based upon the algorithm that was created. Each statement in an algorithm may require one or more lines of programming code.

Desk-check the program—Check the program code by employing the desk-check method and make sure that the sample data selected produces the expected output.

Evaluate and modify, if necessary, the program—Based on the outcome of desk-checking the program, make program code changes, if necessary, or make changes to the original algorithm, if need be.

Do not reinvent the wheel—If the design code already exists, modify it, do not remake it.

Points to Note

1. An algorithm can be traced by verifying every procedure one by one to determine and confirm the corresponding result that is to be obtained.
2. The general procedure to convert an algorithm into a program is to code the algorithm using a suitable programming language, check the program code by employing the desk-check method and finally evaluate and modify the program, if needed.

Because the reader has not yet been introduced to the basics of the C language, the reader has to accept the use of certain instructions like #include <stdio.h>, int main(), printf(), scanf(), and return without much explanation at this stage in the example program being demonstrated below.

However, on a very preliminary level, the general form of a C program and the use of some of the necessary C language instructions are explained briefly as follows:

1. All C programs start with:

```
#include <stdio.h>
    int main ()
    {
```

2. In C, all variables must be declared before using them. So the line next to the two instruction lines and {, given in step 1, above, should be any variable declarations that are needed.

   For example, if a variable called " a " is supposed to store an integer, then it is declared as follows:

   ```
   int a;
   ```

3. Here, scanf() is used for inputting data and printf() is used to output data on the monitor screen.

4. The C program has to be terminated with a statement given below:

   ```
   return 0;
       }
   ```

Here is an example showing how to convert some pseudocode statements into C language statements:

Pseudocode

```
LOOP {

EXIT LOOP

IF (conditions) {

ELSE IF (conditions) {

ELSE {

INPUT a

OUTPUT "Value of a:" a

+ - * / %

=

<-

!=

AND

OR

NOT
```

C language Code

```
while(1) {

break;

if (conditions) {

else if (conditions) {

else

scanf("%d",&a);

printf("Value of a: %d",a);

(same)

==

=

!=
```

```
&&

||

!
```

To demonstrate the procedure of conversion from an algorithm to a program in C, an example is given below.

Problem statement Write an algorithm and the corresponding program in C for adding two integer numbers and printing the result.

Solution

Algorithm

1. START

2. DECLARE A AND B AS INTEGER VARIABLES

3. PRINT " ENTER TWO NUMBERS "

4. INPUT A, B

5. R = A + B

6. PRINT " RESULT = "

7. PRINT R

8. STOP

Program in C

```c
int main( )
{
  int A, B, R;
  printf("\n ENTER TWO NUMBERS:");
  scanf("%d%d",&A,&B);
  R = A + B;
  printf("\n RESULT = ");
  printf("%d",R);
  return 0;
}
```

SUMMARY

A program is a sequence of instructions and the process of writing a program is called programming. Programs are broadly categorized as system programs and application programs. Different programming languages have evolved. High-level languages are easy to use while low-level languages are complex. Therefore, writing programs in low-level languages is difficult and time consuming.

Compilers and interpreters are language translators that convert program instructions to machine code. A linker attaches utilities routines to the translated source code. A loader is responsible for physically placing this code in the main memory.

An algorithm is a statement about how a problem will be solved and almost every algorithm exhibits the same features. There are many ways of stating algorithms; three of them have been mentioned here. These are step-form, pseudo code, and flowchart method. Of these flowchart is a pictorial way of representing the algorithm. Here, the START and STOP are represented by an ellipse-like figure, ⬭, decision construct by the rhombus-like figure, ◇, the processes by rectangles, ▭ and input/output by parallelograms, ▱. Lines and arrows connect these blocks. Every useful algorithm uses data, which might vary during the course of the algorithm. To design algorithms, it is a good idea to develop and use a design strategy.

Generally the design strategy consists of three stages. The first stage is investigation activity followed by the top-down development approach stage and eventually a stepwise refinement process. Once the design strategy is decided the algorithm designed is traced to determine whether it represents the logic. Eventually, the designed and checked algorithm is transformed into a program.

KEY-TERMS

Algorithm Specifies a procedure for solving a problem in a finite number of steps.

Application software A collection of programs that enables the computer to solve a specific data processing task.

Assembler A translator that takes input in the form of the assembly language and produces machine language code as its output.

Assembly language A low-level programming language.

Compiler A language translator that takes the high-level language program as input and produces the executable machine language code.

Correctness Means how easily its logic can be argued to meet the algorithm's primary goal.

Data A symbolic representation of value.

Debug To search and remove errors in a program.

High-level programming language A programming language similar to human languages that makes it easy for a programmer to write programs and identify and correct errors in them.

Interpreter A language translator that translates and executes a program line by line.

Investigation step A step to determine the input, output and processing requirements of a problem.

Linker A program that resolves references between programs.

Loader A program that physically places the machine instructions and data in main memory.

Low-level programming language Closer to the native language of the computer, which is 1's and 0's.

Machine language Language that provides instructions in the form of binary numbers consisting of 1's and 0's to which the computer responds directly.

Operating system System software that manages the computer's resources effectively.

Portability language Programming language that is not machine dependent and can be used in any computer.

Program A set of logically related instructions arranged in a sequence that directs the computer in solving a problem.

Programming languages A language composed of a set of instructions understandable by the programmer.

Programming The process of writing a program.

System software A collection of programs that interfaces with the computer hardware.

Termination Closure of a procedure.

Top-down analysis Breaking up a problem solution into smaller modules and defininig their interconnections to provide the total solution to a problem.

Variable A container for a value that may or may not vary during the execution of the program.

FREQUENTLY ASKED QUESTIONS

1. What is a programming language?

A programming language is an artificial formalism in which algorithms can be expressed. More formally, a *computer program* is a sequence of instructions that is used to operate a computer to produce a specific result.

A programming language is the communication bridge between a programmer and a computer. A programming language allows a programmer to create sets of executable instructions called programs that the computer can understand. This communication bridge is needed because computers understand only machine language, which is an instruction language in which data are represented by binary digits.

2. What is a token?

A token is any word or symbol that has meaning in the language, such as a keyword (reserved word) such as if or while. The tokens are *parsed* or grouped according to the rules of the language.

3. What is syntax?

Syntax is the 'grammar' of a programming language. It specifies the formal rules governing the way the vocabulary elements of the language can be combined to form instructions. The syntax of a programming language defines exactly what combinations of letters, numbers, and symbols can be used in a programming language. During compilation, all syntax rules are checked. If a program is not syntactically correct, the compiler will issue error messages and will not produce object code.

4. What is a variable?

A *variable* is a name given to the area of computer memory that holds the relevant data. Each variable has a data type, which might be number, character, string, a collection of data elements (such as an array), a data record, or some special type defined by the programmer.

5. What are the difficulties faced in procedural programming?

The main drawback of procedural programming is that it breaks down when problems become very large especially when it is highly complex, making it somewhat more difficult for a team of people to work with it. There are limits to the amount of detail one can cope with. Non-procedural programming like object-oriented programming can help the programmer compartmentalize and manage that detail. Various forms of non-procedural programming are vastly more effective for many large real-world problems.

6. What is Spaghetti code?

Non-modular code is normally referred to as spaghetti code. It is named so because it produces a disorganized computer program using many GOTO statements.

7. What is structured programming?

Structured programming is a style of programming designed to make programs more comprehensible and programming errors less frequent. This technique of programming enforces a logical structure on the program being written to make it more efficient and easier to understand and modify. It usually includes the following characteristics:

Block structure The statements in the program must be organized into functional groups. It emphasizes clear logic.

Avoidance of jumps A lot of GOTO statements makes the programs more error-prone. Structured programming uses less of these statements. Therefore it is also known as 'GOTO less programming'.

Modularity It is a common idea that structuring the program makes it easier for us to understand and therefore easier for teams of developers to work simultaneously on the same program.

8. What are the advantages and disadvantages of structured programming?

Structured programming provides options to develop well-organized codes which can be easily modified and documented.

Modularity is closely associated with structured programming. The main idea is to structure the program into functional groups. As a result, it becomes easier for us to understand and therefore easier for teams of developers to work simultaneously on the same program.

Another advantage of structured programming is that it *reduces complexity*. Modularity allows the programmer to tackle problems in a logical fashion. This improves the programming process through better organization of programs and better programming notations to facilitate correct and clear description of data and control structure.

Structured programming also *saves time* as without modularity, the code that is used multiple times needs to be written every time it is used. On the other hand, modular programs need one to call a subroutine (or function) with that code to get the same result in a structured program.

Structured programming *encourages stepwise refinement*, a program design process described by Niklaus Wirth. This is a top-down approach in which the stages of processing are first described in high-level terms, and then gradually worked out in their details, much like the writing of an outline for a book.

The disadvantages of structured programming include the following:

Firstly, error control may be harder to manage. Managing modifications may also be difficult.

Secondly, debugging efforts can be hindered because the problem code will look right and even perform correctly in one part of the program but not in another.

9. What is pseudocode?

Pseudocode is an informal description of a sequence of steps for solving a problem. It is an outline of a computer program, written in a mixture of a programming language and English. Writing pseudocodes is one of the best ways to plan a computer program.

The advantage of having pseudocodes is that it allows the programmer to concentrate on how the program works while ignoring the details of the language. By reducing the number of things the programmer must think about at once, this technique effectively amplifies the programmer's intelligence.

10. What is top-down programming?

Top-down programming is a technique of programming that first defines the overall outlines of the program and then fills in the details.

This approach is usually the best way to write complicated programs. Detailed decisions are postponed until the requirements of the large program are known; this is better than making the detailed decisions early and then forcing the major program strategy to conform to them. Each part of the program (called a *module*) can be written and tested independently.

11. What is an error? Describe different types of error that may occur in a program.

An error that occurs during the compilation stage is called a *compiler error*. A compiler error occurs when a given program does not follow the grammatical rules of a C program.

An error that occurs during the linking stage is called a *linker error*. A linker error typically occurs when the linker cannot locate the file to be linked.

Finally, an error that occurs during the execution of a program is called a *runtime error*. These are the most troublesome errors to correct.

Logical errors are errors in a program that execute without performing the intended action. In this case, the program compiles and executes without complaints, but it produces incorrect results. It occurs when the logic of the program as written is different from what was actually intended. A compiler cannot find such errors, and it must be flushed out when the program runs, by testing it and carefully looking at its output. The programmer is responsible for inspecting and testing the program to guard against logical errors.

12. What is a debugger?

A debugger is a programming tool that is used to debug a program, i.e., to correct the logical errors. Using a debugger, one can control a program while it is running. The execution of the program can be stopped at some point and the values in the different variables can be checked and these values can be amended if desired. In this way, the logical errors can be traced in the program and it can be seen whether the program is producing correct results. This tool is very powerful and complex.

13. What is the function of a loader?

After an executable program is linked and saved on the disk, it is ready for execution. A program called *loader* is needed to load the program into memory and then instruct the processor to execute the program from the first instruction (the starting point of every C program is from the main function). This processor is known as a loader. Linkers and loaders are the parts of development environment. In fact, these are the parts of system software.

14. What do you mean by high-level and low-level programming languages? Differentiate between them.

Both assembly language and machine language are considered as *low-level languages.* The instructions in these languages have to take into account the physical characteristics of the machine. Maybe these features are completely irrelevant to the algorithm, but they have to be considered while writing programs or developing algorithms.

High-level programming languages, on the other hand, are those which support the use of constructs that use appropriate abstraction mechanisms to ensure that they are independent of the physical characteristics of the computer. The term 'high-level' refers to the fact that the programming statements are expressed in a form approaching natural language, far removed from the machine language that is ultimately executed.

The difference between high-level languages and low-level languages is summarized in the following table.

High-level Language	Low-level Language
One instruction = many machine code instructions	One instruction = one machine code instruction
Portable, task-oriented	Machine specific, machine-oriented
More English-like	Less easy to write and debug

EXERCISE

1. What do you mean by a program?
2. Distinguish between system software and application software.
3. State the advantages and disadvantages of machine language and assembly language.
4. Compare and contrast assembly language and high-level language.
5. Differentiate between 3GL and 4GL.
6. What is a translator?
7. What are the differences between a compiler and an interpreter?
8. Briefly explain the compilation and execution of a program written in high-level language.
9. Briefly explain linker and loader? Is there any difference between them?
10. Explain linking loader and linkage editor?
11. Classify the programming languages.
12. What is a functional language?
13. What is an object-oriented language? Name five object-oriented programming languages. State the most common features of object-oriented programming.
14. What do you mean by structured programming? State the properties of structured programming.
15. What is top-down analysis? Describe the steps involved in top-down analysis.
16. What is a structured code?
17. What is an algorithm?
18. Write down an algorithm that describes making a telephone call. Can it be done without using control statements?
19. Write algorithms to do the following:
    (a) Check whether a year given by the user is a leap year or not.
    (b) Given an integer number in seconds as input, print the equivalent time in hours, minutes, and seconds as output. The recommended output format is something like:

    7,322 seconds is equivalent to 2 hours 2 minutes 2 seconds.
    (c) Print the numbers that do not appear in the Fibonacci series. The number of terms to be printed should be given by the user.
    (d) Convert an integer number in decimal to its binary equivalent.
    (e) Find the prime factors of a number given by the user.
    (f) Check whether a number given by the user is a Krishnamurty number or not. A Krishnamurty number is one for which the sum of the factorials of its digits equals the number. For example, 145 is a Krishnamurty number.
    (g) Print the second largest number of a list of numbers given by the user.

(h) Print the sum of the following series:

(i) $1 - \dfrac{x^2}{2!} + \dfrac{x^4}{4!} - \cdots$ up to n terms where n is given by the user

(ii) $1 - \dfrac{1}{2} + \dfrac{1}{3} - \cdots$ up to n terms where n is given by the user

(iii) $1 + \dfrac{1}{2!} + \dfrac{1}{3!} + \cdots$ up to n terms where n is given by the user

20. By considering the algorithmic language that has been taught, answer the following:

   (a) Show clearly the steps of evaluating the following expressions:

   (i) $x - y + 12 * 3/6 + k \wedge x$ where $x = 2, y = 6, k = 5$

   (ii) a AND b OR (m < n) where a = true, b = false, m = 7, n = 9

   (b) State whether each of the following is correct or wrong. Correct the error(s) where applicable.

   (i) The expression ('35' = '035') is true.

   (ii) $x_1 - x_2 * 4$ value

   (iii) INPUT K, Y – Z

21. Write an algorithm as well as draw a flowchart for the following:

Input

- the item ID number
- the Number On Hand
- the Price per item
- the Weight per item in kg
- the Number Ordered
- the Shipping Zone (1 letter, indicating the distance to the purchaser)

Processing

The program will read each line from the user and calculate the following:

Total Weight = Weight Per Item * Number Ordered

Weight Cost = 3.40 + Total Weight / 5.0

Shipping cost is calculated as follows:

```
If Shipping Zone is 'A'
   Then Shipping Cost is 3.00
If Shipping Zone is 'B'
   Then Shipping Cost = 5.50
If Shipping Zone is 'C'
   Then Shipping Cost = 8.75
Otherwise Shipping Cost is 12.60
```

Handling Charges = 4.00, a constant

New Number On Hand = Number On Hand Number Ordered

Discount is calculated as follows:

```
If New Number On Hand < 0
   Then Discount = 5.00
   Else Discount = 0
```

Here the purchaser is being given a discount if the item has to be repeat ordered. Total cost is calculated as follows:

```
Total Cost
   = Price of Each * Number Ordered +
   Handling Charge + Weight Cost +
   Shipping Cost - Discount
```

For each purchase, print out the information about the purchase in a format approximately like this:

```
Item Number:    345612
Number Ordered: 1
Number On Hand: 31
Price of Each:  19.95
Weight of Each: 3
Shipping Zone:  A
Total Cost:     30.95
```

After all the purchases are finished, print two lines stating the total number of purchases and the total cost of all purchases.

22. Fill in the blanks.

   (i) A program flowchart indicates the _____ to be performed and the _____ in which they occur.

   (ii) A program flowchart is generally read from _____ to _____.

   (iii) Flowcharting symbols are connected together by means of _____.

   (iv) A decision symbol may be used in determining the _____ or _____ of two data items.

   (v) _____ are used to join remote portions of a flowchart.

   (vi) _____ connectors are used when a flowchart ends on one page and begins again on another page.

   (vii) A _____ symbol is used at the beginning and end of a flowchart.

   (viii) The flowchart is one of the best ways of _____ a program.

   (ix) To construct a flowchart, one must adhere to prescribed symbols provided by the _____.

   (x) The programmer uses a _____ to aid him in drawing flowchart symbols.

23. Define a flowchart. What is its use?

24. Are there any limitations of a flowchart?

25. Draw a flowchart to read a number given in units of length and print out the area of a circle of that radius. Assume that the value of pi is 3.14159. The output should take the form: The area of a circle of radius _____ units is _____ units.

26. Draw a flowchart to read a number N and print all its divisors.

27. Draw a flowchart for computing the sum of the digits of any given number.

28. Draw a flowchart to find the sum of N odd numbers.

29. Draw a flowchart to compute the sum of squares of integers from 1 to 50.

30. Write a program to read two integers with the following significance.

The first integer value represents a time of day on a 24-hour clock, so that 1245 represents quarter to one mid-day.

The second integer represents a time duration in a similar way, so that 345 represents three hours and 45 minutes.

This duration is to be added to the first time and the result printed out in the same notation, in this case 1630 which is the time 3 hours and 45 minutes after 1245.

Typical output might be: start time is 1415. Duration is 50. End time is 1505.

CASE STUDY

Problem Statement

Write an algorithm to compute and print the sum of the following series:

$$x - \frac{x^3}{3!} + \frac{x^5}{5!} - \frac{x^7}{7!} + \cdots$$

Analysis

From the problem statement, it is evident that the value of x and the number of terms to be summed up should be taken as input and the sum has to be printed.

Analyzing the expression for the above series, it is seen that the powers and the factorials vary in the sequence 1, 3, 5, 7, ... Thus,

$$\frac{x}{1!}$$

$$\frac{x^3}{3!} = \frac{x\ x\ x}{3\ 2\ 1} = \frac{x}{1!}\frac{x^2}{3\ 2}$$

$$\frac{x^5}{5!} = \frac{x\ x\ x\ x\ x}{5\ 4\ 3\ 2\ 1} = \frac{x^3}{3!}\frac{x^2}{5\ 4}$$

$$\frac{x^7}{7!} = \frac{x\ x\ x\ x\ x\ x\ x}{7\ 6\ 5\ 4\ 3\ 2\ 1} = \frac{x^5}{5!}\frac{x^2}{7\ 6}$$

and so on.

Therefore each term in the given series can be described as $T_k = T_{k-1} \times t$,

where T_k is the kth term and T_{k-1} is the $(k-1)^{th}$ term, while the variable t for each of the terms are:

$$\frac{x^2}{3\ 2}, \frac{x^2}{5\ 4}, \frac{x^2}{7\ 6}, \frac{x^2}{9\ 8},$$

respectively. So t can be described by the general form

$$\frac{x^2}{i.(i-1)} \text{ for } i = 3, 5, 7, 9, \cdots$$

The following expression can be used repetitively to generate the positive and negative sign for the alternative terms:

```
sign = -1 × sign
```

The initial value of k should be 1. At each iteration, 2 is added to k so that the values of k is generated as 3, 5, 7, ... and so on. For each iteration, the term is given by the following statement.

```
T = (-1) * T * x * x / (i * (i - 1))
```

The initial value of T is x. The sum of terms should be calculated by the statement S = S + T.

The initial value of S is 0.

Having evolved the above expressions, the following statements should be repeated for N times, where N is the number of terms to be summed up to give the final sum of the series.

```
S = S + T
i = i + 2
T = (1) * T * x * x / (i * (i - 1))
```

The number of iterations can be controlled by using a counter variable c. It may be initialized to 1 and the iterations should continue for the values 1, 2, 3, 4, ... N.

Here i can be used to control the iteration. The value of i varies in the sequence 1, 3, 5, 7, ... It is therefore clear that to repeat the iteration twice, the values of i should be 1 and 3. To iterate thrice, the values of i should be 1, 3 and 5. To repeat the statements four times, the values of i should be 1, 3, 5, and 7. Thus it is obvious that the final value of i is just one short of the twice the number of repetitions. Therefore, the condition for which iteration should continue is given by the expression i < N * 2. Finally the algorithm is created as shown below.

Algorithm

```
1.  START
2.  PRINT "ENTER THE VALUE OF X"
3.  INPUT X
4.  PRINT "HOW MANY TERMS?"
5.  INPUT N
6.  I ← 1
7.  T ← X
8.  S ← 0
9.  S ← S + T
10. I ← I + 2
11. T ← (-1)*T*X*X/(I*(I-1))
12. IF I < N*2 THEN GOTO 9
13. PRINT S
14. STOP
```

C

Basics of C

Chapter 3

Learning Objectives

After reading this chapter, the readers will be able to

- understand the basic structure of a program in C
- learn the commands used in Unix/Linux and MS-DOS for compiling and running a program in C
- obtain a preliminary idea of the keywords in C
- learn the data types, variables, constants, operators, and expressions in C
- understand and grasp the precedence and associativity rules of operators in C
- get acquainted with the rules of type conversions in C

3.1 INTRODUCTION

The story of C started with the Common Programming Language (CPL) which Martin Richards at the University of Cambridge turned into Basic Combined Programming Language (BCPL). This was essentially a type-less language, which allowed the user direct access to the computer memory. This made it useful to system programmers.

Ken Thompson at Bell Labs, USA, wrote his own variant of this language and called it B. In due course, the designers of Unix modified it to produce a programming language called C. Dennis Ritchie, also at Bell Labs, is credited for designing C in the early 1970s. Subsequently, Unix was rewritten entirely in C. In 1983, an ANSI standard for C emerged, consolidating its international acceptance.

Ninety percent of the code of the Unix operating system and of its descendants is written in C. The name C is doubly appropriate being the successor of B and BCPL. It has often been said, and with some justification, that C is the FORTRAN of system software. Just as FORTRAN compilers liberated programmers from creating programs for specific machines, the development of C has freed them to write system software without having to worry about the architecture of the target machine. Where architecture-dependent code, i.e., assembly code is necessary, it can usually be invoked from within the C environment. Today it is the chosen language for system programming, for the development of 4GL packages such as dbase, and also for the creation of user-friendly interfaces for special applications. But application programmers admire C for its elegance, brevity, and the versatility of its operators and control structures. C may be termed as a mid-level language, not as low-level as assembly and not as high-level as BASIC.

C is a high-level language which also provides the capabilities that enable the programmers to 'get in close' with the hardware and allows them to interact with the computer on a much lower level.

3.1.1 Why Learn C?

There are a large number of programming languages in the world today—C++, Java, Ada, BASIC, COBOL, Perl, Pascal, Smalltalk, FORTRAN, etc. Even so, there are several reasons to learn C, some of which are stated as follows.

- *C is a core language*   In computing, C is a general-purpose, cross-platform, block structured, procedural, imperative computer programming language. A number of common and popular computer languages are based on C. Having learnt C, it will be much easier to learn languages that are largely or in part based upon C. Such languages include C++, Java, and Perl.

- *C is a small language*   C has only 32 keywords and only about 20 of them are in common use. This makes it relatively easy to learn compared to bulkier languages.

- *C is quick*   We can write codes which run quickly, and the program can be very 'close to the hardware'. which mean you can access low level facilities in your computer quite easily, without the compiler or run-time system stopping you from doing something potentially dangerous.

- *C is portable*   C programs written on one system can be run with little or no modification on other systems. If modifications are necessary, they can often be made by simply changing a few entries in a header file accompanying the main program. The use of compiler directives to the pre-processor makes it possible to produce a single version of a program which can be compiled on several different types of computer. In this sense C is said to be very portable. The function libraries are standard for all versions of C so they can be used on all systems.

3.1.2 The Future of C

The story of C is not yet over. During the time when the X3J11 committee moved steadily towards producing the ANSI C standard, another researcher, Bjarne Stroustrup of Bell Laboratories began experimenting with an object-oriented flavour of C that he called C++ (pronounced C *plus plus*). C++ extended C, and according to Stroustrup, refined the language, making C++, in his words, 'a better C'.

Apparently, the X3J11 committee agreed, if not completely, and they adopted some of Stroustrup's proposals into the ANSI C standard. Subsequently, a new committee was formed to investigate a standard for ANSI C++ that is now ready. Does this new standard mean that ANSI C is destined to join its ancestors BCPL, B, and K&R C on the heap of discarded programming languages?

The answer is a solid no. Frankly, C++ is not for everyone. When learning C, it is best to stick to the basics, and readers would be well advised to ignore some of the more advanced elements found in C++. For example, C++ provides classes for *object-oriented programming*, or OOP as it is known. Until one knows C, one is not ready for OOP.

On the other hand, because C++ is based on ANSI C, one may as well use modern next-generation C++ compilers to write C programs. That way, one can take advantage of both worlds. After learning C, one is ready to tackle OOP and other advanced C++ subjects.

3.2 STANDARDIZATIONS OF C LANGUAGE

Both Unix and C were created at AT&T's Bell Laboratories in the late 1960s and early 1970s. During the 1970s the C programming language became increasingly popular. Many universities and organizations began creating their own variations of the language for their own projects.

During the late 1970s and 1980s, various versions of C were implemented for a wide variety of mainframe computers, minicomputers, and microcomputers, including the IBM PC. In the early 1980s, a need was realized to standardize the definition of the C language which in turn would help C become more widespread in commercial programming.

In 1983 the American National Standards Institute (ANSI) formed a committee to establish a standard specification of C known as 'ANSI C'. This work ended in the creation of the so-called C89 standard in 1989. Part of the resulting standard was a set of software libraries called the ANSI C standard library. This version of the language is often referred to as ANSI C, Standard C, or sometimes

C89. ISO/IEC standard was thereafter adopted by ANSI and people referred to this common standard as simply 'standard' or simply 'C89'.

In 1990, the ANSI C standard (with a few minor modifications) was modified by the International Organization for Standardization (ISO) as ISO/IEC 9899:1990. This version is sometimes called C90. Therefore, the terms 'C89' and 'C90' refer to essentially the same language.

Changes included in C89 are as follows:

- The addition of truly standard library.
- New preprocessor commands and features.
- Function prototypes which specify the argument types in a function declaration.
- Some new keywords `const`, `volatile` and `signed`.
- Wide characters, wide strings and multi-byte characters.
- Many smaller changes and clarification to conversion rules, declarations and type checking.

C89 is supported by current C compilers, and most C code being written nowadays is based on it. In 1995, amendments to C89 include:

- Three new library headers: `iso646.h`, `wctype.h` and `wchar.h`.
- Some new formatting codes for the `printf` and `scanf` family of functions.
- A large number of functions plus some types and constants for multi-byte and wide characters.

With the evolution of C++, the standardization of C language began to be revised again. Some amendments and corrections to C89 standard were made and a new standard for the C language was created in 1995. In 1999, a more extensive revision to the C standard began. It was completed and approved in 1999. This new version is known as 'ISO/IEC 9899:1999' or simply 'C99' and has now become the official standard C. The following features were included:

- Support for complex arithmetic
- inline functions
- several new data types, including `long long int`, optional extended integer types, an explicit `boolean` data type, and a `complex` type to represent complex numbers
- Variable length arrays
- Better support for non-English characters sets
- Better support for floating-point types including math functions for all types

- C++ style comments (//)
- new header files, such as `stdbool.h` and `inttypes.h`
- type-generic math functions (`tgmath.h`)
- improved support for IEEE floating point
- variable declaration no longer restricted to file scope or the start of a compound statement

GCC and other C compilers now support many of the new features of C99. However, there has been less support from vendors such as Microsoft and Borland that have mainly focused on C++, since C++ provides similar functionality improvement. According to Sun Microsystems, Sun Studio (which is freely downloadable) now supports the full C99 standard.

In 2007, a new version known as ISO/IEC 9899:2011 or C11 standardization was released. It was designed to promote the portability of C programs among different platforms and computing environments. It has been revised by ISO/IEC 9899:2018 which was released in June 2018.

Most C implementations are actually C/C++ implementations giving programmers a choice of which language to use. It is possible to write C code in the common subset of the standard C/C++ language compiler so that code can be compiled either as a C program or a C++ program.

3.3 DEVELOPING PROGRAMS IN C

While developing a program in C, three distinct steps are involved. These steps are executed in the sequence given below:

1. Writing the C program,
2. Compiling the program and
3. Executing the program.

For these steps, some software components are required, namely an operating system, a text editor, a C compiler, an assembler, and a linker. The editor is used to create and modify the program code while the compiler transforms the source program to object code. Operating system is responsible for the execution of the program. There are several editors which provide a complete environment for writing, managing, developing, and testing the C programs. This is sometimes called an integrated development environment, or IDE.

Figure 3.2 depicts the sequential implementation of the program development stages or processes, regardless of the operating system or compiler. A brief explanation of each of the processes involved in the compilation model is given in the following sections.

Writing or Editing: This activity consists of writing a new program code or editing an existing source program using a text editor or an IDE and saving it with .c extension.

Programming Environment Most programming language compilers come with a specific editor that can provide facilities for managing the programs. Such an editor offers a complete environment for writing, developing, modifying, deploying, testing, and debugging the programs. Such software is referred to as an **integrated development environment** or **IDE**. An IDE is typically dedicated to a specific programming language. It thus incorporates features compatible with the particular programming paradigm.

Many IDEs have a Build option, which compiles and links a program in one step. This option will usually be found, within an IDE, in the Compile menu; alternatively, it may have a menu of its own. In most IDEs, an appropriate menu command allows one to run or execute or debug the compiled program. In Windows, one can run the .exe file for the corresponding source program like any other executable program. The processes of editing, compiling, linking, and executing are essentially the same for developing programs in any environment and with any compiled language.

A simple programming environment specially designed for C and C++ programming on Windows is the Quincy IDE. Figure 3.1(a) shows a screenshot of the Quincy environment. Quincy can be freely downloaded from http://www.codecutter.net.

Figure 3.1(a)   Screenshot of quincy

There are many other IDEs available. DevC++ is one of the most popular C++ IDEs amongst the student community. DevC++ is a free IDE distributed under the GNU General Public License for programming in C/C++. It is bundled with MinGW, a free compiler. It can be downloaded from the URL http://www.bloodshed.net.

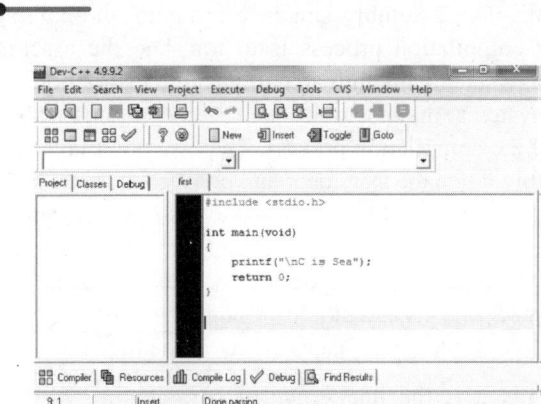

Figure 3.1(b)   Screenshot of Dev C++

In Unix or Linux, the most common text editor is the vi editor. Alternately, one might prefer to use the emacs editor. The vi editor is simpler, smaller, and faster, and has limited customization capabilities, whereas emacs has a larger set of commands and is extensible and customizable. On a PC, a user could use one of the many freeware and shareware programming editors available. These will often provide a lot of help in ensuring the code to be correct with syntax highlighting and auto-indenting of the code.

Preprocessing: It is the first phase of C compilation. It processes include-files, conditional compilation instructions, and macros. The C preprocessor is used to modify the program according to the preprocessor directives in the source code. A preprocessor directive is a statement (such as #define) that gives the preprocessor specific instructions on how to modify the source code. The preprocessor is invoked as the first part of the compiler program's compilation step. It is usually hidden from the programmer because it is run automatically by the compiler.

Compilation: It is the second step of the compiling process. It takes the output of the preprocessor, and the source code, and generates assembler source code. The compiler examines each program statement contained in the source program and checks it to ensure that it conforms to the syntax and semantics of the language. If any mistakes are discovered by the compiler during this phase, they are reported to the user. The errors then have to be corrected in the source program (with the use of an editor), and the program has to be recompiled.

Assembly: It is the third stage of compilation. It takes the assembly source code and produces an assembly listing with offsets. The assembler output is stored in an object file. After the program has been translated into an equivalent assembly language program, the next step in the compilation process is to translate the assembly language statements into actual machine instructions. On most systems, the assembler is executed automatically as part of the compilation process. The assembler takes each assembly language statement and converts it into a binary format known as *object code*, which is then written into another file on the system. This file typically has the same name as the source file under Unix, with the last letter an 'o' (for *object*) instead of a 'c'. Under Windows, the suffix letter 'obj' typically replaces the 'c' in the filename.

Linking: It is the final stage of compilation. After the program has been translated into object code, it is ready to be linked. The purpose of the linking phase is to get the program into a final form for execution on the computer. The functions are the part of the standard C library, provided by every C compiler. The program may use other source programs that were previously processed by the compiler. These functions are stored as separate object files which must be linked to the object file. Linker handles this linking.

The process of compiling and linking a program is often called *building*. The final linked file, which is in an *executable object* code format, is stored in another file on the system, ready to be run or *executed*. Under Unix, this file is called 'a.out' by default. Under Windows, the executable file usually has the same name as the source file, with the .c extension replaced by an .exe extension.

When the program is executed, each of the statements of the program is sequentially executed. If the program requests any data from the user, known as *input*, the program temporarily suspends its execution so that the input can be entered. Or, the program might simply wait for an *event*, such as a mouse being clicked, to occur. Results that are displayed by the program, known as *output*, appear in a window, sometimes called the *console*. Or, the output might be directly written to a file on the system.

If all goes well the program performs its intended task. If the program does not produce the desired results, it is necessary to go back and reanalyze the program. There are three types of errors that may occur:

- *Compiler errors* These are given by the compiler and prevent the program from running.
- *Linking errors* These are given by the linker or at runtime and ends the program. The linker can also detect and report errors, for example, if part of the program is missing or a non-existent library component is referenced.
- *Runtime errors* These are given by the operating system.

Removing errors from a program is called *debugging*. Any type of error in a program is known as *bug*. During *debugging*, an attempt is made to remove all the known problems or *bugs* from the program. By tracing the program step-by-step, keeping track of each variable, the programmer monitors the program state. The *program state* is simply the set of values of all the variables at a given point in program execution. It is a snapshot of the current state of computation.

A *debugger* is a program that enables the programmer to run another program step-by-step and examine the value of that program's variables. Debuggers come in various levels of ease of use and sophistication. The more advanced debuggers show which line of source code is being executed.

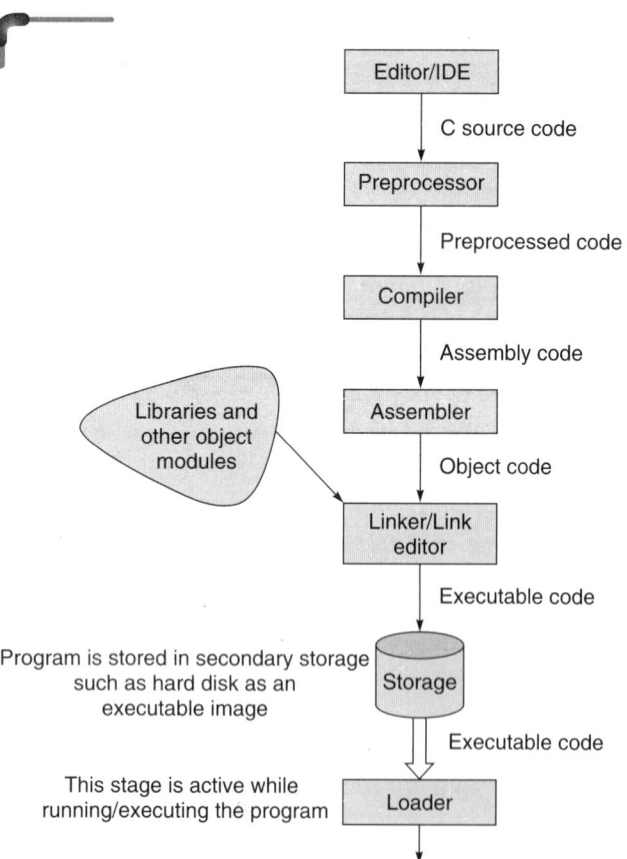

Figure 3.2 Typical steps for entering, compiling, and executing C programs

In the Unix/Linux operating system environment, the program is stored in a file, the name of which ends in '.c'. This means that the extension of the file will be '.c'. This identifies it as a C program. The easiest way to enter text is by using a text editor such as vi, emacs, or xedit. The editor is also used to make subsequent changes to the program. To create or edit a file called 'first.c' using vi editor, the user has to enter vi first.c.

Most of the Windows-based C compilers have an inbuilt context-sensitive editor to write C programs. The program filename should have a '.c' extension.

To compile a C program in Unix simply invoke the command cc. The command must be followed by the name of the C program that has to be compiled. A number of compiler options can be specified also. But only some useful and essential options would be dealt with here; these are introduced below.

In the Unix operating system, to compile a C source program, where first.c is the name of the file, the command is

```
cc first.c
```

In the Linux operating system, a C source program, where first.c is the name of the file, can be compiled by the command

```
gcc first.c
```

The GNU C compiler GCC is popular and available for many platforms. If there are syntax errors in the program due to wrong typing, misspelling one of the keywords, or omitting a semicolon, the compiler detects and reports them. There may, of course, still be logical errors that the compiler cannot detect. The program code may be directing the computer to do the wrong operations.

When the compiler has successfully translated the program, the compiled version, or the executable program code is stored in a file called a.out or if the compiler option −o is used, the executable program code is put in the file listed after the −o option specified in the compilation command.

It is more convenient to use −o and file name in the compilation as shown.

```
cc -o program first.c
```

This puts the compiled program into the file program or any filename following the −o argument, instead of putting it in the file a.out.

PC users may also be familiar with the Borland C compiler. Borland International has introduced many C compilers such as Turbo C, Turbo C++, and Borland C++.

It should be noted here that C++ is the superset of C and has the same syntax. A C program can be compiled by a C++ compiler. In all these cases, the actual computer program development environment comes in two forms.

To run the executable file, the command for both Unix and Linux operating system is

```
./a.out
```

To run an executable program in Unix, simply type the name of the file that contains it; in this case first instead of a.out. This executes the program, displaying the results on the screen. At this stage there may be run-time errors, such as division by zero, or it may become evident that the program has produced incorrect output. If so, the programmer must return to edit the source program, recompile it, and run it again.

Now, to run a C program in the Borland environment, if the MS-DOS prompt obtained while compiling has not been closed.

1. The following prompt would be visible on the screen:
   ```
   c:\borland\bcc55\bin>
   ```
2. Enter
   ```
   c:\borland\bcc55\bin> cd c:\cprg
   ```
3. Press **<Enter>**. This changes the directory to one where the following MS-DOS prompt would be seen:
   ```
   c:\cprg>
   ```
4. Enter first.exe or simply first, and the screen would display
   ```
   c:\cprg>first.exe or c:\cprg>first
   ```
5. Press **<Enter>** to run the program and its output would be available.

For compiling a C program in the Borland C compiler, the given steps must be followed.

1. Open MS-DOS prompt.
2. At the prompt
   ```
   c:\windows>
   ```
   give the following command:
   ```
   c:\windows>cd c:\borland\bcc55\bin
   ```
   Press **<Enter>**.

   This changes the directory to c:\borland\bcc55\bin and the following prompt appears:
   ```
   c:\borland\bcc55\bin>
   ```
   Now, enter
   ```
   bcc32 -If:\borland\bcc55\include
        -Lf:\borland\bcc55\Lib c:\cprg\first.c
   ```
3. Press **<Enter>**.

3.4 A SIMPLE C PROGRAM

The best way to learn C or any programming language is to begin writing programs in it.

Let us write the first program named first.c as follows:

```
/* A Simple C Program */

#include <stdio.h>
int main(void)
{
  printf("C is Sea\n");
  return 0;
}
```

There are a few important points to note about this program. These are common to all C programs.

```
/* A Simple C Program */
```

This is a comment line.

In C, the comments can be included in the program. The comment lines start with /* and terminate with */. These statements can be put anywhere in the program. The compiler considers these as non-executable statements.

The comment lines are included in a program to describe the variables used and the job performed by a set of program instructions or an instruction. Comment lines may also be written to record any other information that may be necessary for the programmer and relevant to the program.

According to C99, a comment also begins with // and extends up to the next line break. So the above comment line can be written as follows:

```
// A Simple C Program
```

// comments were added to C99 due to their utility and widespread existing practice, especially in dual C and C++ translators.

```
#include <stdio.h>
```

In C, all lines that begin with # are directives for the preprocessor, which means that all these directives will be processed before the program is actually compiled. The #include directive includes the contents of a file during compilation. In this case, the file stdio.h is added in the source program before the actual compilation begins. stdio.h is a header file that comes with the C compiler and contains information about input and output functions e.g. printf().

For now it may be noted that there are two ways in which the preprocessor directives differ from program statements: (a) they must begin in the first column and no spaces are allowed between '#' and include and (b) they are not terminated by a semicolon.

```
int main(void)
```

Every C program contains a function called main. This is the starting point of the program. A C program may contain one or more functions one of which must be main(). Functions are the building blocks of a C program. For now the functions may be recognized by the presence of parentheses after their names. When a C program is executed, main() is where the action starts. Then, other functions maybe 'invoked' or called.

A function is a sub-program that contains instructions or statements to perform a specific computation or processing. When its instructions have been executed, the function returns control to the calling point, to which it may optionally return the results of its computations. Since main() is also a function from which control returns to the operating system at program termination, in ANSI C it is customary, although not required, to include a statement in main() which explicitly returns control to the operating environment.

For the Watcom C/C++, IBM VisualAge C/C++, and Microsoft Visual C/C++ compilers, the function main can also be declared to return void. The compilers MetaWare High C/C++ and EMX C/C++ do not allow main to have a return type void. For these compilers, the return type of main has to be declared as int. Borland C/C++, Comeau C/C++, and Digital Mars C/C++ compilers do not explicitly list void main() as a legal definition of main, but somewhat ironically there are example codes using this non-conforming definition on main.

```
{}
```

This is a *brace*. As the name implies, braces come in packs of two, i.e. for every open brace there must be a close brace. Braces allow to lump pieces of program together. Such a lump of program is often called a *block*. A block can contain the declaration of variables used within it, followed by a sequence of program statements which are executed in order. In this case the braces enclose the working parts of the function main. When the compiler sees the matching close brace at the end it knows that it has reached the end of the function and can look for another (if any).

By enclosing the program instructions, printf() and return 0 within the opening brace '{' and the closing brace '}', a block of program instruction is formed. Such a block of program instructions, within these braces, form the body of the function main().

```
printf("C is Sea\n");
```

printf() is a 'library function'

The \n (pronounced backslash n) in the string argument of the function printf()

```
"C is Sea\n"
```

is an example of an escape sequence. It is used to print the new line character. If the program is executed, the \n does not appear in the output. Each \n in the string argument of a printf() causes the cursor to be placed at the beginning of the next line of output. Think of an escape sequence as a 'substitute character' for outputting special characters or some positional action on the printing point, known as cursor, when the output device is a visual display unit.

All escape sequences available in C are given in Table 3.1. Placing any of these within a string causes either the indicated action or the related character to be output.

```
return 0;
```

This statement indicates that the value returned by the function main(), after the program instructions in its body are executed, to the operating system is 0. Though the value, recognized by the OS as *status,* is returned using the return 0 statement, the OS may not always use it.

The return statement is not mandatory; if it is missing, the program will still terminate. In C89, the value returned to the operating system is undefined. In C99, if main() is declared to return an int, the program returns 0 (zero) to the operating system or operating environment; otherwise the program returns an unspecified value.

Throughout this book, at the end of every function definition for main(), the return 0 instruction must be written. Function definition means the sequence of instructions that form the body of the function which performs the desired task. Similarly, main() should always be written as int main(void) in every program given in this book.

The above discussion is summarized in Fig. 3.3.

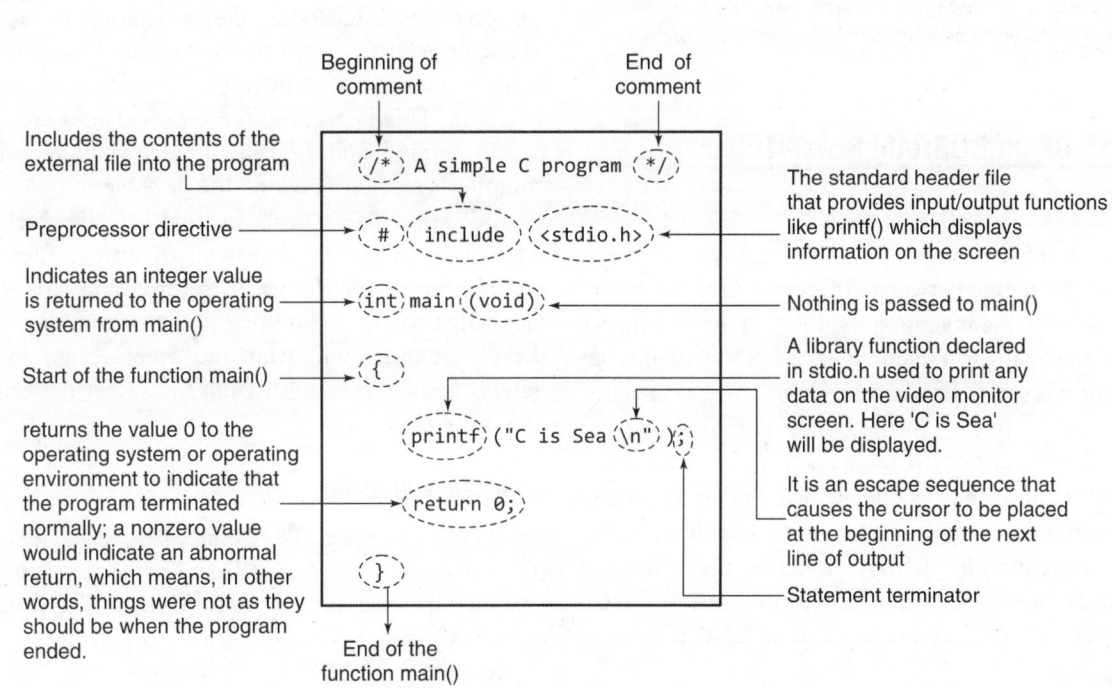

Figure 3.3   An Illustrated version of first.c

Table 3.1 Backslash codes

Code	Meaning
\a	Ring terminal bell (a is for alert) [ANSI extension]
\?	Question mark [ANSI extension]
\b	Backspace
\r	Carriage return
\f	Form feed
\t	Horizontal tab
\v	Vertical tab
\0	ASCII null character
\\	Backslash
\"	Double quote
\'	Single quote
\n	New line
\o	Octal constant
\x	Hexadecimal constant

Points to Note

1. C uses a semicolon as a statement terminator; the semicolon is required as a signal to the compiler to indicate that a statement is complete.

2. All program instructions, which are also called statements, have to be written in lower case characters.

3.5 PARTS OF C PROGRAM REVISITED

Header files

A header file is a file containing C declarations and macro definitions to be shared between different source files.

In C, the usual convention is to give header files names that end with .h. Functions in the ANSI C library are declared in a set of standard headers. This set is self-consistent and is free of name space pollution, when compiling in the pure ANSI mode. The ISO C standard library consists of 24 header files which can be included into a programmer's project with a single directive. Each header file contains one or more function declarations, data type definitions and macros. Later revisions of the C standard have added several new required header files to the library:

- The headers <iso646.h>, <wchar.h>, and <wctype.h> were added with Normative Addendum 1 (hereafter abbreviated as NA1), an addition to the C Standard ratified in 1995.

- The headers <complex.h>, <fenv.h>, <inttypes.h>, <stdbool.h>, <stdint.h>, and <tgmath.h> were added with C99, a revision to the C Standard published in 1999.

The following list contains the set of standard headers:

```
assert.h    inttypes.h  signal.h    stdlib.h
complex.h   iso646.h    stdarg.h    string.h
ctype.h     limits.h    stdbool.h   tgmath.h
errno.h     locale.h    stddef.h    time.h
fenv.h      math.h      stdint.h    wchar.h
float.h     setjmp.h    stdio.h     wctype.h
```

There are two ways of including files in C programs. The first way is to surround the file you want to include with the angled brackets < and > that is like #include <filename>. This method of inclusion tells the preprocessor to look for the file in the predefined default location. This predefined default location is often an INCLUDE environment variable that denotes the path to the include-files. On Unix systems, standard include-files reside under /usr/include.

The second way to include files is to surround the file that is required to be included with double quotation marks like #include "filename". This method of inclusion tells the preprocessor to look for the file in the current directory first, then look for it in the predefined locations the programmer has set up. The #include <filename> method of file inclusion is often used to include standard header files such as stdio.h or stdlib.h. This is because these header files are rarely (if ever) modified, and they should always be read from the compiler's standard include-file directory.

The #include "file" method of file inclusion is often used to include nonstandard header files that the programmer creates for use in the program. This is because these files are often modified in the current directory, and the programmer will want the preprocessor to use the newly modified version of the file rather than the older, unmodified version.

Philosophy of main()

main() is a user-defined function. main() is the first function in the program which gets called when the program executes. The startup code calls main() function. The programmer cannot change the name of the main() function.

According to ANSI/ISO/IEC 9899:1990 International Standard for C, the function called at program startup is named main. The implementation declares no prototype for this function. It can be defined with no parameters:

```
int main(void) { /* ... */ }
```

or with two parameters (referred to here as argc and argv, though any names may be used, as they are local to the function in which they are declared):

```
int main(int argc, char *argv[ ]) { /* ... */ }
```

On many operating systems, the value returned by main() is used to return an exit status to the environment. On Unix, MS-DOS, and Windows systems, the low eight bits of the value returned by main( ) is passed to the command shell or calling program. It is extremely common for a program to return a result indication to the operating system. Some operating systems require a result code. And the return value from main(), or the equivalent value passed in a call to the exit() function, is translated by the compiler into an appropriate code.

There are three and only three completely standard and portable values to return from main() or to pass to exit():

- The plain old ordinary integer value 0.
- The constant EXIT_SUCCESS defined in stdlib.h
- The constant EXIT_FAILURE defined in stdlib.h

If 0 or EXIT_SUCCESS is used, the compiler's run time library is guaranteed to translate this into a result code which the operating system considers as successful.

If EXIT_FAILURE is used, the compiler's run time library is guaranteed to translate this into a result code which the operating system considers as unsuccessful.

main() is MUST

It depends on the environment the program is written for. If it's a hosted environment, then main function is a must for any standard C program. Hosted environments are those where the program runs under an operating system. If it is a freestanding environment, then main function is not required. Freestanding environments are those where the program does not depend on any host and can have any other function designated as the startup function. Freestanding implementation need not support all the standard libraries; usually only a limited number of I/O libraries will be supported and no memory management functions will be supported. Examples of freestanding implementations are embedded systems and the operating system kernel.

The following code will give a linker error in all compilers:

```
MAIN()
{
    printf("hello, world\n");
}
```

Along with the user supplied main() function all C programs include something often called the run-time support package which is actually the code that the operating system executes when starting up your program. The run-time support package then expects to call the user

supplied function main(), if there is no user supplied main() then the linker cannot finish the installation of the run-time support package. In this case the user had supplied MAIN() rather than main(). "MAIN" is a perfectly valid C function name but it isn't "main".

3.6 STRUCTURE OF A C PROGRAM

The general structure of a C program is depicted in the following figure:

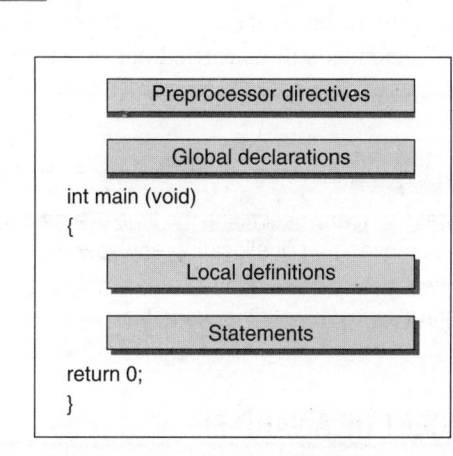

Figure 3.4 Structure of a C program

Declaration is the program statement that serves to communicate to the language translator information about the name and type of the data objects needed during program execution. As discussed before, *preprocessor directives* tell the preprocessor to look for special code libraries, make substitutions in the code and in other ways prepare the code for translation into machine language.

The basic idea behind the *global declaration* is that it is visible to all parts of the program. A more detailed discussion on global declarations has been included in Chapter 7.

All functions including main() can be divided into two sections – local definition and statements. *Local definitions* would be at the beginning of the functions which is followed by statement section. It describes the data that will be used in the function. Data objects in local definitions as opposed to global declarations are visible only to the function that contains them. *Statement section* consists of the instructions that cause the computer to do something.

The difference between a declaration and definition is important. A *declaration* announces the properties of a data object or a function. The main reason for declaring data objects and functions is for type checking. If a variable or function is declared and then later makes reference to it with data objects that do not match the types in the declaration, the compiler will show error. The purpose of the complaint is to catch type errors at compile time rather than waiting until the program is run, when the results can be more fatal.

A *definition*, on the other hand, actually sets aside storage space (in the case of a data object) or indicates the sequence of statements to be carried out (in the case of a function).

Points to Note

1. Declaration means describing the type of a data object to the compiler but not allocating any space for it.
2. Definition means declaration of a data object and also allocating space to hold the data object.

3.7 CONCEPT OF A VARIABLE

Programs operate on data. The instructions that make up the program, and the data that it acts upon, have to be stored somewhere while the computer is executing that program. A programming language must provide a way of storing the data that are to be processed, otherwise it becomes useless. In this context, it may be mentioned that a computer provides a Random Access Memory (RAM) for storing the executable program code and the data the program manipulates.

A computer memory is made up of registers and cells which are capable of holding information in the form of binary digits 0 and 1 (bits). It accesses data as a collection of bits, typically 8 bits, 16 bits, 32 bits or 64 bits. Data is stored in the memory at physical memory locations. These locations are known as memory addresses. Therefore each byte can be uniquely identified by its address (see Fig. 3.5).

The amount of bits on which it can operate simultaneously is known as the *word length* of the computer. A *word* is the natural unit of memory for a given computer design. For 8-bit microcomputers, such as the original Apple computers, a word is just 1 byte. IBM compatibles using the 80286

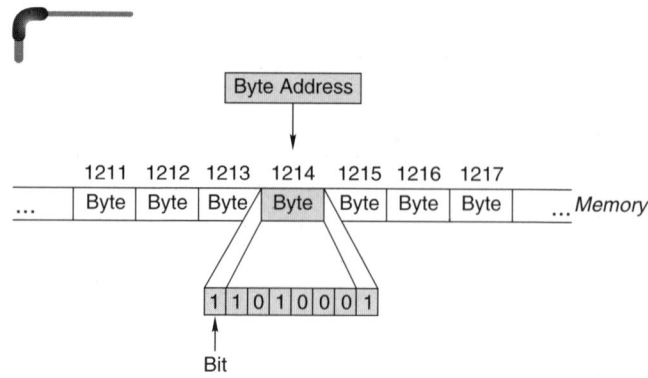

Figure 3.5 Bits and bytes in memory

processor are 16-bit machines. This means that they have a word size of 16 bits, which is 2 bytes. Machines like the Pentium-based PCs and the Macintosh PowerPCs have 32-bit words. More powerful computers can have 64-bit words or even larger. When we say that Pentium 4 is a 32 bit machine, it means that it simultaneously operates on 32 bit of data.

A variable is an identifier for a memory location in which data can be stored and subsequently recalled. Variables are used for holding data values so that they can be utilized in various computations in a program.

Variables are a way of reserving memory to hold some data and assign names to them so that we don't have to remember numbers like 46735; instead we can use the memory location by simply referring to the variable. Every variable is mapped to a unique memory address. Variables are used for holding data values so that they can be utilized in various computations in a program.

The C compiler generates an executable code which maps data entities to memory locations. For example, the variable definition

```
int salary = 65000;
```

causes the compiler to allocate a few bytes to represent salary. The exact number of bytes allocated and the method used for the binary representation of the integer depends on the specific C implementation, but let it be said that two bytes contain the encoded data as a binary number 1111110111101000. The compiler uses the *address* of the first byte at which salary is allocated to refer to it. The above assignment causes the value 65000 to be stored as a binary number in the two bytes allocated (see Fig. 3.6).

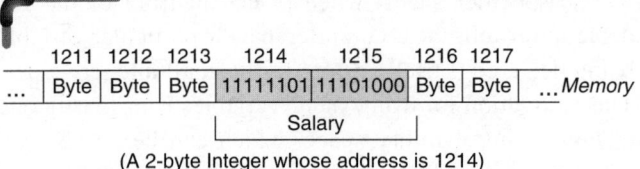

Salary

(A 2-byte Integer whose address is 1214)

Figure 3.6 Representation of an integer in memory

While the exact binary representation of a data item is rarely of interest to a programmer, the general organization of memory and use of addresses for referring to data items is very important.

All variables have three important attributes.

- A *data type* that is established when the variable is defined, e.g., integer, real, character. Once defined, the type of a C variable cannot be changed.

- A *name* of the variable.

- A *value* that can be changed by assigning a new value to the variable. The kind of values a variable can assume depends on its type. For example, an integer variable can only take integer values, e.g., 2, 100, –12.

The number of characters that you can have in a variable name will depend upon your compiler. A minimum of 31 characters must be supported by a compiler that conforms to the C language standard, so you can always use names up to this length without any problem. It is suggested not to make the variable names longer than this, as they become cumbersome and make the code harder to follow. Some compilers will truncate names that are too long.

Variable names are case sensitive, which means that the names `NUM` and `num` are distinct.

In C, a variable must be declared before it can be used. Variables can be declared at the start of any block of code, but these are mostly found at the start of each function. This serves two purposes. First, it gives the compiler precise information about the amount of memory that will be given over to a variable when a program is finally run and what sort of arithmetic will be used on it (e.g., only integer or floating point or none). Secondly, it provides the compiler with a list of the variables in a convenient place so that it can cross check names and types for any errors.

3.8 DATA TYPES IN C

The type, or data type, of a variable determines a set of values that a variable might take and a set of operations that can be applied to those values. Data types can be broadly classified as shown in Fig. 3.7.

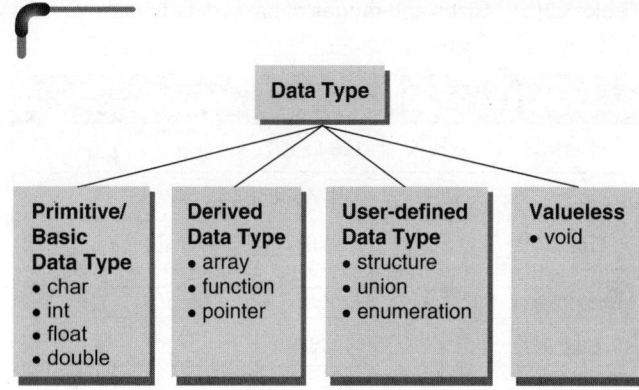

Figure 3.7 Classification of data types

C provides a standard, minimal set of basic data types. Sometimes these are called 'primitive' types. More complex data types can be built up from these basic types. C has five basic data types and they are as follows:

- Character—Keyword used is `char`
- Integer—Keyword used is `int`
- Floating point—Keyword used is `float`
- Double precision floating point—Keyword used is `double`
- Valueless—Keyword used is `void`

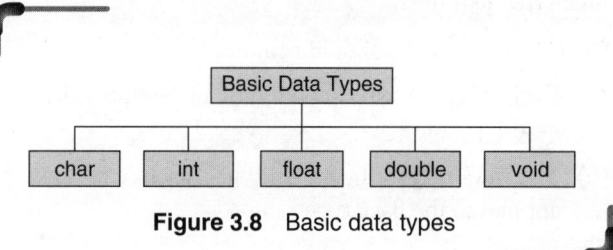

Figure 3.8 Basic data types

Table 3.2(a) lists the sizes and ranges of basic data types in C for a 16-bit computer, and Table 3.2(b) lists the sizes and ranges of basic data types in C for a 32-bit computer.

Table 3.2(a) Sizes and ranges of basic data types in C for a 16-bit computer

Data type	Size (in bits)	Range
char	8	–128 to 127
int	16	–32768 to 32767
float	32	1.17549×10^{-38} to 3.40282×10^{38}
double	64	2.22507×10^{-308} to 1.79769×10^{308}
void	8	valueless

Table 3.2(b) Sizes and ranges of basic data types in C for a 32-bit computer

Data type	Size (in bits)	Range
char	8	−128 to 127
int	32	−2147483648 to 2147483647
float	32	1.17549×10^{-38} to 3.40282×10^{38}
double	64	2.22507×10^{-308} to 1.79769×10^{308}
void	8	valueless

The C standard does not state how much precision the float and double types provide, since different computers may store floating point numbers in different ways. According to IEEE, the precisions for *float* and *double* are 6 and 15 respectively.

The void type has no values and only one operation, assignment. The void type specifies an empty set of values. It is used as the type returned by functions that generate no value. The void type never refers to an object and, therefore, is not included in any reference to object types. According to ISO/IEC draft, "The void type comprises an empty set of values; it is an incomplete type that cannot be completed."

In addition C has four type specifiers or modifiers and three type qualifiers.

The following points should be noted:

(a) Each of these type modifiers can be applied to the base type int.

(b) The modifiers signed and unsigned can also be applied to the base type char.

(c) In addition, long can be applied to double.

(d) When the base type is omitted from a declaration, int is assumed.

(e) The type void cannot be used with these modifiers.

The specifiers and qualifiers for the data types can be broadly classified into three types:

- *Size specifiers*—short and long
- *Sign specifiers*—signed and unsigned
- *Type qualifiers*—const, volatile and restrict

The *size qualifiers* alter the size of the basic data types. There are two such qualifiers that can be used with the data type int; these are short and long.

The specifier short, when placed in front of the int declaration, tells the C compiler that the particular variable being declared is used to store fairly small integer values. The motivation for using short variables is primarily one of conserving memory space, which can be an issue in situations in which the program needs a lot of memory and the amount of available memory is limited.

In any ANSI C compiler, the sizes of short int, int, and long int are restricted by the following rules.

- The minimum size of a short int is two bytes.
- The size of an int must be greater than or equal to that of a short int.
- The size of a long int must be greater than or equal to that of an int.
- The minimum size of a long int is four bytes.

In most of the DOS based compilers that work on 16-bit computers, the size of a short int and an int is the same, which is two bytes. In such compilers, a long int occupies four bytes. On the other hand, in the 32-bit machine compilers such as GNU C (GCC), an int and long int take four bytes while a short int occupies two bytes. For Unix based compilers, a short int takes two bytes, while a long int takes four bytes.

The long qualifier is also used with the basic data type double. In older compilers this qualifier was used with float, but it is not allowed in the popular compilers of today. As mentioned earlier, it may be noted here that the sign qualifiers can be used only with the basic data types int and char.

Table 3.3 lists the sizes of the short int, int and long int data types in different machines.

Table 3.3 Sizes in number of bytes of *short int*, *int* and *long int* data types in different machines

	16-bit Machine	32-bit Machine	64-bit Machine
short int	2	2	2
int	2	4	4
long int	4	4	8

C99 added two additional integer types long long int and unsigned long long int. For long long, the C99 standard specified at least 64 bits to support. Table 3.4 summarizes the size and range of different variations of long long type.

Table 3.4 Size and range of *long long* type

	Size (in bytes)	Range
long long int	8	9,223,372,036,854, 775,808 to +9,223, 372,036,854,775,807
unsigned long int or unsigned long	4	0 to 4,294,967,295
unsigned long long int or unsigned long long	8	0 to +18,446,744,073, 709,551,615

The C89 Committee added to C two *type qualifiers*, const and volatile; and C99 added a third, restrict. Type qualifiers control the way variables may be accessed or modified. They specify the variables that will never (const) change and those variables that can change unexpectedly (volatile).

Both keywords require that an associated data type be declared for the identifier, for example

```
const float pi = 3.14156;
```

specifies that the variable pi can never be changed by the program. Any attempt by code within the program to alter the value of pi will result in a compile time error. The value of a const variable must be set at the time the variable is declared. Specifying a variable as const allows the compiler to perform better optimization on the program because of the data type being known. Consider the following program:

```
#include <stdio.h>
int main(void)
{
const int value = 42;
/* constant, initialized integer variable */
value = 100;
/* wrong! - will cause compiler error */
return 0;
}
```

Point to Note

const does not turn a variable into a constant. A variable with const qualifier merely means the variable cannot be used for assignment. This makes the value read only through that variable; it does not prevent the value from being modified some other ways e.g. through pointer.

The volatile keyword indicates that a variable can unexpectedly change because of events outside the control of the program. This is usually used when some variable within the program is linked directly with some hardware component of the system. The hardware could then directly modify the value of the variable without the knowledge of the program. For example, an I/O device might need to write directly into a program or data space. Meanwhile, the program itself may never directly access the memory area in question. In such a case, we would not want the compiler to optimize-out this data area that never seems to be used by the program, yet must exist for the program to function correctly in a larger context. It tells the compiler that the object is subject to sudden change for reasons which cannot be predicted from a study of the program itself, and forces every reference to such an object to be a genuine reference.

The restrict type qualifier allows programs to be written so that translators can produce significantly faster executable code. Anyone for whom this is not a concern can safely ignore this feature of the language.

Size and range of different combinations of basic data types and modifiers are listed in Table 3.5.

Several new types that were added in C89 are listed below:

- void
- void*
- signed char
- unsigned char
- unsigned short
- unsigned long
- long double

And new designations for existing types were added in C89:

- signed short for short
- signed int for int
- signed long for long

C99 also added new types:

- _Bool
- long long
- unsigned long long
- float _Imaginary
- float _Complex
- double _Imaginary
- double _Complex
- long double _Imaginary
- long double _Complex

Table 3.5 Allowed combinations of basic data types and modifiers in C for a 16-bit computer

Data Type	Size (bits)	Range	Default Type
char	8	−128 to 127	signed char
unsigned char	8	0 to 255	None
signed char	8	−128 to 127	char
int	16	−32768 to 32767	signed int
unsigned int	16	0 to 65535	unsigned
signed int	16	−32768 to 32767	int
short int	16	−32768 to 32767	short, signed short, signed short int
unsigned short int	16	0 to 65535	unsigned short
signed short int	16	−32768 to 32767	short, signed short, short int
long int	32	−2147483648 to 2147483647	long, signed long, signed long int
unsigned long int	32	0 to 4294967295	unsigned long
signed long int	32	−2147483648 to 2147483647	long int, signed long, long
float	32	3.4E−38 to 3.4E+38	None
double	64	1.7E−308 to 1.7E+308	None
long double	80	3.4E−4932 to 1.1E+4932	None

C99 also allows extended integer types `<inttypes.h>` and `<stdint.h>` and a boolean type `<stdbool.h>`.

char A character variable occupies a single byte that contains the *code* for the character. This code is a numeric value and depends on the *character coding system* being used, i.e., it is machine-dependent. The most common coding system is ASCII (American Standard Code for Information Interchange). For example, the character 'A' has the ASCII character code 65, and the character 'a' has the ASCII code 97.

Since character variables are accommodated in a byte, C regards char as being a sub-range of int (the sub-range that fits inside a byte) and each ASCII character is for all purposes equivalent to the decimal integer value of the bit picture that defines it. Thus 'A', of which the ASCII representation is 01000001, has the arithmetical decimal value of 65. This is the decimal value of the sequence of bits 01000001, which may be easily verified. In other words, the memory representation of the char constant 'A' is indistinguishable from that of the int constant, decimal 65.

It may be observed that small int values may be stored in char variables and char values may be stored in int variables. Character variables are therefore signed quantities restricted to the value range [−128 to 127]. However, it is a requirement of the language that the decimal equivalent of each of the printing characters be non-negative.

It may thus be concluded that in any C implementation in which a char is stored in an 8-bit byte, the corresponding int value will always be a non-negative quantity whatever the value of the leftmost (sign) bit. Now, identical bit patterns within a byte may be treated as a negative quantity by one machine and as a positive quantity by another. For ensuring the portability of programs that store non-character data in char variables the unsigned char declaration is useful: it changes the range of char to [0 to 255].

The signedness of characters is an important issue because the standard I/O library routines, which may normally return characters from files, return a negative value when End-of-File is reached.

Let us now discuss these data types in detail.

Signed integer types There are four standard integer types – *short, int, long, long long*.

The precise range of values representable by a signed integer type depends not only on the number of bits used in the representation but also on the encoding techniques.

The most common binary encoding technique for integers is called *2's complement notation* in which a signed integer represented with *n* bits will have a range from (-2^{n-1}) through $(2^{n-1} - 1)$ encoded in the following fashion:

1. The highest order(left-most) bit (of the word) is the sign bit. If the sign bit is 1, the number is negative; otherwise the number is positive.

2. To negate an integer, complement all bits in the word and then add 1 to the result; thus to form the integer -1, start with 1 $(00....001_2)$, complement the bits 11 ..... 110_2 and add 1 giving $11....111_2 = -1$.

3. The maximum negative value, $10.....0000_2$ or -2^{n-1}, has no positive equivalent; negating this value produces the same value.

Other binary integer encoding techniques are 1's complement notation, in which negation simply complements all bits of the word and sign magnitude notation, in which negation involves simply complementing the sign bit. These alternatives have a range from (-2^{n-1}) through $(2^{n-1} - 1)$; they have one less value and two representations for zero (positive and negative). All three notations represent positive integers identically. All are acceptable in standard C.

In C89, information about the representation of integer types is provided in the header file limits.h. In C99, the files stdint.h and inttypes.h contain additional information.

The system file limits.h available in ANSI C-compliant compilers contains the upper and lower limits of integer types. The user may #include it before main() precisely like #include <stdio.h>, as shown

```
#include <limits.h>
```

and thereby give the program access to the constants defined in it.

The permitted minimum and maximum values are shown in Table 3.6.

Unsigned integer types For each signed integer type, there is a corresponding unsigned type that occupies the same amount of storage but has a different integer encoding.

All unsigned types use straight binary notation regardless of whether the signed types use 2's complement, 1's complement, or sign magnitude notation; the sign bit treated as an ordinary data bit. Therefore, an *n*-bit word can represent the integers 0 through $2^n - 1$. Most computers are easily able to interpret the value in a word using either signed or unsigned notation. For example, when the 2's complement notation is used, the bit pattern 11 .....1111_2 (*n* bits long) can represent either -1 (using the signed notation) or $2^n - 1$ (using the unsigned notation). The integers from 0 through $2^{n-1} - 1$ are represented identically in both signed and unsigned notations. The particular ranges of the unsigned types in a standard C implementation are documented in the header file limits.h.

unsigned The declaration of unsigned int variable 'liberates' the sign bit, and makes the entire word

Table 3.6   Constants in limit.h

Name	Meaning	Values
CHAR_BIT	Bits in a char	8
CHAR_MAX	Maximum value of char	UCHAR-MAX or SCHAR_ MAX
CHAR_MIN	Minimum value of char	0 or SCHAR _ MIN
INT_MAX	Maximum value of int	32767
INT_MIN	Minimum value of int	–32767
LONG_MAX	Maximum value of long	2147483647
LONG_MIN	Minimum value of long	–2147483647
SCHAR_MAX	Maximum value of signed char	127
SCHAR_MIN	Minimum value of signed char	–127
SHRT_MAX	Maximum value of short	32767
SHRT_MIN	Minimum value of short	–32767
UCHAR_MAX	Maximum value of unsigned char	255
UINT_MAX	Maximum value of unsigned int	65535
ULONG_MAX	Maximum value of unsigned long	4294967295
USHRT_MAX	Maximum value of unsigned short	65535

(including the freed sign bit) available for the storage of non-negative integers. It should be noted that the sign bit is the left-most bit of a memory word. It determines the sign of the contents of the word: when it is set to 1, the value stored in the remaining bits is negative. Most computers use 2's complement arithmetic in which the sign bit is 'weighted', i.e., it has an associated place value, which is negative. Thus on a 16-bit machine its value is -2^{15}, or $-32,768$. So a 16-bit signed number such as 10000000 00111111 would have the value $2^0 + 2^1 + 2^2 + 2^3 + 2^4 + 2^5 - 2^{15} = -32,705$. As an unsigned integer, this string of bits would have the value $2^{15} + 2^5 + 2^4 + 2^3 + 2^2 + 2^1 + 2^0 = 32831$. On PCs, the unsigned declaration allows for the int variables a range [0 to 65535] and is useful when one deals with quantities which are known beforehand to be both large and non-negative, e.g., memory addresses, a stadium's seating capacity, etc.

short The short int declaration may be useful in instances where an integer variable is known beforehand to be small. The declaration above ensures that the range of short int will not exceed that of int, but on some computers the range may be shorter (e.g., -128 through 127); short int may be accommodated in a byte, thus saving memory. There was a time in the early days of computing when main memory was an expensive resource and programmers tried using such declarations and other methods to optimize core memory usage to the extent possible. The VAX computer uses two bytes to store short int, which is half the amount it uses for int; but for present-day PCs, with cheap and plentiful memory, most compiler writers make no distinction between int and short int.

unsigned short For the unsigned short int variable, the range of values does not exceed that of the unsigned int; it may be shorter.

unsigned long The unsigned long variable declaration transforms the range of long int to the set of 4-byte non-negative integers with values ranging form 0 to 4294967295.

long On most computers, long int variables are 4-byte integers with values ranging over the interval [-2147483648 to 2147483647].

float Integer and character data types are incapable of storing numbers with fractional parts. Depending on the precision required, C provides two variable types for computation with 'floating-point' numbers, i.e., numbers with a decimal (internally a binary) point. Floats are stored in four bytes and are accurate to about seven significant digits;

double Because the words of memory can store values that are precise only to a fixed number of figures, any calculation involving floating-point numbers almost invariably introduces round-off errors. At the same time, scientific computations often demand a far greater accuracy than that provided by single precision arithmetic, i.e., arithmetic with the four-byte float variables. Thus, where large-scale scientific or engineering computations are involved, the double declaration becomes the natural choice for program variables. The double specification allows the storage of double precision floating-point numbers (in eight consecutive bytes) that are held correct to 15 digits and have a much greater range of definition than floats.

boolean data type _Bool A _Bool variable is defined in the language to be large enough to store just the values 0 and 1. The precise amount of memory that is used is unspecified. _Bool variables are used in programs that need to indicate a boolean condition. For example, a variable of this type might be used to indicate whether all data has been read from a file.

By convention, 0 is used to indicate a false value, and 1 indicates a true value. When assigning a value to a _Bool variable, a value of 0 is stored as 0 inside the variable, whereas any nonzero value is stored as 1.

To make it easier to work with _Bool variables in a program, the standard header file stdbool.h defines the values for bool as true and false.

3.9 PROGRAM STATEMENT

A statement is a syntactic construction that performs an action when a program is executed. All C program statements are terminated with a semi-colon (;). A program statement, in C, can be classified as shown in Fig. 3.9.

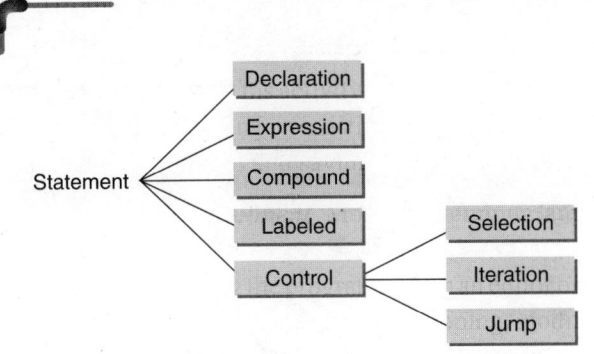

Figure 3.9 Different types of program statements available in C

Declaration is a program statement that serves to communicate to the language translator information about the name and type of the data objects needed during program execution.

Expression statement is the simplest kind of statement which is no more than an expression followed by a semicolon. An *expression* is a sequence of operators and operands that specifies computation of a value.

```
x = 4
```

is an expression (which could be part of a larger expression), but

```
x = 4;
```

is a statement.

Compound statement is a sequence of statements that may be treated as a single statement in the construction of larger statements.

Labeled statements can be used to mark any statement so that control may be transferred to the statement by *switch* statement.

Control statement is a statement whose execution results in a choice being made as to which of two or more paths should be followed. In other words, the control statements determine the 'flow of control' in a program.

The kind of control flow statements supported by different languages varies, but can be categorized by their effect:

- continuation of program execution from a different statement
- executing a set of statements only if some condition is met
- executing a set of statements zero or more times, until some condition is met
- executing a set of distant statements, after which the flow of control usually returns
- stopping the program, preventing any further execution (unconditional halt)

Selection statements allow a program to select a particular execution path from a set of one or more alternatives. Various forms of the *if...else* statement belong to this category.

Iteration statements are used to execute a group of one or more statements repeatedly. *while, for*, and *do...while* statements fall under this group.

Jump statements cause an unconditional jump to some other place in the program. *goto* statement falls in this group.

The first four types of program statements shown in the figure are defined and explained in the next few sections of this chapter. The program control statement, which is of three types, is dealt with in Chapter 5.

3.10 DECLARATION

Declaration introduces one or more variables within a program. Definition, on the other hand, directs the compiler to actually allocate memory for the variable. A declaration statement begins with the type, followed by the name of one or more variables. The general form is

```
data_type variable_name_1, variable_name_2, ...,
variable_name_n;
```

Declaration of multiple variables of the same data type can be done in one statement. For example,

```
int a;
int b;
int c;
```

can be rewritten as

```
int a, b, c;
```

Variables are declared at three basic places. First, when these are declared inside a function, they are called local variables. Second, when the variables are declared in the definition of function parameters, these variables are called formal parameters. And third, when the variables are declared outside all functions, they are called global variables. Variables used in expressions are also referred to as operands.

3.11 HOW DOES THE COMPUTER STORE DATA IN MEMORY?

It is necessary to understand the *word size* of your computer. The word size is the computer's preferred size for moving units of information around; technically it's the width of the processor's *registers*, which are the data holding areas the processor uses to do arithmetic and logical calculations. This is what they mean when people refer to computers as 32 bit or 64-bit computers.

Most computers now have a word size of 64 bits. In the recent past (early 2000s), many PCs had 32-bit words. The old 286 machines, back in the 1980s, had a word size of 16 bits. Old-style mainframes often had 36-bit words.

The computer views your memory as a sequence of words numbered from zero up to some large value dependent on the memory size.

3.11.1 How Integers Are Stored?

Storing *unsigned integers* is a straightforward process. The number is changed to the corresponding binary form and the binary representation is stored.

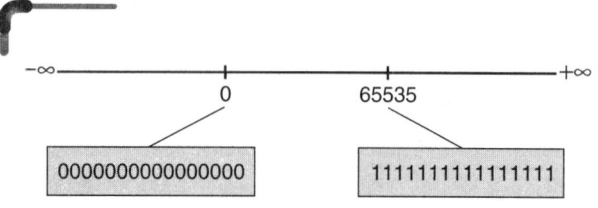

Figure 3.10(a) Range of an unsigned integer stored in a 16-bit word

An unsigned integer can be represented with a circle as shown in Fig. 3.10(b).

0 is placed at the top of the circle and values are placed around the circle clockwise until the maximum value adjacent to the value 0. In other words, storing numbers is a modulo process. The number to be stored is represented as modulus, the maximum value that can be stored plus one, in this case it is 65535.

$$65535 + 1 = 65536 \% 65536 = 0.$$

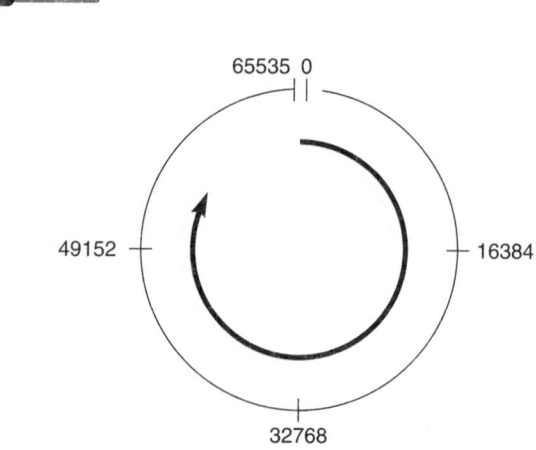

Figure 3.10(b) Cyclic view of the range of an unsigned integer stored in a 16-bit word

For *signed integer* types, the bits of the object representation shall be divided into three groups: *value bits, padding bits*, and the *sign bit*. There need not be any padding bits; there shall be exactly one sign bit. Each bit that is a value bit shall have the same value as the same bit in the object representation of the corresponding unsigned type (if there are M value bits in the signed type and N in the unsigned type, then $M \leq N$). If the sign bit is zero, it shall not affect the resulting value. If the sign bit is one, the value shall be modified in one of the following ways:

- the corresponding value with sign bit 0 is negated (*sign and magnitude*).
- the sign bit has the value $-(2^N)$ (2's complement).
- the sign bit has the value $-(2^N - 1)$ (1's complement).

Which of these applies is implementation-defined, as is whether the value with sign bit 1 and all value bits zero (for the first two), or with sign bit and all value bits 1 (for one's complement), is a trap representation or a normal value. In the case of sign and magnitude and one's complement, if this representation is a normal value it is called a *negative zero*.

Sign and magnitude

In this method, one bit (the left-most) represents sign bit; 0 for positive and 1 for negative. The leftover bits of the word represent the absolute value of the number. Therefore, the maximum positive value is one half of the unsigned value. There are two zero values, a plus zero and a minus zero. This method is not used to store values in computers used these days.

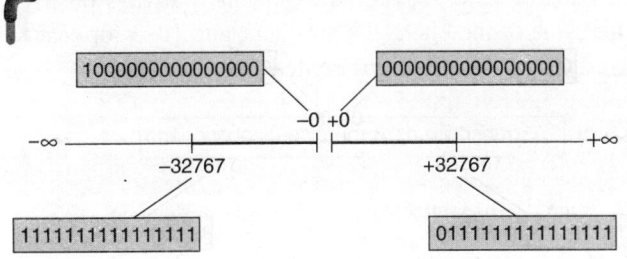

Figure 3.11 Range of a signed integer stored in a 16-bit word in sign and magnitude form

One's complement

In this method, negative numbers are stored in their complemented format. Like sign and magnitude form the 1's complement has two zero values (plus zero and minus zero). Figure 3.12 shows the format for 1's complement values.

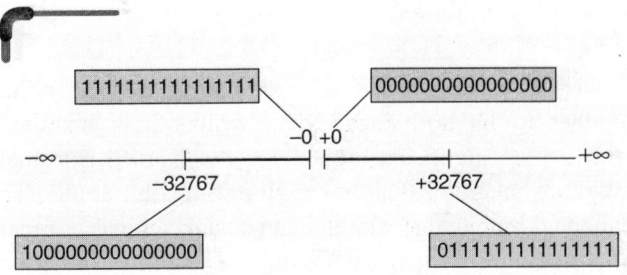

Figure 3.12 Range of a signed integer stored in a 16-bit word in one's complement form

Like sign and magnitude method, this method is not used in general purpose computers.

Two's complement

All bits change when sign of the number changes. So the whole number, not just the most significant bit, takes part in the negation processes. However, we have only one 0.

With a little thought, you should recognize that 0 and –1 are complement of each other. Likewise +32767 and –32768 are the complement to each other. The range of integers in 2's complement format is shown in Fig. 3.14.

32767 is at the bottom of the circle. When we add 10, we move clockwise 10 positions which puts us in the negative portion of the number range. The value at that position is –32759. Thus, the geometric depiction of 2's complement

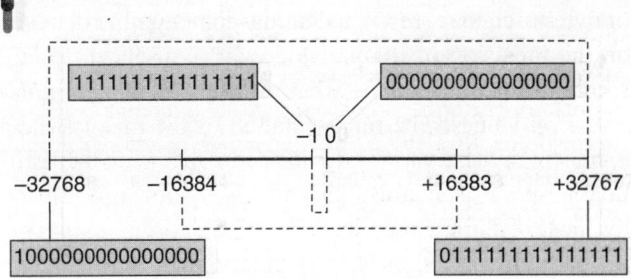

Figure 3.13 Range of a signed integer stored in a 16-bit word in two's complement form

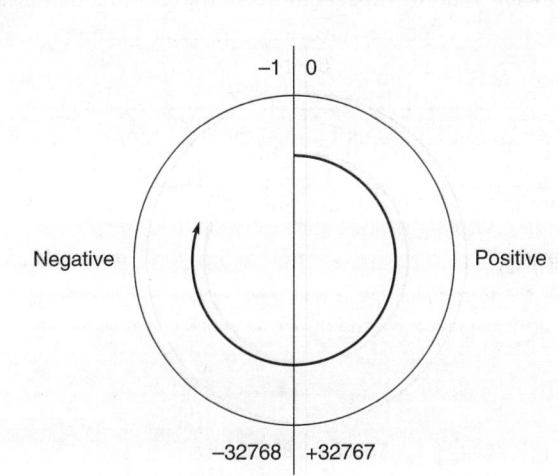

Figure 3.14 Cyclic view of the range of a signed integer stored in a 16-bit word in 2's complement form

numbers may help to understand how overflow conditions can be determined using this representation for negative numbers. Starting at any point on the circle, you can add positive k (or subtract negative k) to that number (the starting point number) by moving k positions clockwise. Similarly, you can subtract positive k (or add negative k) from that number by moving k positions counterclockwise. If an arithmetic operation results in traversal of the point where the endpoints are joined, an incorrect answer will result.

3.11.2 How Floats and Doubles are Stored?

Floating point and double integers are stored in *mantissa* and *exponent* form except that instead of the exponent representing the power of 10, it represents a power of 2, since base 2 is the computer's natural format. The number of bytes used to represent a floating-point number depends on the precision of the variable. float is used to declare *single-precision* variables, whereas double denotes *double-precision* values. The representation of the mantissa and exponent in these variables is in accordance with the IEEE floating-point standards. This representation is followed by most of the C compilers. The IEEE format expresses a floating-point number in a binary form known as a *normalized* form. Normalization involves adjusting the exponent so that the *binary point* (the binary analog of the decimal point) in the mantissa always lies to the right of most significant non-zero digit. In binary representation, this means that the most significant digit of the mantissa is always 1. This property of the normalized representation is exploited by the IEEE format when storing the mantissa. Consider an example of generating the normalized form of a floating-point number. For instance, the binary equivalent to represent the decimal number 5.375 can be obtained as shown in the following example.

Example

Integer part conversion to binary

```
2 | 5
2 | 2   1
2 | 1   0
    0   1
```
Quotient ⌐ ⌐ Remainder

Writing the remainders in reverse order, the integer part in binary is 101

Fraction part conversion to binary

```
.375 × 2 = 0.750   0
.750 × 2 = 1.500   1
.500 × 2 = 1.000   1
```
Whole numbers

Writing the whole numbers part in the same order in which they are obtained, the fraction part in binary is 011

Thus the binary equivalent of 5.375 would be 101.011. The normalized form of this binary number is obtained by adjusting the exponent until the decimal point is to the right of the most significant 1. In this case the result is 1.01011×2^2. The IEEE format for floating-point storage uses a sign bit, a mantissa, and an exponent for representing the power of 2. The sign bit denotes the sign of the number: 0 represents a positive value and 1 denotes a negative value. The mantissa is represented in binary. Converting the floating point number to its normalized form results in a mantissa whose most significant bit is always 1. The IEEE format takes advantage of this by not storing this bit at all. The exponent is an integer stored in unsigned binary format after adding a positive integer bias.

This ensures that the stored exponent is always positive. The value of the bias is 127 for float and 1023 for double. Thus, 1.01011×2^2 is represented as follows:

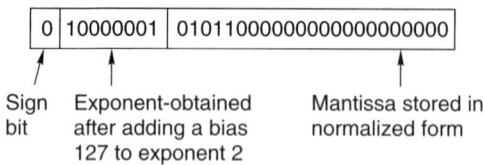

Consider another example. Suppose, the number –0.25 has to be represented in IEEE format. On conversion to binary, this number would become –0.01 and in its normalized form it would be -1.0×2^{-2}. This normalized form when represented in IEEE format would look like

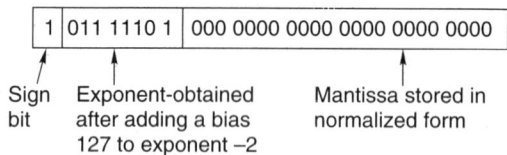

Now it is known that converting the floating point number to its normalized form results in a mantissa whose most significant bit is always 1. The IEEE format takes advantage of this by not storing this bit at all. The exponent is an integer stored in an unsigned binary format after adding a positive integer bias. This ensures that the stored exponent is always positive. The value of the bias is 127 for float and 1023 for double. Figure 3.15 shows how any general float and double numbers are represented in the IEEE format.

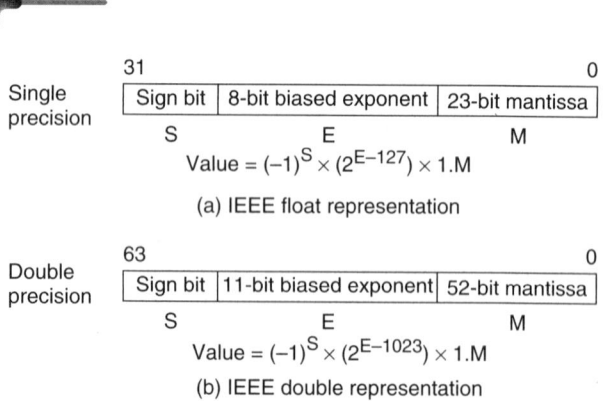

Figure 3.15 IEEE format for representing float and double

According to most C literature, the valid range for float is 10^{-38} to 10^{38}. But, how is such an odd range used? Well, the answer lies in the IEEE representation. Since the exponent of a float in IEEE format is stored with a positive bias of 127, the smallest positive value that can be stored in a float variable is 2^{-127}, which is approximately 1.175×10^{-38}. The largest positive value is 2^{128}, which is about 3.4×10^{38}. Similarly, for a double variable the smallest possible value is 2^{-1023}, which is approximately 2.23×10^{-308}. The largest positive value that can be held in a double variable is 2^{1024}, which is approximately 1.8×10^{308}.

There is one more quirk. After obtaining the IEEE format for a float, when the time comes to actually store it in memory, it is stored in the reverse order. That is, if the user calls the four-byte IEEE form as ABCD, then while storing in memory it is stored in the form DCBA. This can be understood with an example. Suppose the floating point number in question is 5.375. Its IEEE representation is 01000000101011000000000000000000 0000. Expressed in Hex this is 40 AC 00 00. While storing this in memory, it is stored as 00 00 AC 40.

The representation of a long double (10-byte entity) is also similar. The only difference is that unlike float and double, the most significant bit of the normalized form is specifically stored. In a long double, 1 bit is occupied by the sign, 15 bits by the biased exponent (bias value 16383), and 64 bits by the mantissa.

3.12 TOKENS

Tokens are the basic lexical building blocks of source code. In other words, one or more symbols understood by the compiler which help it interpret the program code. Characters are combined into tokens according to the rules of the programming language. The compiler checks the tokens so that they can be formed into legal strings according to the syntax of the language. There are five classes of tokens: *identifiers, reserved words, operators, separators,* and *constants.*

An *identifier* is a sequence of characters used by the programmer to identify or name a specific object, and the name is formed by a sequence of letters, digits, and underscores.

Keywords are explicitly reserved words that have a strict meaning as individual tokens to the compiler. They cannot be redefined or used in other contexts. Use of variable names with the same name as any of the keywords will cause a compiler error.

Operators are tokens used to indicate an action to be taken (usually arithmetic operations, logical operations, bit operations, and assignment operations). Operators can be simple operators (a single character token) or compound operators (two or more character tokens).

Separators are tokens used to separate other tokens. Two common kinds of separators are indicators of an end of an instruction and separators used for grouping.

A *constant* is an entity that doesn't change.

Consider the following piece of code,

```
if(x<5)

    x = x + 2;
else
    x = x + 10;
```

Here the tokens that will be generated are

```
Keywords   : if , else
Identifier : x
Constants  : 2, 10,5
Operators  : +,=
Separator  : ;
```

3.12.1 Identifiers

An identifier or name is a sequence of characters created by the programmer to identify or name a specific object. In C, variables, arrays, functions, and labels are named. Some rules must be kept in mind when naming identifiers. These are stated as follows.

1. The first character must be an alphabetic character (lower-case or capital letter) or an underscore '_'.

2. All characters must be alphabetic characters, digits, or underscores.

3. The first 31 characters of the identifier are significant. Identifiers that share the same first 31 characters may be indistinguishable from each other.

4. An identifier cannot duplicate a keyword. A keyword is a word which has special meaning in C.

Some examples of proper identifiers are employee_number, box_4_weight, monthly_pay, interest_per_annum, job_number, and tool_4.

Some examples of incorrect identifiers are 230_item, #pulse_rate, total~amount, /profit margin, and ~cost_per_item.

3.12.2 Keywords

Keywords form the vocabulary of C. Because they are special to C, one cannot use them for variable names.

There are 32 words defined as keywords in C. These have predefined uses and cannot be used for any other purpose in a C program. They are used by the compiler to compile the program. They are always written in lowercase letters. A complete list of these keywords is given in Table 3.7.

Table 3.7 Keywords in C

auto	double	int	struct
break	else	long	switch
case	enum	register	typedef
char	extern	return	union
const	float	short	unsigned
continue	for	signed	void
default	goto	sizeof	volatile
do	if	static	while

Several keywords were added in C89: *const, enum, signed, void* and *volatile*. The new keywords in C99 are *inline, restrict, _Bool, _Complex* and *_Imaginary*.

Table 3.8 Full set of keywords upto C99

auto	enum	restrict	unsigned
break	extern	return	void
case	float	short	volatile
char	for	signed	while
const	goto	sizeof	_Bool
continue	if	static	_Complex
default	inline	struct	_Imaginary
do	int	switch	
double	long	typedef	
else	register	union	

Note that compiler vendors (like Microsoft, Borland) provide their own keywords apart from the ones mentioned above. These include extended keywords like **near**, **far** and **asm**. Though it has been suggested by the ANSI committee that every such compiler-specific keyword should be preceded by two underscores (as in **__asm**), not every vendor follows this rule.

3.12.3 Constants

A constant is an explicit data value written by the programmer. Thus, it is a value known to the compiler at compiling time. The compiler may deal with this value in any of several ways, depending on the type of constant and its context. For example, the binary equivalent of the constant may be inserted directly into the output code stream. The value of the constant may be stored in a special data area in memory. The compiler may decide to use the constant's value for its own immediate purpose, e.g., to determine how much storage it should allocate to a data array.

C permits integer constants, floating-point constants, character constants, and string constants. Table 3.9 depicts the types of constants that C allows. An integer constant consists of a sequence of digits. It is normally interpreted as a decimal value. Thus, 1, 25, and 23456 are all decimal integer constants.

A literal integer (e.g., 1984) is always assumed to be of type int, unless it has an L or l suffix, in which case it is treated as a long. Also, a literal integer can be specified to be unsigned using the suffix U or u. For example,

```
1984L  1984l  1984U  1984u  1984LU  1984ul
```

Literal integers can be expressed in decimal, octal, and hexadecimal notations. The decimal notation is the one that has been used so far. An integer is taken to be octal if it is preceded by a zero (0), and hexadecimal if it is preceded by a 0x or 0X. For example,

```
92    /* decimal           */
0134  /* equivalent octal   */
0x5C  /* equivalent hexadecimal */
```

Point to Note

In ANSI C, a decimal integer constant is treated as an unsigned long if its magnitude exceeds that of the signed long. An octal or hexadecimal integer that exceeds the limit of int is taken to be unsigned; if it exceeds this limit, it is taken to be long; and if it exceeds this limit, it is treated as an unsigned long. An integer constant is regarded as unsigned if its value is followed by the letter u or U, e.g., 0x9999u; it is regarded as unsigned long if its value is followed by u or U and l or L, e.g., 0xFFFFFFFFul.

A floating-point constant consists of an integer part, a decimal point, a fractional part, and an exponent field containing an e or E followed by an integer. Both integer and fractional parts are digit sequences. Certain portions of this format may be missing as long as the resulting number is distinguishable from a simple integer. For example, either the decimal point or the fractional part, but not both, may be absent. A literal real (e.g., 0.06) is always assumed to be of type double, unless it has an F or f suffix, in which case it is treated as a float, or an L or l suffix, in which case it is treated as a long double. The latter uses more bytes than a double for better accuracy (e.g., 10 bytes on the programmer's PC). For example,

```
0.06F    0.06f    3.141592654L    3.1415926541
```

In addition to the decimal notation used so far, literal reals may also be expressed in *scientific* notation. For example, 0.002164 may be written in scientific notation as

```
2.164E-3    or    2.164e-3
```

The letter E (or e) stands for *exponent*. The scientific notation is interpreted as follows.

$$2.164E-3 = 2.164 \times 10^{-3}$$

The following are examples of *long long*:

```
12345LL
1234511
```

The following are examples of *unsigned long long*:

```
123456ULL
123456ull
```

A character constant normally consists of a single character enclosed in single quotes. Thus, for example, 'b' and '$' are both character constants. Each takes on the numeric value of its character in the machine's character set. Unless stated otherwise, it will henceforth be assumed that the ASCII code is used. Thus, for example, writing down the character constant 'A' is equivalent to writing down the hex value 41 or the octal value 101. The 'A' form is preferable, of course, first, because its meaning is unmistakable, and second, because it is independent of the actual character set of the machine.

In C, certain special characters, in particular, non-printing control characters are represented by special, so-called escape character sequences, each of which begins with the special backslash (\) escape character. Most of these escape codes are designed to make visible, on paper, any of those characters whose receipt by a printer or terminal causes a special, non-printing control action.

Character constants can also be defined using their octal ASCII codes. The octal value of the character is preceded by a backslash and enclosed in single quotes.

```
char terminal_bell = '\07';
            /* 7 = octal ASCII code for beep */
char backspace = '\010';
            /* 10 = octal code for backspace */
```

For ANSI C compilers, character constants may be defined by hex digits instead of octals. Hex digits are preceded by x, unlike 0 in the case of octals. Thus, in ANSI C

```
char backspace = '\xA';
```

is an acceptable alternative declaration to

```
char backspace = '\0101';
```

Any number of digits may be written but the value stored is undefined if the resulting character value exceeds the limit of char.

On an ASCII machine both '\b' and '\010' are equivalent representations. Each will print the backspace character. But the latter form, the ASCII octal equivalent of '\b', will not work on an EBCDIC machine, typically an IBM mainframe, where the collating sequence of the characters (i.e., their gradation or numerical ordering) is different. In the interests of portability it is therefore preferable to write '\b' for the backspace character rather than its octal code. Then the program will work as faultlessly on an EBCDIC machine as it will on an ASCII.

Note that the character constant 'a' is not the same as the string "a". A string is really an array of characters that is a bunch of characters stored in consecutive memory locations, the last location containing the null character; so the string "a" really contains two char, an 'a' immediately followed by '\0'. It is important to realize that the null character is not the same as the decimal digit 0, the ASCII value of which is 00110000.

A string constant is a sequence of characters enclosed in double quotes. Whenever the C compiler encounters a string constant, it stores the character sequence in an available data area in memory. It also records the address of the first character and appends to the stored sequence an additional character, the null character '\0', to mark the end of the string.

The length of a character string is the number of characters in it (again, excluding the surrounding double quotes). Thus, the string "messagen" has a length of eight. The actual number of stored characters is one more as a null character is added.

The characters of a string may be specified using any of the notations for specifying literal characters. For example,

```
"Name\tAddress\tTelephone" /* tab-separated words */
"ASCII character 65: \101"/* 'A' specified as '101' */
```

A long string may extend beyond a single line, in which case each of the preceding lines should be terminated by a backslash. For example,

```
"Example to show \
the use of backslash for \
writing a long string"
```

The backslash in this context means that the rest of the string is continued on the next line. The preceding string is equivalent to the single-line string

```
"Example to show the use of backslash for writing
a long string"
```

Point to Note

A common programming error results from confusing a single-character string (e.g., "A") with a single character (e.g., 'A'). These two are *not* equivalent. The former consists of two bytes (the character 'A' followed by the character '\0'), whereas the latter consists of a single byte.

The shortest possible string is the null string (" "). It simply consists of the null character. Table 3.9 summarizes the different constants.

Table 3.9 Specifications of different constants

Type	Specification	Example
Decimal	nil	50
Hexadecimal	Preceded by 0x or 0X	0x10
Octal	Begins with 0	010
Floating constant	Ends with f/F	123.0f
Character	Enclosed within single quotes	'A' 'o'
String	Enclosed within double quotes	"welcome"
Unsigned integer	Ends with U/u	37u
Long	Ends with L/l	37L
Unsigned long	Ends with UL/w	37UL

C89 added the suffixes **U** and **u** to specify unsigned numbers. C99 added **LL** to specify **long long**.

More than one `\n` can be used within a string enabling multi-line output to be produced with a single use of the printf() function. Here's an example.

```
int main()
{
    printf("This sentence will \n be printed\nin\
    multi-line \n");
    return 0;
}
```

When the program was compiled and run it produced the following output.

```
This sentence will
be printed
in multi-line
```

However if the string is too long to fit on a single line then it is possible to spread a string over several lines by escaping the actual new-line character at the end of a line by preceding it with a backslash. The string may then be continued on the next line as shown in the following program:

```
int main()
{
    printf("hello,\
    world\n");
    return 0;
}
```

The output is

```
hello, world
```

The indenting spaces at the start of the string continuation have been taken as part of the string. A better approach is to use *string concatenation* which means that two strings which are only separated by *whitespaces* are regarded by the compiler as a single string. Space, newline, tab character and comment are collectively known as *whitespace*. The use of string concatenation is shown by the following example.

```
int main()
{
    printf("hello," "world\n");
    return 0;
}
```

3.12.4 Assignment

The assignment operator is the single equal to sign (=). The general form of the assignment statement is

```
variable_name = expression;
```

Some examples are given below.

```
i = 6;
i = i + 1;
```

The assignment operator replaces the content of the location 'i' with the evaluated value of the expression on its right-hand side. The assignment also acts as an expression that returns the newly assigned value. Some programmers use the feature to write statements like the following:

```
y = (x = 2 * x);
```

This statement puts x's new value in y. The operand to the left of the assignment operator must be a variable name. C does not allow any expression, constant, or function to be placed to the left of the assignment operator. Thus, its left operand should be a variable and its right operand may be an arbitrary expression. The latter is evaluated and the outcome is stored in the location denoted by the variable name. For example, the mathematical expression x + 2 = 0 does not become an assignment expression in C by typing x + 2 = 0. It is wrong in C, as the left-hand side of the 'equal to' operator (assignment operator) must not have an expression, value, or constant.

The operand to the left of the assignment operator is an lvalue that denotes left value. An lvalue is anything that denotes a memory location in which a value may be stored. The only kind of lvalue identified so far in this book is a variable. It will be discussed in detail later in this chapter. Other kinds of lvalues, based on pointers and references, will be described later in the book.

3.12.5 Initialization

When a variable is declared, the C compiler does not assign any value to the variable, unless it is instructed to do so. Such declaration is called a *tentative declaration*. For example,

```
int i; /* This declaration is tentative */
int x;
x = i + 5;
/* variable i is not assigned any known value, and
therefore the value of x is undefined. This is a
bug */
```

To prevent such pitfalls, always assign a value to the variable during the declaration of variables. This is known as initialization. The value of initialization is called the initializer. The general form of the initialization statement is

```
data type variable_name=constant;
```

For example,

```
int i = 100; /* 100 is an initializer */

int x;

x = i + 5;

/* since i has been given a value during its
declaration, x is evaluated to hold a value 105 */
```

Check Your Progress

1. What will be the output of the following program?

   (a)
   ```
   #include <stdio.h>
   int main()
   {
       int a=010;
       printf("\n a=%d",a);
       return 0;
   }
   ```
   Output: a = 8

   (b)
   ```
   #include <stdio.h>
   int main()
   {
       int a=010;
       printf("\n a=%o",a);
       return 0;
   }
   ```
   Output: a = 10

Explanation: In (a), the integer constant 010 is taken to be octal as it is preceded by a zero (0). Here the variable 'a' is printed with %d specifier. The decimal equivalent of the octal value 10, which is 8, will be printed. Whereas in (b) the same variable is printed with %o format specifier, so 10 is printed on the screen.

   (c)
   ```
   #include <stdio.h>
   int main()
   {
       int a=010;
       printf("\n a=%x",a);
       return 0;
   }
   ```
   Output: a = 8

Explanation: In (c), the octal value 10 is printed with %x format specifier. That is hexadecimal equivalent of 10, which is 8, will be printed.

   (d)
   ```
   #include <stdio.h>
   int main()
   ```

```
{
    int a=53;
    printf("\n a=%o",a);
    return 0;
}
```

Output: a = 65

Explanation: In (d), an integer constant 53 is stored in the variable 'a' but is printed with %o. The octal equivalent of 53, which is 65, will be printed.

```
(e)  #include <stdio.h>
     int main()
     {
         int a=53;
         printf("\n a=%X",a);
         return 0;
     }
```
Output: a = 35

Explanation: In (e), an integer constant 53 is stored in the variable 'a' but is printed with %x. The hexadecimal equivalent of 53, which is 35, will be printed.

3.13 OPERATORS AND EXPRESSIONS

An operator is a symbol that specifies the mathematical, logical, or relational operation to be performed. This section introduces the built-in C operators for composing expressions with variables. An expression is any computation that yields a value. Figure 3.16 gives the classification of operators in C language. Table 3.10 gives the different types of operators.

When discussing expressions, the term evaluation is often used. For example, it is said that an expression evaluates to

Table 3.10   Different operators

Type of operator	Operator symbols with meanings	
Arithmetical	Unary	
	+	Unary
	−	Unary
	++	Increment
	−−	Decrement
	Binary	
	+	Addition
	−	Subtraction
	*	Multiplication
	/	Division
	%	Modulo
	Ternary	
	?:	Conditional operator
Assignment	Simple Assignment	
	=	
	Compound Assignment	
	+=, −=, *=, /=, %=, &=, ^=, |=	
	Expression Assignment	
	A= 5+(b=8 + (c=2)) −4	
Relational	>, <, >=, <=	
Equality	= =	Equal to
	!=	Not equal to
Logical	&&	Logical AND
	||	Logical OR
	!	Logical NOT
Bitwise	&	Bitwise AND
	|	Bitwise OR
	~	Complement
	^	Exclusive OR
	>>	Right Shift
	<<	Left Shift
Others	,	Comma
	*	Indirection
	.	Membership operator
	->	Membership operator

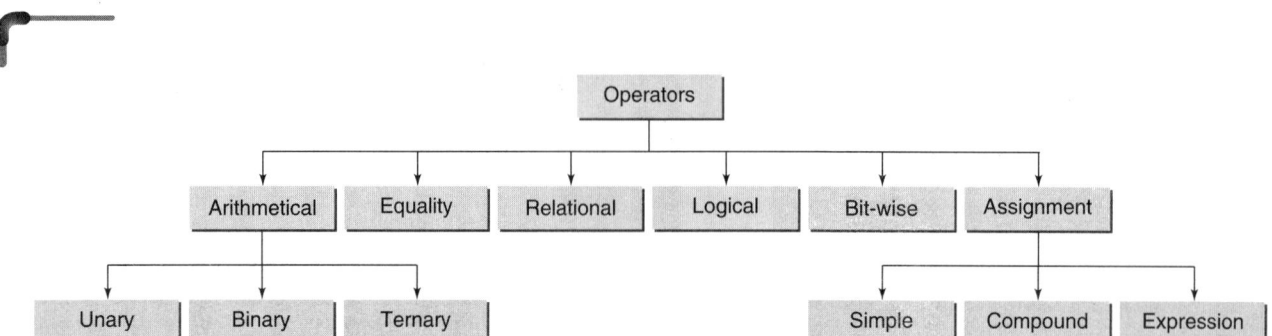

Figure 3.16   Classification of operators in C language

a certain value. Usually the final value is the only reason for evaluating the expression. However, in some cases, the expression may also produce side effects. These are permanent changes in the program state. In this sense, C expressions are different from mathematcal expressions.

C provides operators for composing arithmetic, relational, logical, bitwise, and conditional expressions. It also provides operators that produce useful side effects, such as assignment, increment, and decrement. Each category of operators will be discussed in turn. The precedence rules that govern the order of operator evaluation in a multi-operator expression will also be discussed.

3.13.1 Arithmetic Operators

There are three types of arithmetic operators in C: binary, unary, and ternary.

Binary operators C provides five basic arithmetic binary operators. These are summarized in Table 3.11.

Table 3.11 Arithmetic binary operators

Operator	Name	Example
+	Addition	12 + 4.9 /* gives 16.9*/
-	Subtraction	3.98 - 4 /* gives -0.02*/
*	Multiplication	2 * 3.4 /* gives 6.8 */
/	Division	9 / 2.0 /* gives 4.5 */
%	Remainder	13 % 3 /* gives 1 */

Except for remainder (%), all other arithmetic operators can accept a mix of integer and real operands. Generally, if both operands are integers, the result will be an integer. However, if one or both of the operands are reals, the result will be a real (or double to be exact).

When both operands of the division operator (/) are integers, the division is performed as an integer division and not the normal division. Integer division always results in an integer outcome, i.e., the result is always rounded off by ignoring the remainder. For example,

```
9/2   /* gives 4, not 4.5 */
-9/2  /* gives -4, not 4 */
```

Unintended integer divisions are a common source of programming errors. To obtain a real division when both operands are integers, cast one of the operands to be real, which means forcing the data type of the variable to real. Typecasting will be explained in detail later in this chapter. The following example demonstrates the case of real division.

```
int    cost = 100;
int    volume = 80;
double unitPrice;
unitPrice = cost/(double) volume; /* gives 1.25 */
```

The remainder operator (%) always expects integers for both of its operands. It returns the integer part of the remainder obtained after dividing the operands. For example, 13%3 is calculated by integer division of 13 by 3 to give a remainder of 1; the result is therefore 1.

It is possible for the outcome of an arithmetic operation to be too large for storing in a designated variable. This situation is called an overflow. The outcome of an overflow is machine-dependent and therefore undefined. For example,

```
unsigned char k = 10 * 92;  /* overflow: 920 > 255  */
```

It is not possible to divide a number by zero. This operation is illegal and results in a run-time *division-by-zero* exception that typically causes the program to terminate.

The effects of attempting to divide by zero are officially undefined. The ANSI standard does not require compiler writers to do anything special, so anything might happen. We tried by using a statement y = x, where x and y were declared as integers in a program. Turbo C spotted what was going on and displayed the message

```
Divide error
```

The Unix systems were slightly less informative producing the following messages

```
Arithmetic exception (core dumped)
Breakpoint - core dumped
```

A few examples on the use of various arithmetic operators are given below.

Example

```
1.  #include <stdio.h>
    int main( )
    {
       int a = 100;
       int b = 2;
       int c = 25;
       int d = 4;
       int result;
```

```
result = a-b;                    /*subtraction */
printf("a - b = %d \n", result);
result = b * c;          /* multiplication */
printf("b * c = %d \n", result);
result = a / c;                  /* division */
printf("a / c = %d \n", result);
result = a + b * c;
printf("a + b * c = %d \n", result);
printf("a * b + c * d = %d\n", a* b+c*d);
return 0;
}
```

Output:

```
a - b = 98
b * c = 50
a / c = 4
a + b * c = 150
a * b + c * d = 300
```

2.
```
#include <stdio.h>
int main()
{
    int a = 25;
    int b = 2;
    int result;
    float c = 25.0;
    float d = 2.0;
    printf("6 + a / 5 * b = %d \n", 6 + a / 5 * b);
    printf("a / b * b = %d\n", a / b * b);
    printf("c / d * d = %f\n", c / d * d);
    printf("-a = %d\n",-a);
    return 0;
}
```

Output:

```
6 + a / 5 * b = 16
a / b * b = 24
c / d * d = 25.000000
-a = -25
```

Note the difference between this and the previous program. When we evaluate 6 + a / 5 * b, we have not stored its value in any variable, but it is evaluated in the printf statement itself and printed straight away.

Points to Note

```
op1/op2
op1%op2
```

For / and %, op2 must be non-zero; op2 = 0 results in an error. (We cannot divide by zero.) When op1 and op2 are integers and the quotient is not an integer then the following points have to be noted:

- If op1 and op2 have the same sign, op1/op2 is the largest integer less than the true quotient, and op1%op2 has the sign of op1.
- If op1 and op2 have opposite signs, op1/op2 is the smallest integer greater than the true quotient, and op1%op2 has the sign of op1.

It is to be noted that rounding off is always towards zero.

- % operator returns the remainder of an integer division. i.e., x%y = x - (x/y)*y where x and y both are of integer types. This operator can be applied only to integer operands and cannot be applied to operands of type float or double. The following example shows the occurrence of compiler error when the % operator is applied on a floating point number:

```
#include <stdio.h>
int main()
{
    float c= 3.14;
    printf("%f", c%2);
    return 0;
}
```

Check Your Progress

1. What will be the output of the following programs:

   (a)
   ```
   #include <stdio.h>
   int main()
   {
       int x = 5, y = 7, z;
       z = x + y;
       printf("The value of x is: %d\n", x);
       printf("The value of y is: %d\n", y);
       printf("Their sum, z, is: %d\n", z);
       return 0;
   }
   ```

   Output:

   ```
   The value of x is: 5
   The value of y is: 7
   Their sum, z, is: 12
   ```

(b)
```
#include <stdio.h>
int main()
{
    int a, b, c; /* a, b and c are undefined. */
    c= a + b ;
    printf("The value of a is: %d\n", a);
    printf("The value of b is: %d\n", b);
    printf("Their sum, c, is: %d\n", c);
    return 0;
}
```
Output:
```
The value of a is: 2146744409
The value of b is: 2146744417
Their sum, c, is: -1478470
```

Now, look at the output of this program. Is it possible to predict the values of a, b, and c? Never assume a variable to have a meaningful value, unless a value is assigned to it.

Unary operators The unary '–' operator negates the value of its operand (clearly, a signed number). A numeric constant is assumed positive unless it is preceded by the negative operator. That is, there is no unary '+'. It is implicit. Remember that -x does not change the value of x at the location where it permanently resides in memory. Apart from this, there is another group of unary operators available in C that are described next.

Unary increment and decrement operators The unary '++' and '--' operators increment or decrement the value in a variable by 1. There are 'pre' and 'post' variants for both operators that do slightly different things as explained below.

var++ increment 'post' variant; var-- decrement 'post' variant

++var increment 'pre' variant; --var decrement 'pre' variant

The following examples illustrate the use of increment and decrement operators on a variable not placed in an expression.

```
int i = 42;
i++; /* increment contents of i, same as i = i + 1;*/
                                /* i is now 43 */
i--; /* decrement contents of i, same as i = i - 1;*/
                                /* i is now 42 */
```

```
++i; /* increment contents of i, same as i = i + 1;*/
                                /* i is now 43 */
--i; /* decrement contents of i, same as i = i - 1; */
                                /* i is now 42 */
```

Basic rules for using ++ and -- operators

- The operand must be a variable but not a constant or an expression.
- The operator ++ and -- may precede or succeed the operand.

1.
```
#include <stdio.h>
int main()
{
    int a=5, b=3;
    printf("\n %d", ++(a*b+2));
    return 0;
}
```
Output:
```
Compiler error - Lvalue required
```
2.
```
#include <stdio.h>
int main()
{
    printf("\n %d", ++2));
    return 0;
}
```
Output:
```
Compiler error - Lvalue required
```

It is to be noted that i++ executes faster than i = i + 1 because the expression i++ requires a single machine instruction such as INR to carry out the increment operation whereas i = i + 1 requires more instructions to carry out this operation.

Pre- and post-variations of ++ and -- operators The pre- and post- (++ and --) operators differ in the value used for the operand n when it is embedded inside expressions.

If it is a 'pre' operator, the value of the operand is incremented (or decremented) before it is fetched for computation. The altered value is used for computation of the expression in which it occurs.

A few examples are shown here to demonstrate the use of the increment and decrement operators for postfix and prefix operations in expressions.

Examples

3. Postfix operation

(a) x = a++;

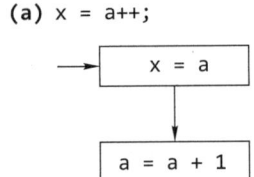

First action: store value of a in memory location for variable x.

Second action: increment value of a by 1 and store result in memory location for variable a.

(b) y = b--;

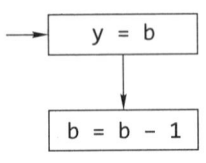

First action: put value of b in memory location for variable y.

Second action: decrement value of b by 1 and put result in memory location for variable b.

4. Prefix operation

(a) x = ++a;

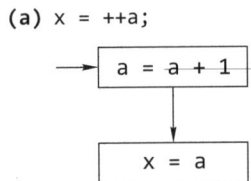

First action: increment value of a by 1 and store result in memory location for variable a.

Second action: store value of a in memory location for variable x.

(b) y = --b;

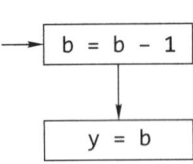

First action: decrement value of b by 1 and put result in memory location for variable b.

Second action: put value of b in memory location for variable y.

To clarify, suppose that an int variable a has the value 5. Consider the assignment

    b = ++a;

Pre-incrementation implies

> *Step 1:*　increment *a*;　　　　/* *a* becomes 6 */
> *Step 2:*　assign this value to *b*;　/* *b* becomes 6 */
> Result:　*a* is 6, *b* is 6

If it is a 'post' operator, the value of the operand is altered after it is fetched for computation. The unaltered value is used in the computation of the expression in which it occurs.

Suppose again that a has the value 5 and consider the assignment

    b = a++;

Post-incrementation implies

> *Step 1:* assign the unincremented *a* to *b*;
> 　　　　/* *b* becomes 5 */
> *Step 2:* increment *a*; /* *a* becomes 6 */
> Result: *a* is 6, *b* is 5

The placement of the operator before or after the operand directly affects the value of the operand that is used in the computation. When the operator is positioned before the operand, the value of the operand is altered before it is used. When the operator is placed after the operand, the value of the operand is changed after it is used. Note in the examples above that the variable a has been incremented in each case.

Suppose that the int variable n has the value 5. Now consider a statement such as

    x = n++ / 2;

The post-incrementation operator, possessing a higher priority than all other operators in the statement, is evaluated first. But the value of n that is used in the computation of x is still 5. Post-incrementation implies using the current value of n in the computation and incrementing it immediately afterwards.

So x gets the value 5/2 = 2, even though n becomes 6. The rule is repeated; in an expression in which a post-incremented or post-decremented operand occurs, the current (unaltered) value of the operand is used; only then, is it changed. Accordingly, in the present instance, 5 is the value of n that is used in the computation. n itself becomes 6.

Now consider the following statement.

    x = ++n / 2;

where n is initially 5.

Pre-incrementation or pre-decrementation first alters the operand n; it is this new value that is used in the evaluation of x. In the example, n becomes 6, as before; but this new value is the value used in the computation, not 5. So x gets the value 6/2 = 3.

Now, consider the following program:

```c
int main()
{
    int x=5;
    printf("Values are %d and %d\n",x++,++x);
    return 0;
}
```

Before revealing the results, let us see if we can work out what the output of the program will be. Here it is needed to consider the values passed to the `printf()` function. The first part of the expression is "x++". This is a post-increment (use-and-increment) expression so the value of the expression is 5 and as a side effect of evaluating the expression the value of x is increased to 6. Next the value of the expression "++x" is calculated. This is the pre-increment (increment-and-use) expression so the value of the expression is clearly 7. Thus the expected output is

```
Values are 5 and 7
```

Some compilers give this expected output but trying the same program using the Turbo C as well as GCC based compiler for example in Quincy 2005 resulted in the output

```
Values are 6 and 7
```

This is rather surprising but it can easily be explained. The C programming language standard rules quite specifically allow the parameters to be passed to a function to be evaluated in any convenient order. Some compilers worked left to right, which seems more natural, whereas others worked right to left which may be more efficient in some circumstances.

This must be remembered when writing programs that are to be compiled on many different machines. A similar difficulty arises when considering the output of a program such as

```
int main()
{
    int x = 4;
    printf("Result = %d\n",x++ + x);
    return 0;
}
```

Since the standard allows expressions involving commutative associative operators such as "+" to be evaluated in any order, a moment's thought shows that the value printed out would be 8 for right-to-left evaluation and 9 for left-to-right evaluation. On the Quincy 2005 the output was

```
Result = 8
```

whereas the Turbo C compiler gave the result

```
Result = 9
```

Strictly the behaviour of the program is undefined, which means the C standard fails to define what the result

should be.

The following statements are undefined

```
i = ++i + 1;
a[i++] = i;
```

while allowing the following statements

```
i = i + 1;
a[i] = i;

#include <stdio.h>
int main(void)
{
    int number = 5;
    printf("the number is: %d\n", number);
    return 0;
}
```

When compiled and executed, this program should display the following onto the screen:

```
the number is: 5
```

If the %d specifier is omitted the value 5 vanishes from the output.

The values of several variables of different types in a single statement as shown in the following example:

```
#include <stdio.h>
int main(void)
{
    int i = 5;
    char ch= 'A';
    float f=12.345;
    printf("\n i = %d ch = %c f = %f", i, ch, f);
    return 0;
}
```

Output:

```
i = 5 ch = A f = 12.345000
```

The conversion specifiers are replaced in order by the values of the variables that appear as the second and subsequent arguments to the `printf()` function, so the value of i corresponds to the first specifier %d, and the value of ch corresponds to the second one, i.e. %c and so on.

One important point to note is that when a variable is not initialized with some values then what is printed on the screen if the following program is compiled and run –

```
#include <stdio.h>
int main(void)
{
    int number;
    printf("the number is: %d\n", number);
    return 0;
}
```

The output will be anything in that the values are indeterminate; this means that one cannot make any assumptions about what values are initially in a location. On many systems we will find that the initial value is zero but you must not rely on this.

Abbreviated (compound) assignment expressions It is frequently necessary in computer programs to make assignments such as

```
n = n + 5;
```

C allows a shorter form for such statements, as shown.

```
n += 5;
```

Assignment expressions for other arithmetic operations may be similarly abbreviated as shown.

```
n -= 5; /* is equivalent to n = n - 5; */
n *=5;  /* is equivalent to n = n * 5; */
n /= 5; /* is equivalent to n = n / 5; */
n %= 5; /* is equivalent to n = n % 5; */
```

The priority and direction of association of each of the operators +=, -=, *=, /=, and %= is the same as that of the assignment operator.

3.13.2 Relational Operators

C provides six relational operators for comparing numeric quantities. These are summarized in Table 3.12. Relational operators evaluate to 1, representing the *true* outcome, or 0, representing the *false* outcome.

Table 3.12 Relational operators

Operator	Action	Example
==	Equal	5 == 5 /* gives 1 */
!=	Not equal	5 != 5 /* gives 0 */
<	Less than	5 < 5.5 /* gives 1 */
<=	Less than or equal	5 <= 5 /* gives 1 */
>	Greater than	5 > 5.5 /* gives 0 */
>=	Greater than or equal	6.3 >= 5 /* gives 1 */

Note that the <= and >= operators are only supported in the form shown. In particular, =< and => are both invalid and do not mean anything.

The operands of a relational operator must evaluate to a number. Characters are valid operands since they are represented by numeric values. For example (assuming ASCII coding),

```
'A' < 'F'          /* gives 1 (is like 65 < 70) */
```

The relational operators should not be used for comparing strings because this will result in string *addresses* being compared, not string contents. For example, the expression

```
"HELLO" < "BYE"
```

causes the address of "HELLO" to be compared to the address of "BYE". As these addresses are determined by the compiler (in a machine-dependent manner), the outcome may be 0 or may be 1, and is therefore undefined.

C provides library functions (e.g., strcmp) for the lexicographic comparison of strings. These will be described later in the book.

3.13.3 Logical Operators

C provides three logical operators for forming logical expressions. These are summarized in Table 3.13. Like the relational operators, logical operators evaluate to 1 or 0.

Logical *negation* is a unary operator that negates the logical value of its single operand. If its operand is non-zero, it produces 0, and if it is 0, it produces 1. Logical AND produces 0 if one or both its operands evaluate to 0. Otherwise, it produces 1. Logical OR produces 0 if both its operands evaluate to 0. Otherwise, it produces 1.

Table 3.13 Logical operators

Operator	Action	Example	Result
!	Logical Negation	!(5 == 5)	0
&&	Logical AND	5 < 6 && 6 < 6	0
||	Logical OR	5 < 6 || 6 < 5	1

Note that here, zero and non-zero operands are mentioned, not zero and 1. In general, any non-zero value can be used to represent the logical *true*, whereas only zero represents the logical *false*. The following are, therefore, all valid logical expressions.

```
!20        gives 0
10 && 5    gives 1
10 || 5.5  gives 1
10 && 0    gives 0
```

C does not have a built-in Boolean type. It is customary to use the type int for this purpose instead. For example,

```
int   sorted = 0;     /* false */
int   balanced = 1;   /* true  */
```

Exceptions in the evaluation of logical expressions containing && and || If the left operand yields a false value, the right operand is not evaluated by a compiler in a logical expression using &&. If the left operand evaluates true value, the right operand is not evaluated by the compiler in a logical expression with the || operator. The operators && and || have left to right associativity. Hence the left operand is evaluated first and, depending on the output, the right operand may or may not be evaluated.

Example

```
5.#include <stdio.h>
  int main()
  {
    int i=0, j=1;
    printf("\n %d", i++ && ++j);
    printf("\n %d %d", i,j);
    return 0;
  }
```

Output:

```
0
1 1
```

3.13.4 Bitwise Operators

C provides six bitwise operators for manipulating the individual bits in an integer quantity. These are summarized in Table 3.14.

Bitwise operators expect their operands to be integer quantities and treat them as bit sequences. Bitwise *negation* is a unary operator that complements the bits in its operands. Bitwise AND compares the corresponding bits of its operands and produces a 1 when both bits are 1, and 0 otherwise. Bitwise OR compares the corresponding bits of its operands and produces a 0 when both bits are 0, and 1 otherwise. Bitwise *exclusive* OR compares the corresponding bits of its operands and produces a 0 when both bits are 1 or both bits are 0, and 1 otherwise.

Table 3.14 Bitwise operators

Operator	Action	Example
~	Bitwise Negation	~'\011' /* gives '\066' */
&	Bitwise AND	'\011' & '\027' /* gives '\001' */
|	Bitwise OR	'\011' | '\027' /* gives '\037' */
^	Bitwise Exclusive OR	'\011' ^ '\027' /* gives '\036' */
<<	Bitwise Left Shift	'\011' << 2 /* gives '\044' */
>>	Bitwise Right Shift	'\011' >> 2 /* gives '\002' */

Bitwise *left shift* operator and bitwise *right shift* operator both take a bit sequence as their left operand and a positive integer quantity n as their right operand. The former produces a bit sequence equal to the left operand but which has been shifted n bit positions to the left. The latter produces a bit sequence equal to the left operand but which has been shifted n bit positions to the right. Vacated bits at either end are set to 0. The general form of the right shift statement is

variable_name >> number of bit positions;

and that of the left shift statement is

variable_name << number of bit positions;

Table 3.15 illustrates bit sequences for the sample operands. To avoid worrying about the sign bit (which is machine dependent), it is common to declare a bit sequence as an unsigned quantity

```
unsigned char x = '\011';
unsigned char y = '\027';
```

Table 3.15 Effect of bit-wise operator implementation

Example	Octal value	Bit sequence							
x	011	0	0	0	0	1	0	0	1
y	027	0	0	0	1	0	1	1	1
~x	366	1	1	1	1	0	1	1	0
x & y	001	0	0	0	0	0	0	0	1
x | y	037	0	0	0	1	1	1	1	1
x ^ y	036	0	0	0	1	1	1	1	0
x << 2	044	0	0	1	0	0	1	0	0
x >> 2	002	0	0	0	0	0	0	1	0

3.13.5 Conditional Operator

The conditional operator has three expressions. It has the general form

expression1 ? expression2 : expression3

First, *expression1* is evaluated; it is treated as a logical condition. If the result is non-zero, then *expression2* is evaluated and its value is the final result. Otherwise, *expression3* is evaluated and its value is the final result. For example,

```
int m = 1, n = 2, min;
min = (m < n ? m : n); /* min is assigned a value 1 */
```

In the above example, because m is less than n, m<n expression evaluates to be true, therefore, min is assigned the value m, i.e., 1.

The same code can also be written using the if-else construct, described in Chapter 5.

```
int m=1, n=2, min;
if(m<n)
   min=m;
else min=n;
```

Note that out of the second and the third expressions of the conditional operator, only one is evaluated. This may be significant when one or both contain side effects, that is, their evaluation causes a change to the value of a variable. For example, in

```
min = (m < n ? m++ : n++);
```

m is incremented because m++ is evaluated but n is not incremented because n++ is not evaluated.

3.13.6 Comma Operator

The comma operator allows the evaluation of multiple expressions, separated by the *comma*, from left to right in order and the evaluated value of the rightmost expression is accepted as the final result. The general form of an expression using a *comma* operator is

```
expressionM = (expression1, expression2, …,
               expressionN);
```

where the expressions are evaluated strictly from left to right and their values discarded, except for the last one, whose type and value determine the result of the overall expression. Here, it may be stated that in the preceding general form, the left hand side expression, expressionM, may be omitted. In such a case, the right hand side expressions exist and the *comma* operator evaluates these from left to right. Finally, the value of the last expression is returned as the outcome. The application of the comma operator is best explained by the following examples.

Examples

6.
```
int i = 0;
int j;
j = (i += 1, i += 2, i + 3);
```
In this example, the *comma* operator is used with three expressions on the right hand side of the assignment operator. Hence, the comma operator takes these three expressions and evaluates them from left to right and returns the value of the rightmost expression. Thus, in this example, the operator first evaluates "i += 1" which increments the value of i. Then the next expression "i += 2" is evaluated which adds 2 to i, leading to a value of 3. The third expression is evaluated and its value is returned as the operator's result. Thus, j is assigned a value of 6.

7.
```
int m = 1;
int n;
n = (m = m+3, m%3);
```
Here, the comma operator takes two expressions. The operator first evaluates "m = m+3" which assigns a value 4 to m. Then the expression m%3 is evaluated to 1. Thus n is assigned a value of 1.

8.
```
int m, n, min;
int mCount = 0, nCount = 0;
⋮
min = (m < n ? mCount++, nCount++, n);
```
Here when m is less than n, mCount++ is evaluated and the value of m is stored in min. Otherwise, nCount++ is evaluated and the value of n is stored in min.

9. Swapping of two integer variables using the comma operator:
```
#include <stdio.h>
int main()
{
    int a=2,b=3,c;
    c=a,a=b,b=c;  /* comma operator is used */
    printf("\n a=%d b=%d",a,b);
    return 0;
}
```
Output: a=3 b=2

From these examples, it may be concluded that the comma operator is used to ensure that parts of an expression are performed in a left to right sequence. The comma allows for the use of multiple expressions where normally only one would be allowed. It is used most often in the `for` loop statement where one statement is called for, but several actually need to be coded.

The comma operator forces all operations that appear to the left to be fully completed before proceeding to the right of the comma. This helps eliminate any inaccuracy in the evaluation of the expression. For example,

```
num1 = num2 + 1, num2 = 2;
```

The comma operator ensures that `num2` will not be changed to a 2 before `num2` has been added to 1 and the result placed in `num1`. The other similar operators that are also considered to be sequence points like the comma operator are as follows:

```
&&
||
?:
```

When any of these operators are encountered all activity associated with any operator to the left is completed before the new operator begins executing. Both the semicolon and the comma also perform this service, ensuring that there is a way to control the order of executions in a program. The commas that separate the actual arguments in a function call are punctuation symbols, not sequence points. A punctuation symbol, in a function, does not guarantee that the arguments are either evaluated or passed to the function in any particular order.

3.13.7 sizeof Operator

C provides a useful operator, `sizeof`, for calculating the size of any data item or type. It takes a single operand that may be a type name (e.g., `int`) or an expression (e.g., 100) and returns the size of the specified entity in bytes. The outcome is totally machine-dependent. The following program illustrates the use of `sizeof` on the built-in types we have encountered so far.

```c
#include <stdio.h>
int main()
{
    printf("char size = %d bytes\n", sizeof(char));
    printf("short size = %d bytes\n", sizeof(short));
    printf("int size = %d bytes\n", sizeof(int));
    printf("long size = %d bytes\n", sizeof(long));
    printf("float size = %d bytes\n", sizeof(float));
    printf("double size = %d bytes\n", sizeof(double));
    printf("1.55 size = %d bytes\n", sizeof(1.55));
    printf("1.55L size = %d bytes\n", sizeof(1.55L));
    printf("HELLO size = %d bytes\n", sizeof("HELLO"));
    return 0;
}
```

When run, the program will produce the following output (dependent on the programmer's PC):

```
char size = 1 bytes
short size = 2 bytes
int size = 2 bytes
long size = 4 bytes
float size = 4 bytes
double size = 8 bytes
1.55 size = 8 bytes
1.55L size = 10 bytes
HELLO size = 6 bytes
```

3.13.8 Expression Evaluation—Precedence and Associativity

Evaluation of an expression in C is very important to understand. Unfortunately there is no 'BODMAS' rule in C language as found in algebra. Operators have rules of precedence and associativity that are used to determine how expressions are evaluated.

When there is more than one operator in an expression, it is the relative priorities of the operators with respect to each other that will determine the order in which the expression will be evaluated. This priority is known as precedence. The *precedence* of operators determines the order in which different operators are evaluated when they occur in the same expression. Operators of higher precedence are applied before operators of lower precedence.

Consider the following expression:

```
4 + 3 * 2
```

the operator '*' has higher precedence than '+', causing the multiplication to be executed first, then the addition. Hence, the value of the expression is 10. An equivalent expression is

```
4 + (3 * 2)
```

But what happens when an expression consists of operators with same precedence. For example

```
4 / 2 *3
```

The *associativity* of operators determines the order in which operators of equal precedence are evaluated when they occur in the same expression. The associativity defines the direction, left-to-right or right-to-left, in which the operator acts upon its operands.

Both * and / have the same precedence. Here division operation will be executed first followed by multiplication. The value of the expression is 6.

Table 3.16 lists the operators in order of decreasing operator priority and states their direction of grouping.

Let's illustrate a statement as written below. Assume that n is a variable of type int:

```
n = 5 - 2 * 7 - 9;
```

The '*' has a higher precedence than '–' so it is evaluated first, and the statement is equivalent to:

```
n = 5 - 14 - 9;
```

The minus has left-to-right associativity, so the statement is equivalent to:

```
n = -18;
```

Also, the '=' has lower precedence than either '–' or '*' or any other arithmetic, logical, or relational operator, and this is how C enforces the rule that the expression to the right of the '=' gets evaluated first and then the resulting value gets assigned to the variable to the left of the '='. Here is another valid statement in C language:

```
x = x + 1;
```

The expression to the right of the equal sign is evaluated first, and its value is then assigned to the variable to the left. So let's assume the value stored in x is equal to 5. When this statement is executed, the expression to the right of '=' evaluates to 6, and the value of 6 is assigned back to x.

It makes sense for the priority of the assignment operator to be lower than the priorities of all the arithmetic operators, and for it to group from right to left. Naturally it is very important for programmers to become familiar with the precedence and grouping properties of all C operators. But if programmers are not sure of the order in which operators will be evaluated in a computation, they may use the parentheses operator, (), to override default priorities. Yes, even the parentheses is an operator in C. The parentheses operator has a priority higher than any binary operator, such as that for multiplication; it groups from left to right. Thus in the statement

```
w = x * (y * z);
```

the product y * z will be computed first; the value obtained will then be multiplied by x; lastly, the result will be assigned to w. Had the parentheses been absent, the order of the computation would first be, the multiplication of x by y, with the result stored as an intermediate quantity; second, the multiplication of this quantity by z; and third, the assignment of the result to w.

The parentheses are an example of a primary operator. C has in addition three other primary operators: array [], the dot (.), and arrow (→), which will be encountered in later chapters. All these operators have the same priority, higher than that of any other operator. They all group from left to right.

Aside from the primary operators, C operators are arranged in priority categories depending on the number of their operands. Thus a unary operator has a single operand and a higher priority than any binary operator, which has two operands. Binary operators have a higher priority than the ternary operator, which has three operands. The comma operator may have any number of operands, and has the lowest priority of all C operators. Table 3.16 illustrates this rule.

One readily available example of a unary operator is the operator for negation, the (-). It changes the sign of the quantity stated on it. Since the unary operators have higher priority than the assignment operator, in the statement

```
x = -3;
```

the 3 is first negated, and only then is this value assigned to x. The negation operator has a priority just below that of the parentheses operator; it groups from right to left. Right to left association is a property the operator for negation shares in common with all unary operators. In the following statement

```
x = -(3 * 4);
```

the presence of the parentheses ensures that the expression 3 * 4 is evaluated first. It is then negated. Finally x is assigned the value -12.

A question that might be asked is: Does C have a unary plus operator, +? In other words, can an assignment of the form a = + 5 be made? Not in compilers conforming to the K&R standard, though ANSI C does provide a unary plus operator. See Table 3.16.

Table 3.16 Precedence and associativity of operators

Operaors	Associativity
( ) [ ] . ++ (postfix) -- (postfix)	L to R
++ (prefix) -- (prefix) !~ sizeof(type) + (unary) - (unary) & (address) * (indirection)	R to L
* / %	L to R
+ -	L to R
<< >>	L to R
< <= > >=	L to R
== !=	L to R
&	L to R
^	L to R
|	L to R
&&	L to R
||	L to R
?:	R to L
= += -= *= /= %= >>= <<= &= ^= |=	R to L
, (comma operator)	L to R

Point to Note

In the division of one integer by another, the remainder is discarded. Thus 7/3 is 2, and 9/11 is 0. The % operator can only be used with the integer variables. It can not be used with the variables of float or double.

Multiplication, division, and residue-modulo operators have the same priority. Addition and subtraction operators also have equal priority, but this is lower than that of the former three operators, *, /, and %. All these operators group from left to right. In a C program, is the value of 3/5 + 2/5 the same as (3 + 2)/5? Is 3 * (7/5) the same as 3 * 7/5? The answer to both questions is 'No'.

Examples

In the examples below let x be an integer variable.

10. x = 2 * 3 + 4 * 5;

The products 2 * 3 and 4 * 5 are evaluated first; the sum 6 + 20 is computed next; finally the assignment of 26 is made to x.

11. x = 2 * (3 + 4) * 5;

The parentheses guarantee that 3 + 4 be evaluated first. Since multiplication groups from left to right, the intermediate result 7 will be multiplied by 2 and then by 5, and the assignment of 70 will finally be made to x.

12. x = 7*6 % 15/9;

Each of the operators above has equal priority; each groups from left to right. Therefore, the multiplication 7 * 6 (= 42) is done first, then the residue-modulo with respect to 15 (42 % 15 = 12), and finally the division (of 12) by 9. Since the division of one integer by another yields the integer part of the quotient and truncates the remainder, 12/9 gives the value 1. x is therefore assigned the value 1.

13. x = 7 * (6 % 15)/9;

The parentheses ensure that 6 % 15 is evaluated first. The remainder, when 6 is divided by 15, is 6. In the second step this result is multiplied by 7, yielding 42. Integer division of 42 by 9 gives 4 as the quotient, which is the value assigned to x.

14. x = 7*6 % (15/9);

Here, 15/9 is performed first and yields 1. The next computation in order is 7 * 6 % 1, i.e., the remainder, on division of 42 by 1, is 0. x gets the value 0.

15. x = 7 * ((6 % 15)/9);

The innermost parentheses are evaluated first: 6 % 15 is 6. The outer parentheses are evaluated next—6/9 is 0. x gets the value 7 * 0 = 0.

16. An example of the use of precedence of operators

```c
#include <stdio.h>
int main()
  {
    int a;
    int b = 4;
    int c = 8;
    int d = 2;
    int e = 4;
    int f = 2;
    a = b + c / d + e * f;
            /* result without parentheses */
    printf("The value of a is = %d \n", a);
    a = (b + c) / d + e * f;
            /* result with parentheses */
    printf("The value of a is = %d \n", a);
    a = b + c / ((d + e) * f);
            /* another result with parentheses */
    printf("The value of a is = %d \n", a);
    return 0;
}
```

Output:
```
The value of a is = 16
The value of a is = 14
The value of a is = 4
```

3.14 EXPRESSIONS REVISITED

An expression in C consists of a syntactically valid combination of operators and operands that computes to a value. An expression by itself is not a statement. Remember, a statement is terminated by a semicolon; an expression is not. Expressions may be thought of as the constituent elements of a statement, the 'building blocks' from which statements may be constructed. The important thing to note is that every C expression has a value. The number 7 as we said a while ago, or any other number by itself, is also an expression, the value of the number being the value of the expression. For example,

    3 * 4 % 5

is an expression with value 2.

    x = 3 * 4

is an example of an assignment expression. Note the absence of the semicolon in the assignment above. The terminating semicolon would have converted the expression into a statement. Like any other C expression, an assignment expression also has a value. Its value is the value of the quantity on the right-hand side of the assignment operator. Consequently, in the present instance, the value of the expression (x = 3 * 4) is 12. Consider a C statement such as

    z = (x = 3 * 4) / 5;

Here the parentheses ensure that x is assigned the value 12 first. It is also the value of the parenthetical expression (x = 3 * 4), from the property that every expression has a value. Thus the entire expression reduces to

    z = 12/5

Next in order of evaluation, the integer division of 12 by 5 yields 2. The leftmost assignment operator finally gives the value 2 to z. x continues to have the value 12. Consider the expression

    x = y = z = 3

The assignment operator groups from right to left. Therefore the rightmost assignment

    z = 3

is made first. z gets the value 3; this is also the value of the rightmost assignment expression, z = 3. In the next assignment towards the left the expression is

    y = z = 3

Since the sub-expression z = 3 has the value 3, so

    y = (z = 3)

i.e., y = 3

The assignment to y is again of the value 3. Equally then the entire expression

    y = z = 3

gets the value 3. In the final assignment towards the left, x gets the value of this latter expression

    x = (y = (z = 3))

Each parenthetical expression is 3. Thus x is 3. One statement that often confuses novice programmers is

    x = x * x;

For those who have studied algebra, the immediate reaction may well be, 'This cannot be right, unless x is 0 or x is 1; and x is neither 0 nor 1 in the program.' However, the statement

    x = x * x;

is not an algebraic equation. It is an instruction to the computer, which in English translates to the following:

> Replace x by x times x.

Or, more colloquially, after its execution

> (new value of x) is (old value of x) * (old value of x)

3.15 LVALUES AND RVALUES

An lvalue is an expression to which a value can be assigned. An rvalue can be defined as an expression that can be assigned to an lvalue. The lvalue expression is located on the *left side* of an assignment operator, whereas an rvalue is located on the *right side* of an assignment operator.

The address associated with a program variable in C is called its lvalue; the contents of that location are its rvalue, the quantity that is supposed to be the value of the variable. The rvalue of a variable may change as program execution proceeds; but never its lvalue. The distinction between lvalues and rvalues becomes sharper if one considers the assignment operation with variables a and b.

    a = b;

b, on the right-hand side of the assignment operator, is the quantity to be found at the address associated with b, i.e., an rvalue. a is assigned the value stored in the address associated with b. a, on the left-hand side, is the address at which the contents are altered as a result of the assignment. a is an lvalue. The assignment operation deposits b's rvalue at a's lvalue.

An `lvalue` cannot be a constant. For example, consider the following statements:

```
1 =  x;
x + y = a + b;
x + b = 5;
```

In each of the above cases, the left side of the statement evaluates to a constant value that cannot be changed because constants do not represent storable locations in memory. Therefore, these two assignment statements *do not* contain lvalue and will generate compiler errors.

Unlike an lvalue, an rvalue can be a constant or an expression, as shown here:

```
int x, y;
x = 5; /* 5 is an rvalue; x is an lvalue */
y = (x + 1); /* (x + 1) is an rvalue; y is an
lvalue */
```

The difference between lvalue and rvalue is given in Table 3.17.

Table 3.17   Lvalue versus rvalue

Lvalue	Rvalue
Consider the following assignment statement: a = b;	
Refers to the address that 'a' represents.	Means the content of the address that b represents.
Is known at compile time.	Is not known until runtime.
Says where to store the value.	Tells what is to be stored.
Cannot be an expression or a constant.	Can be an expression or a constant.

3.16 TYPE CONVERSION IN C

Though the C compiler performs *automatic type conversions*, the programmer should be aware of how casting is done as to understand how C evaluates expressions.

3.16.1 Type Conversion in Expressions

When a C expression is evaluated, the resulting value has a particular data type. If all the variables in the expression are of the same type, the resulting type is of the same type as well. For example, if x and y are both of int type, the expression x + y is of int type as well.

What if the variables of an expression are of different types? In that case, the expression has the same data type as that of the variable with the largest size data type present in it. The smallest to the largest data types with respect to

size are given as follows:

```
char
int
long
float
double
```

Thus, an expression containing an int and a char evaluates to type int, an expression containing a long and a float evaluates to type float, and so on. Within expressions, individual operands are promoted as necessary to match the associated operands in the expression. Operands are promoted in pairs for each binary operator in the expression. If both operands are of the same type, promotion is not needed. If they are not, promotion follows these rules:

- float operands are converted to double.
- char or short (signed or unsigned) are converted to int (signed or unsigned).
- If any one operand is double, the other operand is also converted to double, and that is the type of the result.
- If any one operand is long, the other operand is treated as long, and that is the type of the result.
- If any one operand is of type unsigned, the other operand is converted to unsigned, and that is the type of the result; or the only remaining possibility is that both operands must be int, and that is also the type of the result.

Figure 3.17 illustrates the rule for data type promotion in an expression.

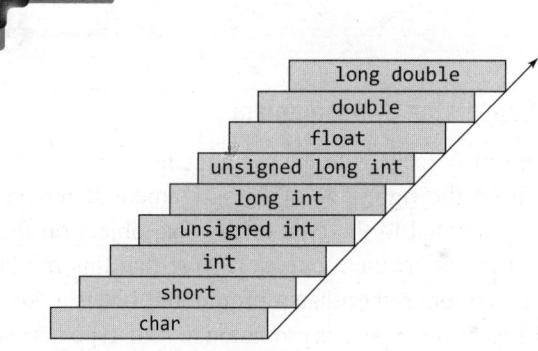

Figure 3.17   Rule for data type promotion in an expression

For example, if x is an int and y is a float, evaluating the expression x/y causes x to be promoted to float type before the expression is evaluated. This does not mean that the type of variable x is changed. It means that a float type copy of x is created and used in the evaluation of the expression. The value of the expression is the float type. Likewise, if x is a double type and y is a float type, y will be promoted to double.

Figure 3.18 shows how the rule of type promotion is followed in a typical expression containing variables of mixed types. The data type of r evaluates to double.

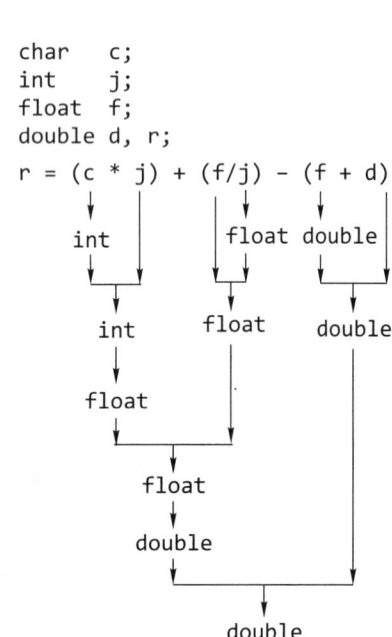

```
char   c;
int    j;
float  f;
double d, r;
r = (c * j) + (f/j) - (f + d)
```

Figure 3.18 Conversion of types in a mixed expression

3.16.2 Conversion by Assignment

Promotions also occur with the assignment operator. The expression on the right side of an assignment statement is always promoted to the type of the data object on the left side of the assignment operator. Note that this might cause a 'demotion' rather than a promotion. If f is a float type and i is an int type, i is promoted to float type in this assignment statement:

```
f = i;
```

In contrast, the assignment statement

```
i = f;
```

causes f to be demoted to type int. Its fractional part is lost on assignment to i. Remember that f itself is not changed

at all; promotion affects only a copy of the value. Thus, after the following statements are executed

```
float f = 1.23;
int i;
i = f;
```

the variable i has the value 1, and f still has the value 1.23. As this example illustrates, the fractional part is lost when a floating point number is converted to an integer type.

The programmer should be aware that when an integer type is converted to a floating point type, the resulting floating point value might not exactly match the integer value. This is because the floating point format used internally by the computer cannot accurately represent every possible integer number.

In most cases, any loss of accuracy caused by this would be insignificant. To be sure, however, keep integer values in int type or long type variables.

Conversions of characters and integers

There are six basic methods of converting values from one type to another. The methods are.

1. **Sign extension** This technique is adopted when converting a signed object to a wider signed object. For example converting a short int to a long int. It preserves the numerical value by filling the extra leading space with 1's or 0's.

2. **Zero extension** This is used when converting an unsigned object to a wider unsigned object. It works by simply prefixing the value with the relevant number of zeroes.

3. **Preserve low order data - truncate** This is used when converting an object to a narrower form. Significant information may be lost.

4. **Preserve bit pattern** This is used when converting between signed and unsigned objects of the same width.

5. **Internal conversion** This uses special hardware to convert between floating point types and from integral to floating point types.

6. **Truncate at decimal point** This is used to convert from floating point types to integral types, it may involve loss of significant information.

The basic conversions listed above are those that take place on assignment.

Conversion of a shorter integer to a longer integer preserves the sign. Traditional C uses 'unsigned preserving integer promotion' (unsigned short to unsigned int), while ANSI C uses 'value preserving integer promotion' (unsigned short to int).

A longer integer is truncated on the left when converted to a shorter integer or to a char. Excess bits are discarded.

When an unsigned integer is converted to a longer unsigned or signed integer, the value of the result is preserved. Thus, the conversion amounts to padding with zeros on the left.

When an unsigned integer is converted to a shorter signed or unsigned integer, the value is truncated on the left. If the result is signed, this truncation may produce a negative value.

Consider the following program which illustrates the above facts:

```c
#include <stdio.h>
int main()
{
  short    int    si;
  long     int    li;
  unsigned        short   int    usi;
  unsigned        long    int    uli;
  si = -10;
  li = si; /* sign extension - li should be -10 */
  printf("si = %8hd li = %8ld\n",si,li);
  usi = 40000U; /* unsigned decimal constant */
  uli = usi;
       /* zero extension - uli should be 40000 */
  printf("usi = %8hu uli = %8lu\n",usi,uli);
  uli = 0xabcdef12;        /* sets most bits ! */
  usi = uli;
                  /* will truncate - discard more
                            sigficant bits */
  printf("usi = %8hx uli = %8lx\n",usi,uli);
  si = usi;           /* preserves bit pattern */
  printf("si = %8hd usi = %8hu\n",si,usi);
  si = -10;
  usi = si;           /* preserves bit pattern */
  printf("si = %8hd usi = %8hu\n",si,usi);
  return 0;
}
```

Output:
```
si = -10     li = -10
usi = 40000  uli = 40000
usi = ef12   uli = abcdef12
si = -4334   usi = 61202
si = -10     usi = 65526
```

It may be interesting to note that the difference between the pairs of values on the last two lines is 65536. Conversions between signed long and unsigned short are typically undefined. The next program shows conversions to and from floating point types.

There is an extra complication concerning variables of type char. The conversion rules to be applied depend on whether the compiler regards char values as signed or unsigned. Basically the ANSI C standard says that variables of type char are promoted to type unsigned int or type signed int depending on whether the type char is signed or unsigned. An unsigned int may then be further converted to a signed int by bit pattern preservation. This is implementation dependent. The following program shows what might happen.

```c
#include <stdio.h>
int main()
{
  int si;
  unsigned int usi;
  char ch = 'a';
              // Most significant bit will be zero
  si = ch;    // will give small +ve integer
  usi = ch;
  printf("c = %c\n  si = %d\n usi = %u\n", ch,
              si,usi);
  ch = '\377';             /* set all bits to 1 */
  si = ch;    /* sign extension makes negative */
  usi = ch;
  printf("si = %d\n usi = %u\n",si,usi);
  return 0;
}
```

Output:
```
  c = a
 si = 97
usi = 97
 si = -1
usi = 4294967295
```

The Turbo C compiler regarded char as a signed data type applying sign extension when assigning the signed char c to the signed int si. The conversion from signed char c to unsigned int usi is more interesting. This took place in two stages, the first being sign extension and the second being bit pattern preservation. On the IBM 6150 char is treated as an unsigned data type, both assignments using bit pattern preservation.

The conversion of the unsigned char to either the signed int si or the unsigned int usi is by bit pattern preservation.

Conversion of float and double

ANSI C considers all floating point constants to be implicitly double precision, and operations involving such constants therefore take place in double precision. To force single precision arithmetic in ANSI C, use the `f` or `F` suffix on floating point constants. To force long double precision on constants, use the `l` or `L` suffix. For example, `3.141` is long double precision, `3.14` is double precision, and `3.14f` is single precision in ANSI C.

What happens if you try to make a float variable exceed its limits? For example, suppose you multiply `1.0e38f` by `1000.0f` (overflow) or divide `1.0e-37f` by `1.0e8f` (underflow)? The result depends on the system. Either could cause the program to abort and to print a runtime error message. Or overflows may be replaced by a special value, such as the largest possible float value; underflows might be replaced by 0. Other systems may not issue warnings or may offer you a choice of responses. If this matter concerns you, check the rules for your system. If you cannot find the information, do not be afraid of a little trial and error.

Conversion of floating and integral types

When a floating value is converted to an integral value, the rounded value is preserved as long as it does not overflow. When an integral value is converted to a floating value, the value is preserved unless a value of more than 6 significant digits is being converted to single precision, or 15 significant digits is being converted to double precision.

Whenever a floating-point value is assigned to an integer variable in C, the decimal portion of the number gets truncated. Assigning an integer variable to a floating variable does not cause any change in the value of the number; the value is simply converted by the system and stored in the floating variable. The following program shows conversions to and from floating point types.

```
#include <stdio.h>
int main()
{
  double  x;
  int     i;
  i = 1400;
  x = i;  /* conversion from int to double */
  printf("x = %10.6le i = %d\n",x,i);
  x = 14.999;
```

```
  i = x;   /* conversion from double to int */
  printf("x = %10.6le i = %d\n",x,i);
  x = 1.0e+60;    /* a LARGE number */
  i = x;  /* won't fit - what happens ?? */
  printf("x = %10.6le i = %d\n",x,i);
  return 0;
}
```

Producing the output

```
x = 1.445000e+03 i = 1445
x = 1.499700e+01 i = 14
x = 1.000000e+60 i = 2147483647
```

The loss of significant data, a polite way of saying the answer is wrong, in the final conversion should be noted.

3.16.3 Casting Arithmetic Expressions

Casting an arithmetic expression tells the compiler to represent the value of the expression in a certain way. In effect, a cast is similar to a promotion, which was discussed earlier. However, a cast is under the programmer's control, not the compiler's. For example, if `i` is a type `int`, the expression

```
(float)i
```

casts `i` to float type. In other words, the program makes an internal copy of the value of `i` in floating point format. When is a typecast used with an arithmetic expression? The most common use is to avoid losing the fractional part of the answer in an integer division. Consider the following example.

Example

17. When one integer is divided by another, any fractional part of the answer is lost.

```
#include <stdio.h>
int main()
{
  int a = 100,b = 40;
  float c;
  ...
  ...
  c = a/b;
  return 0;
}
```

If the value of c is printed, the output will be 2.000000. The answer displayed by the program is 2.000000, but 100/40 evaluates to 2.5. What happened? The expression a/b contains two int type variables. Following the rules explained earlier in this chapter, the value of the expression is int type itself. As such, it can represent only whole numbers, so the fractional part of the answer is lost.

It may be assumed that assigning the result of a/b to a float type variable promotes it to float type. This is correct, but it is too late; the fractional part of the answer is already gone.

To avoid this sort of inaccuracy, one of the int type variables must be cast to float type. If one of the variables is cast to type float, the previous rules say that the other variable is promoted automatically to float type, and the value of the expression is also float type. The fractional part of the answer is thus preserved. To demonstrate this, change the statement

```
c = a/b;
```

in the source code so that the assignment statement reads as follows:

```
c = (float)a/b;
```

The program will then display the correct answer.

Rounding a floating point value to a whole number

A floating point value can be rounded to an integer simply by adding 0.5 before storing it in an integer storage location. Normally, when a floating point value is assigned to an integer storage location, the fractional value (digits to the right of the decimal point) is 'truncated' (chopped-off). If we declare an integer variable named N with the statement

```
int N;
```

and then attempt to assign a floating point value into it with the statement

```
N = 2.8;
```

the variable N would receive the whole value 2, not the value 2.8 or the rounded value 3. Therefore, to assign the rounded result of 2.8 into variable N, we would use the simple expression

```
N = 2.8 + 0.5;
```

which would increase the value to 3.3 and then truncate the .3 portion, resulting in the rounded value 3.

If you had a floating point value stored in a variable named A and you wanted to round it to a whole number and store that in an integer variable named B, the statement would be

```
B = A + 0.5;
```

If you had a complex formula such as

```
(X + 8.5) / (Y - 4.2)
```

that would result in a floating point value and if you want to round off the result to a whole number and store that in an integer variable named C, the statement would be

```
C = (X + 8.5) / (Y - 4.2) + 0.5;
```

Rounding a floating point value to a specific decimal precision

A floating point value can be rounded to a specific decimal precision by following the four major steps described above, but with special care given to production of the appropriate data type during each part of the process. Using casting, we can force a value into an integer data type during a calculation. This would be done just before the step in which we truncate unwanted digits to the right of the offset decimal point. Normally, when a floating point value is converted into an integer, the fractional value (digits to the right of the decimal point) is 'truncated' (chopped-off).

Consider the following example in which a stored floating point value is rounded to 2 decimal places, as are the results of most monetary calculations.

Given the following floating point variables

```
float F;  /* A floating point value that needs to
             be rounded */
float R;  /* A floating point value that has been
             rounded */
```

If we assign a floating point value into F with the statement

```
F = 2.468;
```

the variable F would receive the value 2.468, not the rounded value of 2.47 which would be appropriate for most monetary uses. To assign the rounded result of 2.47 into variable R, we would use the expression

```
R = (int) (F*100+0.5) / 100.0;
```

which would offset the decimal point two places by multiplying F by 100 (resulting in 246.8), then bump the value to 247.3, and then truncate the .3 portion by casting the value into integer form, and finally reposition the decimal point by dividing the result by 100.0. It is essential to write the value 100 in floating point notation (with the .0 attached) to prevent C from performing integer division which would corrupt the results.

When rounding the results of a floating point calculation, simply substitute that expression in place of F in the expression above. But pay careful attention to data types and the order of precedence of operators in the larger expression. For example, if the expression was

```
X+Y;
```

where X and Y were double precision floating point values (long floats), then the larger expression made by inserting X+Y in place of F in the rounding formula above would be

```
R = (long int) ((X+Y)*100+0.5) / 100.0;
```

Notice the enclosure of the X+Y inside of parentheses to force the weak addition operator to be performed before the stronger multiplication by 100. Notice also the use of the long int data type in the casting to allow for the high precision floating point result required by double precision floating point values.

If our intention was to round the floating point value F to three decimal places, then we would use a factor of 1000 (10 raised to the 3rd power) as in

```
R = (int) (F*1000+0.5) / 1000.0;
```

Check Your Progress

All the programs will have #include <stdio.h> preceding the main().

1. Which of the following is an incorrect assignment statement?

    (a) n = m = 0
    (b) value += 10
    (c) mySize = x < y ? 9 : 11
    (d) testVal = (x > 5 || x < 0)
    (e) none of the above

    Answer: (e)

2. What will be the output:

    (a) int main()
    ```
    {
        float c= 3.14;
        printf("%f", c%2);
        return 0;
    }
    ```
    Output: Compiler error

Explanation: In example (a), % operator is applied on a variable of type float. The operands of the % opearator cannot be of float or double. This is why it causes a compiler error.

(b) int main()
```
{
    printf("%d", 'A');
    return 0;
}
```
Output: 65

Explanation: In example (b), 'A' is a character constant and it is printed with format specifier %d. The ASCII equivalent of the character A is 65. So 65 will be printed.

(c) int main()
```
{
    double d= 1/2.0 - 1/2;
    printf("d=%.2lf", d);
    return 0;
}
```
Output: d=0.50

Explanation: The value of 1/2.0 is evaluated as 0.50 as one of the operands is of type double and the result would be in double. Whereas in case of 1/2, both operands are of type int. The result of this expression is 0 as an integer division of 1/2 gives 0. So the value of d is equal to 0.50 - 0, i.e. 0.50. Now, the value of d is printed with %g format specifier; so 0.50 will be printed instead of 0.500000.

(d) int main()
```
{
    unsigned int c= -2;
    printf("c=%u", c);
    return 0;
}
```
Output: c=65534

(Considering Turbo C compiler)

Explanation: An overflow occurs during an operation on unsigned integers, though the result is defined. A signed integer constant –2 is assigned to an unsigned integer variable. Such an operation on numbers is a modulo process. The number to be stored is represented as the maximum value that can be stored plus one, in this case it is 65535+1 i.e 65536, minus the signed value, here is –2. (65535+1) – 2 = 65534. Hence the output.

```
(e) int main()
    {
        char c = 'A';
        printf("%c", c + 10);
        return 0;
    }
```
Output: K

Explanation: The chatracter constant 'A' is stored in the variable c. When 10 is added with c, then 10 is added to the ASCII value of 'A' (i.e., 65). The result is 75. As the result is printed with %c, the character equivalent of 75, which is 'K', is printed on the screen.

```
(f) int main()
    {
        int a=5;
        a=printf("Good")+ printf("Boy");
        printf("%d",a);
        return 0;
    }
```
Output: GoodBoy7

Explanation: printf() function returns the number of characters printed on the screen. 'Good' and 'Boy' will be printed consecutively. The first printf () returns 4 and the second one returns 3. So 4+3=7 is stored in a. When it is printed 7 would be printed at the end of 'GoodBoy'.

```
(g) void int main()
    {
        printf("Work" "Hard");
        return 0;
    }
```
Output: WorkHard

Explanation: In example (g), adjacent string literals will automatically be joined together as one at compile time. So "WorkHard" will be printed on the screen.

```
(h) int main()
    {
        int c= - -2;
        printf("c=%d", c);
        return 0;
    }
```
Output: c = 2;

Explanation: In example (h) unary minus (or negation) operator is used twice. Here math-rule 'minus * minus = plus' is to be applied. However, one cannot give --2 instead of - -2 because the -- operator can only be applied to variables as a decrement operator (eg., i--). 2 is a constant and not a variable.

```
(i) int main()
    {
        int a=5;
        i=!a >10;
        printf("i=%d",i);
        return 0;
    }
```
Output: i = 0

Explanation: In the expression !a>10, the NOT (!) operator has more precedence than the '>' symbol. ! is a unary logical operator. !a (!5) is 0 (NOT of true is false). 0>10 is false (zero).

```
(j) int main()
    {
        printf("\nab");
        printf("\bsi");
        printf("\rha");
        return 0;
    }
```
Remember that   \n - newline
                \b - backspace
                \r - linefeed

Output: hai

Explanation: The escape sequences \n, \b and \r stand for newline, backspace and line feed respectively. At first 'ab' is printed on console. The \b deletes the character 'b' of 'ab' and appends 'si'. Therefore 'asi' is printed. Then \r causes to position the cursor at 'a' of 'asi' and replace 'as' with 'ha'. As a result finally 'hai' is printed on the screen.

```
(k) int main()
    {
        int i=5;
        printf("%d%d%d",i++, i, ++i);
        return 0;
    }
```
Output: 666

Explanation: The arguments in a function call are pushed into the stack from left to right. The evaluation is by popping out from the stack and the evaluation is from right to left, hence the result.

(l)
```c
int main()
{
    int i;
    printf("%d",scanf("%d",&i));
        /* value 10 is given as input here */
    return 0;
}
```
Output: 1

Explanation: `scanf` returns the number of items successfully read. Here 10 is given as input that should have been scanned successfully. So the number of items read is 1.

(m)
```c
int main()
{
    char n;
    n=!2;
    printf("%d",n);
    return 0;
}
```
Output: 0

Explanation: ! is a logical operator. In C, the value 0 is considered to be FALSE, and any non-zero value including negative value, is considered to be the Boolean value TRUE. Here 2 is a non-zero value, so TRUE. !TRUE is FALSE (0), so it prints 0.

(n)
```c
int main()
{
    int i=-2;
    printf("-i = %d \n",-i,);
    return 0;
}
```
Output: -i = 2

Explanation: –i is executed and this execution does not affect the value of i. In `printf` first just print the value of i. After that the value of the expression -i = -(-2) is printed.

(o)
```c
int main()
{
    int x=10,y=15,a,b;
    a=x++;
    b=++y;
    printf("%d%d\n",a,b);
    return 0;
}
```
Output: 1016

Explanation: a = x++ is evaluated as a =x then x = x + 1. So the value of a is 10 and the value of x is 11. The statement b= ++y, ++y is incremented before it is assigned to b. Hence b = ++y is evaluated as y = y+1 followed by b = y. So the value of b is 16; hence the output.

(p)
```c
int main()
{
    int x=10,y=15;
    x=x++;
    y=++y;
    printf("%d%d\n",x,y);
    return 0;
}
```
Output: 1116

Explanation: In this example, x = x++ is evaluated as x = x followed by x = x + 1. That is value of x will be 11. Same thing happens with y also.

(q)
```c
int main()
{
    int x=1,y=5;
    printf("%d ",++(x+y));
    return 0;
}
```
Output: Compiler error - Lvalue required

Explanation: The increment operator (++) cannot be used with expressions. The expression ++(x+y) stands for (x+y) = (x+y) +1. We cannot write expression in the left-hand side of the assignment operator (=).

(r)
```c
int main()
{
    int x=1,y=5;
    printf("%d ",++x+y);
    return 0;
}
```
Output: 7

Explanation: In the expression ++x+y, before addition ++x is evaluated first. The ++x yields 2 and the value of y is 5. The result of x + y is 7; hence the output.

3. How do we round numbers?

Answer: The simplest and most straightforward way is with a code like (int)(x + 0.5). This technique will not work properly for negative numbers, though.

4. Use the following values for the next four questions.

```
int a = 8, b = 3, x1, x2, x3, x4;
x1 = a * b;          x2 = a / b;
x3 = a % b;          x4 = a && b;
```

(a) The value of x1 is

   (i) 0

   (ii) 1

   (iii) 2

   (iv) 3

   (v) none of these

Output: (v)

(b) The value of x2 is

   (i) 0

   (ii) 1

   (iii) 2

   (iv) 3

   (v) none of these

Output: (iii)

(c) The value of x3 is

   (i) 0

   (ii) 1

   (iii) 2

   (iv) 3

   (v) none of these

Output: (iii)

(d) The value of x4 is

   (i) 0

   (ii) 1

   (iii) 2

   (iv) 3

   (v) none of these

Output: (ii)

5. Find the output:

(a)
```
int main()
{
    int a = 7, b = 2;
    float c;
    c = a/b;
    printf("\n%f",c);
    return 0;
}
```
Output: 3.000000

(b)
```
int main()
{
    int c = 1;
    c=c+2*c++;
    printf("\n%f",c);
    return 0;
}
```
Output: 4.000000

(c) Is i % 2 == 0

equivalent to (i % 2) == 0?

Output: Yes,

== has lower precedence than %

(d)
```
int main()
{
    int a=2,b=3, c=3;
    a=b==c;
    printf("a=%d", a);
    return 0;
}
```
Output: a=1

3.17 WORKING WITH COMPLEX NUMBERS

A *complex number* is a number with a real part and an imaginary part. It is of the form a + bi where i is the square root of minus one, and a and b are real numbers. Here a is the real part, and bi is the imaginary part of the complex number. A complex number can also be regarded as an ordered pair of real numbers (a, b).

According to C99, three complex types are supported:

```
float complex
double complex
long double complex
```

C99 implementations support three imaginary types also:

```
float imaginary
double imaginary
long double imaginary
```

To use the complex types, the complex.h header file must be included. The complex.h header file defines some macros and several functions that accept complex numbers and return complex numbers. In particular, the macro I represents the square root of −1. It enables to do the following:

```
double complex c1 = 3.2 + 2.0 * I;
```

```
float imaginary c2= -5.0 * I;
```

The following program illustrates the use of complex and imaginary types:

```
#include <stdio.h>

#include <limits.h>

#include <complex.h>

int main(void)

{

double complex cx = 3.2 + 3.0*I;

double complex cy = 5.0 - 4.0*I;

printf("Working with complex numbers:");

printf("\nStarting values: cx = %g  + %gi cy =
  %g  + %gi",creal(cx), cimag(cx), creal(cy),
  cimag(cy));
```

```
double complex sum = cx+cy;

printf("\n\nThe sum cx + cy = %g + %gi",
  creal(sum),cimag(sum));

return 0;

}
```

Output

```
Working with complex numbers:

Starting values: cx = 3.2  + 3i cy = 5  + -4i

The sum cx + cy = 8.2 + -1i
```

The creal() function returns the real part of a value of type that is passed as the argument, and cimag() returns the imaginary part. For details of the functions that can be applied on these types, the header file complex.h that is supplied with the compiler may be explored.

SUMMARY

C is a programming language that can be used to solve problems. Each of the 32 keywords of C has a fixed meaning and forms the building block for program statements. Variables are given names.

Variables hold data at memory locations allocated to them. There are five basic data types in C, namely, char, int, float, double, and void. Except type void, the basic data types can have various modifiers such as signed, unsigned, long, and short that precedes them. The computer and the data type determine the memory space allocated to a variable. Constants in C have fixed values. There are

several operators in C that can be classified as arithmetic, relational, logical, assignment, increment and decrement, conditional, bit-wise, and special. Expressions are formed with variables and operators. Operators in C have certain precedence and associativity rules that are followed while evaluating expressions. Automatic type conversion takes place according to set rules in expressions with mixed types. Forced type conversion is also possible in C. For handling complex number the complex.h leader file should be included while writing the program

---

KEY-TERMS

ASCII A standard code for representing characters as numbers which is used on most microcomputers, computer terminals, and printers. In addition to printable characters, the ASCII code includes control characters to indicate carriage return, backspace, etc.

Assembler The *assembler* creates the object code.

Associativity The *associativity* of operators determines the order in which operators of equal precedence are evaluated when they occur in the same expression. Most operators have a left-to-right associativity, but some have right-to-left associativity.

Compiler It is a system software that translates the source code to assembly code.

Constant A *constant* is an entity that does not change.

Data type The type, or *data type*, of a variable determines a set of values that the variable might take and a set of operations that can be applied to those values.

Debugger A *debugger* is a program that enables you to run another program step-by-step and examine the value of that program's variables.

IDE An Integrated Development Environment or *IDE* is an editor which offers a complete environment for writing, developing, modifying, deploying, testing, and debugging the programs.

Identifier An *identifier* or name is a sequence of characters used by the programmer to identify or name a specific object.

Keyword *Keywords* are explicitly reserved words that have a strict meaning as individual tokens to the compiler. They cannot be redefined or used in other contexts.

Linker If a source file references library functions or functions defined in other source files, the *linker* combines these functions to create an executable file.

Lvalue   An *lvalue* is an expression to which a value can be assigned.

Precedence   The *precedence* of operators determines the order in which different operators are evaluated when they occur in the same expression. Operators of higher precedence are applied before operators of lower precedence.

Preprocessor   The C preprocessor is used to modify the source program before compilation according to the preprocessor directives specified.

Rvalue   An *rvalue* can be defined as an expression that can be assigned to an lvalue.

Token   A *token* is one or more symbols understood by the compiler that help it interpret the code.

Variable   A *variable* is a named memory location. Every variable has a type, which defines the possible values that the variable can take, and an identifier, which is the name by which the variable is referred.

Whitespace   Space, newline, tab characters and comment are collectively known as *whitespace*.

Word   A *word* is the natural unit of memory for a given computer design. The word size is the computer's preferred size for moving units of information around; technically it is the width of the processor's *registers*.

FREQUENTLY ASKED QUESTIONS

1. What is the difference between compiling and linking?

Compiler converts each source file into an object file. Linker takes all generated object files, as well as the system libraries that are relevant, and builds an executable file that is stored on disk.

2. What is bug?

Any type of error in a program is known as *bug*. There are three types of errors that may occur:

Compiler errors   These are given by the compiler and prevent the program from running.

Linking errors   These are given by the linker or at runtime and end the program. The linker can also detect and report errors, for example, if part of the program is missing or a non-existent library component is referenced.

Runtime errors   These are given by the operating system.

3. Why do we need header files?

The header files primarily contain declarations relating to standard library functions and macros that are available with C. During compilation, the compilers perform type checking to ensure that the calls to the library and other user-defined functions are correct. This form of checking helps to ensure the semantic correctness of the program. The header files, which usually incorporate data types, function declarations and macros, resolve this issue. The file with .h extension is called header file, because it's usually included at the head of a program. Every C compiler that conforms to the international standard (ISO/IEC 9899) for the language will have a set of standard header files supplied with it.

4. What is a library?

A library is a collection of functions. A library file stores each function individually. When the program uses a function contained in a library, the linker looks for the function and adds its code to the program. Note the contents of the entire library are added to the executable file.

5. What is the difference between declaring a variable and defining a variable?

Declaring a variable means informing the compiler about its type without allocating any space for it. To put it simply, a declaration says to the compiler, "Somewhere in the program there will be a variable with this name, and this is the kind of data type it will have". Defining a variable means declaring it as well as allocating space to hold the variable. Here is a declaration of a variable and a variable definition:

```
extern int x; /* this is a declaration */
int y; /* this is a definition */
```

The following is a definition of a variable with initialization.

```
int y=10;
```

It is to be noted that a variable can be declared many times, but it must be defined exactly once. For this reason, definitions do not belong in header files, rather are placed in library files.

6. Why is data type specified for a variable declaration?

The type, or data type, of a variable determines the set of values that the variable might take and the set of operations that can be applied to those values.

7. What are the uses of `void` in C?

It has three uses. When it specifies the return type of a function, it means the function returns no value to the calling function. It is also used to declare that a function has no parameters. Moreover, it can create a generic pointer.

8. Which one is correct: `main()` or `void main()` or `int main()`?

Under C89, `main()` is acceptable, although it is advisable to use the C99 standard, under which only `int main(void)` is acceptable. There are some compilers where `void main()` is allowed, but these are on specialized systems only. If the programmer is not sure of whether he/she is using one of these specialized systems, then the programmer should simply avoid using `void main()`.

9. Is `main()` must?

It depends on the environment your program is written for. If it is a hosted environment, then main function is a must for any standard C program. Hosted environments are those where the program runs under an operating system. If it is a freestanding environment, then main function is not required. Freestanding environments are those where the program does not depend on any host and can have any other function designated as start up function. Freestanding implementation need not provide complete support of the standard libraries; usually only a limited number of I/O libraries will be supported and no memory management functions will be supported. Examples of freestanding implementations are embedded systems and the operating system kernel.

10. Can the prototype for `main()` be included?

Absolutely; it is legal in C though it is not required.

11. Should `main()` always return a value?

Yes, unless it encounters a call for `exit()`. When a program runs, it usually terminates with some indication of success or some error code. The return statement is not mandatory; if it is missing, the program will still terminate. In C89, the value returned to the operating system is undefined. In C99, if `main()` is declared to return an `int`, the program returns 0 (zero) to the operating system or operating environment; otherwise the program returns an unspecified value.

12. How can you check what value is returned from `main()`? Is the executed program terminated normally or not?

A "batch file" or "shell script" can be used for this purpose.

In Unix, each shell has its own method for testing the status code. In the Bourne shell, after executing the C program, the variable $? contains the status of the last program executed. The C shell has similar variable, but its name is $status.

13. What is the need of `unsigned char`?

The signedness of characters is an important issue because the standard I/O library functions which normally read characters from files return a negative value (-1 or its symbolic constant EOF) when the end of file is reached.

14. In some compilers like Turbo C the size occupied by an integer variable is 2 bytes; again in most of the compilers an integer variable takes 4 bytes of memory. What is the size of an integer variable?

The size of an `int` is usually the same as the word length of the execution environment of the program.

15. Both `%d` and `%i` can be used to read and print integers. What is the difference between `%d` and `%i`?

If `%d` is used in `scanf()`, it can only match an integer in decimal form. On the other hand if `%i` is used with `scanf()`, it can match an integer expressed in octal, decimal or hexadecimal form. If the input number is prefixed with a `0`, `%i` treats it as an octal number; if it is prefixed with `0x` or `0X`, it will be treated as a hexadecimal number.

With `printf()`, there is no such difference between these two format specifiers. The aforesaid facts are evident from the following program:

```c
#include <stdio.h>
int main(void)
{
        int n;
        printf("\n Enter an integer: ");
        scanf("%d",&n);
        printf("\n n = %d", n);
        printf("\n Enter the same integer again: ");
        scanf("%i",&n);
        printf("\n n = %i", n);
        return 0;
}
```

Output:
```
Enter an integer: 023
n = 23
Enter the same integer again: 023
n = 19
```

16. What is the difference between %f, %g and %e format specifiers when used to display a real value?

The `%f` characters are used to display values in a standard manner. Unless size and width are specified, `printf()` always displays a float or double value rounded up to six decimal places.

The `%e` characters are used to display the value of a float or double variable in scientific notation.

With the `%g` characters, `printf()` automatically removes from displaying any trailing zeroes. If no digits follow the decimal point, it does not display that either. For illustration consider the following program:

```c
#include <stdio.h>
int main()
{
  float x=12.34;
  printf("\n %f", x);
  printf("\n %g", x);
  printf("\n %e", x);
  return 0;
}
```

Output:
```
12.340000
12.34
1.234000+e001
```

17. What is lvalue and rvalue?

An `lvalue` is an expression to which a value can be assigned. An `rvalue` can be defined as an expression that can be assigned to an `lvalue`. The `lvalue` expression is located on the *left side* of an assignment statement, whereas an `rvalue` is located on the *right side* of an assignment statement.

The address associated with a program variable in C is called its `lvalue`; the contents of that location are its `rvalue`, the quantity that is supposed to be the value of the variable. The `rvalue` of a variable may change as program execution proceeds; but never its lvalue. The distinction between lvalues and rvalues becomes sharper if one considers the assignment operation with variables a and b.

a = b;

b, on the right-hand side of the assignment operator, is the quantity to be found at the address associated with b, i.e., an rvalue. a is assigned the value stored in the address associated with b. a, on the left-hand side, is the address at which the contents are altered as a result of the assignment. a is an lvalue. The assignment operation stores b's rvalue at a's lvalue.

18. What are the difference between l-value and r-value?

l-value	r-value
An l-value expression is located on the *left side* of an assignment statement.	An r-value is located on the *right side* of an assignment statement.
An l-value means the address that it represents.	An r-value means the contents of the address that it represents which is a value.
An l-value says where to store the result.	An r-value says what is to be stored.
An l-value is known at compile time.	An r-value is not known until run time.

19. Why does the statement a + b = c + d is not legal in C?

The given statement is not valid in C becouse the left side of the statement evaluates to a constant value that cannot be changed and does not represent storable locations in memory. Therefore, this assignment statement does not contain an lvalue and will generate compiler errors.

20. Why should we use i++ instead of i = i + 1?

Most C compilers produce very fast and efficient object code for increment and decrement operations. For these reason, we should use the increment and decrement operators when we can.

21. Can we apply ++ and –– operators on floating point numbers?

++ and –– operators can be applied to floating point numbers as well as integers.

22. What is the difference between the prefix and postfix forms of the ++ operator?

The prefix form increments first, and the incremented value goes on to participate in the surrounding expression (if any). The postfix form increments later; the previous value goes on to participate in the surrounding expression.

23. The % operator fails to work on float numbers. Can we get the remainder of a floating point division?

The % operator cannot be used with floating point values. But if it is required to get the remainder of floating point division, one may use the function fmod(). The fmod() function returns the remainder as a floating-point division. Following program illustrates the use of fmod() function.

```
#include <math.h>
int main( )
{
    printf ("%f", fmod (7.25, 3.0));
    return 0;

}
```

The above code snippet would give the output as 1.250000.

24. What is precedence of operators?

Operator precedence determines the sequence in which operators in an expression are evaluated. In fact, each operator in C has a precedence associated with it. The operator with the higher precedence is evaluated first. In the expression

a + b * c

the operation of multiplication is given precedence over the operation of addition. Therefore, the expression

a + b * c

is evaluated as

(a + (b * c))

25. What is associativity?

The sequence of execution for operators of equal precedence is determined by their associativity, which determines whether they are selected from left to right or from right to left.

In the expression

a * b / c

the operations of multiplication and division are of same precedence. Here associativity breaks the tie. Therefore, the expression

a * b / c

is evaluated as

((a * b) / c)

26. What's short-circuiting in C expressions?

Short-circuiting in an expression means that the right hand side of the expression is not evaluated if the left hand side determines the outcome. This means that if the left hand side is true for || or false for &&, the right hand side will not be evaluated.

27. What does the term cast refer to? Why is it used?

Casting is a mechanism built into C language that allows the programmer to force the conversion of data types. This may be needed because most C functions are very particular about the data types they process. A programmer may wish to override the default way the C compiler promotes data types. An example of a type cast which ensures that an expression evaluates to type float is as follows:

    x = (float) x / 2;

28. When should a type cast be used?

There are two situations in which the type casting may be used.

To change the type of an operand so that the arithmetic operation will be performed properly.

To cast pointer types to and from void * in order to port with functions that return void pointers e.g. `malloc()` has to be casted to the return type of the pointer in which allocated address is stored.

29. When should a type cast not be used?

There are two cases where type casting should not be used to override a `const` or `volatile` declaration. Overriding these type modifiers can cause the program to fail to run correctly. To turn a pointer to one type of structure into another.

30. Why is the output of `sizeof('a')` 2 and not 1?

Character constants in C are of type `int`, hence `sizeof ('a')` is equivalent to `sizeof(int)`, i.e. 2. Hence the output comes out to be 2 bytes.

EXERCISE

1. What is the purpose of a header file? Is the use of a header file absolutely necessary?

2. What is the return type of a program's `main()` function?

3. What is meant by a variable? What is meant by the value of a variable?

4. Name and describe the basic data types in C.

5. What is ASCII? How common is its use?

6. How can values be assigned to variables?

7. How can the % symbol be printed using a `printf()` statement?

8. What is an escape sequence? What is its purpose?

9. Describe the different types of operators that are included in C.

10. What are unary operators? State the purpose of each.

11. Describe two different ways of using the increment and decrement operators.

12. What is meant by precedence? Explain with an example.

13. What is meant by associativity? Explain with an example. What is the associativity of arithmetic operators?

14. What is the order of precedence and associativity of arithmetic operators?

15. What are bit-wise operators? Explain.

16. What is the difference between prefix and postfix of -- and ++ operators?

17. Describe the use of the conditional operator to form a conditional expression.

18. Which of the algebraic expressions matches the C expression given below?

    sqrt(x*x + y*y)/sqrt(x*x - 1)

    (a) $\sqrt{\dfrac{x^2 + y^2}{x^2 + 1}}$

    (b) $\sqrt{\dfrac{x^2 + y^2}{x^2 - 1}}$

    (c) $\sqrt{\dfrac{x^2 + y^2}{x^2 - 1}}$

    (d) $\sqrt{\dfrac{x^2 + y^2}{x^2 - y^2}}$

    (e) none of the above

19. Find the value that is assigned to the variables x, y, and z when the following program is executed.

```
int main()
{
int x, y, z;
x = 2 + 3 - 4 + 5 - (6 - 7);
y = 2 * 33 + 4 * (5 - 6);
z = 2 * 3 * 4 / 15 % 13;
x = 2 * 3 * 4 / (15 % 13);
y = 2 * 3 * (4 / 15 % 13);
z = 2 + 33 % 5 / 4;
x = 2 + 33 % - 5 /4;
y = 2 - 33 % - 5 /- 4;
z =-2*-3/-4%-5;
x =50 % (5 * (16 % 12 * (17/3)));
Y=-2*-3%-4 /-5-6+-7;
z = 8 /4 / 2*2*4*8 %13 % 7 % 3;
return 0;
}
```

By inserting appropriate calls to `printf()`, verify the answers obtained.

20. Give the output of the following program:

```
#include <stdio.h>
int main( )
{
int x = 3,y = 5,z = 7,w;
w = x % y + y % x - z % x - x % z;
printf("%d \n", w);
w = x / z + y / z + (x + y) / z;
printf("%d\n", w);
```

```
w = x / z * y / z + x * y / z;
printf("%d\n", w);
w = x % y % z + z % y % (y % x);
printf("%d\n", w);
w = z / y / y / x + z / y / (y / x);
printf("%d\n", w);
return 0;
}
```

21. What does the following program print?

```
#include <stdio.h>
int main()
{
printf("%d\n", - 1 + 2 - 12 * -13 / -4);
printf("%d\n", - 1 % - 2 + 12 % -13 % - 4);
printf("%d \n",-4/2 - 12/4 - 13 % -4);
printf("%d\n", (- 1 + 2 - 12) * (- 13 / - 4));
printf("%d\n", (- 1 % - 2 + 12) %(- 13 % - 4));
printf("%d\n", (- 4 /2 - 12) / (4 - 13 % - 4));
return 0;
}
```

22. Find the output of the following programs:

(a)
```
#include <stdio.h>
int main()
{
int x = 3, y = 5, z = 7, w =9;
w += x;
printf("w = %d\n", w);
w -= y;
printf("w = %d\n", w);
x *= z;
printf("x = %d\n", x);
w += x + y - (z -= w);
printf("w = %d, z=%d\n",w,z);
w += x -= y %= z;
printf("w = %d, x = %d, y = %d\n", w, x, y);
w *= x / (y += (z += y));
printf("w = %d, y = %d, z = %d\n", w, y, z);
w /= 2 + (w %= (x += y - (z -= -w)));
printf("w = %d, x = %d, z = %d\n", w, x, z);
return 0;
}
```

(b)
```
#include <stdio.h>
int main()
{
int x = 7, y = -7, z = 11,
    w =- 11, s = 9, t = 10;
x += (y -= (z *= (w /= (s %= t))));
printf("x = %d, y = %d, z = %d, w = %d,
        s = %d, t = %d\n", x, y, z, w, s, t);
```

```
t += s -= w *= z *= y %= x;
printf("x = %d, y %d, z = %d, w = %d,
        s = %d, t = %d\n", x, y, z, w, s, t);
return 0;
}
```

(c)
```
#include <stdio.h>
int main()
{
int amount = 7;
printf("If I give you");
printf("Rs.%05d\n", amount);
printf("You will owe me");
printf("Rs.%-05d\ n", amount);
return 0;
}
```

23. Given that x, y, z, and w are integers with the respective values 100, 20, 300, and 40, find the output from the following printf() statements.

```
printf("%d\n%d\n%d\n%d", x,*y, z, w);
printf("\t%d\n\t%d\n\t%d\n\t%d", x, y, z, w);
printf("%d %d %d %d %d %d %d %d", x, y,
        w, z, y, w, z, x);
printf("%d %d", x + z - y * y,
        (y - z % w) * x);
```

24. Execute the following program to verify the rules stated above for the output of floating point variables.

```
#include <stdio.h>
int main()
{
double pi = 3.14159265;
printf("%15f\n", pi);
printf("%15.12f\n", pi);
printf("%-15.12f\n", pi);
printf("%15.4f\n", pi);
printf("%15.0f\n", pi);
printf("%15.3g\n", pi);
printf("%15g\n", pi);
printf("%15.4e\n", pi);
printf("%15e\n", pi);
return 0;
}
```

25. What does the following program print?

```
#include <stdio.h>
int main()
{
printf("%-40.24s", "Left
        justified printing.\n");
printf("%-40.20s", "Left
        justified printing.\n");
```

```
printf("%-40.16s", "Left
        justified printing.\n");
printf("%-40.12s", "Left
        justified printing.\n");
printf("%-40. 8s", "Left
        justified printing.\n");
printf("%-40.4s", "Left
        justified printing.\n");
printf("%-40.0s", "Left
        justified printing.\n");
printf("%40.25s", "Right
        justified printing.\n");
printf("%40.20s", "Right
                                        justified printing.\n");
                             printf("%40.15s", "Right
                                        justified printing.\n");
                             printf("%40.10s", "Right
                                        justified printing.\n");
                             printf("%40.5s", "Right
                                        justified printing.\n");
                             printf("%40.0s", "Right
                                        justified printing.\n");
                             printf("%40.0s", "Right
                                        justified printing.\n");
                             return 0;
                             }
```

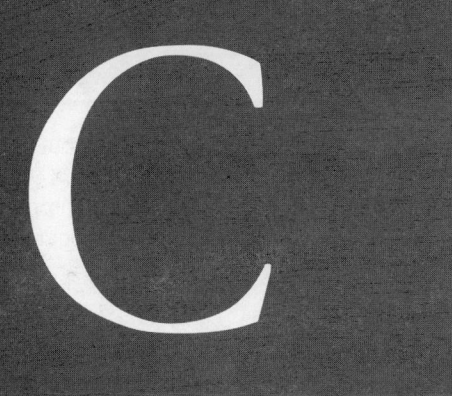

C

Input and Output

Chapter 4

Learning Objectives

After reading this chapter, the readers will be able to

- Understand what C considers as standard input and output devices
- get to know the input and output streams that exist in C to carry out the input and output tasks
- understand that C provides a set of input and output functions
- learn the use of single character unformatted input and output functions `getchar()` and `putchar()`
- learn to use the formatted input and output functions `scanf()` and `printf()` for handling multiple input and output

4.1 INTRODUCTION

For carrying out an arithmetic calculation using C, there is no way other than writing a program, which is equivalent to using a pocket calculator. Different outcomes are obtained when different values are assigned to variables involved in the arithmetic calculation.

Hence, there is a need to read values into variables as the program runs. Notice the words here: 'as the program runs'. Values can be stored in variables using the assignment operator. That is, for example, `a=100;` stores 100 in the variable 'a' each time the program is run, no matter what the program does. Without some sort of input command, every program would produce exactly the same result every time it is run. This would certainly make debugging easy. But in practice, of course, the user may need programs to do different jobs that give different outcomes each time they are run. For this purpose, C has been provided with some input instructions that are in fact a set of functions. For the present, it may be said that a function is a code segment that is complete in itself and does some particular task as and when it is called. Functions will be dealt in greater detail in Chapter 7.

When a program is in execution, each of its statements are executed one after the other or in a particular order. When this process of execution reaches an input instruction, also referred to as an input statement, the most popular being the scanf() function, the program execution pauses to give the user time to enter something on the keyboard. The execution of the program continues only after the user enters some data (or nothing) and presses <**Enter**> or <**Return**> to signal that the procedure of entering input data has been completed. The program execution then continues with the inputted value stored in the memory location reserved for the variable. In this way, each time the program is run, users get a chance to type in different values for the variable and the program also gets a chance to produce different results.

The final missing piece in the jigsaw is using an output command or statement, the commonly used one being the printf() function, the one that has already been used in some example programs in the previous chapter, to print the value currently stored in a variable.

In the context of the above example, it should be understood that the input function, scanf(), is used to read data entered through the keyboard. On the other hand, the printf() function is used to display data on the screen.

The original C specification did not include commands for input and output. Instead, the compiler writers were supposed to implement library functions to suit their machines. In practice, all chose to implement printf() and scanf() and, after a while, C programmers started to think of these functions as I/O keywords. It sometimes helps to remember that they are functions like any other function.

To make C a more uniform language, it has been provided with standard libraries of functions that perform common tasks. Though these libraries are termed standard but until the ANSI committee actually produced a standard, there was, and still is, some variation in what the standard libraries contained and exactly how the functions worked. However, in practice, the situation is not that bad; most of the functions that are used frequently are standard on all implementations. In particular the input and output functions vary very little.

This chapter will, therefore, primarily consider input functions that read data from the keyboard and output functions that display data on the screen.

> **Point to Note**
>
> The scanf() function does not prompt for an input. It is a good programming practice to always use a printf() function before a scanf() function for users of the program to know what they should enter through the keyboard.

4.2 BASIC SCREEN AND KEYBOARD I/O IN C

C provides several functions that give different levels of input and output capability. These functions are, in most cases, implemented as routines that call lower-level input/output functions.

The input and output functions in C are built around the concept of a set of standard data streams being connected from each executing program to the basic input/output devices. These standard data streams or files are opened by the operating system and are available to every C and assembler program for use without having to open or close the files. These standard files or streams are called

- stdin : connected to the keyboard
- stdout : connected to the screen
- stderr : connected to the screen

The following two data streams are also available on MS-DOS based computers, but not on Unix or other multi-user-based operating systems.

- stdaux : connected to the first serial communications port
- stdprn : connected to the first parallel printer port

A number of functions and macros exist to provide support for streams of various kinds. The <stdio.h> header file contains the various declarations necessary for the functions, together with the macros and type declarations needed for the input and output functions. The input/output functions fall into two categories: non-formatted read (input) and display (output) functions and formatted read (input) and display (output) functions.

> **Points to Note**
>
> 1. The input and output functions in C are implemented through a set of standard data streams which connect each executing program to the basic input/output devices.
> 2. The input/output functions are of two kinds: non-formatted and formatted functions.

4.3 NON-FORMATTED INPUT AND OUTPUT

Non-formatted input and output can be carried out by standard input-output library functions in C. These can handle one character at a time. For the input functions it does not require <**Enter**> to be pressed after the entry of the character. For output functions, it prints a single character on the console.

4.3.1 Single Character Input and Output

A number of functions provide for character-oriented input and output. The declaration format of two of these are given as follows:

```
int getchar(void);
//function for character input

int putchar(int c);
//function for character output
```

getchar() is an input function that reads a single character from the standard input device, normally a keyboard. putchar() is an output function that writes a single character on the standard output device, the display screen.

There are two other functions, gets() and puts(), that are used to read and write strings from and to the keyboard and the display screen respectively. A string may be defined as an arranged collection of characters. These two functions will be dealt with in greater detail in the chapter on arrays and strings.

4.3.2 Single Character Input

The getchar() input function reads an unsigned char from the input stream stdin. The character, obtained from the input stream, is treated as an unsigned char and is converted to an int, which is the return value. On 'End of File', the constant EOF is returned, and the end-of-file indicator is set for the associated stream. On error, the error indicator is set for the stream. Successive calls will obtain characters sequentially.

To read a single character from the keyboard, the general form of the statement used to call the getchar() function is given as follows:

```
char_variable = getchar();
```

where char_variable is the name of a variable of type char. The getchar()input function receives the character data entered, through the keyboard, and places it in the memory location allotted to the variable char_variable The following code

```
int ch;
ch = getchar();
```

places the character read from the keyboard in the lower byte of the variable named 'ch'.

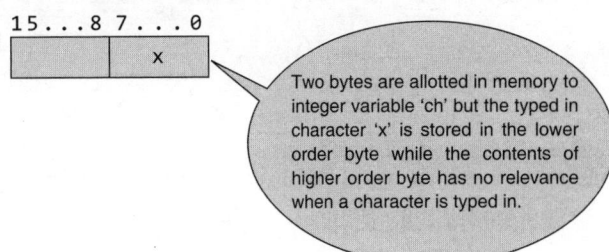

Two bytes are allotted in memory to integer variable 'ch' but the typed in character 'x' is stored in the lower order byte while the contents of higher order byte has no relevance when a character is typed in.

It has to be noted here that getchar() reads a single character from the input data stream; but does not return the character to the program until the '\n' (<**Return**> or <**Enter**>) key is pressed.

There is an important observation that has to be made about the ch = getchar(); function. Though the data entered through the keyboard is perceived to be of character type, the data is actually stored in an integer. Here, this integer is the variable ch. This is because every time ch = getchar(); reads a data from the keyboard it checks whether it is a character data or an 'EOF'. The problem is distinguishing the end of input from valid data. The solution is that getchar() returns a distinctive value when there is no more input, a value that cannot be confused with any real character. This value is called EOF, i.e., end of file. So ch must be declared to be of a type big enough to hold any value that getchar() returns. Therefore, char cannot be used since ch must be big enough to hold EOF in addition to any possible char. Therefore, int is used.

4.3.3 Single Character Output

The putchar() function is identical in description to the getchar() function except the following difference. putchar() writes a character to the stdout data stream. On success, putchar() returns the character. On error, putchar() returns EOF. There is no equivalent to 'End of File' for an output file. To write a single character on the screen, the general form of the statement used to call the putchar() function is given as follows:

```
putchar(char_variable);
```

where char_variable is the name of a variable that is of type char. The character data stored in the memory location, allotted to the variable char_variable, is displayed on the display screen.

The following program code displays the character entered through getchar() on the screen.

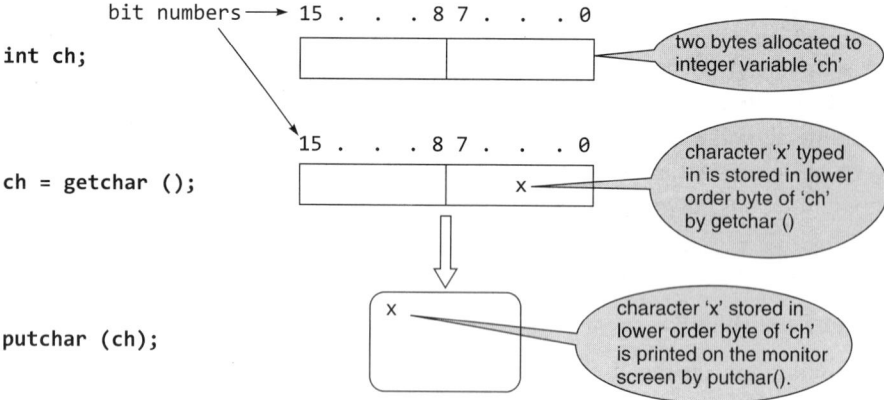

It has to be noted that the character 'x' remains stored in the lower order byte of ch even after putchar(ch) copies it and displays it on the monitor screen.

4.3.4 Additional Single Character Input and Output Functions

Other than getchar() and putchar(), there are some more single character input and output functions that are available in Turbo C only. These are as follows:

getch() This input function reads, without echoing on the screen, a single character from the keyboard and immediately returns that character to the program. General statement form:

```
ch = getch(); /* 'ch' is a character variable */
```

getche() This input function reads, with echo on the screen, a single character from the keyboard and immediately returns that character to the program. General statement form:

```
ch = getche(); /* 'ch' is a character variable */
```

putch() This output function writes the character directly to the screen. On success, the function putch() returns the character printed. On error, it returns EOF. General statement form:

```
putch(ch); /* 'ch' is a character variable */
```

When used in programs, the above functions require the header file conio.h to be included. It should be noted here that the data held by the variable in all the input and output functions are in ASCII value.

Points to Note

1. getchar(), the single character input function, reads a one byte character input from the keyboard and stores it in the lower order byte of an integer variable.

2. putchar(), the single character output function, displays a one byte character on the monitor screen.

Examples

1. Display a given character.

   Solution
   ```
   #include<stdio.h>
   int main(void)
   {
       int ch;
       ch='A';
       putchar(ch);
       return 0;
   }
   ```

   Output: A

Explanation: In this example, the variable ch is declared as an integer. In the next statement the character "A" is assigned to this variable, which results in the ASCII equivalent of the character "A" being stored in the lower order byte of the integer variable ch as shown below :

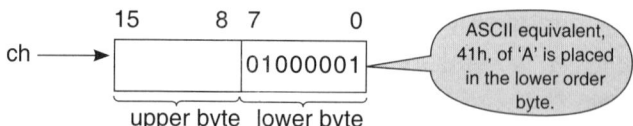

Next, when the output statement `putchar( )`, actually an output function, is executed, the ASCII equivalent of 'A' is taken from the lower order byte of the integer variable `ch` and displayed on the monitor screen.

2. Display a keyed-in character.

Solution
```
#include<stdio.h>
int main(void)
{
  int ch;
  ch=getchar();
  putchar(ch);
  return 0;
}
```

Input: A

Output: A

Explanation: Here, the typed in character is read and stored in the lower order byte allocated to the integer `ch` by the input function `getchar()`. This character is then copied on to the monitor screen by the output function `putchar(ch)`.

3. Accept a given character and display the next character from the ASCII table.

Solution
```
#include<stdio.h>
int main(void)
{
  int ch;
  ch='A';
  ch=ch + 1;
  putchar(ch);
  return 0;
}
```

Output: B

Explanation: Here, the character "A" is assigned to the integer variable `ch`. This results in the ASCII equivalent, 41h, of the character "A" being stored in the lower order byte of the integer variable `ch`. As 1 is added to the contents of `ch`, it becomes 42h, which is the ASCII representation for the character "B". So when `putchar(ch)` is executed the character displayed on the screen is "B". The figure below illustrates the contents of the variable `ch` as it changes from "A" to "B".

4. Display the keyed-in character and the next character from the ASCII table for the keyed in character.

Solution
```
#include<stdio.h>
int main(void)
{
  int ch;
  ch=getchar();
  ch=ch++;
  putchar(ch);
  return 0;
}
```

Input: a

Output: b

Explanation: This example is similar to the previous one excepting for the fact that the integer variable `ch` is assigned a character read in by `getchar()` from the keyboard. Hence, the output obtained after executing this program is similar to the previous example.

5. Double the output of next two characters from the ASCII table.

Solution
```
#include<stdio.h>
int main(void)
{
  int ch;
  ch=getchar();
  putchar(++ch); /* first putchar() */
  putchar(ch++); /* second putchar()*/
  putchar(ch);   /* third putchar() */
  putchar(ch--); /* fourth putchar()*/
  putchar(ch);   /* fifth putchar() */
  return 0;
}
```
(i) **Input**: a

 Output: bbccb

(ii) **Input**: h

 Output: iijji

Explanation: Here when the program is executed, `getchar()` obtains the typed in character and places its ASCII equivalent in the integer variable `ch`. As shown, the typed in character is chosen to be "a". Next, in the first `putchar()`, at the beginning, the content of `ch` is incremented by 1 to represents "b", then this is displayed on the monitor screen. In the second `putchar()`, the content of `ch`, which is "b", is displayed on the monitor screen and then its content is incremented by 1 to represent "c" in ASCII. In the third `putchar()`, the content of `ch`, which is "c", is displayed on the monitor screen and the contents in `ch` does not get altered. During the fourth `putchar()`, the content in `ch`, which is "c", is first displayed on the monitor screen and then the content in `ch` is decremented to represent "b" in ASCII. Therefore, during the fifth `putchar()` the content of `ch` is displayed as "b" on the monitor screen.

Similar result is obtained when the program is run for the second time with "h" as the input data.

6. Print a keyed character.

   Solution

   ```
   #include<stdio.h>
   int main(void)
   {
       int ch;
       putchar(ch=getchar());
       return 0;
   }
   ```

   Input: x

   Output: x

   Explanation: The program in this example is similar to Example 2 shown above except for the fact that the statement `ch=getchar()` is placed as a parameter of the output function `putchar()`. So when `putchar()` is executed `getchar()` gets invoked and it obtains the character data from the keyboard which is passed to `putchar()`. Then `putchar()` displays the data entered through the keyboard.

7. Print a keyed character.

   Solution

   ```
   #include<stdio.h>
   int main(void)
   {
       putchar(getchar());
       return 0;
   }
   ```

   Input: y

   Output: y

   Explanation: This example is almost similar to that of Example 6. The only difference is that the integer variable `ch` has been omitted. But otherwise this program executes similarly as that in Example 6.

8. Get an ASCII number that is ahead by two positions from the keyed number.

   Solution

   ```
   #include<stdio.h>
   int main(void)
   {
   ```

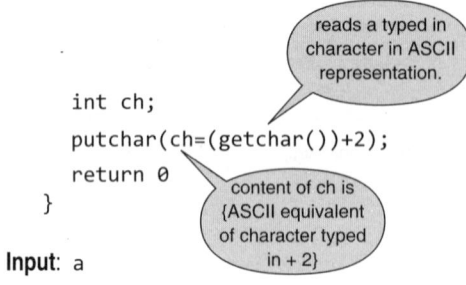

   ```
       int ch;
       putchar(ch=(getchar())+2);
       return 0
   }
   ```

   Input: a

   Output: c

   Explanation: Here, the ASCII equivalent of the typed in character "a", read in by `getchar()`, is 61h. To this 2 is added to make it 63h. The alphabetic character represented by 63h is "c". Therefore, `putchar()` displays this character on the monitor screen.

9. Compare two numbers.

   Solution

   ```
   #include<stdio.h>
   #include<conio.h>
   int main(void)
   {
     int a=2,b=5;
     int t,f,x;
     t=getchar();
     fflush(stdin);   /* the fflush() function clears */
                      /* the input stream stdin       */
     f=getchar();
     x=((a>b)?t:f);
     putchar(x);
     putch(x);
     return 0;
   }
   ```

   Input: 1
              0

   Output: 00

   Explanation: In this example, the character entered in variable "t" is 1 while that for "f" is 0. During evaluation of the expression `x=((a>b)?t:f)` the relation a > b is found to be false, so "f" is assigned to x. Since f contains 0, thus x is assigned this character 0. Therefore, `putchar(x)` displays a 0 on the monitor screen. Since there is no new-line command following the display of 0, the cursor positions itself next to this character. Now, when `putch(x)` is executed it displays the value in x at the cursor positioned next to the earlier display. So the output finally appears as 00.

10. Convert alphabets from lowercase letters to capital letters.

Solution

```c
#include<stdio.h>
int main(void)
{
  int ch,n;
  ch=getchar();
  n=(ch>='a')&&(ch<='z')?
                    putchar(ch+'A'-'a'): putchar(ch);
  putchar(n);
  return 0;
}
```

   (i) **Input**: m

   Output: MM

   (ii) **Input**: b

   Output: BB

   (iii) **Input**: $

   Output: $$

Explanation: In this example program, once the typed in character is read in by getchar(), it's ASCII equivalent is stored in the integer variable ch. Next, the expression (ch>='a')&&(ch<='z') is evaluated. The ASCII equivalent value in ch is compared with the ASCII equivalent value of the beginning (means 'a') and ending(means 'z') characters of the alphabet. In short, this expression checks to find whether the character entered is one among the characters 'a' to 'z' of the alphabet. If this is true, then the function putchar(ch+'A'-'a') is executed and its return value is assigned to "n"; otherwise the function putchar(ch)is executed. Here, it may be noted that on evaluating the expression (ch +'A'-'a') an ASCII value representing the upper-case alphabet corresponding to the lower-case value is obtained. So putchar(ch+'A'-'a') displays the upper-case alphabet and assigns this character to "n". On the otherhand, if the typed in character is none among the alphabets a to z, then the typed in character is displayed. In any case, the output function putchar(n) displays the character once again.

The following two programs depict what happens when getch() and getche() are used.

11. Write a program to show the usefulness of getch().

Solution

```c
#include <stdio.h>
int main()
{
  int ch;
  printf("\nContinue(Y/N)?");
  ch = getch();
  putch(ch);
  return 0;
}
```

This typed-in character is read in by getch() and kept in variable ch. putch(ch) just displays ch content.

Output: Continue(Y/N)? Y

Explanation: Upon pressing the Y or N keys, the character is stored in ch, but the character pressed is not automatically shown on the screen.

The functions getch() and putch(ch) are available only with turbo C compilers.

12. Write a program to show the usefulness of getche().

Solution

```c
#include <stdio.h>
int main()
{
  int ch;
  printf("\nContinue(Y/N)?");
  ch = getche();
  return 0;
}
```

This typed in character is read in by getche() which keeps it in variable ch and displays it.

Result: Continue(Y/N)?N

Explanation: Upon pressing the Y or N key, the character is stored in ch and is also displayed on the screen without using any output function like putch(ch). Such input and output functions are available only with Turbo C compilers.

4.4 FORMATTED INPUT AND OUTPUT FUNCTIONS

When input and output is required in a specified format the standard library functions scanf() and printf() are used. The scanf() function allows the user to input data in a specified format. It can accept data of different data types. The printf() function allows the user to output data of different data types on the console in a specified format.

4.4.1 Output Function printf ( )

The printf() (and scanf()) functions differ from the kind of functions that are created by the programmer as they can take a variable number of parameters. In the case of printf(), the first parameter is always a *control string*, for example 'Hello World', but after that the programmer can include any number of parameters of any type. The general form of a call to the printf() function is

```c
printf("control_string",variable1,variable2,
variable3,...);
```

where the '...' means a list of variables that can be written separated by commas and this list may be as long as is desired. The control string is all-important because it specifies the type of each variable in the list and how the user wants it printed. The control string is also called the *format string*.

The *control string*, which is written within "and", contains *data type* with *format specifiers* indicated by the characters that follow the % symbol. These are arranged in order so that they correspond to the respective variables. In between the % symbol with the specifiers, character strings may be inserted. When the printf() function executes, it scans the control string from left to right and prints out the character string as it is while printing the values of the listed variables according to the information specified with the respective format specifiers. For example,

```
printf("Hello World");
```

has a control string only and has no % characters. The above statement displays Hello World only. The format specifier %d means convert the next value to a signed decimal integer, and hence

```
printf("Total = %d",total);
```

will print Total = and then the value passed by the variable named total as a decimal integer.

The C view of output is at a lower level than one might expect. The %d is known as a format specifier, while it also acts as a *conversion code*. It indicates the data type of the variable to be printed and how that data type should be converted to the characters that appear on the screen. That is, %d says that the next value to be printed is a signed integer value, i.e., a value that would be stored in a standard int variable, and this should be converted into a sequence of characters, i.e., digits representing the value in decimal. If by some accident the variable that is to be displayed happens to be a float or a double, then the user will still see a value displayed but it will not correspond to the actual value of the float or a double.

The reason for this is twofold.

- An int uses two bytes (considering 16-bit machine) to store its value, while a float uses four and a double uses eight. If an effort is made to display a float or a double using %d, then only the first two bytes of the value are actually used.
- Even if there was no size difference, int, float, and double use a different binary representation and %d expects the bit pattern to be a simple signed binary integer.

This is all a bit technical, but that is in the nature of C. These details can be ignored as long as two important facts are remembered.

- The conversion code following % indicates the type of variable to be displayed as well as the format in which that value should be displayed.
- If the programmer uses a conversion code with the wrong type of variable, then some strange things will

be seen on the screen and the error often propagates to other items in the printf() list.

Though this appears a bit complicated, it should also be pointed out that the benefit lies in being able to treat what is stored in a variable in a more flexible way than other languages allow. In fact the programmer need not know that the numeric number stored in a variable is in binary form. But while printing this number, using the printf() function, it would appear to be a decimal number. Of course, whether this is viewed as an advantage depends on what the programmer is trying to do. It certainly brings the user closer to the way the machine works.

The *format string* in printf(), enclosed in quotation marks, has three types of objects:

- *Ordinary characters*: these are copied to output
- *Conversion specifier field*: denoted by % containing the codes listed in Table 4.1 and by optional modifiers such as *width*, *precision*, *flag*, and *size*
- *Control code*: optional control characters such as \n, \b, and \t

% *Format specifiers in printf ( )*

The % format specifiers, also termed here as the conversion code, that can be used in ANSI C are given in Table 4.1.

Table 4.1 Format specifiers for printf()

Conversion code	Usual variable type	Display
%c	char	single character
%d (%i)	int	signed integer
%e (%E)	float or double	exponential format
%f	float or double	signed decimal
%g (%G)	float or double	use %f or %e, whichever is shorter
%o	int	unsigned octal value
%p	pointer	address stored in pointer
%s	array of char	sequence of characters (string)
%u	int	unsigned decimal integer
%x (%X)	int	unsigned hex value
%%	none	no corresponding argument is converted, prints only a %
%n	pointer to int	the corresponding argument is a pointer to an integer into which the number of characters displayed is placed.

Formatting the output in printf ()

The type conversion code only does what is asked of it. This means that it converts a given bit pattern into a sequence of characters that a human can read. If the programmer wants to format the characters, then more needs to be known about the `printf()` function's *control string* or *format string*.

The *format string* in `printf()` has the following general form:

```
"<control    code><character    string><%conversion
specifier field> <control code>"
```

The programmer has the option of changing the order of the objects, such as 'character string', the '% conversion specifier field', and the 'control code' within the *format string*. Except for the '% conversion specifier field', the other two objects, that is, the 'character string' and the 'control code', are optional when the list of variables is present in `printf()`. Figure 4.1 shows the parts of a conversion specifier field for `printf()`.

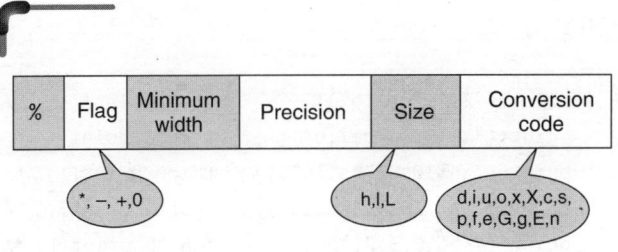

%	Flag	Minimum width	Precision	Size	Conversion code

*, −, +,0   h,l,L   d,i,u,o,x,X,c,s, p,f,e,G,g,E,n

Figure 4.1 Parts of conversion specifier field for `printf()`

The character string is a sequence of ordinary characters that is to be printed without any alteration. The 'control code' and 'conversion specifier' may be embedded within the 'character string'. Each conversion specifier field is coded as follows:

```
%<flag(s)><width><precision><size><conversion-
code>
```

The percent sign and conversion code are required but the other modifiers such as **width** and **precision** are optional. The width modifier specifies the total number of characters used to display the value and precision indicates the number of characters used after the decimal point. The precision option is only used with floats or strings. Its

use with strings will be discussed in a later chapter; for now, its use with floats will be considered.

When used to modify a float, precision indicates how many digits should be printed after the decimal point. If the precision option is used, the number of digits must be preceded by a period. Extra digits will be omitted, and zero digits will be added at the right if necessary. If precision is not specified, the default value of 6 is assumed.

So, the width option is used to specify the minimum number of positions that the output will take. If the output would normally take less than the specified number, the output is padded, usually with empty spaces to the left of the value. If the output requires more space than the specified number, it is given the space that it needs. For example, `%10.3f` will display the float using ten characters with three digits after the decimal point. Notice that the ten characters include the decimal point and a '−' sign if there is one.

Here are some examples.

```
printf("number=%3d\n", 10);
printf("number=%2d\n", 10);
printf("number=%1d\n", 10);
printf("number=%7.2f\n", 5.4321);
printf("number=%.2f\n", 5.4391);
printf("number=%.9f\n", 5.4321);
printf("number=%f\n", 5.4321);
```

The output of these five statements in order are:

number =				1	0

number =	1	0

number =	1	0

number =				5	.	4	3

number =	5	.	4	4

number =	5	.	4	3	2	1	0	0	0	0	0

number =	5	.	4	3	2	1	0	0

Output screen snapshot:

```
Quincy 2005
number= 10
number=10
number=10
number=   5.43
number=5.44
number=5.432100000
number=5.432100
```

The first example prints one space to the left of 10 since a width of 3 was specified. The second case adds no spaces, since 10 takes up the entire width of 2. In the third case, the specified width is just 1, but the value of 10 requires two spaces so it is given.

In the fourth case, a precision of 2 is specified for a float, so only two digits are printed after the decimal place, and a width of 7. So the value, which would normally contain four characters including the decimal point, has three additional spaces. In the fifth case, no width is specified, so the value of width is taken to be exactly what it needs, and a precision of 2 is specified, but this time, the hundredth digit is rounded up.

In the sixth case, a precision of 9 is specified, so five zeros are added to the end of the value, and in the final case, a default precision of 6 is used, so two zeros are added to the end of the value.

The flag option allows one or more print modifications to be specified. The flag can be any one of the characters shown in Table 4.2.

The specifier %-10d will display an int left justified in a ten-character space. The specifier %+5d will display an int using the next five character locations and will add a '+' or '–' sign to the value.

Table 4.2 flag characters used in printf()

flag	Meaning
–	Left justify the display
+	Display positive or negative sign of value
space	Display space if there is no sign
0	Pad with leading zeros
#	Use alternate form of specifier

Here are a couple of examples using the flag options.

```
printf("number=%06.1f\n", 5.5);
printf("%-+6.1f=number\n", 5.5);
```

The output of these two statements in order is:

number = | 0 | 0 | 0 | 5 | . | 5 |

| + | 5 | . | 5 | | | = number

In the first statement, a float is printed with a precision of 1 and width of 6. Because the 0 flag is used, the three extra positions that need to be filled are occupied by zeros instead of spaces. In the second statement, the minus sign causes the value to be left justified, spaces are added to the right instead of the left, and the positive sign causes the sign of the number to be printed with the number.

Similarly, for

```
printf("%-6.3f\n",17.23478);
```

the output on the screen will show

| 1 | 7 | . | 2 | 3 | 5 |

which is left justified and the total width being 6, only three digits after the decimal point are printed. Also, for

```
printf("VAT=17.5%%\n");
```

the output on the screen will be

| V | A | T | = | 1 | 7 | . | 5 | % |

Strings will be discussed later but for now it is enough to remember that if a string is printed using the %s specifier, then all of the characters stored in the array up to the first null will be printed. If a width specifier is used, the string will be right justified within the space. If a precision specifier is included, only that number of characters will be printed.

For example, consider the program given as follows:

```
#include <stdio.h>
int main()
{
    printf("%s","hello");        /* first printf()  */
    printf("\n%3s","hello");     /* second printf() */
    printf("\n%10s","hello");    /* third printf()  */
    printf("\n%-10s","hello");   /*fourth printf() */
    printf("\n%10.3s","hello");  /* fifth printf() */
    return 0;
}
```

The output for the respective printf() functions would be as follows:

| h | e | l | l | o | ← output from first printf()

| h | e | l | l | o | ← output from second printf()

| | | | | | h | e | l | l | o | ← output from third printf()

| h | e | l | l | o | | | | | | ← output from fourth printf()

| | | | | | | | h | e | l | ← output from fifth printf()

The third printf() prints 10 characters with hello right justified, while the fourth printf() prints 10 characters with hello left justified. The fifth printf() prints only the first three characters, considered from the left, of hello because the precision specifier has been given as 3. Also notice that it is normal to pass a constant value to printf() as in printf("%s", "hello").

Output screen:

Among the flags, the only complexity is in the use of the # modifier. What this modifier does depends on the type of format specifier, that is, the conversion code it is used with.

Table 4.3 depicts the actions that take place when this flag is used with the different allowed format specifiers.

Table 4.3 Uses of # flag with format specifier

flag with format specifier	Action
%#o	Adds a leading 0 to the octal number printed
%#x or X	Adds a leading 0x or 0X to the hex number printed
%#f or e	Ensures that the decimal point is printed
%#g or G	Displays trailing zeros in g or G type conversion and ensures decimal point is printed in floating-point number, even though it is a whole number

The effects of the size modifiers that transform the conversion code are shown in Table 4.4.

Table 4.4 Size modifiers used in printf()

Size modifier	Conversion code	Converts to
l	d i o u x	long int
h	d i o u x	short int
l	e f	double
L	e f	long double

Examples of the use of size are as follows:

```
%hd /* short integer */
%ld /* long integer  */
%Lf /* long double   */
```

Adding an 'l' in front of a conversion code will mean a long form of the variable type and an 'h' will indicate a short form. For example, %ld means a long integer variable, usually four bytes, and %hd means a short int. Notice that there is no distinction between a four-byte float and an eight-byte double. The reason is that a float is automatically converted to a double precision value when passed to printf. Therefore, the two can be treated in the same way. In pre-ANSI, all floats were converted to double when passed to a function but this is no longer true.

Finally there are the *control codes* also known as escape sequences that have already been described and listed in Chapter 3. Some of the commonly used ones are listed in Table 4.5.

Table 4.5 List of commonly used control codes

Control code	Action
\b	Backspace
\f	Form feed
\n	New line
\r	Carriage return
\t	Horizontal tab
\'	Single quote
\0	Null

If any of these are included in the format string, the corresponding ASCII control code is sent to the screen, or output device, which should produce the effect listed. In most cases, the programmer only needs to remember \n for new line.

The conversion specifier field is used to format printed values, often to arrange things nicely in columns. Here are some illustrations of the use of printf() with brief explanations.

Examples

13. `printf( "Hello there" );`

Puts Hello there on the screen. The cursor remains at the end of the text, which is where the next printf() statement will place its text.

14. `printf("Goodbye.\n");`

prints Goodbye. on the screen. The \n does not show on the screen; it means 'new line'; it moves the cursor to the next line downwards and to the left.

15. `int int_var;`
    `int_var = 10;`
    `printf("Integer is: %d", int_var);`

Integer variable int_var contains a value of 10. This prints "Integer is: 10" on the screen, as the %d is replaced by the contents of the int_var variable.

16. `int i1, i2; i1 = 2; i2 = 3;`
    `printf( "Sum is: %d", i1 + i2);`

Integer variable i1 contains 2 and i2 contains 3. This prints Sum is: 5 on the screen.

The result of i1+i2 is calculated (2+3=5) and this replaces the %d in the string.

17. ```
    printf( "%3d\n%3d\n%3d\n", 5, 25, 125 );
    ```
    This displays three values on the screen, each followed by a new line. The %3d means 'replace this with an integer, but ensure it takes up at least three spaces on the screen'. This is good for lining up columns of data. There are three of these, so we need three extra parameters to fill them in (5, 25, and 125). So the output is
    ```
    5
    25
    125
    ```

18. ```
    float pi;
    pi = 3.1415926535;
    printf( "Pi is %4.2f to 2dp\n", pi);
    ```
    This example sets a floating-point variable pi to be 3.1415926535. The %4.2f is replaced by this value, but the 4.2 part indicates that the number can be a maximum of four characters wide (including the decimal point), and has two decimal places (i.e., digits after the decimal point). This means that only 3.14 will show. Note that if pi had been 3.146, then 3.15 would have been shown due to rounding off. In this case, what shows is pi which is 3.14, followed by a new line.

19. ```
    char color[11] = "red";
    printf( "Color is: %s\n", color );
    ```
    The %s is replaced by a character array (or string) – in this case, Color is: red is displayed, followed by a new line.

    Note: After the printf() function is executed, the output is printed out on the standard device, which is normally the Video Display Unit (VDU); it returns a number that is equal to the number of characters printed.

To illustrate that the printf() function returns a number that is equal to the number of characters printed, the following program is given below :

```
#include<stdio.h>
int  main( )
{
  int chent
= printf ("Oxford University");
  printf("\n number of character = %d",chent);
  return 0;
}
```

There are 17 characters, including one space in this string

Output:
```
Oxford University
number of character = 17
```

Runtime adjustment and precision in printf()

The correct way to adjust field *width* and *precision* at run time is to replace the *width* and/or precision with a star (*) and include appropriate integer variables in the parameter list. The values of these integer variables representing width and precision will be used before the actual variable to be converted is taken from the parameter list. Here is a program showing the described feature in use.

```
#include <stdio.h>
int main()
{
  double x=1234.567890;
  int i=8,j=2;
  while(i<12)
  {
    j=2;
    while(j<5)
    {
      printf("width = %2d precision = %d display \
>>%*.*lf<<\n",i,j,i,j,x);
      j++;
    }
    i++;
  }
  return 0;
}
```

total number of digit positions provided for output

total number of digit positions provided for decimal part in the output

. takes the values assigned to i and j as width and precision for outputting the value in x

The program displays the effects of various widths and precisions for output of a double variable. Here is the output.

```
width =  8 precision = 2 display >> 1234.57<<
width =  8 precision = 3 display >>1234.568<<
width =  8 precision = 4 display >>1234.5679<<
width =  9 precision = 2 display >>  1234.57<<
width =  9 precision = 3 display >> 1234.568<<
width =  9 precision = 4 display >>1234.5679<<
width = 10 precision = 2 display >>   1234.57<<
width = 10 precision = 3 display >>  1234.568<<
width = 10 precision = 4 display >> 1234.5679<<
width = 11 precision = 2 display >>    1234.57<<
width = 11 precision = 3 display >>   1234.568<<
width = 11 precision = 4 display >>  1234.5679<<
```

The >> and << symbols are used to indicate the limits of the output field. Note that the variables i and j appear twice in the parameter list, the first time to give the values in the annotation and the second time to actually control the output.
```

1. A control string, also termed as format string, and variable names are specified for the prinf() output function to display the values in the variables in the desired form on the monitor screen.
2. The format string in printf(), enclosed in quotation marks, has three types of objects: (i) Characters string (ii) Conversion specifier (iii) Control code, with the programmer's option of changing the order of these three objects within the format string.
3. Except for the % conversion specifier field, the other two objects, that is, the character string and the control code, are optional when the list of variables is present in printf().
4. The control code and conversion specifier may be embedded within the character string.

4.4.2 Input Function scanf ( )

The scanf() function works in much the same way as the printf(). It has the general form

```
scanf("control_string",variable1_address,
variable2_address,...);
```

where the *control string,* also known as *format string* is a list of *format specifiers* indicating the format and type of data to be read from the standard input device, which is the keyboard, and stored in the corresponding address of variables. There must be the same number of format specifiers and addresses as there are input fields.

scanf() returns the number of input fields successfully scanned, converted, and stored. The return value does not include scanned fields that were not stored. If scanf() attempts to read end-of-file, the return value is EOF. If no fields were stored, the return value is 0. However, there are a number of important differences as well as similarities between scanf() and printf().

The most obvious is that scanf() has to change the values stored in parts of the computer's memory associated with variables. Until functions are covered in more detail, understanding this fully has to wait. But, just for now, understand that to store values in memory locations associated with variables, the scanf() function should have the addresses of the variables rather than just their values. This means that simple variables have to be passed with a preceding &.

There is no need to use '&' for strings stored in arrays because the array name is already a pointer. This issue will be dealt with in the chapter on arrays and strings. Moreover, the format string has some extra attributes to cope with

the problems of reading and data writing, which are described below. However, almost all of the conversion specifiers, or format specifiers, listed in connection with printf() can be used with scanf() also.

As with printf(), the format string in scanf() is enclosed in a set of quotation marks and it may contain the following:

- *White space* This causes the input stream to be read up to the next non-white-space character.
- *Ordinary character string* Anything except white space or % characters. The next character in the input stream must match this character.
- *Conversion specifier field* This is a % character, followed by an optional * character, which suppresses the conversion, followed by an optional non-zero decimal integer specifying the maximum field width, an optional h, l, or L to control the length of the conversion, and finally a non-optional conversion specifier. Note that use of h, l, or L will affect the type of pointer which must be used.

Format specifiers in scanf ( )

The format string in scanf() has the following general form:

```
"< character string >< % conversion specifier field >"
```

Here character string is optional and has to be used with care. Each 'conversion specifier field' is coded as follows:

```
%[*]<width><size><conversion-code>
```

Each *conversion* (or *format*) *specifier* begins with the per cent character, **%**, after which comes the following, in the given order.

1. An optional assignment-suppression character, *, which states that the value being read will not be assigned to an argument, but will be dropped.
2. An optional *width specifier*, <width>, which designates the maximum number of characters to be read that compose the value for the associated argument.

   Encountering white space, before the entire width is scanned, terminates the input of this value and moves to the next.
3. An optional conversion-code modifier, <size>, which modifies the conversion code to accept format for a type of :

   h = short int,

l = long int, if the format specifiers provide for an integer conversion,

l = double, if the format specifiers provide for a floating-point conversion, and

L = long double, which is valid only with floating-point conversions.

The format specifiers in scanf() are shown in Fig. 4.2.

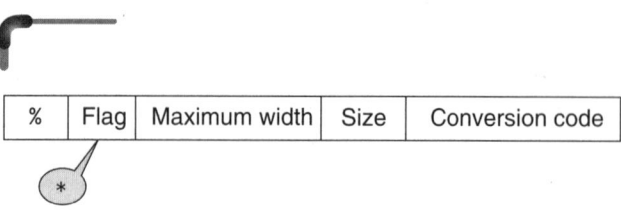

%	Flag	Maximum width	Size	Conversion code

*

Figure 4.2 Parts of conversion specifier field for scanf()

The format specifiers, or the conversion code, that apply to scanf() are given in Table 4.6.

Table 4.6 Format Specifiers for scanf()

Conversion code	Usual variable type	Action
%c	char	Read a single character
%d(%i)	int	Read a signed decimal integer
%e(%E)	float or double	Read signed decimal
%f	float or double	Read signed decimal
%g(%G)	float or double	Read signed decimal
%o	int	Read octal value
%p	pointer	Read in hex address stored in pointer
%s	array of char	Read sequence of characters (string)
%u	int	Read unsigned decimal integer
%x(%X)	int	Read unsigned hex value
%%	none	A single % character in the input stream is expected. There is no corresponding argument.
%n	pointer to int	No characters in the input stream are matched. The corresponding argument is a pointer to an integer into which the number of characters read is placed.
[...]	array of char	Read a string of matching characters

Formatted input in scanf ()

Typically, the format string for a scanf() will not contain constant text. If it does, that means the input must contain the same text in the same position. For example, consider the following simple program.

Example

```
20.  #include <stdio.h>
     int main(void)
     {
         int x;
         scanf("Number=%d", &x);
         printf("The value of x is %d.\n", x);
         return 0;
     }
```

If the user wants the value of x to be 25, the user would have to type "Number=25" exactly, or the behavior of this little program is unpredictable. To avoid this type of problem, it is usually a good idea not to include constant text in format strings when using scanf().

When reading in integers or floats, the scanf() function skips leading white space.

That is, all spaces, tabs, and new line characters will be ignored, and scanf() will keep reading input until it reaches a number. When reading in a character, scanf() will read exactly one character, which can be any valid ASCII character or other valid character for the system. If the user wants to skip a space before a character, the space has to be explicitly included in the character string. For example, consider the following code, assuming that a, b, and c are integers and x is a character.

```
scanf("%d%d%d%c", &a, &b, &c, &x);
```

Assume that the user wants a, b, c, and x to be 1, 2, 3, and z. The user would have to type

```
1 2 3Z
```

If, instead, the user types

```
1 2 3 Z
```

then the value of x will be a space because z has been typed with a space preceding it.

If the user wants to be able to enter the line this way, the scanf() needs to be coded as follows:

```
scanf("%d%d%d %c", &a, &b, &c, &x);
```

Using spaces between integer field specifications is optional. For example, while reading integers x, y, and z

```
scanf("%d%d%d", &x, &y, &z);
```

is equivalent to

```
scanf("%d %d %d", &x, &y, &z);
```

Normally, when reading a numeric value, scanf() reads until it sees trailing white space. The rule is that scanf()

processes the format string from left to right and each time it reaches a specifier it tries to interpret what has been typed as a value. If multiple values are input, these are assumed to be separated by white space, i.e., spaces, new line, or tabs. This means the user can type

```
3 4 5
```
or
```
3
4
5
```

and it does not matter how many spaces are included between items. For example,

```
scanf("%d %d",&i,&j);
```

will read in two integer values into i and j. The integer values can be typed on the same line or on different lines as long as there is at least one white space character between them. The only exception to this rule is the %c specifier that always reads in the next character typed no matter what it is.

If a width modifier is used, it specifies the maximum number of characters to be read. Then scanf() will read either as many characters as specified by the width modifier or until it sees white space, whichever happens first. In this case its effect is to limit the number of characters accepted to the width. For example,

```
scanf("%10d",&i)
```

would use at most the first ten digits typed as the new value for i. There are two other reasons that can cause scanf() to stop. One is if an end-of-file character is encountered. When reading from an actual disk file, there is automatically an end-of-file character at the end of the file. When reading from a keyboard, the user can simulate one by pressing a specific character sequence. On Unix machines, the user can enter an end-of-file character by pressing <**Ctrl-d**>.

The other reason scanf() may stop is when it encounters an invalid input. For instance, if scanf() is expecting to read a numeric value and it comes across a non-numeric character, this is an error.

The following are the reasons because of which scanf() will stop reading a value for a variable.

- A white space character is found after a digit in a numeric sequence.
- The maximum number of characters has been processed.
- An end-of-file character is reached.
- An error is detected.

The scanf() function returns the number of variables successfully read in. For example, consider the following program.

Example

```
21. #include <stdio.h>
    int main(void)
    {
      int a, b, c;
      int num;
      num = scanf("%d %d %d", &a, &b, &c);
      printf("I have read %d values.\n", num);
      return 0;
    }
```
When run, the user must type 10 20 30 for the program to output

```
I have read 3 values.
```
If the user types 10 20 hello the program will output

```
I have read 2 values.
```
If the user types hello 10 20 30 the program will output

```
I have read 0 values.
```

When reading standard input from the keyboard, the input is buffered. In other words, the program is not seeing the text directly as it is typed in; the characters are being temporarily stored in a buffer somewhere. When the user hits <**Enter**>, the buffer is sent to the program. Until then, the user can edit the buffer by adding (typing) new characters, or by hitting the backspace or delete key to remove the last character from the buffer. The program will never see these deleted characters. Consider the following simple program.

Example

```
22. #include <stdio.h>
    int main(void)
    {
      int x;
      scanf("%d", &x);
      printf("You typed %d.\n", x);
      return 0;
    }
```

If an input 45 is given to this program, the printed output will be

```
You typed 45.
```

Another thing to note about scanf() is that the format string should *never* end with a new line character. This will always lead to some form of error. For example,

```
scanf("%d\n", &x);
```

This code will not work correctly because of the `\n` at the end of the `scanf()` format string. The last thing to remember about `scanf()` is that each variable must be preceded by the & symbol. This symbol is the address operator. It takes the address in memory of the variable following the symbol. If the values of the variables are passed to `scanf()`, it would be unable to change the values of the variables. By passing the memory address where these values are stored, the function is able to write new values into memory.

At this point it must be clear that both the functions `scanf()` and `printf()` use the `stdin` and `stdout` streams respectively and require the header file `stdio.h` to be included in the program when they are used.

Points to Note

1. In `scanf()`, the control string or format string, that consists of a list of format specifiers, indicates the format and type of data to be read in from the standard input device, which is the keyboard, for storing in the corresponding address of variables specified.

2. There must be the same number of format specifiers and addresses as there are input variables.

3. The format string in `scanf()` is enclosed in a set of quotation marks and it may contain the following:

    (a) white space

    (b) ordinary character string

    (c) conversion specifier field

Examples

23. Add two integer numbers and print the input numbers and result.

    Solution

    ```c
    #include <stdio.h>
    int main()
    {
      int a,b,c;
      printf("\nThe first number is ");
      scanf("%d",&a);
      printf("\nThe second number is ");
      scanf("%d",&b);
      c=a+b;
      printf("The answer is %d \n",c);
      return 0;
    }
    ```

    Output:
    ```
    The first number is 5
    The second number is 9
    The answer is 14
    ```

24. Print formatted numbers.

    Solution

    ```c
    #include <stdio.h>
    int main()
    {
      printf("/%d/\n",336);
      printf("/%2d/\n",336);
      printf("/%10d/\n",336);
      printf("/%-10d/\n",336);
      return 0;
    }
    ```

    Output:
    ```
    /336/
    /336/
    /.......336/
    /336......./
    ```

25. Print formatted floating-point number.

    Solution

    ```c
    #include <stdio.h>
    int main()
    {
      printf("/%f/\n",1234.56);
      printf("/%e/\n",1234.56);
      printf("/%4.f/\n",1234.56);
      printf("/%3.1f/\n",1234.56);
      printf("/%-10.3f/\n",1234.56);
      printf("/%10.3f/\n",1234.56);
      printf("/%10.3e/\n",1234.56);
      return 0;
    }
    ```

    Output:
    ```
    /1234.560000/
    /1.234560e+003/
    /1235/
    /1234.6/
    /1234.560   /
    /   1234.560/
    /1.235e+003/
    ```

26. Print character strings.

    Solution

    ```c
    #include <stdio.h>
    #define BLURB "Outstanding Program!"
    int main()
    {
      printf("/%2s/\n",BLURB);
      printf("/%22s/\n",BLURB);
      printf("/%22.5s/\n",BLURB);
      printf("/%-22.5s/\n",BLURB);
      return 0;
    }
    ```

    Output:
    ```
    /Outstanding Program!/
    /  Outstanding Program!/
    /Outst                 /
    /                 Outst/
    ```

27. Write a program that prints the next character for the corresponding three characters given to the program.

Solution
```c
#include <stdio.h>
int main()
{
  char a,b,c;
  scanf("%c%c%c",&a,&b,&c);
  a++;
  b++;
  c++;
  printf("a=%c b=%c c=%c",a,b,c);
  return 0;
}
```
Input: PQR
Output: a=Q b=R c=S

28. Determine how much money is in a piggy bank that contains several 50, 25, 20, 10 , and 5 paise coins. Use the following values to test the program: five 50 paise coins, three 25 paise coins, two 20 paise coins, one 10 paise coin, and fifteen 5 paise coins.

Solution
```c
/* To determine how much money there is in a
        piggy bank */
#include <stdio.h>
#include <string.h>
int main(void)
{
  float coin1=0.50,coin2=0.25,coin3=0.20,\
         coin4=0.10, coin5=0.05,total=0.0;
  int ncoins;
  printf("How many 50 paise coins : ");
  scanf("%d",&ncoins);
  total += (ncoins * coin1);
  printf("** %.2f **",total);

  printf("\nHow many 25 paise coins : ");
  scanf("%d",&ncoins);
  total += (ncoins * coin2);
  printf("** %.2f **",total);

  printf("\nHow many 20 paise coins : ");
  scanf("%d",&ncoins);
  total += (ncoins * coin3);
  printf("** %.2f **",total);

  printf("\nHow many 10 paise coins : ");
  scanf("%d",&ncoins);
  total += (ncoins * coin4);
  printf("** %.2f **",total);

  printf("\nHow many 5 paise coins : ");
  scanf("%d",&ncoins);
  total += (ncoins * coin5);
```

```c
  printf("\n\nThe total amount is
            Rs.%.2f",total);
  return 0;
}
```
Output:
```
How many 50 paise coins : 5
** 2.50 **
How many 25 paise coins : 3
** 3.25 **
How many 20 paise coins : 2
** 3.65 **
How many 10 paise coins : 1
** 3.75 **
How many 5 paise coins : 15
The total amount is Rs 4.50
```

29. Modify the program given in Example 28 to accept the total amount (in rupees) and convert them into paise (vice-versa of Example 28).

Solution
```c
#include <stdio.h>
#include <string.h>
int main(void)
{
  int nc1,nc2,nc3,nc4,nc5,temp;
  float total;
  printf("Enter the amount : ");
  scanf("%f",&total);
  temp = total * 100;
  nc1 = temp / 50;
  temp = temp % 50;

  nc2 = temp / 25;
  temp = temp % 25;

  nc3 = temp / 20;
  temp = temp % 20;

  nc4 = temp / 10;
  temp = temp % 10;

  nc5=temp;

  printf("\n\nNo. of 50 paise coins = %d",nc1);
  printf("\nNo. of 25 paise coins = %d",nc2);
  printf("\nNo. of 20 paise coins = %d",nc3);
  printf("\nNo. of 10 paise coins = %d",nc4);
  printf("\nNo. of 5 paise coins = %d",nc5);
  return 0;
}
```
Output:
```
Enter the amount: 7.65
No. of 50 paise coins = 15
No. of 25 paise coins = 0
No. of 20 paise coins = 0
No. of 10 paise coins = 1
No. of 5 paise coins = 5
```

30. Write a program for computing product cost. The program should output the computed cost and the delivery date of the product.

Solution

```c
#include <stdio.h>

int main()
{
  int quantity, day, month, year;
  float cost, total;
  int prod_code;

  printf("Enter quantity: ");
  scanf("%d", &quantity);

  printf("Enter cost: ");
  scanf("%f", &cost);
  total = cost * quantity;

  printf("Enter product code: ");
  scanf("%d", &prod_code);

  printf("Enter date in format dd/mm/yyyy: ");
  scanf("%d/%d/%d", &day, &month, &year);

  month+=1;
  if( month > 12 )
  {
    month = 1; year++;
  }

  printf("Order for %d should be with you by\
    %d/%d/%d at a total cost of %6.2f\n",prod_\
    code, day, month, year, total);
  return 0;
}
```

Result:

```
                                        Inputs
Enter quantity: 3
Enter cost: 1.25
Enter product code: 1 2
Enter date in format dd/mm/yy: 17/12/2003
```

Output: Order for 1 should be with you by 17/1/2004 at a total cost of 3.75

Points to Note

1. The `scanf()` function returns the number of variables successfully read in.
2. The `printf()` function returns a number that is equal to the number of characters printed.

SUMMARY

Generally, input and output in C, from and to standard devices, are managed through standard streams. The standard input and output devices are the keyboard and the screen. To carry out the input and output, a number of standard functions such as `getchar()`, `putchar()`, `scanf()`, and `printf()` are in-built in C.

`getchar()` and `putchar()` functions are single- character input and output functions respectively. So, these do not need any formatted inputs or outputs.

The functions `scanf()` and `printf()` handle multiple variables of all the allowed data types in C. These, therefore, require formatted inputs and outputs.

KEY-TERMS

Character string   A chain of characters placed one after another that is dealt as one unit.

Control code   Special characters that specify some positional action on the printing point, also known as cursor.

Conversion specifier   Same as format specifier.

Flag modifier   It is a character that specifies one or more of the following:

- display space if no sign symbol precedes the output
- inclusion of + or – sign symbol preceding the output
- Padding the output with leading 0s.

- the positioning of the output to be displayed
- Use of alternate form of specifier.

Format specifier   Identifies the data type, along with width, precision, size and flag, for the respective variables to be outputted to or read in from a standard device.

Format string   A group of characters that contain ordinary character string, conversion code, or control characters arranged in order so that they correspond to the respective control string variables placed next to it in printf( ) function.

Precision modifier   Indicates the number of characters used after the decimal point in the output displayed. The precision option is only used with floats or strings.

Size modifier   Precedes the conversion code and specifies the kind of data type thereby indicating the number of bytes required for the corresponding variable.

White space   Blank space that causes the input stream to be read up to the next non-white-space character.

Width modifier   When used in context to the format string, specifies the total number of characters used to display the output or to be read in.

FREQUENTLY ASKED QUESTIONS

1. How can you print % character using `printf()`?

Conversion specifiers always start with a % character so that the `printf()` function can recognize them. Because a % in a control string always indicates the start of a conversion specifier, if one wants to output a % character you must use the sequence %%.

2. What is the return type of `printf()` ?

The return value for `printf()` is incidental to its main purpose of printing output, and it usually isn't used. The return type of `printf()` function is `int`: Under ANSI C, `printf()` function returns the number of characters it printed. If there is an output error, `printf()` returns a negative value. The following program illustrates the fact.

```
#include <stdio.h>
int main(void)
{
    int c;
    c=printf("One");
    printf("\nc = %d",c);
    return 0;
}
```
Output:
```
One
c = 3
```

3. What is the return type of `scanf()`?

The `scanf()` function returns the number of variables that it successfully reads. If it reads no variables, which happens if you type a non-numeric string when it expects a number, `scanf()` returns the value 0. It returns EOF if it detects "end of file". This condition would happen if we press CTRL-z in Windows or CTRL-d in Unix/Linux.

```
#include <stdio.h>
int main(void)
{
    int a,b,c;
    c=scanf("%d %d",&a,&b);
    printf("\nc = %d",c);
    return 0;
}
```

Output:
```
Sample run 1:
2 3
c = 2

Sample run 2:
2 a
c = 2

Sample run 3:
a b
c = 0

Sample run 4:
^z
c = -1
```

4. How do I write `printf()` so that the width of a field can be specified at runtime?

This is shown in following program.

```
int main( )
{
    int w, no;
    printf ("Enter number and the width for the\
            number field:");
    scanf ("%d%d", &no, &w);
    printf ("%*d", w, no);
    return 0;
}
```

Here, an '*' in the format specifier in `printf()` indicates that an `int` value from the argument list should be used for the field width.

5. What is EOF?

EOF is a special character called the end-of-file character. In fact, the symbol EOF is defined in `<stdio.h>` and is usually equivalent to the value −1. However, this isn't necessarily always the case, so one should use EOF in the programs rather than an explicit value. EOF generally indicates that no more data is available from a stream. Incidentally EOF can be entered manually from the keyboard by pressing CTRL + D on a Unix/Linux type machine or by pressing CTRL + Z on a Windows type machine.

1. What will be the value of each variable after the following input command?

   data input: Tom 34678.2 AA4231

   ```
   scanf("%s %3d %f %c %*c %1d",
           name,&m,&x,&ch,&i,&j);
   ```

   (a) name: _____

   (b) m: _____

   (c) x: _____

   (d) ch: _____

   (e) i: _____

   (f) j: _____

2. What output does each of the following produce?

   (a) `putchar('a');` _____

   (b) `putchar('\007');` _____

   (c) `putchar('\n');` _____

   (d) `putchar('\t');` _____

   (e) `n = 32; putchar(n);` _____

   (f) `putchar('\"');` _____

3. For the different values of n, what is the output?

   ```
   printf("%x %c %o %d",n,n,n,n);
   ```

   (a) n = 67 _____

   (b) n = 20 _____

   (c) n = 128 _____

   (d) n = 255 _____

   (e) n = 100 _____

4. What is wrong with each of the following?

   (a) `scanf("%d",i);` _____

   (b) `#include stdio.h` _____

   (c) `putchar('/n');` _____

   (d) `printf("\nPhone Number:(%s) %s", phone);`
       _____

   (e) `getch(ch);` _____

   (f) `putch() = ch;` _____

   (g) `printf("\nEnter your name:", name);`
       _____

5. Which numbering system is not handled directly by the `printf()` conversion specifiers?

   (a) decimal

   (b) binary

   (c) octal

   (d) hexadecimal

6. What are formatted input and output statements in C? Give suitable examples.

7. What do the `getchar()` and `putchar()` functions do?

8. How can a % character be printed with `printf()`?

9. How can `printf()` use %f for type double if `scanf()` requires %lf?

10. How can a variable field width be implemented with `printf()`?

11. How can numbers be printed with commas separating the thousands?

12. Will the call `scanf("%d", i)` work? Give reasons for your answer.

13. Explain why the following code is not going to work.

    ```
    double d;
    scanf("%f",&d);
    ```

14. How can a variable width be specified in a `scanf()` format string?

15. When numbers are read from the keyboard with scanf "%d\n", they seem to hang until one extra line of input is typed. Explain.

16. Why does everyone advise against using `scanf()`? What should be used instead?

17. On the screen write the words

    she sells   seashells by the seashore

    (a) all in one line

    (b) in three lines

18. Write a program that asks interactively the users name and age and responds with

    Hello name, next year you will be next_age.

    where next_age is age + 1.

19. Write programs to read the values of the variables and print the results of the computed expressions given below:

    (a) a = (b+c)*(b-c)

    (b) y = ax^2 + bx + c

    (c) I = (P*R*T)/100

    (d) C = (F-32)/100

    (e) A = -(R1/R2+R3)

    (f) a = 0.5*float1 + 0.25*integer1 + integer2/0.4 + integer3

20. What will be printed by the code given below?

    ```
    int value = 5;
    printf("%s", !(value % 2) ? "yes": "no" );
    ```

21. What will be the output of the following program?
```
int main()
{
    char a,b,c;
    scanf("%c %c %c",&a,&b,&c);
    printf("a=%c b=%c c=%c",a,b,c);
    return 0;
}
```
[Note: The user input is:ABC DEF GHI]

(a) a=ABC b=DEF c=GHI

(b) a=A b=B c=C

(c) a=A b=D c=G

(d) None of these

22. What will be the output of the following program?
```
int main()
{
    int a,b,c;
    scanf("%1d %2d %3d",&a,&b,&c);
    printf("Sum=%d",a+b+c);
    return 0;
}
```
[Note: The user input is: 123456 44 544]

(a) Sum=480

(b) Sum=594

(c) Sum=589

(d) None of these

23. What will be the output of the following program?
```
int main()
{
    int x=20,y=35;
    x = y++ + x++;
    y = ++y + ++x;
    printf("x=%d,y= %d\n",x,y);
    return 0;
}
```

24. What will be the output of the following program?
```
int main()
{
    int x=5;
    printf("%d %d %d\n",x,x<<2,x>>2);
    return 0;
}
```

25. What will be the output of the following program?
```
int main()
{
    int a=2, b=3;
```
```
    printf(" %d ", a+++b);
    printf("a=%d,b=%d",a,b);
    return 0;
}
```

26. What does the following program give as output?
```
int main()
{
    int a,b;
    printf("\n enter integer values");
    printf("for a and b within 0");
    printf("to 100\n");
    scanf("%d%d",&a,&b);
    b=b^a;
    a=b^a;
    b=b^a;
    printf("a=%d, b=%d\n",a,b);
    return 0;
}
```
Note: The user input is 23 67

27. What will be the output of the following program?
```
int main(void)
{
    int var1,var2,var3,minmax;
    var1=5;
    var2=5;
    var3=6;

    minmax=(var1>var2)?(var1>var3)?\
            var1:var3:(var2>var3)? var2:var3;
    printf("%d\n",minmax);
    return 0;
}
```

28. What will be the output of the following program?
```
int main(void)
{
    int a=19,b=4;
    float c,d;
    c=a/b;
    d=a%b;
    printf("/c=%f/\n/d=%\-12.4f/",c,d);
    return 0;
}
```

29. Pick the correct output of the given program.
```
int main(void)
{
    int i=5;
```

```
    printf("%d %d %d %d %d",i, i++, i++, i++, ++i);
    return 0;
}
```
(a) Compile-Time Error
(b) 10 9 8 7 6
(c) 9 8 7 6 5
(d) 10 8 7 6 6

Answers to objective type questions and problems

20. no, **21.** (b), **22.** (a), **23.** x=57, y=94,
24. 5 201, **25.** 5 a=3, b=3 *Explanation*: Here
it evaluates as a+++b. **26.** a=67, b=23, **27.** 6,
28. /c= 4.000000/
/d= 3.0000.../
29. (c)

INCREMENTAL PROBLEM

Starting with this chapter, we will develop an incremental problem chapter by chapter, which will grow complex by the end of Chapter 10. As we go through the chapters, we will add to or modify the program code that we start writing in this section, based on what we learn in the following chapters.

Problem Statement

Write a C program that would find the length of a straight line formed by two end points, whose co-ordinates would be given as inputs.

Solution

To start with, the program for solving this problem needs to take inputs from the user. The inputs are the values of x and y coordinates of the two end points of the straight line. Two basic I/O functions have already been described in this chapter. Four variables of type float are used to store the coordinates of the two endpoints of the straight line joining them. Then the length of this straight line formed by the two end points is given by the following formula:

$$\sqrt{(x_2 - x_1)^2 + (y_2 - y_1)^2}$$

The program for solving the given problem is given as follows:

Program

```
#include<stdio.h>
#include<math.h>
int main()
{
    float x1, y1, x2, y2, lin_len;
    printf("\n\n Enter x-coordinate of first point:");
    scanf("%f", &x1);
    printf("\n Enter y-coordinate of first point:");
    scanf("%f", &y1);
    printf("\n\n Enter x-coordinate of second point:");
    scanf("%f", &x2);
    printf("\n Enter y-coordinate of second point:");
    scanf("%f", &y2);
    lin_len = sqrt((x2-x1)*(x2-x1) + (y2-y1)*(y2-y1));
    printf("\n The length of the straight line joining\
        the two points is %f", lin_len);
    return 0;
}
```

Output

```
Enter x-coordinate of first point: 1
Enter y-coordinate of first point: 2
Enter x-coordinate of second point: 3
Enter y-coordinate of second point: 4

The length of the straight line joining the two
points is 2.828427
Press Enter to return to Quincy...
```

Problem Statement

The packing department of a television set manufacturer has to prepare a requisition note listing the number of different boxes required for the different TV models that it has received from the production department. The list prepared has to be forwarded to the stores department so that the required boxes are issued to the packing department. The category and the number of boxes required for each type of TV model is given as follows:

Model type	Box type	Numbers
TV-LCD 17	1	98
TV-LCD 22	2	79
TV-LCD 26	3	65
TV-LCD 32	4	43
TV-LCD 37	5	17

Analysis

This problem provides some data based on which a requisition note has to be prepared and printed. The note should specify the type and number of box required for each kind of TV model.

The program, written for accomplishing the task specified by the problem, accepts the number of sets of different TV models for each of which a particular type of packing box is required. The box type for each model is of standard dimensions and is pre-assigned a unique type number. Using the data provided by the problem, a requisition note is printed by the program as shown below.

Solution

```c
#include<stdio.h>
int main()
{
int tv17box,tv22box,tv26box,tv32box,tv37box;
    /* Box Types */
int tv17num,tv22num,tv26num,tv32num,tv37num;
    /* Number of TV sets to be packed */

/* Box Types */

tv17box = 1;
tv22box = 2;
tv26box = 3;
tv32box = 4;
tv37box = 5;
```

Assigning type number to packing boxes

```c
printf("\nEnter number of TV-LCD 17 model to be packed:");
scanf("%d",&tv17num);

printf("\nEnter number of TV-LCD 22 model to be packed:");
scanf("%d",&tv22num);

printf("\nEnter number of TV-LCD 26 model to be packed:");
scanf("%d",&tv26num);

printf("\nEnter number of TV-LCD 32 model to be packed:");
scanf("%d",&tv32num);

printf("\nEnter number of TV-LCD 37 model to be packed:");
scanf("%d",&tv37num);

printf("\n **** Requisition Note **** ");
printf("\n ==================================");

printf("\n TV Model |Box type| Numbers ");
printf("\n          |required|         ");

printf("\n ==================================");

printf("\n\n TV-LCD 17 %d %d",tv17box,tv17num);
printf("\n TV-LCD 22 %d %d",tv22box,tv22num);
printf("\n TV-LCD 26 %d %d",tv26box,tv26num);
printf("\n TV-LCD 32 %d %d",tv32box,tv32num);
printf("\n TV-LCD 37 %d %d",tv37box,tv37num);
printf("\n ==================================");

return 0;
}
```

Ouput

```
Enter number of TV-LCD 17 model to be packed:98
Enter number of TV-LCD 22 model to be packed:79
Enter number of TV-LCD 26 model to be packed:65
Enter number of TV-LCD 32 model to be packed:43
Enter number of TV-LCD 37 model to be packed:17
```

**** Requisition Note ****

TV Model	Box type required	Numbers
TV-LCD 17	1	98
TV-LCD 22	2	79
TV-LCD 26	3	65
TV-LCD 32	4	43
TV-LCD 37	5	17

Chapter 5

Control Statements

Learning Objectives

After reading this chapter, the readers will be able to

- understand the meaning of a statement and a statement block
- learn about decision type control constructs in C and the way these are used
- learn about looping type control constructs in C and the technique of putting them to use
- learn the use of special control constructs such as goto, break, continue, and return
- learn about nested loops and their utility

5.1 INTRODUCTION

So far, every program in this book has executed sequentially in the order in which they appear, i.e., statements in a program are normally executed one after another until the last statement completes. A C application begins executing with the first line of the main() function and proceeds statement by statement until it gets to the end of the main() function.

In C, any sequence of statements can be grouped together to function as a syntactically equivalent single statement by enclosing the sequence in braces. This grouping is known as *statement block* or *compound statement*. Compound statements were originally designed to make control structures simpler.

In C89, one must declare all local variables at the start of the block prior to any executable statements. However in C99, local variables can be declared at any point within the block prior to their first use.

Consider the following program that illustrates variable declaration at the beginning of a statement block.

```
#include <stdio.h>
int main(void)
{
    int a=5;
```

```
  printf("\n a = %d", a);
  /* A statement block follows */
  {
    int b=10;
    printf("\n a = %d", a);
    printf("\n b = %d", b);
  }
  printf("\n a = %d", a);
  return 0;
}
```

'b' is visible only within this block

Output:
```
a = 5
a = 5
b = 10
a = 5
```

In C99 compliant compiler, the above program can be written as follows giving the same output:

```
#include <stdio.h>
int main(void)
{
  int a=5;
  printf("\n a = %d", a);
  /* A statement block follows */
  {
    printf("\n a = %d", a);
    int b=10;
    printf("\n b = %d", b);
  }
  printf("\n a = %d", a);
  return 0;
}
```

Take a note of the highlighted line. The visibility or accessibility of the variable 'b' is limited to the block in which it was declared. Consider the modified version of the above program. Here an attempt is made to access the variable out of the block. Definitely we should get a compilation error.

```
#include <stdio.h>
int main(void)
{
  int a=5;
  printf("\n a = %d", a);
  {
    int b=10;
    printf("\n b = %d", b);
  }
  printf("\n b = %d", b);
  return 0;
}
```

Every function has a function body consisting of a set of one or more statements, i.e., a statement block. For that reason, every function body including main() is confined within a set of curly braces and may optionally include variable declarations after the open curly brace. Inside a function, execution proceeds from one statement to the next, top to bottom. However, depending on the requirements of a problem, it might be required to alter the normal sequence of execution in a program. The order in which statements are executed in a running program is called the *flow of control*. Controlling the flow of a program is a very important aspect of programming. Control flow relates to the order in which the operations of a program are executed.

Control statements embody the decision logic that tells the executing program what action to carry out next depending on the values of certain variables or expression statements. The control statements include *selection*, *iteration*, and *jump statements* that work together to direct program flow.

A *selection statement* is a control statement that allows choosing between two or more execution paths in a program. The selection statements in C are the *if* statement, the *if-else* statement, and the *switch* statement. These statements allow us to decide which statement to execute next. Each decision is based on a *boolean expression* (also called a *condition* or *test expression*), which is an expression that evaluates to either true or false. The result of the expression determines which statement is executed next.

The programming mechanism that executes a series of statements repeatedly a given number of times, or until a particular condition is fulfilled, is called a *loop*. The construct used for loop is known as *iteration statement*. C language offers three language elements to formulate iteration statements: *while, do-while,* and *for*.

Jump statements transfer the control to another point of the program. Jump statements include *goto, break, continue* and *return*.

After a very brief introduction to the different types of control structures, it is explained how each type can be used. The subsequent sections will discuss the use of control statements in C. It is also explained how these statements can be used to write efficient programs by using

- Selection or branching statements
- Iteration or loop statements
- Jump statements

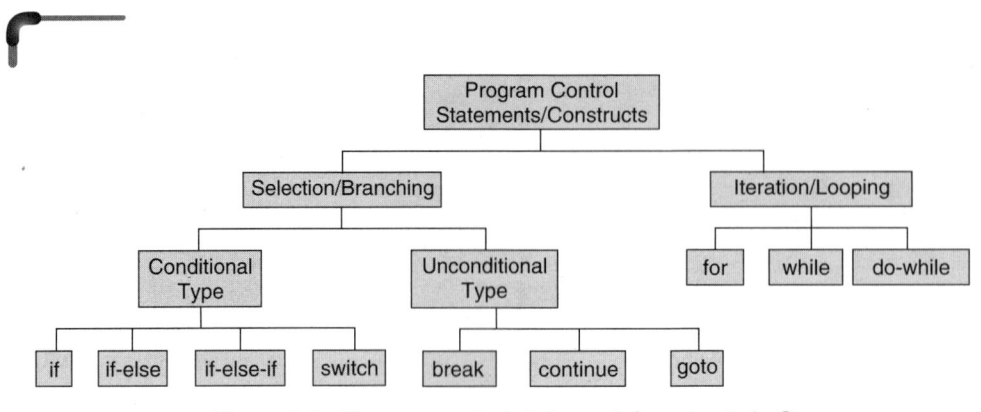

Figure 5.1 Program control statements/constructs in C

5.2 SPECIFYING TEST CONDITION FOR SELECTION AND ITERATION

A test condition used for selection and iteration is expressed as a test expression. If an expression evaluates to true, it is given the value of 1. If a test expression evaluates to false, it is given the value of 0. Similarly, if a numeric expression is used to form a test expression, any non-zero value (including negative) will be considered as true, while a zero value will be considered as false.

Test expression is a Boolean expression that is either true or false. It is formed in terms of relational expression or logical expression or both. The expressions used to compare the operands are called *boolean expressions* in terms of relational operators. In addition to using simple relational expressions as conditions, compound conditions can be formed using the logical operators.

Several relational and logical operators are available to specify the test condition used in the control constructs of C. Relational operators are used to specify individual test expression. More than one test expression can be connected through the logical operator. Tables 5.1 and 5.2 list the several relational, equality, and logical operators used in C.

When the AND operator, &&, is used between two relational expressions, the result is true only if each of both the expressions are true by themselves. When using the OR operator, ||, the condition is true if either one or both of the two individual expressions is true.

The NOT operator, !, is used to change any expression to its opposite state. That is, if the expression has any nonzero value (true), !expression produces a zero value (false). If an expression is false to begin with (has a zero value), !expression is true and evaluates to 1.

Table 5 .1 Relational operators

To Specify	Symbol Used
less than	<
greater than	>
less than or equal to	< =
greater than or equal to	>=

Among the relational, equality, and logical operators only the '!' operator is unary; the rest are binary operators.

Table 5.2 Equality and logical operators

To specify	Symbol used
Equal to	==
Not equal to	! =
Logical AND	&&
Logical OR	||
Negation	!

5.3 WRITING TEST EXPRESSION

Relational expression can be formed using relational operators. A relational operator takes two operands and compares them to each other, resulting in a value of true (1) or false (0). The syntax for relational expression is as follows:

Variable		Variable
OR		OR
Expression	Relational_Operator	Expression
OR		OR
Constant		Constant

The relational operators may be used with integer, float, double, or character operands.

Examples

1. Some examples of expressions are given below.

   - a>2
   - a < b + c
   - a == 3
   - a! = 0
   - a <= b
   - a >= 2

   A test expression involving relational and/or equality and/or logical operators, yields either integer 1 or 0 after evaluation. Consider the following examples of programs.

2. **(a)**
   ```c
   #include <stdio.h>
   int main()
   {
     int a=3;
     printf("\n%d",a>3);
     return 0;
   }
   ```

   Output: 0

   (b)
   ```c
   #include <stdio.h>
   int main()
   {
     int a=3;
     printf("\n%d",a>2);
     return 0;
   }
   ```
   Output: 1

   The reason for the above output is that in C, false is represented by the value 0 and true is represented by the value 1 as the expression is a relational expression. In C, if such a value is zero, it is interpreted as a logical value false. If such a value is not zero, it is interpreted as the logical value true. The value for false may be any zero value, e.g., 0, 0.0, '\0' (null character) or the NULL pointer value, discussed later.

3. The following declarations and initializations are given.

   ```c
   int x=1, y=2,  z=3;
   ```
   Then,

   - The expression x>=y evaluates to 0 (false).
   - The expression x+y evaluates to 3 (true).

     The expression x+y is basically a concise syntax for the full relational expression (x+y != 0), written for coding convenience, as it is only a relational expression which can be used for testing. When x+y evaluates to 3, (x+y !=0) evaluates to true, as it should be.

   - The expression x=y evaluates to 2 (true).

     The expression x=y would again be translated by the compiler to a relational expression ((x=y)!= 0). When x=y evaluates to 2, ((x=y)!= 0) evaluates to true.

   - The expression x==y evaluates to 0 (false).
   - The expression z%2==0 evaluates to 0 (false).
   - The expression x<=y evaluates to 1 (true).

5.3.1 Understanding How True and False is Represented in C

C does not have pre-defined true and false values. The value zero (0) is considered to be *false* by C. Any positive or negative value is considered to be *true*. Conventionally, it is assumed that only positive one is *true* but C evaluates any non-zero value to be *true*.

- The following expressions have the resulting value of *true*, assuming that the integer variables a, b, and c have the values a = 1, b = 2, and c = 3.

  - (a < 2)
  - (a + 1 == b)
  - 1==a
  - a + b >=c
  - c <= (a + b)
  - (a > 0)
  - (a)
  - (-a)
  - (a = 3)

  Note that in the expression (a = 3) where the assignment operator is sometimes accidentally used instead of the relational operator '=='. C evaluates the expression as true even if the variable 'a' is previously assigned some value other than zero (0).

  It is better to develop the habit of writing the literal first, e.g., (3==i). Then, if an equal sign is accidently left out, the compiler will complain about the assignment, as lvalue can never be constant.

  The expression (a) where the variable 'a' was previously assigned the value 1 is true since C considers any expression that evaluates to a non-zero value to be true. Even if the variable 'a' were assigned the value -3, the expression (a) would evaluate to true.

- The following expressions evaluate to *true* where a = 1, b = 2, and c = 3.

  - (b)
  - (c+a)
  - (2*b)
  - (c-2*-30)
  - (0+b)
  - (c-a+b)

- The following expressions evaluate to *false* where a = 1, b = 2, and c = 3.

  - (a - 1)
  - (!(a))
  - (0 * c)
  - (c - a - b)

  Note that the ! symbol, the logical NOT operator, changes a true to a false.

- The following expressions have the resulting value of *false* assuming that the integer variables a, b, and c have the values a = 1, b = 2, and c = 3.

- `(a > 1)`
- `(b == 1)`
- `(a/b + a/b)= = 1`
- `(c % 3)`
- `(a > 0 + 4)`

Care should be taken when one compares two values for equality. Due to truncation, or rounding up, some relational expressions, which are algebraically true, may return 0 instead of 1.

For example, look at the relational expression: `(a/b + a/b)==1` which is `1/2 + 1/2==1`.

This is algebraically true and is supposed to return 1 . The expression, however, returns 0 , which means that the equal-to relationship does not hold. This is because the integer division `1/2` produces 0, not 0.5. The following program proves this.

```
#include <stdio.h>
int main()
{
  int a=1,b=2;
  printf("\n (a/b + a/b) == 1 evaluates %d",
     (a/b + a/b) == 1);
  return 0;
}
```

Output:

`(a/b+a/b) == 1 evaluates to 0`

Another example is `1.0/3.0`, which produces `0.33333....` This is a number with an infinite number of decimal places. But the computer can only hold a limited number of decimal places. Therefore, the expression `1.0/3.0 + 1.0/3.0 + 1.0/3.0 == 1.0` might not return 1 on some computers, although the expression is theoretically true.

- Consider a relational expression such as a < b. If 'a' is less than 'b', then the expression has the integer value 1, which is true. If 'a' is not less than 'b', then the expression has the integer value 0, which is false. Mathematically, the value of a < b is the same as the value of a - b < 0. Because the precedence of the relational operators are less than that of the arithmetic operators, the expression a - b < 0 is equivalent to `(a - b) < 0`

On many machines, an expression such as a < b is implemented as a - b < 0. The usual arithmetic conversions occur in relational expressions.

Let a and b be the arbitrary arithmetic expressions. Table 5.3 shows how the value of a-b determines the values of relational expressions.

Table 5.3 Values of relational expressions

a - b	a < b	a > b	a <= b	a >= b
Positive	0	1	0	1
Zero	0	0	1	1
Negative	1	0	1	0

An equality expression like a == b evaluates to either true or false. An equivalent expression is a - b == 0. If a equals b then a - b evaluates to 0 and 0 == 0 is true. In this case a == b results in the integer value 1 which is true in C. If a is not equal to b, then the expression yields 0, which might be thought of as false.

Points to Note

- If an expression, involving the relational operator, is true, it is given a value of 1. If an expression is false, it is given a value of 0. Similarly, if a numeric expression is used as a test expression, any non-zero value (including negative) will be considered as true, while a zero value will be considered as false.
- Space can be given between operand and operator (relational or logical) but space is not allowed between any compound operator like <=, >=, ==, !=. It is also compiler error to reverse them.
- a == b and a = b are not similar, as == is a test for equality, a = b is an assignment operator. Therefore, the equality operator has to be used carefully.
- The relational operators have lower precedence than all arithmetic operators.

C has three logical operators for combining logical values, which are listed in Table 5.2. && and || are used to connect two or more expressions to form a test condition. && means a conjunction, i.e., all the expressions connected by it must be true to satisfy the test condition. || means a disjunction, i.e., either of the expressions connected by it must be true to satisfy the test condition.

Like arithmetical operators, the relational, equality and logical operators have rules of precedence and associativity for evaluating expression involving these operators. Logical operators may be mixed within relational expressions but one must abide by their *precedence rules which is as follows* (see Table 5.4 for complete list).

```
NOT operator (!), AND operator (&&), OR operator (||)
```

One must remember that the && operation is always performed before the || operation because && is similar to multiplication in normal arithmetic while || is similar to addition.

The == (equal to) and != (not equal to) operators are analogous to the relational operators except for their lower precedence.

Table 5.4 Operators semantics

Operators	Associativity
() ++ (postfix) – (postfix)	left to right
+ (unary) – (unary)	right to left
++ (prefix) – (prefix) * / %	left to right
+ -	left to right
< <= > >=	left to right
== !=	left to right
&&	left to right
||	left to right
?:	right to left
= += –= *= /=	right to left
, (comma operator)	left to right

Given the following declarations and initializations:

```
int a=3,  b=-5,   c=0;
```

consider Table 5.5 which illustrates the use of the logical operators.

Table 5.5 Illustration of the use of logical operators

Expression	Result
a>0 && c>0	0(false)
a>=0 && c>=0	1(true)
a && c	0(false)
a && b	1(true)
a || c	1(true)
!a && c	0(false)
5 && !c	1(true)

In addition to numerical operands, character data can also be compared using relational operators.

```
'a' < 'e'    returns 1(true)
'9' > '1'    returns 1(true)
'A' > 'a'    returns 0 (false)
```

as ASCII value of 'A' is 65 and that of 'a' is 97.

Consider the following declaration:

```
char ch = 'A';
```

To check whether ch contains upper case letter the conditional expression can be written as follows:

```
ch>='A' && ch<='Z'
```

It is also possible to use the ASCII value corresponding to a character in relational expression. The above expression can also be written as

```
ch >= 65 && ch <= 90.
```

- Although C does not have an exclusive OR (XOR) logical operator, outcome of XOR is true if and only if one operand is true but not both. It can be implemented by the following expression:

```
(a || b) && !(a && b)
```

Short-circuiting evaluation in C

It is to be noted that in case of && when the first operand is false, it is evident that the result must be false. So the other operand of the expression will not be evaluated. Likewise, in case of ||, when the first operand is true, there is no need to evaluate the other operand of the expression, so the resulting value is set to true immediately. C uses this short-circuit method which is summarized as follows:

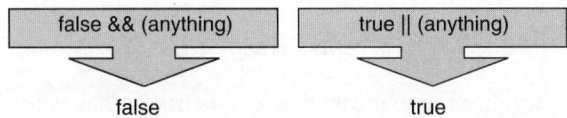

Sometimes, it can cause problems when the second operand contains side effects. For instance, consider the following example:

```
r= a && b++;
```

When the first operand is non-zero, that is if a=2, b=3 then the expression evaluates to give r=2, a=2, and b=4. But if the first variable is zero, then the second variable will never be evaluated. That is, if a=0, b=3; then r=0, a=0, and b=3. Same thing would happen in case of

```
r = a  || b++;
```

If the first operand is non-zero, then the second operand would never be incremented. It is important to understand the complement of relational and equality operators. Table 5.6 illustrates the complements.

Table 5.6 Relational operator complement

Operator	Complement
>	< =
<	>=
==	! =

For example, `!(a<b)` is equivalent to `a>=b`, `!(a>=b)` is equivalent to `a<b`.

- An expression such as `a < b < c` is syntactically correct but often confusing. This is illustrated with an example. In mathematics,

  `3 < j < 5`

  indicates that the variable *j* has the property of being greater than 3 and less than 5. It can also be considered as a mathematical statement that, depending on the value of *j*, may or may not be true. For example, if *j* = 4, then the mathematical statement is true. But if *j* = 7, then the mathematical statement is false. Now consider the C code

  ```
  j =7;
  printf("%d\n",  3 < j < 5);
                        /* 1 gets printed, not 0 */
  ```

  By analogy with mathematics, it might be expected that the expression is false and that 0 is printed. However, that is not the case because relational operators associate from left to right.

  `3 < j < 5` is equivalent to `(3 < j) < 5`

  Because the expression `3 < j` is true, it has value 1. Thus,

  `(3 < j) < 5` is equivalent to `1 < 5`

  which has value 1 . In C, the correct way to write an expression for testing both `3 < j` and `j < 5` is

  `3 < j && j < 5`

  Because relational operators have higher precedence than binary logical operators, this is equivalent to

  `(3 < j)  &&  (j < 5)`

  and, as will be seen later, this expression is true if and only if both operands of the `&&` expression are true.

- Like arithmetic operators, the relational and logical operators have rules of precedence and associativity

for evaluating expressions involving these operators (shown in Table 5.4).

The precedence of the relational operators is less than that of the arithmetic operators, including unary + and –, and greater than that of assignment operators. Thus, `a > b + 5` means the same as `a > (b + 5)`. The expression `a = b > 5` means `a = (b > 5)`. That is, `a` is assigned 1 if `b` is greater than 5 and 0 otherwise; `a` is not assigned the value of `b`.

The relational operators are themselves organized into two different priorities:

Higher-priority group: `<,<=, >,>=`
Lower-priority group: `= =, !=`

Like most other operators, the relational operators associate from left to right. Therefore,

`expr1 != expr2 == expr3`

is the same as

`(expr1 != expr2) == expr3`

First, C checks to see if `expr1` and `expr2` are unequal. Then the resulting value of 1 or 0 (true or false) is compared to the value of `expr3`. It is not recommended to write a relational expression like this but this has been pointed out for a clearer understanding of the precedence and associativity of the relational operator.

Initially C language did not provide any Boolean data type. As in C99, a new data type `_Bool` has been provided which remedied the lack of Boolean type in C language. In this version of C, a Boolean variable can be declared as follows:

`_Bool isPrime;`

`_Bool` is actually an `integer` type (More precisely an `unsigned integer` type). Unlike an ordinary integer variable, `_Bool` variable can only be assigned 0 or 1. When converting any scalar values to type `_Bool`, all non-zero values are converted to 1 while zero values are converted to 0. Consider the following program:

```
#include <stdio.h>
int main(void)
{
  _Bool isPrime =5;
  printf("\n isPrime = %d", isPrime);
  return 0;
}
```

Output: `isPrime = 1`

Because a relational operator produces a Boolean result, it is possible to store the result in a variable of type _Bool. For example

```
_Bool result = 5 < 4; /* result will be false */
```

In addition to _Bool type, C99 also provides a new header file stdbool.h for working with Boolean values. This header file provides a macro bool which to be synonym for _Bool and defines false and true to be 0 and 1 respectively.

If stdbool.h is included then the following declaration can be written:

```
bool flag;
```

This header file also provides macros like true, false which stands for 1 and 0 respectively making it possible to write the following statements:

```
flag=true;
```

5.4 CONDITIONAL EXECUTION AND SELECTION

Uses of selection and iteration statements are the basic tools of thought when designing a logical process. The ability to control the order in which the statements are executed adds enormous value to the programming. The uses of selection in various forms have already been discussed in the previous sections. In this section the concept of iteration or looping will be discussed.

A loop allows one to execute a statement or block of statements repeatedly. There are mainly two types of iterations or loops – *unbounded iteration* or *unbounded loop* and *bounded iteration* or *bounded loop*. In bounded iteration, repetition is implemented by constructs that allow a determinate number of iterations. That is, bounded loops should be used when we know, ahead of time, how many times we need to loop. C provides for construct as bounded loop.

There are also many occasions when one doesn't know, ahead of time, how many iterations may be required. Such occasions require *unbounded loops*. C provides two types of unbounded loop: while loop and do... while loop. These types of loops are also known as indeterminate or indefinite loop.

5.4.1 Selection Statements

When dealing with selection statements, there are generally three versions: *one-way, two-way, and multi-way*. One-way decision statements do a particular thing or they do not. Two-way decision statements do one thing or do another. Multi-way decision statements can do one of many different things depending on the value of an expression.

One-way decisions using if statement

One-way decisions are handled with an if statement that either do some particular thing or do nothing at all. The decision is based on a 'test expression' that evaluates to either true or false. If the test expression evaluates to true, the corresponding statement is executed; if the test expression evaluates to false, control goes to the next executable statement. Figure 5.2 demonstrates this. The form of this one-way decision statement is as follows:

```
if(TestExpr)
    stmtT;
```

TestExpr is the test expression. stmtT can be a simple statement or a block of statements enclosed by curly braces {}.

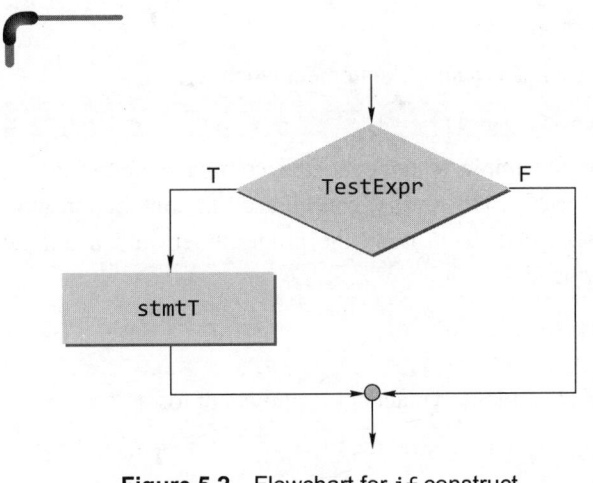

Figure 5.2   Flowchart for if construct

The if construct can be illustrated with the help of the following example.

4. Write a program that prints the largest among three numbers.

   Solution:

Algorithm	C Program
1. START	`#include <stdio.h>`
2. PRINT "ENTER THREE NUMBERS"	`int main()`
	`{`
3. INPUT A, B, C	`int a, b, c, max;`
4. MAX=A	`printf("\nEnter 3 numbers");`
	`scanf("%d %d %d", &a, &b, &c);`
	`max=a;`
5. IF B>MAX THEN MAX=B	`if(b>max)`
	`    max=b;`
6. IF C>MAX THEN MAX=C	`if(c>max)`
7. PRINT "LARGEST NUMBER IS", MAX	`    max=c;`
	`printf("Largest No is %d", max);`
8. STOP	`return 0;`
	`}`

if and the comma operator

Normally, the comma operator is used to combine statements. For example, the statements:

```
x = 1;
y = 2;
```

are treated as a single statement when written as:

```
x = 1, y = 1;
```

With simple statements, the comma operator is not very useful. However it can be used in conjunction with if statement to provide the programmer with a unique shorthand.

```
if (flag)
    x =1, y = 1;
```

This example is syntactically equivalent to:

```
if (flag)
{
    x = 1;
    y = 1;
}
```

The problem with the comma operator is that when you use it you break the rule of one statement per line, which obscures the structure of the program. Therefore never use the comma operator when you can use braces instead.

Two-way decisions using if-else statement

Two-way decisions are handled with if-else statements that either do one particular thing or do another. Similar to one-way decisions, the decision here is based on a test expression. The form of a two-way decision is as follows:

```
if(TestExpr)
    stmtT;
else
    stmtF;
```

If the test expression TestExpr is true, stmtT will be executed; if the expression is false, stmtF will be executed. stmtT and stmtF can be single or a block of statements. Remember that a block of statements are always enclosed with curly braces {}. Figure 5.3 depicts a flowchart of the if-else construct.

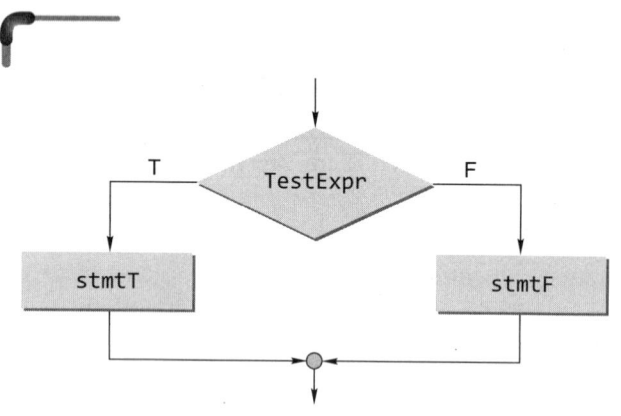

Figure 5.3 Flowchart of if-else construct

The if-else construct is illustrated with the help of an example.

5. Write a program in C to check whether a number given by the user is odd or even.

Algorithm	C Program
1. START	`#include <stdio.h>`
2. PRINT "ENTER THE NUMBER"	`int main()`
3. INPUT N	`{`
4. Q←N/2 (Integer Division)	`int n,r;`
5. R←N-Q*2	`printf("\nEnter the number");`
6. IF R=0 THEN PRINT "EVEN" ELSE PRINT "ODD"	`scanf("%d", &n);`
	`r=n%2;`
7. STOP	`if(r==0)`
	`  printf("EVEN");`
	`else`
	`  printf("ODD");`
	`return 0;`
	`}`

An absolutely classic pitfall is to use assignment (=) instead of comparison (==). This is probably the single most common error made by beginners in C programming. The problem is that in such a case the compiler is of no help—it is unable to distinguish this non-syntax error. Consider the following example program.

6. Check whether the two given numbers are equal.

(a)
```
#include <stdio.h>
int main()
{
  int a=2, b=3;
  if(a == b)
    printf("EQUAL");
  else
    printf("UNEQUAL");
  return 0;
}
```
Output: UNEQUAL

(b)
```
#include <stdio.h>
int main()
{
  int a=2, b=3;
  if(a = b)
    printf("EQUAL");
  else
    printf("UNEQUAL");
  return 0;
}
```
Output: EQUAL

The explanation for the above outputs is that when a condition is specified with = instead of ==, the C compiler checks the value of the test expression. If it is non-zero including negative, it evaluates the test condition as true; otherwise it evaluates the test condition as false. Example 6(a) simply checks the equality and gives the result as expected. But in Example 6(b), the value of b is assigned to a first. Since the value assigned to a is 3, which is non-zero, the condition will be true and the program outputs EQUAL. If the value of b was assigned as zero, then following the above explanation, the second program would print UNEQUAL and now a would be zero.

So the test expression using the equality operator must be specified carefully. If the value of a variable is assigned a constant value, the same thing may not occur. The example statement,

```
if(x = 3) stmT;
```

does not test whether x is 3. This sets x to the value 3, and then returns x to the if construct for testing. Now, 3 is not 0, so it is deduced as true. The actual test expression should be x==3. Such a problem can be overcome by writing the expression as 3==x. It is safe to write. If the expression is written 3=x by mistake, then the compiler will complain because 3 cannot be a lvalue.

In case it is desired to test whether variable x has a non-zero value, one could write

```
if(x)
```

rather than

```
if(x != 0)
```

However, this can sometimes be confusing. In general, it is better to write whatever is meant rather than writing something that has the same effect.

The following three `if()` statements are functionally equivalent.

```
if(x)
   printf("true\n");
if(x!=0)
   printf("true\n");
if(!(x==0))
   printf("true\n");
```

The *unsigned preserving* approach (K&R C) says that when an unsigned type mixes with an `int` or smaller signed type, the result is an unsigned type. This is the simple rule independent of hardware but as in the following example, it does something to force a negative result to lose its sign. The value preserving approach (ANSI C) says that when an integral operand type is mixed like this, the result type is signed or unsigned depending on the relative sizes of the operand type. Consider the following example.

```
#include <stdio.h>
int main()
{
  int i=-1;
  unsigned int u=1;
  if(i<u)
    printf("\n i is less than u");
  else
    printf("\n i is not less than u");
  return 0;
}
```

Output: `i is not less than u (in GCC compiler)`

Depending on whether this program is compiled and executed under K&R or ANSI C, the expression `i<u` will be evaluated differently. The same bit patterns are compared but interpreted as either a negative number or as unsigned (hence positive number).

If either operand is unsigned, the result is unsigned, and is defined to be modulo 2^n, where n is the word size. If both operands are signed, the result is *undefined*.

Suppose, for example, `a` and `b` are two integer variables, known to be non-negative, and you want to test whether `a+b` might overflow. One obvious way to do it looks something like this:

```
if (a + b < 0)
   printf("\OVERFLOW");
```

In general, this does not work. The point is that once a + b has overflowed, all bits are off as to what the result will be. If the operation overflowed, the register would be in overflow state, and the test would fail. One correct way of doing this particular test relies on the fact that unsigned arithmetic is well-defined for all values, as are the conversions between signed and unsigned values:

```
if ((int) ((unsigned) a + (unsigned) b) < 0)
   printf("\OVERFLOW");
```

Examples

7. Suppose a C code has to be written that will calculate the earnings by workers who are paid an hourly wage, with weekly hours greater than 40 being paid 'time and a half'. Suppose weekly hours and hourly rate are known in the program. Two options of the code to handle this situation are as follows.

Option 1 Using simple statements:

```
if(weeklyHours <= 40)
    earnings = hourlyRate * weeklyHours;
else
    earnings = 40 * hourlyRate + (weeklyHours
        - 40) *hourlyRate* 1.5;
```

Option 2 Using a simple and compound statement:

```
if(weeklyHours <= 40)
    earnings = hourlyRate * weeklyHours;
else
    {
       offHours = weeklyHours - 40;
       regpay = 40 * hourlyRate;
       earnings = regpay + offHours * hourlyRate
           * 1.5;
    }
```

A complete program in C is illustrated as follows.

8. Write a program that determines if a year is a leap year.

```
#include<stdio.h>
int main()
{
    int year, rem_4,rem_100,rem_400;
    printf("Enter the year to be tested:");
    scanf("%d", &year);
    rem_4 = year % 4;
    rem_100 = year % 100;
    rem_400 = year % 400;
    if( (rem_4 == 0 && rem_100 != 0) || rem_400 = = 0)
      printf("It is a leap year.\n");
    else
      printf("It is not a leap year.\n");
    return 0;
}
```

Given below are the outputs obtained for different inputs from the above program executed in a computer.

Test run no. 1

```
Enter the year to be tested: 1955
It is not a leap year.
```

Test run no. 2

```
Enter the year to be tested: 2000
It is a leap year.
```

Test run no. 3

```
Enter the year to be tested: 1800
It is not a leap year.
```

Multi-way decisions

Multi-way decision statements use if-else-if nested if or switch statements. They are used to evaluate a test expression that could have several possible values. if-else-if statements are often used to choose between ranges of values. Switch statements are discussed in the next section.

- if-else-if ladder

  The form of a multi-way decision construct using if-else if statements is as follows:

```
if(TestExpr1)
      stmtT1;
  else if(TestExpr2)
          stmtT2;
      else if(TestExpr3)
              stmtT3;
              :
              :
          else if(TestExprN)
              stmtTN;
              else
              stmtF;
```

If the first test expression TestExpr1 is evaluated to true, then stmtT1 is executed. If the second test expression TestExpr2 is true, then stmtT2 is executed, and so on. If none of the test expressions are true, then the statement stmtF is executed. The flow chart of the above construct is shown in Fig. 5.4.

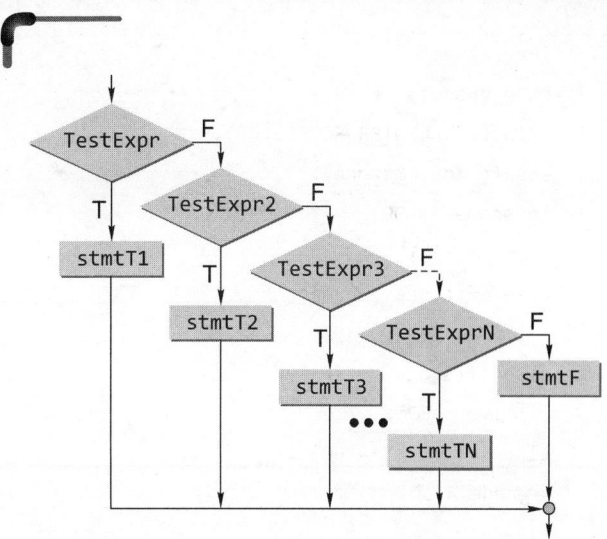

Figure 5.4 Flowchart of an if-else-if construct

9. The following program checks whether a number given by the user is zero, positive, or negative.

```c
#include <stdio.h>
int main()
{
  int x;
  printf("\n ENTER THE NUMBER:");
  scanf("%d", &x);
  if(x > 0)
    printf("x is positive \n");
  else if(x == 0)
    printf("x is zero \n");
      else
        printf("x is negative \n");
  return 0;
}
```

10. This program prints the grade according to the score secured by a student.

```c
#include <stdio.h>
int main()
```

```
{
  int score;
  char grade;
  printf("\n ENTER SCORE : ");
  scanf("%d", &score);
  if(score >= 90)
    grade = 'A';
  else if(score >= 80)
    grade = 'B';
  else if(score >= 70)
    grade = 'C';
  else if(score >= 60)
    grade = 'D';
  else
    grade = 'F';
  printf("GRADE IS:%c", grade);
  return 0;
}
```

Nested if

When any `if` statement is written under another `if` statement, this cluster is called a nested `if`. A simple illustration of a nested `if` is given below.

The `if` statement that tests for divisibility by 5 is located inside the `if` statement that tests for divisibility by 3 therefore it is considered to be a nested if statement.

```
if (number % 3 == 0)
{
  printf("number  is divisible by 3. \n");
  if (number % 5 == 0)
  {
    printf("number  is divisible by 3 and 5. \n");
  }
}
```

Another example is given below.

```
if(a > b)
  if(a > c)
    printf("%d", a);
```

Here `a` will be printed in case both `if` conditions are true. The indentation makes the logic of the statements explicitly clear. Next, the nested loop is further explained with the example given below.

```
if(a > b)
  if(a > c)
    printf("%d",  a);
  else
    printf("%d",  c);
```

An important fact to be noted here is that an `else` always associates itself with the closest (innermost) `if`. In the above example, the `else` part corresponds to the inner `if`, that is, `if(a > c)`. If another `else` is added, the last `else` corresponds to `if(a > b)`. The syntax for the nested `if` is as follows.

Construct 1	Construct 2
`if(TestExprA)`	`if(TestExprA)`
`if(TestExprB)`	`if(TestExprB)`
`stmtBT;`	`stmtBT;`
`else`	`else`
`stmtBF;`	`stmtBF;`
`else`	`else`
`stmtAF;`	`if(TestExprC)`
	`stmtCT;`
	`else`
	`stmtCF;`

`stmtBT`, `stmtBF`, `stmtCT`, and `stmtCF` can be a simple statement or a block of statements. It is to be remembered that a block of statement is always enclosed with curly braces {}.

In construct 1, `stmtBT` will be executed if both `TestExprA` and `TestExprB` evaluate to true. `stmtBF` will be executed if `TestExprA` evaluates to true and `TestExprB` evaluates to false. `stmtAF` will be executed if `TestExprA` is false and does not check for `TestExprB`.

In construct 2, `stmtBT` will be executed if both `TestExprA` and `TestExprB` evaluate to true. `stmtBF` will be executed if `TestExprA` evaluates to true and `TestExprB` evaluates to false. If `TestExprA` is false, then the test expression `TestExprC` will be checked. If it is true, then `stmtCT` will be executed, otherwise `stmtCF` will be executed.

Finally, a program to find the largest among three numbers using the nested loop follows. The required flowchart is shown in Fig. 5.5. The C code is given as follows:

```c
#include <stdio.h>
int main()
{
    int a, b, c;
    printf("\nEnter the three numbers");
    scanf("%d %d %d", &a, &b, &c);
    if(a > b)
      if(a > c)
        printf("%d", a);
      else
        printf("%d", c);
    else
      if(b > c)
        printf("%d", b);
      else
        printf("%d", c);
    return 0;
}
```

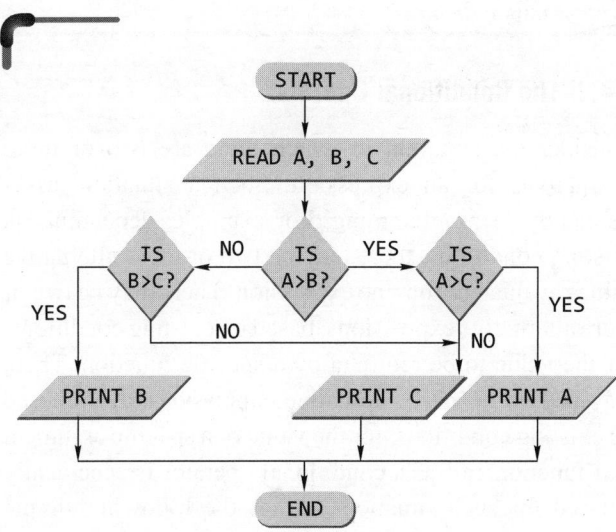

Figure 5.5 Flowchart for finding the largest of three numbers

Dangling else Problem

This classic problem occurs when there is no matching else for each if. To avoid this problem, the simple C rule is that always pair an else to the most recent unpaired if in the current block. Consider the following illustration.

```c
if(TestExprA)

    if(TestExprB)
        stmtBT;
    else
        stmtAF;
```

If TestExprA is evaluated to true, then execution moves to the nested if and evaluates TestExprB. If TestExprB is evaluated to true then stmtBT will be executed. If TestExprA is evaluated to false, then stmtAF is executed. But in the code above, the else is automatically paired with the closest if. But, it is needed to associate an else with the outer if also. The solution is either of the following:

- Use of a null else
- Use of braces to enclose the true action of the second if

Each of these has the following form:

With null else	With braces
`if(TestExprA)`	`if(TestExprA)`
`  if(TestExprB)`	`{`
`    stmtBT;`	`  if(TestExprB)`
`  else`	`    stmtBT;`
`    ;`	`}`
`else`	`else`
`  stmtAF;`	`  stmtAF;`

Now, in both the solutions, if the expression TestExprA evaluates to false then the statement stmtBF will be executed. If it evaluates to true, then it checks for TestExprB. If TestExprB evaluates to true then statement stmtBT will be executed. Consider the following C program with a dangling else problem.

```c
#include <stdio.h>
int main()
{
    int a = 2,b = 2;
    if (a == 1)
      if (b == 2)
        printf("a was 1 and b was 2\n");
      else
        printf("a wasn't 1\n");
    return 0;
}
```

When compiled and run, this program did not produce any output. With the program in its original form it is quite likely that the programmer thought the else statement

```
else
    printf("a wasn't 1\n");
```

would be associated with the first if but it was not. An else always associates with the immediately preceding if as is clear by the alternatively laid out version of the program. The reason for the complete absence of output is the fact that there is no else statement associated with the first if.

In order to achieve the effect that the programmer probably originally intended, it is necessary to re-arrange the program in the following form.

```
int main()
{
    int a = 2;
    int b = 2;
    if (a == 1)
    {
        if (b == 2) printf("a was 1 and b was 2\n");
    }
    else printf("a wasn't 1\n");
    return 0;
}
```

Points to Note

- Multi-way decision statements are used to evaluate a test expression that could have several possible values.
- An else is always associated with the closest unmatched if.

Check Your Progress

1. What will be the output of the following programs?

(a)
```
int main()
{
    printf("Hi!");
    if(-1)
        printf("Bye");
    return 0;
}
```
Output: Hi!Bye

(b)
```
int main()
{
    printf("Hi!");
    if(!1)
        printf("Bye");
    return 0;
}
```
Output: Hi!

(c)
```
float x = 199.9;
if( x < 100)
    printf("one ");
if(x < 200)
    printf("two ");
if(x < 300)
    printf("three ");
```
Output: two three

(d)
```
int main()
{
    int i= -1;
    unsigned int j =1;
    if(i<j)
        printf("Less");
    else
        printf("Greater");
    return 0;
}
```
Output: Greater

5.4.2 The Conditional Operator

Consider the situation in which there are two or more alternatives for an expression. Such a situation arises frequently in programming. For example, depending on existing conditions, there may be two or more alternative values evaluated from the expression. There may be two or more alternative expressions, based on existing conditions, for the value to be returned by a specific function. There may be two or more alternative expressions, again based on existing conditions, for the value of a specific argument in a function call. C's conditional operator is specifically tailored for such situations. It has the following simple format:

```
expr1 ? expr2  :  expr3
```

It executes by first evaluating expr1, which is normally a relational expression, and then evaluates either expr2, if the first result was true, or expr3, if the first result was false.

For instance, if the larger of two integer numbers has to be printed, the program using conditional operator will be

```c
#include <stdio.h>
int main()
{
  int a,b,c;
  printf("\n ENTER THE TWO NUMBERS: ");
  scanf("%d %d", &a, &b);
  c=a>b?a:b;
  printf("\n LARGER NUMBER IS %d",c);
  return 0;
}
```

The following is a more refined version of the program. Here the conditional operator has to be nested.

```c
#include <stdio.h>
int main()
{
  int a,b,c;
  printf("\n ENTER THE TWO NUMBERS: ");
  scanf("%d %d", &a, &b);
  c=a>b? a : b>a ? b :-1;
  if(c==-1)
    printf("\n BOTH NUMBERS ARE EQUAL");
  else
    printf("\n LARGER NUMBER IS %d",c);
  return 0;
}
```

For illustration, let us consider the program that will print the largest among three integer numbers. If the program is written using the nested if construct, it will be as follows:

```c
#include <stdio.h>
int main()
{
  int a,b,c;
  printf("\n ENTER THE THREE NUMBERS: ");
  scanf("%d %d %d", &a, &b, &c);
  if(a>b)
    if(a>c)
      printf("\n LARGEST NUMBER IS: %d", a);
    else
```

```c
      printf("\n LARGEST NUMBER IS: %d", c);
  else
    if(b>c)
      printf("\n LARGEST NUMBER IS: %d", b);
    else
      printf("\n LARGEST NUMBER IS: %d", c);
  return 0;
}
```

Now the above program is converted into one that uses the nested conditional operator.

```c
#include <stdio.h>
int main()
{
  int a,b,c, max;
  printf("\n ENTER THE THREE NUMBERS: ");
  scanf("%d %d %d", &a, &b, &c);
  max=a>b ? a>c ? a : c: b>c? b : c;
  /* This statement is equivalent to
     max= a>b? (a>c? a: c):(b>c? b: c)*/
  printf("\n LARGEST NUMBER IS: %d", max);
  return 0;
}
```

Similarly, the following program finds the largest number among four integer numbers.

```c
#include <stdio.h>
int main()
{
  int a, b, c, d, e;
  printf("\n Enter the four numbers one by one \n");
  scanf("%d %d %d %d", &a, &b, &c, &d);
  e=a>b?(a>c?(a>d?a:d):(c>d?c:d)):(b>c?(b>d?b:d):
      (c>d?c:d));
  printf("\nLargest number is %d\n", e);
  return 0;
}
```

The use of the conditional expression frequently shortens the amount of source code that must be written. For example, a lengthy function call, which has several argument expressions, one of which is conditional, needs to be written only once.

The conditional expression is not only a shorthand; it may also result in less object code than would be generated by other alternative means, e.g., by the use of one or more `if` statements.

Observe that parentheses are normally not needed around the expressions that are separated by the characters '?' and because, as the operator precedence table shows, the '?:' operator has a very low precedence, i.e., it is usually applied last.

5.4.3 The switch Statement

When there are a number of `else` alternatives as above, another way of representing this multi-way selection is by the `switch` statement (shown in Fig. 5.6). The general format of a `switch` statement is

```
switch(expr)
{
  case constant1: stmtList1;
                  break;
  case constant2: stmtList2;
                  break;
  case constant3: stmtList3;
                  break;
  ..........................
  ..........................
  default: stmtListn;
}
```

When there is a `switch` statement, it evaluates the expression and then looks for a matching `case` label. If none is found, the `default` label is used. If no `default` is found, the statement does nothing.

The expanded flowchart of the `switch` statement is shown in Fig. 5.6.

This construct evaluates the expression `expr` and matches its evaluated value with the `case` constants and then the statements in the corresponding statement list are executed. Otherwise if there is a `default` (which is optional) then the program branches to its statement list when none of the `case` constants match with the evaluated value of `expr`. The `case` constants must be integer or character constants. The expression must evaluate to an

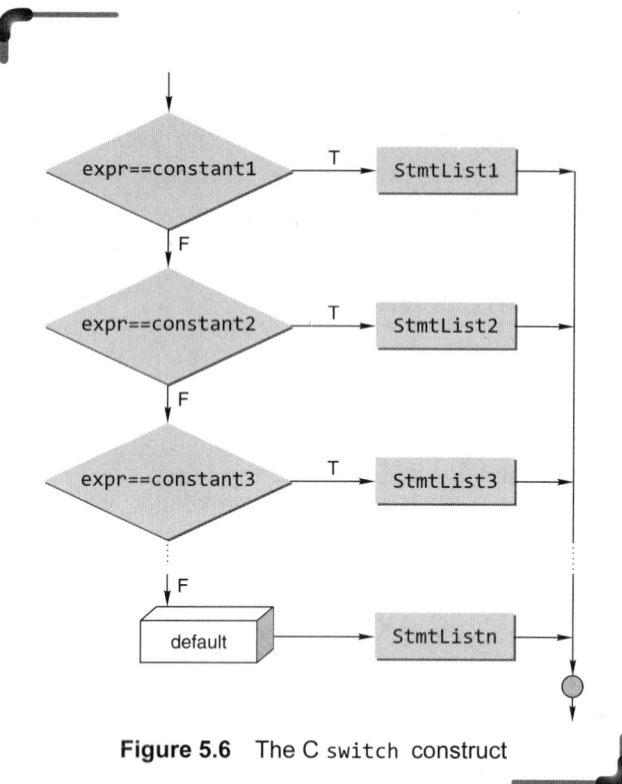

Figure 5.6 The C `switch` construct

integral type. Single quotes must be used around `char` constants specified with each `case`.

Once again, it is emphasized that the `default` case, if present, will be selected if none of the prior cases are chosen. A default case is not required but it is good programming practice to include one.

Perhaps the biggest defect in the `switch` statement is that cases do not break automatically after the execution of the corresponding statement list for the case label. Once the statement list under a case is executed, the flow of control continues down, executing all the following cases until a `break` statement is reached.

The `break` statement must be used within each case if one does not want the following cases to execute once one case is selected. When the break statement is executed within a `switch`, C executes the next statement outside the `switch` construct. However, sometimes it may be desirable not to use the `break` statement in a particular case.

Examples

The following is an example where the control expression is a char variable ch. Notice the use of single quotes around the character variable in each case.

11.
```c
switch(ch)
{
    case 'A':
        printf("You entered an A");
        break;
    case 'B':
        printf("You entered a B");
        break;
    default:
        printf("Illegal entry");
        break;
}
```

Another example is depicted where the variable 'Choice' is an int variable. Note that single quotes are not used around the integer values in each of the case statements.

12.
```c
switch(Choice)
{
    case 1:
        printf("You entered menu choice #1");
        break;
    case 2:
        printf("You entered menu choice #2");
        break;
    case 3:
        printf("You entered menu choice #3");
        break;
    default:
        printf("You failed to enter a valid menu choice");
        break;
}
```

13.
```c
switch(donationLevel)
{
    case 1:
        printf("You donated over Rs 1,000.");
    case 2:
        printf("You donated over Rs 500.");
    case 3:
        printf("You donated over Rs 250.");
    case 4:
        printf("You donated over Rs 100.");
        break;
    default:
        printf("Please be a little more generous.");
        break;
}
```

The break statement causes flow of control to exit from the entire switch block and resume at the next statement outside the switch. Technically, the break statement is optional, although most applications of the switch will use it. If a break statement is omitted in any case of a switch statement, the compiler will not issue an error message. The flow of control continues to the next case label.

The redundancy in the code can be minimized by placing the cases next to each other, as in the following example. That is, several case values can be associated with one group of statements.

14.
```c
switch(number)
{
    case 1:
    case 3:
    case 5:
    case 7:
    case 9:
        printf(" %d is an odd number.", number);
        break;
    case 2:
    case 4:
    case 6:
    case 8:
        printf(" %d is an even number\n", number);
        break;
    default:
        printf(" %d is a value not between or
                including 1 and 9.", number);
        break;
}
```

Points to Note

- The switch statement enables you to choose one course of action from a set of possible actions, based on the result of an integer expression.
- The case labels can be in any order and must be constants.
- No two case labels can have the same value.
- The default is optional and can be put anywhere in the switch construct.
- The case constants must be integer or character constants. The expression must evaluate to an integral type.
- The break statement is optional. If a break statement is omitted in any case of a switch statement, the program flow is followed through the next case label.
- C89 specifies that a switch can have at least 257 case statements. C99 requires that at least 1023 case statements be supported. The case cannot exist by itself, outside of a switch.

Switch vs. nested if

The switch differs from the else-if in that switch can test only for equality, whereas the if conditional expression can be of a test expression involving any type of relational operators and/or logical operators. A switch statement is usually more efficient than nested ifs.

The switch statement can always be replaced with a series of else-if statements. One may only use switch and case statements if an expression is required to check against a finite amount of constant, integral, or character values. If there are too many values and if any of the values depend on variables, or if the values are not integers or characters, one must use a series of else-if statements. Even when one can use switch efficiently, it is just a matter of personal preference whether one decides to use a switch statement or else-if statements.

Examples

15. Writing a program using a switch statement to check whether a number given by the user is odd or even.

    Solution:
    ```c
    #include <stdio.h>
    int main()
    {
      int n;
      printf("\n Enter the number:");
      scanf("%d",  &n);
      switch(n%2)
      {
        case 0: printf("\n EVEN");
          break;
        case 1: printf("\n ODD");
          break;
      }
      return 0;
    }
    ```

16. Write a program to carry out the arithmetic operations addition, subtraction, multiplication, and division between two variables.

    Solution: Use the switch construct to choose the operations.
    ```c
    #include<stdio.h>
    int main()
    {
      int value1, value2;
      char operator;
      printf("Type in your expression. \n");
      scanf("%d %c %d ",&value1,&operator,&value2);
      switch(operator)
      {
        case '+':
          printf("%d \n", value1 + value2);
          break;
        case '-':
          printf("%d \n", value1 - value2);
          break;
        case '*':
          printf("%d \n", value1 * value2);
          break;
        case '/':
          if(value2 == 0)
          printf("division by zero. \n");
          else
          printf("%d \n", value1 / value2);
          break;
        default:
    ```

```
        printf("Unknown Operator \n");
        break;
    }
    return 0;
}
```

17. Write a program that checks whether a character entered by the user is a vowel or not.

    Solution:

    ```c
    #include <stdio.h>
    int main(void)
    {
      char c;
      printf("Enter a character: ");
      scanf("%c", &c);
      switch(c)
      {
        case 'a': case 'A':
        case 'e': case 'E':
        case 'i': case 'I':
        case 'o': case 'O':
        case 'u': case 'U':
        printf("%c is always a vowel!\n", c);
        break;
        case 'y': case 'Y':
        printf("%c is sometimes a vowel!\n", c);
        break;
        default:
        printf("%c is not a vowel!\n", c);
        break;
      }
      return 0;
    }
    ```

    ### Check Your Progress

1. What will be printed by the code below?

    ```c
    float x =  123.4;
    if( x < 100)
        printf("one ");
    ```

    ```c
    if(x < 200)
        printf("two ");
    if(x < 300)
        printf("three ");
    ```

    Output: two three

2. What will the following switch statement print?

    ```c
    char c =  'Y'; switch(c)
    {
      case 'Y': printf("Yes/No");
      case 'N': printf("No/Yes"); break;
      default: printf("Other");
    }
    ```

    Output: Yes/NoNo/Yes

3. What will the following switch statement print?

    (a)
    ```c
    char c =  'y';
    switch(c)
    {
      case 'Y': printf("Yes/No");
      break;
      case 'N': printf("No/Yes");
      break;
      default: printf("Other");
    }
    ```

    Output: Other

    (b)
    ```c
    int main()
    {
      int choice=3; switch(choice)
      {
        default:
          printf("Default");
        case 1: printf("Choice1");
        break;
        case 2: printf("Choice2");
        break;
      }
      return 0;
    }
    ```

    Output: DefaultChoice1

5.5 ITERATION AND REPETITIVE EXECUTION

Selection and iteration statements are the basic tools of thought when designing a logical process. The ability to control the order in which the statements are executed adds enormous value to programming. The uses of selection in various forms have already been discussed in the previous sections. In this section, the concept of iteration or looping will be discussed.

A loop allows one to execute a statement or block of statements repeatedly. There are mainly two types of iterations or loops – *unbounded iteration* or *unbounded loop* and *bounded iteration* or *bounded loop*. In bounded iteration, repetition is implemented by constructs that allow a determinate number of iterations. That is, bounded loops should be used when we know, ahead of time, how many times we need to loop. C provides `for` construct as bounded loop.

There are also many occasions when one doesn't know, ahead of time, how many iterations may be required. Such occasions require *unbounded loops*. C provides two types of unbounded loop: `while` loop and `do...while` loop. These types of loops are also known as *indeterminate* or *indefinite* loop.

A loop can either be a *pre-test loop* or be a *post-test loop*. In a *pre-test loop*, the condition is checked before the beginning of each iteration. If the test expression evaluates to true, the statements associated with the pre-test loop construct are executed and the process is repeated till the test expression becomes false. On the other hand, if the test expression evaluates to false, the statements associated with the construct are skipped and the statement next to the loop is executed. So for such a construct, the statements associated with the construct may not be executed even once.

In the *post-test loop*, the code is always executed once. At the completion of the loop code, the test expression is tested. If the test expression evaluates to true, the loop repeats; if the expression is false the loop terminates. The flowcharts in Fig. 5.7 illustrate these loops.

C has three loop constructs: `while`, `for`, and `do-while`. The first two are pre-test loops and `do-while` is a post-test loop.

In addition to the test expression, two other processes are associated with almost all loops. These are initialization and updating. The test expression always involves a variable, which is known as a *loop control variable*.

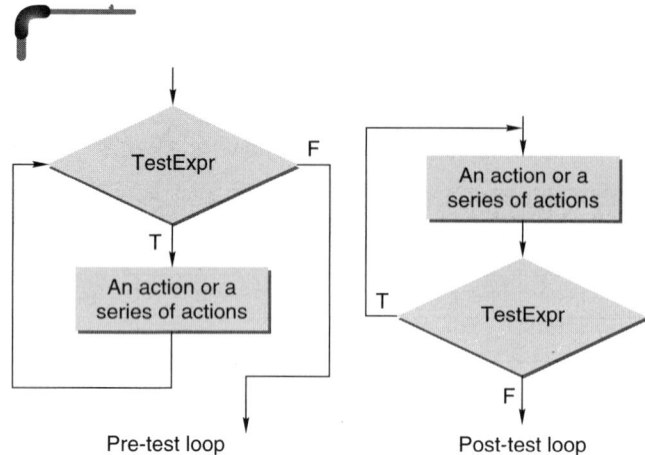

Figure 5.7 Loop variations: pre-test and post-test loops

Initialization is something that initializes the loop. That is the statement that assigns the initial value of the loop control variable. Now, how can the test expression, that controls the loop, be true for a while then changes to false? The answer is that something must happen inside the loop so that the test expression becomes false. The action that changes the test expression from true to false so that the loop is terminated is the updating statement. This involves updating the value of the control variable. *Updating* is done in each iteration. Comparison between a pre-test and post-test loop is given in Table 5.7.

Table 5.7 Comparison between a pre-test and post-test loop

	Pre-test loop	Post-test loop
Initialization	once	once
Number of tests	n+1	n
Actions executed	n	n
Updating executed	n	n
Minimum iteration	not even once	at least once

A loop can be characterized as either event controlled or counter controlled. In an event-controlled loop, an event changes the test expression of the loop from true to false. When the number of repetitions is known, then a counter-controlled loop is used. Here it is needed to initialize the counter, test it, and update it. All the loops used in C are either event controlled or counter controlled.

5.5.1 While **Construct**

while statement is a pre-test loop. It uses a test expression to control the loop. Since it is a pre-test loop, it evaluates the test expression before every iteration of the loop. The basic syntax of the while statement is shown in Fig. 5.8.

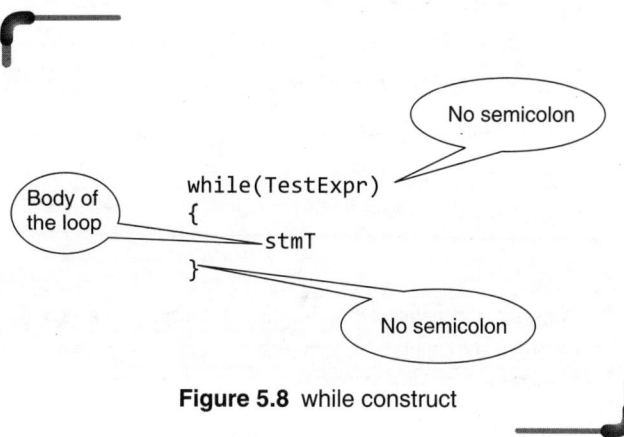

No semicolon

```
while(TestExpr)
{
    stmT
}
```

Body of the loop

No semicolon

Figure 5.8 while construct

stmT will be executed repeatedly till the value of TestExpr becomes 0. stmT may be a single statement or multiple statements terminated by a semicolon.

To use the while statement, the test expression should contain a loop control variable. The initialization of the loop control variable has to be done before the loop starts and updating must be included in the body of the loop. The expanded form of the while statement is given in Fig. 5.9.

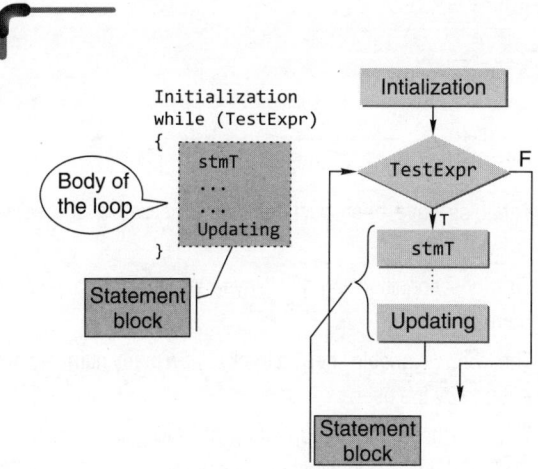

```
Initialization
while (TestExpr)
{
    stmT
    ...
    ...
    Updating
}
```

Body of the loop

Statement block

Intialization

TestExpr

stmT

Updating

Statement block

Figure 5.9 Expanded syntax of while and its flowchart representation

18.
```c
#include <stdio.h>
int main()
{
    int c;
    c=5;            // Initialization
    while(c>0)
    {               // Test Expression
    printf(" \n %d",c);
    c=c-1;          // Updating
    }
    return 0;
}
```

This loop contains all the parts of a while loop. When executed in a program, this loop will output

5
4
3
2
1

The operation of the looping construct in the above example is traced step by step as follows. First, the loop initialization, with 'c' being assigned the value of 5, is carried out. Then, the instructions within the while construct are executed repetitively so long as the test expression, c > 0, is true. The moment the test expression in the while construct evaluates as false, the program is terminated.

Now, when the while statement is encountered, the test expression, similar to an if-test expression, is evaluated. In this case, since c is 5 and c > 0, the test expression evaluates to true. Hence the statement body of the loop is executed sequentially. A printf statement writes the current value of c on the screen. After this c is updated by subtracting 1. Thus c now has the value of 4. On reaching the end of the loop, the loop condition is checked again. If it is true, which it is because 4 > 0, the loop is executed once again. In a similar way, the loop is executed five times.

At the end of the fifth iteration, c has the value of 0 for which the condition will fail since 0 is not greater than 0. Thus the term loop being applied to this repeating control structure can be understood since all statements inside the while loop construct will be executed several times until the condition has failed.

19. Program to print a horizontal row of 50 asterisks

The program is written using `while` loop. Here are three versions of same program. They only differ in the use of test expression and the initialization of the control variable.

Version 1
```c
#include <stdio.h>
int main()
{
  int times = 0;
  while (times < 50)
  {
    printf( "*");
    times++;
  }
  return 0;
}
```

Version 2
```c
#include <stdio.h>
int main()
{
  int times = 1;
  while (times <= 50)
  {
    printf( "*");
    times++;
  }
  return 0;
}
```

Version 3
```c
#include <stdio.h>
int main()
{
  int times = 50;
  while (times > 0)
  {
    printf("*");
    times--;
  }
  return 0;
}
```

Notice the various ways of accomplishing the same task. Run the above three versions and see the output. If a loop is to be executed for a specified number of times and the counter variable is used within the loop, the loop may be written as given in version 3 using countdown instead of count up. This is called *loop inversion*.

The following program takes `age` as input from user and quits when a −1 is entered:

```c
int main()
{
  int count = 0;
```
```c
  int age;
  printf("\n Please enter an age(enter -1 to quit)");
  scanf("%d",&age);
  while(age != -1)
  {
    count++;
    printf("\n Age # %d is %d",count, age);
    printf("\n Enter an age(enter -1 to quit)");
    scanf("%d",&age);
  }
  return 0;
}
```

20. Consider a general `while` loop that accepts input from the keyboard and counts the positive integers until a negative number is entered.

Solution:
```c
#include <stdio.h>
int main( )
{
  int x = 1;
  int count = 0;
  printf("\n Enter the Number:");
  while(x >= 0)
  {
    scanf("%d",&x);
    count += 1;
  }
  return 0;
}
```

The following are some observations on the above `while` loop.

- Variables have been declared and initialized at the same time.
- The loop condition logically says, 'While x is a positive number, repeat.'
- The `count` variable keeps a track of how many numbers are entered by the user.
- This can be a useful loop when accepting input from the keyboard until a negative input is entered.

21. Consider a more extensive example of a program that asks the user to enter some numbers and then find their average.

Solution: The program that would be written would either ask the user in advance how many numbers will be supplied or ask the user to enter a special value after the last number is entered, e.g., negative for test scores. This special value is known as *sentinel* value.

The algorithm of the C program using the first approach is given as follows:

Algorithm

```
1.  START
2.  PRINT  "HOW MANY NUMBERS:"
3.  INPUT N
4.  S ← 0
5.  C ← 1
6.  PRINT  "ENTER THE NUMBER"
7.  INPUT A
8.  S ← S + A
9.  C ← C + 1
10. IF C<=N THEN GOTO STEP 6
11. AVG ← S/N
12. PRINT  ":AVERAGE"   IS AVG;
13. STOP
```

C Program

```c
#include <stdio.h>
int main()
{
  int n, a, c=1,s=0;
  float avg;
  printf("\n HOW MANY NUMBERS?");
  scanf("%d",  &n);
  while(c<=n)
  {
   printf("\n Enter the number:   ");
   scanf("%d",  &a);
   s+=a;
   c++;
  }
  avg=(float)s/n;
  printf(" \n AVERAGE IS %f  ", avg);
  return 0;
}
```

In this example, typecasting is needed as both s and n are integers and avg is a float. Otherwise the program evaluates avg as an integer.

A better way to implement the program in Example 21 is given as follows.

22. *Algorithm*

```
1.  START
2.  S ← 0
3.  N ← 0
4.  ANS ← 'Y'
5.  PRINT "ENTER THE NUMBER"
6.  INPUT A
7.  S ← S + A
8.  N ← N + 1
9.  PRINT "WILL U ADD MORE (Y/N)?"
10. INPUT ANS
11. IF ANS='Y' THEN GOTO STEP 5
12. AVG ← S/N
13. PRINT: AVERAGE IS "AVG"
14. STOP
```

C Program

```c
#include <stdio.h>
int main()
{
  int n=0, a, s=0;
  float avg;
  char ans='y';
  while(ans == 'y' || ans == 'Y')
  {
   printf("\n Enter the number: ");
   scanf("%d", &a);
   s+=a;
   n++;
   printf("\n will U add more(y/ n)?");
   scanf("%c",&ans);
  }
  avg=(float)s/n;
  printf(" \n AVERAGE IS %f", avg);
  return 0;
}
```

23. Consider the two versions of the same program that prints the sum of digits of a number.

Version 1

```c
#include <stdio.h>
int main()
{
  int n, s=0, r;
  printf("Enter the Number");
  scanf("%d", &n);
  while(n>0)
  {
    r=n%10;
    s=s+r;
    n=n/10;
  }
  printf("\nSum of digits %d", s);
  return 0;
}
```

Version 2

```c
#include <stdio.h>
int main()
{
  int n, s=0, r;
  printf("Enter the Number");
  scanf("%d", &n);
  while(n)
  {
    r=n%10;
    s=s+r;
    n=n/10;
  }
  printf("\nSum of digits %d", s);
  return 0;
}
```

Notice the conditions specified in the two versions—in version 1 while(n>0), in version 2 while(n). When an arithmetie expression or variable is used instead of a relational expression, if the result of the expression or the value of the variable is non-zero (including negative), the statements within the while loop will be executed. Both versions will run fine.

Care must be taken in using expressions in a while loop. It should be noted that that there is no semicolon after the right parenthesis ending the expression that 'while' is checking. If there were, it would mean that the program would repeat the null statement until the condition becomes false.

Consider the use of the scanf() function in a loop. Suppose one needs to read and process a list of numbers from the keyboard. The loop ends when EOF is reached (when **<Ctrl+d>** in Unix/Linux or **<Ctrl+z>** in DOS is pressed). The loop logic is shown in the following example:

```c
r=scanf("%d",&a);
while(r!=EOF)
{
  _____
  _____
  r=scanf("%d",&a);
}
or
while((r=scanf("%d",&a))!=EOF)
{
  _____
  _____
}
```

Developing infinite loop using while construct Consider the following programs.

```c
#include <stdio.h>
int main()
{
  int c=5;
  while(c)
  {
    printf("\t %d",c);
    c--;
  }
  return 0;
}
```

Here the output will be

```
5    4    3    2    1
```

Now, the above program is rewritten to print the odd numbers between 5 and 0.

```c
#include <stdio.h>
int main()
{
  int c=5;
  while(c)
  {
    printf("\t %d",c);
    c=c-2;
  }
  return 0;
```

```
}
```
It will print

```
5    3    1    -1    -3    -5    ...
```

That is, it leads to an infinite loop. This is so because after printing 1, the value of 'c' will be -1 and while(c) evaluates true as the value of ' c' is non-zero. As a result, the program will print -1, -3, -5, and so on.

An infinite loop can also be built using the following construct:

```
while(1)
{
    ...
    ...
}
```

The while(1) loop will iterate forever because the while will exit only when the expression 1 is 0. The only way to exit this loop is through a break statement.

It should be noted that any non-zero value including a negative value may be used instead of 1 in the condition expression of the while construct.

Some do's and don'ts for testing floating point 'equality'

- ### Representation error

  Consider the following program fragment that uses C's floating-point arithmetic.

  ```
  double hundred = 100.0;
  double number = 95.0;
  if(number == number / hundred * hundred)
    printf("Equal\n");
  else
    printf("Not equal\n");
  ```

  On some machines, the above fragment prints 'Not equal', because 95.0/100.0 cannot be accurately represented in binary. It might be 0.94999999999, 0.9500000001, or some other value, and when multiplied by 100 it does not exactly equal 95.0.

- ### Compiler optimizations

  In the case of Borland compilers used on PCs, the following program fragment, identical to the above except that the variables have been replaced with their constant values, prints 'Equal'.

```
if(95.0 == 95.0 / 100.0 * 100.0)
    printf("Equal\n");
else
    printf("Not equal\n");
```

The best guess is that the compiler 'optimizes' the constant division and multiplication, causing the statement to appear as "95.0 == 95.0", which is trivially true.

- ### Testing for floating-point 'equality'

  As the preceding examples show, floating-point numbers cannot be compared for exact equality. Here is a second example. Using a floating-point number as an 'exact' terminating condition in a loop is not a good idea. Since floating-point numbers are approximations, a test for exact equality will often be wrong. An example of a program code is given as follows:

```
float x;
x = 0.0;
while(x != 1.1)
{
    x = x + 0.1;
    printf("1.1 minus %f equals %.20g\n", x, 1.1 - x);
}
```

The above loop never terminates on many computers, because 0.1 cannot be accurately represented using binary numbers. Each time through the loop, the error increases, and the sum of eleven 'tenths' never quite equals 1.1. Never test floatingpoint numbers for exact equality, especially in loops. Since floating-point numbers are approximations, the correct way to make the test is to see if the two numbers are 'approximately equal'.

The usual way to test for approximate equality is to subtract the two floating-point numbers and compare the absolute value of the difference against a very small number, *epsilon*. Such an approach is shown in the following program code.

```
#define EPSILON 1.0e-5   /* a very small value */
double hundred=100.0;
double number=95.0;
double n1, n2;
n1 = 95.0;
n2 = number / hundred * hundred;
```

```
if(fabs(n1-n2) < EPSILON)
   printf("Equal\n");
else
   printf("Not equal\n");
```

`fabs()` is the C library function that returns the floating-point absolute value of its argument.

Epsilon is chosen by the programmer to be small enough so that the two numbers can be considered 'equal'. The larger the numbers being compared, the larger will be the value of epsilon. For example, if the floating-point numbers are in the range 1.0e100, epsilon will probably be closer to 1.0e95, which is still a very big number but small compared to 1.0e100. (1.0e95 is ten-thousandth of 1.0e100.) If two numbers of magnitudes 1.0e100 and 1.0e95 differ by only 0.0e05, they may be close enough to be considered equal.

Note that just as adding a very small floating-point value to a very large floatingpoint value may not change the latter, subtracting floating-point numbers of widely differing magnitudes may have no effect. If the two numbers differ in magnitude by more than the *precision* of the data type used, the addition or the subtraction will not affect the larger number. For the float data type on most microcomputers, the precision is about six to seven decimal digits. An example of a program code follows:

```
float big, small, sum;
big = 1.0e20;
small = 1.0;
sum = big - small;
if(sum == big)
   printf("Equal\n");
else
   printf("Not Equal\n");
```

On executing the program code, the computer would print 'Equal', as observed earlier.

5.5.2 for Construct

A loop formed by using the for statement is generally called a determinate or definite loop because the programmer knows exactly how many times it will repeat. The number of repetitions can be determined mathematically by manually checking the logic of the loop. The general form of the for statement is as follows:

```
for(initialization; TestExpr; updating)
   stmT;
```

Initialization This part of the loop is the first to be executed. The statement(s) of this part are executed only once. This statement involves a loop control variable.

TestExpr TestExpr represents a test expression that must be true for the loop to continue execution.

stmT stmT is a single or block of statements.

Updating The statements contained here are executed every time through the loop before the loop condition is tested. This statement also involves a loop control variable.

C allows the updating of a loop control variable to be written inside the body of the loop. An example of a for loop is shown as follows:

```
int main(void)
{
   int i;
   for(i = 0; i < 10; i++)
      printf("%d",i);
   return 0;
}
```

The program continues. The above for loop operates as follows:

1. Set i equal to 0

2. If i is less than 10, execute the body of the loop, that is, 'printf' statement and go to step 3; otherwise, go to the next instruction after the for loop.

3. Increment i
4. Go to step 2

The following figure explains the three expressions in the for loop used in the above program that are separated by semicolons and that control the operation of the loop.

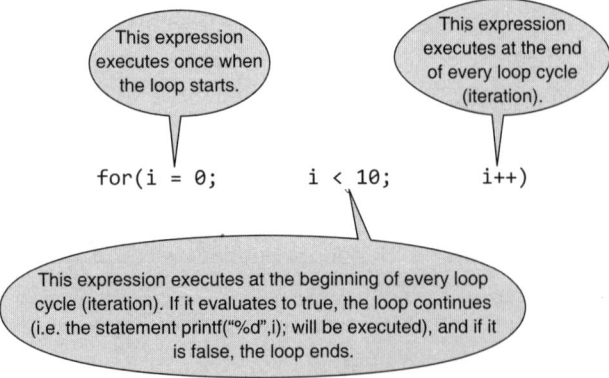

This loop would produce the following output:

```
0123456789
```

Note that 'running the loop' from 0 to 9 executes the body of the loop 10 times. The flowchart of the `for` construct is given in Fig. 5.10.

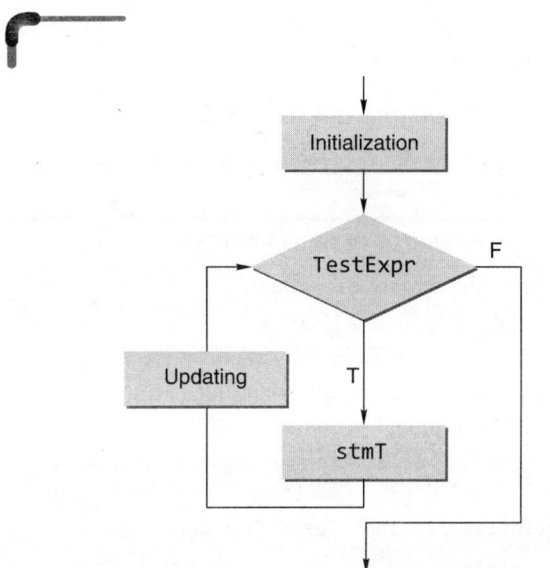

Figure 5.10 `for` construct flow chart

It is to be noted that all four parts of the previous loops are present in the `for` loop, although they are compressed into one line. In general, a `for` loop can be written as an equivalent `while` loop and vice versa.

The equivalence of bounded and unbounded loops

We should now be able to understand that the for, while control flow statements are each closely related. To fully understand this, however, one needs to interpret, that the three 'pieces' of the for construct, are not always *initialization, condition, modification.*

In general, a `for` loop can be written as an equivalent `while` loop and vice versa. The `for` loop

```
for(initialization; TestExpr; updating)
{
   stmT;
}
```

is equivalent to the following while construct:

```
initialization;
while (TestExpr)
{
   stmT;
   updating;
}
```

The following example illustrates a `for` loop that prints 1, 2, 3, 4, 5.

In both cases, we are expecting `TestExpr` to produce a Boolean value, either true or false, as we need that truth value to determine if our loops should 'keep going'.

Let us illustrate the similarities between '`while`' and '`for`' loop constructs an example which prints 1, 2, 3, 4, and 5.The algorithm for the above problem is given below:

1. START
2. C ← 1
3. PRINT C
4. C ← C+1
5. IF C<=5 THEN GO TO STEP 3
6. STOP

The C program corresponding to the problem can use either "while" or "for" construct. The two versions, one using "for" construct and another using "while" construct, and their equivalence are shown below:

```
#include <stdio.h>          #include <stdio.h>
int main(void)              int main(void)
{                           {
int c; Initialization         int c;  TestExpr

for(c=1; c<=5; c++)           c=1;
{                             while(c<=5)
   printf("%d", c);           {
}                                printf("%d", c);
   return 0;                     c++;
}              Updating       }
                              return 0;
                           }
```

To test the understanding of the `while` and `for` loops, conversion of one to the other would be implemented. Suppose, a `while` loop, given in the following illustration, has to be converted to a well constructed `for` loop.

```
float C = 2.0;
char chr = 'F';
while(C > 0.01) {
  printf("%f \n",C);
  C /= 10;
}
```

To make this an easy conversion, note the four parts of a loop.

```
float C = 2.0;         /* initialization */
char chr = 'F';
while(C > 0.01){       /* test expression */
printf("%f \n",C);     /* body of the loop */
  C /= 10;             /* updating */
}
```

Given such information, the transition to the for loop is made. The for loop is

```
float C;
char chr = 'F';
for(C = 2.0; C > 0.01; C /= 10)
{
  printf("%f \n",C);
}
```

There was a small trick in this case. Even though two variables were declared and initialized, only one was used in the while loop. Therefore, only that specific variable, C, is initialized in the for loop.

Now, consider the conversion of the following for loop to its respective while loop.

```
int index;
int Total;
for(Total = 0, index = 0; index < 10; index += 1)
{
  if(index > 5)
      Total += index;
  else if(index < 5)
      Total -= index;
}
```

Again, noting the four parts of the loop, the conversion is given as follows:

```
int index = 0;
int Total = 0;
while(index < 10)
{
  if(index > 5) Total += index;
    else if(index < 5)
```

```
      Total -= index;
  index += 1;
}
```

It must be emphasized that in a for construct, the condition is tested before the statements contained in body and updating are executed; it is possible that the body of the loop is never executed or tested.

The sequence of events that generate the iteration using the for loop are as follows.

1. Evaluate the *initialization* expression.

2. If the value of the *test expression* is false, terminate the loop.

3. Execute the statement or blocks of statements.

4. Evaluate the *update* expression.

5. Go to step 2.

An execution cycle for a for construct is drawn to help understand the concept.

```
      1              2           4
for(initialization; TestExpr; updating)
      stmT;
           3
```

Here is a program that adds a sequence of integers. Assume that the first integer read with scanf() specifies the number of input values to be summed. The program should read only one value each time scanf() is executed. A typical input sequence might be

```
5  102  125  352  54  9
```

where 5 indicates that the subsequent five values are to be summed.

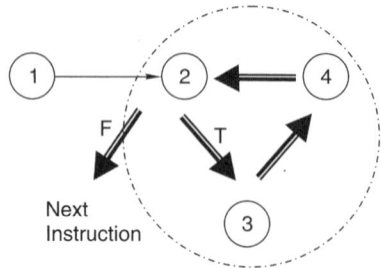

```
#include <stdio.h>
int main()
{
    int sum = 0, number, value, i;
```

```
printf("Enter no. of values to be processed: \n");
scanf("%d", &number);
for(i = 1; i <= number; i++)
{
  printf("Enter a value: \n");
  scanf("%d", &value);
  sum += value;
}
printf("Sum of %d values is: %d\n", number, sum);
return 0;
}
```

In general, how many times does the body of a for() loop execute?

(a) The following loop is executed (n-m)+1 times.

```
for(i=m;  i<=n;  i++)
    ...
```

(b) The following loop is executed (n-m) times.

```
for(i=m;  i<n;  i++)
    ...
```

(c) The following loop is executed (n-m)/x times.

```
for(i=m;  i<n;  i+=x)
    ...
```

Considering the above, the previous program may be rewritten as follows:

```
#include <stdio.h>
int main()
{
    int sum = 0, number, value, i;
    printf("Enter no. of values to be processed: \n");
    scanf("%d", &number);
    for(i = 0; i < number; i++)
    {
      printf("Enter a value: \n");
      scanf("%d", &value);
      sum += value;
    }
    printf("Sum of %d values is: %d\n", number, sum);
    return 0;
}
```

Now, let us calculate the factorial of a number given by the user. The factorial of a positive integer n, written as n!,
is equal to the product of the positive integers from 1 to n. The following is an example of a program.

```
int main()
{
    int n, c;
    long int f=1;
    printf("\n Enter the number: ");
    scanf("%d",&n);
    for(c=1;c<=n;++c)
      f*=c;
    printf("\n Factorial  is %ld",f);
    return 0;
}
```

It can be implemented in another way too. Here the variable 'c' is not required. The alternate program is shown as follows:

```
int main()
{
    int n;
    long int f=1;
    printf("\n Enter the number: ");
    scanf("%d",&n);
    for(;n>0;n--)
      f*=n;
    printf("\n Factorial  is %ld",f);
    return 0;
}
```

The following program inputs a series of ten integer numbers and determines and prints the largest of them.

```
#include <stdio.h>
int main()
{
    int counter = 2, number, max;
    printf("Enter an integer number\n");
    scanf("%d", &max);
    while(counter <= 10)
    {
      printf("Enter an integer number\n");
      scanf("%d", &number);
      if(number > max)
```

```
    max = number;
    counter++;
  }
  printf("The maximum number is %d\n", max);
  return 0;
}
```

There must be no semicolon after a `for` statement or it will lead to a different output. Consider the following program.

```
#include <stdio.h>
int main()
{
  int c;
  for(c=1; c<=5; c++);
    printf("%d", c);
    return 0;
}
```

A semicolon before the `printf` statement implies that the loop only increments the value of `c`. No executable statement is included in this `for` loop, i.e., there is no statement in the statement block. The output will be 6, as the loop continues up to `c=5`. When the value of `c` is 6, the loop terminates as the test expression evaluates false.

Some variations of for loop

From a syntactic standpoint, all the three expressions (`initialization`, `test expression`, and `updating`) need not be present in a `'for'` statement, though semicolon must be present. However, the criteria and consequences of an omission should be clearly understood.

Any initialization statement can be used in the first part of the `for` loop. Multiple initializations should be separated with a comma operator.

Example

24. Print the sum of the series 1+2+3+4+... up to n terms.
    Program 1
```
    #include <stdio.h>
    int main()
    {
      int c, s=0, n;
      printf("\n Enter the No. of terms");
      scanf("%d", &n);
      for(c=1;    c<=n;    c++)/*    Here    c    is
        initialized*/
```

```
      s+=c;
      printf("\n Sum is %d", s);
      return 0;
    }
```

Program 2 Equivalent to Program 1
```
    #include <stdio.h>
    int main()
    {
      int c=1, s, n;
      printf("\n Enter the No. of terms");
      scanf("%d", &n);
      for(s=0;    c<=n;    c++)/*    Here    s    is
        initialized*/
      s+=c;
      printf("\n Sum is %d", s);
      return 0;
    }
```

Program 3
```
    #include <stdio.h>
    int main()
    {
      int c, s, n;
      printf("\n Enter the No. of terms");
      scanf("%d", &n);
      for(c=1, s=0; c<=n; c++)/* Here both c ans s are*\
        * initialized*/
      s+=c;
      printf("\n Sum is %d", s);
      return 0;
    }
```

- If initialization is not required or is done before the `for` loop, the initialization statement can be skipped by giving only a semicolon. This is illustrated using the previous program.

```
    #include <stdio.h>
    int main()
    {
      int c=1, s=0, n;
      printf("\n Enter the No. of terms");
      scanf("%d", &n);
      for(; c<=n; c++)
        s+=c;
      printf("\n Sum is %d", s);
      return 0;
    }
```

- Multiple conditions in the test expression must be connected using the logical operator && or ||.

- In the third expression of the for statement, the increment or decrement statement may contain any expression which involves unary and/or assignment operator. It is not true that increment or decrement statements must be used with ++ or −− only. This is illustrated in the following example where the sum of digits of a given number has to be found.

Example

25. ```c
#include <stdio.h>
int main()
{
  int n, s=0, r;
  printf("\n Enter the Number");
  scanf("%d", &n);
  for(;n>0;n/=10)
  {
    r=n%10;
    s=s+r;
  }
  Printf("\n Sum of digits %d", s);
  return 0;
}
```

- If the increment or decrement is done within the statement block, then the third part can be skipped. The following is the equivalent variation of the program in Example 25 (sum of digits of a number).

  ```c
  #include <stdio.h>
  int main()
  {
    int n, s=0, r;
    printf("\n Enter the Number");
    scanf("%d", &n);
    for(;n>0;)
    {
      r=n%10;
      s=s+r;
      n=n/10;
    }
    printf("Sum of digits %d", s);
    return 0;
  }
  ```

- Multiple statements can be written in the third part of the for statement with the help of the comma operator. The preceding program can be rewritten as follows:

  ```c
  #include <stdio.h>
  int main()
  {
    int n, s=0, r;
    printf("\n Enter the Number");
    scanf("%d", &n);
    for(;n>0;s+=r, n=n/10)
      r=n%10;
      printf("\n Sum of digits %d", s);
      return 0;
  }
  ```

It is to be noted that comma operator associates from the left to right. The code

```c
for(s=0,i=1;i<=n;++i)
  s+=i;
```

can be written as

```c
for(s=0,i=1;i<=n; s+=i, ++i);
```

but not as

```c
for(s=0,i=1;i<=n; ++i, s+=i);
```

Because, in the comma expression ++i, s+=i, the expression ++i is evaluated first and this will cause s to have a different value.

- If ++ or −− operators are used in the increment or decrement part of the for loop, pre-increment or post-increment and post-decrement or pre-decrement has the same effect. So, both the following codes yield the same output 1, 2, 3, 4, 5.

Version 1

```c
#include <stdio.h>
int main()
{
  int c;
  for(c=1; c<=5; c++)
    printf("%d", c);
    return 0;
}
```
```

Version 2

```c
#include <stdio.h>
int main()
{
  int c;
  for(c=1; c<=5; ++c)
    printf("%d", c);
    return 0;
}
```

But the post- and pre-operations play a different role when they are specified in the test_expression.

```c
#include <stdio.h>
int main()
{
  int c;
  for(c=0; c++; c++)
    printf("%d", c);
    return 0;
}
```

Output: Prints nothing as c has been initialized as zero and the post-increment of c makes a difference. The condition is evaluated first, followed by increment. The condition is evaluated false as c contains zero at that moment. The printf() statement will not be executed as the condition becomes false.

```c
#include <stdio.h>
int main()
{
  int c;
  for(c=0;++c; ++c)
    printf("%d", c);
return 0;
}
```

Output: This is an infinite loop. As the first pre-increment takes place, it results in c=1. Then the test expression evaluates to 1 as c contains a non-zero value. Thus the loop continues.

- It is possible to have a variable increase by a value other than one. For example, the following loop would iterate four times with the variable num taking on the values 1, 4, 7, and 10. The step expression adds 3 to the value of num on each iteration.

```c
for(num = 1; num <= 10; num = num + 3)
```

It is a common error for students to use the following for statement, which causes a compilation error:

```c
for(num = 1; num <= 9 ; num + 3)
```

Consider the following program where the increment operator is used at a place other than the third part of the for statement.

```c
#include <stdio.h>
int main()
{
  int c;
  for(c=1; c<=5; )
  printf("%d", c++);
  return 0;
}
```
Output: 12345

```c
#include <stdio.h>
int main()
{
  int c;
  for(c=1; c<=5;)
  printf("%d", ++c);
  return 0;
}
```
Output: 23456

- Any or all of the three expressions in a for loop can be omitted, but the two semicolons must remain. When all three expressions in a for loop are omitted, it acts as a infinite loop. For example,

```c
for(;;)
{
  printf("hello\n");
}
```

This loop will run forever. Although there are some programming tasks, such as operating system command processors, which require an infinite loop, most 'infinite loops' are really just loops with special termination requirements.

- Often, the variable that controls a for loop is needed only for the purposes of the loop and is not used elsewhere. When this is the case, it is possible to declare the variable inside the initialization portion of the for loop in modern compiler. Some compilers, however, do not. You will need to check this feature in the environment you are using. Consider the following program which print the sum of the following series

```c
#include <stdio.h>
int main()
{
    int s=0, n;
    printf("\n Enter the No. of terms");
    scanf("%d", &n);
    for(int c=1; c<=n; c++)
    s+=c;
    printf("\n Sum is %d", s);
    return 0;
}
```

Here c is declared inside the for loop

The variable c is only known throughout the execution of the for loop (it's called a local variable) and cannot be accessed outside the loop. the ANSI/ISO Standard restricts the variable to the scope of the for loop

Points to Note

- If the `test expression` is omitted, however, it will be assumed to have a permanent value of true; thus the loop will continue indefinitely unless it is terminated by some other means, such as a break or a return statement (see Section 5.8).
- Multiple initializations should be separated with a comma operator.
- Multiple relational expressions in the test expression must be connected using logical operators && or ||.
- Do not use a floating-point variable as the control variable because floating-point values are sometimes approximated and may result in imprecise counter values and inaccurate test for termination.

Check Your Progress

1. Is there any difference between the following for statements? Explain.

   (a) `for(x = 1; x < 100; x++)`

   (b) `for(x = 1; x < 100; ++x)`

   (c) `for(x = 1; x < 100; x = x + 1)`

   (d) `for(x = 1; x < 100; x += 1)`

   Output: There is no difference between these for statements. This is because x is incremented in the same manner at the end of the for structure. One

may, equivalently, use the `while` structure to represent these `for` statements.

```c
x = 1;
while(x < 100)
{
    ...
    ++x; /* This can be replaced with x++ or x += 1 or*/
        /* x = x + 1 */
}
```

2. What would be the output from the given program?

```c
int main()
{
    int i=9;
    for(i--; i--; i--)
        printf("%d", i);
    return 0;
}
```

   Output: 7 5 3 1

3. What would be the output from the given program?

```c
int main()
{
    int i;
    for(i=5; ++i; i-=3)
        printf("%d", i);
    return 0;
}
```

   Output: 6 4 2

4. What would be the output from the given program?

```c
int main()
{
    for(;printf("C");); 
    return 0;
}
```

   Output: This is an infinite loop and it will repeatedly print 'c'.

5. Examine the given program and predict the output.

```c
int main()
{
    int i;
    for(i=5; --i;)
```

```
printf("%d",i);
return 0;
}
```
Output: 4321

6. What output is obtained from the given program?

```
int main()
{
  int i=3;
  for(i--; i<7; i=7)
      printf("%d",i++);
      return 0;
  }
```
Output: 2

7. Read the program code and guess what the output could be.

```
int main()
{
  int i;
  for(i=-10; !i; i++);
    printf("%d",-i);
    return 0;
  }
```
Output: No output

5.5.3 do-while Construct

Another construct that is very closely related to the while construct is the do-while construct.

The do keyword is placed on a line of code at the top of the loop. A block of statements follows it with a test expression after the keyword while, at the bottom of the loop. Figure 5.11 illustrates this. The form of this loop construct is as follows:

```
do
{
    stmT;   /* body of statements would be placed here*/
}while(TestExpr);
```

The test expression TestExpr must evaluate to 'true' for the do-while loop to iterate after the first time. StmT may be a single statement or a block of statements. The main difference between the while and do-while loop is the placement of the test expression. Since the do-while has

the test expression at the end of the loop, it is guaranteed that the body of the loop will execute at least once.

In the while loop, it is possible to come upon a condition that is not satisfied and hence does not enter the loop. What are the reasons of placing the condition at the end of the loop in terms of coding? They are few but important. The order of the statements may have to change to reflect the effect of the condition being at the end.

Consider the simple while loop illustrated in Example 22. It can be rewritten as a do-while loop as follows:

```
#include <stdio.h>
int main()
{
  int x = 1;
  int count = 0;
  do {
    scanf("%d", &x);
    if(x >= 0)
        count += 1;
  } while(x >= 0);
  return 0;
}
```

Notice that an extra if statement was added to the loop.

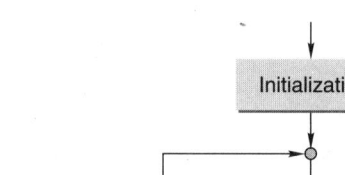
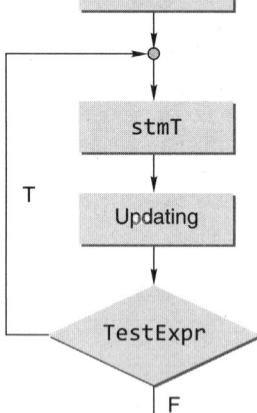

Figure 5.11 The C do-while loop

Explanation: Consider the case when the first number entered is a negative number. Without the if statement, the count would be 1. Beware of the ramifications of allowing at least one execution of the loop when using the `do-while` loop. The following examples will help understand this loop.

```c
#include <stdio.h>
int main()
{
  int c=5;
  while(c<5)
  {
    printf(" Hello");
    c++;
  }
  return 0;
}
```

Output: The program will print nothing. As the condition `c<5` fails, neither the `printf()` statement nor `c++` will be executed.

```c
#include <stdio.h>
int main()
{
  int c=5;
    do
    {
      printf("Hello");
      c++;
    } while(c<5);
  return 0;
}
```

Output: Hello

Here the statements within the loop are executed at least once.

Suppose, one wants to write a code that reads in a positive integer only. The following code will serve the purpose.

```c
do
{
  printf("\n INPUT A POSITIVE INTEGER:  ");
  scanf("%d",&n);
  if(error=(n<=0))
    printf("\n ERROR Do it again\n");
}while(error);
```

while and do-while Loop

Like a `while` loop, a `do-while` loop is considered to be an indeterminate or unbound loop. The important difference between the `while` and `do-while` loops lies with the question '*when* the loop controlling `test expression` is checked?'. A `do-while` loop is considered to be a *post-test loop*, since the `test expression` is located after the body of the loop and after the `while` keyword. A `do-while` loop is guaranteed to execute at least once even if the test expression evaluates to false.

With a `while` statement, the Boolean expression is checked *before* the loop body is executed. If the `test expression` evaluates to false, the body is not executed at all.

Point to Note

With a `do-while` statement, the body of the loop is executed first and the `test expression` is checked after the loop body is executed. Thus, the `do-while` statement always executes the loop body at least once.

Example

26. Euler's number *e* is used as the base of natural logarithms. It may be approximated using the following formula:

$$e = \frac{1}{0!} + \frac{1}{1!} + \frac{1}{2!} + \frac{1}{3!} + ... + \frac{1}{(n-1)!} + \frac{1}{n!}$$

where *n* is sufficiently large. Write a program that approximates *e* using a loop that terminates when the difference between the two successive values of *e* is less than 0.0000001.

```c
#include <stdio.h>
int main()
{
  double term = 1.0;
  double sum = 1.0;
  int n = 0;
  while (term >= 0.0000001)
    {
      n++;
      term = term/n;
      sum = sum + term;
    }
  printf("\n Approximate value of e is: %lf ",sum);
  return 0;
}
```

1. How many times will the following while-loop repeat, i.e., how many xs are printed?

```
int i = 5; while(i-- > 0) printf("x");
```

Output: 5

2. How many xs are printed by the following code?

```
int i = 5;
while(i-- > 0)
  printf("x");
  printf("x");
```

Output: 6

3. What does the following do-while loop print?

```
int i = 0; char c = '0';
do {
  putchar(c + i);
  ++i;
} while(i < 5);
```

Output: 01234

4.
```
int main()
{
  float s=1.0;
    int a=4;
      while(a<=10)
      {
        s = a*1.2;
        printf("%f",s);
      }
    return 0;
}
```

Output: It never ends because 'a' is always 4, an infinite loop!

5. What will be the output of the following program?

```
int main()
{
  while(1);
  printf("DONE");
  return 0;
}
```

Output: None

Explanation: The while(1) in main ends with ';'. So the loop will not reach an end; and the DONE too will not print.

5.6 WHICH LOOP SHOULD BE USED?

A question that must be asked is why are there while, do-while, and for loops? Is it a matter of style?

The while and for constructs are pre-test loops and the do-while construct is post-test loop. The while and do-while loops are event-controlled whereas the for loop is counter-controlled. The for loop is appropriate when one knows in advance how many times the loop will be executed. The while and do-while loops are used when it is not known in advance when the loop should terminate; the while loop is used when one may not want to execute the loop body even once, and the do-while loop when one wants to execute the loop body at least once. These criteria are somewhat arbitrary and there is no hard-and-fast rule regarding which type of loop should be used.

Points to Note

When using loops, always ask
- under what condition(s) will the loop body be executed?
- under what condition(s) will the loop terminate?
- what is the value of the loop control variable(s) when the loop halts?

Some methods of controlling repetition in a program are being discussed in the following subsections. There are three ways of doing this: sentinel values, prime reads, and counters.

5.6.1 Using Sentinel Values

A sentinel value is a value that is not a legitimate data value for a particular problem, but is of a proper type, that is used to check for a 'stopping' value. It is like a flag or an indicator. There may be times when users of the program must be allowed to enter as much information as they want to about something. When the user has finished entering all the information, the user can enter a sentinel value that would let the program know that the user has finished with inputting information.

Examples

27. [-1] may be used as a sentinel value.
```
int main()
{
  int age;
  printf("\n Enter an age(-1 to stop ):");
```

```
      scanf("%d",&age);
      while(age != -1)
      {
        ⋮
        printf("\n Enter an age(-1 to stop ):");
        scanf("%d",&age);
      }
      return 0;
    }
```

28. [-99] may also be used as a sentinel value. Read a list of text scores and calculate their average. An input of -99 for a score denotes end-of-data for the user.

```
    #include <stdio.h>
    int main()
    {
      int n, sum, score;
      float average;
      sum = 0;
      n = 0;
      printf("\n Enter a test score(-99 to quit):");
      scanf("%d", &score);
      while(score != -99)
      {
        sum += score;
        n++;
        printf("\n Enter a test score(-99 to quit):");
        scanf("%d",&score);
      }
      average = (float)sum/ n;
      printf("\n The average is %f", average);
      return 0;
    }
```

5.6.2 Using Prime Read

Another method of controlling repetition is to use a prime read. A prime read and sentinel value often go hand in hand. A prime read is a data input before the loop statement that allows the first actual data value to be entered so that it can be checked in the loop statement. The variable that is inputted by the user and being tested by the expression in the loop is the prime read; the value of the prime read is what one calls a sentinel value [see Section 5.6.1].

29. [age] is used as a prime read.

```
    #include <stdio.h>
    int main()
    {
      int age;
      printf("\n Enter an age(-1 to stop):");
      scanf("%d",&age);
      while(age != -1)
      {
        ⋮
        printf("\n Enter an age(-1 to stop):");
        scanf("%d",&age);
      }
      ⋮
      return 0;
    }
```

30. [score] is used as a prime read. Read a list of text scores and calculate their average. An input of -99 for a score denotes end-of-data for the user.

```
    #include <stdio.h>
    int main()
    {
      int n, sum, score;
      float average;
      sum = 0;
      n = 0;
      printf("\n Enter a test score(-99 to quit):");
      scanf("%d", &score);
      while(score != -99)
      {
        sum += score;
        n++;
        printf("\n Enter a test score(-99 to quit):");
        scanf("%d", &score);
      }
      average = (float)sum / n;
      printf("\n The average is %f", average);
      return 0;
    }
```

EOF can also be used in prime read. Consider the following program.

```c
#include <stdio.h>
#include <stdlib.h>
int main()
{
  int n, sum, score;
  float average;
  sum = 0;
  n = 0;
  printf("\n Enter test scores one by one(EOF\
          to quit): ");
  while(scanf("%d", &score) != EOF)
  {
    sum += score;
    n++;
  }
  average = (float)sum / n;
  printf("\n The average is %f", average);
  return 0;
}
```

5.6.3 Using Counter

Yet another method for controlling repetition during the execution of a program is by using a counter. Using a counter requires knowledge of the exact number of times something needs to be repeated. For example, if a user of the program had to be instructed to input ten numbers, a counter variable could be set to 0, and then a loop set up to continue cycles while the value of the counter is less than ten (this loop would equal ten cycles: 0, 1, 2, 9).

Examples

31. Write a section of code that would output the numbers from 1 to 10.

```c
#include <stdio.h>
int main()
{
  int count;
  count = 0;
  int numTimesNeeded = 10;
  while(count < numTimesNeeded)
  {
    printf("\n%d", (count + 1)) ;
    count++;
  }
  return 0;
}
```

32. Write a section of code that will allow the user to input ten test scores in order to find the average of the scores.

```c
#include <stdio.h>
int main()
{
  int count, score;
  float average;
  count = 0;
  int numTimesNeeded = 10;
  int total = 0;
  while(count < numTimesNeeded)
  {
    printf("\n Enter a test score");
    scanf("%d", &score);
    total += score;
    count++;
  }
  average = (float)total/ numTimesNeeded;
  printf("\n The average is %f" , average);
  return 0;
}
```

5.7 GOTO STATEMENT

The goto statement is another type of control statement supported by C. The control is unconditionally transferred to the statement associated with the label specified in the goto statement. The form of a goto statement is

```c
goto label_name;
```

Because the goto statement can interfere with the normal sequence of processing, it makes a program more difficult to read and maintain. Often, a break statement, a continue statement, or a function call can eliminate the need for a goto statement.

A *statement label* is defined in exactly the same way as a variable name, which is a sequence of letters and digits, the first of which must be a letter. The statement label must be followed by a colon (:) just like a CASE label in a SWITCH. Like other statements, the goto statement ends with a semicolon.

Some examples of goto statements are in order:

Example

33. The following program is used to find the factorial of a number.

```c
#include <stdio.h>
int main()
{
  int n, c;
  long int f=1;
  printf("\n Enter the number:");
  scanf("%d",&n);
  if(n<0)
    goto end;
  for(c=1; c<=n; c++)
      f*=c;
  printf("\n FACTORIAL IS %ld", f);
  end:
    return 0;
}
```

The goto statement can be used for looping as follows. Here the goto statement is used in conjunction with an if statement.

```c
#include <stdio.h>
int main()
{
  int n, c;
  long int f=1;
  printf("\n Enter the number:");
  scanf("%d",&n);
  if(n<0)
    goto end;
  c=1;
  loop:
  f=f*c;
  c++;
  if(c<=n)
    goto loop;
  printf("\n FACTORIAL IS %ld", f);
  end:
    return 0;
}
```

In theory it's always possible to avoid using the goto statement, but there are one or two instances in which it's a useful option. But the goto statement is not considered a good programming statement when overused. Because the goto statement can interfere with the normal sequence of processing, it makes a program more difficult to read and maintain. When too many goto statement are used in a program then the program branches all over the place, it becomes very difficult to follow. Some authors call programs with many goto statements 'spaghetti code'. So it's best to avoid the goto statement as far as possible. Often, a break statement, a continue statement, or a function call can eliminate the need for a goto statement.

5.8 SPECIAL CONTROL STATEMENTS

There are certain control statements, which terminate either a loop or a function. There are three such statements namely: return, break, and continue.

return statements The return type is used in the definition of a function to set its returned value and the return statement is used to terminate execution of the function. The return statement has two forms. Functions with return type void use the following form:

```c
return;
```

Functions with non-void return type use the following form:

```c
return expression;
```

Here, expression yields the desired return value. This value must be convertible to the return type declared for the function. This will be explained in more detail in Chapter 7.

break statements The break statement is used in loop constructs such as for, while and do-while, and switch statement to terminate execution of the loop or switch statement. The form of a break statement is

```c
break;
```

After a break statement is executed within a loop or a case in a switch construct, execution proceeds to the statement that follows the loop construct or switch statement. The following is an example of the use of a break statement.

```c
#include <stdio.h>
int main( )
{
  int c=1;
  while(c<=5)
  {
    if(c==3)
      break;
    printf("\t %d", c);
    c++;
  }
  return 0;
}
```

Or

```c
#include <stdio.h>
int main( )
{
  int c=1;
  for(;c<=5;c++)
  {
    if(c==3)
      break;
    printf("\t %d", c);
  }
  return 0;
}
```

The program will print 1 2 instead of 1 2 3 4 5.

The statement while(1) leads to an infinite loop but by using the break statement it can be made a finite loop. This is illustrated in the following example.

Example

34. **Program 1**

```c
#include <stdio.h>
int main( )
{
  int c=1;
  while(1)
  {
    printf("\t %d", c);
    c++;
  }
  return 0;
}
```

It is an infinite loop. It will print
1   2   3   4...

Program 2

```c
#include <stdio.h>
int main( )
{
  int c=1;
  while(1)        Note this
  {
    if(c==5)
      break;
    printf("\t %d", c);
    c++;
  }
  return 0;
}
```

Or

```c
#include <stdio.h>
int main( )
{
  int c;
  for(;;)          Note this
  {
    if(c==5)
      break;
    printf(" \t.%d", c);
    c++;
  }
  return 0;
}
```

It is a finite loop. It will print
1   2   3   4

A break statement may be used to check whether a number is a prime number or not. The following program illustrates this.

```c
#include <stdio.h>
int main( )
{
  int n, r, d=2;
  printf( "\n Enter the number :");
  scanf("%d", &n);
  r = n%d;
```

```
while(d <=n/2)
{
   r = 1;
   if(r ==0)
      break;
   d++;
}
if(r==0)
   printf("\n IT IS NOT A PRIME NUMBER");
else
   printf("\n IT IS A PRIME NUMBER");
return 0;
}
```

A break used in a switch statement will affect only that switch, and not the loop the switch happens to be in.

continue statements The `continue` statement does not terminate the loop but goes to the test expression in the `while` and `do-while` statements and then goes to the updating expression in a `for` statement. The form of a `continue` statement is

`continue;`

The jumps by `continue` in different pre-test and post-test loops are shown here.

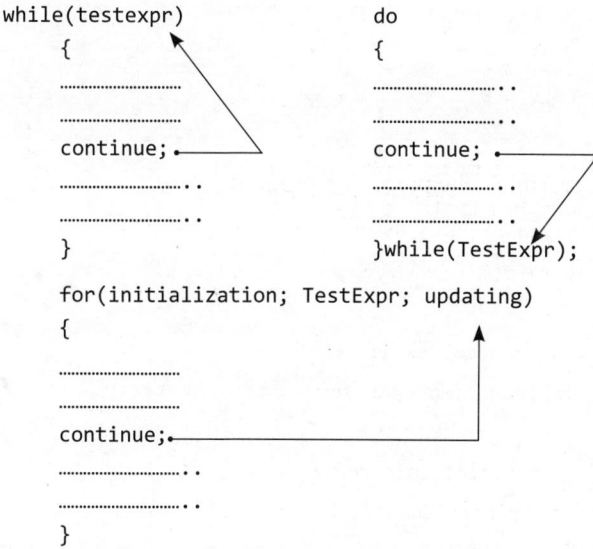

The difference between `break` and `continue` statements is summarized in Table 5.8.

Table 5.8 Break and continue statements

Break	Continue
It helps to make an early exit from the block where it appears.	It helps in avoiding the remaining statements in a current iteration of the loop and continuing with the next iteration
It can be used in all control statements including switch construct.	It can be used only in loop constructs.

This can be illustrated by the following programs.

Program code with break

```
#include <stdio.h>
int main( )
{
   int c=1;
   while(c<=5)
   {
      if(c==3)
         break;
      printf("\t %d", c);
      c++;
   }
   return 0;
}
```

Output: 1 2

Program code with continue

```
#include <stdio.h>
int main()
{
   int c=1;
   while(c<=5)
   {
      if(c==3)
         continue;
      printf("\t %d", c);
      c++;
   }
   return 0;
}
```

Output: 1 2   4 5

5.9 NESTED LOOPS

A nested loop refers to a loop that is contained within another loop. If the program has to repeat a loop more than once, it is a good candidate for a nested loop. In nested loops, the inside loop (or loops) executes completely before the outside loop's next iteration. It must be remembered that each inner loop should be enclosed completely in the outer loop; overlapping loops are not allowed. Thus, the following is not allowed.

```
for(count = 1; count < 100; count++)

{

    do

    {

        /* the do...while loop */

    } /* end of for loop */

}while(x != 0);
```

If the do-while loop is placed entirely in the for loop, there is no problem. For example,

```
for(count = 1; count < 100; count++)

{

    do

    {

        /* the do...while loop */

    }while(x != 0);

} /* end of for loop */
```

An example of the nested loop is to print the following:

```
*
* *
* * *
* * * *
```

In each row, there are several '*' to be printed. In row one, one star has to be printed; in row two, two stars have to be printed; in row three, three stars have to be printed, and so on. So an outer loop is required to keep track of the number of rows to be printed and in each iteration of the outer loop, an inner loop is required to keep track of the printing of stars that corresponds to the row. The program will then read as follows:

```c
#include <stdio.h>
int main()
{
    int row,col;
    for(row=1;row<=4;++row)
    {
        for(col=1;col<=row;++col)
            printf("* \t");
        printf("\n");
    }
    return 0;
}
```

If the following output has to be obtained on the screen

```
1
2 2
3 3 3
4 4 4 4
```

then the corresponding program will be

```c
#include <stdio.h>
int main()
{
    int row,col;
    for(row=1;row<=4;++row)
    {
        for(col=1;col<=row;++col)
            printf("%d \t", row);
        printf("\n");
    }
    return 0;
}
```

The variant of the preceding program is

```c
#include <stdio.h>
int main()
{
    int row,col, k=1;
    for(row=1;row<=4;++row)
    {
        for(col=1;col<=row;++col)
            printf("%d \t", k++);
        printf("\n");
    }
    return 0;
}
```

It will print the following on the screen.

```
1
2  3
4  5  6
7  8  9  10
```

When nested loops are used, remember that changes made in the inner loop might affect the outer loop as well. Note, however, that the inner loop might be independent of any variables in the outer loop; in the above examples, they are not.

Good indenting style makes a code with nested loops easier to read. Each level of loop should be indented one step further than the last level. This clearly identifies the code associated with each loop.

Let us take a look at a trace of two nested loops. In order to keep the trace manageable, the number of iterations has been shortened.

```
for(num2 = 0; num2 <= 3;  num2++)
{
  for(num1 = 0; num1 <= 2; num1++)
  {
    printf("\n %d  %d",num2,num1);
  }
}
```

Memory		Screen
num 2	**num 1**	
0	0	0 0
	1	0 1
	2	0 2
	3 (end)	
1	0	1 0
	1	1 1
	2	1 2
	3 (end)	
2	0	2 0
	1	2 1
	2	2 2
	3 (end)	
3	0	3 0
	1	3 1
	2	3 2
	3 (end)	
4 (end)		

Remember that, in the memory, for loops will register a value one beyond (or the step beyond) the requested ending value in order to disengage the loop.

Here is an example of nested loops which prints out a multiplication table.

Example

```
35. #include <stdio.h>
    int main ()
    {
    int i,j;
    for (i = 1; i <= 10; i++)
      {
      for (j = 1; j <= 10; j++)
        {
          printf ("%5d",i * j);
        }
      printf ("\n");
      }
      return 0;
    }
```

Output:

1	2	3	4	5	6	7	8	9	10
2	4	6	8	10	12	14	16	18	20
3	6	9	12	15	18	21	24	27	30
4	8	12	16	20	24	28	32	36	40
5	10	15	20	25	30	35	40	45	50
6	12	18	24	30	36	42	48	54	60
7	14	21	28	35	42	49	56	63	70
8	16	24	32	40	48	56	64	72	80
9	18	27	36	45	54	63	72	81	90
10	20	30	40	50	60	70	80	90	100

Note that after the inner for loop (at the end of each iteration of the outer for loop), a '\n' is used which causes the next line of the output to be printed in a fresh line.

If a break statement is encountered in a nested loop, the control of the program jumps to the first statement after the innermost loop. For instance, to print the diagonal lower half of the multiplication table (below the diagonal line from the top left to the bottom right), for each row(denoted by i here), once the column(denoted by j) equals the row, the rest of the inner for loop has to be skipped and the line that prints the newline character should be executed. Similarly, the next row has to be printed. The output would be as follows.

```
 1
 2    4
 3    6    9
 4    8   12   16
 5   10   15   20   25
 6   12   18   24   30   36
 7   14   21   28   35   42   49
 8   16   24   32   40   48   56   64
 9   18   27   36   45   54   63   72   81
10   20   30   40   50   60   70   80   90  100
```

The C program to achieve the preceding output is as follows.

```c
#include <stdio.h>
int main()
{
    int i,j;
    for (i = 1; i <= 10; i++)
    {
        for (j = 1; j <= 10; j++)
        {
            printf ("%5d",i * j);
            if(i==j)
                break;
        }
        printf ("\n");
    }
    return 0;
}
```

To put everything together as well as demonstrate the use of the break statement, here is a program for printing prime numbers between 1 and 100.

```c
#include <stdio.h>
#include <math.h>
int main()
{
int i, j;
printf("%d\n", 2);
for(i = 3; i <= 100; ++i)
    {
    for(j = 2; j < i; ++j)
        {
        if(i % j == 0)
            break;
        if(j > sqrt(i))
```

```c
        {
            printf("%d\n", i);
            break;
        }
        }
    }
    return 0;
}
```

The outer loop steps the variable 'i' through the numbers from 3 to 10 0; the code tests to see if each number has any divisors other than 1 and itself. The trial divisor 'j' increments from 2 to 'i'. 'j' is a divisor of 'i' if the remainder of 'i' divided by 'j' is 0, so the code uses C's 'remainder' or 'modulus' operator % to make this test. Remember that i % j gives the remainder when 'i' is divided by 'j'.

If the program finds a divisor, it uses break to come out of the inner loop, without printing anything. But if it evaluates that 'j' has risen higher than the square root of 'i', without its having found any divisors, then 'i' must not have any divisors. Therefore, 'i' is prime, and its value is printed. Once it has been determined that 'i' is prime by noticing that j > sqrt(i), there is no need to try the other trial divisors. Therefore, a second break statement can be used to break out of the loop in that case, too. The following program is a simplified form of the previous program.

```c
#include <stdio.h>
#include <math.h>
main()
{
    int i, j,r;
    for(i = 2; i <= 100; ++i)
    {
        r=1;
        for(j = 2; j <= sqrt(i); ++j)
        {
            r=i%j;
            if(r == 0)
                break;
        }
        if(r!=0)
        printf("%d\n", i);
    }
}
```

Nested loops and the goto statement

Occasionally it is needed to come out of all the nested loops from the innermost loop and then continue with the statement following the outermost loop. A break statement in the innermost loop will only break out of that loop, and execution will continue with the loop which is the immediate outer loop. To escape the nested loops completely using break statements therefore requires quite complicated logic to break out of each level until you escape the outermost loop. This is one situation in which the goto can be very useful (as shown below) because it provides a way to avoid all the complicated logic.

Consider the following code segment:

```
for (i = 0; i < n; ++i)
  for (j = 0; j < m; ++j)
    for (k = 0; k < s; ++k)
    {
      scanf("%d", &n);
      if (n == 0)
        goto GoOut;
      x= n*(i+j+k)
      … … … … … … … … … … … … .
      … … … … … … … … … … … … .
    }
  GoOut:
```

A naive attempt is as follows:

```
for (done = 0, i = 0; !done && i < n; ++i)
  for (j = 0; !done && j < m; ++j)
    for (k = 0; !done && k < s; ++k)
    {
      scanf("%d", &n);
      if (n == 0)
        done = 1;
      x= n*(i+j+k)
      … … … … … … … … … … … … .
      … … … … … … … … … … … … .
    }
```

C89 specifies that at least 15 levels of nesting must be supported by the compiler. C99 raises this limit to 127. In practice, most compilers allow substantially more levels. However, nesting beyond a few levels is seldom necessary, and excessive nesting can quickly confuse the meaning of an algorithm.

Common programming errors

- *Writing expressions like a<b<c or a==b==c etc.*

  These expressions are legal in C but do not have meaning that might be expected. For example, in a<b<c, the operator < is left associative, this expression is equivalent to (a<b) < c.

- *Use of = instead of ==*

  a == b and a = b are not similar as == is a test for equality a = b is an assignment operator. Be careful when writing the equality operator.

- *Forgetting to use braces for compound statement*

  If the number of statements to be executed is more than one i.e. compound statement and those statements are to be executed if the test expression is true for once (if used with if...else) or repeatedly (if used with while or for or do-while), then the compound statement must be enclosed within braces.

- *Dangling else*

  An else is always associated with the closest un-matched if. If this is not the wanted branching impose the proper association between if and else by means of braces. One should be careful when framing if-else-if ladder.

- *Use of semicolon in loop*

  Also, remember not to put a semicolon after the close parenthesis at the end of the for loop (this immediately ends the loop). As an illustration the following code segment will print 12345.

  ```
  for (int c = 1; c <= 5; ++c)
      printf("%d",c);
  ```

  But the following code would print 6.

  ```
  for (int c = 1; c <= 5; ++c);
      printf("%d",c);
  ```

  This same sort of problem can arise with a *while* loop. Be careful not to place a semicolon after the closing parenthesis that encloses the test expression at the start of a *while* loop. A do-while loop has just the opposite problem. You must remember always to end a do-while loop with a semicolon.

- *Floating point equality*

  Do not use the equality operator with a floating point number. When equality of floating point value is desired it would be better if the absolute value of the difference between operands be less than some extremely small value. When it is needed to test for equality such as a == b use

```
if(fabs(a-b) < 0.000001)
```

where the value 0.000001 can be altered to any other acceptably small value. Thus, if the difference between the two operands is less than 0.000001 (or any other user selected amount), the two operands are considered essentially equal.

SUMMARY

A statement is a syntactic construction that performs an action when a program is executed. It can alter the value of variables, generate output, or process input. In C, any sequence of statements can be grouped together to function as a syntactically equivalent single statement by enclosing the sequence in braces. These groupings are called *statement blocks,* which mean a final semicolon after the right brace is not needed.

The program statements in C fall into three general types: assignment, input/output, and control. C has two types of control structures: *selection (decision)* and *repetition (loops).* The decision control constructs are of two types: conditional and unconditional. The conditional control constructs are if, if-else, if-else-if, and switch. The unconditional control constructs are break, continue, and goto. The loop control constructs are for, while, and do-while. Relational and logical operators are used to specify test conditions used in the control constructs of C. The test conditions give shape to test expressions, which are evaluated to give a value of zero or non-zero, irrespective of its sign. In C, the zero value is taken as *false* and any non-zero value, either positive or negative, is taken as *true.*

One-way decisions are handled with an if statement that either does some particular thing or does nothing at all. The decision is based on a test expression that either evaluates to true or false. Two-way decisions are handled with if-else statements that either do one particular thing or do another. Similar to one-way decisions, the decision is based on a test expression. Multi-way decision statements use if-else-if, nested if, or switch statements. They are all used to evaluate a test expression that can have several possible values selecting different actions.

The while statement is a pre-test loop declaration construct. This is a top-driven loop. The *condition* is tested *before* the execution of the code in the body of the loop. It is tested before the body is executed the very first time and if it is false, the body of the loop will not be executed at all. So the loop may execute zero times. A while loop is considered to be an *indeterminate* or *indefinite loop* because it is usually only at run time that it can be determined how many times it will iterate.

A loop formed by using the for statement is generally called a *determinate* or *definite* loop because the programmer knows exactly how many times it will repeat. The number of repetitions can be determined mathematically by manually checking the logic of the loop.

A do-while loop is considered to be a bottom-checking loop since the control expression is located after the body of the loop and after the while keyword. A do-while loop is guaranteed to execute at least once even if the control expression evaluates to false.

A goto statement causes control to be transferred unconditionally to the statement associated with the label specified in the statement. There are some special statements such as break, return, and continue that are used with the control constructs. The break statement is used in loop constructs, such as for, while, and do-while, and switch statement to terminate execution of the loop or switch statement.

The return statement has two forms. In one instance, it is used in the definition of a function to set its returned value and in other instance it is used to terminate the execution of the function. The continue statement is used in while, for, or do-while loops to terminate an iteration of the loop.

A *nested loop* refers to a loop that is contained within another loop. It must be remembered that each inner loop should be enclosed completely in the outer loop; overlapping loops are not allowed.

KEY-TERMS

Block Any sequence of statements can be grouped together to function as a syntactically equivalent single statement by enclosing the sequence in braces.

Boolean expression An expression that evaluates to either true or false.

Loop A programming construct in which a set of statements in a computer program can be executed repeatedly.

Sentinel A sentinel value is a value that is not a legitimate data value for a particular problem, but is of a proper type, that is used to check for a 'stopping' value.

Spaghetti code Programs with many goto statements.

FREQUENTLY ASKED QUESTIONS

1. Is the relational expression a < b < c legal in C?

Yes. It is legal but does not have the meaning that might be expected. Since the operator < is left associative, this expression is equivalent to (a < b) < c. The result from the evaluation of these expression would either be 0 or 1 depending on the values of a, b and c.

2. There is no logical exclusive OR operator in C; can it be simulated by anyway?

The result of the logical exclusive OR operation on two integers is true if and only if one operand (but not both) is true. It can be simulated by the following expression.

```
(a||b) && !(a && b)
```

where a and b are both of type int.

3. The floating point numbers are seldom equal to required value or variable; then how can two floating point values or variables be tested for equality?

The following code segment may be used.

```
float a, b;
if(fabs(a-b) < 0.000001)
        printf("equal");
else
        printf("\n not equal ");
```

4. What is a null statement?

A null statement is an expression statement consisting solely of the terminating semicolon. A null statement can appear on its own, or (most frequently) as the statement body of an iteration statement. "0;"or "1;" can also be used as null statements. Note that {}(which contains nothing within braces, i.e., it is empty) is not a null statement. {} is a compound statement. An empty block (called a null block) is not the same as a null statement.

5. Which form of loop should you use- while or for or do-while?

The decision of selecting while or do-while depends on the situation. It is to be decided whether one needs a pre-test loop or a post-test loop. In such situation where either of while or do-while can be used, the computer scientists usually consider a pre-test loop superior. Because, a general principle is that prevention is better than cure. A program is easier to read if the test for iteration (i.e. loop) is found at the beginning of the loop. In many uses, it is important that the loop be skipped entirely if the test is not initially met.

The choice between a for or a while is partly a matter of taste.

6. What is the difference between a break and continue statement?

Sometimes when executing a loop, it becomes desirable to leave the loop as soon as a certain condition occurs. The break statement can be used for this purpose. Execution of the break statement causes the program to immediately exit from the loop it is executing, whether it's a for, while, or do-while loop. Subsequent statements in the loop are skipped, and execution of the loop is terminated.

The continue statement causes the next iteration of the enclosing for, while, or do loop to begin. In the while and do-while, this means that the test part is executed immediately; in the for, control passes to the increment step. The continue statement applies only to loops, not to switch. A continue inside a switch causes the next loop iteration if it is placed within a loop.

EXERCISE

1. What do you mean by control statements in C?

2. What is the purpose of the if-else statement?

3. Compare the use of the if-else statement with the use of the '?:' operator. In particular, in what way can the '?:' operator be used in place of an if-else statement?

4. What is the purpose of the switch statement? What are labels, i.e., case prefixes? What type of expression must be used to represent a case label?

5. What is the purpose of the comma operator? Within which control statement does the comma operator usually appear?

6. Why is the use of the goto statement generally discouraged? Under what conditions might the goto statement be helpful? What types of usage should be avoided and why?

7. Differentiate between a for loop and a while loop. Discuss the usage of each.

8. Distinguish between the following:
   (a) do-while and while loop
   (b) break and continue

9. Write a program using conditional operators to determine whether a year entered through the keyboard is a leap year or not.

10. The factorial of an integer n is the product of consecutive integers from 1 to n. That is, factorial n = n! = n x (n - 1) x (n - 2) x (n - 3) x ... x 3 x 2 x 1. Write a C program to find the factorial value of n.

11. Write a C program to print the quotient of an integer number without using '/'.

12. Write a program to print all the even and odd numbers of a certain range as indicated by the user.

13. Write a C program to convert the binary equivalent of an integer number without using array.

14. Write a C program to find the prime factors of a number given by the user.

15. Write a C program to check whether a number is a power of 2 or not.

16. Write a program to find the GCD of two numbers.

17. Write a program to find the sum of digits of a number given by the user.

18. Write a C program to calculate the sum of prime numbers in a range.

19. Write a C program to print the sum of the following series up to n terms where n is given by the user.

    $1 + x + x^2/2! + x^3/3! + \dots$ (The value of x is also given by the user.)

20. Write a C program to print the sum of the following series up to n terms where n is given by the user.

    $x - x^3/3! + x^5/5! - \dots$ (The value of x is given by the user.)

21. Write a C program to print the following series: 0 1 1 2 3 5 8 13 .... The number of terms to be printed should be given by the user.

22. Write a C program to print the numbers that do not appear in the Fibonacci series. The number of such terms to be printed should be given by the user.

23. Write a program to convert a decimal number into any base.

24. Write a program to check whether a number is a Krishnamurty number or not. A Krishnamurty number is one whose sum of factorial of digits equals the number.

25. Write a program to print the second largest number among a list of numbers without using array.

26. Write programs to print the sum of the following series (with and without `pow()` library function).

    (a) $S = 1 + x + x^2 + x^3 + \dots$ n terms

    (b) $S = -x + x^2 - x^3 + x^4 + 1 \dots$ n terms

    (c) $1 + x + \dfrac{x^2}{2!} + \dfrac{x^3}{3!} + n$ terms

    (d) $S = 1 + (1+2) + (1+2+3) + \dots$ n terms

    (e) $1 - x + \dfrac{x^2}{2!} - \dfrac{x^3}{3!} + \dots n$ terms

    (f) $x - \dfrac{x^3}{3} + \dfrac{x^5}{5} - \dfrac{x^7}{7} + \dots n$ terms

    (g) $S = 2 + 22 + 222 + 2222 + \dots$ n terms

    (h) $S = 1 + \dfrac{x}{4} + \dfrac{x^2}{8} + \dots$ n terms

    (i) $x - \dfrac{x^2}{2} + \dfrac{x^3}{3} - \dfrac{x^4}{4} \dots n$ terms

27. Write a program to print the prime numbers in a range.

28. Given a number, write a program using `while` loop to reverse the digits of the number. For example, the number 12345 should be written as 54321.

29. Write a program to print the following triangle.

    (a) *
      * *
      * * *
      * * * * ... up to nth line

    (b)   *
           * *
         * * *
       * * * *
        ... up to nth line

    (c) 1
      1 2
      1 2 3
      1 2 3 4 ... up to nth line

    (d)   1
       2 1 2
      3 2 1 2 3 ... up to nth line

    (e) 1
      2 2
      3 3 3
      4 4 4 4
      5 5 5 5 5 ... up to nth line

30. Write a program to check whether a number is a prime number or not.

31. Write a program to print all the prime numbers of a certain range given by the user.

32. Write a program to print the Floyd's triangle.

33. Write a program to add the prime numbers of a certain range given by the user.

Project Questions

1. Write a C program that prompts the user to enter the date as three integer values for the month, the day in the month, and the year. The program should then output the date in the form 31st December 2003 when the user enters 12 31 2010, say. The program has to work out when superscripts "th", "nd", "st", and "rd" need to be appended to the day value. The programmer should not forget 1st, 2nd, 3rd, 4th; and then 11th, 12th, 13th, 14th; and 21st, 22nd, 23rd, and 24th.

2. This is a well-known game with a number of variants. The following variant has an interesting winning strategy. Two players alternately take marbles from a pile. In each move, a player chooses how many marbles to take. The player must take at least

one but at most half of the marbles. Then the other player takes a turn. The player who takes the last marble loses. Write a C program in which the computer plays against a human opponent. Generate a random integer between 10 and 100 to denote the initial size of the pile. Generate a random integer between 0 and 1 to decide whether the computer or the human takes the first turn. Generate a random integer between 0 and 1 to decide whether the computer plays *smart* or *stupid*. In stupid mode the computer simply takes a random legal value (between 1 and *n*/2, where *n* is the total number of marbles) from the pile whenever it has a turn.

In smart mode the computer takes off enough marbles to make the size of the pile a power of two minus 1—that is, 3, 7, 15, 31, or 63. That is always a legal move, except when the size of the pile is currently one less than a power of two. In that case, the computer makes a random legal move. It should be noted that the computer cannot be beaten in smart mode when it has the first move, unless the pile size happens to be 15, 31, or 63. Of course a human player who has the first turn and knows the winning strategy can win against the computer.

INCREMENTAL PROBLEM

In the earlier chapter, a program was developed to determine the length of a straight line joining two points. The program code already developed in the earlier chapter is not repeated here. The program code developed here starts with the assumption that the length has already been determined and that the length of three sides of a triangle are stored in three variables. Considering this fact, the program is further developed to solve the problem stated by using the decision making or looping constructs.

Problem statement

Get the lengths of three sides of a triangle. Check whether the triangle can be formed or not. If possible then classify the triangle as equilateral, isosceles or scalene. Otherwise, if the triangle cannot be formed give the user a chance to re-enter the lengths of the sides or terminate the program.

Solution

To solve this problem, lengths of three sides of a triangle are stored in three variables say sideOne, sideTwo and sideThree. If the sum of the lengths of any two sides is greater than the length of the third side then a triangle can be formed. Therefore to find out whether a triangle can be formed or not, the following test expression has to be evaluated.

```
sideOne+sideTwo > sideThree && sideTwo + sideThree > sideOne && sideOne + sideThree > sideTwo
```

If the above test expression evaluates to false then to give the user a chance to re-enter the lengths of the sides or to terminate the program, a loop has to be used. However, in case the triangle can be drawn, the said loop as well as the program would terminate. For this purpose, the variable ans is used.

Program

```c
#include <stdio.h>
int main(void)
{
    int sideOne,sideTwo,sideThree;
    char ans ='y';
    while(ans == 'y' || ans == 'Y')
    {
        printf("\n Enter the lengths of threesides
            of a triangle:");
        scanf("%d %d %d",&sideOne,&sideTwo,&side Three);
        if(sideOne+sideTwo>sideThree && sideTwo+side
            Three>sideOne && sideOne+sideThree>side
            Two)
        {
            printf("\n Triangle can be drawn");
            if(sideOne==sideTwo && sideTwo==sideThree)
            printf("\n It is a Equilateral Triangle");
            else if(sideOne==sideTwo || sideTwo==side
            Three ||sideOne==sideThree)
            printf("\n It is a Isosceles Triangle");
             else
                printf("\n It is a scalene Triangle");
            ans='n'; // break; can also be used.
        }
        else
        {
            printf("\n Triangle cannot be drawn");
            printf("\n Do you want to reenter the\
lengths again(y/n)? ");
            fflush(stdin);
            scanf("%c",&ans);
        }
    }
    return 0;
}
```

Problem Statement

Write a program to compute the square root of a given number, without using `sqrt()` function of the math library.

Analysis

Let the square root of a number *m* be *n*. i.e. $e = \dfrac{1}{0!}$. Therefore, n * n = m. To devise the algorithm for this problem, consider that m = 49. Suppose one might guess 9 could be the square root of 49. But 9 × 9 = 81 which is larger than 49. As 9 is too large, so next let us try 8. The square of 8 is 64. It is still greater than 49, but more closer to 49. However, the right guess for *n* should be 7. In some case it may be possible that the value of m may not be a perfect square of n. Then the obvious question is how one should choose the initial guess value. The number of iterations is critically dependent on the initial guess. As a consequence, the approach to square root value is another question. If one opted for 4 instead of 9 as the initial guess value, then 4 × 4 is equal to 16 which is too small compared to 49. As the square root of 49 lies between 9 and 4, the average of 9 and 4 might be the next estimate. The average of 9 and 4 is (9 + 4) = 13/2 = 6.5. The square of 6.5 is 42.25, which is less than 49. If 49 is divided by 6.5, the next complimentary value can be found which is 49/6.5=7.5384. Following the same computation method, the next complementary value is given by

$$\frac{49}{7.5384} = 6.5$$

The last two estimates i.e. 7.5384 and 6.5 are closer to the actual result but one is slightly greater than 7 and the other is slightly less than 7. To get the better estimate, the average of most two recent guesses may be considered as a next guess.

$$\frac{7.5384 + 6.500}{2} = 7.0192$$

The square of 7.0192 is 49.2691, which is closer to 49.
To summarize the above analysis, let the previous guess be f, then the complementary value is given by m/f. The next improved estimate of the square root, s, is given by

$$s = \frac{f + (m/f)}{2} \qquad (1)$$

The above averaging process can be repeated by replacing f with s followed by (1). That is the values of f and s furnish most recent estimates for the square root of m. Obviously, the successive repetitions gradually produce better estimates as the iterations decrease the difference between square roots estimated and with successive iterations would become progressively smaller. This is evident from the estimated square roots found out in successive iterations.

$$7.538 \rightarrow 7.0192 \rightarrow 7.0000$$

Because the successive guesses that are derived by repeated application of the formula (1) gets closer and closer to the true value of the square root, one can set a limit that can be used for deciding when to terminate the process. The repetition should be terminated when the difference between recent two successive estimates, f and s, becomes significantly small, preferably less than 0.000001 as the floating-point numbers cannot be compared for exact equality. The usual way to test for approximate equality is to subtract the two floating-point numbers and compare the absolute value of the difference against a very small number. This 'very small number' is chosen by the programmer to be small enough so that the two numbers can be considered 'equal'.

The most important question here is about the initial guess. One may assume that the initial guess might be m/2. This fact would be sorted out from the following table, in which the number and their square roots are listed.

Number	Square root (up to 4 digit after decimal point)
1	1.0000
2	1.4142
2.5	1.5811
3	1.7320
3.5	1.8708
4	2
4.5	2.1213
5	2.2360
5.5	2.3452
6	2.4494
6.5	2.5495
7	2.6457
7.5	2.7386
8	2.8284
8.5	2.9154
9	3.0000

If m is negative then it is safer to display an error message and then immediately terminate without performing any calculations. The square root routine in the standard C library is called `sqrt()` and it returns a 'domain error' if a negative argument is supplied. The actual value that is returned is implementation-defined. On some systems, if you try to display such a value, it displays as NAN, which means Not A Number.

Design

Algorithm for the above problem may be formulated as follows-

```
1. START
2. PRINT "ENTER THE NUMBER:  "
3. INPUT M
4. IF M < 0 THEN PRINT "NEGATIVE VALUE IS NOT
   A VALID INPUT": GOTO 10
5. S ← M/2
6. F ← S
```

```
7. S ← (F+M/F)/2
8. IF (F-S) >= 0.000001 THEN GOTO 6
9. PRINT S
10. STOP
```

Implementation

The corresponding C program following the above algorithm is demonstrated below.

```
/* C progarm to compute the square root of a given
number */

#include <stdio.h>
#include <math.h>
int main(void)
{
  float m, f,s;
  printf("\n Enter the number:");
  scanf("%f", &m);

  /* Checking for negative input */

  if (m < 0)
  {
    printf("\n Negative Input For Computing Square\
          Root Is Not Allowed");
```

```
    return 0;
  }
  s = m/2;                    /* Set the initial guess */
  do
  {
    f = s;
    s = (f + m / f) / 2;
                        /* Compute the next estimate
                            for the square root */

  } while(fabs(f-s) >= 0.000001);
  printf("\n Square root of %g is %g\n", m, s);
  return 0;
}
```

N.B. `fabs()` is the C library function that returns the floating-point absolute value of its argument.

Sample Run

```
Enter the number:  9
Square root of 9 is 3

Enter the number:  5
Square root of 5 is 2.23607

Enter the number:  2.5
Square root of 2.5 is 1.58114
```

Chapter 6

Arrays and Strings

Learning Objectives

After reading this chapter, the readers will be able to

- understand what an array is
- learn about one-dimensional array, their declaration, initialization, ways to access individual array elements, representation of array elements in memory, and other possible operations
- learn about one-dimensional strings and the way they are declared, initialized, manipulated, inputted, and displayed
- learn about two-dimensional arrays, initialization of sized and unsized two-dimensional arrays, accessing elements in such arrays, and how this kind of an array can be used
- know about array of strings, its declaration, initialization, other operations, manipulations, and uses
- get a brief idea of three-dimensional arrays or even larger ones

6.1 INTRODUCTION

The variables used so far have all had a common characteristic: each variable can only be used to store a single value at a time. For example, each of the variables ch, n, and price declared in the statements

```
char ch;
int n;
float price;
```

are of different data types and each variable can only store one value of the declared data type. These types of variables are called *scalar variables*. A scalar variable is a single variable whose stored value is an atomic type. This means that the value cannot be further subdivided or separated into a legitimate data type.

In contrast to atomic types, such as integer, floating point, and double precision data, there are aggregate types. An aggregate type, which is referred to as both a *structured type* and a *data structure*, is any type whose values can be decomposed and are related by some defined structure. Additionally, operation must be available for retrieving and updating individual values in the data structure. Such a *derived data type* is an array.

Why array?

Consider a brand-new problem: a program that can print its input in reverse order. If there are two values, this is easy and the program is

```c
#include <stdio.h>
int main()
{
  int v1, v2;
  printf("Enter two values:");
  scanf("%i %i", &v1, &v2);
  printf("%i\n%i\n", v2, v1);
  return 0;
}
```

If there are three values, this is still relatively easy and the program is

```c
#include <stdio.h>
int main()
{
  int v1, v2, v3;
  printf("Enter three values: ");
  scanf("%d %d %d", &v1, &v2, &v3);
  printf("%d\n %d\n %d \n", v3, v2, v1);
  return 0;
}
```

But what if there are ten or twenty or one hundred values? Then it is not so easy.

Besides that, the solutions work only if the number of inputs exactly matches with those expected by the user.

Consider another problem: the average of n integer numbers given by the user can easily be computed as follows:

```c
#include <stdio.h>
int main()
{
  int count,s=0, n, num;
  float avg;
    printf("\n How many numbers?");
    scanf("%d", &n);
  for(count=1;count<=n;++count)
  {
    printf("\n Enter the Number:");
    scanf("%d", &num);
    s+=num;
  }
  avg=(float)s/n;
  printf("Average is %f", avg);
  return 0;
}
```

Now if the problem is given as 'Print the numbers that are greater than the average', then one solution is to read the numbers twice. That is,

- read in all the numbers and calculate the average.
- read in all the numbers again, this time checking each as it is read against a previously calculated average.

If input is from the keyboard, then the user has to enter each number twice and accurately, with no mistakes. This is not a viable solution. Because, for 25 numbers entered, the user has to remember all the numbers. But what if there are 50 or 100 numbers? Then, it is not so easy. To solve this problem, an array is required. It is a collection of numbered elements.

An array is a fundamental data structure that enables the storing and manipulation of potentially huge quantities of data. An array stores an *ordered* sequence of *homogeneous* values. Homogeneous means that all the values are of the same data type. The order of the values are also preserved, i.e., the integer array {1, 2, 3, 4} is different from {1, 4, 3, 2}.

An array can be defined as a data structure consisting of an ordered set of data values of the homogeneous (same) type. An array is a collection of individual data elements that is

- Ordered—one can count off the elements 0, 1, 2, 3, ...
- Fixed in size
- Homogeneous—all elements have to be of the same type, e.g., int, float, char, etc.

In C, each array has two fundamental properties: the data type and the size. Individual array elements are identified by an integer index. In C, the index begins at zero and is always written inside square brackets.

> **Points to Note**
>
> 1. A scalar variable is a single variable whose stored value is an atomic data type.
> 2. An array is a collection of individual data elements that is ordered, fixed in size, and homogeneous.
> 3. An array is considered to be a derived data type.
> 4. Array enables the storing and manipulation of potentially huge quantities of data.

6.2 ONE-DIMENSIONAL ARRAY

There are several forms of an array used in C: one-dimensional or single-dimensional and multidimensional array. In this section, one-dimensional arrays will be discussed.

Since the array is one dimensional, there will be a single subscript or index whose value refers to the individual array element which ranges from 0 to $(n-1)$, where n is the total number of elements in the array.

6.2.1 Declaration of a One-dimensional Array

To use an array variable in a program, it must be declared. When defining an array in a program, three things need to be specified.

- the type of data it can hold, i.e., int, char, double, float, etc.
- the number of values it can hold, i.e., the maximum number of elements it can hold
- a name

A one-dimensional array declaration is a data type followed by an identifier with a bracketed constant integral expression. The value of the expression, which must be positive, is the *size* of the array. It specifies the number of elements in the array. The array subscripts can range from 0 to (size –1). The lower bound of the array subscripts is 0 and the upper bound is (size –1). Thus, the following relationships hold.

```
int a[size]; /* memory space for a[0],a[1],…, a[size -1]
                allocated */

lower bound = 0
upper bound = size -1
size = upper bound + 1
```

The syntax for declaration of a one-dimensional array is
data_type array_name [SIZE];

- All the array elements hold values of type <data type>
- The size of the array is indicated by <SIZE>, the number of elements in the array. <SIZE> must be an int constant or a constant expression.

For example, to declare an array that can hold up to 10 integers, the following statement has to be written.

```
int ar[10];
```

This reserves *space* for 10 integers. Similarly,

```
int a[100]; /* an array with 100 int elements */
```

declares an array 'a' that can hold 100 integers. Once declared, an array element can be referenced as

```
<array name>[<index>]
```

where <index> is an integer constant or variable ranging from 0 to <SIZE> – 1.

In the above example, the array index starts at 0, so for this array there are elements named a[0], a[1], ..., a[99]. The idea is that if there is an array variable named a, its elements can be accessed with a[0], a[1], ..., a[99]. That is, a particular element of the array can be accessed by its 'index', a number that specifies which element is needed.

In a single-dimensional array of integers, the array is composed of individual integer values where integers are referred to by their position in the list. Indexed variables provide the means of accessing and modifying the specific values in the array. For instance, in an array named 'number'

number[0]	refers to the first number stored in the 'number' array
number[1]	refers to the second number stored in the 'number' array
number[2]	refers to the third number stored in the 'number' array
number[3]	refers to the fourth number stored in the 'number' array
number[4]	refers to the fifth number stored in the 'number' array

Figure 6.1 illustrates the number array in memory with the correct designation for each array element. Each individual array element is called an *indexed variable* or a *subscripted variable*, since both a variable name and an index or a subscript value must be used to reference the element. Remember that the index or subscript value gives the position of the element in the array. Internally, unseen by the programmer, the computer uses the index as an offset from the array's starting position.

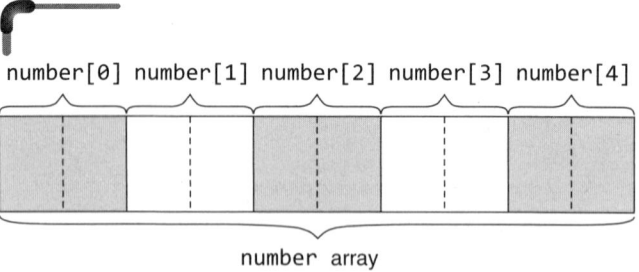

number[0] number[1] number[2] number[3] number[4]

number array

Figure 6.1 Identifying individual array elements

As illustrated in Fig. 6.2, the index indicates how many elements to skip over, starting from the beginning of the array, to get the desired element. At the time of declaration, the size of the array must be given; it is mandatory. Otherwise the compiler generates an error.

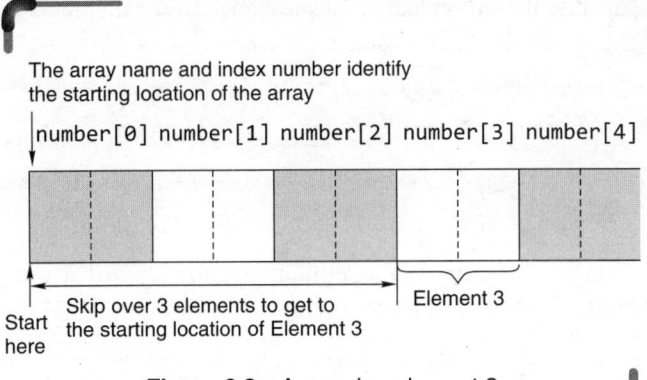

The array name and index number identify
the starting location of the array

number[0] number[1] number[2] number[3] number[4]

Start here ⟶ Skip over 3 elements to get to the starting location of Element 3 ⟶ Element 3

Figure 6.2 Accessing element 3

The following declaration is invalid.

```c
#include <stdio.h>
int main()
{
  double x[], y[];
  ...
  return 0;
}
```

No value is assigned for array size

C does not allow declaring an array whose number of elements (i.e. size after of the array) is unknown at compile time. So the above declaration statement is not valid. Now, consider the following code:

```c
#include <stdio.h>
int main()
{
  int N;
  double x[N], y[N];
  ...
  scanf("%d",&N);
  return 0;
}
```

A variable of integer data Type specified as size of the arrays

Here, the variable size array declaration, e.g.,

```c
double x[N], y[N];
```

is used where N is an integer variable. This kind of a declaration is illegal in C and results in a compile-time error.

It is sometimes convenient to define an array size in terms of a symbolic constant, rather than a fixed integer quantity. This makes it easier to modify a program that utilizes an array, since all references to the maximum array size can be altered by simply changing the value of the symbolic constant. This approach is used in many of the sample programs given in this book. Consider the following sample program, which uses this approach.

```c
/* Define a symbolic constant for the size of
the array */
#include <stdio.h>
#define N 100
int main()
{
  double x[N], y[N];
  ...
  return 0;
}
```

The symbolic constant N is assigned the value 100

N is replaced with the assigned value 100

It is a good programming practice to define the size of an array as a symbolic constant.

Hence, it may be observed that a literal number or a previously declared '#defined symbolic constant' must be used in an array declaration for the size of the array. No variables are allowed for the size of the array.

Since the number of array elements can also be given by an expression, the declarations depicted below can be used.

```c
int x[N+1];
double y[M+5*N];
```

However, the C compiler must be able to evaluate the expression, which implies that all components of the expression must be available for evaluation of the expression when the program is compiled—there must be no unknowns. This means that the expression must be composed of constants. In the preceding examples, identifiers consisting of capital letters have been used, which is the convention for symbols defined with #define directives.

Thus the following expressions accessing elements of array arr are valid.

```c
/* Give N a value so that the examples are concrete! */
#define N 20
int i = 1, j = 3, k = 2;
float arr[N];

arr[0]
arr[3]
arr[9]
arr[i*j+k] /* given values of i,j,k evaluates i*j+k to 5 */
arr[N-10]
arr[N-1]
```

The evaluated value of this expression is the index of arr here

The following array references are not valid.

```
arr[-1]
arr[N-21]
arr[N+20]
arr[N]
```

In the previous example, `arr[N-1]` is the cause of many problems for new C programmers. It must be remembered that C array indices start at 0. Thus for an array with N elements, the index of the last element is N-1. It may be of help to think of the array index as an offset from the beginning of the array, so that the first element, at offset 0 from the beginning, is `arr[0]` and the last, at offset N-1, must be `arr[N-1]`.

Thus, expressions such as `arr[N]` are happily accepted by the compiler. (C compilers usually make the assumption that programmers know what they are doing.) The results of running such programs are entirely unpredictable, since the space at the end of the array may have arbitrary data in it. The results from a program may even vary from one run to another, as the memory space in which the compiler assumes the (N+1)th object to be stored may well have been allocated to some other object.

Points to Note

1. In C, arrays are of two types: one-dimensional and multidimensional.

2. An array must be declared with three attributes: *type of data* it can hold, the number of data it can hold(*size*), and an identifier(*name*) before it is used.

3. The array *size* must be a positive integer number or an expression that evaluates to a positive integer number that must be specified at the time of declaration with the exception that it may be unspecified while initializing the array.

4. In C, the array index starts at 0 and ends at (size−1) and provides the means of accessing and modifying the specific values in the array.

5. C never checks whether the array index is valid—either at compile time or when the program is running.

6.2.2 Initializing Integer Arrays

Variables can be assigned values during declaration like the following example.

```
int x = 7;
```

Arrays can be initialized in the same manner. However, since an array has multiple elements, braces are used to denote the entire array of values and commas are used to separate the individual values assigned to the elements in the array initialization statements as shown.

(a) `int A[10] = {9, 8, 7, 6, 5, 4, 3, 2, 1, 0};`

| 9 | 8 | 7 | 6 | 5 | 4 | 3 | 2 | 1 | 0 | ← values stored in array elements

0 1 2 3 4 5 6 7 8 9 ← index values of array elements

(b) `double a[5] = {3.67, 1.21, 5.87, 7.45, 9.12}`

Automatic sizing While initializing, the size of a one-dimensional array can be omitted as shown.

```
int arr[] = {3,1,5,7,9};
```

Here, the C compiler will deduce the size of the array from the initialization statement.

From the above initialization statement, the size of the array is deduced to be 5.

6.2.3 Accessing Array Elements

Single operations, which involve entire arrays, are not permitted in C. Thus, if x and y are similar arrays (i.e., of the same data type, dimension, and size), then assignment operations, comparison operations, etc., involving these two arrays must be carried out on an element-by-element basis. This is usually accomplished within a loop, or within nested loops for multidimensional arrays.

For initializing an individual array element, a particular array index has to be used. For example, in an array A, for initializing elements 0 and 3, the following statements are used,

```
A[0] = 3;
A[3] = 7;
```

Subscripted variables can be used at any place where scalar variables are valid. Examples using the elements of an array named numbers are shown here:

```
numbers [0] = 98;
numbers [1] = numbers [0] - 11
numbers [2] = 2 * (numbers [0] - 6);
numbers [3] = 79;
numbers [4] = (numbers [2] + numbers [3] - 3)/2;
total = numbers[0] + numbers[1] + numbers[2] +
        numbers[3] + numbers[4];
```

One extremely important advantage of using integer expressions as subscripts is that it allows sequencing through an array using a for loop. This makes statements such as

```
total = numbers[0] + numbers[1] + numbers[2] +
        numbers[3] + numbers [4];
```

unnecessary. The subscript value in each of the subscripted variables in this statement can be replaced by the counter in a for loop to access each element in the array sequentially. For example, the C statements,

```
total = 0;            /*initialize total to zero */
for(i = 0; i <5; ++i)
total = total + numbers[i]; /* add in a number */
```

sequentially retrieve each array element and adds the element to the total. Here the variable i is used both as the counter in the for loop and as a subscript. As i increases by one each time through the for loop, the next element in the array is referenced. The procedure for adding the array elements within the for loop is the same as that used before.

The following code

```
/* Initialization of all of the elements of the
sample array to 0 */

for(i = 0; i < 5; i++)
{
  a[i] = 0;
}
```

would cause all the elements of the array to be set to 0. Consider the following program that would use the above code segment.

```
#include <stdio.h>
#define ARRAY_SIZE 10
int main()
{
  int index, a[ARRAY_SIZE];
  for(index = 0; index < ARRAY_SIZE; index++)
  {
    a[index] = 0;
    printf("a[%d] = %d\n", index, a[index]);
  }
  printf("\n");
  return 0;
}
```

The output from the above example is as follows:

```
a[0] = 0
a[1] = 0
a[2] = 0
a[3] = 0
a[4] = 0
a[5] = 0
a[6] = 0
a[7] = 0
a[8] = 0
a[9] = 0
```

The same can be achieved in C99 by defining an array as follows- int a [ARRAY-SIZE] = {0};

Arrays are a real convenience for many problems, but there is not a lot that C can do with them automatically. In particular, neither can all elements of an array be set at once nor can one array be assigned to another. Both assignments

```
a = 0;    /* WRONG */
```

and

```
int b[10];
b = a;    /* WRONG */
```

are illegal, where a is an array.

So, for example, to assign values to (i.e., store values into) an array, ar[10], the following program statements may be used.

```
ar[0] = 1;
ar[1] = 3;
ar[2] = 5;
...
ar[9] = 19;
```

Or

```
for(i = 0; i < 10; i++)
  ar[i] = (i*2) + 1;
```

Notice how the variable i, used as a subscript, increments from 0 to 'less than' 10, i.e., from 0 to 9. To access values in an array, the same subscripted notation has to be utilized as shown.

```
printf("%d", ar[2]);
thirdOdd = ar[2];
nthOddSquared = ar[n-1] * ar[n-1];
```

6.2.4 Other Allowed Operations

These operations include the following, for an array named ar.

(a) To increment the ith element, the given statements can be used:
```
ar[i]++;
ar[i] += 1;
ar[i] = ar[i] + 1;
```

(b) To add n to the ith element, the following statements may be used:
```
ar[i] += n;
ar[i] = ar[i] + n;
```

(c) To copy the contents of the `ith` element to the `kth` element, the following statement may be written.

```
ar[k] = ar[i];
```

(d) To copy the contents of one array `ar` to another array `br`, it must again be done one by one.

```
int ar[10],br[10];
for(i = 0; i < 10; i = i + 1)
br[i] = ar[i];
```

(e) To exchange the values in `ar[i]` and `ar[k]`, a 'temporary' variable must be declared to hold one value, and it should be the same data type as the array elements being swapped. To perform this task, the following C statements are written

```
int temp;
temp = ar[i]; /* save a copy of value in ar[i] */
ar[i] = ar[j]; /* copy value from ar[j] to ar[i]  */
ar[j] = temp; /* copy saved value of ar[i] to ar[j]  */
```

Storing values given by the user in an array Reading the input into an array is done as shown.

```
int a[10]; /* an array with 10 "int" elements */
int i;
for(i=0 ; i< 10; i++)
    scanf("%d", &a[i]);
```

The idea is that first a value must be read and copied into a[0], then another value read and copied into a[1], and so on, until all the input values have been read.

Printing an array The following code segment prints the elements of an array, `a[10]`.

```
for(i=0 ; i< 10; i++)
    printf("%d", a[i]);
```

Now the problem posed earlier can be solved. For printing of numbers entered by the user in the reverse order, the program will be as follows:

```
#include <stdio.h>
#include <stdlib.h>
int main()
{
    int a[30],n,i;
```

```
/* n = number of array elements and i=index */
    printf("\n Enter the number n");
    scanf("%d",&n);
    if(n>30)
    {
      printf("\n Too many Numbers");
      exit(0);
    }
    for(i=0 ; i< n; i++)
      scanf("%d", &a[i]);
      printf("\n Numbers entered in reverse order \n");
    for(i=n-1 ; i>=0; i--)
      printf("%d", a[i]);
      return 0;
}
```

A program for printing numbers that are greater than the average is as follows:

```
#include <stdio.h>
#include <stdlib.h>
int main()
{
    int a[30],n,i,s=0;
    float avg;
    printf("\n Enter the number of numbers");
    scanf("%d",&n);
    if(n>30)
    {
      printf("\n Too many Numbers");
      exit(0);
    }
    for(i=0 ; i< n; i++)
    {
      scanf("%d", &a[i]);
      s+=a[i];
    }
    avg=(float)s/n;
    printf("\n Numbers greater than the average: \n");
    for(i=0 ; i< n; i++)
      if(a[i]>avg)
      printf("%d",a[i]);
      return 0;
}
```

6.2.5 Internal Representation of Arrays in C

Understanding how arrays work in C requires some understanding of how they are represented in the computer's memory. In C, an array is implemented as a single block of memory, with element 0 occupying the first 'slot' in that block. That is, arrays are allocated contiguous space in memory. As a result, C subscripts are closely related to actual memory addresses and to the notion of 'pointer' that will be discussed in the chapter on pointers.

The possible consequences of the misuse of arrays should motivate one to pay close attention to the array indices.

For a simple variable (e.g., `int`, `double`, etc.) of data type `X`, the compiler allocates `sizeof(X)` bytes to hold it. For an array of length `L` and data type `X`, the compiler allocates `L* sizeof (X)` bytes.

Given an array like `int scores[100]`, the compiler allocates 200 bytes starting at some location, say `64789`. Given an expression like `scores[5]`, the compiler accesses the value stored at the memory location starting with byte `64789+(5*2)`. In general, `a[i]` is located at byte: base address of `a + i * sizeof` (type of array).

References to elements outside of the array bounds It is important to realize that there is no array bound checking in C. If an array `x` is declared to have `100` elements, the compiler will reserve `100` contiguous, appropriately sized slots in computer memory on its behalf. The contents of these slots can be accessed via expressions of the form `x[i]`, where the integer `i` should lie in the range `0` to `99`. As seen, the compiler interprets `x[i]` to mean the contents of the memory slot which is `i` slots away from the beginning of the array. Obviously, accessing elements of an array that do not exist is going to produce some sort of error. Exactly what sort of error is very difficult to say—the program may crash, it may produce an absurdly incorrect output, it may produce plausible but incorrect output, it may even produce correct output—it all depends on exactly what information is being stored in the memory locations surrounding the block of memory reserved for x. This type of error can be extremely difficult to debug, since it may not be immediately apparent that something has gone wrong when the program is executed. It is, therefore, the programmer's responsibility to ensure that all references to array elements lie within the declared bounds of the associated arrays.

A bit of memory allocation It has been seen how arrays can be defined and manipulated. It is important to learn how to do this because in more advanced C programs it is necessary to deal with something known as dynamic memory management. This is where the memory management of the programs is taken over by the programmer so that they can do more advanced things. To understand this, it is important to have a rough idea of what is going on inside the computer's memory when the program runs. Basically, it is given a small area of the computer's memory to use. This memory, which is known as the *stack*, is used by variables in the program

```
int a = 10;
float values[100];
```

The advantage of this is that the memory allocation is very simple. When a variable or array is required, the user can declare it. When the variable or array goes out of scope, it is destroyed and the memory is freed up again. A variable goes out of scope when the program control (the place of the program in the code) gets to the next closing curly bracket. This is normally at the end of a function or even at the end of an `if-else/for/while` structure.

This is why it is necessary to be careful when getting functions to fill in arrays. If the function declares the array and then returns it, what actually happens is that only the pointer is kept safe (copied back to the calling function); all the memory allocated for the array is de-allocated. This is a disadvantage.

Another disadvantage is that the size of memory allocated from the stack must be fixed at compile time. For example, it is impossible to declare an array using a variable for the size because at compile time the compiler does not know how big the array will be. For this reason, the following code will not work.

```
int size;
printf("How big do you want the array?\n");
scanf("%d", &size);
int array[size];
```

Therefore, doing things dynamically is a real problem. Perhaps the biggest problem with using memory from the stack is that the stack is not very big. It is typically only

64k in size, even on a machine with tens of megabytes of memory. The rest of this memory is left alone by the compiler but the user can access it explicitly; it is called the *heap*.

6.2.6 Variable Length Arrays and the C99 Changes

With the earlier version of C (C89) compilers, an array's size must be a *constant integral expression* so that it can be calculated at compile-time. This has already been mentioned in earlier sections. But in the C99 compilers, an array size can be an *integral expression* and not necessarily a constant one. This allows the programmer to declare a *variable-length array* or an array whose size is determined at runtime. However, such arrays can exist within a block or a function, thereby signifying its scope to be limited within a set of instructions contained within a pair of left ({) and right (}) braces. This means that storage allocation to such an array is made at run-time and during its existence within the scope of a block or a function and relinquishes this storage the moment it exits its scope.

The following program illustrates the concept:

```
#include <stdio.h>
int main(void)
{
  int n,i;
  printf("\n enter the value of n: ");
  scanf("%d", &n);
  int a[n];
  printf("\n enter the values one by one\n");
  for(i=0;i<n; ++i)
    scanf("%d", &a[i]);
  printf("\n entered numbers are.....\n");
  for(i=0;i<n;++i)
    printf("\n %d",a[i]);
  return 0;
}
```

Some changes in initializing an array has been made in C99. Here, the element number of an array can be specified explicitly by using a format called a *specification initializer*. When an array is initialized in C89, each element needs to be initialized in order from the beginning.

In C99, initial values can be set only for certain elements, with uninitialized elements being initialized as 0. In C99, initial values can be set only for specific members, with uninitialized members being initialized as 0. This is useful when the elements requiring initialization are limited, or when arrays have large element counts.

Example

1. `int arr[6] = { [2] =3, [5] = 7 };`

   Here array element `arr[2]` and `arr[5]` is assigned the value 3 and 7 respectively, while all other elements in arr are assigned the value 0.

6.2.7 Working with One-Dimensional Array

Printing binary equivalent of a decimal number using array Here the remainders of the integer division of a decimal number by 2 are stored as consecutive array elements.

The division procedure is repeated until the number becomes 0.

```
#include <stdio.h>
int main()
{
  int a[20],i,m,n,r;
  printf("\n Enter the decimal integer");
  scanf("%d",&n);
  m=n;
  for(i=0;n>0;i++)
  {
    r=n%2;
    a[i]=r;
    n=n/2;
  }
  printf("\n Binary equivalent of %d is \t",m);
  for(i--;i>=0;i--)
  printf("%d",a[i]);
  return 0;
}
```

Fibonacci series using an array This example will introduce another application of the array. The program prints out an array of Fibonacci numbers. These are defined by a series in which any element is the sum of the previous two elements. This program stores the series in an array, and after calculating the terms, prints the numbers out as a table.

```
#include <stdio.h>
int main()
{
  int fib[15];
  int i;
  fib[0] = 0;
  fib[1] = 1;
  for(i = 2; i < 15; i++)
  fib[i] = fib[i-1] + fib[i-2];
  for(i = 0; i < 15; i++)
  printf("%d\n", fib[i]);
  return 0;

}
```

Output:
```
0
1
1
2
3
5
8
13
21
34
55
89
144
233
377
```

Behaviour of rolling dice Here is a slightly bigger example of the use of arrays. Suppose one wants to investigate the behaviour of rolling a pair of dice. The total roll value can range from 2 to 12, and how often each roll comes up is to be counted. An array is to be used to keep track of the counts: a[2] will count how many times 2 have been rolled, etc.

The simulation of the roll of a dice is done by calling C's random number generation function, rand(). Each time rand() is called, it returns a different, pseudo-random integer. The values that rand() returns typically span a large range, so C's *modulus* (or remainder) operator % will be used to produce random numbers in the required range. The expression rand() % 6 produces random numbers in the range 0 to 5, and rand() % 6 + 1 produces random numbers in the range 1 to 6.

Here is the program.

```
#include <stdio.h>
#include <stdlib.h>
int main()
{
  int i;
  int d1, d2;
  int a[13]; /* uses a[2]*/
  for(i = 2; i <= 12; i = i + 1)
    a[i] = 0;
  for(i = 0; i < 100; i = i + 1)
  {
    d1 = rand() % 6 + 1;
    d2 = rand() % 6 + 1;
    a[d1 + d2] = a[d1 + d2] + 1;
  }
  for(i = 2; i <= 12; i = i + 1)
    printf("%d: %d\n", i, a[i]);
  return 0;
}
```

The header file <stdlib.h> has to be included because it contains the necessary declarations for the rand() function. The array of size 13 has to be declared so that its highest element will be a[12]. Space for a[0] and a[1] will be wasted; this is no great loss. The variables d1 and d2 contain the roll values of the two individual dice; they are added together to decide which cell of the array to increment in the line

```
a[d1 + d2] = a[d1 + d2] + 1;
```

After 100 rolls, the array is printed out. Typically, mostly 7's are seen as output, and relatively few 2's and 12's. However, using the % operator to reduce the range of the rand() function is not always a good idea.

Check Your Progress

1. Given the array declaration
   ```
   int myArray[] = {0, 2, 4, 6, 8, 10};
   ```
   What is the value of myArray[myArray[2]];
   Output: 8

2. ```
   #include <stdio.h>
   int main()
   {
     float a[10];
     printf("%d", sizeof(a));
   ```
   ```

```
    return 0;
}
```

What is the output of this program?

Output: 40

3.
```
#include <stdio.h>
int main()
{
    int a[5],i;
    for(i=0;i<5;++i)
    printf("%d",a[i]);
    return 0;
}
```

What is the output of this program?

Output: Garbage

4. An array has been declared as `int a[] = {1, 2, 3, 4, 5, ...};` How can you find the number of elements (i.e., size) of the array without manually counting them?

Output: `printf("%d",sizeof(a)/sizeof(a[0]));`

Points to Note

1. Single operations, which involve entire arrays, are not permitted in C.
2. Neither can all elements of an array be set at once nor can one array be assigned to another.
3. For an array of length L and data type X, the compiler allocates L* sizeof (X) bytes of contiguous space in memory.
4. It is not possible to declare an array using a variable for the *size*.

6.3 STRINGS: ONE-DIMENSIONAL CHARACTER ARRAYS

Strings in C are represented by arrays of characters. The end of the string is marked with a special character, the *null character*, which is a character all of whose bits are zero, i.e., a NUL (not a NULL). (The null character has no relation except in name to the *null pointer*. In the ASCII character set, the null character is named NUL.) The null or string-terminating character is represented by another character escape sequence, `\0`.

Although C does not have a string data type, it allows string constants. For example,"hello students" is a string constant.

6.3.1 Declaration of a String

Strings can be declared like one-dimensional arrays. For example,

```
char str[30];
char text[80];
```

illustrates this feature.

6.3.2 String Initialization

Character arrays or strings allow a shorthand initialization, for example,

```
char str[9] = "I like C";
```

which is the same as

```
char str[9] = {'I',' ','l','i','k','e',' ','C','\0'};
```

Whenever a string, enclosed in double quotes, is written, C automatically creates an array of characters containing that string, terminated by the `\0` character. C language allows the alternative notation

```
char msg[] = "Hello";
```

that is always used in practice. The rules for writing string constants are exactly the same as those that were discussed earlier in this book when the use of `printf()` was introduced. It should be noted that the size of the aggregate msg is six bytes, five for the letters and one for the terminating NUL.

There is one special case where the null character is not automatically appended to the array. This is when the array size is explicitly specified and the number of initializers completely fills the array size. For example,

```
char c[4] = "abcd";
```

Here, the array c holds only the four specified characters, a, b, c, and d. No null character terminates the array.

Points to Note

1. An array formed by characters is a string in C.
2. The end of the string is marked with the null character.
3. When the character array size is explicitly specified and the number of initializers completely fills the array size, the null character is not automatically appended to the array.

6.3.3 Printing Strings

The conversion type s may be used for output of strings using `printf()`. Width and precision specifications may be used with the `%s` conversion specifier. The width specifies the minimum output field width; if the string is shorter, then space padding is generated. The precision specifies the maximum number of characters to display. If the string is too long, it is truncated. A negative width implies left justification of short strings rather than the default right justification. For example,

```
printf("%7.3s",name)
```

This specifies that only the first three characters have to be printed in a total field width of seven characters and right justified in the allocated width by default. We can include a minus sign to make it left justified (`%-7.3`). The following points should be noted.

- When the field width is less than the length of the string, the entire string is printed.
- The integer value on the right side of the decimal point specifies the number of characters to be printed.
- When the number of characters to be printed is specified as zero, nothing is printed.
- The minus sign in the specification causes the string to be printed as left justified.

The following program illustrates the use of the `%s` conversion specifier.

```
#include <stdio.h>
int main()
{
    char s[]="Hello, World";
    printf(">>%s<<\n",s);
    printf(">>%20s<<\n",s);
    printf(">>%-20s<<\n",s);
    printf(">>%.4s<<\n",s);
    printf(">>%-20.4s<<\n",s);
    printf(">>%20.4s<<\n",s);
    return 0;
}
```

producing the output

```
>>Hello, World<<
>>         Hello, World<<
>>Hello, World        <<
>>Hell<<
>>Hell                <<
>>                Hell<<
```

The `>>` and `<<` symbols are included in this program so that the limits of the output fields are clearly visible in the output.

There is another way to print a string. The library function `puts()` writes a line of output to the standard output. It terminates the line with a new line, `'\n'`. It returns an EOF if an error occurs. It will return a positive number upon success. The use of `puts()` is given as follows:

```
#include <stdio.h>
int main()
{
    char s[]="Hello, World";
    puts(s);
    return 0;
}
```

The library function `sprintf()` is similar to `printf()`. The only difference is that the formatted output is written to a memory area rather than directly to a standard output. It is particularly useful when it is necessary to construct formatted strings in memory for subsequent transmission over a communications channel or to a special device. Its relationship with `printf()` is similar to the relationship between `sscanf()` and `scanf()`. The library function `puts()` may be used to copy a string to the standard output, its single parameter is the start address of the string. `puts()` writes a new-line character to standard output after it has written the string.

The following is a simple example of the use of `sprintf()` and `puts()`.

```
#include <stdio.h>
int main()
{
    char buf[128];
    double x = 1.23456;
    int i = 0;
    sprintf(buf,"x = %7.5lf",x);
    while(i<10)
    puts(buf+i++);
    return 0;
}
```

The output produced is as follows:

```
x = 1.23456
```

```
= 1.23456
= 1.23456
1.23456
1.23456
.23456
23456
3456
456
56
```

If \n had been incorporated in the format string of the sprintf(), the output would have been double-spaced because the function would have put a new-line character in the generated string and puts() would then generate a further new line.

6.3.4 String Input

The following sections will describe the methods of taking input from the user.

Using %s control string with scanf()

Strings may be read by using the %s conversion with the function scanf() but there are some irksome restrictions. The first is that scanf() only recognizes a sequence of characters delimited by white space characters as an external string. The second is that it is the programmer's responsibility to ensure that there is enough space to receive and store the incoming string along with the terminating null which is automatically generated and stored by scanf() as part of the %s conversion. The associated parameter in the value list must be the address of the first location in an area of memory set aside to store the incoming string.

Of course, a field width may be specified and this is the maximum number of characters that are read in, but remember that any extra characters are left unconsumed in the input buffer. A simple use of scanf() with %s conversions is illustrated in the following program.

```
int main()
{
    char str[50];
    printf("Enter a string");
    scanf("%s",str);
    printf("The string was :%s\n",str);
    return 0;
```

```
}
```

Output of sample runs:

```
(a) Enter a string    manas
    The string was  :manas
(b) Enter a string    manas ghosh
    The string was  :manas
(c) Enter a string  "manas and ghosh"
    The string was : "manas"
```

Dissimilar to the integer, float, and characters, the %s format does not require the ampersand before the variable str.

It will also be observed that attempts to quote a string with internal spaces or to escape the internal spaces (both of which normally work in the Unix command environment) did not work. C supports variable field width or precision, e.g.,

```
printf("%*.*s",w,d,str);
```

prints the first d characters of the string in the field width of w. For example,

```
int main()
{
    char str[50];
    printf("\n Enter a string:");
    scanf("%s",str);
    printf("\n %*.*s\n",2,3,str);
    return 0;
}
```

> Specifies that the first three characters of the string will be printed.

Sample run:

```
Enter a string:Manas
```

Man—

> First three characters of entered string "Manas" is displayed on the screen.

As an illustration, the following program converts a decimal number into its hexadecimal equivalent.

```
#include <stdio.h>
int main(void)
{
    int n, r, i, a[50];
    char hexdigit[]="0123456789ABCDEF";
    printf("\n Enter the decimal number: ....\t");
    scanf("%d", &n);
    i=0;
    while(n>0)
```

```
    {
      r=n%16;
      a[i]=r;
      i++;
      n=n/16;
    }
    printf("\n Hexadecimal equivalent is...: \t");
    for(--i;i>=0;--i)
    printf("%c", hexdigit[a[i]]);
    return 0;
}
```

Here, at each iteration, remainder of the integer division of n by 16 is stored as an element of the array variable a. It continues until the number n becomes 0. After storing the remainders as elements of the array a, it is needed to print the elements in reverse order. When the control comes out of the while loop the value of i would be an incremented value.

So it is needed to decrement i by one and it has been performed at the initialization part of the for loop. The expression hexdigit[a[i]] would print the corresponding hexadecimal digit at each iteration. If the value stored in a[i] is 5, then printf("%c", hexdigit[5]) would print 5. If the value stored in a[i] is 13, then printf("%c", hexdigit[13]) would print D. The trace of the above program is given below.

```
n= 28
n=28  i=0   r=12  a[0]=12
n=1   i=1   r=1   a[1]=1
n=0   i=2
```

The value of i is 2 when the control is outside the while loop. i becomes 1 at the initialization step. In the first iteration, hexdigit[1] that is 'C' will be printed because the value stored in a[1] is 12. In the second iteration, hexdigit[0] that is '1' will be printed because the value stored in a[0] is 1.

The above program can be rewritten where the remainders are stored in the string hexdigit.

```
#include <stdio.h>
#include <string.h>
int main(void)
{
  int n, r, i;
  char hexdigit[50];
  printf("\n Enter the decimal number: ....\t");
  scanf("%d", &n);
```

```
  i=0;
  while(n>0)
  {
    r=n%16;
    if(r<10)
      hexdigit[i]=r+48;
    else
      hexdigit[i]=r%10+65;
    i++;
    n=n/16;
  }
  hexdigit[i]='\0';
  printf("\n Hexadecimal equivalent is...: \t");
  for(i=strlen(hexdigit)-1;i>=0;--i)
  printf("%c", hexdigit[i]);
  return 0;
}
```

Using scanset

The scanset conversion facility provided by scanf() is a useful string input method. This conversion facility allows the programmer to specify the set of characters that are (or are not) acceptable as part of the string. A scanset conversion consists of a list of acceptable characters enclosed within square brackets. A range of characters may be specified using notations such as 'a-z', meaning all characters within this range. The actual interpretation of a range in this context is implementation-specific, i.e., it depends on the particular character set being used on the host computer. If an actual '-' is required in the scanset, it must be the first or last character in the set. If the first character after the '[' is a '^' character, then the rest of the scanset specifies unacceptable characters rather than acceptable characters.

The following program shows the use of scansets.

```
int main()
{
  char str[50];
  printf("Enter a string in lower case:");
  scanf("%[a-z]",str);
  printf("The string was : %s\n",str);
  return 0;
}
```

Three sample runs are given below.

```
(a) Enter a string in lower case: hello world
    The string was: hello world
```

(b) Enter a string in lower case: hello, world
   The string was: hello

(c) Enter a string in lower case: abcd1234
   The string was : abcd

In the second case, the character, ',' (comma) is not in the specified range. Note that in all cases, conversion is terminated by the input of something other than a space or lowercase letter.

Single-line input using scanset with ^

The circumflex (^) plays an important role while taking input. For a single-line text input, the user presses the <**Return**> or <**Enter**> key to terminate the string. The maximum number of characters typed by the user might be 80 because the screen can print a maximum of 80 character in a line. All characters are allowed to be typed as input except \n. In the example that follows, the computer takes this (\n) as a clue indicating that the string has ended. Look at the example given below.

```c
#include <stdio.h>
int main()
{
  char str[80];
  printf("Enter a string in lower case");
  scanf("%[^\n]",str);
  printf("The string was : %s\n", str);
  return 0;
}
```

Multiline input using scanset

One can use a bracketed string read, %[..] where the square brackets [] are used to enclose all characters which are permissible in the input. If any character other than those listed within the brackets occurs in the input string, further reading is terminated. Reciprocally, those characters may be specified with the brackets which, if found in the input, will cause further reading of the string to be terminated. Such input terminators must be preceded by the caret (^). For example, if the tilde (~) is used to end a string, the following scanf() shows how it is coded.

```c
char string [200];
scanf("%[^~]", string);
```

Then, if the input for string consists of embedded spaces, no matter what, they will all be accepted by scanf();

and reading will stop when a tilde (~) is entered. This is illustrated in the following program and its output.

```c
#include <stdio.h>
int main( )
{
  char string [80];
  printf("Enter a string, terminate with a tilde\
        (~)...");
  scanf("%[^~]", string);
  printf("%s", string);
  return 0;
}
```

Output:

```
Enter a string, terminate with a tilde (~) ... I
am a string. ~
I am a string.
```

Though the terminating tilde is not itself included as an element of the string read, it stays in the 'read buffer'—the area of memory designated to store the input—and will be picked up by the next call to scanf(), even though it is not required. This is illustrated by the following program and its output. Here, when the second call to scanf() is executed automatically, the tilde (~) character is assigned to the character variables x. The call to putchar() prints the value of x.

```c
#include <stdio.h>
int main( )
{
  char string [80];
  char x;
  printf("Enter a string, terminate with a tilde
        (~)...");
  scanf("%[^~]", string);
  scanf("%c", &x); /* The leftover from the last
        scanf is read here. This scanf() does not
        wait for the user to enter another char.*/
  printf("%s", string);
  putchar(x);
  return 0;
}
```

Output:
```
Enter a string, terminate with a tilde (~) ... I am a
string. ~
I am a string. ~
```

Compile and execute the program. It will be found that the machine executes the second `scanf()` without much fuss. Such dangling characters must be 'absorbed away' by a subsequent call to `scanf()` with %c, or to `getchar()` or they may interfere in unexpected ways with subsequent calls to `scanf()` or `getchar()`.

String input using scanf() with conversion specifier %c

An alternative method for the input of strings is to use `scanf()` with the `%c` conversion which may have a count associated with it. This conversion does not recognize the new-line character as special. The count specifies the number of characters to be read in. Unlike the `%s` and `%[ ]` (scanset) conversions, the `%c` conversion does not automatically generate the string terminating NUL and strange effects will be noted if the wrong number of characters is supplied. The following program demonstrates its use.

```
int main()
{
  char str[10];
  int i;
  while(1)
  {
    printf("Enter a string of 9 characters:");
    scanf("%10c",str);
    str[9]='\0';              /* Make it a string */
    printf("String was :%s\n",str);
    if(str[0] == 'Z') break;
  }
  return 0;
}
```

The output of the sample runs is given below.

    (a) Enter a string of 9 characters: 123456789
         String was : 123456789

    (b) Enter a string of 9 characters: abcdefghi
         String was : abcdefghi

    (c) Enter a string of 9 characters: abcdefghijklmnopqr
         String was :abcdefghi

    (d) Enter a string of 9 characters: 123456789
         String was :klmnopqr

    (e) Enter a string of 9 characters: ttttttttt
         String was :23456789

There are some rather odd things going on here. The first point to note is that, contrary to the prompt, 10 characters are being converted. This is done so that the new-line character at the end of the input line is also read in; otherwise it would be left in the input buffer to be read in as one of the input characters the next time round. The effect of providing too many input characters is that 'unconsumed' input characters (including new-line characters) are left in the input buffer. These will be 'consumed' by the next call to `scanf()`. If too few input characters are provided, `scanf()` hangs (or blocks) until it gets enough input characters. Both types of behavior can be seen in the above example.

The complexities in using the `scanf()` function suggest that it is not really suitable for a reliable, general-purpose string input.

Using gets()

The best approach to string input is to use a library function called `gets()`. This takes the start address of an area of memory suitable to hold the input as a single parameter. The complete input line is read in and stored in the memory area as a null-terminated string. Its use is shown in the program below.

```
int main()
{
  char str[150];
  printf("Enter a string");
  gets(str);
  printf("The string was :%s\n",str);
  return 0;
}
```
Sample run:

    (a) Enter a string   manas
         The string was :manas

    (b) Enter a string   manas ghosh
         The string was :manas ghosh

`gets()` can be implemented using `getchar()` or `scanf()` with %c conversion specifier as follows:

```
#include <stdio.h>
int main()
{
  char s[80], ch;
```

```
int i;
printf("\n Enter the text:");
for(i=0; i<80 ;i++)
{
  ch=getchar();
  if(ch=='\n')
  break;
  s[i]=ch;
}
s[i]='\0';
printf("\n Entered text is:");
puts(s);
return 0;
}
```

Be careful not to input more characters than can be stored in the string variable used because C does not check array bounds. gets() and puts() functions can be nested. The following statements can be written in C.

```
printf("%s", gets(s));
puts(gets(s));
```

sscanf()

There are a variety of library functions for handling input data. The most useful include sscanf() and the function atoi(). The function sscanf() applies scanf() type conversions to data held in a program buffer as a single string but not to read data from standard input. The atoi() function converts a character string from external decimal form to internal binary form.

The use of sscanf() in conjunction with gets() is illustrated by the following program. The purpose of the program is to read in an integer. Unlike simple uses of scanf(), input errors are detected and the prompt repeated until a valid integer is entered.

```
#include <stdio.h>
int main()
{
  int error;
  char inbuf[256];
  int i;
  char c;
  while(1)
  {
    error = i = 0;
```

```
    printf("Enter an integer");
    gets(inbuf);           /* get complete input line */
    while(inbuf[i] == ' ')
    i++;                   /* skip spaces */
    if(inbuf[i] == '-' || inbuf[i] == '+')
    i++;
    while((c = inbuf[i++])!='\0')
                           /* while string end with NUL */
    {
      if(c>'9' || c<'0')   /* non-digit ? */
      {
        printf("Non-Numeric Character %c\n",c);
        error = 1;
        break;
      }
    }
    if(!error)             /* was everything OK ? */
    {
      int num;             /* local variable */
      sscanf(inbuf,"%d",&num);   /* conversion */
      printf("Number was %d\n",num);
      break;
    }
  }
  return 0;
}
```

Sample outputs are shown below:

(a) Enter an integer a123
    Non-Numeric Character a
(b) Enter an integer 123a
    Non-Numeric Character a
(c) Enter an integer 1234.56
    Non-Numeric Character .
(d) Enter an integer   1234
    Number was 1234
(e) Enter an integer   +43
    Number was 43

There are some interesting points about this program. The main processing loop first skips any leading spaces pointing to the first non-blank character in the input text. An initial sign is also skipped. After the optional initial sign, all input characters must be digits until the input string terminating NUL is encountered. If anything other than a digit, including trailing blanks, is encountered, the loop is broken and an error indicator is set. The condition

```
c = inbuf[i++]
```

associated with the loop that checks for digits is a typical piece of C code that does several things in one go. The value of the expression `inbuf[i++]` is the next character from the input buffer `inbuf`. In the course of shifting of the character, the variable `i` is incremented as a side effect. The character value is assigned to the variable `c` to be used in the test for being a digit on the following line, the value of the assignment expression being, of course, the value assigned. The value of this expression becomes zero and terminates the loop when the character in question is the string terminating NUL.

In practice the code of this program would be incorporated into a user-defined function that might return the value of the entered integer.

The function `sscanf()` is similar to `scanf()` except that it has an extra parameter, which is the address of the start of the memory area that holds the character string to be processed. The library function `atoi()` could have been used instead of `sscanf()` in this example by changing the appropriate line to read.

```
num = atoi(inbuf);
```

The function `atoi()` takes the address of an area of memory as parameter and converts the string stored at that location to an integer using the external decimal to internal binary conversion rules. This may be preferable to `sscanf()` since `atoi()` is a much smaller, simpler, and faster function. `sscanf()` can do all possible conversions whereas `atoi()` can only do single decimal integer conversions. This type of function will be discussed in later sections.

String input and output using fscanf() and fprintf()

`stdin`, `stdout`, and `stderr`: Each C program has three I/O streams.

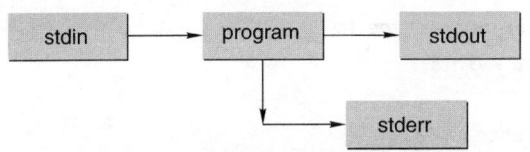

The input stream is called standard-input (`stdin`); the usual output stream is called standard-output (`stdout`); and the side stream of output characters for errors is called standard error (`stderr`). Internally they occupy file descriptors 0, 1, and 2 respectively.

Now one might think that calls to `fprinf()` and `fscanf()` differ significantly from calls to `printf()` and `scanf()`. `fprintf()` sends formatted output to a stream and `fscanf()` scans and formats input from a stream. See the following example.

```
#include <stdio.h>

int main()
{
    int first, second;
    fprintf(stdout,"Enter two ints in this line:  ");
    fscanf(stdin,"%d %d", &first, &second);
    fprintf(stdout,"Their sum is: %d.\n", first + second);
    return 0;
}
```

There is a third defined stream named `stderr`. This is associated with the standard error file. In some systems such as MS-DOS and Unix, one can redirect the output of the programs to files by using the redirection operator. In DOS, for example, if `fl.exe` is an executable file that writes to the monitor, then it can be redirected to output to a disk file. Output that would normally appear on the monitor can thus be sent to a file. Writing error messages to `stderr` can be done by

```
fprintf(stderr,"Unable  to  open  newfile.dat  for
        writing");
```

This ensures that normal output will be redirected, but error messages will still appear on the screen. Observe the following program.

```
#include <stdlib.h>
#include <stdio.h>
int main()
{
    int i;
    printf("Input an integer:");
    /* read an integer from the standard input stream */
    if(fscanf(stdin,"%d", &i))
    printf("The integer read was: %i\n", i);
    else
    {
        fprintf(stderr,"Error reading an integer from\
            stdin.\n");
```

```
   exit(1);
}
   return 0;
}
```

Points to Note

1. One special case, where the null character is not automatically appended to the array, is when the array size is explicitly specified and the number of initializers completely fills the array size.
2. printf() with the width and precision modifiers in the %s conversion specifier may be used to display a string.
3. The %s format does not require the ampersand before the string name in scanf().
4. If fewer input characters are provided, scanf() hangs until it gets enough input characters.
5. scanf() only recognizes a sequence of characters delimited by white space characters as an external string.
6. While using scanset with scanf(), dangling characters must be 'absorbed away' by a subsequent call to scanf() with %c or to getchar().

6.3.5 Character Manipulation in the String

In working with a string, one important point to be remembered is that it must be terminated with NUL (\0). The following program removes all the blank spaces in the character string.

```
#include <stdio.h>
#include <string.h>
int main()
{
  char a[80],t[80];
  int i,j;
  printf("\n enter the text\n");
  gets(a);
  for(i=0,j=0; a[i]!='\0';++i)
  if(a[i]!= ' ')
  t[j++]=a[i];
  t[j]='\0';
  printf("\n the text without blank spaces\n");
  puts(t);
  return 0;
}
```

Table 6.1 lists the character-handling functions of the header file. Notice that except for the toupper() and tolower() functions, all these functions return values indicating true or false. It may be recalled that in C, true is any non-zero number and false is zero. The character is seemingly typed as an integer in these functions. This is because the character functions are really looking at the ASCII values of the characters, which are integers.

Table 6.1 Character functions in <ctype.h> where c is the character argument

Function	Description
ialnum(c)	Returns a non-zero if c is alphabetic or numeric
isalpha(c)	Returns a non-zero if c is alphabetic
scntrl(c)	Returns a non-zero if c is a control character
isdigit(c)	Returns a non-zero if c is a digit, 0 – 9
isgraph(c)	Returns a non-zero if c is a non-blank but printing character
islower(c)	Returns a non-zero if c is a lowercase alphabetic character, i.e., a – z
isprint(c)	Returns a non-zero if c is printable, non-blanks and white space included
ispunct(c)	Returns a non-zero if c is a printable character, but not alpha, numeric, or blank
isspace(c)	Returns a non-zero for blanks and these escape sequences: '\f', '\n', '\r', '\t', and '\v'
isupper(c)	Returns a non-zero if c is a capital letter, i.e., A – Z
isxdigit(c)	Returns a non-zero if c is a hexadecimal character: 0 – 9, a – f, or A – F
tolower(c)	Returns the lowercase version if c is a capital letter; otherwise returns c
toupper(c)	Returns the capital letter version if c is a lowercase character; otherwise returns c

To see the actual effect of some of these character manipulation functions write and run the following program on the computer. This program counts the number of words in a string.

```
#include <stdio.h>
#include <ctype.h>
int main()
{
  char s[30];
  int i=0,count=0;
  printf("\n Enter the string\n");
  scanf("%[^\n]",s);
  while(s[i]!='\0')
```

```
{
  while(isspace(s[i]))
  i++;
  if(s[i]!='\0')
  {
    ++count;
    while(!isspace(s[i]) && s[i] != '\0')
    i++;
  }
}
printf("\n NO. of words in the string is %d:", count);
return 0;
}
```

Here is a short program which illustrates the effect of the `tolower()` and `toupper()` functions. Notice that if a character is not lowercase, the `toupper()` function does not change the character; the effect is similar if a character is not a capital letter. The following program converts a given text into a capital letter using `toupper()` function.

```
#include <stdio.h>
#include <string.h>
int main()
{
  char a[30];
  int i=0;
  printf("\n Enter the string\n");
  gets(a);
  while(a[i]!='\0')
  {
    a[i]=toupper(a[i]);
    i++;
  }
  a[i]='\0';
  puts(a);
  return 0;
}
```

It should be remembered that there is a difference between characters and integers. If the character `'1'` is treated as an integer, perhaps by writing

```
int i = '1';
```

it will probably not get the value `1` in `i`; it will produce the value of the character `'1'` in the machine's character set. In ASCII, it is 49. When the numeric value of a digit character has to be found (or to put it in another way, to get the digit character with a particular value) it is useful to remember that in any character set used by C, the values for the digit characters, whatever they are, are contiguous.

In other words, no matter what values `'0'` and `'1'` have, `'1'` - `'0'` will be `1` (and, obviously, `'0'` - `'0'` will be 0). So, for a variable `c` holding some digit character, the expression

```
c - '0'
```

gives its value. Similarly, for an integer value i, i + '0' gives us the corresponding digit character, as long as `0 <= i <= 9`.

Just as the character `'1'` is not the integer 1, the string `'123'` is not the integer 123. When a string of digits is available, it can be converted to the corresponding integer by calling the standard function `atoi`.

```
char string[] ="123";
int i = atoi(string);
int j = atoi("456");
```

6.3.6 String Manipulation

C has the weakest character string capability of any general-purpose programming language. Strictly speaking, there are no character strings in C, just arrays of single characters that are really small integers. If `s1` and `s2` are such 'strings' a program cannot

- assign one to the other: `s1 = s2;`
- compare them for collating sequence: `s1 < s2`
- concatenate them to form a single longer string: `s1 + s2`
- return a string as the result of a function

A set of standard C library functions that are contained in `<string.h>` provides limited support for the first three. By convention, the end of a string is delimited by the non-printable null character (0 value), but there is no indication of the amount of memory allocated. Consequently, both user code and standard library functions can overwrite memory outside the space allocated for the array of characters.

The string header, `string.h`, provides many functions useful for manipulating strings or character arrays. Some of these are mentioned in Table 6.2.

Counting number of characters of a string

The first of these, `strlen()`, is particularly straightforward. Its single parameter is the address of the start of the string and its value is the number of characters in the string excluding the terminating NUL.

To demonstrate the use of `strlen()`, here is a simple program that reads in a string and prints it out reversed, a useful thing to do. The repeated operation of this program

Table 6.2 String manipulation functions available in `string.h`

Function	Description
`strcpy(s1,s2)`	Copies `s2` into `s1`
`strcat(s1,s2)`	Concatenates `s2` to `s1`. That is, it appends the string contained by `s2` to the end of the string pointed to by `s1`. The terminating null character of `s1` is overwritten. Copying stops once the terminating null character of `s2` is copied.
`strncat(s1,s2,n)`	Appends the string pointed to by `s2` to the end of the string pointed to by `s1` up to n characters long. The terminating null character of `s1` is overwritten. Copying stops once n characters are copied or the terminating null character of `s2` is copied. A terminating null character is always appended to `s1`.
`strlen(s1)`	Returns the length of `s1`. That is, it returns the number of characters in the string without the terminating null character.
`strcmp(s1,s2)`	Returns 0 if `s1` and `s2` are the same Returns less than 0 if `s1<s2` Returns greater than 0 if `s1>s2`
`strchr(s1,ch)`	Returns pointer to first occurrence ch in `s1`
`strstr(s1,s2)`	Returns pointer to first occurrence `s2` in `s1`

is terminated by the user by entering a string of length zero, i.e., by hitting the <**Return**> key immediately after the program prompt.

```c
#include <stdio.h>
#include <string.h>
int main()
{
  char s[100];
  int   len;    /* holds length of string */
  while(1)
  {
    printf("Enter a string");
    gets(s);
    len = strlen(s);   /* find length */
    if(len == 0) break; /* termination condition */
    while(len > 0)
    {
      len--;
      printf("%c",s[len]);
    }
    printf("\n");
  }
  return 0;
}
```

The program operates by printing the characters one by one, starting with the last non-NUL character of the string. Notice that len will have been decremented before the output of the character. This is correct since the length returned by strlen() is the length excluding the NUL but the actual characters are aggregate members, 0, ..., length–1. The outputs of this program for different sample runs are

(a) Enter a string 1234

    4321

(b) Enter a string   manas

    sanam

(c) Enter a string abc def ghi

    ihg fed cba

Look at the following program that reads a line of text, stores it in a string, and prints its length (excluding the new line at the end).

```c
#include <stdio.h>
int main()
{
  int n, c;
  char line[100];
  n = 0;
  while((c=getchar()) != '\n')
  {
    if(n < 100)
    line[n] = c;
    n++;
  }
  line[n]='\0';
  printf("length = %d\n", n);
  return 0;
}
```

Lastly, here is another version of strlen().

```c
int mystrlen(char str[])
{
  int i;
    for(i = 0; str[i] != '\0'; i++);
    return i;
}
```

In this case, all one has to do is find the \0 that terminates the string. It turns out that the three control expressions of the for loop do all the work; there is nothing left to do in the body. Therefore, an empty pair of braces {} are used as the loop body. Equivalently, a null statement could be used, which is simply a semicolon as shown.

```c
for(i = 0; str[i] != '\0'; i++);
```

Empty loop bodies can be a bit startling at first, but they are not unheard of.

Copying a string into another

Since C never lets entire arrays to be assigned, the strcpy() function can be used to copy one string to another. strcpy() copies the string pointed to by the second parameter into the space pointed to by the first parameter. The entire string, including the terminating NUL, is copied and there is no check that the space indicated by the first parameter is big enough. The given code shows the use of the strcpy() function.

```c
#include <string.h>
int main()
{
    char s1[] ="Hello, world!";
    char s2[20];
    strcpy(s2, s1);
    puts (s2);
    return 0;
}
```

The destination string is strcpy's first argument, so that a call to strcpy mimics an assignment expression, with the destination on the left-hand side. Note that string s2 must be allocated sufficient memory so that it can hold the string that would be copied to it. Also, at the top of any source file, the following line must be included

```c
#include <string.h>
```

that contains external declarations for these functions.

Since a string is just an array of characters, all string-handling functions can be written quite simply, using no technique more complicated than the ones that are already known. In fact, it is quite instructive to look at how these functions might be implemented. Here is a version of the code that simulates the same effect as strcpy();.

```c
#include <stdio.h>
int main()
{
    char src[30], dest[30];
    int i = 0;
    printf("\n Enter the source string: ");
    scanf("%[^\n]",src);
    while(src[i] != '\0')
    {
        dest[i] = src[i];
        i++;
    }
    dest[i] = '\0';
    printf("\n Source string is :%s\n", src);
    printf("\n Destination string is : %s\n", dest);
    return 0;
}
```

Its operation is simple. It looks at characters in the src string one at a time, and as long as they are not \0, assigns them, one by one, to the corresponding positions in the dest string. On completion, it terminates the dest string by appending a \0. After exiting the while loop, i is guaranteed to have a value one greater than the subscript of the last character in src. For comparison, here is a way of writing the same code, using a for loop instead of while loop.

```c
for(i = 0; src[i] != '\0'; i++)
    dest[i] = src[i];
dest[i] = '\0';
```

The above statements can be rewritten using the following expression:

```c
for(i=0;(dest[i] = src[i]) != '\0';i++);
```

This is actually the same sort of combined operation.

Comparing strings

Another function, strcmp(), takes the start addresses of two strings as parameters and returns the value zero if the strings are equal. If the strings are unequal, it returns a negative or positive value. The returned value is positive if the first string is greater than the second string and negative if the first string is lesser than the second string. In this context, the relative value of strings refers to their relative values as determined by the host computer character set (or collating sequence).

It is important to realize that two strings cannot be compared by simply comparing their start addresses although this would be syntactically valid. The following program illustrates the comparison of two strings.

```c
#include <stdio.h>
#include <string.h>
int main()
{
    char x[50],y[]="a programming example";
    strcpy(x,"A Programming Example");
    if(strcmp(x,"A Programming Example") == 0)
        printf("Equal \n");
```

```
  else
    printf("Unequal \n");
  if( strcmp(y,x) == 0)
    printf("Equal \n");
  else
    printf("Unequal \n");
  return 0;
}
```

It produces the following output.

```
Equal
Unequal
```

Putting strings together

The arithmetic addition cannot be applied for joining of two or more strings in the manner

```
string1 = string2 + string3; or
string1 = string2 +"RAJA";
```

For this, the standard library function, strcat(), that concatenates strings is needed. It does not concatenate two strings together and give a third, new string. What it really does is append one string at the end of another. Here is an example.

```
#include <stdio.h>
#include <string.h>
int main()
{
  char s[30] ="Hello,";
  char str[] ="world!";

  printf("%s\n", s);
  strcat(s, str);

  printf("%s\n", s);
  return 0;

}
```

The first call to printf prints "Hello,", and the second one prints "Hello,world!", indicating that the contents of str have been appended to the end of s. Notice that s was declared with extra space, to make room for the appended characters.

Note that in arithmetic, char variables can usually be treated like int variables. Arithmetic on characters is quite legal, and often makes sense.

```
c = c + 'A' - 'a';
```

converts a single, lowercase ASCII character stored in c to a capital letter, making use of the fact that corresponding ASCII letters are a fixed distance apart. The rule governing this arithmetic is that all chars are converted to int before the arithmetic is done. Be aware that conversion may involve a sign-extension; if the leftmost bit of a character is 1, the resulting integer might be negative.

Therefore, to convert a text into lowercase, the following program can be used

```
#include <stdio.h>
int main()
{
  char c;
  while((c=getchar()) != '\n')
  if('A'<=c && c<='Z')
  putchar(c+'a'-'A');
      /* equivalent statement in putchar(C+32);*/
  else
    putchar(c);
  return 0;
}
```

Sample run:

```
TIMES OF INDIA
times of india
```

The following program will demonstrate the strncat() library function.

```
#include <string.h>
#include <stdio.h>
int main()
{
  char aString1[80] ="RCC Institute of Information
          Technology" ,
  aString2[80] ="Oxford University Press";

  printf("\n Before the concatenation...\n");
  puts(aString1);
  puts(aString2);

  strncat(aString1, aString2, 6);

   printf("\n After the concatenation...\n");
  puts(aString1);
  puts(aString2);
  return 0;

}
```

Output:

```
Before the copy...
RCC Institute of Information Technology
Oxford University Press
Before the copy...
RCC Institute of Information Technology Oxford
Oxford University Press
```

> **Points to Note**
>
> 1. Since C never lets entire arrays to be assigned, the `strcpy()` function can be used to copy one string to another.
> 2. Strings can be compared by the help of `strcmp()` function.
> 3. The arithmetic addition cannot be applied for joining two or more strings; this can be done by using the standard library function, `strcat()`.

Some sample programs

One interesting thing: This program tries to prove that a string really is an array of characters. Note the explicit placement of the string terminator at the end of the string. Note the `&str[2]`. Remember that `str[2]` is the third character, so `&str[2]` is the address of the third character. Since `str` is the address of the first character, `&str[2]` effectively is `str` but with the first two characters removed. Try replacing `&str[2]` with str+2. Does this work? Lastly, notice the use of the `strcpy` (string copy) function from the `string.h` library.

```
#include <stdio.h>
#include <string.h>
int main()
{
  char str[30];
  str[0]='M';
  str[1]='A';
  str[2]='D';
  str[3]='A';
  str[4]='M';
  str[5]= '\0'; /* terminate string with a null */
  printf("String is %s\n",str);
  printf("Part of string is %s\n",&str[2]);
  strcpy(str,"SIR");
  printf("String is %s\n",str);
```

```
  return(0);
}
```

Sample run:

```
String is MADAM
Part of string is DAM
String is SIR
```

To make sure that what is going on is understood, consider the following table:

Code	Format	Output
`printf("%?", str);`	"%s"	MADAM
`printf("%?", str[1]);`	"%s"	Error
`printf("%?", &str[1]);`	"%s"	ADAM
`printf("%?", &str);`	"%s"	MADAM

Some of the following programs will illustrate the manipulation of strings. The following program toggles the case of every character in the input string.

```
#include <stdio.h>
#include <string.h>
int main()
{
  char istr[128];   /* input buffer */
  char tstr[128];   /* translated string here */
  int i;
  int slen;         /* string length */
  while(1)
  {
    printf("Enter a string");
    gets(istr);
    if((slen=strlen(istr))==0) break;/* terminate */
    strcpy(tstr,istr);            /* make a copy */
    i = 0;
    while(i < slen)          /* translate loop */
    {
      if(tstr[i] >= 'A' && tstr[i] <= 'Z')
                              /* upper case */
        tstr[i] += 'a'-'A';
      else if(tstr[i] >= 'a' && tstr[i] <= 'z')
                              /* lower case */
        tstr[i] += 'A'-'a';
      i++;                    /* to next character */
    }
```

```
  printf("Original string = %s\n",istr);
  printf("Transformed string = %s\n",tstr);
  }
  return 0;
}
```

Output

```
Enter string aBDefgXYZ
Original string = aBDefgXYZ
Transformed string = AbdEFGxyz
Enter string ab   CD    123
Original string = ab   CD    123
Transformed string = AB   cd    123
```

This program can also be written as follows where `'\0'` character is used as a tool.

```
#include <stdio.h>
#include <string.h>
int main()
{
  char istr[128]; /* input buffer */
  char tstr[128]; /* translated string here */
  int i;
                  /* string length */
  while(1)
  {
    printf("Enter a string");
    gets(istr);
    if(strlen(istr)==0) break;  /* terminate */
    strcpy(tstr,istr);          /* make a copy */
    i = 0;
    while(tstr[i]!='\0')        /* translate loop */
    {
      if(tstr[i] >= 'A' && tstr[i] <= 'Z')
                                /* upper case */
        tstr[i] += 'a'-'A';
      else if(tstr[i] >= 'a' && tstr[i] <= 'z')
                                /* lower case */
        tstr[i] += 'A'-'a';
      i++;                      /* to next character */
    }
    printf("Original string = %s\n",istr);
    printf("Transformed string = %s\n",tstr);
  }
  return 0;
}
```

The following program checks whether a string given by the user is a palindrome or not. In this program, the first character `s[0]` and the last character `s[n-1]` are compared. Then the second character `s[1]` and last but one character `s[n-2]` are compared, and so on. This process will be continued up to half the length of the string. If characters are found to be different during any comparison, then the string is not a palindrome. Else it is a palindrome.

```
#include <stdio.h>
#include <string.h>
int main()
{
  int n,i,j,chk=1;
  char s[30];
  printf("\n Enter the string:");
  scanf("%[^\n]",s);
  n=strlen(s)-1;
  for(i=0,j=n;i<n/2;i++,j--)
  if(s[i]!=s[j])
    {chk=0;
    break;}
  if(chk==1)
    printf("String is Palindrome");
  else
    printf("String is not Palindrome");
  return 0;
}
```

Here the variable `chk` is used to check the result of the comparison. Alternatively, the preceding program can be implemented as follows:

```
#include <stdio.h>
#include <string.h>
int main()
{
  int n,i,j;
  char s[30],t[30];
  printf("\n Enter the string:");
  scanf("%[^\n]",s);
  n=strlen(s)-1;
  for(i=0,j=n;j>=0;i++,j--)
  t[i]=s[j];
  t[i]='\0';
  if(strcmp(s,t)==0)
  printf("String is Palindrome");
```

```
else
    printf("String is not Palindrome");
    return 0;
}
```

In the above example, the string given by the user is reversed and is stored in another array. Then using the strcmp() library function, two strings are compared to test whether they are equal or not. If the outcome of strcmp() is 0, then the string entered by the user is a palindrome.

Sample runs:

```
(a)  Enter the string : madam
     String is Palindrome
(b)  Enter the string: india
     String is not Palindrome
```

The following program deletes a word of a sentence. Here the logic used is that each word is extracted from the sentence into the string w. The words are separated by a space except the last word, which is terminated by the NUL character. Each word is compared with the word to be deleted. If there is a match, then that word will not be concatenated at the target string t, else it is.

```
#include <stdio.h>
#include <string.h>
int main(void)
{
    char line[80],wrd[50],t[80]=" ",d[50];
    int i,j;found = 0;
    printf("\n Enter the line of text ....\n");
    gets(line);
    printf("\n Enter the word to be deleted:");
    scanf("%s",d);
    i=j=0;
    while(line[i]!='\0')
    {
      if(line[i]==' '|| line[i]=='.'||line[i]==';');
      {
        wrd[j]='\0';
        j=0;
        if (strcat (wrd,d)! = 0)
        {
            strcat(t,wrd);
            if(line[i]==' ')
                strcat(t, " ");
            else if (line [i]==',')
                strcat(t,",");
                else if (line [i]==';')
                    strcat(t,";");
```

```
        }
        else
                found=1;
      ++1;
      // printf ("\n ====== %s", wrd);
    }
    else
    {
      wrd[j]=line[i];
      ++j;
      ++i;
    }
}
wrd[j]='\0';
if(strcmp(wrd,d)! = 0)
{
    strcat (t,wrd);
    strcat(t," ");
}
    else
      found=1;
    if(found==0)
      printf("\n word not present");
    else
      puts(t);
    return 0;
}
```

Sample run:

```
Enter the sentence: Ram is a good boy
Enter the word to be deleted:good
After deletion the sentence is as follows...
Ram is a boy
```

The following program takes the name of a person as input and prints the first letters of the first name and middle name (if any), and the title as it is. For example, printing Raj Kumar Santoshi as R.K. Santoshi.

```
#include <stdio.h>
#include <string.h>
int main(void)
{
    char line[80],wrd[50];
    int i,j;
    printf("\n Enter the line of text ...\n");
    gets(line);
    i=j=0;
    while(line[i]!='\0')
    {
```

```c
if(line[i]==' ' || line[i]=='.')
{
  wrd[j]='\0';
  j=0;
  ++i;
  printf("%c. ",wrd[0]);
}
else
  wrd[j]=line[i];
  ++j;
  ++i;

}
}
wrd[j]='\0';
printf("%s.",wrd);
return 0;
}
```

The logic as applied in the previous program is used here too. Each word is extracted and the first letter of the word w[0] is printed. If '\0' is encountered, that word must be the title and it is printed as it is.

──────────── **Check Your Progress** ────────────

1. What is the index of the element 'A' in the array below?

```c
char myArray[] = {'m', 'y', 'A', 'r', 'r', 'a', 'y'};
```

Output: 2

2. What will be the output for the following programs?

(a)
```c
#include <stdio.h>
int main()
{
  char s1[]="Oxford";
  char s2[]="University";
  s1=s2;
  printf("%s",s1);
  return 0;
}
```

Output: There is a compilation error that states "it cannot be a modifiable 'lvalue'". Or "Incompatible types in assignment"

(b)
```c
#include <stdio.h>
#include <string.h>
int main()
```

```c
{
  char p[]="string";
  char t;
  int i,j;
  for(i=0,j=strlen(p);i<j;i++)
  {
    t=p[i];
    p[i]=p[j-i];
    p[j-i]=t;
  }
  printf("%s",p);
  return 0;
}
```

Output: No output

(c)
```c
#include <stdio.h>
int main()
{
  char names[5][20]={"pascal","ada","cobol",
    "fortran","perl"};
  int i;
  char *t;
  t=names[3];
  names[3]=names[4];
  names[4]=t;
  for(i=0;i<=4;i++)
  printf("%s",names[i]);
  return 0;
}
```

Output: Compiler error:"Lvalue required"
                    Or
"Incompatible types in assignment"

(d)
```c
#include <stdio.h>
int main()
{
  int i;
  char a[]="\0";
  if(printf("%s\n",a))
    printf("Ok here \n");
  else
    printf("Forget it\n");
  return 0;
}
```

Output: Ok here

(e)
```c
#include <stdio.h>
int main()
{
  char p[ ]="%d\n";
  p[1] = 'c';
  printf(p,65);
```

```
  return 0;
}
```
Output: A

(f)
```c
#include <stdio.h>
#include <string.h>
int main()
{
  char str1[] = {'s','o','m','e'};
  char str2[] = {'s','o','m','e','\0'};
  while(strcmp(str1,str2))
  printf("Strings are not equal\n");
  return 0;
}
```
Output:
```
"Strings are not equal"
"Strings are not equal"
        ...
```

(g)
```c
#include <stdio.h>
#include <ctype.h>
int main()
{
  char p[]="The Matrix Reloaded";
  int i=0;
  while(p[i])
  {
    if( !isupper(p[i]++) )
    ++i;
  }
  printf("%d", i);
  return 0;
}
```
Output: 19

6.4 MULTIDIMENSIONAL ARRAYS

Arrays with more than one dimension are called multidimensional arrays. Although humans cannot easily visualize objects with more than three dimensions, representing multidimensional arrays presents no problem to computers.

6.4.1 Declaration of a Two-dimensional Array

An array of two dimension can be declared as follows:

```
data_type array_name[size1][size2];
```

Here, data_type is the name of some type of data, such as int. Also, size1 and size2 are the sizes of the array's first and second dimensions, respectively.

Here is an example of defining an eight-by-eight array of integers, similar to a chessboard. Remember, because

C arrays are zero-based, the indices on each side of the chessboard array run from zero through seven, rather than one through eight. The effect is the same. However, it is a two-dimensional array of 64 elements which has the following declaration statement.

```
int arr[8][8];
```

6.4.2 Declaration of a Three-dimensional Array

A three-dimensional array, such as a cube, can be declared as follows:

```
data_type array_name[size1][size2][size3]
```

Arrays do not have to be shaped like squares and cubes; each dimension of the array can be given a different size, as follows:

```
int non_cube[2][6][8];
```

Three-dimensional arrays, and higher, are stored in the same basic way as are two-dimensional ones. They are kept in computer memory as a linear sequence of variables, and the last index is always the one that varies fastest (then the next-to-last, and so on).

6.4.3 Initialization of a Multidimensional Array

The number of subscripts determines the *dimensionality* of an array. For example, x[i] refers to an element of a one-dimensional array, x. Similarly, y[i][j] refers to an element of a two-dimensional array, y, and so on.

Multidimensional arrays are initialized in the same way as are single-dimension arrays. For example,

(a)
```c
int a[6][2] = {
                1,1,
                2,4,
                3,9,
                4,16,
                5,25,
                6,36
              };
```

(b)
```c
int b[3][5] = {{1,2,3,4,5},
               {6,7,8,9,10},
               {11,12,13,14,15}
              };
```

The same effect is achieved by

```c
int b[3][5]={1,2,3,4,5,6,7,8,9,10,11,12,13,14,15};
```

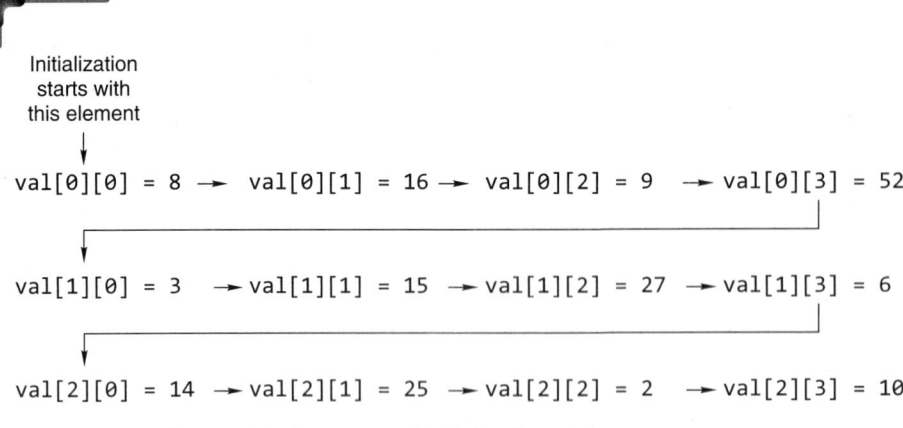

Initialization
starts with
this element

val[0][0] = 8 → val[0][1] = 16 → val[0][2] = 9 → val[0][3] = 52

val[1][0] = 3 → val[1][1] = 15 → val[1][2] = 27 → val[1][3] = 6

val[2][0] = 14 → val[2][1] = 25 → val[2][2] = 2 → val[2][3] = 10

Figure 6.3 Storage and initialization of the `val[]` array

Although the commas in the initialization braces are always required, the inner braces can be omitted. Thus, the initialization for an array `val` may be written as

```
int val[3][4] = {8, 16, 9, 52,
                 3, 15, 27, 6,
                 14, 25, 2, 10};
```

The separation of initial values into rows in the declaration statement is not necessary since the compiler assigns values beginning with the `[0][0]` element and proceeds row by row to fill in the remaining values. Thus, the initialization

```
int val [3][4] = {8, 16, 9, 52, 3, 15, 27, 6, 14,
                  25, 2, 10};
```

is equally valid but does not clearly illustrate to another programmer where one row ends and another begins.

As illustrated in Fig. 6.3, the initialization of a two-dimensional array is done in row order. First the elements in the first row are initialized, then the elements in the second row are initialized, and so on, until the initializations are completed. This row ordering is also the same as the ordering used to store two-dimensional arrays. That is, array element `[0][0]` is stored first, followed by element `[0][1]`, followed by element `[0][2]`, and so on. Following the first row's elements is the second row's elements, and so on for all the rows in the array.

Using the following rules, braces can be omitted when initializing the members of multidimensional arrays.

- When initializing arrays, the outermost pair of braces cannot be omitted.
- If the initializer list includes all the initializers for the object being initialized, the inner braces can be omitted.

Consider the following example.

```
int x[4][2] = {
               { 1, 2 },
               { 3, 4 },
               { 5, 6 }
              };
```

In this example, 1 and 2 initialize the first row of the array `x`, and the following two lines initialize the second and third rows, respectively. The initialization ends before the fourth row is initialized, so the members of the fourth row default to 0 or garbage depending on the compiler. Here is the result.

```
x[0][0] = 1;
x[0][1] = 2;
x[1][0] = 3;
x[1][1] = 4;
x[2][0] = 5;
x[2][1] = 6;
x[3][0] = 0;
x[3][1] = 0;
```

The following declaration achieves the same result.

```
int x[4][2] = { 1, 2, 3, 4, 5, 6 };
```

Here, the compiler fills the array row by row with the available initial values. The compiler places 1 and 2 in the first row (x[0]), 3 and 4 in the second row (x[1]), and 5 and 6 in the third row (x[2]). The remaining members of the array are initialized to zero or garbage value.

6.4.4 Unsized Array Initializations

If unsized arrays are declared, the C compiler automatically creates an array big enough to hold all the initializers. An array declared with a blank as its size is called an unsized array. The following are examples of declarations with initialization.

(a) `char e1[] ="read error\n";`

(b) `char e2[] ="write error\n";`

(c) `int sgrs[][2] =`
```
    {
        1,1,
        2,4,
        3,9,
        4,16,
    };
```

6.4.5 Accessing Multidimensional Arrays

The elements of a multidimensional array are stored contiguously in a block of computer memory. In scanning this block from its start to its end, the order of storage is such that the last subscript of the array varies most rapidly whereas the first varies least rapidly. For instance, the elements of the two-dimensional array `x[2][2]` are stored in the order: `x[0][0]`, `x[0][1]`, `x[1][0]`, `x[1][1]`. Take a look at the following code.

```c
#include <stdio.h>
int main()
{
    int i,j;
    int a[3][2] = {{4,7},{1,0},{6,2}};
    for(i = 0; i < 3; i++)
    {
        for(j = 0; j < 2; j++)
        {
            printf("%d", a[i][j]);
        }
        printf("\n");
    }
    return 0;
}
```

Since computer memory is essentially one-dimensional with memory locations running straight from 0 up through the highest, a multidimensional array cannot be stored in memory as a grid. Instead, the array is dissected and stored in rows. Consider the following two-dimensional array.

Row 0	1	2	3
Row 1	4	5	6
Row 2	7	8	9

Note that the numbers inside the boxes are not the actual indices of the array, which is two-dimensional and has two indices for each element, but only arbitrary placeholders to enable the reader to see which elements correspond in the following example. The row numbers correspond to the first index of the array, so they are numbered from 0 to 2 rather than 1 to 3.

In the computer, the above array actually 'looks' like this.

1	2	3	4	5	6	7	8	9
row 0			row 1			row 2		

Another way of saying that arrays are stored by rows and that the second index varies fastest, a two-dimensional array is always thought of as follows:

```
array_name[row][column]
```

Every row stored will contain elements of many columns. The column index runs from 0 to `[size - 1]` inside every row in the one-dimensional representation where `size` is the number of columns in the array. So the column index changes faster than the row index as the one-dimensional representation of the array inside the computer is traversed.

To illustrate the use of multidimensional arrays, the elements of the array `a2` might be filled in or initialized using this piece of code.

```c
int i, j;
for(i = 0; i < 5; i = i + 1)
{
    for(j = 0; j < 7; j = j + 1)
    a2[i][j] = 10 * i + j;
}
```

This pair of nested loops sets `a[1][2]` to `12`, `a[4][1]` to `41`, etc. Since the first dimension of `a2` is `5`, the first subscripting index variable, `i`, runs from `0` to `4`. Similarly, the second subscript varies from `0` to `6`.

The array `a2` could be printed out in a two-dimensional way suggesting its structure, with a similar pair of nested loops.

```c
for(i = 0; i < 5; i = i + 1)
```

```
{
    for(j = 0; j < 7; j = j + 1)
    printf("%d\t", a2[i][j]);
    printf("\n");
}
```

The character `\t` in the `printf()` string is the tab character, which is itself an escape sequence or control code. To understand this more clearly, the 'row' and 'column' subscripts could be made explicit by printing them too. So, the following code could be used.

```
for(j = 0; j < 7; j = j + 1)
    printf("\t%d:", j);
printf("\n");
for(i = 0; i < 5; i = i + 1)
{
    printf("%d:", i);
    for(j = 0; j < 7; j = j + 1)
    printf("\t%d", a2[i][j]);
    printf("\n");
}
```

This last fragment would print

```
      0:   1:   2:   3:   4:   5:   6:
0:    0    1    2    3    4    5    6
1:    10   11   12   13   14   15   16
2:    20   21   22   23   24   25   26
3:    30   31   32   33   34   35   36
4:    40   41   42   43   44   45   46
```

Finally, there is no reason to loop over the rows first and the columns second; depending on what the user wanted to do, the two loops could be interchanged, like this.

```
for(j = 0; j < 7; j = j + 1)
{
    for(i = 0; i < 5; i = i + 1)
    printf("%d\t", a2[i][j]);
    printf("\n");
}
```

Notice that `i` is still the first subscript and it still runs from `0` to `4`, and `j` is still the second subscript and it still runs from `0` to `6`.

It will be found that the program still runs without any problems. This is because a multidimensional array is implemented as a big, single-dimensional array. When an element of the array is referenced, the two indices used are modified into a single index for the array.

6.4.6 Working with Two-dimensional Arrays

The most important application of the two-dimensional array is with a matrix. A matrix is defined as an ordered rectangular array of numbers. They can be used to represent systems of linear equations.

Transpose of a matrix

The transpose of a matrix is found by exchanging rows for columns, i.e., for

$$\text{Matrix } A = (a_{ij})$$

the transpose of A is $A^T = (a_{ji})$, where i is the row number and j is the column number.

For example, the transpose of a matrix A would be given by

$$A = \begin{pmatrix} 5 & 2 & 3 \\ 4 & 7 & 1 \\ 8 & 9 & 9 \end{pmatrix} \quad A^T = \begin{pmatrix} 5 & 4 & 8 \\ 2 & 7 & 9 \\ 3 & 1 & 9 \end{pmatrix}$$

In the case of a square matrix ($m = n$), the transpose can be used to check if a matrix is symmetric. For a symmetric matrix, $A = A^T$.

$$A = \begin{pmatrix} 1 & 2 \\ 2 & 3 \end{pmatrix} \quad A^T = \begin{pmatrix} 1 & 2 \\ 2 & 3 \end{pmatrix} = A$$

The following program finds the transpose of a matrix.

```
#include <stdio.h>
int main()
{
    int row,col;
    int i, j, value;
    int mat[10][10], transp[10][10];
    printf("\n Input the number of rows:");
    scanf("%d", &row);
    printf("Input number of cols:");
    scanf("%d", &col);
    for(i = 0 ; i < row; i++)
    {
        for(j = 0 ; j < col; j++)
        {
            printf("Input Value for : %d: %d:",
                i+1,j+1);
            scanf("%d", &value);
            mat[i][j] = value;
        }
}
```

```
}
printf("\n Entered Matrix is as follows:\n");
for(i = 0; i < row; i++)
{
  for(j = 0; j < col; j++)
  {
    printf("%d", mat[i][j]);
  }
  printf("\n");
}
for(i = 0; i< row; i++)
{
  for(j = 0; j < col; j++)
  {
    transp[i][j]= mat[j][i];
  }
}
printf("\n Transpose of the matrix is as\
      follows:\n");
for(i = 0; i < col; i++)
{
  for(j = 0; j < row; j++)
  {
    printf("%d", transp[i][j]);
  }
  printf("\n");
}
return 0;
}
```

In the above example, it should be remembered that the number of both rows and columns must be less than or equal to 10.

Matrix addition and subtraction

Two matrices A and B can be added or subtracted if and only if their dimensions are the same, i.e., both matrices have an identical amount of rows and columns. Take the matrices,

$$A = \begin{pmatrix} 1 & 2 & 3 \\ 1 & 0 & 2 \end{pmatrix} \qquad B = \begin{pmatrix} 2 & 1 & 2 \\ 1 & 0 & 3 \end{pmatrix}$$

Addition If A and B above are matrices of the same type, then their sum is found by adding the corresponding elements $a_{ij} + b_{ij}$.

Here is an example of adding A and B together.

$$A + B = \begin{pmatrix} 1 & 2 & 3 \\ 1 & 0 & 2 \end{pmatrix} + \begin{pmatrix} 2 & 1 & 2 \\ 1 & 0 & 3 \end{pmatrix} = \begin{pmatrix} 3 & 3 & 5 \\ 2 & 0 & 5 \end{pmatrix}$$

Subtraction If A and B are matrices of the same type, then their difference is found by subtracting the corresponding elements $a_{ij} - b_{ij}$.

Here is an example of subtracting matrices.

$$A - B = \begin{pmatrix} 1 & 2 & 3 \\ 1 & 0 & 2 \end{pmatrix} - \begin{pmatrix} 2 & 1 & 2 \\ 1 & 0 & 3 \end{pmatrix} = \begin{pmatrix} -1 & 1 & 1 \\ 0 & 0 & -1 \end{pmatrix}$$

The following program pertains to matrix addition.

```
#include <stdio.h>
#include <stdlib.h>
#define row 10
#define col 10
int main()
{
  int row1, col1;
  int row2, col2;
  int i,j;
  float mat1[row][col];
  float mat2[row][col];
  float mat_res[row][col];
  printf("\n Input the row of the matrix->1:");
  scanf("%d", &row1);
  printf("\n Input the col of the matrix->1:");
  scanf("%d", &col1);
  printf("\n Input data for matrix-> 1\n");
  for(i = 0; i< row1; i++)
  {
    for(j = 0; j<col1; j++)
    {
      printf("Input Value for: %d: %d:", i+1, j+1);
      scanf("%f", &mat1[i][j]);
    }
  }
  printf("\n Input the row of the matrix ->2:");
  scanf("%d", &row2);
  printf("\n Input the col of the matrix->2:");
  scanf("%d", &col2);
  printf("\n Input data for matrix-> 2\n");
  for(i = 0; i< row2; i++)
```

```
      for(j = 0; j<col2; j++)
      {
        printf("Input Value for: %d: %d:", i+1, j+1);
        scanf("%f", &mat2[i][j]);
      }
    printf("\n Entered Matrix First is:\n");
    for(i = 0; i < row1; i++)
    {
      for(j = 0; j < col1; j++)

        printf("%f", mat1[i][j]);

      }
      printf("\n");

    printf("\n Entered Matrix Two is:\n");
    for(i = 0; i < row2; i++)
    {
      for(j = 0; j < col2; j++)

        printf("%f", mat2[i][j]);

      printf("\n");
    }
    if((row1 == row2) && (col1 == col2))
    {
      printf("\n Addition is possible and");
      printf("the result is: \n");
      for(i = 0; i<row1; i++)
      for(j = 0; j<col1; j++)
      mat_res[i][j] = mat1[i][j]+mat2[i][j];
      for( i = 0; i < row1; i++)
      {
        for( j = 0; j < col1; j++)

          printf("%f", mat_res[i][j]);

        printf("\n");
      }
    }
    else
    printf("\n Addition is not possible");
    return 0;
}
```

Matrix subtraction can be implemented in a similar way.

Matrix multiplication

When the number of columns of the first matrix is the same as the number of rows in the second matrix, then matrix multiplication can be performed.

Here is an example of matrix multiplication for two 2×2 matrices.

$$\begin{pmatrix} a & b \\ c & d \end{pmatrix}\begin{pmatrix} e & f \\ g & h \end{pmatrix} = \begin{pmatrix} (ae+bg) & (af+bh) \\ (ce+dg) & (ef+dh) \end{pmatrix}$$

Here is an example of matrix multiplication for a 3×3 matrix.

$$\begin{pmatrix} a & b & c \\ d & e & f \\ g & h & i \end{pmatrix}\begin{pmatrix} j & k & l \\ m & n & o \\ p & q & r \end{pmatrix}$$
$$= \begin{pmatrix} (aj+bm+cp) & (ak+bn+cq) & (al+bo+cr) \\ (dj+em+fp) & (dk+en+fq) & (dl+eo+fr) \\ (gj+hm+ip) & (gk+hn+iq) & (gl+ho+ir) \end{pmatrix}$$

Now let us look at the $n \times n$ matrix case, where A has dimensions $m \times n$ and B has dimensions $n \times p$. The product of A and B is the matrix C, which has dimensions $m \times p$. The ijth element of matrix C is found by multiplying the entries of the ith row of A with the corresponding entries in the jth column of B and summing the n terms. The elements of matrix C are

$$c_{11} = a_{11}b_{11} + a_{12}b_{21} + \ldots + a_{1n}b_{n1}$$
$$c_{12} = a_{11}b_{12} + a_{12}b_{22} + \ldots + a_{1n}b_{n2}$$
$$c_{mp} = a_{m1}b_{1p} + a_{m2}b_{2p} + \ldots + a_{mn}b_{np}$$

Note $A \times B$ is not the same as $B \times A$.

```
#include <stdio.h>
#include <stdlib.h>
#define row 10
#define col 10
int main()
{
  int row1, col1;
  int row2, col2;
  int i,j,k;
  float mat1[row][col];
  float mat2[row][col];
  float mat_res[row][col];
  printf("\n Input the row of the matrix->1:");
  scanf("%d", &row1);
  printf("\n Input the col of the matrix->1:");
  scanf("%d", &col1);
  printf("\n Input data for matrix-> 1\n");
  for(i = 0 ; i< row1; i++)
```

```
    for(j = 0 ; j<col1; j++)
    {
      printf("Input Value for: %d: %d:", i+1, j+1);
      scanf("%f", &mat1[i][j]);
    }

printf("\n Input the row  of the matrix->2:");
scanf("%d", &row2);
printf("\n Input the col of the matrix ->2:");
scanf("%d", &col2);
printf("\n Input data for matrix-> 2\n");
for(i = 0 ; i< row2; i++)

    for(j = 0 ; j<col2; j++)
    {
      printf("Input Value for: %d: %d:", i+1, j+1);
      scanf("%f", &mat2[i][j]);
    }

printf("\n Entered Matrix First is:\n");
for(i = 0; i < row1; i++)
{
  for(j = 0; j < col1; j++)

    printf("%f", mat1[i][j]);

  printf("\n");
}
printf("\n Entered Matrix Two is: \n");
for(i = 0; i < row2; i++)
{
  for(j = 0; j < col2; j++)

    printf("%f", mat2[i][j]);

  printf("\n");
}
if(col1 == row2)
{
  printf("\n Multiplication is possible and the
          Result is as follows\n");
  for(i=0; i<row1; i++)
  for(j=0; j<col2; j++)
```

```
  {
    mat_res[i][j] = 0;
    for(k = 0; k < col1; k++)

      mat_res[i][j] += mat1[i][k] * mat2[k][j];

  }
  for(i = 0; i < row1; i++)
  {
    for(j = 0; j < col2; j++)

      printf("%f", mat_res[i][j]);

    printf("\n");
  }
}
else
printf("\n Multiplication is not possible");
return 0;
}
```

Finding norm of a matrix

The norm of a matrix is defined as the square root of the sum of the squares of the elements of a matrix.

```
#include <stdio.h>
#define row 10
#define col 10
int main()
{
  float mat[row][col], s;
  int i,j,r,c;
  printf("\n Input number of rows:");
  scanf("%d", &r);
  printf("\n Input number of cols:");
  scanf("%d", &c);
  for(i = 0 ; i< r; i++)

    for(j = 0 ;j<c; j++)
    {
      printf("\nInput Value for: %d: %d:", i+1, j+1);
      scanf("%f", &mat[i][j]);
```

```
}

printf("\n Entered 2D array is as follows:\n");
for(i = 0; i < r; i++)
{
  for(j = 0; j < c; j++)

    printf("%f", mat[i][j]);

  printf("\n");
}
s = 0.0;
for(i = 0; i < r; i++)
{
  for(j = 0; j < c; j++)

    s += mat[i][j] * mat[i][j];

}
printf("\n Norm of above matrix is: %f", sqrt(s));
return 0;
}
```

Points to Note

- Multi-dimensional arrays are kept in computer memory as a linear sequence of variables.
- The elements of a multi-dimensional array are stored contiguously in a block of computer memory.
- The number of subscripts determines the *dimensionality* of an array.
- The separation of initial values into rows in the declaration statement is not necessary.
- If unsized arrays are declared, the C compiler automatically creates an array big enough to hold all the initializers.

6.5 ARRAYS OF STRINGS: TWO-DIMENSIONAL CHARACTER ARRAY

A two-dimensional array of strings can be declared as follows:

```
<data_type> <string_array_name>[<row_size>]
        [<columns_size>];
```

Consider the following example on declaration of a two-dimensional array of strings.

```
char s[5][30];
```

6.5.1 Initialization

Two-dimensional string arrays can be initialized as shown

```
char s[5][10] ={"Cow","Goat","Ram","Dog","Cat"};
```

which is equivalent to

s[0]	C	o	w	\0					
S[1]	G	o	a	t	\0				
S[2]	R	a	m	\0					
S[3]	D	o	g	\0					
S[4]	C	a	t	\0					

Here every row is a string. That is, s[i] is a string. Note that the following declarations are invalid.

```
char s[5][] ={"Cow","Goat","Ram","Dog","Cat"};

char s[][] ={"Cow","Goat","Ram","Dog","Cat"};
```

6.5.2 Manipulating String Arrays

The following program demonstrates how an individual string of an array of strings can be used to take input from the user. As mentioned before, each row (i.e., s[i], if 's' is the array of strings) of an array of strings is a string.

```
#include <stdio.h>
int main()
{
  int i;
  char s[10][30];
  for(i=0;i<10;i++)
    scanf("%s",s[i]);
    for(i=0;i<10;i++)
      printf("\n%s",s[i]);
  return 0;
}
```

The following codes show how arrays of strings may be manipulated. This program checks whether a number is odd or even without using any control statement.

```
#include <stdio.h>

int main()
{
  char s[2][5]={"EVEN","ODD"};
```

```
int n;
printf("\n Enter the number:");
scanf("%d",&n);
printf("\n The number is %s",s[n%2]);
return 0;
}
```

The following program accepts one line of text and prints the words in reverse order. For example, if input is 'Today is Tuesday', then output will be 'Tuesday is Today'.

```
#include <stdio.h>
#include <string.h>
int main()
{
  char st[25][30],s[80],w[20],d[20];
  int i,j, k=0;
  printf("\n Enter the Sentence :");
  gets(s);
  i=0;
  while(s[i]!='\0')
  {
    j=0;
    while(1)
    {
     if(s[i]==' '||s[i]=='\0')
     break;
     w[j++]=s[i++];
    }
    w[j]='\0';
    strcpy(st[k],w);
    k++;
    if(s[i]!='\0')
    i++;
```

```
}
for(k--;k>=0;k--)
printf("%s ",st[k]);
return 0;
}
```

The following program sorts an array of strings using bubble sort. Note here that strcmp() is used to compare the string. strcpy() is used for interchanging the strings.

```
#include <stdio.h>
#include <string.h>
int main()
{
  char s[10][30], t[30];
  int i,j,n;
  printf("\n How many strings:");
  scanf("%d",&n);
  printf("\n Enter the strings:\n");
  for(i=0;i<n;i++)
  scanf("%s",s[i]);
  printf("\n **Starting comparing and sorting**");
  for(i=0;i<n-1;i++)
    for(j=i+1; j<n; ++j)
      if(strcmp(s[i],s[j])>0)
      {
        strcpy(t,s[i]);
        strcpy(s[i],s[j]);
        strcpy(s[j],t);
      }
  printf("\n **Sorted array**\n");
  for(i=0;i<n;i++)
    printf("\n%s",s[i]);
  return 0;
}
```

SUMMARY

An array is a collection of individual data elements that is *ordered, fixed in size,* and of *homogeneous* data type. When defining an array in a program, three things need to be specified: what *kind of data* it can hold, *how many values* it can hold, and a *name* for it.

A one-dimensional array declaration is a *type* followed by an *array name* with a bracketed constant integral expression. The value of the expression, which must be positive, is the *size* of the array. It specifies the number of elements in the array.

The array subscripts (index) can range from 0 to (*size*–1). The lower bound of the array subscripts is 0 and the upper bound is (*size* –1). An element can be referenced by the array name and index. At the time of declaration, the size of the array has to be given; it is mandatory. Otherwise the compiler generates an error. No variables are allowed as the size of the array.

C never checks whether the array index is valid—either at compile time or when the program is running. Array elements are initialized using the assignment operator, braces, and commas. Single operations, which involve entire arrays, are not permitted in C.

Strings are an array of characters terminated by '\0'. Character arrays or strings allow a shorthand initialization. Although C does not have a string data type, it allows string constants. There are a set of input and output functions in C suitable for handling strings. The manipulation of strings can be carried out with the help of several functions provided in the `string.h` file. Arrays can also be formed with strings. These are categorized as two-dimensional arrays.

Arrays with more than one dimension are called multidimensional arrays. An array of two dimensions can be declared by specifying the data type, array name, and the size of the rows and columns.

KEY-TERMS

Aggregate data type   It is an agglomeration of data, of any data type, that is identified with a single name and can be decomposed and related by some defined structure.

Array identifier   A name assigned to an array.

Array initialization   The procedure of assigning numerical value or character to each element of an array.

Array of strings   An array that contains strings as its elements.

Array   It is a collection of individual data elements that is ordered, fixed in size and homogeneous.

Concatenation of strings   A kind of string manipulation where one string is appended to another string.

Homogeneous data   Data of same kind or same data type.

Index of an array   It is an integer constant or variable ranging from 0 to (*size* – 1).

Library functions   Pre-written functions, provided with the C compiler, which can be attached to user written programs to carry out some task.

Multidimensional array   An array that is represented by a name and more than one index or subscript.

One-dimensional array   An array that is represented by a name and single index or subscript.

Scalar variable   It is a single variable whose stored value is an atomic data type.

Scanset   It is a conversion specifier that allows the programmer to specify the set of characters that are (or are not) acceptable as part of the string.

Size of array   The number of elements in an array.

stderr   The side stream of output characters for errors is called standard- error

stden   Standard input stream that is used to receive and hold input data from standard input device.

stdout   Standard output stream that is used to hold and transfer output data to standard output device.

String compare   A kind of string manipulation where two strings are compared to primarily find out whether they are similar or not.

String copy   A kind of string manipulation where one string is copied into another.

String manipulation   Carrying out various operations like comparing, appending, copying, etc. among strings.

String   One-dimensional array of characters that contain a NUL at the end.

FREQUENTLY ASKED QUESTIONS

1. Why is it necessary to give the size of an array in an array declaration?

When an array is declared, the compiler allocates contiguous memory for all the elements of the array. The size is to be known to allocate the required space at compile time. Thus, the size must be specified.

2. Why do array subscripts start at 0 instead of 1?

It can make array subscripting somewhat faster. Two facts are known about an array. Firstly, an array name say `arr` always designates the base address of the array. Secondly, address of ith element of `arr` is given by `&arr[i]`, which is eventually `(arr + i)`. The base address is the address of the first element which is nothing but address of the first element `&a[0]`. That means that both `arr` and `&a[0]` holds the same value which is the address of the first element of the array. To carry the expression `(arr+i)` same equivalence for all the elements of the array, subscript of the first element must be 0. Having the subscript to start at 0 simplifies scaling a bit for the compiler.

3. Why do we have a null character ('\0' or NUL) at the end of a string?

A string is not a data type but a data structure. This means that its implementation is logical not physical. The physical data structure is the array in which string is stored. Since string, by definition, is a variable length structure, it is needed to identify the logical end of the data within the physical structure. This is done by using \0 or NUL.

4. If a string `str` contains a string literal "Oxford University Press", then is it legal to print the string using the statement `printf(str);`?

Yes. It prints Oxford University Press on the screen.

EXERCISE

1. What is an array? What type and range must an array subscript have?
2. What does the array name signify?
3. Can array indexes be negative?
4. Illustrate the initialization of one-dimensional arrays, two-dimensional arrays, and strings.
5. Demonstrate the storage of two-dimensional arrays in memory with the help of a diagram.
6. Write a program to find the inverse of a square matrix.
7. Write a program to find the determinant of a matrix.
8. What is null character?
9. What is the difference between `strcat()` and `strncat()`?
10. Write the characteristics of array in C.
11. In what way does an array differ from an ordinary variable?
12. Take input from the user in a two-dimensional array and print the row-wise and column-wise sum of numbers stored in a two-dimensional array.
13. What is the difference between `scanf()` with %s and `gets()`?
14. What is the difference between character array and string?
15. Write C programs for the following.
    (a) Store a list of integer numbers in an array and print the following:
        (i) the maximum value
        (ii) the minimum value
        (iii) the range
             Hint This is computed as maximum-minimum.
        (iv) the average value
             Hint To compute this, add all the numbers together into Sum and count them all in Count. The average is Sum/Count.
    (b) Swap the kth and (k+1)th elements in an integer array. k is given by the user.
    (c) Find the binary equivalent of an integer number using array.
    (d) Find similar elements in an array and compute the number of times they occur.
    (e) Find the intersection of two sets of numbers.
    (f) Enter n numbers and store in an array and rearrange the array in the reverse order.
    (g) Find the frequency of digits in a set of numbers.
    (h) Remove the duplicates from an array.
    (i) Merge two sorted arrays into another array in a sorted order.
    (j) Compare two arrays containing two sets of numbers.
    (k) Rearrange an array in reverse order without using a second array.
16. Write a C program to read a text and count all the occurrences of a particular letter given by the user.
17. Write a C program that will capitalize all the letters of a string.
18. Write a C program to check whether a string given by the user is a palindrome or not.
19. Write a C program that counts the total numbers of vowels and their frequency.
20. Write a C program to remove the white spaces (blank spaces) from a string.
21. Write a C program to print a sub-string within a string.
22. Write a C program that will read a word and rewrite it in alphabetical order.
23. Write a C program that deletes a word from a sentence. Note that the word may appear any number of times.
24. Write a C program that will analyze a line of text and will print the number of words, the number of consonants, and the number of vowels in the text.
25. Write a C program to find a string within a sentence and replace it with another string.
26. Write a C program that will insert a word before a particular word of a sentence.
27. Write a C program that takes the name of a person as input and prints the name in an abbreviated fashion, e.g., Manas Ghosh as M.G.
28. Write a C program that reads in a string such as '20C' or '15F' and outputs the temperature to the nearest degree using the other scale.
29. Write a C program that takes the name of a person as input and prints the first letter of the first name and middle name (if any), and the title as it is, e.g., Raj Kumar Santoshi as R.K. Santoshi.
30. Write a C program that reads a line of text and counts all occurrences of a particular word.
31. Write a program to convert each character of a string into the next alphabet and print the string.

32. Write a program that accepts a word from the user and prints it in the following way:

    For example, if the word is COMPUTER, the program will print it as

    C
    C O

    C O M
    C O M P
    C O M P U
    C O M P U T
    C O M P U T E
    C O M P U T E R

Project Questions

1. Write a program that performs the following: The user inputs a number and then enters a series of numbers from 1 to that number. Your program should determine which number (or numbers) is missing or duplicated in the series, if any. For example, if the user entered 5 as the initial number and then entered the following sequences, the results should be as shown.

Input Sequence	Output
1 2 3 4 5	Nothing bad

   However, if 7 were the highest number, the user would see the results on the right for the following number entries:

Input Sequence	Output
1 3 2 4 5	Missing 6
	Missing 7

   And if 10 were the highest number and the user entered the numbers shown on the left, note the list of missing and duplicate numbers:

Input Sequence	Output
1 2 4 7 4 4 5 10 8 2 6	Duplicate 2 (2 times)
	Missing 3
	Duplicate 4 (3 times)
	Missing 9

   The program should check the highest number that the user inputs to ensure that it does not exceed the size of any array you might be using for storage.

2. Given an array of integers, find subarray with largest sum

---

INCREMENTAL PROBLEM

Continuing with what has been done earlier, the program for incremental problem solving now uses arrays to represent the vertices of a triangle. So there is a change in the program code, though, as in the earlier case, the objective is to test and obtain an equilateral triangle.

Problem statement

Using arrays to represent the three vertices of a triangle, calculate the length of the three sides of a triangle formed with these vertices. Then determine whether an equilateral triangle can be formed with the given vertices.

Solution

The x and y co-ordinates of the three vertices of the triangle are represent by two one-dimensional arrays. The x and y co-ordinates for each vertex, entered by the user, are stored in the two arrays. Using these values, the program computes the value of the length of each side, which are in turn stored in an array. The length of the sides of the triangle is then considered to find whether the sum of lengths of any two sides is greater than the length of the third side. Only if the test evaluates to be true, it is considered that a triangle can be formed with the chosen vertices and the next test for evaluating whether the triangle is an equilateral triangle conducted. If it is found that neither a triangle can be formed nor an equilateral triangle be obtained, then the program is terminated; otherwise it is considered that an equilateral triangle can be obtained.

Program

```c
#include<stdio.h>
#include<math.h>
int main(void)
{
    double x[3],y[3],len[3];
    int i;
    char run ='y';
     while(run=='y' || run=='Y')
    {
        printf("\n Enter the coordinates of the\
                vertices of a triangle");
        for(i=0;i<3;++i)
        {
            printf("\n Enter x[%d]:",i);
```

```
        scanf("%f",&x[i]);
        printf("\n Enter y[%d]: ",i);
        scanf("%f",&y[i]);
    }
    for(i=0; i<3; ++i)
    len[i]= sqrt((x[(i+1)%3]-x[i])*(x[(i+1)%3]-x[i])\
        + (y[(i+1)%3]-y[i])*(y[(i+1)%3]-y[i]));
    if(((len[0]+len[1])>len[2])&&((len[1]+len[2])\
        >len[0])&& ((len[2] + len[0]) >len[1]))
    {
        printf("\n Triangle can be drawn");
        if((len[0]=len[1])&&(len[1]=len[2])
            &&(len[2]=len[0]))
```

```
            printf("\n Triangle is equilateral");
        else
            printf("\n Triangle is not equilateral");
    }
    else
        printf("Triangle cannot be drawn");
        fflush(stdin);
        printf("\n\n Run once more? \n Enter y or n:");
        scanf("%c", &run);
    }
    return 0;
}
```

Problem Statement

A company manufactures three types of UPS models. At the end of any month serial numbers are to be generated for each of the models manufactured. The last serial number for each type of model has to be taken into consideration for generating the new set of serial number for each set of models. At the end of a particular month the following data is available for generating the new serial numbers model-wise:

Model type	Units manufactured	Last serial number
Ups1	3	24
Ups2	4	19
Ups3	5	9

A program has to be written that generates the new serial numbers for each model type for the month under consideration taking the above data as input.

Analysis

The problem consists of calculating the serial number for each model type by taking into consideration the serial number that was allotted to the last unit of each type manufactured the previous month. The above given data pertaining to each type has to be fed to the program. Depending on the number of units manufactured and the last serial number, the new set of serial numbers are computed for each model type. At the end a report is printed depicting the serial numbers allotted to each of the model units manufactured.

The algorithm for solving this problem is given as follows:

```
1.  START
2.  PRINT "MODEL OPTIONS:  1 FOR  UPS1,  2  FOR
    UPS2, 3 FOR UPS3"
3.  WHILE  1
4.  BEGIN
5.  PRINT"ENTER MODEL OPTION"
6.  INPUT  OPTION
7.  IF  OPTION NOT  ENTERED  EARLIER  THEN  GOTO 13
8.  ELSE PRINT"OPTION ENTERED EARLIER AND DO YOU
    WANT TO AMEND ENTERED DATA?"
9.  IF YOU WANT TO AMEND ENTERED DATA  THEN  GOTO 11
10. ELSE GOTO  22
11. IF  OPTION = 1  THEN  FLAG1=1
    ELSE
    IF  OPTION = 2  THEN  FLAG2=1
    ELSE
    IF  OPTION = 3  THEN  FLAG3=1
    ELSE
    PRINT "WRONG OPTION"  AND  EXIT
12. PRINT "ENTER LAST SERIAL NUMBER"
13. INPUT  LAST_SERIAL_NUMBER
14. PRINT "ENTER NUMBER_OF_UNITS PRODUCED"
15. INPUT NUMBER_OF_UNITS
16. I = 0
17. J = 0
18. NEW_SERIAL_NUMBER[J] = LAST_SERIAL_NUMBER  + 1 + I
19. I = I + 1
20. J = J + 1
21. IF  I < NUMBER_OF_UNITS  THEN   GOTO 19
22. PRINT "WANT TO ENTER DATA FOR ONE MORE MODEL ?"
23. IF  NO  THEN  GOTO 25
24. END
25. PRINT "REPORT"
26. PRINT "ITEM NUMBER MODEL TYPE SERIAL NUMBER"
```

```
27. I = 0
28. PRINT "ITEM_NUMBER MODEL_TYPE[ I ] NEW_
    SERIAL_NUMBER[ I ]"
29. I = I + 1
30. IF  I < NUMBER_OF_UNITS  GOTO  28
31. STOP
```

C Implementation

```c
#include<stdio.h>
#include<string.h>
#include<stdlib.h>

int main()
{
    int i,j,k,last_sn[3],new_sn[3][50],op;
    int units[3];
    char model[3][6] = {"ups01","ups02","ups03"};
    char str[3][6];
    int flag[3] = {0};

    printf("\n Model options:");
    printf("\n  1: ups01, 2: ups02, 3: ups03");

    while(1)
    {
        printf("\n Enter model option:");
        scanf("%d", &op);

        if (flag[op - 1] != 0)
        {
            printf("\n\n model option %d already
                   entered", op);
            printf("\n\n want to correct erroneous\
                   entry, enter 1 for yes and 2 for no");
            scanf("%d",&k);
            if(k==2)
            goto label1;
        }

        switch(--op)
        {
         case 0:
            flag[0] = 1;
            strcpy(str[op],model[op]);
            break;
         case 1:
            flag[1] = 1;
            strcpy(str[op],model[op]);
            break;
         case 2:
            flag[2] = 1;
            strcpy(str[op],model[op]);
            break;
         default:
            printf("\n\n wrong option");
            exit(0);
        }
        printf("\n\n Enter last serial number:");
        scanf("%d",&last_sn[op]);

        printf("\n\n:%d",last_sn[op]);
                    /* test  if entry is correct */

        printf("\n\n Enter no. of units produced:");
        scanf("%d",&units[op]);

        for(i=0;i<units[op];i++)
            new_sn[op][i]= last_sn[op]+1+i;

        for(i=0;i<units[op];i++)
                    /* test  if  entry is correct */
        printf("\n serial number: %d",new_sn[op][i]);
label1:
        printf("\n\n Want to enter data for one\
                more model:\
                enter 1 for yes and 2 for no:");
        scanf("%d",&k);
        if(k==2)break;
    }

    printf("\n\n REPORT");

    printf("\\n-------------------------------");
    printf("\n\n ITEM NUMBER  MODEL TYPE  SERIAL\
            NUMBER");
    printf("\\n-------------------------------");

    k=1;

    for(i=0; i<3; i++)
    {
        for(j=0; j<units[i]; j++)
        {
            printf("\n\n %d %s %d", (j+k),\
                   str[i],new_sn[i][j]);
            printf("\\n------------------");
        }
        k = j + k;
    }
    printf("\n\n done");
    return 0;
}
```

Sample run result:

Model options:
1: ups01, 2: ups02, 3: ups03
Enter model option:1
Enter last serial number: 24
:24

Enter number of units produced: 3
        serial number: 25
        serial number: 26
        serial number: 27

Want to enter data for one more model:enter 1 for
yes and 2 for no: 1
Enter model option:2
Enter last serial number: 19
:19

Enter number of units produced: 4
        serial number: 20
        serial number: 21
        serial number: 22
        serial number: 23

Want to enter data for one more model:enter 1 for
yes and 2 for no: 1
        Enter model option:3
        Enter last serial number: 9
        :9

Enter number of units produced: 5
        serial number: 10
        serial number: 11
        serial number: 12
        serial number: 13
        serial number: 14

Want to enter data for one more model:enter 1 for
yes and 2 for no: 2

REPORT

ITEM NUMBER	MODEL TYPE	SERIAL NUMBER
1	ups01	25
2	ups01	26
3	ups01	27
4	ups02	20
5	ups02	21
6	ups02	22
7	ups02	23
8	ups03	10
9	ups03	11
10	ups03	12
11	ups03	13
12	ups03	14

done

Press Enter to return to Quincy...

C

Functions

Chapter 7

Learning Objectives

After reading this chapter, the readers will be able to

- understand what a function is and how its use benefits a program
- learn how a function declaration, function call, and function definition are constructed
- understand how variables and arrays are passed to functions
- understand what scope rules mean in functions and blocks and learn about global and local variables
- learn about storage class specifiers for variables
- understand the basic concept of recursion and learn the technique of constructing recursive functions
- learn various searching and sorting alogorithms

7.1 INTRODUCTION

Software engineering is a discipline that is concerned with the construction of robust and reliable computer programs. Just as civil engineers use tried and tested methods for the construction of buildings, software engineers use accepted methods for analysing a problem to be solved, a blueprint or plan for the design of the solution and a construction method that minimizes the risk of error. The discipline has evolved as the use of computers has spread. In particular, it has tackled issues that have arisen as a result of some catastrophic failures of software projects involving teams of programmers writing thousands of lines of program code. Just as civil engineers have learnt from their failures so have software engineers.

One of the most important barriers to the development of better computer software is the limited ability of human beings to understand the programs that they write. To design a program we often use some method of software engineering. Each approach to software engineering divides the required task into sub-tasks, modules, sub-systems or processes of various types. Functions are a natural way of implementing such designs in C.

A particular method or family of methods that a software engineer might use to solve a problem is known as a *methodology*. During the 1970s and into the 80s, the primary software engineering methodology was *structured programming*. Dijkstra introduced the term structured programming to refer to a set of principles (e.g. sequence, selection or branching, iteration or looping, etc.) for writing well-organized programs that could be more easily shown to be correct. Structured programming is a style of programming designed to make programs more comprehensible and programming errors less frequent. Other computer scientists added further principles, such as *modularization* (breaking down a program into separate procedures, such as for data input, different stages of processing, and output or printing). Modularization makes it easier to figure out which part of a program may be causing a problem, and to fix part of a problem without affecting other parts. It enables programmers to break problems into small and easily understood components that eventually will comprise a complete system.

The structured programming approach to program design was based on the following method:

- To solve a large problem, break the problem into several pieces and work on each piece separately;

- To solve each piece, treat it as a new problem that can itself be broken down into smaller problems;

- Repeat the process with each new piece until each can be solved directly, without further decomposition.

Structured programming also encourages stepwise refinement, a program design process described by Niklaus Wirth, creator of Pascal. This is a *top-down approach* in which the stages of processing are first described in high-level terms (like pseudocode), and then gradually elaborated in their details. That is, the planning activities of problem solving are carried out in the direction from general to specific. Structured programming refers to the implementation of the resulting design. It requires planning and organization, but a good design will often save much time when it comes to actual implementation, and the resulting code will be more elegant and readable. Functions form an important part of top-down design and structured programming. Using functions removes the need to repeat identical groups of statements within programs when the same task must be performed several times. Also, the use of functions allows libraries of frequently used software to be built up and re-used in different programs thus allowing the creation of compact and efficient programs.

7.2 CONCEPT OF FUNCTION

A *function* is a self-contained block of program statements that performs a particular task. It is often defined as a section of a program performing a specific job. In fact, the concept of functions, which were originally a subset of a concept called subroutine, came up because of the following deliberation.

Imagine a program wherein a set of operations has to be repeated often, though not continuously, *n* times or so. If they had to be repeated continuously, loops could be used. Instead of inserting the program statements for these operations at so many places, write a separate program segment and compile it separately. As many times as it is needed, keep 'calling' the segment to get the result. The separate program segment is called a function and the program that calls it is called the 'main program'.

C went one step further; it divided the entire concept of programming to a combination of functions. C has no procedures, only functions. `scanf()`, `printf()`, `main()`, etc. that have been used in programs so far, are all functions. C provides a lot of library functions; in addition, the programmers can write their own functions and use them. The special function called `main()` is where program execution begins. When a function is called upon, with or without handing over of some input data, it returns information to the main program or calling function from where it was called.

7.2.1 Why are Functions Needed?

The use of functions provides several benefits.

- *First*, it makes programs significantly easier to understand and maintain by breaking up a program into easily manageable chunks. Even without software engineering, functions allow the structure of the program to reflect the structure of its application.

- *Secondly*, the main program can consist of a series of function calls rather than countless lines of code. It can be executed as many times as necessary from different points in the main program. Without the ability to package a block of code into a function, programs would end up being much larger, since one would typically need to replicate the same code at various points in them.

- The *third* benefit is that well written functions may be reused in multiple programs. The C standard library is an example of the reuse of functions. This enables code sharing.

- Fourthly, functions can be used to protect data. This is related with the concept of local data. Local data is the data described within a function. They are available only within a function when the function is being executed.
- The *fifth* benefit of using functions is that different programmers working on one large project can divide the workload by writing different functions.

7.3 USING FUNCTIONS

Referring back to the Introduction, all C programs contain at least one function, called `main()` where execution starts. Returning from this function the program execution terminates and the returned value is treated as an indication of success or failure of program execution.

When a function is called, the code contained in that function is executed, and when the function has finished executing, control returns to the point at which that function was called. The program steps through the statements in sequence in the normal way until it comes across a call to a particular function. At that point, execution moves to the start of that function—that is, the first statement in the body of the function. Execution of the program continues through the function statements until it hits a return statement or reaches the closing brace marking the end of the function body. This signals that execution should go back to the point immediately after where the function was originally called.

Functions are used by *calling* them from other functions. When a function is used, it is referred to as the '*called function*'. Such functions often use data that is passed to them from the calling function. Parameters provide the means by which you pass information from the calling function into the called function. Only after the called function successfully receives the data can the data be manipulated to produce a useful result.

7.3.1 Function Prototype Declaration

All the header files contain declarations for a range of functions, as well as definitions for various constants. In a C program, a user-written function should normally be declared prior to its use to allow the compiler to perform type checking on the arguments used in its call statement or calling construct. The general form of this function declaration statement is as follows:

```
return_data_type function_name (data_type variable1,
...);
```

Or

```
return_data_type function_name (data_type_list);
```

There are three basic parts in this declaration.

- `function_name` This is the name given to the function and it follows the same naming rules as that for any valid variable in C.
- `return_data_type` This specifies the type of data given back to the calling construct by the function after it executes its specific task.
- `data_type_list` This list specifies the data type of each of the variables, the values of which are expected to be transmitted by the calling construct to the function.

The following are some examples of declaration statements.

(a) `float FtoC(float faren);`

(b) `double power(double, int);`

(c) `int isPrime(int);`

(d) `void printMessage(void);`

(e) `void fibo_series(int);`

A function has a name that both identifies it and is used to call it for execution in a program. The name of a function is global. Functions, which perform different actions, should generally have different names. The names are, generally, created to indicate the particular job that the function does, as is seen in examples (a) to (e).

There are two ways for prototyping functions. The most common method is simply to write the function declaration with the arguments typed, with or without identifiers for each, such as example (a) can be written as either of the following:

```
float FtoC(float);
float FtoC(float faren);
```

The ANSI standard does not require variable names for the prototype declaration parameters. In fact, readability and understandability are improved if names are used.

In modern properly written C programs, all functions must be declared before they are used. This is normally accomplished using a function prototype. Function prototypes were not part of the original C language, but were added by C89. Although prototypes are not technically required, their use is strongly encouraged.

If there are no parameters to a function, you can specify the parameter list as `void`, as you have been doing in the case of the `main()` function. Actually, when a function takes no parameters, the inclusion of the word "void" inside the parentheses is optional, since it is the default.

When a function returns no value, however, it is required to include void as the function type, since the default is int. If you are writing a function that returns an int, technically speaking you could leave out the type and you should always include it.

> **Points to Note**
>
> - The name of a function is global.
> - It should not be forgotten that a semicolon is required at the end of a function prototype. Without it, the compiler will give an error message. And no function can be defined in another function body.
> - If the number of arguments does not agree with the number of parameters specified in the prototype, the behavior is undefined.
> - The function return type cannot be an array or a function type. These two cases must be handled by returning pointers to the array or function.

7.3.2 Function Definition

The collection of program statements in C that describes the specific task done by the function is called a function definition. It consists of the *function header* and a *function body*, which is a block of code enclosed in parentheses. The definition creates the actual function in memory. The general form of the function definition is as follows-

```
return_data_type function name(data_type variable1,
data_type variable2,……)
{
    /* Function Body */
}
```

The *function header* in this definition is

```
return_data_type function name(data_type variable1,
data_type variable2,……)
```

and the portion of program code within the braces is the *function body*. Notice that the function header is similar to the function declaration but does not require the semicolon at the end. The list of variables in the function header is also referred to as the *formal parameters*.

One point to be noted here is that the names of the parameters do not need to be the same in the prototype declaration and the function definition. If the types are not the same then the compiler will generate an error. The compiler checks the types in the prototype statements with the types in the call to ensure that they are the same or at least compatible.

A value of the indicated data type is returned to the calling function when the function is executed. The return data type can be of any legal type. If the function does not return a value, the return type is specified by the keyword void. The keyword void is also used to indicate the absence of parameters. So a function that has no parameters and does not return a value would have the following header.

```
void function_name(void)
```

A function with a return type specified as void should not be used in an expression in the calling function. Since it does not return a value, it cannot sensibly be part of an expression. Therefore, using it in this way will cause the compiler to generate an error message.

There is no standard guideline about the number of parameters that a function can have. Every ANSI C compliant compiler is required to support at least 31 parameters in a function. However, it is considered bad programming style if a function contains an inordinately high (eight or more) number of parameters. The number of parameters a function has also directly affects the speed at which it is called—the more parameters, the slower the function call. Therefore, if possible, one should minimize the number of parameters to be used in a function.

The statements in the function body, following the function header, perform the desired computation in a function. To understand this, consider the following examples.

> **Example**

1. Write a function that computes x^n, where x is any valid number and n an integer value.

```
/*********************************************
 Function to compute integral powers of any valid
 number. First argument is any valid number,
 second argument is power index.
**********************************************/

double power(double x, int n)
                            /* function header */
{
                /* function body starts here... */
    double result = 1.0;
            /* declaration of variable result */
    for(int i = 1; i<=n; i++)
                            /* computing x^n */
        result *= x;
                        /*      :        */
    return result;
            /* return value in 'result' to
                            calling function*/
}
            /* function body ends here...      */
```

In Example 1, the first statement in the function body declares a variable `result` that is initialized with the value `1.0`. The variable `result` is local to the function, as are all automatic variables declared within a function body. This means that the variable `result` ceases to exist after the function has completed execution.

The calculation is performed in the `for` loop. A loop control variable `i` is declared in the `for` loop which will assume successive values from `1` to `n`. The variable `result` is multiplied by `x` once for each loop iteration. Thus this occurs `n` times to generate the required value. If `n` is `0`, the statement in the loop will not be executed at all because the loop continuation condition will immediately fail, and so `result` will be left as `1.0`.

Example

2. Function for converting a temperature from Fahrenheit scale to Celsius scale.

```
float FtoC(float faren) /*function header */
{                /* function body starts here…….*/
    float factor = 5.0/9.0;  /*  :              */
    float freezing = 32.0;   /*  :              */
    float celsius;           /*  :              */
    celsius = factor *(faren - freezing);
    return celsius;      /*      :          */
}                /* function body ends here……. */
```

Again, refer to Example 2. Here, several variables have been declared within the function `FtoC()`. They are declared just like any other variable. They are called automatic local variables, because: Firstly, they are local: their effect is limited to the function. Secondly, they are automatic since they are automatically created whenever the function is called. Also their value can be accessed only inside the function, not from any other function; some authors also use `auto` to indicate that they are automatically created.

The scope of variables declared within a function is limited to its use in the function only. Any change made to these variables, internally in the function, is made only to the local copies of the variables. Such variables are created at the point at which it is defined and ceases to exist at the end of the block containing it. There is one type of variable that is an exception to this – those declared as `static`. Discussions on static variables will be carried out a little later in this chapter.

return Statement

The general form of the return statement is as follows:

```
return expression;
```

or

```
return(expression);
```

where `expression` must evaluate to a value of the type specified in the function header for the return value. The expression can be any desired expression as long as it ends up with a value of the required type. In Example 1, the `return` statement returns the value of `result` to the point where the function was called. What might strike immediately is that the variable `result`, as stated earlier, ceases to exist on completing the execution of the function. So how is it returned? The answer is that a copy of the value being returned is made automatically, and this copy is available to the return point in the program.

The `expression` can also include function calls, if those functions return a numeric value! The following is a valid calling statement:

```
x = power(power(2, 5), 2);
```

The inner call to power returns 32, which is then used as an argument for the outer call to power. This call to power passes 32 and 2, and power will return the value 1024 which would get assigned to x.

If a function returns a value, usually it has to be assigned to some variable since a value is being returned. If there is no assignment specified, then is it a valid statement in C? The answer is yes but may fire a warning message. It is allowed as the returned value is simply discarded. Let us consider the following example.

Example

3.
```
#include <stdio.h>
int sum(int, int);
int main()
{
    int a=5, b=10;
    sum(a,b);          The statement is
    return 0;          valid but may elicit
}                      warning message
int sum(int x, int y)
{
    return x+y;
}
```

The following statement may be used instead of the statement sum(a,b) to avoid the warning message.

```
(void)sum(a,b)
```

Thus the returned value is purposely discarded in this manner.

If the type of return value has been specified as void, there must be no expression appearing in the return statement. It must be written simply as

```
return;
```

For such a case the return statement may be omitted, if desired. Also, note that when a function doesn't return a value, the return statement is not followed by an expression, just a semicolon right away. Actually, if there is not a return statement at the end of a function, and execution gets to the end of the function, a return statement is assumed and control goes back to the caller.

A function can only return one value. A function with return type void does not return any values. There may be more than one return statement in a function, but only one return statement will be executed per calling to the function. As an illustration, the following function definition checks whether a given year is a leap year or not. The year passed to that function as an argument. It returns 1 if the year is a leap year, otherwise it returns 0.

Example

4. Function definition to checks whether a given year is a leap year or not.

```
void leap_yr(int yr)
{
  if((yr%4==0)&&(yr%100!=0)||yr%400 ==0)
    return 1;
  else
    return 0;
}
```

Points to Note

- If a program is compiled that contains a function defined with a void return type and tries to return a value, an error message will occur.
- An error message will be fired by the compiler if a bare return is used in a function where the return type was specified to be other than void.

Standard C permits main to be defined with zero or two parameters as demonstrated below:

(a)
```
int main(void)
{
  ................
  return 0;
}
```

(b)
```
int main()
{
  ................
  return 0;
}
```

(c)
```
int main(int argc, char *argv[])
{
  ................
  return 0;
}
```

The value returned by the function main(), after the program instructions in its body are executed, is 0. Prior to C99, the return type of main was often omitted, defaulting to int. This is no longer used. In Microsoft based compiler, C programs use void main(void). Most of the C compilers like Borland and GCC always recommend main() properly returning an int.

According to the newly ratified update to the C standard in 1999, main() should be defined with a return type of int. The practical reason to return an int from main() is that on many operating systems, the value returned by main() is used to return an exit status to the environment. On Unix, MS-DOS, and Windows systems, the low eight bits of the value returned by main() is passed to the command shell or calling program. This is often used to change the course of a program, batch file, or shell script.

7.3.3 Function Calling

It may be concluded that a function will carry out its expected action whenever it is invoked (i.e. whenever the function is called) from some portion of a program which means the program control passes to that of the called function. Once the function completes its task, the program control is returned back to the calling function. Generally, a function will process information passed to it from the calling statement of a program and return a single value. A function with returned type void does not return any value. It only returns the control from called function to calling function. The general form of the function call statement (or construct) is

```
function_name(variable1, variable2,…);
```

or

```
variable_name = function_name(var1, var2,…);
```

If there are no arguments to be passed in the function, i.e., the argument is void, then the calling statement would be

```
function_name();
```

or

```
variable_name = function_name();
```

Information will be passed to the function via special identifiers or expression called *arguments* or *actual parameters* and returned via the return statement.

Points to Note

One thing to notice here is that even when there are no parameters, you need to include left and right parentheses after the name of the function when you call it. If you leave them out, the code will still compile, but the function never actually gets called. What happens is that C interprets a function name without parentheses as the memory address where the function is stored, and it is actually legal to have a number by itself as a statement. The statement is useless, but valid.

There are certain rules for parameters which must be keep in mind while writing a C program which uses one or more functions. These are listed below -

- The number of parameters in the actual and formal parameter lists must be consistent.
- Parameter association in C is *positional*. This means that the first actual parameter corresponds to the first formal parameter, the second matches the second and so on.
- Actual parameters and formal parameters must be of compatible data types.
- Actual (input) parameters may be a variable, constant, or any expression matching the type of the corresponding formal parameter.

Concepts described above have been taken together in the following complete program.

Example

5. Write C a program that uses a function to convert a temperature from Fahrenheit scale to Celsius scale.

```
#include <stdio.h>
float FtoC(float);          Function prototype declaration
int main(void)
{
  float tempInF;
  float tempInC;
  printf("\n Temperature in Fahrenheit scale: ");
  scanf("%f", &tempInF);
  tempInC = FtoC(tempInF);          Function calling
  printf("%f Fahrenheit equals %f Celsius \n",
      tempInF,tempInC);
  return 0;
}
/* FUNCTION DEFINITION */
float FtoC(float faren)          Function header
{
  float factor = 5.0/9.0;
  float freezing = 32.0;
  float celsius;                          Function body
  celsius = factor *(faren - freezing);
  return celsius;
}
```

Points to Note

The values passed to a function are referred to as *arguments*. The *parameters* of the called function can be thought of as declared local variables that get initialized with the values of the arguments. Some text books use the terms formal parameters and actual parameters instead of parameters and arguments.

Finally, there are some points which are very relevant as well as crucial here. When function prototypes are used

- The number and types of arguments must match the declared types otherwise the program causes an error message.
- The arguments are converted as if by assignment, to the declared types of the formal parameters. The argument is converted according to the following default argument promotions:

- Type float is converted to double.
- Array and function names are converted to corresponding pointers.
- When using traditional C, types unsigned short and unsigned char are converted to unsigned int, and types signed short and signed char are converted to signed int.
- When using ANSI C, types short and char, whether signed or unsigned, are converted to int.

7.4 CALL BY VALUE MECHANISM

The technique used to pass data to a function is known as parameter passing. Data are passed to a function using one of the two techniques: *pass by value* or *call by value* and *pass by reference* or *call by reference*.

In call by value, a copy of the data is made and the copy is sent to the function. The copies of the value held by the arguments are passed by the function call. Since only copies of values held in the arguments are passed by the function call to the formal parameters of the called function, the value in the arguments remains unchanged. In other words, as only copies of the values held in the arguments are sent to the formal parameters, the function cannot directly modify the arguments passed. This can be demonstrated by deliberately trying to do so in the following example.

Example

```
6. #include <stdio.h>
   int mul_by_10(int num); /* function prototype */
   int main(void)
   {
     int result,num = 3;
     printf("\n num = %d before function call", num);
     result = mul_by_10(num);
     printf("\n result = %d after return from\
         function", result);
     printf("\n num = %d", num);
     return 0;
   }
   /* function definition follows */
   int mul_by_10(int num)
   {
     num *= 10;
     return num;
   }
```
Output
```
num = 3, before function call
result = 30, after return from function
num = 3
```

The sample result obtained from this program shows that the attempt to modify the arguments of the function has failed. This confirms that the original value of num remains untouched. The multiplication occurred on the copy of num that was generated, and was eventually discarded on exiting from the function. Some more examples have been furnished on function calls and the passing of arguments using the 'pass by value' or 'call by value' technique.

The second technique, *pass by reference*, sends the address of the data rather than a copy. In this case, the called function can change the original data in the calling function. Unfortunately, C does not support pass by reference. Whenever the data in the calling function have to be changed, one must pass the variable's address explicitly and use it to change the value. Here values are passed by explicitly handing over the addresses of arguments to the called function, it is possible to change the values held within these arguments by executing the function. This appears as if multiple values are returned by the called function. Details on call by reference will be presented in the chapter on pointers.

Points to Note

C supports only call by value mechanism which means the values of the actual arguments are conceptually copied to the formal parameters. If it is required to alter the actual arguments in the called function, the addresses of the arguments must be passed explicitly.

7.5 WORKING WITH FUNCTIONS

Functions can be used in a program in various ways:

(a) Function that perform operations on their parameters and return a value:
(b) Function that manipulates information on their parameters and returns a value that simply indicates the success or failure of that manipulation.
(c) Function having no return type that is strictly procedural

Function that perform operations on their parameters and return a value Functions in this category may be classified into two types.

1. A function with fixed number of parameters.
2. A function with variable number of parameters such as printf(). Writing a function with variable arguments will not be explored in this book.

As an illustration of a function with fixed number of parameters, the following example may be sited.

Example

7. Write a function that uses a function to find the greatest common divisor (GCD) of two integers.

To find the GCD using a function, two integers should be passed as parameters. Let they are x and y. It is needed to check whether k (for k = 2, 3, 4 and so on) is a common divisor for x and y until k is greater than x or y. The common divisor is to be stored in a variable named result. Initially result is 1. Whenever a new common divisor is found, the value of result is updated with the new common divisor. When all the possible common divisors from 2 to up to x or y, are checked the value in the variable result is the greatest common divisor and it is returned to the calling function. Here is the implementation.

```
#include <stdio.h>
int GCD(int,int);
int main(void)
{
  int nOne, nTwo, n;
  printf("\n Enter two numbers: ");
  scanf("%d %d", &nOne, &nTwo);
  n=GCD(nOne,nTwo);
  printf("\n GCD of %d and %d is %d \n",
         nOne,nTwo,n);
  return 0;
}
int GCD(int x,int y)
{
  int result=1, k=2;
  while(k<=x && k<=y)
  {
      if(x%k==0 && y%k == 0)
        result=k;
      k++;
  }
  return result;
}
```

Function that manipulates information on their parameters and returns a value that simply indicates the success or failure of that manipulation For example, using function we can determine whether a number is a prime number or not. If the number is a prime then the function returns 1 and returns 0 otherwise. Definition of the function may be implemented as follows:

```
int isPrime(int x)
{
  int d;
  for(d=2;d<=x/2;++d)
    if(x%d==0)
      return 0;
  return 1;
}
```

In C99 compliant compiler, the above function can be rewritten using standard header file stdbool.h. The return type of the function is bool.

```
bool isPrime(int x)
{
  int d;
  for(d=2;d<=x/2;++d)
    if(x%d==0)
      return false;
  return true;
}
```

Using the above function, it is possible to solve the following problem.

Example

8. Print the prime factors of a given number using a function.

A number can always be divided by 1 and the number itself. The logic behind this program is we have to divide the number starting from 2 to n/2 where n is the given number. In any case if the number becomes divisible by any number in the range 2 to n/2, then that is considered to be a factor of the number. If that factor is a prime number then the factor is a prime factor. We can use the function isPrime() to determine whether the factor is a prime factor or not.

```
#include <stdio.h>
#include <stdbool.h>
bool isPrime(int);
int main(void)
{
  int n, d=2;
  printf("\n Enter the Number:  ");
  scanf("%d",&n);
  printf("\n Prime factors of %d is....\n",n);
```

```
    for(d=2;d<=n/2;++d)
      if(n%d==0 && isPrime(d))
        printf("%d ",d);
    return 0;
  }
  bool isPrime(int x)
  {
    int d;
    for(d=2;d<=x/2;++d)
      if(x%d==0)
        return false;
    return true;
  }
```

Sample run:

```
  Enter the Number:  51
  Prime factors of 51 is....
    3  17
```

Function having no return type that is strictly procedural
The function may or may not have parameters. Unlike some other languages, C makes no distinction between subroutines (procedures) and functions. In C, there is only the function, which can optionally return a value. A function with void as return type simulates the procedure in C.

We've seen that when we pass the value of a typical variable to a function, a copy of that value gets assigned to the parameter. Changing the value of the parameter within the called function does not affect the value of the local variable in the calling function. Things are different when an array is passed to a function. What we are actually passing is the memory address of the array (this may seem more clear after we learn about pointers), and if the called function changes specific entries in the array, these entries remain changed when control gets back to the calling function. So when arrays or strings are passed to a function, call by value mechanism is not followed. That means any modification made in the array or string parameter within the called function will be reflected in the original array or string in the calling function that was passed to the function. This concept will be understood more clearly in Chapter 8. As a result in most of the cases, it is not required to return anything. Here is an example:

Example

9.
```c
#include <stdio.h>
void change(int []);
int main(void)
{
  int arr[3] = {1, 2, 3};
  change(arr);
  printf("Elements  are  %d,  %d,  and  %d.\n",
      arr[0], arr[1], arr[2]);
  return 0;
}
void change(int my_array[])
{
  my_array[0] = 10;
  my_array[2] = 20;
  return;
}
```

This program will print Elements are 10, 2, and 20. to the screen.

As a further illustration, Example 10 sorts a set of numbers stored in an array using a function.

Example

10. Write a C program that uses a function to sort an array of integers using bubble sort algorithm.

Sorting an array in ascending order means that rearranging the values in the array so that the elements progressively increase in value from the smallest to the largest. By the end of such a sort, the minimum value is contained in the first location of the array, whereas the maximum value is found in the last location of the array, with values that progressively increase in between.

This example implements the bubble sort algorithm, which we will discuss later in this chapter. A function called sort, takes two arguments: the array to be sorted and the number of elements in the array.

```c
#include <stdio.h>
void sort (int [], int);
int main (void)
{
  int i;
  int arr[10] = {3,2,7,0,6,4,9,8,1,5};
```

```
printf ("The array before the sort:\n");
for (i = 0; i < 10; ++i)
  printf ("%i", arr[i]);
sort (array, 10);
printf ("\n\nThe array after the sort:\n");
for (i = 0; i < 10; ++i)
  printf ("%i", arr[i]);
return 0;
}
void sort (int a[], int n)
{
  int i, j, temp;
  for(i = 0; i < n-1; ++i)
    for(j = 0; j < n-i-1; ++j)
                      if (a[j] > a[j+1])
                      {
                        temp = a[j];
                        a[j] = a[j+1];
                        a[j+1] = temp;
                      }
}
```

Output

```
The array before the sort:
3 2 7 0 6 4 9 8 1 5
The array after the sort:
0 1 2 3 4 5 6 7 8 9
```

7.6 PASSING ARRAYS TO FUNCTIONS

Arrays can also be arguments of functions. When an array is passed to a function, the address of the array is passed and not the copy of the complete array. Therefore, when a function is called with the name of the array as the argument, address to the first element in the array is handed over to the function. Hence when an array is a function argument, only the address of the array is passed to the function called. This implies that during its execution the function has the ability to modify the contents of the array that is specified as the function argument. Therefore array is not passed to a function by value. This is an exception to the rule of passing the function arguments by value. Consider the following example.

```
11. #include <stdio.h>
    void doubleThem(int [], int);
                        /* declaration of function */
    int main(void)
    {
      int myInts[10] = {1,2,3,4,5,6,7,8,9,10};
      int size=10;
      printf("\n\n The given numbers are :");
      for (i = 0; i < size; i++)
        printf("%d,",myInts[i]);
      doubleThem(myInts,size);   /* function call */
      printf("\n\n The double numbers are : ");
      for (i = 0; i < size; i++)
        printf("%d,",myInts[i]);
      return 0;
    }
    /******* function definition *******/
    void doubleThem(int a[], int size)
    {
      int i;
      for(i = 0; i < size; i++)

        a[i] = 2 * a[i];

    }
```

Output

```
The given numbers are :1, 2, 3, 4, 5, 6, 7, 8,
9, 10,
The double numbers are : 2, 4, 6, 8, 10, 12, 14,
16, 18, 20,
```

It is to be noted that the value of the variable is initialized with 10 as there are 10 values in the array myInts. The value of the variable can also be determined by the expression sizeof(myInts)/sizeof(myInts[0])
That is,

```
size=sizeof(myInts)/sizeof(myInts [0]);
```

12. Write a program that uses a function to find the average age of students of a class chosen for a junior quiz competition.

```
#include <stdio.h>
```

```
#define SIZE 50
float avg_age(int [],int);
int main(void)
{
  int i,b[SIZE],n;
  float average;
  printf("\n How many students? \n%");
  scanf("%d",&n);
  printf("\n Enter the age of students \n");
  for(i=0;i<n;i++)
    scanf("%d",&b[i]);
  average=avg_age(b,n);
  printf("\n The average age of students =%f",
      average);
  return 0;
}
float avg_age(int a[], int n)
{
  int j;
  float sum=0.0;
  for(j=0;j<n;j++)
    sum=sum+a[j];
  return sum/n;
}
```

13. Write a program that uses a function to find the maximum value in an array.

Solution

```
#include <stdio.h>
int maximum(int [],int); /* function prototype */
int main(void)
{
  int values[5], i, max;
  printf("Enter 5 numbers\n");
  for(i = 0; i < 5; ++i)
    scanf("%d", &values[i]);
  max = maximum(values,5); /* function call */
  printf("\nMaximum value is %d\n", max);
  return 0;
}
/**** function definition ****/
int maximum(int values[], int n)
{
```

```
  int max_value, i;
  max_value = values[0];
  for(i = 1; i < n; ++i)
    if(values[i] > max_value)
      max_value = values[i];
  return max_value;
}
```

Output

```
Enter 5 numbers
11 15 8 21 7
Maximum value is 21
```

When an array is passed to a function, actually the address of the first element (called the base address of an array) is passed which is nothing but passing arguments by address. In general, when a one dimensional array is passed to a function, it degenerates to a pointer. This will be explained in the chapter on pointers.

A local variable max_value is set to the first element of values, and a for loop is executed which cycles through each element in values and assigns the maximum item to max_value. This number is then passed back by the return statement, and assigned to max in the main() function.

However, it has to be noted that an array name with an index number as a function argument will only pass that particular array element's value, like all other variables, to the function called.

Strings are passed to functions in the same way as are one-dimensional arrays. By implementing string functions, it will be shown how strings are passed into and out of functions. Some examples involving strings as function arguments follow.

Example

14. Write a program that uses a function to copy one string into another without using the strcpy() function available in the standard library of C.

Solution

```
#include <stdio.h>
void string_copy(char [], char []);
                    /* function prototype */
int main()
{
  char a[100]; /*** source string ***/
  char b[100]; /*** destination string ***/
```

```
printf("\n Input source string :");
scanf("%[^\n]",a); /* read input source string */
string_copy(b,a); /* function call */
printf("\n Destination string : %s\n",b);
return 0;
}
/*** function definition ***/
void string_copy(char d[], char s[])
{
    int i = 0;
    printf("\n Source string : %s\n",s);
                        /* copying the string */
    for (i = 0; s[i] != '\0'; i++)
        d[i] = s[i]; /* Copy NUL character to
                                destination string */

}
```

Multidimensional arrays are also allowed to be passed as arguments to functions. The simplest type of such an array is the two-dimensional array. It may be recalled here that when a two-dimensional array is initialized, the number of rows need not be specified. A similar technique is adopted while specifying the two dimensional array as a formal parameter in a function header. The first dimension value can be omitted when a multidimensional array is used as a formal parameter in a function.

Of course, the function will need some way of knowing the extent of the first dimension. For example, the function header could be written as follows:

```
double yield(double arr[][4], int index);
```

Here, the second parameter, index, would provide the necessary information about the first dimension of the array. The function can operate with a two-dimensional array with any value for the first dimension, but with the second dimension fixed at 4.

Example

15. Write a program that uses a function to perform addition and subtraction of two matrices having integer numbers.

    The computation that is carried out in the function is simply a nested for loop with the inner loop summing elements of a single row and the outer loop repeating this for every row.

    ```
    #include <stdio.h>
    ```

```
#define row 2
#define col 3
void mat_arith(int [][col], int [][col]);
                            /* function prototype */
int main()
{
    int a[row][col], b[row][col],i,j;
    printf("\n Enter elements of the first matrix.\n");
    for(i=0; i<row; i++)
                /** Read first matrix elements **/
        for(j=0; j<col; j++)
            scanf("%d",&a[i][j]);
            printf("\n Enter elements of the second\
                    matrix.\n");
    for(i=0; i<row; i++)
                /** Read second matrix elements **/
        for(j=0; j<col; j++)
            scanf("%d",&b[i][j]);
    mat_arith(a,b);            /** function call **/
}
void mat_arith(int a[][col], int b[][col])
{
    int c[row][col],i,j,choice;
    printf("\n For addition enter: 1 \n")
    printf("For subtraction enter: 2\n");
    printf("\nEnter your choice:");
    scanf("%d",&choice);
    for(i=0; i<row; i++)
    for(j=0; j<col; j++)
    {
        if(choice==1)
            c[i][j]= a[i][j] + b[i][j];
        else if(choice==2)
            c[i][j]= a[i][j] - b[i][j];
        else
        {
            printf("\n Invalid choice. Task not done.");
            return;
        }
    }
    printf("\n The resulting matrix is:\n");
    for(i=0; i<row; i++)
    {
        for(j=0; j<col; j++)
        printf("%d", c[i][j]);
```

```
        printf("\n\n");
    }
    return;
}
```

Output

```
    Enter elements of the second matrix.
    1 3 5 7 9 11
    For addition enter: 1
    For subtraction enter: 2
    Enter your choice: 1
    The resulting matrix is:
    3  7  11
    14 17 21
```

Till now, the function definition was always placed after the main program. In fact, C allows the function definition to be placed ahead of the main program. In such a case, the function prototype is not required.

7.7 SCOPE AND EXTENT

The region of the program over which the declaration of an identifier is visible is called the *scope* of the identifier. The scope relates to the accessibility, the period of existence, and the boundary of usage of variables declared in a statement block or a function. These features in turn define whether a variable is local or global in nature.

7.7.1 Concept of Global and Local Variables

There are two common terms related to the visibility or accessibility of a variable. They are global and local variables. Actually global and local are the terms related with lifetime. *Lifetime* is the period during execution of a program in which a variable or function exists. It will be discussed in details later on in this section.

Variables declared within the function body are called *local variables*. They have local lifetime. Local variables are automatically created at the point of their declaration within the function body and are usable inside the function body. These variables only exist inside the specific function that creates them. They are unknown to other functions and to the main program. The existence of the local variables ends when the function completes its specific task and returns to the calling point. They are recreated each time a function is executed or called.

Variables declared outside of all the functions of a program and accessible by any of these functions are called *global variables*. The existence and region of usage of these variables are not confined to any specific function body. They are implemented by associating memory locations with variable names. Global variables are created at the beginning of program execution and remain in existence all through the period of the execution of the program. These variables are known to all functions in the program and can be used by these functions as many times as may be required. They do not get recreated if the function is recalled. Global variables do not cease to exist when control is transferred from a function. Their value is retained and is available to any other function that accesses them.

All global variables are declared outside of all the functions. There is no general rule, as to where these should be declared outside the functions but declaring them on top of the code is normally recommended, as explained through Example 17. If a variable of the same name is declared both within a function and outside of it, the function will use the variable that is declared within it and ignore the global one. If not initialized, a global variable is initialized to zero by default. Moreover, the use of global variables should be as few as possible. (Please read points to use on page 229). Consider the example below.

Example

16. Write a program that uses a function to swap values stored in two integer variables to understand the concept of local and global variables.

```
#include <stdio.h>
void exchange(int, int);
int main()
{ /* main() program body starts here...*/
  int a, b;          /* local variables */
  a = 5;
  b = 7;
  printf(" In main: a = %d, b = %d\n", a, b);
  exchange(a, b);
  printf("\n Back in main:");
  printf("a = %d, b = %d\n", a, b);
  return 0;
} /* main() program body ends here... */
void exchange(int a, int b)
```

```
{ /* function body starts here...*/
  int temp; /* local variable */
  printf("\n In function exchange() before\
      change: just received from main... a=%d\
      and b=%d",a,b);
  temp = a;
  a = b;
  b = temp; /* interchange over */
  printf("\n In function exchange() after change:");
  printf("a = %d, b = %d\n", a, b);
} /* function body ends here...*/
```

Output:

```
In main: a = 5, b = 7
In function exchange() before change: just
received from main... a=5 and b=7
In function exchange() after change: a = 7, b = 5
Back in main: a = 5, b = 7
```

The results depict that the program code above failed to exchange the numbers between the variables in the function main(). This happened because, firstly, the variables a and b in main() and that within the function exchange() are not the same. The variables a and b within exchange() are local variables and are created when the function is invoked, which means program control is taken over by the function, and these are killed the moment program control returns to the main() program. While calling the exchange() function from main(), copies of the values held by a and b, which are local to main(), are handed over to separate variables a and b that are local to the function exchange(). Within this exchange() function, the task of exchanging the values between its local variables a and b is carried out successfully, as is evident from the messages displayed when the program is run. This in no way affects the values in variables a and b in the main(). Secondly, this exchanged copy of values in the variables is not passed back from the function exchange() to the variables in main(). Hence the values in the variables a and b within main() remained untouched and unchanged. This demonstrates the difference in the accessibitiy or visibility of the local variables in main() and the function exchange(). One way to affect an interchange could be by declaring the variables that are to be exchanged, that is a and b, as global variables only. This is demonstrated by the example program code that follows.

17.
```
#include <stdio.h>
void exchange(void);
int a, b;     /* declaration of global variables */
int main()
{ /* main program starts here...*/
  a = 5;
  b = 7;
  printf(" In main: a = %d, b = %d\n", a, b);
  exchange();   /* function call, no parameters
                    are passed */
  printf("\n Back in main:");
  printf("a = %d, b = %d\n", a, b);
  return 0;
} /* main program ends here */
void exchange(void)
{ /* function body starts here...*/
  int temp; /* decl. of local variable in function*/
  printf("\n In function exchange() before\
      change: just received from\
  main... a=%d and b=%d",a,b);
  temp = a;
  a = b;
  b = temp; /* interchange over */
  printf("\n In function exchange() after change:");
  printf("a = %d, b = %d\n", a, b);
} /* function body ends here*/
```

Output

```
In main: a = 5, b = 7
In function exchange() before change: just
received from main... a=5 and b=7
In function exchange() after change: a = 7, b = 5
Back in main: a = 7, b = 5
```

The example shows that for global variables the interchange is possible by following the scope rules. By using pointers in functions, the same job can be done more effectively and the function call technique is known as call by reference more strictly call by address. This would be discussed in the chapter on pointers.

Rather than passing variables to a function as arguments, it is possible to make all variables global. But it is not recommended, as global variables break the normal safeguards provided by functions. Using parameter passing mechanism and declaring local variables as needed, C offers provision for making functions independent and insulated from each other, including the necessity of carefully designating the type of arguments needed by a function, the variables used in the function, and the value returned. Using only global variables can be especially disastrous in larger programs that have many user-defined functions. Since a global variable can be accessed and changed by any function following the global declaration, it is a time-consuming and frustrating task to locate the origin of an erroneous value.

But it is not always true that use of global variables is always disadvantageous. There are certain instances where use of global variables is advocated. Global variables, however, are extremely useful in creating array of data and constants that must be shared between many functions. If many functions require access to a group of arrays, global variables allow the functions to make efficient changes to the same array without the need for multiple arrays passing.

Now, it is the time to introduce the concept of scope in detail.

7.7.2 Scope Rules

The region of the program over which the declaration of an identifier is accessible is called the *scope* of the identifier. The scope relates to the accessibility, the period of existence, and the boundary of usage of variables declared in a program. Scopes can be of four types.

- block
- file
- function
- function prototype

The following sections describe the scope associated with variables.

Block scope

This means that the identifier can only be used in the block in which it is declared. These variables are created at the point of their declaration inside the *block* and cease to exist outside it. Outside the block, these variables are unknown and non-existent. For blocks within blocks, termed as nested blocks, variables declared outside the inner blocks are accessible to the *nested blocks*, provided these variables are not redeclared within the inner block. The redeclaration of variables within the blocks bearing the same names as those in the outer block, masks the outer block variables while executing the inner blocks.

In general, it is always better to use different names for variables not common to outer and inner blocks to avoid unforced errors. The following are some examples illustrating the scope rules in blocks.

Example

18. Write a program that illustrates the scope rules in blocks.

```c
#include <stdio.h>
int main()
{
  int x= 3;     /* variable declaration in outer
                                        block */
  printf("\n in outer block x = %d before\
      executing inner block", x);
  {
    int x= 45; /* variable declaration in inner
                                        block */
    printf("\n in inner block x = %d", x);
  }
  printf("\n in outer block x = %d after
      executing\ inner block", x);
  return 0;
}
```

Output

```
in outer block x = 3 before executing inner
block
in inner block x = 45
in outer block x = 3 after executing inner
block
```

This program shows that because the variable x has been redeclared as 45 in the inner block, a local variable gets created in the inner block. This variable is only accessible and known to the inner block.

Functions are considered as named block. Variables declared within a function block can be used anywhere within the function in which they are defined. The variable x declared in outer block has the block scope. Like blocks, functions can either be defined in parallel, where the functions are placed one after the other and a function can be called from any other function. But C does not allow functions to be nested, i.e. a function cannot be defined within another function definition.

Function scope

This applies only to labels. Normally labels are used with goto statement. It simply means that labels can be used anywhere within the function in which they are defined. This includes use before definition.

File scope

This means that the identifier can be used anywhere in the current file after the declaration of the identifier. This applies to functions and all variables declared outside functions. File scope variable is same as global variable. The illustration involving global or file scope variables has already been discussed in Section 7.7.1. File scope identifiers may be hidden by the block scope declarations having same name.

Function prototype scope

In order to improve readability and understandabilty, function prototypes are usually written with 'dummy' variable names. For example

```
double max(double x, double y);
```

The identifiers 'x' and 'y' have function prototype scope, which terminates at the end of the prototype. This allows any dummy parameter names appearing in a function prototype to disappear at the end of the prototype. Consider the following program:

```
#include <stdio.h>
int main(void)
{
  void show(int x);
  int x=10;
  show(x);
  return 0;
}
void show(int x)
{
  printf("\n %d",x);
}
```

The int variable name does not conflict with the parameter *name* because the parameter went out of scope at the end of the prototype. However, the prototype is still in scope.

Points to Note

In standard C, formal parameters in the function definition have the same scope as variables declared at the beginning of the block that forms the function body and therefore they cannot be hidden or redeclared by declarations in the body. The following function definition, if used, will give error message at compile time.

```
int sum(int x, int y)
{
    int x=5;
    return x+y;
}
```

Compilation error message displayed

```
In function 'sum':
error: 'x' redeclared as different kind of symbol
note: previous definition of 'x' was here
```

How long memory will be associated with them is known as *extent* or *lifetime* of a data object. The storage duration of the identifier determines its lifetime, either global lifetime or local lifetime. The *lifetime* of an object describes whether its storage is allocated once only, at program start-up, or is more transient in its nature, being allocated and freed as necessary. Global lifetime means that the object has its storage allocated permanently i.e. storage is allocated at or before the beginning of program execution and the storage remain allocated until program termination. Local lifetime means that the storage is allocated and freed as necessary.

The following rules specify whether an identifier has global (static) or local (automatic) lifetime:

- *Global lifetime* All functions have global lifetime. As do the identifiers declared at the top level (that is, outside all blocks in the program at the same level of function definitions).

- *Local lifetime* An object (unless it is declared as static) is said to have local lifetime when it is created on entry to a block or function and destroyed on exit from block or function. Formal parameters and variables declared at the beginning of the block may have local lifetime depending on the place of declaration.

The data object created with the use of special library functions such as malloc() or calloc() etc have *dynamic duration* and the storage remain allocated from the time of creation at run time until program termination or until a call to special library function free().

7.8 STORAGE CLASSES

7.8.1 Storage Class Specifiers for Variables

In C, the variables are declared by the type of data they can hold. The name of a variable is associated with a memory location within the computer where the value assigned to the variable is stored in the form of bits. During the execution of the program, these variables may be stored in the registers of the CPU or the primary memory of the computer. To indicate where the variables would be stored, how long they would exist, what would be their region of existence, and what would be the default values, C provides four storage class specifiers that can be used along with the data type specifiers in the declaration statement of a variable. These four storage class specifiers are *automatic, external, register, and static*.

The storage class specifier precedes the declaration statement for a variable. The general form of the variable declaration statement that includes the storage class specifier is given as follows:

```
storage_class_specifier data_type variable_name;
```

The storage class – auto

By default, all variables declared within the body of any function are automatic. The keyword auto is used in the declaration of a variable to explicitly specify its storage class. For example, the following declaration statement within a function body

```
auto char any_alpha;
```

specifies that any_alpha is a variable that can hold a character and its storage class is automatic. Even if the variable declaration statement in the function body does not include the keyword auto, such declared variables are implicitly specified as belonging to the automatic storage class. In fact, all local variables in a function, by default, belong to automatic storage class. Their region of use is limited within the function body and vanishes when the function completes its specific task and returns to the main program from where the function was invoked. These variables are stored in the primary memory of the computer.

Local variables declared within nested blocks in a function belong by default to the automatic storage class.

19. Write a C program that demonstrates the use of the automatic storage class variable.

```c
#include <stdio.h>
int main(void)
{
    auto int a =5;
    printf("\n a = %d",a);
    {
        int a = 10;
        printf("\n a = %d",a);
        printf("\n i = %d",i);
    }
    printf("\n a = %d",a);
    return 0;
}
```

Output

```
a = 5
a = 10
i = 4199232
a = 5
```

Output shows that because a is declared auto in outer block and a declared in inner block is also auto by default. Since this local variable i is not initialized within the inner block, the value held by it is unpredictable and thus garbage. This is printed as 4199232. When inner block ends, the existence of both the variables a and i go away. So outside the inner block, the value of a is printed as 5. Any attempt to access the variable i outside the inner block causes a compiler error. This example demonstrates the accessibility, existence, effect of initialization, and garbage default value of the automatic storage class or the local variable.

The storage class – register

Values stored in registers of the CPU are accessed in much lesser time than those stored in the primary memory. To allow the fastest access time for variables, the register storage class specifier is used. The keyword for this storage class is register. The variables thus specified are stored in some register of the CPU. In most C compilers, the register specifier can only be applied to int and char type variables; however, ANSI C has broadened its scope.

Arrays cannot be stored in a registers but they may still receive preferential treatment by the compiler depending on C compiler and the operating system under which it is running.

The existence of the variables with the storage class specifier `register` is restricted within the region of a function or a block where it has been declared and exists as long as the function or block remains active. The default value within this variable is unknown, which is interpreted as garbage. Storage class of a global variable cannot be specified as `register`.

Points to Note

- Global variables with register storage class are not allowed.
- In C, it is not possible to obtain the address of a register variable by using '&' operator.
- In addition, the only storage class specifier that can be used in a parameter declaration is register.

The storage class – static

Two kinds of variables are allowed to be specified as static variables: local variables and global variables. The local variables are also referred to as *internal static variables* while the global variables are also known as *external static variables*. The default value of a static variable is zero.

To specify a local variable as static, the keyword `static` precedes its declaration statement.

A *static local variable* is allotted a permanent storage location in the primary memory. This variable is usable within functions or blocks where it is declared and preserves its previous value held by it between function calls or between block re-entries. However, once a function is invoked, the static local variable retains the value in it and exists as long as the main program is in execution.

The *external static variables* in a program file are declared like global variables with the keyword static preceding its declaration statement. These static variables are accessible by all functions in the program file where these variables exist and are declared. The external static variables are not available to functions defined earlier in the same file or not accessible to functions defined in other files although these may use the extern keyword. These variables exist throughout the period of the main program execution. Such variables get stored in the primary memory.

Example

20. Write a C program that illustrates the use local static variables and functions.

```c
#include <stdio.h>
int main()
{
    void show(void);
    printf("\n First Call of show()");
    show();
    printf("\n Second Call of show()");
    show();
    printf("\n Third Call of show()");
    show();
    return 0;
}
void show(void)
{
    static int i;
    printf("\n i=%d",i);
    i++;
}
```

Output

```
First Call of show()
i=0
Second Call of show()
i=1
Third Call of show()
i=2
```

The storage class – extern

A program in C, particularly when it is large, can be broken up into smaller programs. After compiling, each program file can be joined together to form the large program. These small program modules that combine together may need some variables that are used by all of them. In C, such a provision can be made by specifying these variables, accessible to all the small program modules, as an external storage class variable. These variables are global to all the small program modules that are formed as separate files. The keyword for declaring such global variables is extern. Such global variables are declared like any other variable in one of the program modules while the declaration of these variables is preceded with the keyword extern in all other combining program modules. The program modules may also be a function or a block. These variables remain in existence as long as the program is in execution and their existence does not terminate upon the exit of a function or a block or a program module from its state of execution. These variables are stored in the primary memory and their default value is zero. Table 7.1 provides a summary of the salient features of storage class specifiers. The following programs illustrate the use of the external storage class variable.

Example

21.
```
/*********************************************/
/*           Program file: pgm1.c            */
/*********************************************/
#include <stdio.h>
#include "pgm2.c" /*** link program pgm2.c ***/
int i;           /*** external/global decl.**/
void show(void);   /*** function prototype ***/
int main()
{
   i=10;
   show(); /* call to function in program file
                                    pgm2.c */
   printf("\n Value of i in pgm1.c=%d ",i);
   return 0;
}         /****** pgm1.c file ends **********/
/*********************************************/
/*        Program file: pgm2.c               */
/*********************************************/
extern int i;
/***** function definition of show()*********/
void show()            /*** function header ***/
{    /*** fn. body starts..**/
   printf("\n Value of i in pgm2.c=%d",i);
}                      /*** fn. body ends.. **/
```

Output
```
Value of i in pgm2.c=10
Value of i in pgm1.c=10
```

Here is another example where the global variable i is assigned a value in the program file in which the basic declaration statement and main() are absent. There is a minor difference between this example and the previous one.

Table 7.1 Summary of salient features of storage class specifiers

Storage class specifier	Place of storage	Scope	Lifetime	Default value
auto	Primary memory	Within the block or function where it is declared.	Exists from the time of entry in the function or block to its return to the calling function or to the end of block.	garbage
register	Register of CPU	Within the block or function where it is declared.	Exists from the time of entry in the function or block to its return to the calling function or to the end of block.	garbage
static	Primary memory	**For local** Within the block or function where it is declared. **For global** Accessible within the combination of program modules/files that form the full program.	**For local** Retains the value of the variable from one entry of the block or function to the next or next call. **For global** Preserves value in the program file	0
extern	Primary memory	Accessible within the combination of program modules/file that form the full program.	Exists as long as the program is in execution.	0

Example

22.
```
/*********************************************/
/*          Program file: pgm1.c           */
/*********************************************/
#include <stdio.h>
#include "pgm2.c" /*** link program pgm2.c ***/
int i; /*** external/global decl.**/
void show(void);   /*** function prototype ***/
int main()
{
   show(); /* call to function in program file pgm2.c */
   printf("\n Value of i in pgm1.c=%d",i);
   return 0;
} /****** pgm1.c file ends**********/
/*********************************************/
/*          Program file: pgm2.c           */
/*********************************************/
extern int i;
/****** function definition of show() *******/
void show()             /*** function header ***/
{                       /*** fn. body starts..**/
   i = 20;
   printf("\n Value of i in pgm2.c=%d",i);
}                       /*** fn. body ends.. **/
```

Output
```
Value of i in pgm2.c=20
Value of i in pgm1.c=20
```

7.8.2 Storage Class Specifiers for Functions

The only storage class specifiers that may be assigned with functions are extern and static. The extern signifies that the function can be referenced from other files- that is, the function name is exported to the linker. The static signifies that the function cannot be referenced from other files- that is the function name is *not* exported to the linker. If no storage class appears in a function definition, extern is presumed.

7.8.3 Linkage

An identifier's *linkage* determines which of the references to that identifier refer to the same object. An identifier's linkage is determined by whether it appears inside or outside a function, whether it appears in a declaration of a function (as opposed to an object), its storage-class specifier, and the linkage of any previous declarations of the same identifier that have file scope. C defines three types of linkages – external, internal and no linkage. In general,

- Functions and global variables have external linkage. This means they are available to all files that constitute a program.
- Identifiers with file scope declared as static have internal linkage. These are known only within the file in which they are declared.
- Local identifiers have no linkage and are therefore known only within their own block.

Two declarations of the same identifier in a single file that have the same linkage, either internal or external, refer to the same object. The same identifier cannot appear in a file with both internal and external linkage.

Points to Note

It is not always necessary to specify both the storage class and the type of identifiers in a declaration. Storage class specifiers appearing in declarations outside of functions are assumed to be extern. In a declaration inside a function, if a type but no storage class is indicated, the identifier is assumed to be auto. An exception to the latter rule is made for functions because functions with storage class auto do not exist; it is implicitly declared to be extern.

7.9 THE INLINE FUNCTION

C99 has added the keyword *inline*, which applies to functions. By preceding a function declaration with *inline*, the compiler is instructed to optimize calls to the function. Typically, this means that the function's code will be expanded in line, rather than called. Below is a definition of such inline function.

```
inline int sum(int x, int y)
{
   return x+y;
}
```

The inline designation is only a hint to the compiler, suggesting that calls to the inline function should be as fast as possible. The name comes from a compiler optimization called *inline expansion*, whereby a call to a function is replaced by a copy of the function body. This eliminates the overhead of the function call. There is no guarantee in general that the compiler will take note of a function being declared as *inline*. It is free to ignore the request.

7.10 RECURSION

The formal definition is given below:

A recursive function is one that calls itself directly or indirectly to solve a smaller version of its task until a final call which does not require a self-call.

Recursion is like a top–down approach to problem solving; it divides the problem into pieces or selects one key step, postponing the rest. On the other hand, iteration is more of a bottom–up approach; it begins with what is known and from this constructs the solution step by step.

7.10.1 What is Needed for Implementing Recursion?

- Decomposition into smaller problems of same type
- Recursive calls must diminish problem size
- Necessity of base case
- Base case must be reached
- It acts as a terminating condition. Without an explicitly defined base case, a recursive function would call itself indefinitely.
- It is the building block to the complete solution. In a sense, a recursive function determines its solution from the base case(s) it reaches.

Points to Note

What is a base case? An instance of a problem the solution of which requires no further recursive calls is known as a base case. It is a special case whose solution is known. Every recursive algorithm requires at least one base case in order to be valid. A base case has two purposes.

The recursive algorithms will generally consist of an if statement with the following form:

```
if(this is a base case) then
   solve it directly
else
   redefine the problem using recursion.
```

Four questions can arise for constructing a recursive solution. They are as follows.

- How can the problem be defined in terms of one or more smaller problems of the same type?
- What instance(s) of the problem can serve as the base case(s)?
- As the problem size diminishes, will this/these base case(s) be reached?
- How is/are the solution(s) from the smaller problem(s) used to build a correct solution to the current larger problem?

It is not always necessary or even desirable to ask the above questions in strict order. For example, sometimes the solution to a problem is easier to imagine if it is first asked what instance(s) can serve as the base case(s) and then define the problem in terms of one or more smaller problems of the same type which are closer to the base case(s).

The following sections discuss some popular problems where the recursive functions are constructed and used keeping in mind the above approach.

Factorial of a number

Factorial of an unsigned integer n can be expressed as

$$n! = n \times (n-1) \times (n-2) \ldots 3 \times 2 \times 1$$

Thinking about the iterative solution for this problem, a program can be coded as shown in the following example.

Example

23. Write a program in C to determine the factorial of an unsigned integer without using recursion.

```c
#include <stdio.h>
unsigned long int factorial(int);

int main(void)
{
   int n;
   unsigned long int result;
   printf("\n Enter a number to find its Factorial: ");
   scanf("%d", &n);
   if (n < 0)
      printf("\n Factorial of negative number is
      not possible\n");
   else
   {
      result = factorial(n);
      printf("\n The Factorial of %d is %lu.\n",
      n, result);
   }
   return 0;
}

unsigned long int factorial(int num)
   {

      unsigned long int fact=1;
```

```
    while(num>0)
      {
        fact *=num;
        num --;
      }
      return fact;
}
```

Output

```
Enter a number to find its Factorial: 5
The Factorial of 5 is 120.
```

Now, think of finding the factorial of an integer in a recursive way. For example, $5! = 5 \times 4 \times 3 \times 2 \times 1 = 120$. It can also be worked out as:

$$5! = 5 \times 4!$$
$$4! = 4 \times 3!$$
$$3! = 3 \times 2!$$
$$2! = 2 \times 1!$$
$$1! = 1 \times 0!$$

It is known that $0! = 1$. This can be considered as a base case to solve the problem recursively. Hence

$$0! = 1$$
$$1! = 1 \times 0! = 1 \times 1 = 1$$
$$2! = 2 \times 1! = 2 \times 1 = 2$$
$$3! = 3 \times 2! = 3 \times 2 = 6$$
$$4! = 4 \times 3! = 4 \times 6 = 24$$
$$5! = 5 \times 4! = 5 \times 24 = 120$$

Following the above procedure, $n!$ can be stated recursively as follows

$$n! = n \times (n-1)!$$
$$n! = n \times (n-1) \times (n-2)!$$
$$n! = n \times (n-1) \times (n-2) \times (n-3)!$$
$$\vdots$$
$$n! = n \times (n-1) \times (n-2) \ldots\ldots 3 \times 2!$$
$$n! = n \times (n-1) \times (n-2) \ldots\ldots 3 \times 2 \times 1!$$
$$n! = n \times (n-1) \times (n-2) \ldots\ldots 3 \times 2 \times 1 \times 0!$$
$$0! = 1$$

This is the known solution. Formally, the factorial of n, $f(n)$, can be expressed as recursive relationship, which is given below:

$$f(n) = \begin{cases} 1, & \text{if } n = 0 \\ n \times f(n-1), & \text{when } n > 0 \end{cases}$$

Example

24. Write a C program to find the factorial of an unsigned integer number using recursion.

```
#include <stdio.h>
 unsigned long int factorial(int);

int main(void)
{
  int n;
  unsigned long int result;
  printf("\n Enter a number to find its Factorial: ");
  scanf("%d", &n);
  if (n < 0)
    printf("\n Factorial of negative number is
    not possible\n");
  else
  {
    result = factorial(n);
    printf("\n The Factorial of %d is %lu.\n",
    n, result);
  }
  return 0;
}

unsigned long int factorial(int num)
{

  if(num==0)
    return 1;
  else
    return (unsigned long int)num *
    factorial(num-1);
}
```

Output

```
Enter a number to find its Factorial: 4
The Factorial of 4 is 24.
```

The Fibonacci sequence

The Fibonacci numbers are a sequence of numbers that have many varied uses. They were originally intended to model the growth of a rabbit colony. The sequence is as follows:

0, 1, 1, 2, 3, 5, 8, 13, 21, 34, 55, 89, 144, ...

The third term of the sequence is the sum of the first and second terms. The fourth term is the sum of the second and third terms, and so on. The problem is to compute the value of the *n*th term recursively.

Let fib(n) denote the nth term of the Fibonacci sequence. Four questions arise.

- How can the problem be defined in terms of one or more smaller problems of the same type?

  ```
  fib(n) = fib(n-2) + fib(n-1) for n>2
  ```

  This recursive relation introduces a new point. In some cases, one solves a problem by solving more than one smaller problem of the same type.

- What instance of the problem can serve as the base case?

  One must be careful while selecting the base case in this situation. For example if one simply says that fib(1) is the base case, what happens if fib(2) is called?

  ```
  fib(2) is fib(0) + fib(1) but fib(0) is undefined.
  ```

  That makes fib(2) undefined. Therefore, it is necessary to give fib(2) an explicit definition.

  ```
  fib(1) = 0 for n = 1
  fib(2) = 1 for n = 2
  ```

  Two base cases are necessary because there are two smaller problems.

- As the problem size diminishes, will one reach these base cases?

  As n is a non-negative integer and each call to the function will reduce the parameter n by 1 or 2, the base cases n = 1, n = 2 will be reached.

- How are the solutions from the smaller problems used to build a correct solution to the current larger problem?

The recursive step adds the results from the two smaller problems fib(n-2) and fib(n-1) to obtain the solution to the current fib(n) problem. This function uses what is known as 'non-linear' recursion.

In this context, brief definitions of linear, non-linear, and mutual recursions are given as follows.

- **Linear recursion** This term is used to describe a recursive function where at most one recursive call is carried out as part of the execution of a single recursive process.

- **Non-linear recursion** This term is used to describe a recursive function where more than one recursion

can be carried out as part of the execution of a single recursive process.

- **Mutual recursion** In order to check and compile a function call, a compiler must know the type of the function, the number of parameters, and so on. In direct recursion the function header, which contains this information, is seen before any call within the function body or later. In mutual recursion, the functions must be defined in some order. This means that a call of at least one function must be compiled before its definition is seen. Different programming languages approach this problem in various ways. Some use separate *forward* definitions of function headers to give sufficient information to compile a call and *body* definitions to contain those calls.

Coming back to the Fibonacci sequence problem, any number in the sequence can be determined by the definition that follows.

$$\text{fib}(n) = \begin{cases} 0 & \text{when } n = 1 \\ 1 & \text{when } n = 2 \\ \text{fib}(n-1) + \text{fib}(n-2) & \text{otherwise} \end{cases}$$

Considering the definition, the following code may be used in a *recursive function* to generate the numbers in the *Fibonacci sequence*.

```
int fib(int term)
{
    if(term ==1)
        return 0;
    else if(term==2)
        return 1;
    else
        return(fib(term - 1) + fib(term - 2));
}
```

The following example illustrates the use of the preceding recursive function for generating the Fibonacci numbers.

Example

```
25. /*********************************************/
    /* Program for computing the Fibonacci number
    sequence using recursion. */
    /*********************************************/
    #include <stdio.h>
    #include <stdlib.h>
    int fib(int); /* function prototype */
```

```
int main()
{
  int i,j;
  printf("\n Enter the number of terms: ");
  scanf("%d",&i);
  if(i < 0)
  {
    printf("\n Error - Number of terms cannot be\
        negative\n");
    exit(1);
  }
  printf("\n Fibonacci sequence for %d terms is:",i);
  for( j=1; j<=i; ++j)
  printf(" %d",fib(j)); /* function call to return
                            jth Fibonacci term*/
  return 0;
}
/*********************************************/
/*          Recursive function fib()         */
/*********************************************/
int fib(int term)
{
  if(term ==1)
    return 0;
  else if(term==2)
      return 1;
    else
      return(fib(term - 1) + fib(term - 2));
}
```

Output

```
(a) Enter the number of terms: 6
    Fibonacci sequence for 6 terms is: 0 1 1 2 3 5
(b) Enter the number of terms: 4
    Fibonacci sequence for 4 terms is: 0 1 1 2
```

The *non-recursive version* of the Fibonacci function discussed above follows.

```
int fib(int val)

{

  int current = 1;

  int old = 1;

  int older = 1;

  val -=2;

  while(val > 0)

  {

    current = old + older;

    older = old;

    old = current;
```

```
    --val;

  }

  return current;

}
```

Greatest common divisor

The greatest common divisor of two integers is the largest integer that divides them both. The problem is to calculate the GCD of two non-negative integers m and n recursively.

If n divides m, then by definition of what a GCD is, $gcd(m, n) = n$. n divides m if and only if $(m \% n) = 0$. So the base case is when $(m \% n) = 0$. If $m > n$ at the start, then $gcd(n, m \% n)$ is a smaller problem than $gcd(m, n)$. If $m < n$ at the start then $(m \% n) = m$ and the first recursive step $gcd(n, m \bmod n)$ is equivalent to $gcd(n, m)$. This has the effect of exchanging the parameter values m and n. So after the first call, it is back to the situation where the first parameter is greater than the second.

In this function, the result from the smaller problem $gcd(n, m \% n)$ is the solution to the current larger problem $gcd(m, n)$. All the algorithm has to do is find the solution to the base case and return it unchanged until it reaches the original problem.

Using the definition given for gcd(), the following code may be used in a *recursive function* to find the GCD of two integers.

Example

26. Write a C program to find the Greatest Common Divisor using recursion.

```
#include <stdio.h>

int gcd(int, int);     /* function prototype */

int main()

{

  int i,j;

  printf("\n Enter the numbers :");

  scanf("%d% d",&i,&j);

  printf("\n The GCD of %d and %d is\
      %d",i,j,gcd(i,j)); /* function call */

  return 0;

}
/*********************************************/
/* Recursive function gcd() */
/*********************************************/
```

```
int gcd(int a,int b)
{
  int remainder;
  remainder = a % b;
  if(remainder == 0)
    return b;
  else
    return gcd(b, remainder);
}
```

Output

```
Enter the numbers :48 18
The GCD of 48 and 18 is 6
```

The Towers of Hanoi

The Towers of Hanoi problem is a classic case study in recursion. It involves moving a specified number of disks from one tower to another using a third as an auxiliary tower. Legend has it that at the time of the creation of the world, the priests of the Temple of Brahma were given the problem with 64 disks and told that when they had completed the task, the world would come to an end.

Move n disks from peg A to peg C, using peg B as needed. The following conditions apply.

- Only one disk may be moved at a time.
- This disk must be the top disk on a peg.
- A larger disk can never be placed on top of a smaller disk.

The solution should be in the form of a printed list of disk moves. For example, if $n = 3$, then the pegs would look as shown in Fig. 7.1.

The key to the problem is not to focus on the first step (which must be to move the disk 1 from A to somewhere) but on the hardest step, i.e., moving the bottom disk to peg C. There is no way to reach the bottom disk until the top $n-1$ disks have moved. Further, they must be moved to peg B to allow the movement of the bottom disk to peg C. Now $n-1$ disks are on peg B that must be moved to peg C (using peg A). There is no reason why the $n-1$ remaining disks cannot be moved in the same manner; in fact, it must be done in the same manner since there is again a bottom disk that must be moved last. Therefore,

- Move $n-1$ disks from peg A to peg B using peg C
- Move the nth disk from peg A to peg C

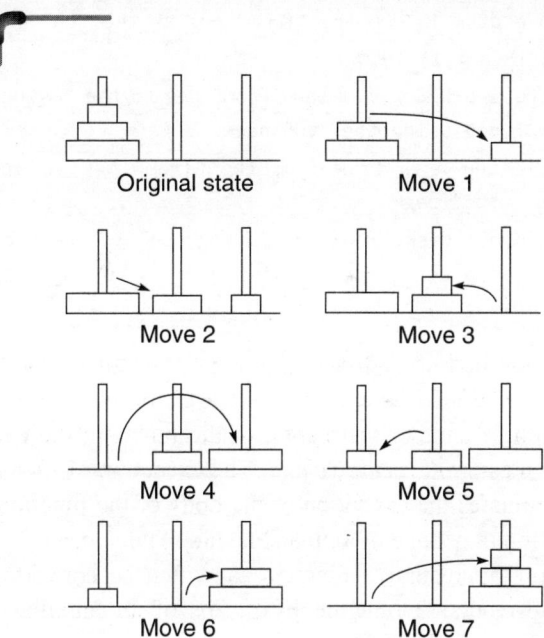

Figure 7.1 Moving of disks from and to different pegs

- Move $n-1$ disks from peg B to peg C using peg A

Notice that the size of the Towers of Hanoi problem is determined by the number of disks involved. This implies that the problem has been redefined in terms of three smaller problems of the same type.

- What instance(s) of the problem can serve as the base case(s)?

  If $n = 1$, then the problem consists of moving one disk from peg A to peg C, which can be clearly solved immediately.

- As the problem size diminishes, will the base case be reached?

  Since each call to the function will reduce the parameter n by 1, and n is nonnegative, the base case $n = 1$ will always be reached.

- How is the solution from the smaller problem used to build a correct solution to the current larger problem?

As seen in the first question, when each of the three smaller problems are solved, then the solution to the current problem is completed. The following is a summary of the algorithm described earlier.

Algorithm

```
FUNCTION MoveTower(disk, from, to, using):
IF(n is 1) THEN
```

```
move disk 1 from the "from" peg to the "to" peg
ELSE IF(n > 1) THEN
    move n-1 disks from the "from" peg to the "using"
        peg using the "to" peg
    move the n'th disk from the "from" peg to the
        "to" peg
    move n-1 disks from the "using" peg to the "to"
        peg using the "from" peg
ENDIF
```

If in the body of a function, a recursive call is placed in such a way that its execution is *never* followed by the execution of another instruction of the function; the call is known as *a tail recursive call*. The execution of such a call terminates the execution of the body of the function. A function may have more than one tail recursive call.

A non-tail recursive function can often be converted to a tail-recursive function by means of an 'auxiliary' parameter. This parameter is used to form the result. The idea is to attempt to incorporate the pending operation into the auxiliary parameter in such a way that the recursive call no longer has a pending operation. The technique is usually used in conjunction with an 'auxiliary' function. This is simply to keep the syntax clean and to hide the fact that auxiliary parameters are needed.

For example, a tail-recursive Fibonacci function can be implemented by using two auxiliary parameters for accumulating results. It should not be surprising that the tree-recursive fib function requires two auxiliary parameters to collect results; there are two recursive calls. To compute fib(n), call fib_aux(n 1 0)

```
int fib_aux(int n, int next, int result) {
    if (n == 0)
        return result;
    else
        return fib_aux(n - 1, next + result, next);
}
```

A tail recursive call can be eliminated by changing the values of the calling parameters to those specified in the recursive call, and repeating the whole function. Consider, for example, the function used to solve the Towers of Hanoi problem.

```
void MoveTower(int n, char from, char to, char
using){
```

```
    if(n == 1)
        printf("\n Move disk 1 from peg %c to ped %c",
            from, to);
    else if(n > 1) {
    MoveTower( n-1, from, using, to);
    printf("\n Move disk %d from peg %c to ped %c",
            n, from, to);
    MoveTower( n-1, using, to, from);
    }
}
```

By removing *tail recursion,* the function can be rewritten as

```
void MoveTower(int n, char from, char to, char
using){
    char temp;
    if(n > 1) {
    MoveTower( n-1, from, using, to);
    printf("\n Move disk %d from peg %c to ped %c",
            n, from, to);
    n = n - 1;
    temp = from;
    from = using;
    using = temp;
    }
    if(n == 1) then
    printf("\n Move disk 1 from peg %c to ped %c",
            from, to);
}
```

The recursive call, MoveTower(n-1, from, using, to);, is not a tail recursive call because its execution is followed by the execution of other instructions in the function, namely, a printf() statement, various assignment statements, and if n == 1 is true, another printf() statement.

In general, any recursive call placed within a looping statement is not *tail recursive* because when control returns from the recursive call, there may be one or more cycles of the loop yet to be executed.

Elimination of *tail recursion* is simple and can shorten the execution time quite considerably. It is not a necessary stage in the elimination of all recursive calls. In particular, compilers do not normally deal with removal

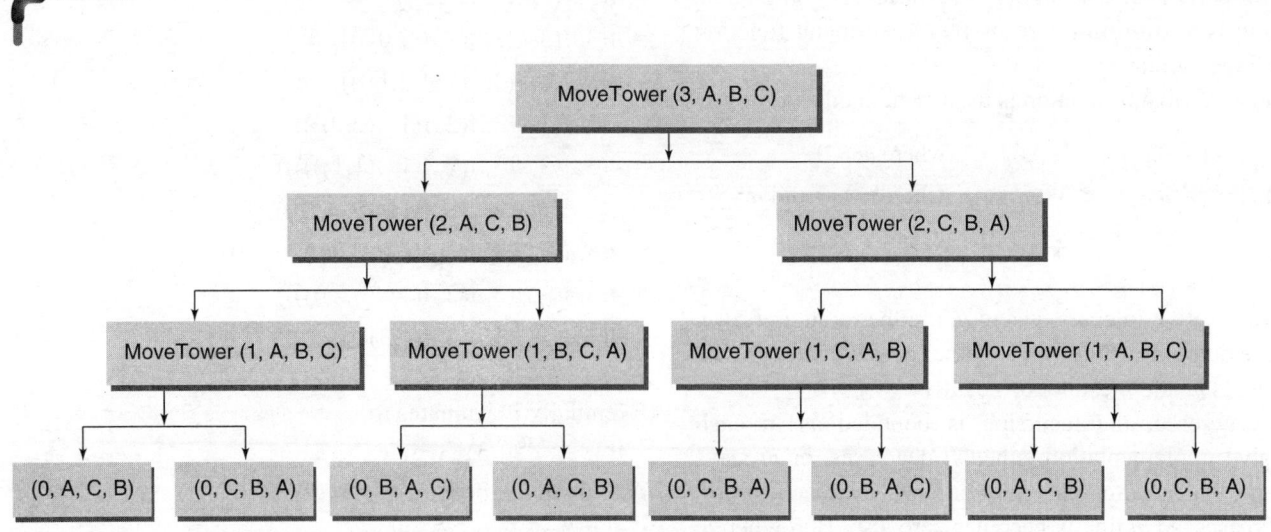

Figure 7.2   Recursion tree for movetower (3,a,b,c)

of *tail recursions* separately, and this explains the gain in efficiency mentioned above.

A key tool for analyzing recursive algorithms is the recursion tree, which portrays the life history of a recursive process (or, equivalently, the life history of the runtime stack). A *recursion tree* can be built according to the following rules.

- Every tree must have a main root from which all branches originate. This principle root will represent the initial call to the function.

- The tree consists of nodes (vertices), with each node representing a particular call to the recursive function.

- A branch of the tree (solid line) represents a call-return path between any two instances of the function.

Figure 7.2 shows a call tree for `MoveTower(3,A,B,C)`.

Ackermann function

In number theory, almost all functions, addition, multiplication, exponentiation, are primitive recursive in nature. This means that these functions can be specified utilizing a certain form of composition and natural recursion.

Ackermann function is the example of *total function*, which is *computable* but not *primitive recursive*.

The word *total* means the function does not violate any of the rules established to define it. The term *computable*

entails that it can, in principle, be evaluated for all possible input values. *Primitive recursive* means that it can be computed using only `for` loops – repeated application of a single operation a predetermined number of times. While implementing Ackermann function, it overshoots the capacity of any `for` loop as the number of loop repetitions is not known beforehand. Rather, this number is itself involved in the calculation, and increases as the computation progresses. The only way to compute the Ackermann function is by using a `while` loop, which goes on repeating an operation until an associated test turns out to be false.

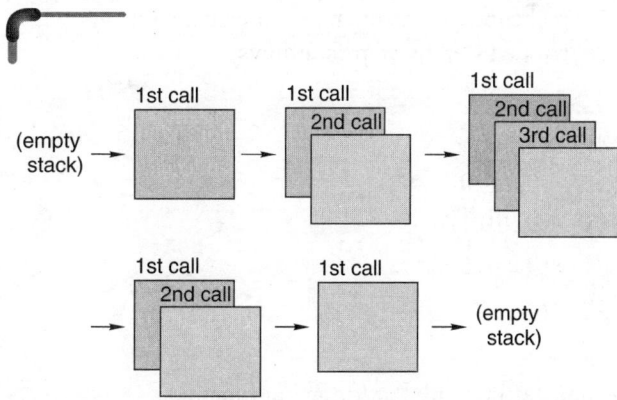

Figure 7.3   The sequence of events that takes place when a stack is used with function calls

In the early 1900s, it was believed that every computable function is also primitive recursive. Ackermann function refuted the belief.

The Ackermann function is usually defined as follows:

$$A(m,n) = \begin{cases} n+1, & \text{where } m = 0 \\ A(m-1,1), & \text{where } m > 0 \text{ and } n = 0 \\ A(m-1, A(m,n-1)), & \text{where } m > 0 \text{ and } n > 0 \end{cases}$$

Two positive integers, m and n, are the input and $A(m, n)$ is the output in the form of another positive integer. The arguments m and n cannot be negative.

In any case, the recursion is bounded as in each recursive implementation either m decreases, or m stays the same and n decreases. Every time when n reaches zero, m decreases, so m finally becomes zero also. But, when m decreases there is no upper bound for the increase of n — and it shall often increase enormously.

The function, stated above, can be expanded with natural positive values for m as follows:

$A(0, n) = n + 1$

$A(1, n) = n + 2$

$A(2, n) = 2n + 3$

$A(3, n) = 2n+3 - 3$

....

$$A(4,n) = \underbrace{2^{2^{\cdot^{\cdot^2}}}}_{n+3} - 3$$

At this point, it should be noted that $2^{2^{2^2}} = 2^{2^4} = 2^{16} = 65536$ not $2^{2 \times 2 \times 2} = 256$. This occurs because it is evaluated right-associatively.

To make the expansion more understandable, let $A(1, 2)$ be expanded step by step as follows:

$A(1,2)$

$= A(0,A(1,1))$

$= A(0,A(0,A(1,0)))$

$= A(0,A(0,A(0,1)))$

$= A(0,A(0,2))$

$= A(0,3)$

$= 4$

Again, starting with the following function

$A(4,3) = A(3,A(4,2))$

$= A(3,A(3,A(4,1)))$

$= A(3,A(3,A(3,A(4,0))))$

$= A(3,A(3,A(3,A(3,1))))$

$= A(3,A(3,A(3,A(2,A(3,0)))))$

$= A(3,A(3,A(3,A(2,A(2,1)))))$

$= A(3,A(3,A(3,A(2,A(1,A(2,0))))))$

$= A(3,A(3,A(3,A(2,A(1,A(1,1))))))$

$= A(3,A(3,A(3,A(2,A(1,A(0,A(1,0))))))) $

$= A(3,A(3,A(3,A(2,A(1,A(0,A(0,1))))))) $

$= A(3,A(3,A(3,A(2,A(1,A(0,2))))))$

$= A(3,A(3,A(3,A(2,A(1,3)))))$

$= ...$

Eventually it evaluates to,

$= A(3, 2^{65536} - 3)$

And finally, it becomes

$= 2^{65536} - 3$

Derivation of $A(1, n)$ and $A(2, n)$ can be shown as follows

$A(1, n) = A(0, A(1, n-1))$

$= A(1, n-1) + 1$

$= A(0, A(1, n-2)) + 1$

$= A(1, n-2) + 2$

$= ....$

$= A(1, 0) + n$

$= A(0, 1) + n$

$= n + 2$

$A(2 , n) = A(1, A(2, n-1))$

$= A(2, n-1) + 2$

$= A(1, A(2, n-2)) + 2$

$= A(2, n-2) + 4$

$= ....$

$= A(2, 0) + 2n$

$= A(1, 1) + 2n$

$= 2n + 3$

The function can be implemented by the following program code:

```c
#include <stdio.h>
unsigned int ackermann(unsigned int m, unsigned
    int n) {
    if(m==0)
    return n + 1;
  if(n==0)
    return ackermann(m - 1, 1);
    return ackermann(m - 1, ackermann(m, n - 1));
}
```

```
int main() {
  unsigned int m, n;
    for (m = 0; m < 4; ++m) {
      for (n = 0; n < 10; ++n) {
        printf("A(%u, %u) = %u\n", m, n,
        ackermann(m, n));
      }
    }
    return 0;
}
```

For small values of m like 1, 2, or 3, the Ackermann function grows relatively slowly with respect to n, which may at most

be exponentially. For $m \geq 4$, however, it grows much more quickly. As a result, the program might stop at run-time. For example, if we replace the nested loop within the main() function as listed below, the program terminates abnormally.

```
for (m = 0; m <= 4; ++m) {
      for (n = 0; n < 10; ++n) {
        printf("A(%u, %u) = %u\n",
        m, n, ackermann(m, n));
      }
}
```

The following table shows the values resulting from the computation of Ackermann function.

		N				
		0	1	2	3	n
m	0	1	2	3	4	$n+1$
	1	2	3	4	5	$n+2$ $=2+(n+3)-3$
	2	3	5	7	9	$2n+3$ $=2\times(n+3)-3$
	3	5	13	29	61	$2^{n+3}-3$
	4	$13 = 2^{2^2} - 3$	65533 $2^{2^{2^2}} - 3$	$2^{65536} - 3$ $2^{2^{2^{2^2}}} - 3$	$2^{2^{65536}} - 3$ $- 3$	$2^{2^{\cdot^{\cdot^{\cdot^2}}}} - 3$
	5	.....	....	....	.....	......

The abnormal behaviour of the program is either because of integer overflow or because of the fact that it may be running out of memory. Considering a 32-bit compiler, on incrementing the value of m and n it may lead to many stack frames on recursive calls, which shall be more evident after studying the following section (7.10.2). The system is bound to run out of memory. Since the Ackermann function is enormously recursive, it is occasionally utilized as a programming language performance benchmark or as a stress test for recursion.

7.10.2 How is Recursion implemented?

The run-time stack For the moment, let it be left to recursion to consider what steps are needed to call any function in a single processor computer system.

Modern languages are usually implemented in a manner such that storage for program code and storage for

data items are allocated separately. The area of store set aside to hold the data items used in the call of a function is called its *data area* or *activation record*.

This data area essentially consists of calling parameters, local variables, and certain system information such as the address of the instruction that must be returned to on leaving the function.

The storage mechanism that most modern languages use is called *stack storage management*. Using this mechanism, storage for the main program's data area is allocated at load time, while storage for a function's data area is only allocated when the function is called. On exit from the function this storage is de-allocated. This mechanism results in a stack of data areas called the '*run-time stack*'. When a function is called, space for its data area is allocated and placed on top of the run-time stack. On exit from the function, its data area is de-allocated and removed from the top of the run-time stack. Basically the principle it follows is Last In First Out (LIFO).

Stack storage management is capable of dealing with recursive functions. In the recursive case, two recursive calls are regarded as being different so that the data areas for one call do not overlap with the other; just like one would not mix the data areas for different sub-functions, one called from within the other. This implies that there may be several data areas in existence simultaneously, one for each recursive call.

In the stack implementation of recursion, the local variables of the function will be pushed onto the stack as the recursive call is initiated. When the recursive call terminates, these local variables will be popped from the stack and thereby restored to their former values.

But doing so is pointless because the recursive call is the last action of the function and so the function now terminates. The just-restored local variables are discarded. It is thus pointless to use the recursion stack since no local variables need to be preserved. All that is needed is to set the calling parameters to their new values and branch to the beginning of the function.

Points to Note

- It may not terminate if the stopping case is not correct or is incomplete (stack overflow: run-time error)
- Make sure that each recursive step leads to a situation that is closer to a stopping case.

7.10.3 Comparing Recursion and Iteration

Recursion is a very powerful tool for solving complex problem, particularly when the underlying problem or data to be treated are already defined in recursive terms. For such problems, recursion can lead to solutions that are much clearer and easier to modify than their iterative counterparts.

However, such recursive definitions do not guarantee that a recursive algorithm is the best way to solve a problem. Depending on the implementation available and the algorithm being used, recursion can require a substantial amount of runtime overhead. Thus, the use of recursion illustrates the classic trade off between time spent in constructing and maintaining a program and the cost in time and memory of execution of that program.

Two factors contribute to the inefficiency of some recursive solutions.

- The overhead associated with function calls
- The inefficient utilization of memory

With most implementations of modern programming languages, a function call incurs a booking overhead in the form of a runtime stack. Recursive functions magnify this bookkeeping overhead because a single initial call to the function can generate a large number of recursive calls.

It makes inefficient utilization of memory, as every time a new recursive call is made a new set of local variables is allocated to function. Moreover it also slows down execution speed, as function calls require jumps, and saving the current state of the calling function onto stack before jump.

Recursion is of value when the return values of the recursive function are used in further processing within the calling version of the function (rather than being immediately passed back to an earlier version of the function). In this case it was *worth* saving the parameter and local variables on the stack because they are used later in some useful way.

If one problem can be solved in both way (recursive or iterative), then choosing iterative version is a good idea since it is faster and doesn't consume a lot of memory.

Points to Note

In general, an iterative version of a program will execute more efficiently in terms of time and space than a recursive version. This is because the overhead involved in entering and exiting a function is avoided in iterative version. However a recursive solution can be sometimes the most natural and logical way of solving a complex problem.

7.11 SEARCHING AND SORTING

7.11.1 Searching Algorithms

We will discuss two of the most important searching algorithms here: sequential search and binary search.

Sequential or linear search algorithm

The idea behind the sequential search is to compare the given number to each of the numbers in the array. If a number in the list matches the given key, we can return the index of that number. If we reach the end of the list, we can indicate that key does not exist in array by returning −1. Here is an implementation of this simple algorithm:

```
int  Lsearch(int ArrayElement[], int key,
                      int ArraySize)
```

```
{
    int i ;
    for (i = 0; i < ArraySize;  i++)
        if (ArrayElement[i] == Key)
                    return (i) ;
    return (-1);
}
```

The function calling statement will be as follows:

```
p=Lsearch(a,k,n);
if(p = = -1)
    printf("\n KEY NOT FOUND");
else
    printf("\n KEY  FOUND AT POSITION %d", p);
```

Binary search algorithm

The drawbacks of sequential search can be eliminated if it becomes possible to eliminate large portions of the list from consideration in subsequent iterations. The binary search method does just that; it halves the size of the list to search in each iteration.

Binary search can be explained simply by the analogy of searching for a page in a book. Suppose a reader is searching for page 90 in a book of 150 pages. The reader would first open the book at random towards the latter half of the book. If the page number is less than 90, the reader would open at a page to the right; if it is greater than 90, the reader would open at a page to the left, repeating the process till page 90 is found. As can be seen, by the first instinctive search, the reader dramatically reduced the number of pages to be searched.

Precondition of binary search is that it requires sorted data to operate on. Basic technique is to compare the search element with the element which is in the middle of the search space and then to restrict further searching into the appropriate half of the search space (this can be done because the search space is sorted). Then at each step, the process is repeated (cutting the remaining search space in half at each step) until either the search element is found or we have run out of elements to compare and the element was not in the search space.

To implement binary search, Variables beg and end keep track of the lower bound and upper bound of the array, respectively. We begin by examining the middle element of the array. If the key we are searching for is less than the middle element, then it must reside in the lower half of the array. Thus, we set end to (mid – 1). If the key we are

searching for is greater than the middle element, then it must reside in the upper half of the array. Thus, we set beg to (mid + 1).This restricts our next iteration through the loop to the top half of the array. In this way, each iteration halves the size of the array to be searched. For example, the first iteration will leave 3 items to test. After the second iteration, there will be 1 item left to test. Therefore it takes only three iterations to find any number.

To Illustrate the algorithm, let us Consider the following array:

3	10	15	20	35	40	60

Suppose we want to search the element "15"

1. We take beg = 0, end = 6 and compute the location of the middle element as

$$min = \frac{(beg + end)}{2} = \frac{(0 + 6)}{2} = 3$$

2. We then compare the search key with mid i.e. a[mid]==a[3] is not equal to 15. Since beg<end, we have to start the next iteration.

3. As a[mid]=20>15, therefore, we take end = mid–1 = 3 – 1 = 2 whereas beg remains the same.. Thus

$$min = \frac{(beg + end)}{2} = \frac{(0 + 2)}{2} = 1$$

4. Since a[mid], i.e. a[1]=10<15, therefore, we take beg=mid+1=1+1=2, while end remains the same.

5. Now beg=end. Compute the mid element:

$$min = \frac{(beg + end)}{2} = \frac{(2 + 2)}{2} = 2$$

Since a[mid], i.e. a[2]=15, the search terminates on success.The C code for binary search is given below.

```
#include <stdio.h>
int binarysearch(int a[], int n, int key)
{
    int beg,mid;
    beg=0; end=n-1;
    while(beg<=end)
    {
        mid=(beg+end)/2;
        if(key==a[mid])
                return mid;
        else if(key>a[mid])
```

```
                beg=mid+1;
        else
                end=mid-1;

    }
    return -1;

}
int main()
{

    int arr[50], n, key, index;
    printf("How many elements?");
    scanf("%d", &n);
    puts("Enter the array elements in ascending\
        order");
    for (index = 0; index < n; index++)
        scanf("%d", &arr[index]);
    printf("Enter the search key: ");
    scanf("%d", &key);
    index = binarysearch(arr, n, key);
    if (index == -1)
      puts("Sorry, the given key was not found");
    else
      printf("The given key was found at index:\
        %d\n", index);
    return 0;

}
```

Binary search in a recursive way

Binary search is often written using recursion, instead of iteration. The key idea is that when the algorithm decides to search the right or left half of the array, which is a simpler version of the original problem. In the recursive Search function below note how the parameters to the recursive calls are adjusted to specify either the right or left half of the array.

```
/* Given:x      Array of integers.
   Low         The low index of the range of integers
               to search.
   High        The top index of the range of integers
               to search.
   k           The integer for which to search.
   Task:       To do a recursive binary search for k
               in the specified range of Array.
   Return:     In the function name, return the index
               of where k was found or -1 if it was
               not found.
```

```
*/
int search(int x[ ], int k, int low, int high)
{
  int mid;
  if(low > high)
    return (-1);
  mid = (low + high) /2;
  return (k= =x[mid] ? mid : k < x[mid] ? search(x,
      k, low, mid – 1):search(x, k, mid+1, high));
}
```

7.11.2 Sorting Algorithms

Arranging elements of an array in a particular order is called sorting. The order of arrangement may be ascending or descending in nature. There are several methods of arranging or sorting arrays. Sorting algorithms are divided into two categories: internal and external sorts.

- *Internal sort* Any sort algorithm, which uses main memory exclusively during the sort. This assumes high-speed random access to all memory.
- *External sort* Any sort algorithm, which uses external memory, such as tape or disk, during the sort.

A sort algorithm is said to be 'stable' if multiple items which compare as equal will stay in the same order they were in after a sort.
Some of the sorting methods include:

- Bubble sort
- Selection sort
- Insertion sort
- Merge sort
- Quick sort

Bubble sort

A bubble sort compares adjacent array elements and exchanges their values if they are out of order. In this way, the smaller values 'bubble' to the top of the array (towards element 0), while the larger values sink to the bottom of the array. This sort continues until no exchanges are performed in a pass. If no exchanges are made, then all pairs must be in order. For this reason, a flag named 'sorted' is used.

The way bubble sort works is that it iterates through the data set comparing two neighbouring items at a time and swapping them if the first item is larger than the second item. The following example depicts the different stages of bubble sort.

	Pass 1	Pass 2	Pass 3	Pass 4	Pass 5
42	42	26	26	26	26
60	26	42	34	28	28
26	55	34	28	34	34
55	34	28	42	42	42
34	28	55	55	55	55
28	60	60	60	60	60

Now the implementation of the above algorithm will be as follows:

```c
#include <stdio.h>
#include <stdlib.h>
int main()
{
int a[30],n,i,j,temp, sorted=0;
printf("\n How many numbers");
scanf("%d",&n);
if(n>30)
{
printf("\n Too many Numbers");
exit(0);
}
printf("\n Enter the array elements \n");
for(i=0 ; i< n; i++)
scanf("%d", &a[i]);
for(i = 0; i < (n-1) && sorted==0; i++)
{
sorted=1;
for(j = 0; j < (n - i) -1; j++)
if(a[j] > a[j+1])
{
temp = a[j];
a[j] = a[j+1];
a[j+1] = temp;
sorted=0;
}
}
printf("\n The numbers in sorted order \n");
for(i=0 ; i<n; ++i)
printf("\n %d", a[i]);
return 0;
}
```

Output

```
How many numbers 6
Enter the array elements
42
60
26
55
34
28
The numbers in sorted order
26
28
34
42
55
60
```

Selection sort

Selection sort is a way of arranging the elements, of a supposedly unsorted array, in an ascending order. It works by finding the smallest element in the whole array and placing it at the first element position. It then finds the 2nd smallest element in the array disregarding the first element and places it in the 2nd position. Next it finds the smallest element in the array disregarding the elements placed in position 1 and 2. This continues until the entire array has been sorted. The implementation algorithm for selection sort may be states as follows:

1. Examine each element in the array or list to find the smallest.
2. Swap the element found in step 1 with the first element in the array or list.
3. Repeat steps 1 and 2, each time ignoring the element at the start of the last sort. Stop when only one element has to be sorted.

The selection sort is, therefore, a combination of searching and sorting. During each pass, the unsorted element with the smallest (or largest) value is moved to its proper position in the array. This sort also uses an incremental approach to sorting the array. The number of times the sort passes through the array depends on the size of the array. The algorithm makes one less pass than the number of elements in the array.

A function for the selection sort can be developed using two loops. There is an inner loop that passes through the array and finds the next smallest (or largest) value, and an outer loop that places that value into its proper position. The selection sort is one of the easiest sorts to implement, but is among the least efficient. It provides no way to end a sort early even if it begins with an already sorted list. A function developed for implementing the selection sort technique for arranging a list of elements in ascending order is shown below:

```
void selectsort(int numbers[], int array_size)

{
    int i, j;

    int min, temp;

    for (i = 0; i < array_size-1; i++)

    {

        min = i;

        for (j = i+1; j < array_size; j++)

        {

            if (numbers[j] < numbers[min])

            min = j;

        }

        temp = numbers[i];

        numbers[i] = numbers[min];

        numbers[min] = temp;

    }

}
```

an array formed with integers

highlighted "for loop" finds the position of the smallest integer

highlighted statements interchange the position of the smallest integer with that at the first position.

For the above algorithm to work, it *must* ignore elements that have already been sorted. For instance, once the smallest element has been placed in its correct position, it must be ignored for the rest of the sort. In practice this means that to implement the algorithm, the already sorted elements have to be skipped, looking only for the smallest element that is not yet sorted. This can be implemented in the function void selectsort() by replacing the encircled portion of the program code with that shown within the box on the right.

```
void selectsort(int numbers[], int array_size)
{
    int i, j;
    int min, temp;
    for (i = 0; i < array_size-1; i++)
    {
        min = i;
        for (j = i+1; j < array_size; j++)
        {
```

```
            if (numbers[j] < numbers[min])
                min = j;
        }

        temp = numbers[i];
        numbers[i] = numbers[min];
        numbers[min] = temp;

    }
```

```
    if(min != i)
    {
        temp = numbers[i];
        numbers[i] = numbers[min];
        numbers[min] = temp;
    }
```

Insertion sort

The primary idea, in insertion sort, is to pick up a data element from a list or array and insert it into its proper place in the partial data list or array considered so far.

The process of insertion sort is started by considering the first element to belong to a sorted sub-array while the remaining array elements to another sub-array which is considered as unsorted. The first step then is to compare the first element of the unsorted array with the sorted array's element. If the sorting is for arranging the elements in ascending order, then the comparison is carried out to find whether the first element of the unsorted array is smaller than that of the sorted array's element. If this is true then the first element of the unsorted array is placed at the first position of the sorted array while the existing element in the sorted array is shifted right by one position. The sorted sub-array will now contain two sorted elements while the unsorted sub-array will contain N-2 elements, where N denotes the size of the whole array. In the second step again the first element of the unsorted sub-array is compared with the elements of the sorted sub-array and the resulting element is placed at the proper position while shifting the larger elements by one position to the right in the sorted sub-array.

The sorted sub-array now contains three elements arranged in order while the rest of the elements form the unsorted sub-array. In the same way, the next step repeats the same procedure of comparison and placing of the appropriate element at the proper position. This process continues till the last element in the array. Thus, in each pass, the first element of the unsorted portion is picked up, transferred to the sorted sub-list, and inserted at the appropriate place. A list of N elements will take at most N–1 passes to sort the data.

Figure 7.4 shows the insertion sort technique. THis illustration demonstrates the way the array is sorted. Every time the first element, which is shown coloured, is compared with the elements of the sorted sub-array and interposed at the proper position in sorted sub-array by suitably shifting the larger value elements.

A function prepared for implementing the insertion sort algorithm for sorting an array in ascending order is given in Fig. 7.4.

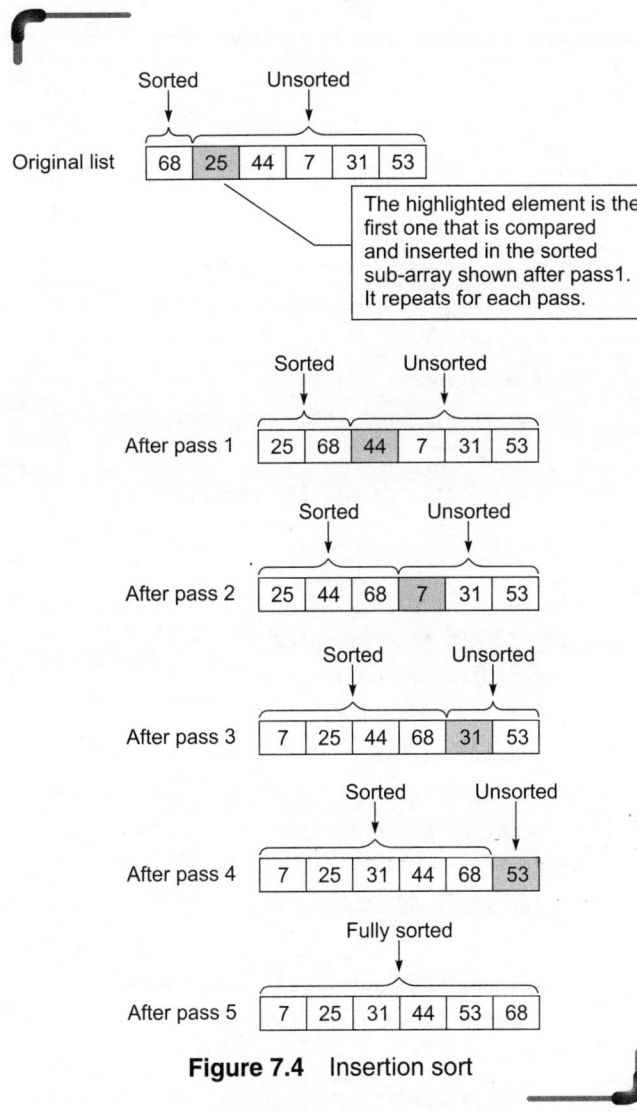

Figure 7.4   Insertion sort

```
void insertSort(int A[], int arr_size)
{
    int i, j,temp;
       for (i=1; i < arr_size; i++)
```

```
{
    temp = A[i];
    j = i;
    while ((j > 0) && (A[j-1] >temp))
     {
        A[j] = A[j-1];
        j = j - 1;
     }
    A[j] = temp;
   }
}
```

An alternate function that can also do insertion sorting is shown below.

```
void insort(int A[], int size)
{
    int i, j, temp;
    for (i = 1 ; i < size; i++)
    {
        temp = A[i];
        for (j = i - 1; j >= 0 && temp < A[j] ; j--)
            A[ j + 1] = A[ j ];
        A[ j + 1] = temp;
    }
}
```

An advantage of this procedure is that it sorts the array only when it is really necessary. If the array is already in order, no moves for sorting are performed. However, it overlooks the fact that the elements may already be in their proper positions. When an element has to be inserted, all elements greater than this have to be shifted. There may be large number of redundant shifts, as an element, which is properly located, may be shifted but later brought back to its position.

The best case is when the data are already in order. Only one comparison is made for each position and the data movement is 2N – 1, where N is the size of the array. The worst case is when the data are in reverse order. Each data element is to be moved to new position and for that each of the other elements have to be shifted. When the elements are in random order, it turns out that both number of comparisons and movements turn out to be closer to the worst case .

Merge sort

The merge sort splits a data list to be sorted into two equal halves, and places them in separate arrays.

This sorting method uses the divide-and-conquer paradigm. It separates the list into two halves and then sorts the two half data sets recursively. Finally, these are merged to obtain the complete sorted list.

To be more specific, the merge sort breaks an array down into smaller and smaller pieces until the individual pieces are just one item in size. Since a single item is always considered to be sorted, two contiguous items can be merged. The merge sort algorithm therefore breaks the array down into smaller chunks on the way down the recursion tree. On the way back up, it merges these smaller pieces of the array into larger pieces. One could say that the sorting is done on the way back up the tree.

Figure 7.5 shows a typical example of the merge sort algorithm for an unsorted array A of size 8 that contains the following data elements 32 45 26 15 25 91 30 73.

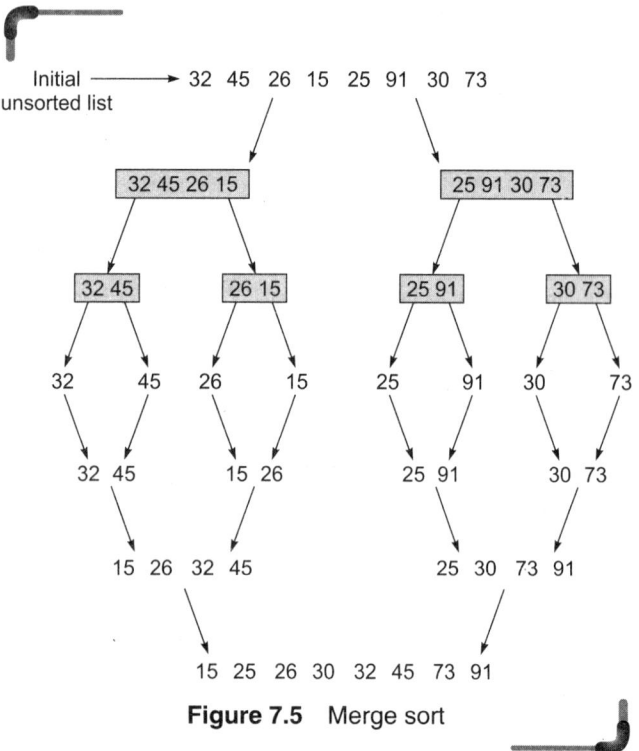

Initial unsorted list → 32 45 26 15 25 91 30 73

Figure 7.5 Merge sort

In the example shown above the original array is kept on splitting in two halves till it reduces to array of one element. Then these are merged in the following steps:

1. Elements 32 and 45 are compared and merged to form the array [32 45] .

2. Elements 26 and 15 are compared and merged to form the array [15 26].

3. Next sub-arrays [32 45] and [15 26] are compared and merged to form the array [15 26 32 45].

4. Elements 25 and 91 are compared and merged to form the array [25 91].

5. Elements 30 and 73 are compared and merged to form the array [30 73].

6. Next sub-arrays [25 91] and [30 73] are compared and merged to form the array [25 30 73 91].

7. Finally the sorted and merged sub-arrays in steps 3 and 6 are sorted and merged to form the array [15 25 26 30 32 45 73 91].

A function that implements the merge sort algorithm discussed above is given as follows:

```c
void mergesort(int array[], int n)
{
    int j,n1,n2,arr1[n],arr2[n];
        if (n<=1)return;
    n1=n/2;
    n2 = n - n1;
    for(j = 0; j<n1; j++)
        arr1[j]= array[j];
    for(j = 0; j<n2; j++)
        arr2[j]= array[j+n1];
    mergesort(arr1, n1);
    mergesort(arr2, n2);
    merge(array, arr1, n1, arr2, n2);
}
void merge (int array[], int arr1[], int n1,
                        int arr2[], int n2)
{
    int j, p=0, p1=0,p2=0;
    printf("\n After merging [");
    for(j=0; j<n1; j++)
    printf("%d ",arr1[j]);
      printf("] [");
    for(j=0; j<n2; j++)
      printf("%d",arr2[j]);
    printf("]");
    while (p1 < n1 && p2 < n2)
    {
      if(arr1[p1] < arr2[p2])
        array [p++] = arr1[p1++];
      else
        array[p++] = arr2[p2++];
    }
    while (p1 < n1)
      array [p++] = arr1[p1++];
    while (p2 < n2)
```

```
      array[p++] = arr2[p2++];
  printf("merged array is [");
  for(j=0; j<n1+n2; j++)
    printf("%d", array[j]);
  printf("]\n");
}
```

Quick sort

Quick sort is a recursively defined procedure for rearranging the values stored in an array in ascending or descending order. Suppose an array a of 11 integers is given as shown in Fig.7.6(a).

| 14 | 3 | 2 | 11 | 5 | 8 | 0 | 2 | 9 | 4 | 20 |
a[0]   a[10]

(a) Array of 11 elements containing integers

| 4 | 3 | 2 | 2 | 5 | 0 | | 8 | | 11 | 9 | 14 | 20 |
a[0]   a[10]

(b) Separation of elements with values less or more than the pivot, 8

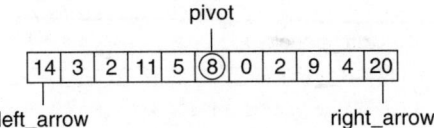

(c) Choosing the index of the pivot

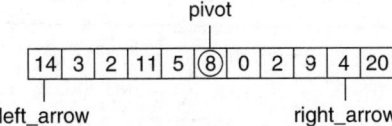

(d) Moving the right_arrow to the left until 'value <= pivot'

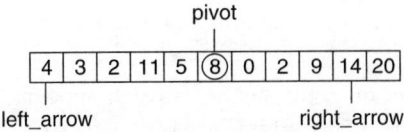

(e) Swapping of the values in the a[left_arrow] and a[right_arrow] elements

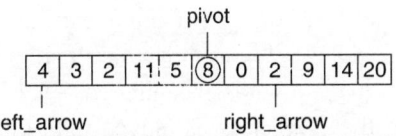

(f) Position of the right_arrow after a[right_arrow] <=pivot condition becomes true as the right_arrow is moved left

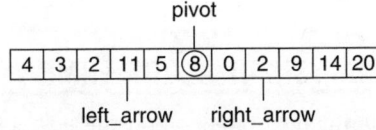

(g) Position of left_arrow after a[left_arrow]>=pivot condition becomes true as the left_arrow is moved right

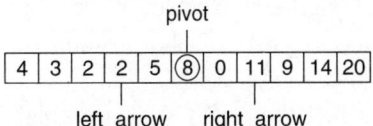

(h) Exchanging a[left_arrow] and a[right_arrow]

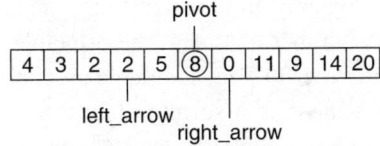

(i) Moving right_arrow to the Left till a[right_arrow]<=pivot

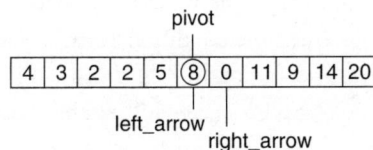

(j) Moving left_arrow right till a[left_arrow]>= pivot

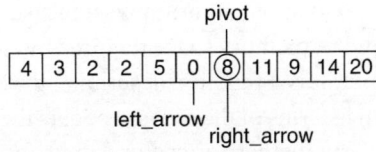

(k) Exchanging pivot with right_arrow content

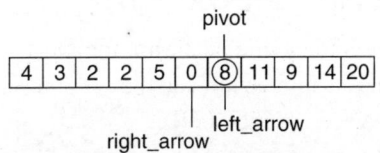

(l) The right_arrow is moved left and the left_arrow is moved right

Figure 7.6 Step-by-step depiction of how quick sort works

The idea is to use a process that separates the list into two parts, using a distinguishedvalue in the list called a *pivot*. At the end of the process, one part will contain only values less than or equal to the pivot, and the other will contain only values greater than or equal to the pivot. So, if 8 is picked as the pivot, Fig. 7.6(b) shows the result at the end of the process.

The same process can then be reapplied exactly to the left-hand and right-hand parts separately. This reapplication of the same procedure leads to a recursive definition. The detail of the rearranging procedure is as follows. The index of the pivot value is chosen simply by evaluating

```
(first + last) / 2
```

where first and last are the indices of the initial and final elements in the arrayrepresenting the list. A left_arrow and a right_arrow are then identified on the farleft and the far right respectively, as can be seen in Fig. 7.6(c), where left_arrow and right_arrow initially represent the lowest and highest indicesof the array components. Starting from the right, the right_arrow is moved left until a value less than or equal to the pivot is encountered. See Fig. 7.6(d).

Similarly, the left_arrow is moved right until a value greater than or equal to the pivot is encountered. Now the contents of the two array components are swapped as can be seen in Fig. 7.6(e).

Now continuing the movement of the right_arrow left till a[right_arrow]<=pivot, the position of the right_arrow is as shown in Fig. 7.6(f).

Having reached the status shown in Fig. 7.6(g), the contents of the a[left_arrow] and a[right_arrow] are interchanged. After this interchange the contents of the elements are shown in Fig. 7.6(h).

The process of movement of the left_arrow and right_arrow only stops when the condition left_arrow > right_arrow becomes true. Since in Fig. 7.6(h), this condition is still False, move right_arrow left again as seen in Fig. 7.6(i).

Having reached the status shown in Fig. 7.6(k), the contents of the a[left_arrow] and a[right_arrow] are inter-changed. It is acceptable to exchange the pivot because pivot is the value itself, not the index. As before, the right_arrow is moved left and the left_arrow is moved right as can be seen in Fig. 7.6(l).

The procedure's terminating condition left_arrow > right_arrow is now true,and the first sub-division of the list (i.e., array) is now complete.

Here the quick sort procedure is coded as a recursive C function. This can be seen asfollows.

```c
void quick_sort(int list[], int left, int right)
{
    int pivot, left_arrow, right_arrow;
    left_arrow = left;
    right_arrow = right;
    pivot = list[(left + right)/2];
    do
    {
        while(list[right_arrow] > pivot)
            right_arrow--;
        while(list[left_arrow] < pivot)
            left_arrow++;
        if(left_arrow <= right_arrow)
        {
            swap(list[left_arrow], list[right_arrow]);
            left_arrow++;
            right_arrow--;
        }
    }
    while(right_arrow >= left_arrow);
    if(left < right_arrow)
        quick_sort(list, left, right_arrow);
    if(left_arrow < right)
        quick_sort(list, left_arrow, right);
}
```

7.12 ANALYSIS OF ALGORITHMS

One significant factor considered while designing algorithms is the algorithm's efficiency. The efficiency of an algorithm is determined by the amount of time it takes to run the program and the memory space the program requires. In analyzing an algorithm, rather than a piece of code, the number of times 'the principle activity' of that algorithm is performed, should be predicted. For example, if one is analyzing a sorting algorithm, one might count the number of comparisons performed, and if it is an algorithm to find an optimal solution, one might count the number of times it evaluates a solution.

Complexity of an algorithm is a measure of the amount of time and/or memory space required by an algorithm for a given input. It is a function describing the efficiency of the algorithm in terms of the amount of data the algorithm must process. Usually there are natural units for the domain and range of this function. The factor or parameters or fields whose values affect the number of operations performed is called the *problem size* or the *input size*. The following are the two main complexity measures of the efficiency of an algorithm:

- **Time complexity** is a function describing the amount of time an algorithm takes with respect to the amount of input provided to the algorithm. 'Time' can mean the number of memory accesses performed, the number of comparisons between integers, the number of times some inner loop is executed, or some other natural unit related to the amount of real time the algorithm will take. It is denoted as $T(n)$ where n is the size of the input.

- **Space complexity** is a function describing the amount of memory (space) an algorithm takes with respect to the amount of input provided to the algorithm. Space complexity is sometimes ignored because the space used is minimal and/or obvious, but sometimes it becomes as important an issue as time. It is denoted as $S(n)$ where n is the size of the input.

Complexity analysis attempts to characterize the relationship between the number of data elements and resource usage (time or space) with a simple formula approximation. Using the RAM model of computation, one can count how many steps our algorithm will take for executing a program based on the input provided. However, to really understand how good or bad an algorithm is, one must know how it works over all instances. There are three terms to describe these situations:

- The **worst-case complexity** of the algorithm is the function defined by the maximum number of steps taken on any instance of input size n.
- The **best-case complexity** of the algorithm is the function defined by the minimum number of steps taken on any instance of input size n.
- Finally, the **average-case complexity** of the algorithm is the function defined by the average number of steps taken on any instance of input size n.

Every input instance can be represented as a point on a graph, where the x-axis is the size of the problem (for sorting, the number of items to sort) and the y-axis is the number of steps taken by the algorithm on this instance. Worse case complexity is represented by the curve passing through the highest point of each column. The curve passing through the lowest point of each column represents the best case complexity.

The average case is probably the most important, but it is problematic. One has to make some assumption about the probabilities, and the analysis will only be as accurate as the validity of the assumptions. In simple cases, the average complexity is established by considering possible inputs to an algorithm, for each input, adding the number of steps for all the inputs and dividing by the number of inputs. Here it is assumed that the possibility of the occurrence of each input is the same, which will not always be the case. To consider the probability explicitly, the average complexity is defined as the average over the number of steps executed when processing each input weighted by the probability of occurrence of this input.

If a function is linear, that is, if it contains no loops, then its efficiency is a function of the number of instructions it contains. In this case, its efficiency is dependent on the speed of the computer. On the other hand, functions that contain loops will vary widely in their efficiency. The study of algorithm efficiency is, therefore, largely devoted to the study of loops. The efficiency of an algorithm can be expressed as a function of the number of elements or inputs to be processed. The general format is

```
f(n) = efficiency
```

Loops can be of various types. Let us discuss these in detail.

Linear loops Consider the following simple loop.

```
for(i=1;i<=n;++i)     for(i=0;i<n;++i)
{                     {
  stmTs                 stmTs
}                     }
```

The body of the loop will be repeated for n times. In the following loop,

```
for(i=1;i<=n; i=i+2)
{
  stmTs
}
```

the body of the loop will be executed $n/2$ times. In all of the above cases, the number of iterations is directly proportional to a factor. The higher the factor, the higher will be the number of iterations. If either of these loops were plotted, one would get a straight line. For that reason, they are known as linear loops. Because the efficiency is proportional to the number of iterations, it is

```
f(n) = n
```

Logarithmic loops Now, the following loops are to be considered in which the controlling variable is multiplied or divided in each iteration.

```
Multiply loop          Divide loop
for(i=1; i<n; i=i*2)   for(i=n; i>=1; i=i/2)
{                      {
  stmTs                  stmTs
}                      }
```

Let $n = 10$; the number of iterations in both cases is 4. The reason is that in each iteration the value of i doubles for the multiply loop and is cut in half for the divide loop. The number of iterations is a function of the multiplier or divisor. The loop continues while the following condition is true.

For the multiply loop, $2^{\text{iteration}} < n$

For the divide loop, $n/2^{\text{iteration}} >= 1$

Generalizing the analysis, $f(n) = [\log_2 n]$

Nested loop For the nested loop, the total number of iterations would be the product of the number of iterations for the inner loop and the number of iterations for the outer loop. There are various types of nested loops, namely, quadratic, dependent quadratic, linear logarithmic, etc.

Quadratic loop Here each of the loops iterates the same number of times as shown in the following code.

```
for(i=1;i<=n;i++)
  for(j=1;j<=n;j++)
  {
    stmTs
  }
```

For each iteration of the outer loop, the inner loop will be executed n times. The outer loop will be executed n times. Therefore,

```
f(n) = n²
```

Dependent quadratic Consider the following nested loop:

```
for(i=1;i<=n;i++)
  for(j=1;j<=i;j++)
  {
    stmTs
  }
```

Here, the inner loop is dependent on the outer loop for one of its factors. It is executed only once for the first iteration, twice for second iteration, thrice for third, and so forth. The number of iteration for the inner loop is

```
1+2+3+4+........n = n(n+1)/2
```

The average of this loop is $(n+1)/2$. Multiplying the inner loop by the number of times the outer loop is executed gives the following formula for a dependent quadratic loop.

```
f(n) = n(n+1)/2
```

Linear logarithmic Consider the following nested loop in which the outer loop is linear and the inner loop is logarithmic.

```
for(i=1;i<=n;i++)
  for(j=1;j<=n;j=j*2)
  {
    stmTs
  }
```

Therefore, the number of iterations in the inner loop is $[\log_2 n]$. The outer loop will be executed n times. So,

```
f(n) = [nlog₂ n]
```

It has been shown that the number of statements executed in the function for n elements of data is a function of the number of elements, expressed as `f(n)`. There is a dominant factor in the equation that determines the 'order of magnitude' of the result. Therefore, it is not needed to determine the complete measure of efficiency, only the factor that determines the magnitude. This factor is the Big-O.

7.12.1 Asymptotic Notation

Asymptotic notation is a way of describing functions without having to deal with distracting details. In many ways, asymptotic notation can seem very imprecise and intuitive, but it is important that it is precisely defined; it is also crucial to understand exactly what it means.

Big-O Notation

The most well known symbol in asymptotic notation is the *big-O* (historically, the Greek letter omicron). It is used to give an *upper limit* to the *asymptotic growth* of a function. Order notation, or Big-O notation, is a measure of the running time of an algorithm, as it relates to the size of the input to that algorithm. It is intended, not to measure the performance of the machine on which the algorithm is run, but rather to strictly measure the performance of the algorithm itself.

Formally it can be defined as, if `f(n)` and `g(n)` are functions defined for positive integers then `f(n) = O(g(n))` if there exists a c such that $|f(n)| <= c|g(n)|$ for all sufficiently large positive integers n.

```
f(n) = O(g(n)) is true if
lim f(n)/g(n) is a constant.
n → a
```

It is to be noted that the big-O notation says 'some constant multiple of' without saying what the constant is. This leaves out some information that is sometimes important, but it allows specifying time without reference to the speed of the computer and without measuring exactly how many instructions are in a certain block of code. The properties of the big-O notation are as follows.

1. `O(k*f(n)) = O(f(n))`, therefore, constants can be ignored.

2. `O(f(n)*g(n)) = O(f(n)) * O(g(n))`, i.e., if a function is a product then its order is the product of the orders of the factors.

3. `O(f(n)/g(n)) = O(f(n)) / O(g(n))`, i.e., the order is the same for a function that is a quotient.

4. `O(f(n)) > O(g(n))`, if and only if, f dominates g.

5. `O(f(n)+g(n)) = Max[O(f(n)), O(g(n))]`, i.e., terms of lower degree can be ignored.

6. One should be careful with functions that have subtraction:

   If `f(n) = O(h(n))` and `g(n) = O(h(n))` then

   `f(n)-g(n)` is not equal to `O(h(n)) - O(h(n)) = 0`

7. Big O is transitive. That is, if `f(n) = O(g(n))` and `g(n)` is `O(h(n))`, then `f(n) = O(h(n))`.

8. The powers of n are ordered according to the exponent $n^a = O(n^b)$ iff `a <= b`.

9. The order of log n is independent of the base taken $\log_a n = O(\log_b n)$ for all `a, b > 1`.

10. Logarithms grow more slowly than any power of n
    `log n = O(n^a)` for any a>0 but `n^a != O(log n)`

11. `na = O(bn)`, for all `a, b > 1` but `b^n != O(n^a)` for `b > 1`

The big-O notation can be derived from `f(n)` using the following steps:

1. In each term, set the coefficient of the term to one.

2. Keep the largest term in the function and discard the others. Terms are ranked from lowest to highest as follows:

   `log n, n, nlog n, n², n³, …, n^k, 2^n, n!, …`

For example, to calculate the Big-O notation for

$$f(n) = n(n+1)/2 + 5n^3 = n^2/2 + n/2 + 5n^3$$

we first remove the coefficients. This gives us n2 + n + n3. The largest factor is n3. Therefore, the big-O notation is stated as

$$O(f(n)) = O(n^3)$$

Certain big-O expressions occur so frequently that they are given names. An algorithm is

- constant, if `f(n)` is `O(1)`.
- logarithmic, if `f(n)` is `O(lg n)`.
- linear, if `f(n)` is `O(n)`.
- quadratic, if `f(n)` is $O(n^2)$.
- polynomial, if `f(n)` is $O(n^k)$, where k is constant.
- exponential, if `f(n)` is $O(n^k)$, where k is constant.

Let us now discuss these in detail.

Constant O(1)

An algorithm with the running time O(1) is said to have a 'constant' running time. Basically, this means that the algorithm always takes the same amount of time, regardless of the size of the input. To state it technically, if an algorithm will never performs more than a certain number of steps, no matter how large the input is, then that algorithm is considered to have a constant running time.

Linear O(n)

An algorithm which runs in `O(n)` is said to have a 'linear' running time. This means that the amount of time to run the algorithm is proportional to the size of the input. Alternatively, an algorithm which never performs more than a certain number of steps for each element in the input has a linear running time.

Quadratic O(n²)

This means that whenever one increases the size of the input by a factor of n, the running time increases by a factor of n^2.

Logarithm O(log n)

This means that as the size of the input increases by a factor of n, the running time increases by a factor of the logarithm of n. For example, if one increases the input size of O(logn) algorithm by a factor of 1024, the running time will increase by a factor of 10. This running time is better than O(n), but not as good as O(1). As the input size gets large, however, the behavior becomes comparable to O(1) in many circumstances.

Linear Logarithmic O(nlog n)

An algorithm which when given an input of size n never performs more than cn log n steps (for some c which is always the same regardless of the value of n) has a running time of O(n log n). This running time is better than O(n²).

Exponential O(2ⁿ)

This means that its running time will double every time you add another element to the input. An algorithm with this running time is generally considered to be too slow to be useful for anything but the smallest of problems.

Lower Bounds and Tight Bounds

Big O only gives an upper bound on a function, i.e., if the constant factors are ignored and n gets big enough, it is obvious that some function will never exceed some other function. But this can give too much freedom. For instance, the time for selection sort is easily O(n³), because n² is O(n³). But we know that O(n²) is a more meaningful upper bound. What is required is to be able to describe a *lower bound*, a function that always grows more slowly than f(n), and a *tight bound*, a function that grows at about the same rate as f(n). There is a symmetrical definition of the lower bound in the definition of big-Ω (omega):

The function f(n) is Ω (g(n)), if there exist positive numbers c and N such that f(n) > cg(n) for all n > N. In other words, cg(n) is a lower bound on the size of f(n) or in the long run f grows at least at the rate of g.

There is an interconnection between these two notations expressed by the equivalence.

```
f(n) is Ω (g(n)) iff g(n) is O(f(n)).
```

There is a common ground between big-O and big-Ω notations indicated by the equalities in the definition of these notations. Big-O is defined in terms of ≤ and Big-Ω in terms of >; = is included in both inequalities. This restriction can be accomplished by the following definition of θ (theta) notation:

The function f(n) is θ(g(n)), if there exist positive numbers c1, c2, and N such that c1g(n) < f(n) < c2g(n) for all n > N.

7.12.2 Efficiency of Linear Search

For the linear search algorithm, the number of steps depend on whether the key is in the list, and if so, where in the list or array, as well as on the length of the list (number of elements in the list or array).

For search algorithms, the main steps are the comparisons of values of array elements with the key value. Counting these for data models representing the *best case*, the worst case, and the *average case* produces the following table. For each case, the number of steps is expressed in terms of n, the number of elements in the array.

Case	Comparisons as a function of n
Best Case (fewest comparisons)	1
Worst Case (most comparisons)	n
Average Case (average number of comparisons)	n/2

The best case for sequential search is that it does only one comparison. In the worst case, sequential search does n comparisons, and either matches the last element in the array or does not match anything.

The average case is harder to do. It is known that the number of comparisons depends on the position of key in the array. But what is the typical position of the key? One reasonable assumptionis that if the key is in the array, it is equally likely to be any position. So probability of occurences of position = 1/n. Therefore, average number of comparisons

$$= \sum_{i=1}^{n} (1/n) \times i$$

$$= 1/n \sum_{i=1}^{n} i$$

$$= n(n+1)/2n$$

$$= (n+1)/2$$

But if key is not in the list, the number of comparisons is always n. Suppose for an array, any permutation of the list is equally likely. Then we can average over all possible permutations. Therefore, average number of comparisons

$$= \sum_{i=1}^{n!} \frac{1}{n!} \cdot \text{(position of key in permutation i)}$$

$$= \sum_{p=1}^{n} \frac{1}{n!} \cdot p \cdot \text{(number of permutations with key in position P)}$$

$$= \sum_{p=1}^{n} \frac{1}{n!} \cdot p \cdot (n-1)!$$

$$= \sum_{p=1}^{n} \frac{1}{n!} \cdot p$$

$$= (n+1)/2$$

Hence, this assumption gives the same analysis. A second point to be made about average case analysis is that sometimes it makes sense to analyze different cases separately. The analysis above assumes key is always in the array; if key is not in the array, it requires n comparisons. One could make up a probability p that x is in or out of the array and combine the two numbers above to get a total average number comparisons equal to pn + (1-p)(n+1)/2 but it makes more sense to just mention both numbers separately.

The best-case analysis on an average has no significance. If the first element checked happens to be the target, any algorithm will take only one comparison. The worst and average case analyses give a better indication of algorithm efficiency.

Notice that if the array grows in size, the number of comparisons required to find a key item in both worst and average cases grows *linearly*. In general, for an array of length n, the worst case is n comparisons. The algorithm is called *linear search* because its complexity/efficiency can be expressed as a linear function. The number of comparisons to find a target increases linearly as the size of the array. Therefore, T(n) = O(n).

7.12.3 Binary Search Analysis

To evaluate binary search, count the number of comparisons in the best case and worst case. This analysis omits the average case, which is a bit more difficult, and ignores any differences between algorithms in the amount of computation corresponding to each comparison.

The best case occurs if the middle item happens to be the target. Then only one comparison is needed to find it. As before, the best-case analysis does not reveal much. When does the worst case occur? If the target is not in the array, then the process of dividing the list in half continues until there is only one item left to check. Figure 7.7 shows a pattern of the number of comparisons done after each division, given the simplifying assumption of an initial array length that is an even power of two which gives an exact division in half on each iteration. Consider an array in which the following elements are stored: 1 2 3 4 5 6 7 8 9.

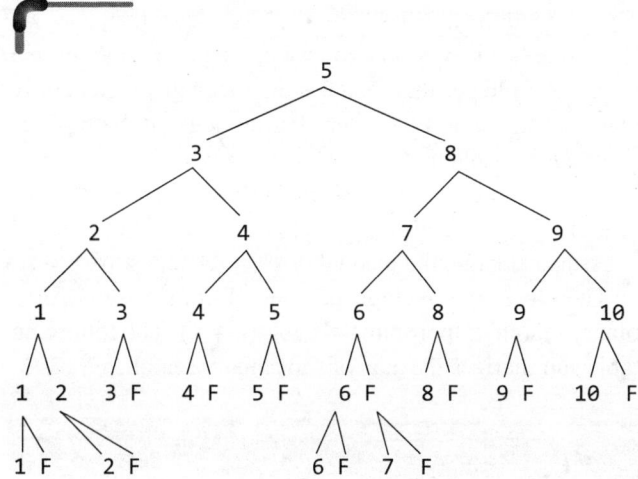

Figure 7.7 Comparison tree for n=10

Every search ends at a leaf whether successful or unsuccessful denoted by F. To find the average number of comparisons for a successful search, one has to find total comparisons for successful searches and divide by number of searches (=n). That is, it is needed to a count number of branches leading from root to each leaf that terminates a successful search. From the comparison tree, the following observations can be made:

1. Height of tree = maximum number of key comparisons possible (height = number of levels below root)

2. Height of tree is at most one more than average number of key comparisons because the levels of leaves can only differ by one, as size of lists when divided by algorithm can only differ by zero or one

3. The number of leaves in a tree expands by a power of two (Fig. 7.8)

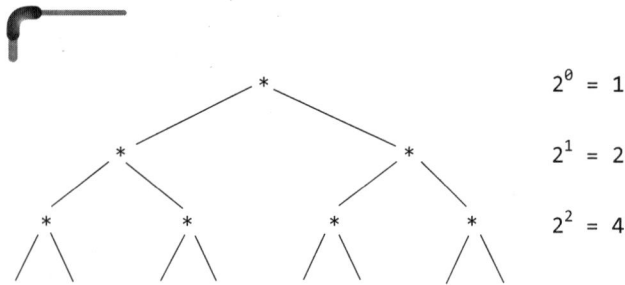

$2^0 = 1$

$2^1 = 2$

$2^2 = 4$

Figure 7.8 Number of leaves in a tree expands by a power of two

Number of leaves $= 2^h$ where h is the height of the tree. Therefore, if the tree has leaves on same level then $2^h = 2n$. If the tree has leaves on two levels, then $2^h > 2n$ (where h is smallest integer that matches the inequality). Generally one can say that $2^h >= 2n$. Taking logs of both sides (base 2) (i.e., given $a^y = x$, we get $\log_a x = y$).

If $2^h >= 2n$ then $h >= 1 + \log_2 n$ {as $\log(2*n)$ becomes $\log(2) + \log(n)$ and $\log_2 2 = 1$}

As n gets large, the inequality $2^h >= 2n$ tends to $2^h = 2n$

Therefore, the average number of comparisons for a binary search is approximately $\log_2(n + 1)$. The following table summarizes the analysis for binary search.

Case	Comparisons as a function of n
Best Case (fewest comparisons)	1
Worst Case (most comparisons)	$\log_2 n$

Hence, the worse case complexity is $T(n) = O(\log_2 n)$ and the best case complexity is $T(n) = O(1)$.

7.12.4 Analysis of Bubble Sort

To analyze bubble sort, it is needed to compare the first and second elements of an array and exchange, if necessary, so that the smaller is in the first position. This is repeated for the second and third pair, third and fourth pair, etc. until a pass through all adjacent pairs has been made. At the end of this first pass, the last item will be in its proper place (i.e., it will be the largest).

A second pass is performed on the first (n-1) items, after which the last two elements will be in place. (n-1) passes will be required to sort an array containing n elements. At the end of the ith pass, the last i elements will be

ordered. If the pass is made in which no exchanges are required, then the array is in order, even if less than (n-1) passes have been made.

For a list containing n items, the number of swaps required for each location in the first half of the array can be shown as follows:

Location	1	2	3	..	..	n/2-2	n/2-1	n/2
Swaps	n-1 +	n-3 +	n-5 +	.. +	.. +	5 +	3 +	1

Each swap is experienced by two elements and the number of swaps is counted, and it is experienced by half the elements. Every swap always moves the elements towards their eventual location and the sum of this series will be the total number of swaps required. Consider the following table.

Pass	Comparisons	Swaps	Moves
First	(n-1)	(n-1)/2 swaps (average)	3(n-1)/2
Second	(n-2)	(n-1)/2 swaps(average)	3(n-2)/2
All passes	= (n-1)+(n-2)...+ 1 = n(n-1)/2 = ~ n2/2	= n(n-1)/4 =~ n2/4 (average)	~3n2/4 moves

Therefore,

$$T(n) = n + (n - 1) + (n - 2) + (n - 3) + (n - 4)$$
$$... (2) + (1)$$
$$= n(n(n-1)/2) = n^2/2$$

Hence, the time complexity of bubble sort is $O(n^2)$. The average case behaviour of the bubble sort algorithm can be shown to be approximately equal to the worst case behaviour. It can be assumed that for the worst case situation, every element is approximately half the list away from its eventual location in the sorted list. This will require each element to experience a minimum of n/2-1 swaps. It cannot be assumed that the other element participating in the swap will benefit from the swap by being moved towards its desired location. It can be assumed that the swaps in the average case situation are only 50% as effective as the swaps in the worst case situation. This leads to the conclusion that each element has to experience approximately n swaps and as each swap moves two elements, the total number of swaps is approximately $n^2/2$. This is the same number of swaps as required in the worst case situation and will need at least as many iterations of the inner loop.

Therefore, the worse case complexity is $T(n) = O(n^2)$ and the average case complexity is also $T(n) = O(n^2)$.

7.12.5 Analysis of Quick Sort

In quick sort, each recursive call could have a different sized set of numbers to sort. Here are the three analyses that must be performed:

- Best case
- Average case
- Worst case

In the best case, a perfect partition is to be set every time. If we let $T(n)$ be the running time of quick sorting n elements, then $T(n) = 2T(n/2) + O(n)$, since partition runs in $O(n)$ time.

Now, consider how bad quick sort would be if the partition element was always the greatest value of the one remaining to be sorted. In this situation, one has to run partition n-1 times, the first time comparing n-1 values, then n-2, followed by n-3, etc. This points to the sum $1+2+3+...+(n-1)$ which is $(n-1)n/2$. Thus, the worst case running time is $O(n^2)$.

Now, lets us calculate the average case running time. This is certainly difficult to ascertain because one cannot get any sort of partition. It is assumed that each possible partition (0 and n-1, 1 and n-2, 2 and n-3, etc.) is equally likely. One way to work out the mathematics is as follows. Assume that you run quick sort n times. In doing so, since there are n possible partitions, each equally likely, on average, each partition occurs once. So, the following recurrence relation is found:

$$nT(n) = T(0)+T(n-1)+T(1)+T(n-2)+...+T(n-1)+T(0) + n*n$$
$$= 2[T(1)+T(2)+...T(n-1)] + n^2 \quad (7.1)$$

Now, putting n-1 in Eqn (7.1),

$$(n-1)T(n-1) = 2[T(1)+T(2)+...T(n-2)] + (n-1)^2 \quad (7.2)$$

Subtracting Eqn (7.2) from Eqn (7.1), gives

$$nT(n) - (n-1)T(n-1) = 2T(n-1) + 2n - 1 \, nT(n)$$
$$= (n+1)T(n-1) + (2n - 1)$$
$$T(n) = [(n+1)/n]T(n-1) + (2n - 1)/n \quad (7.3)$$

Since it is an approximate analysis, the −1 is dropped at the end of this equation. Dividing Eqn (7.3) by n+1, yields

$$T(n)/(n+1) = T(n-1)/n + 2/(n+1) \quad (7.4)$$

Now, substituting different values of n into this recurrence to form several equations, it evaluates to

$$T(n)/(n+1) = T(n-1)/n + 2/(n+1)T(n-1)/(n)$$
$$= T(n-2)/(n-1) + 2/(n)$$
$$T(n-2)/(n-1) = T(n-3)/(n-2) + 2/(n-1)$$

$\vdots$

$$T(2)/3 = T(1)/2 + 2/1 \quad (7.5)$$

Now, adding Eqns (7.5) reveals many identical terms on both sides. In fact, after cancelling identical terms, we are left with

$$T(n)/(n+1) = T(1)/2 + 2[1/1 + 1/2 + 1/3 + ... + 1/(n+1)]$$

The sum on the right hand side of the equation is a harmonic number. The nth harmonic number (H_n) is defined as $1 + 1/2 + 1/3 + ... 1/n$.

Through calculus, it can be shown that $H_n \sim \ln n$ (ln is the natural log with the base e; e ~ 2.718282). Now,

$$T(n)/(n+1) \sim 1/2 + 2\ln n$$
$$T(n) \sim n(\ln n) \text{ (simplifying a bit)}$$

Thus, even in the average case for quick sort, it is found that $T(n) = O(n \log n)$.

Note, in order analysis, any function of the form $\log_b n = O(\log_c n)$, for all positive constants b and c, greater than 1.

Let us look at the best case complexity. The best case occurs when the pivot is the median value, thus the two recursive calls are problems with approximately half the size of the original problem. This recurrence is given by

$$T(n) = 2T(n / 2) + O(n) = O(n \log n)$$

Weiss derives the best case performance figure to be

$$c * n * \log n + n$$

where c represents the constant pivot selection time.

The main consideration is quick sort's average performance. This has been shown (see Kruse et al.) to be $1.39 * n * \log n + c * n$.

For quick sort, best case is $T(n) = O(n \log n)$, worse case is $T(n) = O(n^2)$, and average case is $T(n) = O(n \log n)$.

7.12.6 Disadvantages of Complexity Analysis

Complexity analysis can be very useful, but there are problems with it too. The disadvantages of complexity analysis are as follows.

- Many algorithms are simply too hard to analyze mathematically.
- The average case is unknown. There may not be sufficient information to know what the most important 'average' case really is, therefore analysis is impossible.
- Big-O analysis only specifies how it grows with the size of the problem, not how efficient it is.
- If there are no large amounts of data, algorithm efficiency may not be important.

A *function* is a self-contained block of program statements that performs some particular task. Programs should be built with a large number of small compact *functions* rather than with a small number of large functions. The use of functions in programs makes it more manageable and easy to understand. They may be called as many times as the main program needs to use them. Functions are reusable and can therefore be used in multiple programs.

The linkage with the user-made functions and the main() program is established through three components associated with the user function. These three components are

- the *declaration* statement
- the *function* definition
- the *calling* statement

When a function is called, parameters are passed by value. Depending on its return type specified by its declaration, a function either does not return any value or some value of the type mentioned in its prototype. Another method of passing parameters to function is known as call by reference more strictly 'call by address'. This will be discussed in detail in the chapter on pointers.

Scope rules related to statement blocks and functions basically describe the existence, accessibility, and default values of variables called *local variable*, declared within the function body and those called *global variables*, declared outside all functions.

To indicate where the variables would be stored, how long they would exist, what would be their region of existence, and what would be the default values, C provides four *storage class* specifiers that can be used along with the data type specifiers in the declaration statement of a variable. These four *storage class* specifiers are as follows:

- automatic
- external
- register
- static

Recursion in programming is a technique for defining a problem in terms of one or more smaller versions of the same problem. A function that calls itself directly or indirectly to solve a smaller version of its task until a final call which does not require a self-call is a recursive function. The following are necessary for implementing recursion:

- Decomposition into smaller problems of same type
- Recursive calls must diminish problem size
- Necessity of base case
- Base case must be reached

An instance of the problem whose solution requires no further recursive calls is known as a base case. It is a special case whose solution is known. Every recursive algorithm requires at least one base case in order to be valid.

Some popular problems where the recursive functions can be used have been discussed in this chapter. While developing user-defined functions, the common errors encountered by programmers, ideas on how to choose test data, and the way these can be tracked have also been presented in detail.

The simplest method of searching for an element in an array is called *linear on sequential search*. The drawbacks of sequential search can be eliminated by eliminating large portions of the list from subsequent iterations. *Binary search* halves the size of the list to search in each iteration.

Arranging elements of an array in particular order is called sorting. Some popular internal sorting algorithms have been discussed in this chapter.

Actual parameters Information will be passed to the function via special identifiers or expression called *arguments* or *actual parameters*.

Average-case The average-case complexity of the algorithm is the function defined by the average number of steps taken on any instance of input size.

Base case An instance of a problem the solution of which requires no further recursive calls is known as a base case.

Best-case The best-case complexity of the algorithm is the function defined by the minimum number of steps taken on any instance of input size.

Big-O Big-O notation is a measure of the running time of an algorithm, as it relates to the size of the input to that algorithm. It is intended, not to measure the performance of the machine on which the algorithm is run, but rather to strictly measure the performance of the algorithm itself.

Call by Value Call by value means the values of the actual arguments are conceptually copied to the formal parameters.

Extent How long memory will be associated with them is known as *extent*.

Formal parameters The list of variables in the function header is also referred to as the formal parameters.

Recursion A technique by which a function is called by itself.

Scope The region of the program over which the declaration of an identifier is accessible is called the scope of the identifier.

Space complexity Space complexity is a function describing the amount of memory (space) an algorithm takes with respect to the amount of input provided to the algorithm.

Storage class Storage class specifies where the variables would be stored, how long they would exist, what would be their region of existence, and what would be the default values

Structured programming Structured programming refers to a set of principles for writing well-organized programs that could be more easily shown to be correct.

Time complexity Time complexity is a function describing the amount of time an algorithm takes with respect to the amount of input provided to the algorithm.

Worst-case The worst-case complexity of the algorithm is the function defined by the maximum number of steps taken on any instance of input size.

FREQUENTLY ASKED QUESTIONS

1. Why is a function prototype required?
A function prototype tells the compiler what kind of arguments a function receives and what kind of value a function is going to give back to the calling function. Function prototype helps the compiler ensure that calls to a function are made correctly and that no erroneous type conversions are taking place. If the compiler finds any difference between the prototype and calls to the function or the definition of the function, an error or a warning may be caused.

2. Why is scope important?
In structured programming approach, the program is divided into independent functions that perform a specific task. The key word here is *independent*. For true independence, it is necessary for each function's variables to be isolated from interference caused by other functions. Only by isolating each function's data can you make sure that the function performs its intended task without affecting or being affected by some other part of the program. it is also true that in some situation complete data isolation between functions isn't always desirable. By specifying the scope of variables, a programmer may attain the control over the degree of data isolation.

3. If global variables can be used anywhere in the program, why not make all variables global?
When the program becomes complex and large, it may be needed to declare more and more variables. Variables declared as global take up memory for the entire time the program is running; however, local variables don't. For the most part, a local variable takes up memory only while the function to which it is local is active. Additionally, global variables are subject to unintentional alteration by other functions. If this occurs, the variables might not contain the values one expects when they're used in the functions for which they were created.

4. What is the advantage of using register storage class? What are the restrictions with register storage class?
Access to 'register' identifiers should be as fast as possible, so the compiler may place the value in a machine register. However, the compiler is free to treat a 'register' declaration as an 'auto' declaration because it is only a hint and not a directive.

There are some restrictions with register storage class. They include the following.

The variable must be of a type that can be held in the CPU's register. This usually means a single value of a size less than or equal to the size of an integer. Some machines have registers that can hold floating-point numbers as well.

An array should not be declared with register storage class; doing so is an undefined behavior.

Address-of operator (&) cannot be applied to an identifier with register storage class. An attempt to do so would cause as an error by the compiler.

Register storage class can only be applied to local variables and to the formal parameters in function. Global register variables are not allowed. That is, the 'register' storage class should not occur in an external declaration.

5. What is linkage?
An identifier's *linkage* determines which of the references to that identifier refer to the same object. An identifier's linkage is determined by whether it appears inside or outside a function, whether it appears in a declaration of a function (as opposed to an object), its storage-class, and the linkage of any previous declarations of the same identifier that have file scope.

6. What does linkage intend?
Linkage is used to determine what makes the same name declared in different scopes refer to the same thing. An object only ever has one name, but in many cases we would like to be able to refer to the same object from different scopes.

7. What are the different types of linkages?
C defines three types of linkages – *external, internal and no linkage*. In general,

Functions and global variables have *external linkage*. This means they are available to all files that constitute a program.

Identifiers with file scope declared as static have *internal linkage*. These are known only within the file in which they are declared.

Local identifiers have *no linkage* and are therefore known only within their own block.

Two declarations of the same identifier in a single file that have the same linkage, either internal or external, refer to the same object. The same identifier cannot appear in a file with both internal and external linkage.

8. Differentiate between an internal static and external static variable?
An internal static variable is declared inside a block with static storage class whereas an external static variable is declared outside all the blocks in a file. An internal static variable has persistent storage, block scope and no linkage. An external static variable has permanent storage, file scope and internal linkage

9. What does extern mean in a function declaration?
Using extern in a function declaration the function can be used outside the file in which it is defined.

10. Compare recursion and iteration.

Recursion is a top-down approach to problem solving; it divides the problem into pieces or selects out one key step, postponing the rest. On the other hand, iteration is more of a bottom-up approach; it begins with what is known and from this constructs the solution step by step.

Depending on the implementation available and the algorithm being used, recursion can require a substantial amount of runtime overhead. Thus, the use of recursion illustrates the classic tradeoff between time spent constructing and maintaining a program and the cost in time and memory of execution of that program. For that reason, it is often the case that an iterative version of a solution is considerably more efficient than a recursive one.

11. Can `main()` be called recursively?

This is perfectly legal to call main() recursively if properly written as follows-

```
#include <stdio.h>
int main()
{
   static int c=5;
```

```
if(c-->0)
{
   printf("\t %d", c);
   return main();
}
else
   return 0;
}
```

Output:
```
 4  3  2  1  0
```

If the recursive call does not have base case as the following program then this will go on till a point where runtime error occurs due to stack overflow.

```
#include <stdio.h>
int main()
{
   main();
   return 0;
}
```

EXERCISE

1. A function that returns an integer value and takes a single integer as an argument can be prototyped as
   - `int myFun();`
   - `void myFun( int);`
   - `int myFun(void);`
   - `int myFun(int);`

2. If called by the statement

   `n = myFun(9);`

   what value will `myFun(9)` return for assign-ment to n?

   ```
   int myFun(int val) {
      return(val * (val + 1))/2;
   }
   ```

3. Which of the function prototypes below have no errors?
   - `void myFun1(int)`
   - `int myFun2(void);`
   - `float myFun3(a, b, c);`
   - `double myFun(void a, int b);`
   - `int myFun5(int var1, int );`

4. A function is defined that calculates and returns the hypotenuse of a right triangle with sides a and b. The function prototype is

   `double hypot(double a, double b);`

   Which of the statements below are correct uses of (calls to) this function (assume x, y, and z are double variables and that x and x have been initialized properly)?
   - `z = hypot(4.0, 4.5);`

   - `z = hypot(double x, double y);`
   - `hypot(x, y);`
   - `printf("%f", hypot(x, y));`
   - `z = x + y + hypot(x, y);`

5. A function, sumN, is defined that takes an integer n as argument and returns the sum of the integers from 1 through n. What is the value of the expression shown below?

   `sumN(3456) - sumN(3455);`

6. Choose all the correct ways of calling a function with prototype

   `int f1(int, double);`

   given the variables below and that the math library was included.

   ```
   int val1 = 5, retVal;
   double val2 = 9.8;
   ```
   - `retVal = f1(4, 3.5);`
   - `retVal = f1(int val1, float val2);`
   - `retVal = f1(1000, val2);`
   - `retVal = f1(2*val1, val2/3.5);`
   - `retVal = f1( val1, sqrt(val2));`

7. Given the function definition shown for `f1()` below, what will be printed?

   ```
   int f1(void);
   int main(void) {
   printf("%d", f1());
   printf("%d", f1());
   ```

```
printf("%d", f1());
return 0;
}
int f1(void) {
int val = 1;
return val++;
}
```

8. Given the function definition shown for f1() below, what will be printed?

```
int f1(void);
int main(void) {
    printf("%d", f1());
    printf("%d", f1());
    printf("%d", f1());
    return 0;
}
int f1(void) {
    static int val = 1;
    return val++;
}
```

9. What is printed by the code below?

```
void f1(void);
int val = 6;
int main(void) {
    f1();
    printf("%d", val);
    f1();
    printf("%d", val);
    return 0;
}
void f1(void) {
    ++val;
}
```

10. What is printed by the code below?

```
void f1(int);
int val = 6;
int main(void) {
    f1(val);
    printf("%d", val);
    f1(val);
    printf("%d", val);
    return 0;
```

```
}
void f1(int val) {
    ++val;
}
```

11. Given the array declaration and function prototype below, choose all the correct ways of calling the function from main() and giving it a reference to myarray[].

```
void myFun(int a[]);

int main() {
    int myArray[] =
        {10,20,30,40,50,60,70,80};

    /* function call here */
```
- myFun(myArray);
- myFun(myArray[]);
- myFun(&myArray[0]);
- myFun(myArray[0]);
- myFun(myArray[8]);

12. What will be the output of the following program?

```
#define swap(a,b) temp=a; a=b; b=temp;
int main()
{
    static int a=5,b=6,temp;
    if(a > b)
        swap(a,b);
    printf("a=%d b=%d",a,b);
    return 0;
}
```
(a) a=5 b=6   (b) a=6 b=5
(c) a=6 b=0   (d) None of these

13. The following code is not well written. What is the output?

```
int main()
{
    int a=1,b=2;
    printf("%d",add(a,b));
    return 0;
}
int add(int a,int b)
{
return(a+b);
}
```
(a) Run-time error   (b) Compile-time error
(c) 3   (d) None of these

14. What will be the output of the following program?

```
int add(int a,int b)
{
    int c=a+b;
}
int main()
{
    int a=10,b=20;
    printf("%d %d %d",a,b,add(a,b));
    return 0;
}
```

(a) 10 20 0   **(b)** Compile-time error

(c) 10 20 30   **(d)** None of these

15. What will be the output of the following program?

```
int add(int a,int b)
{
    int c=a+b;
    return;
}
int main()
{
    int a=10,b=20;
    printf("%d %d %d",a,b,add(a,b));
    return 0;
}
```

(a) 10 20 0   **(b)** Compile-time error

(c) 10 20 30   **(d)** None of these

16. What will be the output of the following program?

```
int main()
{
    int add(int,int);
    int a=7,b=13;
    printf("%d",add(add(a,b),
        add(a,b)));
    return 0;
}
int add(a,b)
int a,b;
{
    return(a+b);
}
```

(a) Compile-time error   **(b)** 20

(c) 40   **(d)** None of these

17. What will be the output of the following program?

```
int add(a,b)
{
    int c=a+b;
    return c;
}
int main()
{
    int a=10,b=20;
    printf("%d",add(a,b));
    return 0;
}
```

(a) 30   **(b)** Compile-time error

(c) 0   **(d)** None of these

18. What will be the output of the following program?

```
int funct2(int b)
{
    if(b == 0)
        return b;
    else
        funct1(b--);
}
int funct1(int a)
{
    if(a == 0)
        return a;
    else
        funct2(a--);
}
int main()
{
    int a=7;
    printf("%d",funct1(a));
    return 0;
}
```

(a) 0   **(b)** Compile-time error

(c) Infinite loop   **(d)** 7

19. What will be the output of the following program?

```
int funct2(int b)
{
    if(b == 0)
        return b;
    else
```

```
        funct1(--b);
}
int funct1(int a)
{
   if(a == 0)
      return a;
   else
      funct2(--a);
}
int main()
{
   int a=7;
   printf("%d",funct1(a));
   return 0;
}
```

(a) 0   (b) Compile-time error

(c) Infinite loop   (d) 7

20. What will be the output of the following program?

```
int funct1(int a)
{{;}{{;}return a;}}
int main()
{
   int a=17;
   printf("%d",funct1(a));
   return 0;
}
```

(a) 0   (b) Compile-time error

(c) 17   (d) None of these

21. What will be the output of the following program?

```
int funct1(int a)
{
   if(a)
      return funct1(--a)+a;
   else
      return 0;
}
int main()
{
   int a=7;
   printf("%d",funct1(a));
   return 0;
}
```

(a) 7   (b) 21

(c) 28   (d) None of these

22. What will be the output of the following program?

```
int compute(int a,int b)
int c;
{
   c=a+b;
   return c;
}
int main()
{
   int a=7,b=9;
   printf("%d",compute(a,b));
   return 0;
}
```

(a) Compile-time error   (b) 16

(c) None of these

23. What will be the output of the following program?

```
int a=10;
void compute(int a)
{
   a=a;
}
int main()
{
   int a=100;
   printf("%d",a);
   compute(a);
   printf("%d",a);
   return 0;
}
```

(a) 10 10   (b) Compile-time error

(c) 100 100   (d) 100 10

24. What will be the output of the following program?

```
int funct(char ch)
{
   ch=ch+1;
   return ch;
}
int main()
{
   int a=127;
   printf("%d %d",a,funct(a));
   return 0;
}
```

(a) Compile-time error   **(b)** 127 128

(c) 127–128   **(d)** None of these

25. What will be the output of the following program?

```c
char funct(int val)
{
    char ch=val;
    return ch;
}
int main()
{
    float a=256.25;
    printf("%d",funct(a));
    return 0;
}
```

(a) 0   **(b)** 256.25

(c) 256   **(d)** None of these

26. What will be the output of the following program?

```c
auto int a;
void changeval(int x)
{
    a=x;
}
int main()
{
    a=15;
    printf("%d",a);
    changeval(75);
    printf("%d",a);
    return 0;
}
```

(a) Compile-time error   **(b)** 15 75

(c) 15 15   **(d)** None of these

27. What will be the output of the following program?

```c
int val;
static int funct()
{
    return val*val;
}
int main()
{
    val=5;
    funct();
    val++;
```

```c
    printf("%d",funct());
    return 0;
}
```

(a) Compile-time error   **(b)** 25

(c) 36   **(d)** None of these

28. What will be the output of the following program?

```c
static int funct(int val)
{
    static int sum;
    sum+=val;
    return sum;
}
int main()
{
    int i,n=9;
    for(i=1; i<n-; i++)
        funct(i*2);
    printf("%d",funct(0));
    return 0;
}
```

(a) 20   **(b)** 0

(c) 30   **(d)** None of these

29. What will be the output of the following program?

```c
void print(int a[],...)
{
    while(*a != -1)
        printf("%d",*a++);
}
int main()
{
    int a[]={1,2,3,4,5,-1};
    print(a,5,6,7,8,9,-1);
    return 0;
}
```

(a) Compile-time error   **(b)** Run-time error

(c) 12345   **(d)** 56789

30. What will be the output of the following program?

```c
int main()
{
    int a=19,b=4;
    float c;
    c=a/b;
    printf("%f",c);
    return 0;
```

```
}
```

(a) 4.75   **(b)** 4

(c) 4.750000   **(d)** 4.000000

31. What will be the output of the following program?

```
int main()
{
    int _;
    _=70;
    printf("%d",_);
    return 0;
}
```

(a) Compile-time error   **(b)** Run-time error

(c) 70   **(d)** None of these

32. What will be the output of the following program?

```
#define func(x,y) { func(x,y) }
int main()
{
    int a=5,b=6;
    c=func(x,y);
    printf("%d %d %d",c);
    return 0;
}
```

(a) Compile-time error   **(b)** Linker error

(c) 5 6 11   **(d)** Infinite loop

33. What will be the output of the following program?

```
#define big(a,b) a > b ? a : b
#define swap(a,b) temp=a; a=b; b=temp;
int main()
{
    int a=3,b=5,temp;
    if((3+big(a,b)) > b)
        swap(a,b);
    printf("%d %d",a,b);
    return 0;
}
```

(a) 3 0   **(b)** 5 3

(c) 3 5   **(d)** 5 0

34. Write a function to find the sum of digits of a given number.

35. Write a program that uses a function to search a number within an array.

36. Write a function that takes a decimal number and base as argument and returns the equivalent number of the given base.

37. Write a function that will scan a string that is passed as an argument and convert all characters to capital letters.

38. Write a program that uses a function to add a string to the end of another string without using any library function.

39. Write function to sort an array of integers in ascending order.

40. Write a function to reverse a given string and use it to check whether the given string is a palindrome or not.

41. Write a program to perform addition, subtraction, and multiplication on two matrices depending upon the user's choice.

42. Write a program to print the transpose of that matrix.

43. Write a program that sorts the words of a sentence in alphabetical order.

44. Write a function that will print the longest word written in a line.

45. Write a program to sort the numbers stored in a matrix.

46. Read two integers, representing a rate of pay (pence per hour) and a number of hours. Print out the total pay, with hours up to 40 being paid at basic rate, from 40 to 60 at rate- and-a-half, above 60 at double-rate. Print the pay as pounds to two decimal places.

Hints Construct a loop. Terminate the loop when a zero rate is encountered. At the end of the loop, print out the total pay. The code for computing the pay from the rate and hours is to be written as a function.

The recommended output format is

```
Pay at 200 pence/hr for 38 hours is 76.00 pounds
Pay at 220 pence/hr for 48 hours is 114.40 pounds
Pay at 240 pence/hr for 68 hours is 206.40 pounds
Pay at 260 pence/hr for 48 hours is 135.20 pounds
Pay at 280 pence/hr for 68 hours is 240.80 pounds
Pay at 300 pence/hr for 48 hours is 156.00 pounds
Total pay is 928.80 pounds
```

The 'program features' check that explicit values such as 40 and 60 appear only once, as a #define or an initialized variable value.

47. Write functions to convert feet to inches, convert inches to centimeters, and convert centimeters to meters. Write a program that prompts a user for a measurement in feet and converts and outputs this value in meters. Facts to use: 1 ft = 12 inches, 1 inch = 2.54 cm, 100 cm = 1 meter

1. Write a menu-based program in C that uses a set of functions to perform the following operations
   (a) reading a complex number
   (b) writing a complex number
   (c) addition of two complex numbers
   (d) subtraction of two complex numbers
   (e) Multiplication of two complex numbers

INCREMENTAL PROBLEM

As was done in the earlier chapters, the test for forming a triangle with the given vertices is conducted.

If it is possible to draw a triangle with the given vertices, the area of the triangle is computed. Here, in addition to using arrays, functions are used.

Problem statement

Compute the lengths of three sides of a triangle formed by three points whose co-ordinates are given. Check whether a triangle can be formed or not. Then compute the area of the triangle. Next, take a point as input from the user and check whether it is inside or outside the triangle.

Solution

The problem can be divided into functions. One function named getLength() could be used to compute the length of the side of a triangle from the coordinates of the two vertices. Another function called getArea() could be used to calculate the area of the triangle from the lengths of three sides of the triangle. The area is given by,

$$\text{Area} = \sqrt{s(s-a)(s-b)(s-c)}$$

where a, b, c are the lengths of the three sides and

$$s = (a + b + c)/2.$$

Finally, to check whether a point is located inside or outside a triangle another function should be used. The three vertices of a triangle can be represented by two integer arrays x[3] and y[3] where (x[0],y[0]), (x[1],y[1]) and (x[2],y[2]) make up the vertices of the triangle.

When a point resides inside a triangle, the sum of the areas of the triangles formed by taking two adjacent vertices and the point together must be same as the area of the triangle.(see the figure) That is, sum of areas of the triangles formed by {(x,y), (x_0,y_0), (x_1,y_1)}, {(x,y), (x_1,y_1), (x_2,y_2)} and {(x,y), (x_0,y_0), (x_2,y_2)} must be the same as the area of the triangle formed with {(x_0,y_0),(x_1,y_1),(x_2,y_2)} if the point is located inside the triangle.

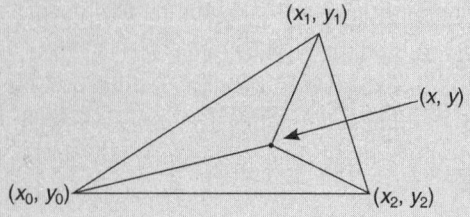

(x_1, y_1)

(x, y)

(x_0, y_0) (x_2, y_2)

Program

```c
#include <stdio.h>
#include <math.h>
double getLength(int, int, int, int);
double getArea(double, double, double);
int insideOrOutside(int[], int[], int, int);
int main(void)
{
    int x[3],y[3];
    int i,xx,yy;
    double a,b,c, area;
    printf("\n Enter the co-ord. of the vertices");
    for(i=0;i<3;++i)
    {
        printf("\n Enter x[%d]:",i);
        scanf("%d",&x[i]);
        printf("\n Enter y[%d]:",i);
        scanf("%d",&y[i]);
    }
    a = getLength(x[0],y[0],x[1],y[1]);
    b = getLength(x[1],y[1],x[2],y[2]);
    c = getLength(x[0],y[0],x[2],y[2]);
    if(a+b>c && b+c>a && c+a>b)
    {
        printf("Triangle can be drawn");
        area = getArea(a,b,c);
        printf("\n Area is %lf sq. units", area);
        printf("\n Enter the co-ord. of the point:");
        printf("\n x co-ordinate:");
        scanf("%d",&xx);
        printf("\n y co-ordinate:");
        scanf("%d",&yy);
        if(insideOrOutside(x,y,xx,yy))
            printf("\n Inside the triangle");
        else
            printf("\n Outside the triangle");
    }
    else
        printf("Triangle cannot be drawn");
    return 0;
```

```
}
double getLength(int xOne, int yOne, int xTwo,int yTwo)
{
    int m, n;
    m = (xOne-xTwo)*(xOne-xTwo);
    n = (yOne-yTwo)*(yOne-yTwo);
    return sqrt((double)(m+n));
}
double getArea(double sA,double sB, double sC)
{
    double s;
    s = (sA+sB+sC)/2.0;
    return sqrt(s*(s-sA)*(s-sB)*(s-sC));
}
int insideOrOutside(int x[],int y[],int xx, int yy)
{
    int i,k;
    double d[3], area, sumArea=0.0,aa,bb;
    for(i=0;i<3;++i)
    {
        d[i] = getLength(x[i],y[i],x[(i+1)%3],
                  y[(i+1)%3]);
    }
    area = getArea(d[0],d[1],d[2]);
    for(i=0;i<3;++i)
    {
        aa = getLength(xx,yy,x[i],y[i]);
        bb = getLength(xx,yy,x[(i+1)%3],y[(i+1)%3]);
        sumArea += getArea(d[i],aa,bb);
    }
    if(fabs(area-sumArea) < 0.00001)
        return 1;
```

```
    else
        return 0;
}
```

Note

The lengths of three sides constituted by vertices {(x[0],y[0]), (x[1],y[1])}, {(x[1],y[1]),(x[2],y[2])} and {(x[0], y[0]), (x[2], y[2])} are stored in d[0], d[1], d[2] respectively.

The following portion of code contained in insideOrOutside() needs to be explained.

```
for(i=0;i<3;++i)
{
    aa = getLength(xx,yy,x[i],y[i]);
    bb = getLength(xx,yy,x[(i+1)%3],y[(i+1)%3]);
    sumArea += getArea(d[i],aa,bb);
}
```

In each iteration, the code within the for loop can be described as follows.

i = 0	`aa = getLength(xx,yy,x[0],y[0]);`
	`bb = getLength(xx,yy,x[1],y[1]);`
	`sumArea += getArea(d[0],aa,bb);`
	
	Here (i+1)%3 evaluates to 1 as (0+1)%3=1

i = 1	`aa = getLength(xx,yy,x[1],y[1]);`
	`bb = getLength(xx,yy,x[2],y[2]);`
	`sumArea += getArea(d[1],aa,bb);`
	
	Here (i+1)%3 evaluates to 2 as (1+1)%3=2

i = 2	`aa=getLength(xx,yy,x[2],y[2]);`
	`bb=getLength(xx,yy,x[0],y[0]);`
	`sumArea+=getArea(d[2],aa,bb);`
	Here (i+1)%3 evaluates to 0 as (2+1)%3 = 0

CASE STUDY

Problem Statement

The functional value at a point has to be determined with only a few given functional values at some points and without any functional expressions being given. Using Lagrange's interpolation technique, find the functional value at a given point.

Analysis and Algorithm

The basic problem of polynomial interpolation is as follows: Given a set of $(n + 1)$ distinct data points (x_i, y_i), where $i = 0, 1, 2, ..., n$, the curve passing through these points is to be found. When the curve is found, the coordinate corresponding to any desired abscissa value is also readily found. Let

$$y = a_0 + a_1 x + a_2 x^2 + ... + a_n x^n$$

be the required curve of degree less than or equal to n, where the constants a_1, where $i = 0, 1, 2, ..., n$, are to be determined; n being a positive integer. Since it passes through the prescribed points (x_i, y_i), it follows that

$$y_0 = a_0 + a_1 x_0^2 + ... + a_n x_0^n$$
$$y_1 = a_1 + a_1 x_1 + a_2 x_1^2 + ... + a_n x_1^n$$
$$\vdots$$
$$y_n = a_0 + a_1 x_n + a_2 x n^2 + ... a_n x_n^n$$

This is a system of $(n + 1)$ linear algebraic equations for the $(n + 1)$ unknowns a_i, where $i = 0, 1, 2, ..., n$. The coefficient determinant of the system is given by

$$= 1/n \sum_{i=1}^{n} i$$

This is known as Van der Monde determinant, which is clearly different from zero, in view of the fact that the given points are distinct. An alternative solution path was suggested by the great mathematician Lagrange, who formulated the problem and solved it in closed form. Following Lagrange, let us define the auxiliary functions

$$P_k(x) = (x - x_0) \ldots (x - x_k - 1)(x - x_k - 1) \ldots (x - x_n)$$

So that the function $P_k(x)$ is a continued product of n-factors of the from $(x - x_i)$, beginning from $i = 0$ to n, from which the factor $(x - x_k)$ is missing. It is to be noted that $P_k(x)$ vanishes for any value $x = x_i$, where $i = 0, 1, \ldots n$. Since there are n factors, the functions $P_k(x)$ are polynomials of degree n. Further let

$$y = \phi(x) = = \sum_{i=1}^{n!} \frac{1}{n!}.$$

where A_k ($k = 0, 1, \ldots n$) are constants to be determined.
Clearly, the function $\phi(x)$ is a polynomial of degree n(or less). Further, it is given that, at $x = x_i$, $y = y_i$ so that

$$= \sum_{p=1}^{n} \frac{1}{n!}.p.$$

Therefore, $A_i = y_i | P_i(x_i)$. Hence,

$$= \sum_{p=1}^{n} \frac{1}{n!}.p.(n-1)!$$

...(1)

Equation (1) is the *Lagrange interpolation formula*. It defines a polynomial of degree $<= n$, which approximates the unknown function $f(x)$ (assumed to be sufficiently smooth) and assumes the prescribed values y_i at the pivotal points x_i.

The algorithm for solving this problem is given as follows:

```
1.  START
2.  PRINT "Enter the no. of data:"
3.  INPUT N
4.  ALLOCATE STORAGE SPACE FOR N NUMBER OF DATA
    VALUES FOR X AND Y
5.  I←0
6.  PRINT "ENTER X AND Y VALUES:"
7.  INPUT X[I], Y[I]
8.  I←I+1
9.  IF(I < N) THEN GO TO 6
10. PRINT "Enter the value of x:"
11. INPUT A
12. RESULT = CALL lagrange(X,Y,A,N)
13. PRINT VALUE OF y
14. STOP

FUNCTION lagrange(X,Y,A,N)
1.  START
2.  J←0
3.  L←1
4.  R←0
5.  I←0
6.  IF(I!=J)THEN
    L*=(A-X[I])/(X[J]-X[I])
7.  I←I+1
8.  IF I<N THEN GOTO 6
9.  R← R + Y[J]*L;
10. L←1;
11. J←J+1
12. IF J<N THEN GOTO 5
13. RETURN R
```

Program

```c
#include <stdio.h>
#include <conio.h>
#include <stdlib.h>
float  lagrange( float *, float *, float, int);
int main(void)
{
  int i,j,n;
  float *x,*y,result,a;
  printf("Enter the no. of data:");
  scanf("%d",&n);

  if(n<1)
  {
    printf("ERROR");
    exit(0);
  }

  x=(float*)malloc(n*sizeof(float));
  y=(float*)malloc(n*sizeof(float));

  for(i=0;i<n;i++)
  {
```

```
    fflush(stdin);
    printf("Enter the value of x%d:",i);
    scanf("%f",(x+i));
    fflush(stdin);
    printf("Enter the value of y%d:",i);
    scanf("%f",(y+i));
  }

  printf("Enter the value of x:");
  scanf("%f",&a);
  result=lagrange(x,y,a,n);
  printf("\n value of y is %f", result);
  return 0;
  }

float lagrange( float *x, float *y, float a, int n)
{
  int i,j;
  float l=1,r=0;

  for(j=0;j<n;j++)
  {
    for(i=0;i<n;i++)
    {
        if(i!=j)l*=(a-x[i])/(x[j]-x[i]);
    }

    r+=y[j]*l;
    l=1;
  }
  return r;
}
```

Sample run:

```
Enter the no. of data:4
Enter the value of x0:-1
Enter the value of y0:9
Enter the value of x1:0
Enter the value of y1:5
Enter the value of x2:2
Enter the value of y2:3
Enter the value of x3:5
Enter the value of y3:15
Enter the value of x:3.4

 value of y is 6.360001
Press Enter to return to Quincy..._
```

Pointers in C

Chapter 8

8.1 INTRODUCTION

In programming with C, there are far too many things that can only be done with pointers. In many cases, C programmers use pointers because they make the code more efficient. But at the same time, pointers seem to make the code harder to understand. However, with increased power, pointers bring increased responsibility.

Pointers allow new and ugly types of bugs, and pointer bugs can crash in random ways, which makes them more difficult to debug. Nonetheless, even with their problems, pointers are a powerful programming construct. The only peculiarity of C, compared to other languages is its heavy reliance on pointers and the relatively permissive view of how they can be used.

Before going on to discuss the concept of pointers, it is necessary to understand the use of memory in a C program.

8.2 UNDERSTANDING MEMORY ADDRESSES

All computers have *primary memory*, also known as RAM or *random access memory*. For example, a computer may have 16, 32, 64, 128, 256, or 512 MB of RAM installed. RAM holds the programs that the computer is currently running along with the data they are currently manipulating (their variables and data structures). All the variables used in a program (and indeed, the program itself) reside in the memory when the program is executed. The organization of the memory is rather straightforward. It is a sequence of a large number of memory locations (cells), each of which has an address. Each memory location is capable of storing a small number (0 to 256), which is known as a byte. A `char` data is 1 byte in size and hence needs one memory location of the memory. Both integer and `float` need four bytes each, or four locations in a 32-bit machine. The size needed for a particular data type varies with the platform in which the program is run. Even if an `int/float` number is small, it will still occupy four locations. When a program in C is written and compiled, the compiler will allocate the memory necessary to run the program. This is part of the reason why declaring variables is so important. For example,

```
int x;
x=1000;
```

will first convey to the C compiler that x is an integer before assigning a value of 1000 to it. The declaration statement informs the compiler to allocate enough memory to store an integer and assign an address to that space in memory. Since an integer requires two or four bytes of memory, the compiler searches for two or four free bytes memory and holds them until a value is assigned to x. It then puts that value in the memory location and stores it there until x is redefined as something else. The same goes for other data types in C. Declaring variables first always allows the compiler to set aside a space in memory which can then be filled up with useful numbers. Figure 8.1 represents these facts.

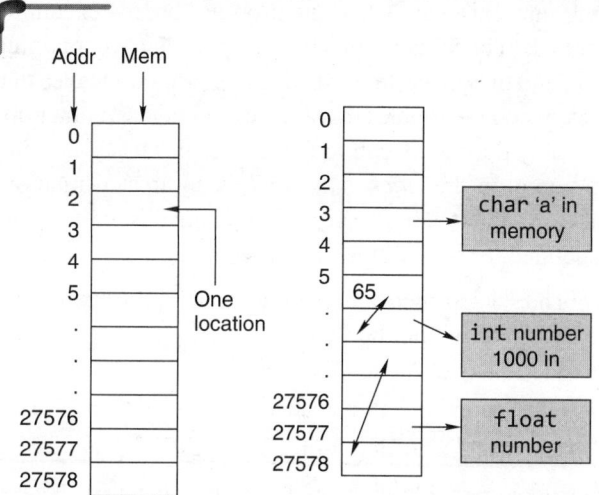

Figure 8.1 The computer memory (16-bit system)

Variables can be stored in several places in memory, depending on their lifetime. Variables that are defined outside any function (whether of global or file static scope), and variables that are defined inside a function as static variables, exist for the lifetime of the program's execution. These variables are stored in the *data segment*. The *data segment* is a fixed-size area in memory set aside for these variables. The data segment is subdivided into two parts, one for initialized variables and another for uninitialized variables.

There may be several global variables declared in the program, but they will not be stored contiguously, since the compiler is not compelled to store them in any order convenient to the programmer. They are randomly stored throughout the available global memory even though it is a fact that every C compiler will probably assign them in some contiguous manner.

There are virtual memory, cache memory, registers, and other kinds of memory that make the system run a little faster or appear to have more memory. The blocks returned to the program from the heap have additional housekeeping memory associated with them and there are byte alignment considerations for both the heap and the stack. Global memory also has some byte alignment considerations. For example, the compiler may require that all float and double type variables start on an even numbered byte boundary, or on a byte boundary that is modulo four. This may require some bytes added as padding to get to the boundary when one of these is encountered. The compiler/linker will take care of these details.

Variables that are defined inside a function as auto variables (that are not defined with the keyword `static`) come into existence when the program begins executing the block of code (delimited by curly braces {}) containing them, and they cease to exist when the program leaves that block of code. Variables that are the arguments to functions exist only during the call to that function. These variables are stored on the *stack*. The *stack* is an area of memory that starts out small and grows automatically up to some predefined limit. The stack has three major functions:

1. The stack provides the storage area for local variables declared within the function.
2. The stack stores *housekeeping* information involved when function call is made.
3. The stack is needed for recursive call.

Once a variable is stored on the stack, it can be referred to by the code that puts it on the stack, so that it is a variable available for use in much the same manner as global variables are available. However, when the program has finished using the data on the stack, it can be discarded to allow the stack to be used for other data when needed. This is probably unclear at this point, but it will make more sense when one gets to the actual usage. It is to be noted that stack would not be needed except for recursive calls. If not, for these a fixed amount of space for local variables, parameters and return addresses would be known at compile time and could be allocated in BSS.

In DOS and other systems without virtual memory, the limit is set either when the program is compiled or when it begins executing. In Unix and other systems with virtual memory, the limit is set by the system, and it is usually so large that the programmer can ignore it.

The third and final area doesn't actually store variables but can be used to store data pointed to by variables.

Pointer variables that are assigned to the result of a call to the `malloc()` function contain the address of a dynamically allocated area of memory. This memory is in an area called the *heap*. When the program requests a block of data, the dynamic allocation scheme carves out a block from the heap and assigns it to the user by returning a pointer to the beginning of the block. When the system has finished using the block, it returns the block to the heap where it is returned to the pool of available memory called the free list. This is called de-allocation. The heap can share a memory segment with either the data segment or the stack, or it can have its own segment. It all depends on the compiler options and operating system. The heap, like the stack, has a limit on how much it can grow, and the same rules apply as to how that limit is determined.

Since readers are interested only in the logical assignment of memory, they can ignore all of these extra considerations, and still write efficient, robust programs. The compiler writers have a big job to do because they must keep track of all of these entities in order to make the programmer's job easier. C uses pointers in three main ways.

1. Pointers in C provide an alternative means of accessing information stored in arrays, which is especially valuable when working with strings. There is an intimate link between arrays and pointers in C.
2. C uses pointers to handle *variable parameters* passed to functions.
3. They are used to create *dynamic data structures*, those that are built up from blocks of memory allocated from the heap at run-time. This is only visible through the use of pointers.

Table 8.1 describes the memory layout of the memory elements of a C program.

Table 8.1 Memory layout summary

Memory Section Name	Description
Text (or the code segment)	This is the area of memory that contains the machine instructions corresponding to the compiled program. This area is READ ONLY and is shared by multiple instances of a running program.
Data	This area in the memory image of a running program contains storage for *initialized global* variables. This area is separate for each running instance of a program.
BSS	This is the memory area that contains storage for *uninitialized global* variables. It is also separate for each running instance of a program.
Stack	This region of the memory image of a running program contains storage for the automatic (local) variables of the program. It also stores context-specific information before a function call, e.g., the value of the instruction pointer (program counter) register before a function call is made. On most architectures, the stack grows from *higher memory to lower memory addresses*.
Heap	This memory region is reserved for dynamically allocating memory for variables at run-time. Dynamic memory allocation is done by using the malloc or calloc functions.
Shared libraries	This region contains the executable image of shared libraries being used by the program.

8.3 ADDRESS OPERATOR (&)

Readers might have noticed that when we call certain functions in C the & sign is used. For example,

```
scanf("%d", &n);
```

takes the input from the terminal and stores it in integer format in the variable named n. The & sign indicates to the address in memory of the integer n, which must be previously declared using

```
int n;
```

where the function stores the inputted data. Just like a house address in a town, the memory address is an integer specifying the location where something resides. scanf needs to know this in order to redirect the data. If one forgets and types n instead, the scanf function interprets the actual integer value of n as an address and tries to send its output there. This address may not exist, it may be used by the operating system or otherwise blocked, or it may be impossible to find again. It is likely to get a

```
segmentation fault
```

error when one compiles, and one will certainly get nonsense values if the program runs.

To recap, the compiler thinks n means the value of n (which will be junk if it has not been assigned yet) and &n means n's address. At the moment when the variable is declared, it must be stored in a concrete location in the succession of cells in the memory. The programs do not decide where the variable is to be placed. That is done automatically by the compiler and the operating system at run-time. But once the operating system has assigned an address there may be cases where it may be of interest to know the location of the variable. This can be done by preceding the variable identifier by an *ampersand* (&), which literally means 'address of'.

Now the above ideas are illustrated with some more details. Consider the declaration,

```
int i = 3;
```

This declaration tells the C compiler to

- reserve space in memory to hold the integer value
- associate the name i with this memory location
- store the value 3 at this location

i's location in the memory may be logically represented with the memory map shown in Fig. 8.2.

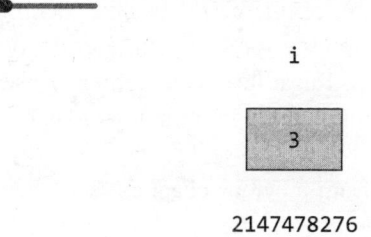

i

3

2147478276

Figure 8.2   Memory map

The computer has selected memory location 2147478276 as the place to store the value 3. This location number 2147478276 is not a number to be relied upon because at some other time the computer may choose a different location for storing the value 3. This address can be printed through the following statement:

```
printf("\n Address of i = %u", &i);
```

The output will be: 2147478276. Look at the printf() statement carefully. The '&' used in this statement is C's address operator. The expression &i returns the address of the variable i, which in this case happens to be 2147478276.

The address is printed using %u control string as it is of type unsigned int. %X can also be used. Actually %p should be used because it prints the input argument as a memory address.

The following statement

```
printf("\n Address of i = %x", &i);
```

will print FFDC in hexadecimal as the address of variable 'i'.

Why an unassigned pointer should not be used?

According to a verse taught in elementary school, "I shot an arrow into the air, where it lands, I don't care." It may rhyme, but its message is really not appropriate for little ones. However, when a pointer is declared and then used without first assigning it a value, it is doing the programming equivalent of the verse.

The following program declares a pointer and then attempts to output its value without first assigning it a value.

```
#include <stdio.h>
int main()
{
  int *ptr;
  printf("\n The value of ptr is %u", ptr);
  return 0;
}
```

The result, depending on the compiler and operating system, may be a compiler error, a run-time error, or a computer that locks up. Regardless, attempting to use a declared pointer without first assigning it a value is not a good idea.

It may be recalled from previous chapters that when a variable is declared and then an attempt is made to output its value without first assigning it a value, the result is a so-called *garbage value* that makes little sense. The reason for this result is that the computer attempts to interpret whatever value is left over from previous programs at the address of the variable.

When the variable is a pointer, that leftover value is interpreted as another memory address, which the pointer then tries to access when we attempt to use it. There are a number of memory address ranges that are not permitted to access programmatically, such as those reserved for use by the operating system. If the leftover value is interpreted as one of those prohibited addresses, the result is an error.

> **Points to Note**
> - After declaring a variable, where the variable is to be located, is decided by the compiler and the operating system at run-time.
> - After declaring a variable, if an attempt is made to output its value without assigning a value, the result is a garbage value.

8.4 POINTER

A pointer provides a way of accessing a variable without referring to the variable directly. The mechanism used for this is the address of the variable. A program statement can refer to a variable indirectly using the address of the variable.

A pointer variable is a variable that holds the memory address of another variable. Put another way, the pointer does not hold a value in the traditional sense; instead, it holds the address of another variable. They are called pointers for the simple reason that, by storing an address, they 'point' to a particular point in memory. A pointer points to that variable by holding a copy of its address. Because a pointer holds an address rather than a value, it has two parts. The pointer itself holds the address. The address points to a value.

Pointers can be used to:

- call by address, thereby facilitating the changes made to a variable in the called function to become permanently available in the function from where the function is called
- return more than one value from a function indirectly
- pass arrays and strings more conveniently from one function to another
- manipulate arrays more easily by moving pointers to them (or to parts of them) instead of moving the arrays themselves
- create complex data structures, such as linked lists and binary trees, where one data structure must contain references to other data structures
- communicate information about memory, as in the function `malloc()` which returns the location of free memory by using a pointer
- compile faster, more efficient code than other derived data types such as arrays

Therefore, a pointer variable is a variable that stores the address of another variable. In C there is an additional restriction on pointers—they are *not* allowed to store *any* memory address, but they can only store addresses of variables of a given type.

8.4.1 Declaring a Pointer

Just as any other variable in a program, a pointer has to be declared; it will have a value, a scope, a lifetime, a name; and it will occupy a certain number of memory locations. The pointer operator available in C is '*', called '*value at address*' operator. It returns the value stored at a particular address. The value at address operator is also called 'indirection' operator. A pointer variable is declared by preceding its name with an asterisk. The syntax for declaring a pointer variable is

```
datatype * pointer_variable;
```

where, *datatype* is the type of data that the pointer is allowed to hold the address of (that is, the type of data that the pointer is allowed to point to) and *pointer_variable* is the pointer variable name that is used to refer to the address of a variable of type datatype.

An example of a pointer declaration would be

```
char *ptr;
```

The above declaration should be evaluated as: `ptr` is a pointer to `char` type data. `char` is not the data type of ptr. ptr is an identifier of type pointer and char is a data specifier that is used to indicate what type of data is at the memory address that ptr is holding. Pointers are variables that hold memory addresses. At the memory address, held in a pointer, is a value; this value has a data type of one of the C data types or a user-defined data type (e.g., structure). In declaring a pointer variable, the programmer is actually declaring a variable that holds a memory address that points to a specific type of data value. Consider the following declaration.

```
int *a;
```

The above declaration indicates that a is a pointer type variable that points to int type data. That is, the int indicates that the pointer variable is intended to store the address of an integer variable. Such a pointer is said to 'point to' an integer.

```
float *t;
```

The above declaration represents the fact that t is a pointer type variable that points to float type data. Some declarations are listed in Table 8.2.

Table 8.2 Meaning of some pointer type variable declarations

Declaration	What it Means
int p	p is an integer
int *p	p is a pointer to an integer
char p	p is a character
char *p	p is a pointer to a character
long p	p is a long integer
long *p	p is a pointer to a long integer
unsigned char p	p is an unsigned character
unsigned char *p	p is a pointer to an unsigned character

Consider the following program.

```
#include <stdio.h>
int main()
{
    int *p;
    float *q;
    double *r;
    printf("\n the size of integer pointer is %d",
           sizeof(p));
    printf("\n the size of float pointer is %d",
           sizeof(q));
    printf("\n the size of double pointer is %d",
           sizeof(r));
    printf("\n the size of character pointer is %d",
           sizeof(char *));
    return 0;
}
```

Output:

In Turbo C

```
the size of integer pointer is 2
the size of float pointer is 2
the size of double pointer is 2
the size of character pointer is 2
```

In GCC

```
the size of integer pointer is 4
the size of float pointer is 4
the size of double pointer is 4
the size of character pointer is 4
```

The output shows that all the pointer type variables (p, q, and r) take up the same storage space. Depending upon the machine architecture, the size of a pointer will range from being a 16-bit field on the IBM PC class of machines, to a 64-bit field on a Cray supercomputer.

Why should pointers have data types

Let it be assumed that an address in a hypothetical machine is 32-bits long. The addressing of a byte or word will, therefore, require a 32-bit address. This suggests that a pointer (as pointers store addresses) should be capable of storing at least, a 32-bit value irrespective of whether it is an integer or a character. This brings in a question. Why should pointers have data types when their size is always four bytes (in a 32-bit machine) irrespective of the target they are pointing to?

Before discussing why pointers should have data types, it would be beneficial to understand the following points about C.

- It has data types of different size, i.e., objects of different types will have different memory requirements.

- It supports uniformity of arithmetic operations across different (pointer) types.

- It does not maintain data type information in the object or executable image.

When objects of a given data type are stored consecutively in the memory (that is, an array), each object is placed at a certain offset from the previous object, if any, depending on its size. A compiler that generates a code for a pointer, which accesses these objects using pointer arithmetic, requires information on generating offset. The data type of the pointer provides this information. This explains the first point.

The second point is reasonable enough to suggest that pointers should have data types. Sizes of various data types are basically decided by the machine architecture and/or the implementation. And, if arithmetic operations were not uniform, then the responsibility of generating proper offset for accessing array elements would completely rest on the programmer. This has the following drawbacks.

- A programmer is likely to commit mistakes such as typographical mistakes and providing wrong offsets.
- Porting the code to other implementations would require changes, if data type sizes differ. This would lead to portability issues.

Point to Note

- Pointers have data types but the size of a pointer variable is always four bytes (in a 32-bit machine) whatever the data type is used in declaring it.

Where is a pointer stored?

A pointer can be stored in any location like any other variable but is generally not stored on the heap. It can be defined and stored globally, or it can be defined local to a function and stored on the stack. The size of the pointer depends on the implementation and for 32-bit operating systems, it generally requires four bytes of storage space. This is, however, not a requirement. A compiler writer can use any number of bytes desired to store a pointer.

Keep in mind, that a pointer is like any other variable in the sense that it requires storage space somewhere in the computer's memory, but it is not like most variables because it contains no data, only an address. Since it is an address, it actually contains a number referring to some memory location. Dynamically allocated arrays can also be expanded during the execution of the program.

8.4.2 Initializing Pointers

It should be noted that, unlike a simple variable that stores a value, a pointer must be initialized with a specified address prior to its use. One of the most common causes of errors in programming by novices and professionals alike is uninitialized pointers. These errors can be very difficult to debug because the effect of the errors is often delayed until later in the program execution. Consider the following program.

```c
#include <stdio.h>
int main()
{
    int *p;          /* a pointer to an integer */
    printf("%d\n",*p);
    return 0;
}
```

This code conveys to the compiler to print the value that p points to. However, p has not been initialized yet; it contains the address 0 or some random address. A pointer must not be used until it is assigned a meaningful address. To use a pointer that has not been initialized properly will cause unpredictable results. When a program starts execution, an uninitialized pointer will have some unknown memory addresses in them. More precisely, they will have an unknown value that will be interpreted as memory addresses. To use a pointer that has not been initialized properly will cause unpredictable results. In most cases, a segmentation fault (or some other run-time error) results, which means that the pointer variable used points to an invalid area of memory. Sometimes the program will appear to run correctly but when the program terminates, the message 'Null Pointer Assignment' will be displayed. This message is produced by the system for notifying the programmer that the program is using an uninitialized pointer. In other cases, the use of an uninitialized pointer will result in a 'Bus Error' or a 'Memory Fault' run-time error. No matter what, the use of an uninitialized pointer is extremely dangerous, especially on PC type systems, and difficult to track down.

Point to Note

- A pointer should be initialized with another variable's memory address, with 0, or with the keyword NULL prior to its use; otherwise the result may be a compiler error or a run-time error.

Now, back to the new pointer variable p declared earlier. Suppose p stores the address of the integer variable i that contains the value 3. To store the address of 'i' in 'p', the unary & address operator is to be used. This is shown as follows:

```c
p = &i;
```

The & operator retrieves the lvalue (address) of i, even though i is on the right-hand side of the assignment operator '=', and copies that onto the contents of the pointer ptr.

Now, `ptr` is said to 'point to' `i`. The `&` operator applies only to objects in memory; that is, variables and array elements. It cannot be applied to expressions, constants, or register variables.

The following program shows how to use the address operator to assign the address of a variable to a pointer. This program also demonstrates that the value of a pointer is the same as the address to which the pointer points.

```c
#include <stdio.h>
int main()
{
    int i = 5;
    int *ptr = &i;
    printf("\nThe address of i using &num is %p", &i);
    printf("\nThe address of i using Ptr is %p", ptr);
    return 0;
}
```

The output (the following addresses might be different on different computers) is

```
The address of i using &num is 0012FED4
The address of i using Ptr is 0012FED4
```

Figure 8.3 shows graphically how the pointer points to the integer variable.

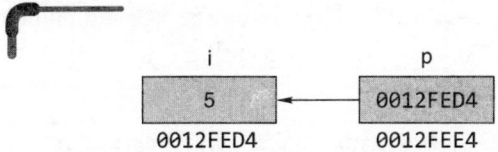

Figure 8.3 Pointer pointing to an integer variable

Another point to be remembered is that a *pointer variable is always bound to a specific data type (except void pointer)*. This means that the type of the pointer and the variable whose address is contained in the pointer must be of the same type. The following pointer initializations are invalid.

```c
int a=3, *ip;
float *p;
char ch='A';
p=&a; ———————— INVALID
ip=&ch; ———————— INVALID
```

Any number of pointers can point to the same address. For example, we could declare `p`, `q`, and `r` as integer pointers and set all of them to point to `i` as shown here.

```c
int i=3;
int *p, *q, *r;
p = &i;
q = &i;
r = p;
```

Note that in this code, `r` points to the same address that `p` points to, which is the address of `i`. We can assign pointers to one another, and the address is copied from the right-hand side to the left-hand side during the assignment. The pictorial representation is given in Fig. 8.4.

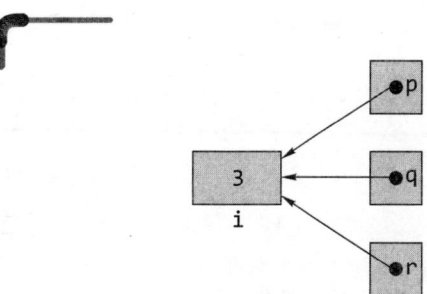

Figure 8.4 Three pointers pointing to the same variable

The variable `i` can be accessed through `i`, `*p`, `*q`, and `*r`. There is no limit on the number of pointers that can hold, and therefore point to, the same address.

> **Point to Note**
>
> - A pointer is bound to a specific data type (except pointer to void). A pointer to an int cannot hold the address of a character variable in which case a compiler error would result.

Printing pointer value

A pointer variable contains a memory address that points to another variable. To print the memory address stored in pointers and non-pointer variables using the `%p` conversion specifier and to learn the use of the `%p` conversion specifier, study the following program.

```c
#include <stdio.h>
int main(void)
{
    int a=10, *p;
    p=&a;
    printf("\n p = %p", p);
    return 0;
}
```

Output:

```
p = 0022FF2C
```

On most systems %p produces a hexadecimal number. On ANSI C systems the %p is preferred. Instead of %p, %x can be used giving the same output. If %u is used the address will be printed in decimal form. Compare the output with the previous program.

```c
#include <stdio.h>
int main(void)
{
  int a=10, *p;
  p=&a;
  printf("\n p = %u", p);
  return 0;
}
```

Output:

```
p = 2293548
```

Point to Note

- Addresses must always be printed using %u or %p or %x. If %p is used, the address is printed in hexadecimal form. If %u is used, address is printed in decimal form.

Is it possible to assign a constant to a pointer variable?

Consider the following code:

```c
int *pi;
pi= (int*)1000;
*pi = 5;
```

Location 1000 might contain the program. Since it is a read only, the OS will throw up a segmentation fault.

What about *pi = 5? Again, it will most likely cause a segmentation fault because lower memory addresses are typically used for program code. This area is read only. It should be known in advance where this constant is located in the memory. This construction is useful when writing an OS or device driver that communicates with the device using memory.

For example, in older PCs, the screen could be updated by directly accessing an array in memory (the address probably started at 0x10000). The array was of integers that were two bytes. The first byte held the ASCII character code and the second byte stored the character attributes. Once again, if one did not know what one were doing, the computer could crash.

Points to Note

- A pointer is a variable that holds the address of a memory location. That is, pointers are variables that *point* to memory locations.
- In C, pointers are not allowed to store any arbitrary memory address, but they can only store addresses of variables of a given type.

8.4.3 Indirection Operator and Dereferencing

The primary use of a pointer is to access and, if appropriate, change the value of the variable that the pointer is pointing to. The other pointer operator available in C is '*', called the 'value at address' operator. It returns the value stored at a particular address. The value at address operator is also called indirection operator or dereference operator.

In the following program, the value of the integer variable num is changed twice.

```c
#include <stdio.h>
int main()
{
  int num = 5;
  int *iPtr = &num;
  printf("\n The value of num is %d", num);
  num = 10;
  printf("\n The value of num after num = 10 is\
      %d", num);
  *iPtr = 15;
  printf("\n The value of num after *iPtr = 15 is\
      %d", num);
  return 0;
}
```

Output:

```
The value of num is 5
The value of num after num = 10 is 10
The value of num after *iPtr = 15 is 15
```

The second change should be familiar, by the direct assignment of a value to num, such as num=10. However, the third change is accomplished in a new way, by using the indirection operator.

```c
*iPtr = 15;
```

The indirection operator is an asterisk, the same asterisk that is used to declare the pointer or to perform multiplication. However, in this statement the asterisk is not being used in a declaration or to perform multiplication.

Therefore, in this context it is being used as an indirection operator. Observe the following statements carefully.

```
int i=5;
int *p;
p = &i;
printf("\nValue of i = %d", i);
```

Output: 5

```
printf("\nValue of i = %d", *(&i));
```

Output: 5

Note that printing the value of *(&i) is same as printing the value of i. * always implies value at address. *(&i) is identical to i. The unary operators & and * bind more tightly than arithmetic operators; they associate right to left, hence *&i is equivalent to *(&i).

The placement of the indirection operator before a pointer is said to *dereference the pointer*. The value of a dereferenced pointer is not an address, but rather the value at that address—that is, the value of the variable that the pointer points to.

For example, in the preceding program, iPtr's value is the address of num. However, the value of iPtr dereferenced is the value of num. Thus, the following two statements have the same effect, both changing the value of num.

```
num = 25;
*iPtr = 25;
```

Similarly, a dereferenced pointer can be used in arithmetic expressions in the same fashion as the variable to which it points. Thus, the following two statements have the same effect.

```
num *= 2;
*iPtr *= 2;
```

In these examples, changing a variable's value using the indirection operator rather than through a straightforward assignment seems like an unnecessary complication. However, there are instances covered later in this chapter, such as looping through an array using a pointer, or using dynamic memory allocation, in which using the indirection operator is helpful or even necessary.

Points to Note

- Address of operator (&): It is used as a variable prefix and can be translated as 'address of'. Thus, &variable can be read as .address of variable.
- Dereference operator (*): It can be translated by .value pointed by or 'value at address'. *ptr can be read as 'value pointed by ptr'. It indicates that what has to be evaluated is the content pointed by the expression considered as an address.

The following example shows how pointers can be used to add numbers given by the user through the use of pointers without using the variable directly.

```
#include <stdio.h>
int main()
{
    int a,b,c;
    int *pa,*pb,*pc;
    pa=&a;
    pb=&b;
    pc=&c;
    printf("\n ENTER THE FIRST NUMBER:");
    scanf("%d",pa);
    printf("\n ENTER THE SECOND NUMBER:");
    scanf("%d",pb);
    *pc=*pa+*pb;
    printf("\n SUM IS %d",*pc);
    return 0;
}
```

Output:

```
ENTER THE FIRST NUMBER 5
ENTER THE SECOND NUMBER 6
SUM IS 11
```

The following statements are also valid.

```
*ptr = *ptr + 10;
```

increments *ptr by 10. The unary operators * and & bind more tightly than arithmetic operators, so the assignment

```
y = *ptr + 1
```

takes whatever ptr points at, adds 1, and assigns the result to y, while

```
*ip += 1
```

increments what ptr points to. A pointer variable does not always points to a particular variable throughout the program. It can point to any variable; the only precondition is that their type must be same because the pointer variable is bound to specific data type. The following program illustrates this fact.

```
#include <stdio.h>
int main()
{
    int a=5, b=10;
    int *p;
    p = &a;
    printf("\na=%d b=%d *p=%d", a, b,*p);
    p=&b;
    printf("\na=%d b=%d *p=%d", a, b,*p);
    return 0;
}
```

Output:

```
a=5 b=10 *p=5
a=5 b=10 *p=10
```

8.5 VOID POINTER

A void pointer is a special type of pointer. It can point to any data type, from an integer value or a float to a string of characters. Its sole limitation is that the pointed data cannot be referenced directly (the asterisk * operator cannot be used on them) since its length is always undetermined. Therefore, *type casting* or assignment must be used to turn the void pointer to a pointer of a concrete data type to which we can refer. Take a look at the following example.

```
#include <stdio.h>
int main()
{
    int a=5,
    double b=3.1415;
    void *vp;
    vp=&a;
    printf("\n a= %d", *((int *)vp));
    vp=&b;
    printf("\n a= %d", *((double *)vp));
    return 0;
}
```

Output:
```
a= 5
b= 3.141500
```

Points to Note

- Void pointer can point to a variable of any data type, from an integer value or a float to a string of characters.
- The type casting or assignment must be used to turn the void pointer to a pointer of a concrete data type to which we can refer.

8.6 NULL POINTER

Suppose a variable, e.g., a, is declared without initialization.
```
int a;
```

If this is made outside of any function, ANSI-compliant compilers will initialize it to zero. Similarly, an uninitialized pointer variable is initialized to a value guaranteed in such a way that it is certain not to point to any C object or function. A pointer initialized in this manner is called a *null* pointer.

A *null pointer* is a special pointer that points nowhere. That is, no other valid pointer to any other variable or array cell or anything else will ever be equal to a null pointer.

The most straightforward way to get a null pointer in the program is by using the predefined constant NULL, which is defined by several standard header files, including <stdio.h>, <stdlib.h>, and <string.h>. To initialize a pointer to a null pointer, code such as the following can be used.

```
#include <stdio.h>
int *ip = NULL;
```

To test it for a null pointer before inspecting the value pointed to, code such as the following can be used.

```
if(ip != NULL)
    printf("%d\n", *ip);
```

It is also possible to refer to the null pointer using a constant 0, and to set null pointers by simply saying
```
int *ip = 0;
```

If it is too early in the code to know which address to assign to the pointer, then the pointer can be assigned to NULL, which is a constant with a value of zero defined in several standard libraries, including stdio.h. The following program does so.

```
#include <stdio.h>
int main()
{
    int *p;
    p = NULL;
    printf("\n The value of p is %u", p);
    return 0;
}
```

Output:
```
The value of p is 0
```

On most operating systems, programs are not permitted to access memory at address 0 because that memory is reserved by the operating system. It is not the case that the pointer points to a memory address that is reserved by the operating system. However, the memory address 0 has special significance; it signals that the pointer is not intended to point to an accessible memory location. Thus, if it is too early in the code to know which address to assign to a pointer, the pointer should first be assigned to NULL, which then makes it safe to access the value of a pointer before it is assigned a 'real' value such as the address of another variable or constant.

Furthermore, since the definition of 'true' in C is a value that is not equal to 0, the following statement tests for non-null pointers with abbreviated code such as

```
if(ip)
    printf("%d\n", *ip);
```

This has the same meaning as our previous example; if(ip) is equivalent to if(ip != 0) and to if(ip != NULL). The value 0 can be used to represent a null pointer in

- assignment and initialization
- comparison

All of these uses are legal, although the use of the constant NULL is recommended for clarity.

Point to Note

NULL is a constant that is defined in the standard library and is the equivalent of zero for a pointer. NULL is a value that is guaranteed not to point to any location in memory.

Consider the following code segment:

```
#include <stdio.h>
int main(void)
{
    char *p=NULL;
    printf("%s",p);
    return 0;
}
```

The C standard lays down that the argument for a %s specifier shall be a pointer to an array of characters. Since NULL is not an array of characters, the statement "printf("%s",p);" shows an undefined behaviour resulting in unpredictable or compiler defined output.

8.7 USE OF POINTERS

Call by address

One of the typical applications of pointers is to support call by reference. However, C does not support call by reference as do other programming languages such as Pascal and FORTRAN. Typically a function call is made to communicate some arguments to the function. C makes use of only one mechanism to communicate arguments to a function: *call by value*. This means that when a function is called, a copy of the values of the arguments is created and given to the function. For example,

```
#include <stdio.h>
void swap(int a, int b)
{
    int temp;
    temp=a;
    a=b;
    b=temp;
}
int main()
{
    int x=5,y=10;
    void swap(int,int);
    printf("%d %d\n",x,y);
    swap(x,y);
    printf("%d %d\n",x,y);
    return 0;
}
```

Output:
```
5 10
5 10
```

No swapping takes place. Now when the function swap is called, the system automatically creates two new variables (called a and b in this case). These will contain a copy of the values that are specified in the function call (i.e., the value of x and the value of y). All the operations performed by the function operate on the copies of the values (a, b), and will not affect the original values (x, y).

Of course, in this particular example, the function will probably not accomplish what is needed. The function swap is used to exchange the content of two variables, but when the call is made, the function will receive and operate on the copies of the variables, leaving the original variables (x, y) untouched. So at the end of the function the effect of the changes done by swap are lost (the copies created when the function is called are destroyed when the function is completed).

This is a common situation in C. Each function always receives copies of values and the function does not have any way of modifying the value of variables that exist outside the function (e.g., x, y in the example).

The way to obtain the desired effect is *call by reference*. This means that when the function is called, we do not create copies of values but the function is allowed to access the original values. This also means that if the function modifies such values, then the modification will affect the original value and will persist once the function execution is finished.

Call by reference does not exist in C, but it can be simulated through the use of pointers. To make a function be able to modify a certain variable, the function must be provided with information about the location of the variable in memory (i.e., its address). If the function knows where the variable is in memory, it will be able to access that area of memory by using pointers and change its content. This is known as *call by address*.

The way to obtain the desired effect is for the calling program to pass pointers to the values to be changed. For example,

```
swap(&x, &y);
```

Since the operator & produces the address of a variable, &x is a pointer to x. In swap itself, this will arrive to the function in the form of a pointer. That is, the parameters are declared as pointers, and the operands are accessed indirectly through them. Now the preceding program is rewritten using call by address.

```
#include <stdio.h>
void swap(int *a, int *b)
{
  int temp;
  temp = *a;
  *a = *b;
  *b = temp;
}
int main()
{
  int x=5,y=10;
  void swap(int *,int *);
  printf("%d %d\n",x,y);
  swap(&x, &y);
  printf("%d %d\n",x,y);
  return 0;
}
```

Output:
```
5 10
10 5
```

The values have been exchanged by the function swap(). Within the main() function, the & operator causes the address of arguments x and y to be passed in the call to swap(). In the swap() function header, the addresses being passed from the calling function are received in pointer type variables (int *a, int *b). Within the swap() function body, the * operator is used to retrieve values held at the addresses that were passed. The following example attempts to demonstrate how identifiers or variables are

assigned locations in memory and how values are stored in those locations. All addressing in the following example is assumed arbitrarily.

```
int main()
{
void swap(int *, int *);
int
  x = 5,
  y = 10
  ;
  /* pass addresses */
  swap(&x, &y);
  return 0;
}
void
swap(int *a, int *b)

{
  int temp;
  temp = *a;
  *a = *b;
  *b = temp;
}
```

Variable name	Memory address	value
x	2000	5
y	2002	10
a	3000	2000
b	3002	2002
temp	4000	0/garbage
temp	4000	5
*a	2000	10
*b	2002	5

In the above code, the addresses of x and y are passed to the function swap(). The parameters of the swap() function, int *a and int *b are pointers to integer type data. These pointers receive the addresses of x and y respectively that are passed in the call to swap(). Within the function swap(), a local variable temp is declared. The pointer a is dereferenced, meaning that the value at the address held in a is retrieved. This value is stored into temp. Then the value at the address held in b is retrieved and assigned to the value at the address held in a, thus exchanging values. The final statement in the function completes the exchange of values. Notice that the function does not return a value because of the void return type. Figure 8.5 presents this diagrammatically.

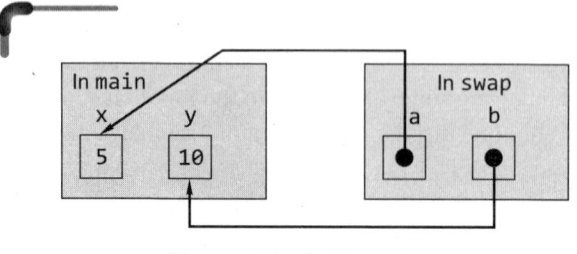

Figure 8.5 Call by address

Suppose one accidentally forgets the & when the swap function is called, and that the swap line accidentally looks like this:

```
swap(x, y);
```

This causes a segmentation fault. When the value of a is passed instead of its address, a points to an invalid location in memory and the system crashes when *a is used.

Point to Note

- C only supports call by value. C does not support call by reference in true sense, but it can be simulated through the use of pointers known as *call by address*.

Returning more than one value from a function

Functions usually return only one value and when arguments are passed by value, the called function cannot alter the values passed and have those changes reflected in the calling function. Pointers allow the programmer to 'return' more than one value by allowing the arguments to be passed by address, which allows the function to alter the values pointed to, and thus 'return' more than one value from a function.

Example

```
1. #include <stdio.h>
   int main()
   {
     float r, area, perimeter;
     float compute(float, float *);
     printf("\n enter the radius of the circle:");
     scanf("%f",&r);
     area=compute(r, &perimeter);
     printf("\n AREA = %f", area);
     printf("\n PERIMETER = %f", perimeter);
     return 0;
   }
   float compute(float r, float *p)
   {
     float a;
     a=(float)3.1415 * r * r;
     *p=(float)3.1415 * 2 * r;
     return a;
   }
```

It must keep the value available until execution reaches a *sequence point*, which in this case means the end of the statement. When the system is notified to assign the value to area, a copy of it is saved. Following that, the compiler writer may delete the memory used to return the value. If it was returned on the stack, it is imperative to remove it from the stack in preparation for the next operation. But that can be done because the value is stored in area and can be used in any way.

Returning pointer from a function

It is also possible to return a pointer from a function. When a pointer is returned from a function, it must point to data in the calling function or in the global variable. Consider the following program. In this program, a pointer would point an integer variable whichever is larger between two variables through a function which returns the address of the larger variable.

```
#include <stdio.h>
int *pointMax(int *, int *);
int main(void)
{
  int a,b,*p;
  printf("\n a = ?");
  scanf("%d",&a);
  printf("\n b = ?");
  scanf("%d",&b);
  p=pointMax(&a,&b);
  printf("\n*p = %d", *p);
  return 0;
}
int *pointMax(int *x, int *y)
{
  if(*x>*y)
    return x;
  else
    return y;
}
```

Output:
```
a = ?5
b = ?7
*p = 7
```

When the function pointMax() is called addresses of two integer variables are passed to it. In the function the pointers x and y are pointing to a and b respectively. If a is greater than b then the function pointMax()returns the address of a; otherwise, it returns the address of b. When the control returns to the main(), p points either to a or b.

Returning a pointer to a local variable in the called function is not effectual or legal as illustrated in the following code segment. Because when function terminates the address of the local variable becomes invalid. Some compilers issue a warning that 'function returns address of local variable'.

```
int *pointMax(void)
{
  int a,b;
  .
  .
  .
  if(a>b)
    return a;
  else
    return b;
}
```

> **WRONG!**
> Never return a pointer to an automatic local variable. In C99, a warning will be issued

But it is legal to write a function that returns a pointer to an external variable or to a static variable that has been declared *static*.

```
include <stdio.h>
int *pointMax(void);
int main(void)
{
  int *p;
  p=pointMax();
  printf("*p = %d", *p);
  return 0;
}
int *pointMax(void)
{
  static int a=5, b=10;
  if(a>b)
    return &a;
  else
    return &b;
}
```

When an array is passed as argument to a function, sometimes it may be useful to return a pointer to one of the elements of the array as shown in the following function.

```
int *findMiddle(int x[], int n)
{
  return &x[n/2];
}
```

8.8 ARRAYS AND POINTERS

Pointers and arrays are inseparably related, but they are not synonymous.

8.8.1 One-dimensional Arrays and Pointers

An array is a non-empty set of sequentially indexed elements having the same type of data. Each element of an array has a unique identifying index number. Changes made to one element of an array does not affect the other elements. An array occupies a contiguous block of memory. The array a is laid out in memory as a contiguous block, as shown.

```
int a[]={10, 20, 30, 40, 50};
```

a[0]	a[1]	a[2]	a[3]	a[4]
10	20	30	40	50

2147478270 2147478274 2147478278 2147478282 2147478286

Elements of array are stored in the successive increasing locations of memory. For example, if the array starts at memory location 2147478270 (considering a 32-bit machine), then with the assumed size of an integer as four bytes, the first element is stored at location 2147478270, the second element at location 2147478274, and so on. Here the locations are taken as arbitrary.

Array notation is a form of pointer notation. The name of an array is the beginning address of the array, called the base address of the array. That is, the base address of an array is the address of the zeroth element of the array. The array name is referred to as an *address constant*. Mentioning the name of the array fetches its base address. Consider the following program.

Example

```
2. #include <stdio.h>
   int main()
   {
     int array[]={10, 20, 30, 40, 50};
     printf("%u %u", array, &array[0]);
     return 0;
   }
```

Output:
```
2147478270 2147478270
```

Again, consider the following program.

```
#incl]ude <stdio.h>
int main()
{
  int array[]={10, 20, 30, 40, 50};
  printf("%u %u", array, &array);
  return 0;
}
```

Output:
```
2147478270 2147478270
```

Both `array` and `&array` would give the base address of the array. Though both `array` and `&array` give the same address, there is a small difference between them. Under ANSI/ISO Standard C, `&array` yields a pointer, of type pointer-to-array-of-T, where T is the data type to the entire array. Under pre-ANSI C, the & in `&array` generally elicited a warning, and was generally ignored. Under all C compilers, an unadorned reference to an array yields a pointer, of type pointer-to-T, to the array's first element.

Points to Note

- Array name is an *pointer constant*. It cannot be used as *lvalue*. That is array names cannot be used as variables on the left of an assignment operator.
- Both `array` and `&array` would give the base address of the array, but the only difference is under ANSI/ISO Standard C, `&array` yields a pointer, of type pointer-to-array of-the data type to the entire array.

An array can be subscripted to get to individual cells of data. With the name of the array actually being a constant that represents a memory address, the name of the array can be used as a pointer and an integer value can be used to represent an offset from the base address. This alternate method can be used to get to individual cells of an array. An element of the array a is addressed as `a[i]` and the address of the ith element of the array a is given by `&a[i]=a+i*` size of the type pointed to by a.

The expression `a + i` (with integer i) means the address of the ith element beyond the one a points to. This is not measured in number of bytes, but in number of `sizeof(type)` bytes. This is known as *scaling*.

The compiler automatically scales a subscript to the size of the object pointed at. The compiler takes care of scaling before adding to the base address. This is the reason why pointers are always typed-constrained to point to objects for only one type – so that the compiler knows how many bytes to retrieve on pointer dereference and it knows by how much to scale a subscript.

As indirection operator '*' implies value at address, `a[i]` is equivalent to `*(a+i)`. Consider the following two versions of the same program.

Example

3.(a)
```c
#include <stdio.h>
int main()
{
  int a[]={10, 20, 30, 40, 50};
  int i;
  for(i=0;i<5;++i)
    printf("\n%d", a[i]);
  return 0;
}
```
Output:
```
10
20
30
40
50
```

(b)
```c
#include <stdio.h>
int main()
{
  int a[]={10, 20, 30, 40, 50};
  int i;
  for(i=0;i<5;++i)
    printf("\n%d", *(a+i));
  return 0;
}
```
Output:
```
10
20
30
40
50
```

The integer identifier i is added to the base address of the array. The C compiler computes the resulting address that will be accessed by taking the value held in i multiplied by the size in bytes of the type of array a and adds the proper offset to a to give the correct memory address. Subscript notation is converted by the compiler into the pointer notation. Hence, pointer notation would work faster since conversion time can be saved by using it.

All the following four expressions are the same when their addresses are considered.

```
a[i]
*(a + i)
*(i + a)
i[a]
```

In the expression a[i], i must be an integer. The other may either be an array name or a pointer. For any one-dimensional array a and integer i, the following relationships are always true.

1. &a[0] == a

   The address of the first element of the array a is the value of a itself. In other words, a is a pointer; it points to the first element in the array.

2. &a[i] == a + i

   The address of the ith element of a is the value of a + i. This is one of the great truths (and a defining characteristic) of C. The first relationship is a special case of this more general relationship.

3. a[i] == *(a + i)

   This is basically the same as the previous relationship but this relationship still holds if both sides of the equality operator are dereferenced.

4. (&a[i] - &a[j]) == (i - j)

   This relationship defines the subtraction of pointers. The subtraction of two pointers of type t is the number of elements of type t that would fit between them.

A pointer variable (of the appropriate type) can also be used to initialize or point to the first element of the array. Then it can also be used as above.

```c
#include <stdio.h>
int main()
{
    int a[]={10, 20, 30, 40, 50};
    int i, *p;
    p=a; /* it can also be written as p=&a[0]; */
    for(i=0;i<5;++i)
        printf("\n%d", p[i]);

    return 0;
}
```

```c
printf ("\n%d", *(p+i));
            OR
printf ("\n%d", *(i+p));
            OR
printf ("\n%d", i[p]);
```

Output:
```
10
20
30
40
50
```

One can define a pointer of the same type as the elements of the array and can assign it the address of any element of the array and use it to access the array elements. In fact, one may add an integer value to it. Such a statement in the program uses the formula given earlier to do the assignment; so it also adjusts the count for the size of the element. Pointers and arrays are so closely related that their notation can be interchanged such that the following terms are identical if p contains the value of a.

```c
a[i]
*(a + i)
*(p + i)
p[i]
where i=0,1,2,...(N-1). N is the size of the array.
```

The similarities between arrays and pointers end up being quite useful, and in fact C builds on the similarities, leading to what is called 'the equivalence of arrays and pointers in C'. This equivalence does not mean that arrays and pointers are the same (they are, in fact, quite different) but that they can be used in related ways, and that certain operations may be used between them. These operations are as follows.

- The first such operation is that it is possible to (apparently) assign an array to a pointer.

  ```c
  int a[10];
  int *p;
  p = a;
  ```

  C defines the result of this assignment to be that p receives a pointer to the first element of a. In other words,

  ```c
  p = &a[0];
  ```

- The second aspect of the equivalence is that the *array subscripting* notation [i] can be applied on pointers, too. p[3] can be written as *(p + 3).

  So a pointer that points to an array or a part of an array can be treated 'as if' it *was* an array, using the convenient [i] notation. In other words, at the beginning of this discussion, the expressions *p, *(p+1), *(p+2), and in general *(p+i), could have been written as p[0], p[1], p[2], and p[i]. This can be quite useful (or at least convenient).

The pointer to an array does not always point to the first element of the array. It can point to any element of the array. For example,

```c
int a[]={10,20,30,40,50};
int *p;
p = a + 3;
```

can also be written as follows

```c
p = &a[0] + 3;
```

which, in turn, gives the same result as

    p = &a[3];

Figure 8.6 depicts the equivalence among array notation and pointer notation.

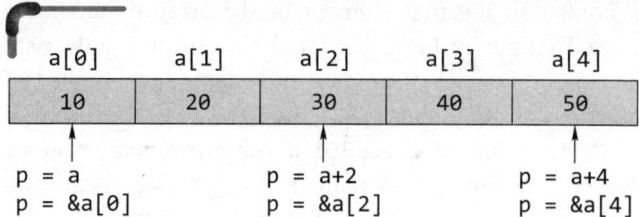

a[0]	a[1]	a[2]	a[3]	a[4]
10	20	30	40	50

    p = a   p = a+2   p = a+4
    p = &a[0]   p = &a[2]   p = &a[4]

Figure 8.6   Pointer notation of array elements

Is it possible to treat an array as if it were a 1-based array?

Although this technique is attractive (and was used in old editions of the book *Numerical Recipes in C*), it does not conform to the C standards. Pointer arithmetic is defined only as long as the pointer points within the same allocated block of memory, or to the imaginary 'terminating' element one past it; otherwise, the behavior is undefined, *even if the pointer is not dereferenced*. The preceding code could fail if, while subtracting the offset, an illegal address were generated (perhaps because the address tried to 'wrap around' past the beginning of some memory segment). Here is a neat trick, the details of which will be discussed in Section 8.18.

    int arr[10];
    int *a = &arr[-1];

Point to Note

For any one-dimensional array a and integer i, the following relationships are always true.

• a[i] ≡ *(a+i) ≡ *(i+a) ≡ i[a].

8.8.2 Passing an Array to a Function

An array may be passed to a function, and the elements of that array may be modified without having to worry about referencing and dereferencing. Since arrays may transform immediately into pointers, all the difficult stuff gets done automatically. A function that expects to be passed with an array can declare that formal parameter in one of the two ways.

    int a[] or int *a

When passing an array name as argument to a function, the address of the zeroth element of the array is copied to the local pointer variable in the function. The values of the elements are *not* copied. The corresponding local variable is considered as a pointer variable, having all the properties of pointer arithmetic and dereferencing. It is *not* an address constant. This is illustrated with an example. The relevant function calls in main() and the corresponding function headers are shown as follows for easy reference.

```
#define MAX 50
int main()
{
    int arr[MAX],n;
    ...
    n = getdata(arr, MAX);
    show(arr, n);
    return 0;
}
int getdata(int a[], int n)
{
    ...
}
void show(int a[], int n)
{
    ...
}
```

When a formal parameter is declared in a function header as an array, it is interpreted as a pointer variable, *not* an array. Even if a size were specified in the formal parameter declaration, only a pointer cell is allocated for the variable, not the entire array. The type of the pointer variable is the specified type. In the preceding example, the formal parameter, a, is an integer pointer. It is initialized to the pointer value passed as an argument in the function call. The value passed from main() is arr, a pointer to the first element of the array, arr[].

Within the function, getdata(), it is now possible to access all the elements of the array indirectly. Since the variable a in getdata() points to the first element of the array arr[], it accesses the first element of the array. In addition, a + 1 points to the next element of the array, so it accesses the next element, i.e., arr[1]. In general, *(a + i) accesses the element arr[i]. To access elements of the array, we can either write *(a + i) or a[i], because dereferenced array pointers and indexed array elements are identical ways of writing expressions for array access.

The functions, getdata() and show() can be used to read objects into any integer array and to print element values of any integer array, respectively. The calling function must simply pass an appropriate array pointer and maximum number of elements as arguments. These functions may also be written explicitly in terms of indirect access. Such an example is as follows:

Example

```
4. #include <stdio.h>
   #define MAX 50
   int main()
   {
     int arr[MAX],n;
     int getdata(int *, int);
     void show(int *, int);
     n = getdata(arr, MAX);
     show(arr, n);
     return 0;
   }
   /* Function reads scores in an array. */
   int getdata(int *a, int n)
   {
     int x, i = 0;
     printf("\n Enter the array elements one by one\n");
     while(i < n)
     {
       scanf("%d", &x);
       *(a + i) = x;
       i++;
     }
     return i;
   }
   void show(int *a, int n)
   {
     int i;
     for(i=0;i<n;++i)
       printf("\n %d", *(a+i));
   }
```

Figure 8.7 illustrates the connection between the calling function main(), and the called functions.

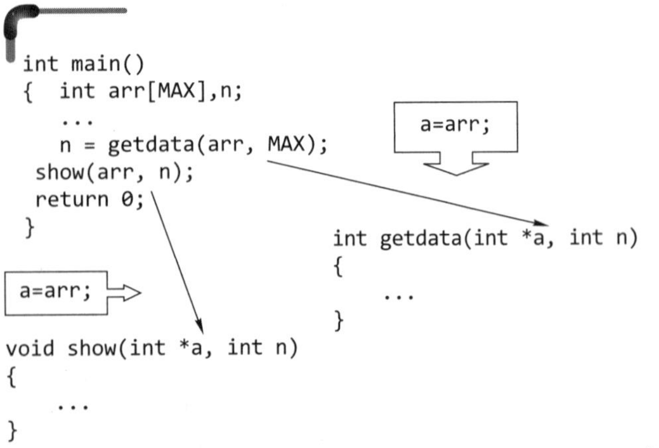

Figure 8.7 Passing array to a function

When an array is passed to a function, the C language allows the programmer to refer the formal parameter as either an array or as a pointer. The compiler knows that whenever a formal parameter is declared as an array, inside the function it will in fact always be dealing with a pointer to the first element of the array of unknown size. That's why the calling function must simply pass an appropriate array pointer and maximum number of elements as arguments.

Parts of an array, called a sub-array, may also be passed to a function. A pointer to a sub-array is also an array pointer; it simply specifies the base of the sub-array. In fact, as far as C is concerned, there is no difference between an entire array and any of its sub-arrays. For example, a function call can be made to print a sub-array by specifying the starting pointer of the sub-array and its size. Suppose we need to print the sub-array starting at arr[3] containing five elements; the expression, &arr[3] is a pointer to an array starting at arr[3]. The function call is,

```
show(&arr[3], 5);
```

Alternately, since arr + 3 points to arr[3], the function call can be

```
show(arr + 3, 5);
```

Points to Note

- When an array is passed to a function, it degenerates to a pointer. All array names that are function parameters are always converted into pointers by the compiler. Because when passing an array to a function, the address of the zero-th element of the array is copied to the pointer variable which is the formal parameter of the function. However, arrays and pointers are processed differently by the compiler, represented differently at runtime.

8.8.3 Differences between Array Name and Pointer

From the above discussion it seems that array name and pointer, which points to the base address of the array, are equivalent. But it is not true. There are a several differences between them. They are as follows.

- When memory is allocated for the array, the starting address is fixed, i.e., it cannot be changed during program execution. Therefore, array name is an address constant; the value contained in it should not be changed. To ensure that this pointer is not changed, in C, array names may not be used as variables on the left of an assignment statement, i.e., they may not be used as an lvalue. Instead, if necessary, separate pointer variables of the appropriate type may be declared and used as lvalues. Here is an example of a common error when an attempt to use an array as an lvalue is made.

```c
#include <stdio.h>
int main()
{
  int i;
  float a[5];
  for(i = 0; i < 5; i++)
  {
    *a = 0.0;
    a++; /* BUG: a = a + 1; */
  }
  return 0;
}
```

In this example, a is fixed and cannot be used as an lvalue; the compiler will generate an error stating that an lvalue is required for the ++ operator. However, a pointer variable can be declared, which can point to the same type as the type of the array, and initialize it with the base address of array. This pointer variable can be used as an lvalue and no error message will be displayed. Here is the difference.

```c
#include <stdio.h>
int main()
{
  int i;
  float *ptr, a[5];
  ptr = a;
  for(i = 0; i < 5; i++)
  {
    *ptr = 0.0; /* *ptr accesses a[i] */
    ptr++;
  }
  return 0;
}
```

Observe that the pointer variable, ptr, is type float*, because the array is of type float. It is initialized to the value of the fixed pointer, a (i.e., the initial value of ptr is set to the same as that of a, namely, &a[0]), and may subsequently be modified in the loop to traverse the array. The first time through the loop, *ptr which points to (a[0]) is set to zero and ptr is incremented

by one so that it points to the next element in the array. The process repeats and each element of the array is set to 0.0.

Following the same concept, an array cannot be assigned to another. The following code

```c
int a[5]={1,2,3,4,5};
int b[5];
b = a;       /* WRONG */
```

is illegal. To copy a into b, something like the following has to be entered.

```c
for(i=0; i<5; i++)
  b[i]=a[i];
```

Or, to put it more succinctly,

```c
for(i=0; i<5; b[i]=a[i], i++);
```

But two pointer variables can be assigned.

```c
int *p1, *p2;
int a[10]={1,2,3,4,5};
p1 = &a[0];
p2 = p1;
```

Pointer assignment is straightforward; the pointer on the left is simply made to point wherever the pointer on the right does. The statement p1=p2 does not copy the data pointed to (there is still just one copy in the same place); it just makes two pointers point to the same location.

- The & (address of) operator normally returns the address of the operand. However, arrays are the exception. When applied to an array (which is an address), it has the same value as the array reference without the operator. This is not true of the equivalent pointers, which have an independent address. The following example shows this.

Example

5. **(a)**
```c
#include <stdio.h>
int main()
{
  int a[]={10, 20, 30, 40, 50};
  printf("%u %u %u", a, &a[0],&a);
  return 0;
}
```
Output:
```
65506 65506 65506
```

(b)
```c
#include <stdio.h>
int main()
{
  int a[]={10, 20, 30, 40, 50};
  int *ptr;
  ptr=a;
  printf("%u %u", &a[0],ptr,&ptr);
  return 0;
}
```
Output:
```
65506 65506 65526
```

- The `sizeof` operator returns the size of the allocated space for arrays. In case of a pointer, the `sizeof` operator returns two or four or more bytes of storage (machine dependent).

Example

6.(a)
```c
#include <stdio.h>
int main()
{
  int a[]={10, 20, 30, 40, 50};
  printf("%d", sizeof (a));
  return 0;
}
```
Output:

In Turbo C
```
10
```
In GCC
```
20
```

(b)
```c
#include <stdio.h>
int main()
{
  int a[]={10, 20, 30, 40, 50};
  int *ptr;
  ptr=a;
  printf("%d", sizeof (ptr));
  return 0;
}
```
Output:

In Turbo C
```
2
```
In GCC
```
4
```

Table 8.3 lists the differences between pointers and arrays.

Table 8.3 Differences between pointers and arrays

Arrays	Pointers
• Array allocates space automatically.	• It is explicitly assigned to point to an allocated space.
• It cannot be resized.	• It can be resized using `realloc()`.
• It cannot be reassigned.	• It can be reassigned.
• `sizeof(arrayname)` gives the number of bytes occupied by the array.	• `sizeof(p)` returns the number of bytes used to store the pointer variable p.

8.9 POINTERS AND STRINGS

Strings are one-dimensional arrays of type `char`. By convention, a string in C is terminated by the end-of-string sentinel `\0`, or null character. The null character is a byte with all bits off; hence, its decimal value is zero. It is useful to think of strings as having a variable length, delimited by `\0`, but with the maximum length determined by the size of the string. The size of a string *must* include the storage needed for the end-of-string sentinel. As with all arrays, it is the job of the programmer to make sure that string bounds are not overrun.

String constants are written between double quotes. For example, `"abc"` is a character array of size 4, with the last element being the null character `\0`. Note that string constants are different from character constants. For example, `"a"` and `'a'` are not the same. The array `"a"` has two elements, the first with value `'a'` and the second with value `'\0'`.

A string constant, like an array name by itself, is treated by the compiler as a pointer. Its value is the base address of the string. Like the numeric array, individual characters contained in a string can be printed.

```c
#include <stdio.h>
int main()
{
  char s[]="Oxford";
  for(i=0;s[i]!='\0';++i)
  putchar(s[i]);
  return 0;
}
```

A string in C is a pointer itself. The following program proves the fact.

```
#include <stdio.h>
int main()
{
  for(i=0;*("I am a pointer" + i)!='\0';++i)
    printf("%c",*("I am a pointer" + i));
  return 0;
}
```

Output:

```
I am a pointer
```

But this is not true for a numeric array. The following program gives an error.

```
#include <stdio.h>
int main()
{
  for(i=0;*({1,2,3,4,5} + i)!='\0';++i)
  putchar(*({1,2,3,4,5} + i));
  return 0;
}
```

Consider the following code.

```
char *p = "abc";
printf("%s %s \n", p, p + 1);   /* abc bc is printed */
```

The variable p is assigned the base address of the character array "abc". When a pointer to char is printed in the format of a string, the pointed-at character and successive characters are printed until the end-of-string sentinel (that is, '\0') is reached. Thus, in the `printf()` statement, the expression p causes abc to be printed, and the expression p + 1, which points to the letter b in the string "abc", causes bc to be printed. Because a string constant such as "abc" is treated as a pointer, expressions such as

```
"abc"[1] and *("abc" + 2)
```

are possible. Such expressions are not used in serious code, but they help to emphasize that string constants are treated as pointers. It should be noted that arrays and pointers have similar uses. They also have differences. Let us consider two declarations

```
char *p = "abcde"; and char s[] = "abcde";
```

In the first declaration, the compiler allocates space in the memory for p, puts the string constant "abcde" in memory somewhere else, and initializes p with the base address of the string constant. Now think of p as pointing to the string. The second declaration is equivalent to

```
char s[] = {'a', 'b', 'c', 'd', 'e', '\0'};
```

Because the brackets are empty, the compiler allocates six bytes of memory for the array s. The first byte is initialized with 'a', the second byte is initialized with 'b', and so on. Here is how these objects are stored in memory.

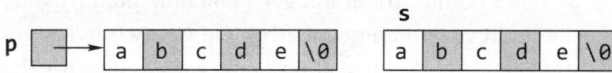

A char is always stored in one byte, and on most machines a pointer is stored in a word. Thus, on the machine, p is stored in four bytes, and s is stored in six bytes of storage. For technical reasons, it is better not to print null characters. However, the printing of null strings is perfectly acceptable.

One question may arise—when an array is passed, how does the function know how many elements the array has?

For a string, the number of elements it has need not be passed because it has the terminating null character. For other types of arrays, the number of elements must be passed as well.

> **Points to Note**
>
> - A string constant is treated by the compiler as a pointer.
> - For a string, the number of elements it has need not be passed to a function because it has the terminating null character.

8.10 POINTER ARITHMETIC

If p is declared as a pointer variable of any type and it has been initialized properly, then, just like a simple variable, any operation can be performed with *p. Because * implies value at address, working with *p means working with the variable whose address is currently held by p. Any expression, whether relational, arithmetic, or logical, can be written, which is valid for a simple value variable. But with only p, operations are restricted as in each case address arithmetic has to be performed. The only valid operations on pointers are as follows.

- Assignment of pointers to the same type of pointers: the assignment of pointers is done symbolically. Hence no integer constant except 0 can be assigned to a pointer.

- Adding or subtracting a pointer and an integer.

- Subtracting or comparing two pointers (within array limits) that point to the elements of an array.
- Incrementing or decrementing the pointers (within array limits) that point to the elements of an array. When a pointer to an integer is incremented by one, the address is incremented by two (as two bytes are used for `int`). Such scaling factors necessary for the pointer arithmetic are taken care of automatically by the compiler.
- Assigning the value 0 to the pointer variable and comparing 0 with the pointer. The pointer with address 0 points to nowhere at all.

These valid address arithmetic are discussed below in detail. Do not attempt the following arithmetic operations on pointers. They will not work.

- Addition of two pointers
- Multiplying a pointer with a number
- Dividing a pointer with a number

8.10.1 Assignment

Pointers with the assignment operators can be used if the following conditions are met.

- The left-hand operand is a pointer and the right-hand operand is a null pointer constant.
- One operand is a pointer to an object of incompatible type and the other is a pointer to `void`.
- Both the operands are pointers to compatible types.

Some of the pointer assignment statements were discussed earlier. For the notion of incompatible types, including the use of `void *`, there are now some complicated rules about how pointers can be mixed and what arithmetic with pointers really permits.

Pointers to `void` can be freely converted back and forth with pointers to any object or incomplete type. Converting a pointer to an object or an incomplete type to `void *` and then back gives a value which is equal to the original one.

Example

```
7. #include <stdio.h>
   int main()
   {
     int i;
     int *ip;
     void *vp;
     ip = &i;
```

```
     vp = ip;
     ip = vp;
     if(ip != &i)
       printf("\n Compiler error\n");
     else
       printf("\n No Compiler error\n");
     return 0;
   }
```

Output:

```
   No Compiler error
```

Now, consider the revised version of the program in Example 7.

```
#include <stdio.h>
int main()
{
  int i=5;
  int *ip;
  void *vp;
  ip = &i;
  vp = ip;
  //printf("\n *vp= %d",*vp); ———— ERROR
  ip = vp;
  printf("\n *ip= %d",*ip);
  return 0;
}
```

This program gives an error in the first `printf` statement stating 'not an allowed type' because no type is associated with a `void` pointer. The `void` pointer can store the address of a variable of any type. But while using the `void` pointer, the right type has to be specified through type casting. The right version of this program is as follows.

```
#include <stdio.h>
int main()
{
  int i=5;
  int *ip;
  void *vp;
  ip = &i;
  vp = ip;
  printf("\n *vp= %d",*((int *)vp));
  ip = vp;
  printf("\n *ip= %d",*ip);
  return 0;
}
```

Output:
```
*vp=5
*ip=5
```

The predefined constant NULL, which is defined by several standard header files, including <stdio.h>, <stdlib.h>, and <string.h> can be assigned.

```
int *p;
p = NULL;
```

It is also possible to refer to the null pointer by using a constant 0 by simply writing

```
int *ip = 0;
```

In fact, NULL is a preprocessor macro that typically has the value, 0.

The only values that can be assigned to pointers apart from 0 are the values of other pointers of the same type. However, one of the things that makes C a useful replacement for assembly language is that it allows one to do the sort of things that most other languages prevent. Try this.

```
int *ip;
ip = (int *)6;
*ip = 0xFF;
```

What does that do? The pointer has been initialized to the value of 6 (notice the cast to turn an integer 6 into a pointer). This is a highly machine-specific operation, and the bit pattern that ends up in the pointer is quite possibly nothing like the machine representation of 6. After the initialization, a hexadecimal FF is written into wherever the pointer is pointing. The int at location 6 has had 0xFF written into it—subject to whatever 'location 6' means on this particular machine.

It may or may not make sense to do that sort of thing; C gives you the power to express it, it is up to the programmer to get it right. As always, it is possible to do things like this by accident, too, and to be very surprised by the output.

8.10.2 Addition or Subtraction with Integers

In a closely related piece of syntax, a '+' between a pointer and an integer does the same offset computation as explained earlier, but leaves the result as a pointer. The square bracket syntax gives the nth element while the '+' syntax gives a pointer to the nth element. So the expression (arr + 3) is a pointer to the integer arr[3]. (arr + 3) is of type (int *) while arr[3] is of type int. The two expressions only differ in whether the pointer is dereferenced or not. So the expression (arr + 3) is equivalent to the expression (&(arr[3])). In fact those two probably compile to exactly the same code. They both represent a pointer to the element at index 3. Any []

expression can be written with the + syntax instead. It just needs the pointer dereference to be added in. So arr[3] is equivalent to *(arr + 3). For most purposes, the [] syntax is the easiest to use and the most readable as well. Every once in a while the + is convenient if one needs a pointer to the element instead of the element itself.

Therefore, expressions can add (or subtract, which is equivalent to adding negative values) integral values to the value of a pointer to any object type. The result has the type of the pointer and if n is added, then the result points n array elements away from the pointer. The most common use is repeatedly to add 1 to a pointer to step it from the start to the end of an array, but addition or subtraction of values other than 1 is possible. Consider the following two versions of same program.

Example

```
8. (a) #include <stdio.h>
    int main(void)
    {
      int a[] = {10, 12, 6, 7, 2};
      int i;
      int sum = 0;
      for(i=0; i<5; i++)
      {
        sum += a[i];
      }
      printf("%d\n", sum);
      return 0;
    }
   (b) #include <stdio.h>
    int main(void)
    {
      int a[] = {10, 12, 6, 7, 2};
      int i;
      int sum = 0;
      for(i=0; i<5; i++)
      {
        sum += *(a + i);
      }
      printf("%d\n", sum);
      return 0;
    }
```

Note that if the pointer resulting from the addition points in front of the array or past the non-existent element just after the last element of the array, then it results in overflow or underflow and the result is undefined.

This is a typical string-processing function. Pointer arithmetic and dereferencing are used to search for various characters or patterns. Often a character pointer is used to march along a string while parsing it or interpreting it in some way.

Declaration and initializations	
char s1[ ] = "India is a beautiful country"; s2[ ] = "C is sea";	
Expression	**Value**
strlen(s1)	28
strlen(s2 + 5)	3
Statements	**What gets printed**
printf("%s", s1 + 10); strcpy(s1 + 10, s2 + 8) strcat(s1, "great country"); printf("%s", s1);	beautiful country India is a great country

If p is a pointer to an element in an array, then (p+1) points to the next element in the array. The statement p++ can be used to step a pointer over the elements in an array. The program in Example 8 can be rewritten as follows.

```
#include <stdio.h>
int main(void)
{
  int a[] = {10, 12, 6, 7, 2};
  int i;
  int sum = 0;
  int *p;
  p = a;
  for(i=0; i<5; i++)
  {
    sum += *p;
    p++;
  }
  printf("%d\n", sum);
  return 0;
}
```

Similarly, since ++p and p++ are both equivalent to p=p + 1, incrementing a pointer using the unary ++ operator, either pre- or post-, increments the address it stores by the amount sizeof(type) where 'type' is the type of the object pointed to (i.e., 4 for an integer in a 32-bit machine).

Example 9 shows that pointers may be incremented and decremented. In either case, if the original pointer points to an object of a specific type, the new pointer points to the next or the previous object of the same type. That is, pointers are incremented or decremented in steps of the

object size that the pointer points to. Thus, it is possible to traverse an array starting from a pointer to any element in the array. Consider the following program.

Example

```
9. #include <stdio.h>
   #define N 5
   int main()
   {
     float arr[N], *ptr;
     int *iptr, a[N], i;
     /* initialize */
     for(i = 0; i < N; i++)
     {
       arr[i] = 0.3;
       a[i] = 1;
     }
     /* initialize ptr to point to element arr[3] */
     ptr = &arr[3];
     *ptr = 1.0;         /* arr[3] = 1.0 */
     *(ptr - 1) = 0.9;  /* arr[2] = .9 */
     *(ptr + 1) = 1.1;  /* arr[4] = 1.1 */
     /* initialize iptr in the same way */
     iptr = &a[3];
     *iptr = 0;
     *(iptr - 1) = -1;
     *(iptr + 1) = 2;
     for(i = 0; i < N; i++)
     {
       printf("arr[%d] = %f", i, *(arr + 1));
       printf("a[%d] = %d\n", i, a[i]);
       return 0;
     }
   }
```

The program is straightforward. It declares a float array of size 5, and an integer array of the same size. The float array elements are all initialized to 0.3, and the integer array elements to 1. The program also declares two pointer variables, one a float pointer and the other an integer pointer. Each pointer variable is initialized to point to the array element with index 3; for example, ptr is initialized to point to the float array element, arr[3]. Therefore, ptr - 1 points to arr[2], and ptr + 1 points to arr[4]. The value of *ptr is then modified, as is the value of *(ptr - 1) and *(ptr + 1). Similar changes are made in the integer array. Finally, the arrays are printed. Here is the output of the program.

```
arr[0] = 0.300000 a[0] = 1
arr[1] = 0.300000 a[1] = 1
```

```
arr[2] = 0.900000 a[2] = -1
arr[3] = 1.000000 a[3] = 0
arr[4] = 1.100000 a[4] = 2
```

Consider the following program.

```
int b[]={10,20,30,40,50};
int i,*p;
  p=&b[4]-4;
for(i=0;i<5;++i)
   {
     printf("%d",*p);
     p++;
   }
```

The expression &b[4] gives the address of b[4]. Let the address of b[4] be 65540. Then the expression p = &b[4]-4 may give either 65536 or 65532 (considering a 16-bit machine). To explain this, consider the following statements assuming the previous array.

```
int *p;
p=&b[4]
p=p-4;
```

The statement p-4 gives the address of 65532 as p-4 evaluates as p-4* sizeof(int) i.e., 65540 - 8 (considering a 16-bit machine). That is, p is pointing to the address of b[0] or &b[0]. The rest of the code is executed as usual.

Consider the following program where the elements of the array a are initialized, and then all elements in array a are copied into b, so that a and b are identical.

Example

10.
```
#define MAX 10
  int main()
  {
    int a[MAX];
    int b[MAX];
    int i;
    for(i=0; i<MAX; i++)
    a[i]=i;
    b=a;
    return 0;
  }
```

If it is compiled, there will be an error. Arrays in C are unusual in that variables a and b are not, technically, arrays themselves but permanent pointers to arrays. Thus, they point to blocks of memory that hold the arrays. They hold the addresses of the actual arrays, but since they are pointer constant or address constant, their addresses cannot be changed. The statement b=a;, therefore, does not work.

To copy array a into another array b, something like the following has to be entered.

```
for(i=0; i<MAX; i++)
  a[i]=b[i];
```

Or, to put it more succinctly,

```
for(i=0; i<MAX; a[i]=b[i], i++);
```

In the statement p++; if p is pointing to an array, the compiler knows that p points to an integer. So this statement increments p by the appropriate number of bytes to move it to the next element of the array. The array a can be copied into b using pointers as well. The following code can replace (for i=0; i<MAX; a[i]=b[i], i++); :

```
int *p *q;
p=a;
q=b;
for(i=0; i<MAX; i++)
{
  *q = *p;
  q++;
  p++;
}
```

This code can be abbreviated as follows.

```
p=a;
q=b;
for(i=0; i<MAX; i++)
  *q++ = *p++;
```

Further abbreviation leads to

```
for(p=a,q=b,i=0; i<MAX; *q++ = *p++, i++);
```

It is important to note that the unary operators ++ and -- have the same priority as *. All unary operators bind from right to left. Therefore, ++*p is equivalent to ++(*p); Notice the difference.

	Equivalent:
(*ip)++;	int temp;
	(temp = *ip, *ip = *ip + 1)
	Equivalent:
*ip++;	*(ip++);
	int* temp;
	(temp = ip, ip = ip + 1)

Since * and ++ have the same precedence and associate from right to left, this is equivalent to *(ip++); the value of ip++ is ip, so this pointer will be dereferenced. After that the pointer ip is incremented by 1. Like always, it is recommended to use parentheses () in order to avoid unexpected results. Since ++ and -- are either prefix or postfix operators, other combinations of * and ++ and -- occur, although less frequently. For example,

```
*--p
```

decrements p before fetching the variable that p points to. Example 11 will clear these facts.

Example

```
11. #include <stdio.h>
    int main()
    {
        int A[] = {10, 20, 30, 40, 50};
        int *p, i;
        p = A;
        printf("*p : %i\n\n", *p);
        i = *(p++);
        printf("i is: %i\n", i);
        printf("*p is: %i\n\n", *p);
        i = (*p)++;
        printf("i is: %i\n", i);
        printf("*p is: %i\n\n", *p);
        i = *(++p);
        printf("i is: %i\n", i);
        printf("*p is: %i\n\n", *p);
        i = ++(*p);
        printf("i is: %i\n", i);
        printf("*p is: %i\n\n", *p);
        return 0;
    }
```

Output:

```
*p : 10
i is: 10
*p is: 20
i is: 20
*p is: 21
i is: 30
*p is: 30
i is: 31
*p is: 31
```

An integer can also be subtracted. This is illustrated in Example 12.

Example

```
12. #include <stdio.h>
    int main(void)
    {
        int a[] = {10, 20, 30, 40, 50};
        int i, *p;
        p=a+4;
        for(i=4; i>=0; i--)
            printf("%d\n", *(p-i));
        return 0;
    }
```

Output:

```
10
20
30
40
50
```

The above code may be replaced by the following code.

```
#include <stdio.h>
int main(void)
{
    int a[] = {10, 12, 6, 7, 2};
    int i, *p;
    p=a+4;
    for(i=4; i>=0; i--)
        printf("%d\n", p[-i]);
    return 0;
}
```

p[-i] is equivalent to *(p-i). Initially p points to the last element. At the beginning, i=4, p-i evaluates as p-i*sizeof(int)= p-16 (in a 32-bit machine) or =p-8(in a 16-bit machine). Now p-i gives the address of the first element of the array. p[-i], which is equivalent to, *(p-i), prints the first element of the array. Then i = 3, so p[-i] prints the second element and so on. Look at Fig. 8.8.

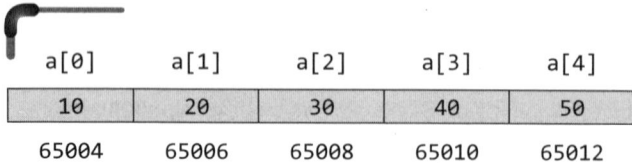

a[0]	a[1]	a[2]	a[3]	a[4]
10	20	30	40	50
65004	65006	65008	65010	65012

Figure 8.8 Subscripted notation value and address of elements of an array

Here a 16-bit machine is assumed. Initially p=65012, i=4. Therefore, p[-i]=*(p-i)= value at address p-i*sizeof(int)

= value at address (p-8)

= value at address (65012-8) = value at address 65004

= 10.

When i=3, p[-i]=*(p-6)=*(65012-6)= value at address 65006 = 20 and so on. If i iterates from 0 to 4, then this code will print the elements of array in reverse order.

Examples

13.
```c
#include <stdio.h>
int main(void)
{
  int a[] = {10, 12, 6, 7, 2};
  int i, *p;
  p=a+4;
    for(i=0; i<5; i++)
    printf("%d\n", p[-i]);
  return 0;
}
```

Output:
```
50
40
30
20
10
```

The reason is very simple. Apply the same calculation as before. The study of strings is useful to further tie in the relationship between pointers and arrays. This discussion is also applicable to strings as strings are nothing but an array of characters. Consider the following program that uses a pointer to shift to the next character of the string.

14.
```c
#include <stdio.h>
int main()
{
  char a[15] = "test string";
  char *pa;
  pa = a;
  while(*pa)
  {
    putchar(*pa);
    pa++;
  }
  printf("\n");
  return 0;
}
```

Output:
```
test string
```

The while loop is equivalent to while(*pa!='\0'). More aspects of pointers and strings are illustrated here by studying versions of some useful functions adapted from the standard library string.h. The first function is strcpy(t,s), which copies the string s to the string t. It would be nice just to write t=s but this copies the pointer, not the characters. To copy the characters, a loop is needed. The array version is as follows.

15.
```c
#include <stdio.h>
int main()
{
  char a[50], b[50];
  void scopy(char *, char *);
  printf("\n Enter the string: ");
  gets(a);
  scopy(b,a);
  printf("\n %s",b);
  return 0;
}
/* scopy: copy s to t; array subscript version */
void scopy(char *t, char *s)
{
  int i;
  i = 0;
  while(s[i]!= '\0')
  {
    t[i] = s[i];
    i++;
  }
  t[i]='\0';
}
```

An equivalent version of scopy() is given as follows.

```c
void scopy(char *t, char *s)
{
  int i;
  i = 0;
  while((t[i] = s[i]) != '\0')
  i++;
}
```

For contrast, here is a version of scopy() with pointers.

```c
/* scopy: copy s to t; pointer version */
void scopy(char *t, char *s)
{
  int i;
  i = 0;
  while((*t = *s) != '\0')
  {
    s++;
    t++;
  }
}
```

Because arguments are passed by value, scopy can use the parameters b and a. Here they are conveniently initialized pointers, marching along the arrays one character at a time, until the '\0' that terminates s has been copied into t. Experienced C programmers would prefer the following version.

```
/* scopy: copy s to t; pointer version 2 */
void scopy(char *s, char *t)
{
    while((*t++ = *s++) != '\0')
    ;
}
```

This moves the increment of s and t into the test part of the loop. The value of *s++ is the character that s pointed to before t was incremented; the postfix ++ does not change s until after this character has been fetched. In the same way, the character is stored into the old t position before t is incremented. This character is also the value that is compared against '\0' to control the loop. The net effect is that characters are copied from s to t, up and including the terminating '\0'.

The C99 standards state that the strcpy() function must return a *copy* of its destination parameter. In both cases, we are returning a copy of the *destination* parameter – that is, we are *returning a pointer* as the function's value. That's why, The strcpy() in the standard library (<string.h>) returns the target string as its function value. It might look like

```
char *strcopy(char *destination, char *source)
{
    char *p = destination;
    while(*source != '\0')
      {
        *p++ = *source++;
      }
    *p = '\0';
    return destination;
}
```

The following is the array subscript version of the strlen library function.

```
int strlen(char s[])
{
    int x;
    x=0;
    while(s[x] != '\0')
      x=x+1;
    return(x);
}
```

Using a pointer-based approach, this function can be rewritten as follows.

```
int strlen(char *s)
{
    int c=0;
    while(*s != '\0')
    {
      c++;
      s++;
    }
    return(c);
}
```

This code can be abbreviated as follows.

```
int strlen(char *s)
{
    int c=0;
    while(*s++)
      c++;
    return(x);
}
```

Now examine strcmp(s,t), which compares the character strings s and t, and returns negative, zero, or positive if s is lexicographically less than, equal to, or greater than t. The value is obtained by subtracting the characters at the first position where s and t disagree.

```
int stcmp(char *s, char *t)
{
    int i;
    for(i = 0; s[i] == t[i]; i++)
      if(s[i] == '\0')
        return 0;
    return s[i] - t[i];
}
```

The pointer version of stcmp is an follows:

```
int stcmp(char *s, char *t)
{
    for(; *s == *t; s++, t++)
    if(*s == '\0')
      return 0;
    return *s - *t;
}
```

To illustrate string processing, a function is written that counts the number of words in a string. It is assumed that words in the string are separated by white space. Here function will use the macro isspace(), which is defined in the standard header file ctype.h. This macro is used to test whether a character is a blank, tab, new line, or some other white-space character. If the argument is a white-space character, then a non-zero (*true*) value is returned; otherwise, zero (*false*) is returned.

Examples

16.
```c
/* Count the number of words in a string. */
#include <stdio.h>
#include <ctype.h>
int word_cnt(char *s)
{
  int cnt = 0;
  while(*s != '\0')
  {
   while(isspace(*s))       /*skip white space */
    ++ s;
   if(*s != '\0')
    {                       /*found a word */
      ++cnt;
      while(!isspace(*s) && *s ! = '\0')
                            /* skip the word */
       ++s;
    }
  }
  return cnt;
}
int main()
{
  char str [80]
  printf("\n ENTER THE SENTENCE");
  scanf("%[^\n]", str);
  printf("\n NO OF WORDS =% d", word_cnt(str));
  return 0;
}
```

As an example, try to write a function that looks for one string within another, returning a pointer to the string if it can, or a null pointer if it cannot. Here is the function (using the obvious brute-force algorithm): at every character of the input string, the code checks for a match to the pattern string.

17.
```c
#include <stddef.h>
#include <stdio.h>
int main()
{
char a[50], b[30];
char *mystrstr(char *, char *);
printf("\n Enter the string:");
  gets(a);
```
```c
printf("\n Enter the substring to search:");
  gets(b);
if(mystrstr(a,b) == NULL)
    printf("NOT FOUND\n");
  else
    printf("FOUND\n");
  return 0;
}
char *mystrstr(char *input, char *pat)
{
  char *start, *p1, *p2;
  for(start = &input[0]; *start != '\0'; start++)
  {  /* for each position in input string... */
   p1 = pat;   /* prepare to check for pattern
                            string there */
   p2 = start;
   while(*p1 != '\0')
    {
      if(*p1 != *p2)    /* characters differ */
       break;
      p1++;
      p2++;
    }
   if(*p1 == '\0')            /* match found*/
   return start;
  }
  return NULL;
}
```

The start pointer steps over each character position in the input string. At each character, the inner while loop checks for a match thereby using p1 to step over the pattern string (pat) and p2 to step over the input string (starting at start). The successive characters are compared until either the end of the pattern string (i.e. *p1 == '\0') is reached or two characters differ. When the end of the pattern string (i.e. *p1 == '\0') is reached it means that all preceding characters matched and a complete match is found for the pattern starting at start, so start is returned. Otherwise, the outer loop is executed again, to try another starting position. It no match is found, a null pointer is returned. Notice that the function is declared as returning (and does in fact return) a pointer-to-char.

mystrstr (or its standard library counterpart strstr) can be used to determine whether one string contains another. Hence, the code is as follows:

```
if(mystrstr(a,b) == NULL)
  printf("NOT FOUND\n");
else printf("FOUND\n");
```

In general, C does not initialize pointers to NULL, and it never tests pointers to see if they are null before using them. If one of the pointers in the programs points somewhere some of the time but not all of the time, an excellent convention to use is to set it to a null pointer when it does not point to any valid location, and test to see if it is a null pointer before using it. But an explicit code must be used to set it to NULL, and to test it against NULL. (In other words, just setting an unused pointer variable to NULL does not guarantee safety; one also has to check for the null value before using the pointer.) On the other hand, if it is known that a particular pointer variable is always valid, it does not have to insert a paranoid test against NULL before using it.

8.10.3 Subtraction of Pointers

As has been seen, an integer can be added to a pointer to get a new pointer, pointing somewhere beyond the original (as long as it is in the same array). For example, one might write

```
p2 = p1 + 3;
```

Applying a little algebra,

```
p2 - p1 = 3
```

Here both p1 and p2 are pointers pointing to the elements of the same array. From this it can be concluded that the two pointers are subtracted, as long as they point into the same array. The result is the number of elements separating them. One may also ask (again, as long as they point into the same array) whether one pointer is greater or less than another; one pointer is 'greater than' another if it points beyond where the other one points.

Therefore, pointer subtraction is also valid: Given two pointers p and q of the same type, the difference p – q is an integer k such that adding k to q yields p. The result is portable and useful only if they point to the elements of the same array. The difference k is the difference in the subscripts of the elements pointed by them. The following code illustrates this.

```
#include <stdio.h>
int main()
{
  double a[2],*p,*q;
  p=a;
```

```
  q=p+1;
  printf("%d\n",q - p);
  return 0;
}
```

Output:

```
1
```

To print the number of bytes resulting from q-p, each pointer may be typecast.

```
#include <stdio.h>
int main()
{
  double a[2],*p,*q;
  p=a;
  q=p+1;
  printf("%d\n",(int)q-(int)p);
  return 0;
}
```

Output:

```
8
```

It has been seen that two pointers to *compatible types* may be subtracted. Actually, the result is stored in the variable type ptrdiff_t, which is defined in the header file <stddef.h>. Both pointers must point into the same array, or one past the end of the array, otherwise the behavior is undefined. The value of the result is the number of array elements that separate the two pointers.

Example

```
18. #include <stdio.h>
int main()
{
int x[100];
int *pi, *cpi = &x[99]; /* cpi points to the last
                                     element of x */
pi = x;
if((cpi - pi) != 99)
  printf("Error\n");
pi = cpi;
pi++;                        /* increment past end of x */
if((pi - cpi) != 1)
  printf("Error\n");
return 0;
}
```

The execution of the above program prints nothing. Consider another version of the standard library function *strlen*.

```c
int stlen(char *s)
{
  char *p = s;
  while(*p != '\0')
  p++;
  return p - s;
}
```

In its declaration, p is initialized to s, that is, to point to the first character of the string. In the while loop, each character in turn is examined until the '\0' at the end is seen. Because p points to characters, p++ advances p to the next character each time, and p-s gives the number of characters advanced over, that is, the string length. The number of characters in the string could be too large to store in an int. The header <stddef.h> defines a variable type ptrdiff_t that is large enough to hold the signed difference of two pointer values. If we were being cautious, however, we would use size_t for the return value of strlen to match the standard library version. size_t is the unsigned integer type returned by the sizeof operator.

Point to Note

The += and -= operators can involve pointers as long as the left-hand side is a pointer to an object and the right-hand side is an integral expression.

8.10.4 Comparing Pointers

C allows pointers to be compared with each other. If two pointers compare equal to each other, then they point to the same thing, whether it is an object or the non-existent element of the end of an array (see arithmetic above). If two pointers point to the same thing, then they compare equal to each other. The relational operators >, <=, and so on give the result that would be expected if the pointers point to the same array: if one pointer compares less than another, then it points nearer to the front of the array. Consider the following program.

Example

```c
19. #include <stdio.h>
   int main(void)
   {
     int a[] = {10, 20, 30, 40, 50};
     int i, *p;
     for(p=a; p<=a+4; p++)
     printf("%d\n", *p);
     return 0;
   }
```

Output:
```
10
20
30
40
50
```

Here each time p is compared with the base address of the array.

One common use of pointer comparisons is for copying arrays using pointers. Here is a code fragment which copies 10 elements from array1 to array2, using pointers. It uses an end pointer, ep, to keep track of when it should stop copying.

```c
int array1[10], array2[10];
int *ip1, *ip2 = &array2[0];
int *ep = &array1[10];
for(ip1 = &array1[0]; ip1 < ep; ip1++)
  *ip2++ = *ip1;
```

As mentioned earlier, there is no element array2[10], but it is legal to compute a pointer to this (non-existent) element as long as it is only used in pointer comparisons like this (that is, it is legal as long as no attempt is made to fetch or store the value that it points to).

The following program will print the line in reverse order. The program uses two pointers pointing to elements of the same array, illustrating the pointer comparison.

Example

```c
20. #include <stdio.h>
   #include <string.h>
   int main()
   {
     char a[50];
     void reverse(char *);
     printf("\n Enter the string:");
     gets(a);
     reverse(a);
     printf("\nAfter reversing the string is :\n");
     puts(a);
     return 0;
   }
   void reverse(char *string)
   {
     char *lp = string;          /* left pointer */
     char *rp = &string[strlen(string)-1];
                                 /* right pointer */
     char tmp;
```

```
   while(lp < rp)
     {
       tmp = *lp;
       *lp = *rp;
       *rp = tmp;
       lp++;
       rp--;
     }
}
```

Output:
```
Enter the string:manas
After reversing the string is:
sanam
```

A null pointer constant can be assigned to a pointer; that pointer will then compare equal to the null pointer constant. A null pointer constant or a null pointer will not compare equal to a pointer that points to anything which actually exists. This has already been discussed and illustrated earlier. A pointer arithmetic summary is given in Table 8.4.

8.11 POINTERS TO POINTERS

So far in the discussion, pointers have been pointing directly to data. C allows the use of pointers that point to pointers, and these, in turn, point to data. For pointers to do that, we only need to add an asterisk (*) for each level of reference. Consider the following declaration.

```
int a=5;
int *p; ← pointer to an integer
int **q; ← pointer to a pointer to an integer
p=&a;
q=&p;
```

- To refer to a using pointer p, dereference it once, that is, *p.
- To refer to a using q, dereference it twice because there are two levels of indirection involved.
- If q is dereferenced once, actually p is referenced which is a pointer to an integer. It may be represented diagrammatically as follows.

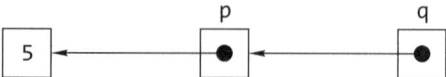

So, *p and **q print 5 if they are printed with a printf statement.

```
#include <stdio.h>
int main()
{
    int a=5;
    int *p,**q;
    p=&a;
    q=&p;
    printf("\n *p=%d",*p);
    printf("\n **q=%d",**q);
    return 0;
}
```

Output:
```
*p=5
**q=5
```

a	p	q
5	65540	65550
65540	65550	65558

Table 8.4 Pointer arithmetic summary

Operation	Condition	Example	Result
Assignment	Pointers must be of same type	int *p,*q ... p = q;	p points to whatever q points to
Addition of an integer		int k,*p; ... p + k	Address of the kth object after the one p points to
Subtraction of an integer		int k,*p; ... p - k	Address of the kth object before the one p points to
Comparison of pointers	Pointers pointing to the members of the same array	int *p,*q; ... q < p	Returns true (1) if q points to an earlier element of the array than p does. Return type is int
Subtraction of pointers	Pointers to members of the same array and q < p	int *p,*q; ... p - q	Number of elements between p & q;

In the preceding figure, the cells contain the content of the variable and its location is given below the cells. In this example, variable q, can be described in three different ways; each one of them would correspond to a different value.

q is a variable of type (int **) with a value of 65550

*q is a variable of type (int *) with a value of 65540

**q is a variable of type (int) with a value of 5

Consider the following declarations.

```
int a;     /*integer variable */
int *p;    /*pointer to integer */
int **q;   /*pointer to pointer to integer */
a = 5;     /*assign value to a */
p = &a;    /*address of a is stored in p */
q = &p;    /*address of pa is stored in q */
```

Memory picture

Variable	Address	Value
a	65540	5
p	65550	65540
q	65558	65550

Consider introducing the following expression in the preceding memory picture.

*p = 7;

Variable	Address	Value
a	65540	5̶ 7
p	65550	65540
q	65558	65550

As p is the address of int a, *p changes the value of a to 7. Now consider introducing the following expression in the same example.

**q = 10;

Variable	Address	Value
a	65540	5̶ 7̶ 10
p	65550	65540
q	65558	65550

Now **q also refers to int a; it changes value of a to 10. It is also possible to change the value of p using q because q points to p. Consider the following table.

Variable	Address	Value
a	65540	10
p	65550	65540
q	65558	65550
b	65512	

Now *q = &b modifies the place where q is pointing, i.e., p. So we get the following table.

Variable	Address	Value
a	65540	10
p	65550	65512
q	65558	65550
b	65512	

The call by value and call by address mechanisms are also applicable to pointers also. Consider the following program:

```
#include <stdio.h>
void change(int *);
int a,b;
int main(void)
{
   int *p;
   a=5;
   b=10;
   p=&a;
   change(p);
   printf("\n *p = %d", *p);
   return 0;
}
void change(int *q)
{
   q=&b;
}
```

Output

*p = 5

Both a and b are global variables. They can be accessible from all the functions of the program. The address of the variable 'a' is assigned in the pointer p. Then p is passed to the function change(). What is intended to be done here is that the address of the variable 'b' is to be assigned to p through the function change(). But the output shows that though pointer is passed to a function still it follows call by value mechanism. The address contained in p is passed to the function and stored in q through the parameter passing. When the address of b is assigned to q, p is still pointing to a because of call by value mechanism. Pointer is not an exception, it should be pass by address as in the following program.

```c
#include <stdio.h>
void change(int **);
int a,b;
int main(void)
{
    int *p;
    a=5;
    b=10;
    p=&a;
    change(&p);
    printf("\n *p = %d", *p);
    return 0;
}
void change(int **q)
{
    *q=&b;
}
```

Output

```
*p = 10
```

As address of p is passed to a function, it follows call by address mechanism. The statement *q = &b is equivalent to p = &b; hence the value at address held by p is printing 10.

The following program explores how pointer to a pointer to an integer and pointer to pointer to pointer can be used to read the value of the same variable.

Example

```c
21. #include <stdio.h>
    int main()
    {
        int a;
        int *p;
        int **dp;
        int ***tp;
        p=&a;
        dp=&p;
        tp=&dp;
        printf("\n ENTER THE VALUE OF a");
        scanf("%d",&a);
        printf("\n a=%d",a);
        printf("\n ENTER THE VALUE OF a");
        scanf("%d",p);
        printf("\n a=%d",a);
        printf("\n ENTER THE VALUE OF a");
```
```c
        scanf("%d",*dp);
        printf("\n a=%d",a);
        printf("\n ENTER THE VALUE OF a");
        scanf("%d",**tp);
        printf("\n a=%d",a);
        return 0;
    }
```

Output:

```
ENTER THE VALUE OF a 5
a=5
ENTER THE VALUE OF a 10
a=10
ENTER THE VALUE OF a 20
a=20
ENTER THE VALUE OF a 25
a=25
```

Now the question is how many levels of indirection can be used in a single declaration?

According to the ANSI C standard, all compilers must handle at least 12 levels. Actually, it depends on the compiler. Some compilers might support more.

8.12 ARRAY OF POINTERS

An array of pointers can be declared very easily. It is done thus.

```c
int *p[10];
```

This declares an array of 10 pointers, each of which points to an integer. The first pointer is called p[0], the second is p[1], and so on up to p[9]. These start off as uninitialized—they point to some unknown point in memory. We could make them point to integer variables in memory thus.

```c
int* p[10];
int a = 10, b = 20, c = 30;
p[0] = &a;
p[1] = &b;
p[2] = &c;
```

It can be seen from the diagram that there is no way of knowing in advance where the compiler is going to put these numbers in memory. They may not even be stored in order.

The obvious thing to do is to sort the numbers in memory, not by moving the numbers themselves around but by altering the order of the pointers to them.

Example

22.
```c
#include <stdio.h>
/* the array of pointers is declared here so that
       the function display can access them */
int *p[10];
void display()
  { int i;
  /* Displaying what each pointer in the array
        points to. */
  for(i = 0; i < 10; i++)
    printf("%d \n",*p[i]);
  }
int main()
  { int a = 46, b = 109, c = 51, d = 66, e = 82, f = 47,
    g = 40, h = 36, k = 70, l = 79;
    int* temp;
    int i,j;
    p[0] = &a;
    p[1] = &b;
    p[2] = &c;
    p[3] = &d;
    p[4] = &e;
    p[5] = &f;
    p[6] = &g;
    p[7] = &h;
    p[8] = &k;
    p[9] = &l;
    display(); /* Displaying the values before
                  sorting */
    for(i = 0; i < 10; i++)
      for(j = 0; j < 9-i; j++)
        if(*p[j] > *p[j+1])
          {
            temp = p[j];
            p[j] = p[j+1];
            p[j+1] = temp;
          }
    display();   /* Displaying after sorting */
    return 0;
  }
```

This program is very clumsy. It can be rewritten. In the following program, an array of pointers contains the base address of three one-dimensional arrays.

```c
{
  int a[]={1,2,3,4,5};
  int b[]={10,20,30,40,50};
  int c[]={100,200,300,400,500};
  int *ap[3]={a,b,c};
  int i;
  for(i=0;i<3;++i)
    printf("%d",*ap[i]);
}
```

In the `for` loop, `printf()` prints the values at the addresses stored in `ap[0]`, `ap[1]`, and `ap[2]`, which are 1, 10, and 100.

The above `for` loop can also be replaced by the following to get the same output.

```c
{
  .
  .
  .
  int *p; p=ap;
  for(i=0;i<3;++i)
  {
    printf("%d",**p);
    p++;
  }
}
```

Another illustration is as follows.

```c
int main()
{
  int a[3][3]={1,2,3,4,5,6,7,8,9};
  int *ptr[3]={a[0],a[1],a[2]};
  int i;
  for(i=0;i<3;++i)
    printf("%d",*ptr[i]);
    printf("\n");
  for(i=0;i<3;++i)
    printf("%d",*a[i]);
    return 0;
}
```

Output:
```
1 4 7
1 4 7
```

In the second `for` loop, the values of the base address stored in the array `a[]` are printed, which are again 1 4 7.

An array of character pointers that is pointed to the strings is declared as follows.

```c
char *nameptr[MAX];
```

The array, `nameptr[]`, is an array of size `MAX`, and each element of the array is a character pointer. It is then possible to assign character pointer values to the elements of the array. For example,

```
nameptr[i] = "Oxford";
```

The string `"Oxford"` is placed somewhere in memory by the compiler and the pointer to the string constant is then assigned to `nameptr[i]`. It is also possible to assign the value of any string pointer to `nameptr[i]`. For example, if `s` is a string, then it is possible to assign the pointer value `s` to `nameptr[i]`.

```
nameptr[i] = s;
```

Again, for example,

```
char *name[] = {"Manas","Pradip","Altaf"};
/* Creates and initializes an array of 3 strings
name[0] is Manas, name[1] is Pradip and name[2]
        is Altaf*/
```

Beginners are often confused about the difference between this example and a multi-dimensional array.

```
char name[3][10] = {"Manas","Pradip","Altaf"};
```

Both of these will behave the same way in most circumstances. The difference can only be seen if we look at the memory locations.

name[0]	→	M	a	n	a	s	\0			
name[1]	→	P	r	a	d	i	p	\0		
name[2]	→	A	l	t	a	f	\0			

This figure shows the first declaration `char *name[]`; `name` contains an array of three pointers to `char`. The pointers to `char` are initialized to point to locations which may be anywhere in memory containing the strings `"Manas"`, `"Pradip"` and `"Altaf"` (all correctly `\0` terminated).

| M | a | n | a | s | \0 | ? | P | r | a | d | i | P | \0 | ? | A | l | t | a | f | \0 | ? | ? | ? | ? | ? | ? | ? | ? | ? |

This represents the second case—the `\0` characters terminate the strings. The `?` represent memory locations which are not initialized. `char *a[]` represents an array of pointers to `char`. This can be used to contain a number of strings.

Look at the following program, which uses an array of pointers.

23.
```
char *rainbow[] = {"red", "orange", "yellow",
        "green", "blue", "indigo", "violet" };
int main()
{
  int color;
  for(color = 0; color <= 6; color++)
  {
    printf("%s", rainbow[color]);
  }
  printf("\n");
  return 0;
}
```

Output:

```
red
orange
yellow
green
blue
indigo
violet
```

The following program would clear the above facts.

24.
```
#include <stdio.h>
char *getday(int);
int main()
{
    int iday;
    char *dayofWeek;
    printf("Enter a number from 1 to 7 for the day\
        of the week:");
    scanf("%d",&iday);
    dayofWeek=getday(iday);
    if(dayofWeek!=NULL)
        printf("\n\nThat day of the week is %s", dayofWeek);
    else
        printf("Invalid entry for day!");
    return 0;
}
char *getday(int iNo)
{
    char *days[7];
    days[0]="Sunday";
    days[1]="Monday";
    days[2]="Tuesday";
    days[3]="Wednesday";
```

```
days[4]="Thursday";
days[5]="Friday";
days[6]="Saturday";
if(iNo >=1 && iNo<=7)
  return days[iNo-1];
else
  return NULL;
}
```

In general, an array of pointers can be used to point to an array of data items, with each element of the pointer array pointing to an element of the data array. Data items can be accessed either directly in the data array, or indirectly by dereferencing the elements of the pointer array. The advantage of an array of pointers is that the pointers can be reordered in any manner without moving the data items. For example, the pointer array can be reordered so that the successive elements of the pointer array point to data items in a sorted order without moving the data items. Reordering pointers is relatively fast compared to reordering large data items such as data records or strings. This approach saves a lot of time, with the additional advantage that the data items remain available in the original order. How such a scheme might be implemented is now discussed here.

Sorting an array of strings requires swapping the strings that can require copying a lot of data. For the sake of efficiency, it is better to avoid actual swapping of data whenever a data item is large, such as a string or an entire database record. In addition, arrays may be needed in more than one order; for example, an exam scores array sorted by ID numbers and by weighted scores; or strings may be needed in both an unsorted form and a sorted form. In either of these cases, either two copies of the data, each sorted differently, must be kept, or a more efficient way to store the data structure must be found. The solution is to use pointers to elements of the array and swap pointers. Consider some examples.

```
int data1, data2, *ptr1, *ptr2, *save;
  data1 = 100; data2 = 200;
  ptr1 = &data1; ptr2 = &data2;
```

The values of the data can be swapped and the swapped values stored in data1 and data2. Or the values of the pointers can be exchanged.

```
temp = ptr1;
  ptr1 = ptr2;
  ptr2 = save;
```

Here, the values in data1 and data2 have not changed; but ptr1 now accesses data2 and ptr2 access data1. The pointer values have been swapped so they point to objects in a different order. The same idea can be applied to strings.

```
char name1[] = "Oxford";
char name2[] = "University";
char *p1, *p2;
  p1 = name1;
  p2 = name2;
```

Pointers p1 and p2 point to strings name1 and name2. Now the pointer values can be swapped so that p1 and p2 point to name2 and name1, respectively. Given an array of strings, the following program uses pointers to order the strings in a sorted form, leaving the array unchanged.

Example

```
25. #include <stdio.h>
    #include <stdlib.h>
    #include <string.h>
    #define COLS 50
    void sort_words(char *a[], int n)
    {
      int i,j;
      char *temp;
      for(i=0;i<n-1;++i)
        for(j=i+1;j<n;++j)
          if(strcmpi(a[i],a[j])>0)
            {
            temp=a[i];
            a[i]=a[j];
            a[j]=temp;
        }
    }
    int main()
    {
    char w[10][COLS];
    char *wdptr[10];
    int i;
    for(i=0; i<10; ++i)
    {
    gets(w[i]);
    wdptr[i]=w[i];
    }
    printf("\n Before sorting the strings\
            are.......\n");
    for(i=0; i<10; ++i)
    puts(w[i]);
```

```
sort_words(wdptr,10);
printf("\n After sorting the strings are....\n");
for(i=0; i<10; ++i)
puts(wdptr[i]);
return 0;
}
```

When an array of pointers to strings is used, the strings can be initialized at the point where the array is declared, but the strings entered by the user cannot be received using scanf(). Consider the following program.

```
int main()
{
  char *name[5];
  int i;
  for(i=0;i<5;++i)
  {
    printf("\n ENTER NAME");
    scanf("%[^\n]",name[i]);
  }
    return 0;
}
```

The program may not work because when an array is declared it contains garbage value, and it would be wrong to send the garbage value to scanf() as address where the string received from the keyboard should be kept.

8.13 POINTERS TO AN ARRAY

Suppose we have an array of unsigned long values called v. We can declare a pointer to a simple integer value and make it point to the array as is done normally.

```
int v[5] = {1004, 2201, 3000, 432, 500};
int *p = v;
printf("%d \n", *p);
```

This piece of code displays the number, which the pointer p points to, that is the first number in the array, namely 1004.

p →	1004	v[0]
	2201	v[1]
	3000	v[2]
	432	v[3]
	500	v[4]

C tends to treat arrays almost as though they were pointers, which is why we can set a pointer to an array straight rather than using the address of operator. The instruction p = v makes the pointer point to the address of the array. The number at this address is the first element of the array; so that is the value produced when we access *p. p++ gives some extra arithmetic instructions that lets us use the pointer to the array more flexibly.

```
      p++
```

This instruction increases the pointer so that it points to the next element of the array. If it is followed by the instruction printf("%d \n", *p); then it would display the number 2201, which is the content of element v[1] (i.e., the second element).

Similarly, we can use instructions such as += and -= to refer to different elements in the array.

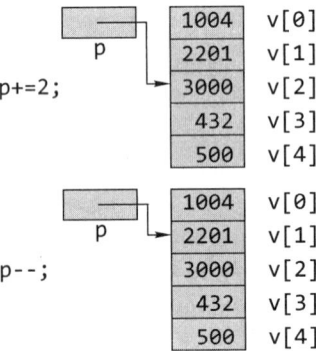

Reference can be made to the different array elements without having to alter the value of p. We have already used *p to refer to the first element of the array (or subsequent elements if p has been updating with += or -=), but *(p+1) can be used to refer to the next element after *p, *(p+2) to refer to the one after that, etc.

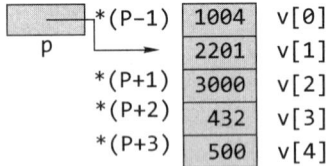

Now it is time to turn to the problem of the two-dimensional array. As stated earlier, C interprets a two-dimensional array as an array of one-dimensional arrays. That being the case, the first element of a two-dimensional array of integers is a one-dimensional array of integers. And a pointer to a two-dimensional array of integers must be a pointer to that data type. One way of accomplishing this is through the use of the keyword 'typedef'. typedef assigns a new name to a specified data type.

For example,

```
typedef unsigned char byte;
```

causes the name *byte* to mean type unsigned char. Hence,

```
byte b[10];
```

would be an array of unsigned characters.

Note that in the typedef declaration, the word *byte* has replaced what would normally be the name of unsigned char. That is, the rule for using typedef is that the new name for the data type is the name used in the definition of the data type. Thus in

```
typedef int Array[10];
```

Array becomes a data type for an array of 10 integers. That is, "Array my_arr"; declares my_arr as an array of 10 integers and Array arr2d[5]; makes arr2d an array of five arrays of 10 integers each.

Also note that Array *ptr2arr; makes ptr2arr a pointer to an array of 10 integers. Because *ptr2arr points to the same type as arr2d, assigning the address of the two-dimensional array arr2d to ptr2arr, the pointer to a one-dimensional array of 10 integers is acceptable. That is, ptr2arr = &arr2d[0]; or ptr2arr = arr2d; are both correct.

Since the data type of the pointer is an array of 10 integers it is expected that incrementing ptr2arr by one would change its value by 10*sizeof(int), which it does. That is, sizeof(*ptr2arr) is 20. It can be proved by writing and running a simple short program.

Now, while using typedef makes things clearer for the reader and easier on the programmer, it is not really necessary. What is needed is a way of declaring a pointer such as ptr2arr without using the typedef keyword. It turns out that this can be done and that

```
int(*ptr2arr)[10];
```

is the proper declaration, i.e., ptr2arr here is a pointer to an array of 10 integers just as it was under the declaration using the array type. Note that this is different from

```
int *ptr2arr[10];
```

which would make ptr2arr the name of an array of 10 pointers to type int.

The elements of a two-dimensional array can be printed using a pointer to an array. The following program illustrates this.

Example

```
26. int main()
    {
      int a[2][3]={{3,4,5},{6,7,8}};
      int i; int(*pa)[3];
      pa=a;
      for(i=0;i<3;++i)
        printf("%d\t",(*pa)[i]);
      printf("\n");
      pa++;
      for(i=0;i<3;++i)
        printf("%d\t",(*pa)[i]);
      return 0;
    }
```

Output:

```
3   4   5
6   7   8
```

Table 8.5 summarizes the differences between array of pointer and pointer to an array.

Table 8.5 Difference between an array of pointers and a pointer to an array

Array of Pointer	Pointer to an Array
Declaration	Declaration
data_type *array_name[SIZE];	data_type(*array_name)[SIZE];
Size represents the number of rows	Size represents the number of columns
The space for columns may be allotted	The space for rows may be dynamically allotted

8.14 TWO-DIMENSIONAL ARRAYS AND POINTERS

A two-dimensional array in C is treated as a one-dimensional array whose elements are one-dimensional arrays (the rows). For example, a 4×3 array of T (where 'T' is any data type supported by C) may be declared by 'T a[4][3]', and described by the following scheme.

Figure 8.9 is the logical layout of a two-dimensional array in memory but it does not give a good picture of what is happening internally. The 'internal pseudo-memory map' works just to display what the two-dimensioned array looks like within the system, and can be used to illustrate how it is actually implemented. Figure 8.10 is the graphical representation of a two-dimensional array. Keep in mind that this may not be an accurate picture of what is actually stored in memory, but it is accurate in terms of the concept of a two-dimensional array.

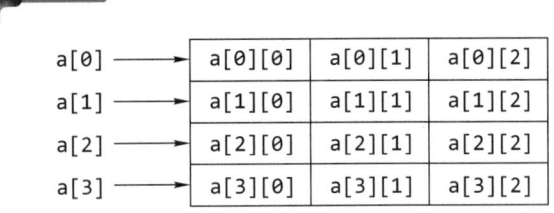

Figure 8.9 Logical representation of a two-dimensional array

The first thing to be noticed is that there is still a single pointer that is the name of the entire array, but in this case it is a constant pointer to a constant pointer. It points to an array of pointers, each of which points somewhere inside of the array. Finally, there is the actual storage for the elements of the array. According to the definition of C, all elements of the array must be contiguous. The elements are drawn in the manner shown to emphasize this fact. One may guess, and properly so, that none of the pointers are necessarily real pointers, but are somehow bound up in the addressing logic of the code, or they may be stored in registers. On the other hand, they could actually all be pointers if the implementers decided to do so. There are no assumptions made about the underlying implementation.

The address arithmetic for the a[n] array of pointers can be used as done earlier, but it is a slightly different case this time. The following formula is used with size being the number of bytes used to store a pointer.

```
byte_address = a + i * size
```

It will, however, be correct to think of these pointers existing somewhere in memory conceptually in order to understand how a two-dimensional array is stored in the computer memory.

Pointer arithmetic can be performed within each row as is done with the one-dimensional array. The constant pointer named a[0] can be considered to be a constant pointer to the first element in the first row and the formula mentioned earlier can be used for pointer arithmetic just as if it were referring to a one-dimensional array. Therefore, the following two expressions,

```
*(a[0] + 3)
```

and

```
a[0][3]
```

are identical as far as the compiler is concerned.

It is possible to keep the first array index set to zero and vary the second array index from zero to eleven, thereby accessing all twelve elements by varying a single subscript. This is considered bad practice in some programming circles and its use is not encouraged, but it does illustrate how the elements are actually stored.

```
for(i = 0; i < 12; i++)
    a[0][i] = i;
```

This trick is possible because C does not do run-time range checking of array subscripts. The following code is also valid for the two-dimensional array a[4][3] of integer type

```
for(i = 0; i < 12; ++i)
    scanf("%d", &a[0][i]);
```

Readers may have noticed that in C the rightmost subscript of a two-dimensional array varies faster than the leftmost (in fact, there are no multidimensional arrays in C, but array of arrays). This fact suggests that the array is stored in a 'row major addressing' format. So the array equation for element 'a[m][n]' of type T is as follows:

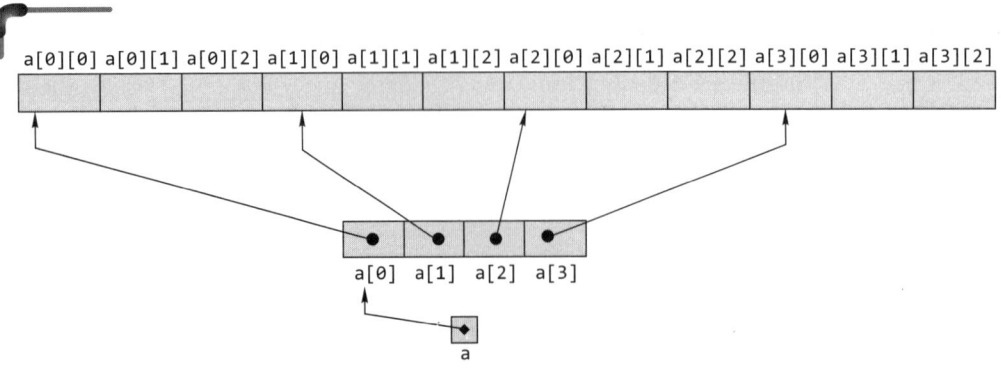

Figure 8.10 Physical representation of a two-dimensional array

```
Address of (a[i][j]) = address of a[0][0] + (i *
                                            n + j)
```

The array equation is important. In C, it is hidden from the programmer; the compiler automatically computes the necessary code whenever an array reference is made. The obvious advantage is that the number of rows is not required in the array equation, the address of an element does not have to be computed. That is why it is not always necessary to specify the first dimension in a function that is being passed a two-dimensional array. But for higher-dimensional arrays, the equation gets more and more complicated.

K&R tried to create a unified treatment of arrays and pointers, one that would expose rather than hide the array equation in the compiler's code. It has been already discussed that a[i] = *(a + i). Therefore, following the same concept, a two-dimensional array can be expressed as follows:

```
a[i][j] = *(a[i]+ j) = (*(a + i))[j] = *(*(a + i) + j)
```

The array equation discussed above is a consequence of the aforesaid notations in the case of a two-dimensional array. The following program illustrates the facts just discussed.

Example

```
27. #include <stdio.h>
    int main()
    {
      int a[2][3]={10,20,30, 40,50,60};
      int i,j;
      for(i=0;i<2;++i)
      {
        printf("\n");
        for(j=0;j<3;++j)
          printf("%d\t",*(*(a+i)+j));
      }
      return 0;
    }
```

Output:
```
10 20 30
40 50 60
```

The same output will result if the statement
```
printf("%d\t",*(*(a+i)+j));
```

is replaced by the following equivalent statements.

```
printf("%d\t",*(a[i]+j));
printf("%d\t",(*(a+i))[j]);
printf("%d\t",*(&a[0][0]+i*3+j));
```

Thus, to evaluate either expression, a total of five values must be known.

- The address of the first element of the array, which is returned by the expression a, i.e., the name of the array
- The size of the type of the elements of the array, in this case sizeof(int)
- The second dimension of the array
- The specific index value for the first dimension, 2 in this case
- The specific index value for the second dimension, 3 in this case

8.14.1 Passing Two-dimensional Array to a Function

The following are several alternative ways in C to handle an array passed to a function. They differ in the formal parameter. For illustration, the following C statements are considered.

```
#define MAX_ROWS   10
#define MAX_COLS   10
int A[MAX_ROWS][MAX_COLS];
```

When data is accessed in our matrix using the notation

```
A[i][j]
```

the location for this data is computed using

```
&A[0][0] + MAX_COLS * i + j
```

Some interesting information about a two-dimensional array A[10][10] is as follows.

- &A[0][0] is the base address
- A[0] is the base address
- A is the base address
- &A[0] is the base address

But these are not interchangeable. For instance,

```
&A[0][0] +1   points to A[0][1]
A[0] + 1      points to A[0][1]
A + 1         points to A[1][0]
              (A + 1 is the same as A[1] and points to row 1)
&A[0] + 1     points to A[1][0]
```

That is, C stores a matrix linearly in rows. The values for the matrix elements are referenced as

```
A[i][j] = (*(A+i))[j] = *((*(A+i))+j) = *(A[i]+j)
```

Therefore,

```
A[0][0] = (*(A))[0] = *((*A)+0) = *(A[0]+0)
A[0][2] = (*(A))[2] = *((*A)+2) = *(A[0]+2)
A[1][2] = (*(A+1))[2] = *((*(A+1))+2) = *(A[1]+2)
```

Thus address equalities will be

```
&A[i][j] = (A+i)[j] = *(A+i)+j = A[i]+j
```

So,

```
&A[0][0] = (A)[0] = *A+0 = A[0]+0
&A[0][2] = (A)[2] = *A+2 = A[0]+2
&A[1][2] = (A+1)[2] = (*A+1)+2 = A[1]+2
```

The following program illustrates the above facts.

```
#include <stdio.h>
int main()
{
int A[2][3] = { {1, 2, 3},{4, 5, 6} };
printf("\nThe value of element A[0][0] is \n");
printf("%d %d %d %d \n", A[0][0], (*(A+0))[0],
        *((*A)+0), *(A[0]+0));
printf("\nThe address of element A[0][0] is \n");
printf("%x  %x  %x  %x\n",&A[0][0],(A)[0],(*A+0),
        (A[0]+0));
return 0;
}
```

Traditional method which uses array notation as a formal parameter—an array with an empty first dimension

```
#include <stdio.h>
int main()
{
  int a[2][3]={10,20,30, 40,50,60};
  void show(int [][3]);
  show(a);
  return 0;
}
void show(int b[][3])
{
  int i,j;
  for(i=0;i<2;++i)
  {
  printf("\n");
  for(j=0;j<3;++j)
    printf("%d\t",*(*(b+i)+j));
  }
}
```

Pointer to an array as a formal parameter Here the second dimension is explicitly specified. A pointer to the array of 10 integers can be declared as follows.

```
int(*ptr)[10] = &a;
```

The following program shows the use of a pointer to an array as a formal parameter.

```
#include <stdio.h>
int main()
{
  int a[2][3]={10,20,30,40,50,60};
  void show(int(*)[3]);
  show(a);
  return 0;
}
void show(int(*b)[3])
{
  int i,j;
  for(i=0;i<2;++i)
  {
    printf("\n");
    for(j=0;j<3;++j)
    printf("%d\t",*(*(b+i)+j));
  }
}
```

A double pointer cannot be used directly as a formal parameter for a two-dimensional array. Consider the following program.

Example

```
28. #include <stdio.h>
  int main()
  {
    int a[2][3]={10,20,30,40,50,60};
  void show(int **);
  show(a);
  return 0;
  }
  void show(int **b)
  {
  int i,j;
  for(i=0;i<2;++i)
  {
    printf("\n");
    for(j=0;j<3;++j)
    printf("%d\t",b[i][j]);
  }
  }
```

It gives the wrong output instead of printing `10,20,30,40,50,60`. The reason is as follows.

Although the compiler may not complain, it is wrong to declare `int **b` and then use `b` as a two-dimensional array. These are two very different data types and by using them you access different locations in memory.

The array decays into pointer when it is passed to a function. The famous *decay convention* is that an array is treated as a pointer that points to the first element of the array. This mistake is common because it is easy to forget that the decay convention must not be applied recursively (more than once) to the same array, so a two-dimensional array is *not* equivalent to a double pointer. A 'pointer to pointer of T' cannot serve as a 'two-dimensional array of T'. The two-dimensional array is equivalent to a 'pointer to row of T', and this is very different from 'pointer to pointer of T'.

When a double pointer that points to the first element of an array is used with subscript notation '`ptr[0][0]`', it is fully dereferenced two times. After two full de-referencings, the resulting object will have an address equal to whatever value was found *inside* the first element of the array. Since the first element contains the data, we would have wild memory accesses.

The extra dereferencing could be taken care of by having an intermediary 'pointer to T'.

```
type a[m][n], *ptr1, **ptr2;
ptr2 = &ptr1;
ptr1 = (type *)a;
```

But that would not work either; the information on the array 'width' (n) is lost. A possible solution to make a double pointer work with a two-dimensional array notation is to have an auxiliary array of pointers, each of them pointing to a row of the original two-dimensional array.

```
type a[m][n], *aux[m], **ptr2;
ptr2 = (type **)aux;
for(i = 0; i < m; i++)
    aux[i] = (type *)a + i * n;
```

Of course, the auxiliary array could be dynamic.

Points to Note

- C does not do run-time range checking of array subscripts.
- In C the rightmost subscript of a two-dimensional array varies faster than the leftmost.
- Multi-dimensional array is stored in a 'row major addressing' format.
- The following expressions are equivalent for a two-dimensional array

```
a[i][j]= *(a[i]+ j)
        = (*(a + i))[j] = *(*(a + i) + j)
```

A single pointer as a formal parameter With this method general-purpose functions can be created. The dimensions do not appear in any declaration, so they can be added to the formal argument list. The manual array indexing will probably slow down the execution.

```
#include <stdio.h>
int main()
{
  int a[2][3]={10,20,30,40,50,60};
  void show(int *);
  show(&a[0][0]);        Can be replaced by
                          show(*a);
  return 0;
}
void show(int *b)
{
  int i,j;
  for(i=0;i<2;++i)
  {
  printf("\n");
  for(j=0;j<3;++j)
  printf("%5.2d", *(b + 3*i + j));
  }
}
```

Passing matrices to a function can be tricky. For more clarity here are some examples of passing a 3 × 4 matrix to functions. Notice each and every program carefully.

Examples

29.
```c
#include <stdio.h>
#define ROWS 3
#define COLS 4
int main()
{
    int i, j;
    int mat[ROWS][COLS];
    int *ptr;
    void show(int [][COLS], int, int);
    printf("\nThe matrix is %d x %d \n",ROWS,COLS);
    printf("The original values using array indices \n");
    for(i=0; i < ROWS; i++)
    {
        printf("%p",mat[i]);
        for(j=0; j < COLS; j++)
        {
        mat[i][j] = i+j;
            printf("%d", mat[i][j]);
        }
        printf("\n");
    }
    printf("\n The first call to show \n");
    show(mat, ROWS, COLS);
    printf("\n The second call to show \n");
    show(&mat[0], ROWS, COLS);
    printf("\nThe original values using a pointer. \n");
    ptr = &mat[0][0];
    for(i=0; i < ROWS; i++)
    {
    printf("%p",ptr);
    for(j=0; j < COLS; j++)
    {
      *ptr = i+j;
      printf("%d", *(ptr++));
    }
    printf("\n");
    }
    printf("\n The first call to show\n");
    show(mat, ROWS, COLS);
    printf("\n The second call to show\n");
    show(&mat[0], ROWS, COLS);
    return 0;
}
void show(int array[][COLS], int rows, int cols)
{
    int i,j;
    for(i=0; i < rows; i++)
    {
    printf("%p",array[i]);
    for(j=0; j < cols; j++)
    printf("%d", array[i][j]);
    printf("\n");
    }
}
```

Output:
```
The matrix is 3 x 4
The original values using array indices
FFDC 0 1 2 3
FFE4 1 2 3 4
FFEC 2 3 4 5
The first call to show
FFDC 0 1 2 3
FFE4 1 2 3 4
FFEC 2 3 4 5
The second call to show
FFDC 0 1 2 3
FFE4 1 2 3 4
FFEC 2 3 4 5
The original values using a pointer
FFDC 0 1 2 3
FFE4 1 2 3 4
FFEC 2 3 4 5
The first call to show
FFDC 0 1 2 3
FFE4 1 2 3 4
FFEC 2 3 4 5
The second call to show
FFDC 0 1 2 3
FFE4 1 2 3 4
FFEC 2 3 4 5
```

In the first call to show() function, the base address is passed implicitly in function.

In the second call, the base address of the element in the first row is passed explicitly. This will run faster because there is no need to compute the location using &mat[0][0] + 4*i + j. A two-dimensional array is actually a one-dimensional array that maps to the storage map for mat; that is why we do not need the first index size.

In the following illustration, the function display() takes pointer to array of four integers. Here a pointer to an array of integers is used and only one index is used.

30.
```c
#include <stdio.h>
#define ROWS 3
#define COLS 4
int main()
{
  int i, j;
  int mat[ROWS][COLS];
  int * ptr;
  void display(int(*)[COLS], int, int);
  printf("\nThe matrix is %d x %d \n",ROWS, COLS);
  printf("The original values for mat and display \n");
  for(i=0; i < ROWS; i++)
  {
    printf("%p",mat[i]);
    for(j=0; j < COLS; j++)
    {
      mat[i][j] = i+j;
      printf("%d", mat[i][j]);
    }
    printf("\n");
  }
  printf("\n The first call to display\n");
  display(mat, ROWS, COLS);
  printf("\n The second call to display\n");
  display(&mat[0], ROWS, COLS);
  printf("\nThe original values using a pointer. \n");
  ptr = &mat[0][0];
  for(i=0; i < ROWS; i++)
  {
    printf("%p",ptr);
    for(j=0; j < COLS; j++)
    {
    *ptr = i+j;
    printf("%d", *(ptr++));
    }
    printf("\n");
  }
  printf("\n The first call to display\n");
  display(mat, ROWS, COLS);
  printf("\n The second call to display\n");
  display(&mat[0], ROWS, COLS);
  return 0;
}
```

```c
void display(int (*array)[COLS], int rows, int cols)
{
  int i,j;
  for(i=0; i < rows; i++)
  {
    printf("%p", array);
    for(j=0; j < cols; j++)
    printf("%d",(*array)[j]);
    array++;
    printf("\n");
  }
}
```

Output:
```
Our matrix is 3 x 4
The original values for mat and display
FFDC 0 1 2 3
FFE4 1 2 3 4
FFEC 2 3 4 5
The first call to display
FFDC 0 1 2 3
FFE4 1 2 3 4
FFEC 2 3 4 5
The second call to display
FFDC 0 1 2 3
FFE4 1 2 3 4
FFEC 2 3 4 5
The original values using a pointer
FFDC 0 1 2 3
FFE4 1 2 3 4
FFEC 2 3 4 5
The first call to display
FFDC 0 1 2 3
FFE4 1 2 3 4
FFEC 2 3 4 5
The second call to display
FFDC 0 1 2 3
FFE4 1 2 3 4
FFEC 2 3 4 5
```

Now let us pass these values to print_mat() function. This will run faster than show and display. pt-array is a pointer that points to the elements in the matrix. This is convenient because C stores two-dimensional arrays in rows.

31.
```c
#include <stdio.h>
#define ROWS 3
#define COLS 4
int main()
{
  int i, j;
  int mat[ROWS][COLS];
  int *ptr;
  void print_mat(int *, int, int);
  printf("\n The matrix is %d x %d \n",ROWS, COLS);
  printf("The original values for the matrix \n");
  for(i=0; i < ROWS; i++)
  {
    printf("%p",mat[i]);
    for(j=0; j < COLS; j++)
    {
      mat[i][j] = i+j;
      printf("%d", mat[i][j]);
    }
    printf("\n");
  }
  printf("\n The first call to print_mat\n");
  print_mat(mat[0], ROWS, COLS);
  printf("\n The second call to print_mat\n");
  print_mat(&mat[0][0], ROWS, COLS);
  printf("\n The third call to print_mat\n");
  print_mat(*mat, ROWS, COLS);
      /* This will run faster as will print_mat.*/
  printf("\nThe original values for print_mat \n");
  ptr = &mat[0][0];
  for(i=0; i < ROWS; i++)
  {
    printf("%p",ptr);
    for(j=0; j < COLS; j++)
    {
      *ptr = i+j;
      printf("%d", *(ptr++));
    }
  printf("\n");
  }
}
  printf("\n The first call to print_mat\n");
  print_mat(mat[0], ROWS, COLS);
  printf("\n The second call to print_mat\n");
  print_mat(&mat[0][0], ROWS, COLS);
  printf("\n The third call to print_mat\n");
  print_mat(*mat, ROWS, COLS);
  return 0;
  }
```

```c
void print_mat(int *pt_array, int rows, int cols)
  {
    int i,j;
    for(i=0; i < rows; i++)
    {
      printf("%p",pt_array);
      for(j=0; j < cols; j++)
        printf(" %d", *(pt_array++));
      printf("\n");
    }
  }
```

Output:
```
The matrix is 3 x 4
The original values for the matrix
FFDC 0 1 2 3
FFE4 1 2 3 4
FFEC 2 3 4 5
The first call to print_mat
FFDC 0 1 2 3
FFE4 1 2 3 4
FFEC 2 3 4 5
The second call to print_mat
FFDC 0 1 2 3
FFE4 1 2 3 4
FFEC 2 3 4 5
The third call to print_mat
FFDC 0 1 2 3
FFE4 1 2 3 4
FFEC 2 3 4 5
The original values for print_mat
FFDC 0 1 2 3
FFE4 1 2 3 4
FFEC 2 3 4 5
The first call to print_mat
FFDC 0 1 2 3
FFE4 1 2 3 4
FFEC 2 3 4 5
The second call to print_mat
FFDC 0 1 2 3
FFE4 1 2 3 4
FFEC 2 3 4 5
The third call to print_mat
FFDC 0 1 2 3
FFE4 1 2 3 4
FFEC 2 3 4 5
```

In the above illustrations, the address of the corresponding rows is printed on the first column.

Consider the problem of date conversion, from day of the month to day of the year and vice versa. For example,

March 1st is the 60th day of a non-leap year, and the 61st day of a leap year. Let us define two functions to do the conversions.

day_of_year converts the month and day into the day of the year and month_day converts the day of the year into the month and day. Since this latter function computes two values, the month and day arguments will be pointers.

month_day(1988, 60, &m, &d) sets m to 2 and d to 29 (February 29th).

Both these functions need the same information, a table of the number of days in each month. Since the number of days per month differs for leap years and non-leap years, it is easier to separate them into two rows of a two-dimensional array than to keep track of what happens to February during computation. The array and the functions for performing the transformations are as follows.

```c
static char daytab[2][13] = {
  {0, 31, 28, 31, 30, 31, 30, 31, 31, 30, 31, 30, 31},
  {0, 31, 29, 31, 30, 31, 30, 31, 31, 30, 31, 30, 31}
};
/* day_of_year: set day of year from month & day */
int day_of_year(int year, int month, int day)
{
  int i, leap;
  leap = year%4 == 0 && year%100 != 0
                     || year%400 == 0;
  for(i = 1; i < month; i++)
    day += daytab[leap][i];
  return day;
}
/* month_day: set month, day from day of year */
void month_day(int year, int yearday,
              int *pmonth, int *pday)
{
  int i, leap;
  leap = year%4 == 0 && year%100 != 0
                     || year%400 == 0;
  for(i = 1; yearday > daytab[leap][i]; i++)
    yearday -= daytab[leap][i];
  *pmonth = i;
  *pday = yearday;
}
```

Recall that the arithmetic value of a logical expression, such as the one for leap, is either zero (false) or one (true), so it can be used as a subscript of the array daytab. The array daytab has to be external to both day_of_year and month_day, so they can both use it. It is made as char to illustrate a legitimate use of char for storing small non-character integers.

In C, a two-dimensional array is really a one-dimensional array, each of whose elements is an array. Hence, subscripts are written as

daytab[i][j]

and elements are stored by rows. So the rightmost subscript, or column, varies fastest as elements are accessed in storage order.

Here the array daytab is started with a column of zero so that month numbers can run from the natural 1 to 12 instead of 0 to 11. Since space is not at a premium here, this is clearer than adjusting the indices.

Ragged arrays It is required to contrast a two-dimensional array of type char with a one-dimensional array of pointers to char. Similarities and differences exist between these two constructs.

Example

```c
32. #include<stdio.h>
    int main(void)
    {
      char a[2][15]= {"abc:", "a is for apple"};
      char *p[2]= {"abc:", "a is for apple"};
      printf("%c %c %c %s %s \n", a[0][0],a[0][1],
          a[0][2], a[0], a[1]);
      printf("%c %c %c %s %s \n", p[0][0],p[0][1],p[0]
          [2],p[0],p[1]);
      return 0;
    }
```

Output:
```
abc abc: a is for apple
abc abc: a is for apple
```

The program and its output illustrate similarities in how the two constructs are used. The identifier a is a two-dimensional array, and its declaration causes 30 chars to be allocated. The two-dimensional initializer is equivalent to

{{'a', 'b', 'c', ':', '\0'}, {'a', ' ', 'i', 's', ...}}

The identifier a is an array, each of whose elements is an array of 15 chars. Thus, a[0] and a[1] are arrays of 15 chars. Because arrays of characters are strings, a[0] and a[1] are strings. The array a[0] is initialized to

{'a', 'b', 'c', ':', '\0'}

and because only five elements are specified, the rest are initialized to zero (the null character). Even though not all elements are used in this program, space has been allocated for them. The compiler uses a storage mapping function to access a[i][j]. Each access requires one multiplication and one addition.

The identifier p is a one-dimensional array of pointers to char. Its declaration causes space for two pointers to be allocated (four bytes for each pointer on the 32-bit machine). The element p[0] is initialized to point at "abc:", a string that requires space for five chars. The element p[1] is initialized to point at "a is ...", a string that requires space for 15 chars, including the null character \0 at the end of the string. Thus, p does its work in less space than a. Moreover, the compiler does not generate code for a storage mapping function to access p[i][j], which means that p does its work faster than a. Note that a[0][14] is a valid expression, but that p[0] [14] is not. The expression p[0][14] overruns the bounds of the string pointed to by p[0]. Of course, a[0][14] overruns the string currently stored in a[0], but it does not overrun the array a[0]. Hence, the expression a[0][14] is acceptable.

Another difference is that the strings pointed to by p[0] and p[1] are constant strings, and, hence, cannot be changed. In contrast to this, the strings pointed to by a[0] and a[1] are modifiable.

An array of pointers whose elements are used to point to arrays of varying sizes is called a *ragged array*. Because, in the preceding program, the rows of p have different lengths, it is an example of a ragged array. If we think of the elements p[i][j] arranged as a 'rectangular' collection of elements in rows and columns, the disparate row lengths give the 'rectangle' a ragged look. Hence, the name ragged array.

The following is a depiction of a ragged array.

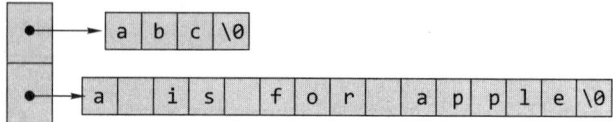

8.15 THREE-DIMENSIONAL ARRAYS

Arrays of dimension higher than two work in a similar fashion. Let us describe how three-dimensional arrays work. If the following is declared

```
int a[7][9][2];
```

then a compiler such as a[i][j][k] is used in a program. The compiler uses the storage-mapping function to generate the object code to access the correct array element in memory.

Initialization   Consider the following initialization.

```
int a[2][2][3] = {
  {{1, 1, 0}, {2, 0, 0}},
  {{3, 0, 0}, {4, 4, 0}}
  };
```

C uses two implementations of arrays, depending on the declaration. They are the same for one dimension, but different for more dimensions. For example, if an array is declared as

```
int array[10][20][30];
```

then there are exactly 6000 ints of storage allocated, and a reference of the form array[i][j][k] will be translated to

```
*(array + i*20*30 + j*30 + k)
```

which calculates the correct offset from the pointer 'array', and then does an indirection on it. To pass an array of this type to a function, the formal parameter must be declared as

```
int arg[][20][30];
```

Here is a function that will sum the elements of the array. Note carefully that all the sizes except the first must be specified.

```
int sum(int a[ ][9][2])
{
  int i, j, k, sum = 0;
  for(i = 0; i < 7; ++i)
    for(j = 0; j < 9; ++j)
      for(k = 0; k < 2; ++k)
        sum + = a[i][j][k];
  return sum;
}
```

In the header of the function definition, the following three declarations are equivalent.

```
int a[ ][9][2] int a[7][9][2] int(*a)[9][2]
```

In the second declaration, the constant 7 acts as a reminder to human readers of the code, but the compiler disregards it. The other two constants are needed by the compiler to generate the correct storage-mapping function.

Point to Note
In case of multi-dimensional arrays all sizes except the first must be specified.

Caution   These three declarations are equivalent only in a header to a function definition.

If a three-dimensional array is declared as

```
int ***array;
```

(and it is assumed for the moment that it has been allocated space for a 10*20*30 array), then there is an array of 10 pointers to pointers to ints, 10 arrays of 20 pointers to ints, and 6000 ints. The 200 elements of the 10 arrays each point to a block of 30 ints, and the 10 elements of the one array each point to one of the 10 arrays. The array variable points to the head of the array with 10 elements.

In short, array points to a pointer to a pointer to an integer, *array points to a pointer to an integer, '**array' points to an integer, and '***array' is an integer.

In this case, an access of the form array[i][j][k] results in an access of the form

```
*(*(*(array+i) + j) + k)
```

This means take a pointer to the main array, add i to offset to the pointer to the correct second dimension array, and indirect to it. Now there is a pointer to one of the arrays of 20 pointers, and j is added to get the offset to the next dimension, and an indirection is done on that. Now a pointer to an array of 30 integers is obtained, and k is added to get a pointer to the desired integer, and an indirection is done to have the integer.

8.16 POINTERS TO FUNCTIONS

One of the power features of C is to define pointers to functions. Function pointers are pointers, i.e., variables, which point to the address of a function. A running program is allocated a certain space in the main memory. The executable compiled program code and the used variables are both put inside this memory. Thus a function in the program code has an address. Like other pointer variables, function pointers can be declared, assigned values, and then used to access the functions they point to.

8.16.1 Declaration of a Pointer to a Function

Function pointers are declared as follows:

```
Return_type(*function_pointer_name
          (argument_type1, argument_type2, ...);
```

In the following example, a function pointer named fp is declared. It points to functions that take one float and two char and return an int.

```
int(*fp)(float, char, char);
```

Some examples include the following.

```
int(*fp)();
  double(*fptr)();
```

Here, fp is declared as a pointer to a function that returns int type, and fptr is a pointer to a function that returns double. The interpretation is as follows for the first declaration: the dereferenced value of fp, i.e., (*fp) followed by () indicates a function that returns integer type. The parentheses are essential in the declarations. The declaration without the parentheses

```
int *fp();
```

declares a function fp that returns an integer pointer.

8.16.2 Initialization of Function Pointers

Like other pointer variables, function pointers must be initialized prior to use. It is quite easy to assign the address of a function to a function pointer. One simply uses the name of a function. It is optional to use the address operator & in front of the function's name. For example, if add() and sub() are declared as follows

```
int add(int, int);
```

and

```
int sub(int, int);
```

the names of these functions, add and sum, are pointers to those functions. These can be assigned to pointer variables.

```
fpointer = add;
fpointer = sub;
```

8.16.3 Calling a Function using a Function Pointer

In C there are two ways of calling a function using a function pointer: use the name of the function pointer instead of the name of the function or explicitly dereference it.

```
result1 = fpointer(4, 5);
result2 = fpointer(6, 2);
```

The following program illustrates the above facts.

Example

```
33. int(*fpointer)(int, int);
              /* Define a pointer to a function */
    int add(int, int);    /* Define a few functions. */
    int sub(int, int);
    int main()
    {
      fpointer = add;
        /* Put the address of 'add' in 'fpointer' */
```

```
printf("%d \n", fpointer(4, 5));
            /* Execute 'add' and print results */
fpointer = sub;              /* Repeat for 'sub' */
printf("%d \n", fpointer(6, 2));
return 0;
}
int add(int a, int b)
{
  return(a + b);
}
int sub(int a, int b)
{
  return(a - b);
}
```

8.16.4 Passing a Function to another Function

A function pointer can be passed as a function's calling argument. The following code shows how to pass a pointer to a function, which returns a double and takes two double arguments. Suppose, a computation can be performed with different functions. Consider

$$\sum_{k=m}^{n} f(K)$$

where in one instance `f(K) = x`^{K}`/K!` and in another instance `f(K) = 1/x`^{K}.

`f(K) = x`^{K}`/K!` can be implemented as follows.

```
double exp_term(double b, double x)
{
  return(pow(x,b)/fact(b));
}
double fact(double a)
  {
    double f=1.0;
    for(;a>0;a--)
      f*=a;
    return f;
  }
```

`f(K) = 1/x`^{K} can be implemented as follows.

```
double by_term(double b, double x)
{
  return(1/pow(x,b));
}
```

Now, the summation function can be implemented as follows.

```
double sum(double f(double,double), int m, int n)
{
```

May be treated as pointer to a function

```
int K;
double s = 0.0;
double x;
printf("\n ENTER THE VALUE OF x");
scanf("%lf",&x);
for(K=m; K<=n;++K)
  s+=f(K,x);
return s;
}
```

When a function appears as an argument, the compiler interprets it as a pointer. The following is an equivalent header to the function.

```
double sum(double(*f)(double), int m, int n)
{
   ... same as above
}
```

Here, `double(*f)(double)` is a pointer to a function that takes an argument of type double and returns a value of type double.

Parentheses is very important as `()` binds more tightly than `*`. If the argument is written as `double f(double)` instead of `double(f)(double)` then it implies that `f` is a function that takes an argument of type double and returns a pointer to a double.

In the body of the sum function, the statement

`s+ = f(K)`

can be replaced by

`s+ = (*f)(K)`

where the pointer to the function is explicitly dereferenced. Here,

`f` implies the pointer to a function

`*f` implies the function itself

`(*f)(K)` the call to the function

Figure 8.11 depicts the meaning of each part in a function pointer notation.

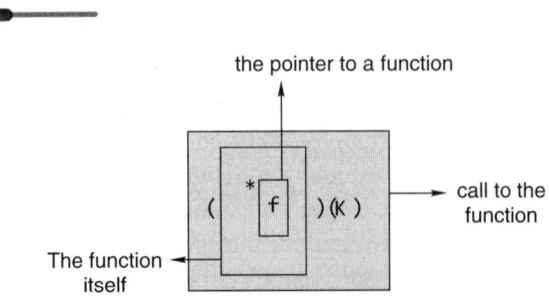

Figure 8.11 Meaning of function pointer notation

Now, what should be the prototype of the functions? The prototypes of the corresponding functions used here are given by

```
double by_term(double);              (i)
double exp_term(double);             (ii)
double fact(double);                 (iii)
double sum(double(*f)(double), int, int);  (iv)
```

There are several equivalent prototype declarations for the function prototype (iv) that show a function as a formal parameter.

```
double sum(double(*)(double), int, int);
double sum(doublef(double), int, int);
double sum(doublef(double x), int m, int n);
```

Now, come to the calling statement of the function that follows.

```
int main()
{
    printf("\n SUM OF COMPUTATION 1: %lf:", sum(exp_
        term,0,3));
    printf("\n SUM OF COMPUTATION 2: %lf", sum(by_
        term,0,4));
    return 0;
}
```

sum(exp_term, 0, 4) computes the sum of the following series.

$$s = \frac{x^0}{0!} + \frac{x^1}{1!} + \frac{x^2}{2!} + \frac{x^3}{3!} + \frac{x^4}{4!}$$

$$= 1 + x + \frac{x^2}{2!} + \frac{x^3}{3!} + \frac{x^4}{4!}$$

sum(by_term, 0, 4) computes the sum of the following series.

$$s = \frac{1}{x^0} + \frac{1}{x^1} + \frac{1}{x^2} + \frac{1}{x^3} + \frac{1}{x^4}$$

$$= 1 + \frac{1}{x} + \frac{1}{x^2} + \frac{1}{x^3} + \frac{1}{x^4}$$

The following is the complete program.

Example

```
34. #include <stdio.h>
    #include <math.h>
    double fact(double a)
    {
        double f=1.0;
        for(;a>0;a--)
            f*=a;
        return f;
    }
```

```
double exp_term(double b, double x)
{
    return(pow(x,b)/fact(b));
}
double by_term(double b, double x)
{
    return(1/pow(x,b));
}
double sum(double f(double,double), int m, int n)
{
    int K;
    double s = 0.0;
    double x;
    printf("\n ENTER THE VALUE OF x ");
    scanf("%lf",&x);
    for(K=m; K<=n;++K)
    s+=f(K,x);
    return s;
}
int main()
{
    printf("\n SUM OF COMPUTATION 1: %lf:",
                        sum(exp_term,0,3));
    printf("\n SUM OF COMPUTATION 2: %lf",
                        sum(by_term,0,4));
    return 0;
}
```

Output:

```
ENTER THE VALUE OF x 2
SUM OF COMPUTATION 1:6.333333
ENTER THE VALUE OF x 2
SUM OF COMPUTATION 2:1.937500
```

8.16.5 How to Return a Function Pointer

It is a little bit tricky but a function pointer can be a function's return value. In the following example there are two solutions of how to return a pointer to a function that takes two float arguments and returns a float. If anyone wants to return a pointer to a function all that needs to be done is to change the definitions/declarations of all function pointers.

```
float Add(float a, float b) { return a+b; }
float Sub(float a, float b) { return a-b; }
```

Add and Sub have been defined. They return a float and take two float values. The function takes a char and returns a pointer to a function that takes two floats and returns a float. <opCode> specifies which function to return.

```
float(*GetPtr1(char opCode))(float, float)
{
  if(opCode == '+') return &Add;
  if(opCode == '-') return &Sub;
}
```

A solution using a typedef defines a pointer to a function that takes two float values and returns a float.

```
typedef float(*ptr2Func)(float, float);
```

The function takes a char and returns a function pointer that is defined as a type above. <opCode> specifies which function to return.

```
ptr2Func GetPtr2(char opCode)
{
  if(opCode == '+') return &Add;
  if(opCode == '-') return &Sub;
}
void Return_A_Function_Pointer()
{
  printf("Executing Return_A_Function_Pointer\n");
  float(*fptr)(float, float);
                      /* define a function pointer*/
  fptr=GetPtr1('+');/* get function pointer from
                      function 'GetPtr1' */
  printf("%f \n",fptr(2, 4));
              /* call function using the pointer */
  fptr=GetPtr2('-');/*get function pointer from
                      function 'GetPtr2'*/
  printf("%f \n",fptr(2, 4));
              /* call function using the pointer */
}
```

8.16.6 Arrays of Function Pointers

As has been seen, there are arrays of pointers to an int, float, string, and structure. Similarly, an array of pointers to a function can also be used. Operating with arrays of function pointers is very interesting. It offers the possibility of selecting a function using an index. It is illustrated in the following program.

Example

```
35. int main()
  {
    void(*p[3])(int, int);
    int i;
    void Add(int, int);
    void Sub(int, int);
    void Mul(int, int);
    p[0] = Add;
    p[1] = Sub;
    p[2] = Mul;
```

```
    for(i = 0; i <= 2; i++)
    (*p[i])(10, 5);
    return 0;
}
void Add(int a, int b)
{
printf("\n Result of Addition = %d",a+b);
}
void Sub(int a, int b)
{
    printf("\n Result of Subtraction = %d",a-b);
}
void Mul(int a, int b)
{
    printf("\n Result of Multiplication = %d",a*b);
}
```

8.17 DYNAMIC MEMORY ALLOCATION

A problem with many simple programs such as those written so far is that they tend to use fixed-size arrays, which may or may not be big enough. There are more problems of using arrays. Firstly, there is the possibility of overflow since C does not check array bounds. Secondly, there is wastage of space—if an array of 100 elements is declared and a few are used, it leads to wastage of memory space.

How can the restrictions of fixed-size arrays be avoided? The answer is dynamic memory allocation. It is the required memory that is allocated at run-time (at the time of execution). Where fixed arrays are used, static memory allocation, or memory allocated at compile time, is used. Dynamic memory allocation is a way to defer the decision of how much memory is necessary until the program is actually running, or give back memory that the program no longer needs.

The area from where the application gets dynamic memory is called heap. The heap starts at the end of the data segment and grows against the bottom of the stack. If both meet, the program is in trouble and will be terminated by the operating system. Thus, C gives programmers the standard sort of facilities to allocate and de-allocate dynamic heap memory. These will be discussed here.

Static memory allocation The compiler allocates the required memory space for a declared variable. By using the address of operator, the reserved address is obtained that may be assigned to a pointer variable. Since most declared variables have static memory, this way of assigning pointer value to a pointer variable is known as static memory allocation.

Dynamic memory allocation A dynamic memory allocation uses functions such as malloc() or calloc() to get memory dynamically. If these functions are used to get memory dynamically and the values returned by these functions are assigned to pointer variables, such assignments are known as dynamic memory allocation. Memory is assigned during run-time.

C provides access to the heap features through library functions that any C code can call. The prototypes for these functions are in the file <stdlib.h>. So any code which wants to call these must #include that header file. The four functions of interest are as follows:

- **void* malloc(size_t size):** Request a contiguous block of memory of the given size in the heap. malloc() returns a pointer to the heap block or NULL if the request is not satisfied. The type size_t is essentially an unsigned long that indicates how large a block the caller would like measured in bytes. Because the block pointer returned by malloc() is a void * (i.e., it makes no claim about the type of its pointee), a cast will probably be required when storing the void pointer into a regular typed pointer.

- **calloc():** works like malloc, but initializes the memory to zero if possible. The prototype is

```
void * calloc(size_t count, size_t eltsize)
```

This function allocates a block long enough to contain an array of count elements, each of size eltsize. Its contents are cleared to zero before calloc returns.

- **void free(void* block):** free() takes a pointer to a heap block earlier allocated by malloc() and returns that block to the heap for reuse. After the free(), the client should not access any part of the block or assume that the block is valid memory. The block should not be freed a second time.

- **void* realloc(void* block, size_t size):** Take an existing heap block and try to reallocate it to a heap block of the given size which may be larger or smaller than the original size of the block. It returns a pointer to the new block, or NULL if the reallocation was unsuccessful. Remember to catch and examine the return value of realloc(). It is a common error to continue to use the old block pointer. realloc() takes care of moving the bytes from the old block to the new block. realloc() exists because it can be implemented using low-level features that make it more efficient than the C code a programmer could write.

To use these functions, either stdlib.h or alloc.h must be included as these functions are declared in these header files.

Points to Note

All of a program's memory is de-allocated automatically when it exits. So a program only needs to use free() during execution if it is important for the program to recycle its memory while it runs, typically because it uses a lot of memory or because it runs for a long time. The pointer passed to free() must be the same pointer that was originally returned by malloc() or realloc(), not just a pointer into somewhere within the heap block.

Let us discuss the functions and their use in detail. Note that if sufficient memory is not available, the malloc returns a NULL. Because malloc can return NULL instead of a usable pointer, the code should *always* check the return value of malloc to see whether it was successful. If it was not, and the program dereferences the resulting NULL pointer, the program will crash. A call to malloc, with an error check, typically looks something like this.

```
int *ip;
*ip =(int *) malloc(sizeof(int));
if(ip == NULL)
{
  printf("out of memory\n");
  exit(0);            /* 'return' may be used*/
}
```

About exit() In the previous example there was a case in which we could not allocate memory. In such cases it is often best to write an error message, and exit the program. The exit() function will stop the program, clean up any memory used, and will close any files that were open at the time.

```
#include <stdlib.h>
void exit(int status);
```

Note that we need to include stdlib.h to use this function.

When memory is allocated, the allocating function (such as malloc() and calloc()) returns a pointer. The type of this pointer depends on whether one using an older K&R compiler or the newer ANSI type compiler. With the older compiler, the type of the returned pointer is char; with the ANSI compiler it is void.

malloc() returns a void pointer (because it does not matter to malloc what type this memory will be used for) that needs to be cast to one of the appropriate types. The expression (int*) in front of malloc is called a 'cast expression'.

Although this is not mandatory in ANSI/ISO C, but it is recommended for portability of the code. Because many compilers yet fully compliant with the standard. The following program illustrates malloc() in action.

Example

36.
```c
#include <stdlib.h>
#include <stdio.h>
int main()
{
  int * ip;
  double * dp;
  float * fp1;
  float * fp2;
  ip = (int *) malloc(sizeof(int));
  if(ip == NULL)
  {
    printf("out of memory\n");
    exit(-1);
  }
  dp =(double *) malloc(sizeof(double));
  if(dp == NULL)
  {
    printf("out of memory\n");
    exit(-1);
  }
  fp1 =(float *) malloc(sizeof(float));
  if(fp1 == NULL)
  {
    printf("out of memory\n");
    exit(-1);
  }
  fp2 = (float *) malloc(sizeof(float));
  if(fp2 == NULL)
  {
    printf("out of memory\n");
    exit(-1);
  }
  *ip = 42;
  *dp = 3.1415926;
  *fp1 = -1.2;
  *fp2 = 0.34;
  printf("ip: address %d; contents %d\n", (int)ip, *ip);
  printf("dp: address %d; contents %f\n", (int)dp, *dp);
  printf("fp1: address %d; contents %f\n", (int)
          fp1, *fp1);
  printf("fp2: address %d; contents %f\n", (int
          fp2, *fp2);
  return 0;
}
```

Output:
```
ip: address 133792; contents 42
dp: address 133808; contents 3.141593
fp1: address 133824; contents -1.200000
fp2: address 133840; contents 0.340000
```

This program declares a number of pointer variables, calls malloc to allocate memory for their contents, stores values into them, and then prints out the addresses that were allocated and the values that were stored there. The size of the memory to be allocated must be specified in bytes as an argument to malloc(). Since the memory required for different objects is implementation-dependent, the best way to specify the size is to use the sizeof operator. Recall that the sizeof operator returns the size of the operand in bytes.

The example above is useless because in each case enough memory is allocated for exactly one object with each call to malloc(). Dynamic memory allocation is really needed when the amount of memory to be allocated will not be known until the program is run. For example, it will be determined on the basis of responses from a user of the program.

The malloc() has one potential error. If malloc() is called with zero size, the result is unpredictable. It may return a NULL pointer or it may return some other implementation dependent value. We should never call malloc() with zero size.

Points to Note

- In dynamic memory allocation, memory is allocated at runtime from heap.
- According to ANSI compiler, the block pointer returned by allocating function is a void pointer.
- If sufficient memory is not available, the malloc()and calloc() returns a NULL.
- According to ANSI compiler, a cast on the void pointer returned by malloc() is not required.
- calloc() initializes all the bits in the allocated space set to zero where as malloc() does not do this. A call to calloc() is equivalent to a call to malloc() followed by one to memset(). calloc(m, n) is essentially equivalent to p = malloc(m * n); memset(p, 0, m * n);
- When dynamically allocated, arrays are no longer needed, it is recommended to free them immediately.

8.17.1 Dynamic Allocation of Arrays

To allocate a one-dimensional array of length N of some particular type where N is given by the user, simply use malloc() to allocate enough memory to hold N elements of the particular type, and then use the resulting pointer as if it were an array. The following program will create an array of N elements, where the value of N is given by the user, and then print the sum of all the elements of the array.

Example

```
37. #include <stdio.h>
    #include <stdlib.h>
    int main()
    {
      int N,*a,i,s=0;
      printf("\n enter no. of elements of the array:");
      scanf("%d",&N);
      a=(int *)malloc(N*sizeof(int));
      if(a==NULL)
      {
        printf("\n memory allocation unsuccessful...");
        exit(0);
      }
      printf("\n enter the array elements one by one");
      for(i=0; i<N;++i)
        {
        scanf("%d",&a[i])); /* equivalent statement
                            scanf("%d",(a+i));*/
        s+=a[i];
        }
      printf("\n sum is %d ",s);
      return 0;
    }
```

Here is a function that allocates memory and then prints out the values that happen to be stored there without initializing them.

```
void show()
{
  float *fp;
  int i;
  fp = (float *) malloc(10 * sizeof(float));
  if(fp == NULL)
  {
    printf("\nout of memory\n");
    exit(0);
  }
  for(i = 0; i < 10; i++)
  printf("%f\n", fp[i]);
}
```

Upon being run, this program gives different results at different times depending on who else is using the computer and how much memory they are using. Usually it just prints out all zeros, but every once in a while it prints something like the following.

```
4334128524874197894168576.000000
0.000000
18495578222950245904.000000
1788256649177597725455364 9152.000000
768233769452934741562518226 86208.000000
757781365851288653266944.000000
735638711504485109754090309 55008.000000
756535199813913309525846261 76.000000
712207053994188380351663964 16.000000
425856950822677896390246 4.000000
```

What happened was that there were non-zero values in the memory that were allocated, and the printf function tried to interpret those values as floating point numbers. Maybe they were floating point numbers, but they could have been characters, integers, pointers, or anything else.

It is a good idea to initialize the memory returned by malloc(). The reason is that the memory may not be 'clean'—it may have been recently used by some other program, and the values stored there might or might not make sense if interpreted as the type of object we expect to be there (in this case, as floating point numbers). Sometimes there will be zeros. Sometimes, odd values. Sometimes, the values will be so weird that the processor will detect what is called a 'bus error', and will dump core. If the memory is initialized to contain legitimate values of the appropriate type, this will not happen.

Here is a useful program that creates an array that can hold floating point numbers.

```
float * make_float_array(int size)
{
  int i;
  float *fa;
  fa = (float *) malloc(size * sizeof(float));
  if(fa == NULL)
  {
    printf("out of memory\n");
    exit(0);
  }
  for(i = 0; i < size; i++)
  fa[i] = 0.0;
  return(fa);
}
```

Another way is to use `calloc()` that allocates memory and clears it to zero. It is declared in stdlib.h.

```
void * calloc(size_t count, size_t eltsize)
```

This function allocates a block long enough to contain a vector of `count` elements, each of size `eltsize`. Its contents are cleared to zero before calloc returns. The sum of all N elements of an array that uses dynamic memory allocation through `malloc()` function can be written as follows.

Example

38.
```
#include <stdio.h>
#include <stdlib.h>
int main()
{
  int N,*a,i,s=0;
  printf("\n enter the number of elements of the
        array:");
  scanf("%d",&N);
  a=(int *)calloc(N,sizeof(int));
  if(a==NULL)
  {
    printf("\n memory allocation unsuccessful...");
    exit(0);
  }
  printf("\n enter the array elements one by one");
  for(i=0; i<N;++i)
    {
      scanf("%d",(a+i));
      s+=a[i];
    }
  printf("\n sum is %d ",s);
  return 0;
}
```

`calloc()` can be defined using `malloc()` as follows.
```
void * calloc(size_t count, size_t eltsize)
{
  size_t size = count * eltsize;
  void *value = malloc(size);
  if(value != 0)
    memset(value, 0, size);
  return value;
}
```

But in general, it is not necessary that `calloc()` calls `malloc()` internally. `memset` sets n bytes of s to byte c where its prototype is given by

```
void *memset(void *s, int c, size_t n);
```

`memset` also sets the first n bytes of the array s to the character c. The following program illustrates the use of the `memset` function.

Example

39.
```
#include <string.h>
#include <stdio.h>
#include <mem.h>
int main(void)
{
  char b[] = "Hello world\n";
  printf("b before memset: %s\n", b);
  memset(b, '*', strlen(b) - 1);
  printf("b after memset: %s\n", b);
  return 0;
}
```

Output:
```
b before memset: Hello world
b after memset: ***********
```

The `malloc()` function has one potential error. If `malloc()` is called with a zero size, the results are unpredictable. It may return some other pointer or it may return some other implementation-dependent value. It is recommended that `malloc()` never be called with a size zero.

Some programmers like to replace `malloc()` as follows.

```
#include <stdlib.h>
void *safe_malloc(size_t, char *);
```

Now the function definition would be as follows.

```
/* Error checking malloc function*/
void *safe_malloc(size_t size, char *location)
{
  void *ptr;
  ptr= malloc(size);
  if(ptr == NULL) {
  fprintf(stderr,"Out of memory at function:\
      %s\n",location);
  exit(-1);
  }
  return ptr;
}
```

This function can then be called like a normal `malloc()` but will automatically check memory as follows.

```
void get_n_ints(int n)
{
  int *array;
  array= (int *) safe_malloc (n * sizeof(int),
       "get_n_ints()");
    ⋮
}
```

Point to Note

Regarding size_t type in the declaration of safe_malloc, it is a type declared in stdlib.h that holds memory sizes used by memory allocation functions. It is the type returned by the sizeof operation.

A final point worth mentioning related to safe_malloc() is the special variables __LINE__ and __FILE__ that are used to indicate a line number and a file name. They are put in by the pre-processor and are replaced by, respectively, an int that is the line number where the __LINE__ tag occurs and a string which is the name of the file. A commonly used version is as follows.

```
#include <stdlib.h>
void *safe_malloc(size_t);
/* Error trapping malloc wrapper */
void *safe_malloc(size_t size)
/* Allocate memory or print an error and exit */
{
  void *ptr;
  ptr= malloc(size);
  if(ptr == NULL) {
  fprintf(stderr, "Out of memory at line %d file\
       %s\n", __LINE__, __FILE__);
  exit(-1);
  }
  return ptr;
}
```

Points to Note

- malloc() requires two parameters, the first for the number of elements to be allocated and the second for the size of each element, whereas calloc() requires one parameters.
- calloc() initializes all the bits in the allocated space set to zero whereas malloc() does not do this. A call to calloc() is equivalent to a call to malloc() followed by one to memset().
- calloc(m, n) is essentially equivalent to p = malloc(m * n); memset(p, 0, m * n);
- If malloc() is called with a zero size, the results are unpredictable. It may return some other pointer or it may return some other implementation-dependent value.

How much amount of memory that the compiler's implementation of malloc() can allocate at one time? The argument to malloc() is of type size_t so the integer type that corresponds to size_t will limit the number of bytes you can specify. If size_t corresponds to a 4-byte unsigned integer, you will be able to allocate up to 4,294,967,295 bytes at one time.

8.17.2 Freeing Memory

Memory allocated with malloc() does not automatically get de-allocated when a function returns, as automatic-duration variables do, but it does not have to remain for the entire duration of the program, either.

In fact, many programs such as the preceding one use memory on a transient basis. They allocate some memory, use it for a while, but then reach a point where they do not need that particular piece any more (when function or main() finishes). Because memory is not inexhaustible, it is a good idea to de-allocate (that is, release or *free*) memory that is no longer being used.

Dynamically allocated memory is de-allocated with the free function. If p contains a pointer previously returned by malloc(), a call such as

```
free(p);
```

will 'give the memory back' to the stock of memory (sometimes called the 'arena' or 'pool') from which malloc requests are satisfied. When the allocated memory is de-allocated with the free() function, it returns the memory block to the 'free list' within the heap.

When thinking about malloc, free, and dynamically-allocated memory in general, remember again the distinction between a pointer and what it points to. If we call malloc() to allocate some memory, and store the pointer which malloc gives us in a local pointer variable, what happens when the function containing the local pointer variable returns? If the local pointer variable has *automatic duration* (which is the default, unless the variable is declared static), it will disappear when the function returns. But for the pointer variable to disappear says nothing about the memory pointed to. That memory still exists and, as far as malloc() and free() are concerned, is still allocated. The only thing that has disappeared is the pointer variable we had which pointed at the allocated memory. Furthermore, if it contained the only copy of the pointer we had, once it disappears, we will have no way of freeing the memory, and no way of using it, either. Using memory and freeing memory both require that we have at least one pointer to the memory.

Look at the following program that is similar to the programs written earlier but differs only in the use of free().

```
#include <stdio.h>
#include <stdlib.h>
int main(void)
{
  int *array;
  int size = 1;
  int i;
  printf("Enter the number of values:");
  scanf("%d", &size);
  array = (int *)calloc(size, sizeof(int));
  for(i=0; i<size; i++) {
  printf("Please enter value #%d: ", i+1);
  scanf("%d", array+i);
  }
for(i=0; i<size; i++) {
printf("Value #%d is: %d\n", i+1, array[i]);
  }
free(array);
return 0;
}
```

Naturally, once some memory has been freed, it must not be used any more. After calling

```
free(p);
```

it is probably the case that p still points at the same memory. However, since it has been given back, it is now available, and a later call to malloc() might give that memory to some other part of the program. If the variable p is a global variable or will otherwise stick around for a while, one good way to record the fact that it is not to be used any more would be to set it to a null pointer.

```
free(p);
p = NULL;
```

Now the question is why NULL should be assigned to the pointer after freeing it. This is paranoid based on long experience. After a pointer has been freed, the pointed-to data can no longer be used. The pointer is said to be a *dangling pointer*; it does not point at anything useful. If a pointer is 'NULL out' or 'zero out' immediately after freeing it, the program can no longer get in trouble by using that pointer. Also, there still might be copies of the pointer that refer to the memory that has been de-allocated; that is the nature of C. Zeroing out pointers after freeing them will not solve all problems.

malloc() and calloc() can also be used in a similar way with strings.

```
include <stdio.h>
#include <alloc.h>
#include <string.h>
int main(void)
{
  char *str = NULL;
  /* allocate memory for string */
  str = (char *)calloc(10, sizeof(char));
  /* copy "Hello" into string */
  strcpy(str, "Hello");
  /* display string */
  printf("String is %s\n", str);
  /* free memory */
  free(str);
  str=NULL;
  return 0;
}
```

How malloc() and free() work Some steps from a typical malloc() call will show how much work is performed here.

- A program does request memory from the heap with

  ```
  int* ptr = (int*) malloc(1024 * sizeof(int));
  ```

  It expects a pointer back that points to a newly allocated area on the heap that is at least big enough to hold 1024 integer values, no matter how big an integer on this platform is. If the program would ask for (1024 * 2) bytes, it would assume 16-bit integer values and would not be portable to other hardware.

- The malloc() function is part of the C run-time library. It will now check the current status of free memory on the heap. It needs to find a piece of memory big enough for 1024 integers. Once it finds it, it will be returned to the application. What could be simpler?

The reason for malloc() being a very expensive call has many facets. First, finding the proper area needs a clever memory organization by malloc() so that it will find those pieces fast. Remember, malloc() does not know how much memory will be requested. The next problem appears when the current heap size becomes too small. The operating system allocates physical memory and maps it into the process address space that belongs to the heap. Frequent allocations are expensive if done in small sizes, but how should malloc() know? And lastly, when the memory is returned, malloc() has to try to reduce fragmentation of memory space. Otherwise it will not find a piece of memory big enough to satisfy a request even though enough small pieces would be available.

8.17.3 Reallocating Memory Blocks

Sometimes it is not known at first how much memory is needed. For example, if a series of items entered by the user has to be stored, the only way to know how many they are totally depends on the user input. Here malloc() will not work. It is the realloc() function that is required. For example, to point ip variable from an earlier example in Section 8.17 at 200 ints instead of 100, try calling

```
ip = realloc(ip, 200 * sizeof(int));
```

Since each block of dynamically allocated memory needs to be contiguous (so that one can treat it as if it were an array), it may be a case where realloc cannot make the old block of memory bigger 'in place', but has to reallocate it elsewhere to find enough contiguous space for the new requested size. realloc() does this by returning a new pointer. If realloc() was able to make the old block of memory bigger, it returns the same pointer. If realloc() has to go elsewhere to get enough contiguous memory, it returns a pointer to the new memory after copying the old data there. (In this case, after it makes the copy, it frees the old block.) Finally, if realloc() cannot find enough memory to satisfy the new request at all, it returns a NULL. Therefore, usually the old pointer is not overwritten with realloc()'s return value until it has been tested to make sure it is not a null pointer.

```
int *np;
np = (int *)realloc(ip, 200 * sizeof(int));
if(np != NULL)
  ip = np;
else {
  printf("out of memory\n");
  exit(0);
}
```

If realloc() returns something other than a null pointer, then memory reallocation has succeeded and ip might be set to what it returned. If realloc() returns a null pointer, however, the old pointer ip still points at the original 100 values.

Putting all this together, here is a program that reads a series of numbers from the user and stores each integer in a dynamically allocated array and prints the sum.

Example

```
40. #include <stdio.h>
    #include <stdlib.h>
    int main()
    {
      int N,*a,*np,i,s=0;
      char ans='Y';
      printf("\n Enter no. of elements of the array:");
      scanf("%d",&N);
      a=(int *)malloc(N*sizeof(int));
      if(a==NULL)
      {
        printf("\n memory allocation unsuccessful");
        exit(0);
      }
      i=0;
      while(toupper(ans)=='Y')
      {
        if(i >= N)
        {  /* increase allocation */
          N *=2;
          np =(int *)realloc(a,N*sizeof(int));
          if(np == NULL)
          {
            printf("out of memory\n");
            exit(1);
          }
          a = np;
        }
        printf("\n Enter the number ...");
        scanf("%d",&a[i]);
        s+=a[i];
        i++;
        printf("\n Do U 12 Continue(y/n)?...");
        fflush(stdin);
        scanf("%c", &ans)
      }
      N=i;
      printf("\n THE NUMBERS ARE:...\n");
      for(i=0;i<N;++i)
        printf("\n%d",a[i]);
      printf("\n Sum is %d",s);
      return 0;
    }
```

Two different variables are used here to keep track of the 'array' pointed to by a. N represents how many elements have been allocated, and i how many of them are in use. Whenever another item is about to store in the array, if i>=N, the old array is full, and it is time to call realloc() to make it bigger.

8.17.4 Implementing Multidimensional Arrays using Pointers

It is usually best to allocate an array of pointers, and then initialize each pointer to a dynamically allocated 'row'. Here is an example.

Example

```
41. #include <stdlib.h>
    #include <stdio.h>
    #define ROW 5
    #define COL 5
    int main()
    {
     int **arr,i,j;
     arr=(int **)malloc(ROW*sizeof(int *));
     if(!arr)
    {
     printf("out of memory\n");
     exit(EXIT_FAILURE);
    }
     for(i=0;i<ROW;i++)
     {
       arr[i]=(int *)malloc(sizeof(int)*COL);
       if(!arr[i])
       {
         printf("out of memory\n");
         exit(EXIT_FAILURE);
       }
     }
     printf("\n Enter the Elements of the matrix\n");
     for(i=0;i<ROW;++i)
       for(j=0;j<COL;++j)
       scanf("%d",&arr[i][j]);
     printf("\n The matrix Is as follows...\n");
     for(i=0;i<ROW;++i)
     {
       printf("\n");
       for(j=0;j<COL;++j)
         printf("%d\t",arr[i][j]);
     }
     return 0;
    }
```

With exit(), status is provided for the calling process as the exit status of the process.

Typically a value of 0 indicates a normal exit and a nonzero value indicates some error.

The following exit status can be used.

Table 8.6 exit() status

Status	Indicates
EXIT_SUCCESS	Normal program termination
EXIT_FAILURE	Abnormal program termination. Signal to operating system that program has terminated with an error

arr is a pointer-to-pointer-to-int. At the first level, it points to a block of pointers, one for each row. That first-level pointer is the first one that is allocated; it has row elements, with each element big enough to hold a pointer-to-int, or int *. If it is successfully allocated, then the pointers (all row of them) are filled in with a pointer (obtained from malloc) to col number of ints, the storage for that row of the array. If this is not quite making sense, a picture should make everything clear:

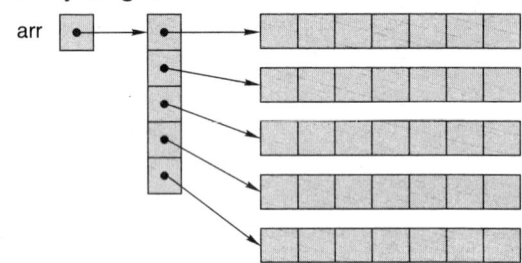

If the double indirection implied by the above schemes is for some reason unacceptable, a two-dimensional array with a single, dynamically allocated one-dimensional array can be simulated.

```
int *arr = (int *)malloc(nrows * ncolumns * sizeof(int));
```

An appropriate block of memory is first allocated for the two-dimensional array size desired. Since array storage in C is in row major form, the block is treated as a sequence of rows with the desired number of columns. The pointer to the allocated block is a pointer to the base type of the array; therefore, it must be incremented to access the next column in a given row. It must also be incremented to move from the last column of a row to the first column of the next row.

The following program asks the user to specify the number of rows and columns for a two-dimensional array. It then dynamically allocates a block of memory to accommodate the array. The block is then treated as a two-dimensional array with the specified rows and columns. Data is read into the array, and then the array is printed.

Example

42.
```c
#include <stdlib.h>
#include <stdio.h>
void getdata(int *,int, int);
void showdata(int *,int,int);
int main()
{
int row, col;
int *a;
printf("\n ENTER THE NUMBER OF ROWS:");
scanf("%d",&row);
printf("\n ENTER THE NUMBER OF COLUMNS:");
scanf("%d",&col);
a=(int *)malloc(row*col*sizeof(int));
getdata(a,row,col);
showdata(a,row,col);
free(a);
a=NULL:
return 0;
}
void getdata(int *p,int r, int c)
{
int i,j;
printf("\n Enter the Numbers one by one....\n");
for(i=0;i<r;++i)
for(j=0;j<c;++j)
{
scanf("%d",p);
p++;
}
}
void showdata(int *p,int r,int c)
{
int i,j;
printf("\n the MATRIX is as follows....\n");
for(i=0;i<r;++i)
{
printf("\n");
for(j=0;j<c;++j)
{
printf("\t %d",*p);
p++;
}
}
}
```

The array's contents can be kept contiguous with the explicit pointer arithmetic.

```c
int **arr = (int **)malloc(nrows * sizeof(int *));
arr[0] = (int *)malloc(nrows * ncolumns * sizeof(int));
for(i = 1; i < nrows; i++)
    arr[i] = arr[0] + i * ncolumns;
```

In either case, the elements of the dynamic array can be accessed with normal-looking array subscripts: arr[i][j] (for 0 <= i < nrows and 0 <= j < ncolumns). Here is the program.

Example

43.
```c
#include <stdlib.h>
#include <stdio.h>
#define ROW 5
#define COL 5
  int main()
  {
    int **arr;
    arr= (int **) malloc(ROW * sizeof(int *));
    if(!arr)
    {
    printf("out of memory\n");
    exit(EXIT_FAILURE);
    }
    arr[0] = (int *)malloc(ROW *COL* sizeof(int));
    if(!arr[0])
    {
    printf("out of memory\n");
    exit(EXIT_FAILURE);
    }
    for(int i=1; i < ROW; i++)
    arr[i] = arr[0] + i * COL;
    return 0;
}
```

One way of dealing with the problem is through the use of the typedef keyword. Consider the following program.

```c
#include <stdio.h>
#include <stdlib.h>
#define COLS 5
typedef int RowArray[COLS];
RowArray *rptr;
int main(void)
{
  int nrows = 10;
  int r, c;
  rptr = malloc(nrows * COLS * sizeof(int));
```

```
for(r = 0; r < nrows; r++)
{
for(c = 0; c < COLS; c++)
{
rptr[r][c] = 0;
}
}
return 0;
}
```

Here it has been assumed that an ANSI compiler has been used, so a cast on the void pointer returned by `malloc()` is not required. If an older K&R compiler is being used, it will have to cast using

```
rptr = (RowArray *)malloc(...);
```

Using this approach, `rptr` has all the characteristics of an array name, (except that `rptr` is modifiable), and array notation may be used throughout the rest of the program. That also means a function has to be written to modify the array contents, `COLS` must be used as a part of the formal parameter in that function, as was done when discussing the passing of two-dimensional arrays to a function.

In the above method, `rptr` turned out to be a pointer to type 'one-dimensional array of `COLS` integers'. It turns out that there is a syntax that can be used for this type without the need of `typedef`. If the following is written

```
int(*ptr)[COLS];
```

the variable `ptr` will have the same characteristics as the variable `rptr` in the method above, and it is not necessary to use the `typedef` keyword. Here `ptr` is a pointer to an array of integers and the size of that array is given by the `#defined` `COLS`. The parentheses placement makes the pointer notation predominate, even though the array notation has higher precedence. That is, if it is written as

```
int *ptr[COLS];
```

it implies that `ptr` is an array of pointers holding the number of pointers equal to that `#defined` by `COLS`. That is not the same thing at all. However, arrays of pointers have their use in the dynamic allocation of two-dimensional arrays. Consider the following program, which creates an array of strings through dynamic memory allocation and sorts the strings alphabetically and also uses pointer to a pointer in swapping by the bubble sort method. Here, instead of swapping the strings, their base addresses are exchanged.

Example

```
44. #include <stdio.h>
    #include <stdlib.h>
    #define COLS 25
    int main()
    {
    char word[50];
    char *w[cols];
    for(i=0; i<COLS; ++i)
    {
    scanf("%s",word);
    w[i]=(char *)calloc(strlen(word)+1, sizeof(char));
    strcpy(w[i],word);
    }
    n=i;
    sort_words(w,n);
    return 0;
    }
    void sort_words(char *a[], int n)
    {
      int i,j;
      for(i=0;i<n-1;++i)
        for(j=i+1;j<n;++j)
          if(strcmpi(a[i],a[j])>0)
            swap(&a[i],&a[j]);
    }
    void swap(char **p, char**q)
    {
      char *tmp;
      tmp=*p;
      *p=*q;
      *q=tmp;
    }
```

In the swap() function, the formal parameters are pointer to a pointer. So it is called with addresses of the successive strings.

With all of these techniques, it is necessary to remember to free the arrays which may take several steps as follows; when they are no longer needed, and one cannot necessarily intermix dynamically allocated arrays with conventional, statically allocated ones, it is recommended to free them immediately.

```
    int i, **a;
      for(i=m;i>=0;++i)
        free(a[i]);
    free(a);
```

Here, m is the number of rows of the dynamically allocated two-dimensional array.

All of the above techniques can also be extended to three or more dimensions. As before, it is assumed that the variable is defined as

```
int ***array;
```

and we want the dimensions to be 10*20*30. All of the following subscripts could be done for an arbitrary i,j,k, which is closer to what is needed.

First, we need an array of 10 int **s, so we use the following.

```
array = (int ***) malloc(10 * sizeof(int **));
```

The sizeof function returns an integer indicating how many bytes are needed by something of type int**, and we need 10 of them. The (int***) is a cast which changes the pointer type from char* to int*** to keep the types correct. Do not forget that after this call to malloc, one should check to see if array==NULL.

Now that there are 10 pointers, the next level of pointers can be obtained with the following code:

```
for(i = 0; i < 10; ++i) {
    array[i] = (int **) malloc(20 * sizeof(int *));
}
```

And finally, each of these pointers can be filled with an array of 30 integers.

```
for(i = 0; i < 10; ++i) {
    for(j = 0; j < 20; ++j) {
        array[i][j] = (int *) malloc(30 * sizeof(int));
    }
}
```

Again, remember that each call to malloc() must check the result. Also note that the preceding two steps can be put together, filling each set of 20 pointers. It is much more efficient to combine all similar allocations and divide the memory after getting it.

Arrays of buffers can also be allocated from the heap. This allows for a dynamically allocated two-dimensional array.

Example

```
45. #include <stdio.h>
    #include <stdlib.h>
    int main()
    {
    char **buf;
    int height, width, i, j;
```

```
    printf("\nEnter number of lines:");
    scanf("%d", &height);
    fflush(stdin);
    printf("\nEnter width of lines:");
    scanf("%d", &width);
    fflush(stdin);
    buf = (char **)malloc(height * sizeof(char *));
    if(buf == (char **)NULL)
    {
    fprintf(stderr, "\nCannot Allocate a Space\n");
    return 1;
    }
    for(i = 0; i < height; ++i)
    {
      buf[i] = (char *)malloc(width);
      if(buf[i] == (char *)NULL)
    {

      fprintf(stderr,"\nCannot allocate text space.\n");
      --i;
      while(i >= 0)
      {
        free(buf[i]);
        --i;
      }
      free(buf);
      return 1;
      }
    }
    for(i = 0; i < height; ++i)
    {
      printf("\nEnter text:");
      gets(buf[i]);
    }
    printf("\n\n\n\n\n");
    for(i = 0; i < height; ++i)
      printf("%s\n",buf[i]);
    for(i = 0; i < height; ++i)
    free(buf[i]);
      free(buf);
    return 0;
}
```

8.18 OFFSETTING A POINTER

In mathematics, the subscript for vectors and matrices starts at 1 instead of 0. There are several ways to achieve it.

In vector (one-dimensional array), the following may be done.

```
double *allot_space(int n)
{
  double *v;
  v=(double *)(n, sizeof(double));
  return(v-1);
}
main()
{
  int n;
  double *a;
  a=allot_space(n);
  ...
  ...
  ...
}
```

Actually what is done here is that the following code segment replaces the function allot_space().

```
v=(double*)calloc(n, sizeof(double));
—v;
```

The following memory diagram may clarify the preceding program statements.

```
 ▨│ │ │ ... │ │
 0 1 2
```

Here a[0] should not be accessed, neither written to nor read. For de-allocating the memory space, the following statement should be used.

```
free(a+1);
```

For matrix, i.e., a two-dimensional array,

```
double **get_matrix_space(int m, int n)
{
  int i;
  double **a;
  a=(double **)calloc(m, sizeof(double*));
  --a;
  for(i=1;i<=m;++i)
    {
      a[i]=(double *)calloc(n, sizeof(double));
      --a[i];
    }
  return a;
}
```

The main() function will be as follows.

```
int main()
{
  int **v;
  int r,c;
  ...
  ...
  ...
  v=get_matrix_space(r,c);
  ...
  ...
  ...
  release_space(v,r);
  return 0;
}
```

The memory allocation can be depicted as follows.

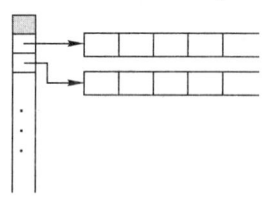

De-allocating of memory space for the above matrix should be through the release_space() function that takes one parameter number of rows.

```
void release_space(double **a, int m)
{
  int i;
  for(i=1;i<=m;++i)
    free(a[i]+1);
  free(a+1);
}
```

There is another way to achieve the above by allocating all the memory at once. Here the pointer that is used to allocate memory would have to be offset. The get_matrix_space() function can be rewritten as follows.

```
double **get_matrix_space(int m, int n)
{
  int i;
  double *p;
  double **a;
  p=(double *)malloc(m*n*sizeof(double));
  a=(double **)malloc(m*sizeof(double *));
    --a;                      /*offset the pointer*/
}
```

```
void release_space(double **a)
{
  double *p;
  p=(double *)a[1]+1;
    free(p);
}
```

8.19 MEMORY LEAK AND MEMORY CORRUPTION

A *memory leak* occurs when a dynamically allocated area of memory is not released or when no longer needed. In C, there are two common coding errors that can cause memory leaks.

Firstly, an area can be allocated but, under certain circumstances, the control path bypasses the code that frees the area. This is particularly likely to occur if the allocation and release are handled in different functions or even in different source files.

Secondly, the address of an area can be stored in a variable (of pointer data type) and then the address of another area stored in the same variable without releasing the area referred to the first time. The original address has now been overwritten and is completely lost. In a reasonably well-structured program, the second type are usually the harder to find. In some programming languages and environments, special facilities known as *garbage collectors* are available to track down and release unreferenced dynamically allocated blocks. But it should be noted that automatic garbage collection is not available in C. It is the programmer's responsibility to deallocate the memory that was allocated through the use of malloc() or calloc(). The following sample codes will cause memory leak.

```
...
char *oldString = "Old String";
char newString;
strcpy(newString, oldString);
...
free(newString);
```

Memory leaks are another undesirable result when a function is written as follows.

```
void my_function(void)
{
  int *a;
  a=(int *)malloc(100*sizeof(int));
  /* Do something with a*/
  /* forgot to free a */
}
```

This function is tested and it will do everything it is meant to. The only problem is that every time this function is called, it allocates a small bit of memory and never gives it back. If this function is called a few times, all will be fine and the difference will not be noticed. On the other hand, if it is called often, then it will gradually eat all the memory in the computer. Even if this routine is only called rarely but the program runs for a long time, it will eventually crash the computer. This can also be an extremely frustrating problem to debug.

Dangling pointer In C, a pointer may be used to hold the address of dynamically allocated memory. After this memory is freed with the free() function (in C), the pointer itself will still contain the address of the released block. This is referred to as a dangling pointer. Using the pointer in this state is a serious programming error. Pointers should be assigned 0, or NULL in C after freeing memory to avoid this bug.

If the pointer is reassigned a new value before being freed, it will lead to a 'dangling pointer' and memory leak. Consider the following example.

```
char *a = malloc(128*sizeof(char));
char *b = malloc(128*sizeof(char));
b = a;
free(a);
free(b);        /* will not free the pointer to the
                     original allocated memory.*/
```

In a programming language such as C, which is weakly typed, garbage collection is not a serious option and the programmer must avoid leaks or take the consequences. Debugging leaky code can be tricky without some assistance. This assistance usually takes the form of variants of the memory allocation and release functions that keep a record of where they were called from (source file name and line number) and maintain a list of all allocated blocks. This list can be inspected or displayed periodically and usually gives a pretty good indication of the data area that is causing the difficulty.

A solution was found using the C pre-processor with declarations such as

```
#ifdef DEBUG
#define malloc(a) mymalloc((a),__LINE__,__FILE__)
#endif
```

The explanation of this code needs some expertise, which can be obtained after reading up pre-processor in detail.

Memory corruption Memory when altered without an explicit assignment due to the inadvertent and unexpected altering of data held in memory or the altering of a pointer to a specific place in memory is known as memory corruption.

The following are some examples of the causes of memory corruption that may happen.

Buffer overflow A case of overflow: Overwrite beyond allocated length

```
char *a = malloc(128*sizeof(char));
memcpy(a, data, dataLen);  /* Error if dataLen is
                                       too long. */
```

A case of index of array out of bounds: (array index overflow—index too large/underflow—negative index)

```
Char *s="Oxford University";
ptr = (char *) malloc(strlen(s));
                /* Should be (s + 1) to account */
                      /* for null termination.*/
strcpy(ptr, s);
  /* Copies memory from string s which is one byte
                 longer than its destination ptr.*/
```
Overflow by one byte

Using an address before memory is allocated and set

```
    int *ptr;
    ptr=5;
```
In this case, the memory location is NULL or random.

Using a pointer which is already freed

```
char *a = (char *)malloc(128*sizeof(char));
...
...
free(a);
puts(a); /* This will probably work but dangerous. */
```

Freeing memory that has already been freed

Freeing a pointer twice:

```
char *a = malloc(128*sizeof(char));
free(a);
... Do Something ...
free(a);
/* A check for NULL would indicate nothing. This
memory space may be reallocated and thus one may
be freeing memory. It does not intend to free or
portions of another block of memory. The size of
the block of memory allocated is often held just
before the memory block itself..*/
```

Freeing memory which was not dynamically allocated

```
double a=6.12345, *ptr;
ptr = &a;
...
free(ptr);
```

8.20 POINTER AND CONST QUALIFIER

A declaration involving a pointer and const has several possible orderings

8.20.1 Pointer to Constant

The const keyword can be used in the declaration of the pointer when a pointer is declared to indicate that the value pointed to must not be changed. If a pointer is declared as follows

```
int n = 10;
const int *ptr=&n;
```

The second declaration makes the object that it points at read-only and of course, both the object and what it points at might be constant. Because we have declared the value pointed to by ptr to be const, the compiler will check for any statements that attempt to modify the value pointed to by ptr and flag such statements as an error. For example, the following statement will now result in an error message from the compiler:

```
*p = 100; /* ERROR */
```

As the declaration asserted that what ptr points to must not be changed. But the following assignment is valid.

```
n = 50;
```

The value pointed to has changed but here it was not tried to use the pointer to make the change. Of course, the pointer itself is not constant, so it is always legal to change what it points to:

```
int v = 100;
ptr = &v;  /* OK - changing the address in ptr */
```

This will change the address stored in ptr to point to the variable v.

It is to be noted that the following declarations are equivalent.

```
const int *ptr=&n;
int const *ptr=&n;
```

8.20.2 Constant Pointers

Constant pointers ensure that the address stored in a pointer cannot be changed. Consider the following statements -

```
int n = 10;
int *const ptr = &n; /* Defines a constant */
```

Here's how one could ensure that a pointer always points to the same object; the second statement declares and initializes ptr and indicates that the address stored must not be changed.

Any attempt to change what the pointer points to elsewhere in the program will result in an error message when you compile:

```
int v = 5;
ptr = &v; /* Error - attempt to change a constant
                                     pointer */
```

It is still legitimate to change the value that ptr points to using ptr though:

```
*ptr = 100;     /* OK - changes the value of v */
```

This statement alters the value stored in v through the pointer and changes its value to 100.

You can create a constant pointer that points to a value that is also constant:

```
int n = 25;
const int *const ptr = &n;
```

ptr is a constant pointer to a constant so everything is fixed. It is not legal to change the address stored in ptr as well as ptr cannot be used to modify what it points to.

8.20.3 Constant Parameters

Remembering that arrays are passed to functions by address and it is also known that function implementations can alter the original array's contents. To prevent an array argument from being altered in a function, use the const qualifier as demonstrated in the next programs.

Version 1

```
#include <stdio.h>
void change(char *);
int main(void)
{
  char s[]="Siva";
  change(s);
  printf("\n The string after calling change():\
        %s", s);
  return 0;
}
```

```
void change(char *t)
{
  *t= 'V';
}
```

Output:

```
The string after calling change():Viva
```

Version 2

```
#include <stdio.h>
void change(const char *);
int main(void)
{
  char s[]="Oxford University";
  change(s);
  printf("\n The string after calling change():\
        %s", s);
  return 0;
}
```

Note the constant parameter

```
void change(const char *t)
{
  *t='V';
}
```

Output:

```
Compiler error: Assignment of read-only location
```

The same error will cause when the following program is compiled.

```
#include <stdio.h>
void change(const int [], int);
int main(void)
{
  int a[]={1,2,3,4,5};
  int n,i;

  n=sizeof(a)/sizeof(a[0]);
  change(a,n);
  printf("\n The array elements after calling
        change()\n");
  for(i=0;i<n;++i)
    printf("\t%d",a[i]);
  return 0;
}
void change(const int b[],int n)
{
  int i;
  for(i=0;i<n;++i)
    b[i]+=10;
}
```

The expression sizeof(a)/sizeof(a[0]) yields 5 as sizeof(a) returns 20 and sizeof(a[0]) returns 4.

In the above program, use of constant parameter protects the elements of the array from being modified within the function change() though arrays passed as arguments are passed by address automatically.

Check Your Progress

What will be the output of the following program?

1.
```c
int main()
{
    int val = 5;
    int *ptr = &val;
    printf("%d %d", ++val, *ptr);
    return 0;
}
```
Output: 6 5

2.
```c
int main()
{
    int val = 5;
    int *ptr = &val;
    printf("%d %d", val, *ptr++);
    return 0;
}
```
Output: 5 5

3.
```c
int main()
{
    int val = 5;
    int *ptr = &val;
    printf("%d %d", val, ++*ptr);
    return 0;
}
```
Output: 6 6

4.
```c
int main()
{
    int a[] = {1,2,3,4,5,6};
    int *ptr = a + 2;
    printf("%d %d", *++a, --*ptr);
    return 0;
}
```
Output: Error: Lvalue required

5.
```c
int main()
{
    int a[] = {1,2,3,4,5,6};
    int *ptr = a + 2;
    printf("%d %d", --*ptr+1,1+*--ptr);
    return 0;
}
```
Output: 2 3

6.
```c
int main()
{
    char myArray[5], *p = myArray;
    int i;
    for(i = 4; i > 0; i--){
    *p++ = i * i; p++;}
    for (i = 4; i >= 0; i--)
    printf("%d", myArray[i]);
    return 0;
}
```
Output: 0 1 4 9 16

7.
```c
int main()
{
    int a = 555, *ptr = &a, b = *ptr;
    printf("%d %d %d", ++a, --b, *ptr++);
    return 0;
}
```
Output: 556 554 555

8.
```c
int main()
{
    int val = 5;
    int *ptr = &val;
    printf("%d %d", val,(*ptr)++);
    return 0;
}
```
Output: 6 5

9.
```c
int main()
{
    int a[100];
    int sum = 0;
    for(k = 0; k < 100; k++)
    *(a+k) = k;
    printf("%d", a[--k]);
    return 0;
}
```
Output: 99

10.
```c
int main()
{
    void F(int *a, int n);
    int arr[5] = {5,4,3,2,1};
    F(arr,5);
    return 0;
}
void F(int *a, int n)
{
    int i;
    for(i = 0; i < n; i++)
    printf("&d", *(a++)+i);
}
```
Output: 55555

11.
```c
int main(void)
{
    int a[10];
    printf("%d", ((a + 9) + (a + 1)));
    return 0;
}
```
Output: Error

12.
```c
int main()
{
    char A[] = {'a','b','c','d','e','f','g','h'};
    char *p = A;
    ++p;
    while(*p != 'e')
    printf("%c", *p++);
    return 0;
}
```
Output: bcd

13.
```c
int main()
{
    char *p1 = "Name";
    char *p2;
    p2 = (char *) malloc(20);
    while(*p2++ = *p1++);
        printf("%s\n", p2);
        return 0;
}
```
Output: An empty string

14.
```c
int main()
{
    int a = 2, b = 3;
    printf("%d", a+++b);
    return 0;
}
```
Output: 5

15.
```c
int main()
{
    int a[] = {1,2,3,4,5,6,7};
    char c[] = {'a','x','h','o','k'};
    printf("%d\t %d", (&a[3]-&a[0]),(&c[3]-&c[0]));
    return 0;
}
```
Output: 3 0

16.
```c
#include#<stdio.h>
int main()
{
    char s1[] = "Manas";
```

```c
    char s2[] = "Ghosh";
    s1 = s2;
    printf("%s", s1);
    return 0;
}
```
Output: Error

17.
```c
int main()
{
    char *ptr = "Mira Sen";
    (*ptr)++;
    printf("%s\n", ptr);
    ptr++;
    printf("%s\n", ptr);
    return 0;
}
```
Output: Nira Sen
          ira Sen

18.
```c
int main()
{
    char *p = "The Matrix Reloaded";
    int i = 0;
    while(*p)
    {
        if(!isupper(*p++))
            ++i;
    }
    printf("%d", i);
    return 0;
}
```
Output: 16

19.
```c
int main()
{
    char str[] = "Test";
    if((printf("%s", str)) == 4)
        printf("Success");
    else
        printf("Failure");
        return 0;
}
```
Output: Test Success

20.
```c
int main()
{
    printf("Hi Friends"+3);
    return 0;
}
```
Output: Friends

21.
```c
int main()
{
    int a[] = {1,2,3,4,5,6};
    int *ptr = a + 2;
    printf("%d", *--ptr);
    return 0;
}
```
Output: 2

22.
```c
int main()
{
    int i = 100, j = 20;
    i++ = j;
    i* = j;
    printf("%d\t %d\n", i,j);
    return 0;
}
```
Output: Error lvalue required

23.
```c
int main()
{
    int a[5], *p;
    for(p = a; p < &a[5]; P++)
    {
        *p = p-a;
        printf("%d", *p);
    }
    return 0;
}
```
Output: 2

24.
```c
int main()
{
    putchar(5["manas"]);
    return 0;
}
```
Output: Nothing will be printed

25.
```c
int main()
{
    int a[] = {1,2,3,4,5};
    int i, s = 0;
    for(i = 0; i < 5; ++i)
      if((a[i]%2) == 0)
        s+ = a[i];
    printf("%d", s);
    return 0;
}
```
Output: 6

26.
```c
int main()
{
    int i;
    char s[] = "Oxford University Press";
    for(i = 0; s[i]!= '\0'; ++i)
      if((i%2) == 0)
        printf("%c %c", s[i], s[i]);
        return 0;
}
```
Output: O Of fr r n nv vr ri iy yP Pe es s

27.
```c
int main()
{
    int i;
    char s[] = "Oxford University Press";
    for(i = 0; s[i]!= '\0'; ++i)
      if((i%2) == 0)
        putchar(s[i]);
    return 0;
}
```
Output: Ofr nvriyPes

28.
```c
int main()
{
    char s[3][6] = {"ZERO", "ONE", "TWO"};
    printf("%s", s[2]);
    printf("%c", s[2][0]);
    return 0;
}
```
Output: TWOT

29.
```c
int main()
{
    int a[][3] = {0,1,2,3,4,5};
    printf("%d", sizeof(a));
    return 0;
}
```
Output: 12

30.
```c
int main()
{
    int a[2][3] = {0,1,2,3,4,5};
    printf("%d", sizeof(a[2]));
    return 0;
}
```
Output: 6 OR 12

31.
```c
int main()
{
  char *str = "This is my string";
    str[3] = 'B';
    puts(str);
    return 0;
}
```

Output: ThiB is my string

32.
```c
int main()
{
int a[5]={1,3,6,7,0};
int *b;
b=&a[2];
printf("%d", b[-1]);
return 0;
}
```

Output: 3

33.
```c
int main()
{
register int x=5, *p;
p=&x
```

```c
printf("%d",*p);
return 0;
}
```

Output: Error

34.
```c
int main()
{
void x(void);
x();
return 0;
}
void x(void)
{
char a[]="HELLO";
char *b="HELLO";
char c[10]="HELLO";
printf("%s %s %s\n", a, b, c);
printf("%d %d %d\n",sizeof(a), sizeof(b), sizeof(c));
}
```

Output: HELLO   HELLO   HELLO
          6 4 10

sizeof(b) gives the bytes required for storing the pointer b. The other two are the array sizes.

SUMMARY

Think of memory as an array of *cells*. Each memory cell has a location/ address/lvalue and contains a value/rvalue. There is a difference between the address and the contents of a memory cell. A pointer is a variable that contains the address in memory of another variable. There can be a pointer to any variable type. The unary or monadic operator '&' gives the 'address of a variable'. The *indirection* or dereference operator '*' gives the 'contents of an object pointed to by a pointer'. A pointer to any variable type is an address in memory, which is an integer address. A pointer is definitely not an integer. When a pointer is declared, it does not point anywhere. It must be set to point somewhere before it can be used. That is, an address must be assigned to the pointer by using an assignment statement or a function call prior to its use. A pointer is bound to a particular data type (void pointer is an exception). For instance, the address of a short int cannot be assigned to a long int. There is a special pointer which is defined to be zero. It is called the NULL pointer.

There are many cases when a passed argument in the function may need to be altered and the new value received back once the function has finished. Other languages do this. C uses pointers explicitly to do this. Other languages mask the fact that pointers also underpin the implementation of this. Pointers provide the solution: Pass the address of the variables to the functions and access address of function.

Pointers and arrays are very closely linked in C. When subscript notation is used, the C compiler generates an executable code that does the following.

- Determines the size of the elements in the array. Let us call that elemSize.

- Multiplies elemSize by the subscript value. Let us call that offset.

- Adds offset to the address that represents the beginning of the array. This is the address of the element that we want to access.

The address of ARRAY[i] is calculated each time again by the compiler as follows.

        address of ARRAY[i] = ARRAY+i*sizeof(int);

The equivalence of arrays and pointers must be understood. Assume that a is an array and i is an integer.

        a[i] == *(a + i) == *(i + a) == i[a]

Although these are equivalent, it is recom-mended that i[a] never be written instead of a[i]. However, pointers and arrays are different.

- A pointer is a variable. We can do

    pa = a and pa++.

- An array *is not* a variable. a = pa and a++ are illegal.

When an array is passed to a function what is actually passed is its initial element's location in memory. Array decays into pointers when passed into function.

The following 'meaningful' arithmetic operations are allowed on pointers.

- Add or subtract integers to/from a pointer. The result is a pointer.
- Subtract two pointers to the same type. The result is an int.
- Assigning NULL or any pointer of same datatype

Multiplying, adding two pointers, etc. does not make sense.

It is also possible to have arrays of pointers since pointers are variables. *Arrays of pointers* are a data representation that will cope efficiently and conveniently with variable length text lines. This eliminates

- complicated storage management
- high overheads of moving lines

Pointers, of course, can be 'pointed at' any type of data object, including arrays.

```
int(*p)[10];
```

is the proper declaration, i.e., p here is a pointer to an array of 10 integers just as it was under the declaration using the array type. Note that this is different from

```
int *p[10];
```

which would make p the name of an array of 10 pointers to type int.

A two-dimensional array is really a one-dimensional array, each of whose elements is itself an array. Array elements are stored row by row. When a two-dimensional array is passed to a function, the number of columns must be specified; the number of rows is irrelevant. The reason for this is pointers again. C needs to know the number of columns in order to jump from row to row in memory.

Consider int a[5][10] to be passed in a function

It is possible to say

```
f(int a[][10]) {.....}
```

or even

```
f(int(*a)[10]) {.....}
```

It needs a parenthesis (*a) since [ ] have a higher precedence than *.

So,

```
int(*a)[10];  declares a pointer to an array of 10 ints.

int *a[10];  declares an array of 10 pointers to ints.
```

Dynamic memory allocation is a way to defer the decision of how much memory is necessary until the program is actually running, get more if it runs out, or give back memory that the program no longer needs it. When memory is allocated, the allocating function (such as malloc() and calloc()) returns a pointer. The type of this pointer depends on the type of compiler, whether it is an older K&R compiler or the newer ANSI type compiler. With the older compiler the type of the returned pointer is char; with the ANSI compiler it is void. When the program finishes using whatever memory it dynamically allocates, it can use the free function to indicate to the system that the memory is available again.

The rules to be followed for deciphering pointer declarations are as follows. These are particularly important for function pointers.

- Start with the name that will identify the pointer, known as the identifier.
- Move to the right until you encounter a right-parenthesis ')' or reach the end. Do not stop if the ( ) brackets are used to pass parameters to a function. Also do not stop on encountering brackets used with arrays: [ ].
- Now go left of the identifier to continue deciphering the declaration. Keep going left until you find a left-parenthesis '(' or reach the end. Do not stop if the brackets are used to pass parameters to a function.
- The whole interpretation should be a single long sentence.

<hr>

KEY-TERMS

Call by address facilitating the changes made to a variable in the called function to become permanently available in the function from where the function is called.

Call-by-value A particular way of implementing a function call, in which the arguments are passed by their value (i.e., their copies).

Dangling pointer A pointer pointing to a previously meaningful location that is no longer meaningful; usually a result of a pointer pointing to an object that is deallocated without resetting the value of the pointer.

Dynamic data structures Those that are built up from blocks of memory allocated from the heap at run-time.

Dynamic memory allocation The process of requesting and obtaining additional memory segments during the execution of a program.

Function pointer A function has a physical location in memory that can be assigned to a pointer. Then it is called function pointer. This address is the entry point of the function and it is the address used when the function is called.

Garbage collection If only implicit dynamic allocation is allowed then deallocation must also be done by implicit means, which is often called garbage collection.

Heap This memory region is reserved for dynamically allocating memory for variables at run-time. Dynamic memory allocation is done by using the malloc() or calloc() functions.

Memory leak A commonly used term indicating that a program is dynamically allocating memory but not properly deallocating it, which results in a gradual accumulation of unused memory by the program to the detriment of other programs, the operating system, and itself.

NULL   A special C constant, defined as macro in stdio.h as or 0, or (void*)), that can be used as the null value for pointers.

Null pointer   A null pointer is a special pointer value that points nowhere. I is initialized with value 0 or NULL.

Pointer   A value or a variable with two attributes: (i) an address and (ii) a data type of what should be found at that address.

Ragged array   An array of pointers whose elements are used to point to arrays of varying sizes is called a ragged array.

Stack   A data structure resembling a deck of cards; a new item can only be put on top of the deck (the push operation) or removed from the top of the deck (the pop operation).

Static memory allocation   Memory layout for static data prepared by the compiler.

Void pointer   A void pointer is a special type of pointer that can point to any data type,

FREQUENTLY ASKED QUESTIONS

1. Why Use Pointers?

C uses pointers in three different ways:

First, pointers allow different sections of code to share information easily. One can get the same effect by copying information back and forth, but pointers solve the problem better.

Secondly, in some cases, C programmers also use pointers because they make the code slightly more efficient. Pointers allow to create complex dynamic data structures like linked lists and binary trees.

Thirdly, pointers in C provide an alternative way to access information stored in arrays. Pointer techniques are especially valuable when you work with strings. There is an intimate link between arrays and pointers in C.

Apart from these, C uses pointers to handle *variable parameters* passed to functions.

2. Why pointers should have data types when their size is always 4 bytes (in a 32-bit machine), irrespective of the variable they are pointing to?

Sizes of various data types are basically decided by the machine architecture and/or the implementation. Considering a 32-bit machine, the addressing of a byte or word will, therefore, require a 32-bit address. This suggests that a pointer (as pointers store addresses) should be capable enough to store, at least, a 32-bit value; no matter if it points to an integer or a character.

For an array, consecutive memory is allocated. Each element is placed at a certain offset from the previous element, if any, depending on its size. The compiler that generates code for a pointer, which accesses these elements using the pointer arithmetic, requires the number of bytes to retrieve on pointer dereference and it knows how much to scale a subscript. The data type of the pointer provides this information. The compiler automatically scales a subscript to the size of the variable pointed at. The compiler takes care of scaling before adding the base address.

3. What is wrong with the following code segment?

```
int *p;
*p=10;
```

The pointer p is an uninitialized pointer which may have some unknown memory address in it. More precisely, it may have an unknown value that will be interpreted as a memory location. Most likely, the value will not be valid for the computer system that are using or if it is, will not be valid for the memory that has been allocated. If the address does not exist, one may get immediate runtime errors.

4. Does C have 'pass by reference' feature?

Not really. Strictly speaking, C always uses pass by value. One can simulate pass by reference by defining functions which accept pointers as formal parameters and then using the & operator when calling the function. The compiler will essentially simulate it when an array to a function is passed (by passing a pointer instead). But truly C has no equivalent to the formal pass by reference feature as C++ provides.

5. What is wild pointer in C?

A pointer in c which has not been initialized is known as wild pointer.

6. Is a null pointer same as an uninitialized pointer?

A null pointer is conceptually different from an uninitialized pointer. An uninitialized pointer may point to anywhere, whereas a null pointer does not point to any object or function. Null pointer points the base address of segment while wild pointer doesn't point any specific memory location.

7. What are the uses of the null pointers?

The null pointer is used for three purposes:

- To stop indirection
- As an error value
- As a sentinel value

8. Is NULL always defined as 0?

NULL is defined as either 0 or (void*)0. These values are almost identical; either a literal zero or a void pointer is converted automatically to any kind of pointer, as necessary, whenever a pointer is needed (although the compiler cannot always tell when a pointer is needed).

9. What is the difference between NULL and NUL?

NULL is a macro defined in <stddef.h> for the null pointer. NUL is the name of the first character in the ASCII character set. It corresponds to a zero value. NULL can be defined as ((void*)0), whereas NUL is '\0'. Both can also be defined simply as 0.

10. Since 0 is used to represent the null pointer, can it be thought of as an address with all zero bits?

Each compiler interprets the null pointers differently and not all compilers use a zero address. For example, some compilers use a nonexistent memory address for the null pointer; that way, attempting to access memory through a null pointer can be detected by the hardware. When NULL is assigned to a pointer, then 0 is converted to the proper internal form by the compiler.

11. What is the difference between arr and &arr where arr is an array name, though both displays the base address of the array?

The array name arr is a pointer to the first element in the array whereas the &arr is a pointer to the array as a whole. Numerically, the values they display are same; however, their interpretation is not same.

12. When would you use a pointer to a function?

Pointers to functions are typically used when it is required to pass them to other functions. The called function takes function pointers as formal parameters. This is known as a "callback." It is frequently used in graphical user interface libraries.

13. What are the uses of dynamic memory allocations?

Typical uses of dynamic memory allocation are:

- Ccreation of *dynamic arrays* – arrays whose sizes are chosen at run time;
- Ccreation of *dynamic data structures* – data collections that grow and shrink with the changing data storage needs of a program or module.

14. Why is it required to cast the values returned by malloc() to the pointer type being allocated?

Before ANSI/ISO Standard C introduced the void * generic pointer type, these casts were typically required to avoid warnings about assignment between incompatible pointer types. Under ANSI/ISO Standard C, these casts are no more required.

15. What happens if malloc(0) is called?

If malloc() is called with zero size, the result is unpredictable. Each compiler is free to define the behavior of malloc()when the size is 0. It may either return NULL or it may return other implementation dependent value.

16. What is the difference between calloc() and malloc() ?

malloc() takes one argument, whereas calloc() takes two. calloc() initializes all the bits in the allocated space set to zero whereas malloc() does not do this.

A call to calloc() is equivalent to a call to malloc() followed by one to memset().

```
calloc(m, n)
```
is essentially equivalent to
```
p = malloc(m * n);
memset(p, 0, m * n);
```

17. What is a dangling pointer?

A dangling pointer arises when you use the address of an object after its lifetime is over. This may occur in situations like returning addresses of the automatic variables from a function or using the address of the memory block after it is freed.

18. Why should NULL be assigned to the pointer after freeing it?

After a pointer has been freed, the pointer can no longer be used. After this memory is freed with the free() function , the pointer itself will still contain the address of the released block. Such a pointer is referred to as a dangling pointer; it doesn't point at anything useful. If the pointer is used without reinitializing it, it may or may not run; merely produces a bug. Such a pointer must be assigned NULL after freeing memory to avoid this bug. The program can no longer get in trouble by using that pointer.

19. Is it legal to return a pointer to a local variable in the called function?

Absolutely not; it is an error to return a pointer to a local variable in the called function, because when the function terminates, its memory gets inaccessible.

20. What is memory leak?

When memory is allocated dynamically, it is the responsibility of the programmer to deallocate the dynamically allocated memory by calling free(). Freeing the memory returns it to the system, where it can be reassigned to another application when needed. When an application dynamically allocates memory, and does not free that memory when it is finished using it, that chunk of memory is still in use to the operating system. The memory is not being used by the application anymore, but it cannot be used by the system or any other program either. This is known as *memory leak*. Memory leaks add up over time, and if they are not cleaned up, the system eventually runs out of memory

EXERCISE

1. What are pointers? Why are they important?

2. Explain the features of pointers.

3. Explain the pointer of any data type that requires four bytes.

4. Explain the use of (*) indirection operator.

5. What is a NULL pointer? Is it the same as an uninitialized pointer?

6. What is a NULL macro? What is the difference between a NULL pointer and a NULL macro?

7. What does the error 'Null Pointer Assignment' mean and what causes this error?

8. Explain the effect of ++ and -- operators with pointer of all types.

9. What is an array of pointer? How is it declared?

10. Explain the relation between an array and a pointer.

11. Why is the addition of two pointers impossible?

12. Which arithmetic operations are possible with pointers?

13. Explain the comparison of two pointers.

14. How does one pointer point to another pointer?

15. How will you recognize pointer to pointer? What does the number of '*'s indicate?

16. How are strings stored in the pointer variables? Is it essential to declare length?

17. What is base address? How is it accessed differently for one-dimensional and two-dimensional arrays?

18. Distinguish between the address stored in the pointer and the value at that address.

19. Why does the element counting of arrays always start from '0'?

20. Write a program to read and display a two-dimensional array of 5 by 2 numbers. Reduce the base address of an array by one and start element counting from one.

21. How is a pointer initialized?

22. Explain the effects of the following statements.

    (a) `int a, *b=&a;`
    (b) `int p, *p;`
    (c) `char *s;`
    (d) `a = (float*) &x;`
    (e) `double(*f)();`

23. Predict the output of each of the following programs (draw the memory diagram so that it will be easy to answer) where memory addresses are to be described. You can assume any six-digit number. Assume numbers starting from 333333.

    (a) `int a;`

```c
int *integer_pointer;
a=222;
integer_pointer=&a;
printf("The value of a is %d\n",a);
printf("The address of a is %d\n",&a);
printf("The address of\
 integer_pointer %d\n", &integer_pointer);
printf("Star integer_pointer\
%d\n", *integer_pointer);
```

(b)
```c
char a;
char *char_pointer;
a='b';
char_pointer=&a;
printf("The value of a %d\n", a);
printf("The address of a %d\n",&a);
printf("The address of\
 char_pointer %d\n", &char_pointer);
printf("Star char_pointer %d\n", *char_pointer);
```

(c) for float
```c
float a;
float *float_pointer;
a=22.25;
float_pointer=&a;
printf("The value of a %d\n", a);
printf("The address of a %d\n", &a);
printf("The address of\
 float_pointer %d\n", &float_pointer);
printf("Star float_pointer %d\n", *float_
            pointer);
```

(d)
```c
int a, b
int *ip1, *ip2;
a=5;
b=6;
ip1=&a;
ip2=ip1;
printf("The value of a is %d\n", a);
printf("The value of b is %d\n", b);
printf("The address of a is %d\n",&a);
printf("The address of b is %d \n"&b);
printf("The address of ip1 is %d\n", &ip1);
printf("The address of ip2 is %d\n", &ip2);
printf("The value of ip1 is %d\n",ip1);
printf("The value of ip2 is %d\n", ip2);
```

```
        printf("ip1 dereferenced %d\n",*ip1);
        printf("ip2 dereferenced %d\n", *ip2);
    (e) int i, j, *ip;
        i=1;
        ip=&i;
        j=*ip;
        *ip=0;
        printf("The value of i %d\n", i);
        printf("The value of j %d\n", j);
    (f) int x, y;
        int *ip1, *ip2;
        y=1;
        ip2=&y;
        ip1=ip2;
        x=*ip1+y;
        printf("The value of x %d\n", x);
        printf("The value of y %d\n",y);
```

24. Distinguish between (*m)[5] and *m[5].

25. Explain the difference between 'call by reference' and 'call by value'.

26. Write a program using pointers to read in an array of integers and print its elements in reverse order.

27. We know that the roots of a quadratic equation of the form

$$ax^2 + bx + c = 0$$

are given by the following equations:

$$x_1 = \frac{-b + \text{squareroot } (b^2 - 4ac)}{2a}$$

$$x_2 = \frac{-b - \text{squareroot } (b^2 - 4ac)}{2a}$$

Write a function to calculate the roots. The function must use two pointer parameters, one to receive the coefficients a, b, and c, and the other to send the roots to the calling function.

28. Does mentioning the array name give the base address in all contexts?

29. Write a C program to read through an array of any type using pointers. Write a C program to scan through this array to find a particular value.

30. Write a function using pointers to add two matrices and to return the resultant matrix to the calling function.

31. Using pointers, write a function that receives a character string and a character as argument and deletes all occurrences of this character in the string. The function should return the corrected string with no holes.

32. Write a function day_name that receives a number n and returns a pointer to a character string containing the name of the corresponding day. The day names should be kept in a static table of character strings local to the function.

33. Write a program to find the number of times that a given word (i.e., a short string) occurs in a sentence (i.e., a long string).

Read data from standard input. The first line is a single word, which is followed by general text on the second line. Read both up to a new-line character, and insert a terminating null before processing. Typical output should be:

```
The word is "the".
The sentence is "the cat sat on the mat".
The word occurs 2 times.
```

34. Write a program to read in an array of names and to sort them in alphabetical order. Use sort function that receives pointers to the functions strcmp, and swap. sort in turn should call these functions via the pointers.

35. Given an array of sorted list of integer numbers, write a function to search for a particular item using the method of *binary search*. Also show how this function may be used in a program. Use pointers and pointer arithmetic.

Hint In binary search, the target value is compared with the array's middle element. Since the table is sorted, if the required value is smaller, we know that all values greater than the middle element can be ignored. That is, in one attempt, we eliminate one half of the list. This search can be applied recursively till the target value is found.

36. Differentiate between p and *p.

37. What is the equivalent pointer notation to the subscript notation pt [0][2]?

38. What is the difference between *p++ and p++?

39. What is the result of adding an integer to a pointer?

40. What are the advantages of using pointers?

41. How do pointers differ from variables in C?

42. Explain the following declaration.

```
    int(*pf) (char *a, int *b);
```

43. What is the purpose of the realloc() function?

44. Differentiate between calloc() and malloc() functions in C.

45. For the version of C available on your particular computer, how many memory cells are required to store a single character? An integer quantity? A long integer? A floating-point quantity? A double-precisions quantity?

46. What is meant by the address of a memory cell? How are addresses usually numbered?

47. How is a variable's address determined?

48. What kind of information does a pointer variable represent?

49. What is the relationship between the address of a variable v and the corresponding pointer variable pv?

50. What is the purpose of the indirection operator? To what type of operand must the indirection operator be applied?

51. What is the relationship between the data item represented by a variable v and the corresponding pointer variable pv?

52. What precedence is assigned to the unary operators compared with the multiplication, division, and module operators? In what order are the unary operators evaluated?

53. Can the address operator act upon an arithmetic expression such as 2* (u + v)? Explain your answer.

54. Can an expression involving the indirection operator appear on the left side of an assignment statement? Explain.

55. What kinds of objects can be associated with pointer variables?

56. How is a pointer variable declared? What is the purpose of the data type included in the declaration?

57. In what way can the assignment of an initial value be included in the declaration of a pointer variable?

58. Are integer values ever assigned to pointer variables? Explain.

59. Why is it sometimes desirable to pass a pointer to a function as an argument?

60. Suppose a function receives a pointer as an argument. Explain how this function is declared within its calling function. In particular, explain how the data type of the pointer argument is represented.

61. Suppose a function receives a pointer as an argument. Explain how the pointer argument is declared within the function definition.

62. What is the relationship between an array name and a pointer? How is an array name interpreted when it appears as an argument to a function?

63. Suppose a formal argument within a function definition is an array. How can the array be declared within the function?

64. How can a portion of an array be passed to a function?

65. How can a function return a pointer to its calling routine?

66. Describe two different ways to specify the address of an array element.

67. Why is the value of an array subscript sometimes referred to as an offset when the subscript is a part of an expression indicating the address of an array element?

68. Describe two different ways to access an array element. Compare your answer to that of Question 62.

69. Can an address be assigned to an array name or an array element? Can an address be assigned to a pointer variable whose object is an array?

70. How is the library function malloc used to associate a block of memory with a pointer variable? How is the size of the memory block specified? What kind of information does the malloc function return?

71. Suppose a numerical array is defined in terms of a pointer variable. Can the individual array elements be initialized?

72. Suppose a character-type array is defined in terms of a pointer variable. Can the individual array elements be initialized? Compare your answer with that of the previous question.

73. Suppose an integer quantity is added to or subtracted from a pointer variable. How will this difference be interpreted?

74. Under what conditions can one pointer variable be subtracted from another? How will this difference be interpreted?

75. Under what conditions can two pointer variables be compared? Under what conditions are such comparisons useful?

76. How is a multidimensional array defined in terms of a pointer to a collection of contiguous array of lower dimensionality?

77. How can the indirection operator be used to access a multidimensional array element?

78. How is a multidimensional array defined in terms of an array of pointers? What does each pointer represent? How does this definition differ from a pointer to a collection of contiguous array of lower dimensionality?

79. How can a one-dimensional array of pointers be used to represent a collection of strings?

80. If several strings are stored within a one-dimensional array of pointers, how can an individual string be accessed?

81. If several strings are stored within a one-dimensional array of pointers, what happens if the strings are reordered? Are the strings actually moved to different locations within the array?

82. Under what conditions can the elements of a multidimensional array be initialized if the array is defined in terms of an array of pointers?

83. What is the relationship between a function name and a pointer?

84. Suppose a formal argument within a function definition is a pointer to another function. How is the formal argument declared? Within the formal argument declaration, what does the data type refer to? Deficient or abundant?

85. Define an integer pointer array of 10 integers. Initialize them to any integer values from the keyboard. Find the sum, average, minimum, and maximum of these 10 integers. Sort the 10 integers in descending order.

86. Write a program to display the starting day and ending day of the week for a project. The user is asked which day (0 to 6) is preferable to begin the project and the expected duration in number of days (a decimal number, e.g., 6.5 refers to 6.5 days)

to complete the project. It then displays the starting and ending day as:

Project starts on Monday and ends on Wednesday—duration is 10.5 days (if the start day number is 1 and duration = 10.5 days). The program allows the user to continue until the start day number is entered as 9 to exit the program.

Project Questions

Write a program that reads in up to 10 strings or to EOF, whichever comes first. Have it offer the user a menu with five choices: print the original list of strings, print the strings in alphabetical order, print the strings in order of increasing length, print the strings in order of the length of the first word in the string, and quit. Have the menu recycle until the user enters the quit request. The program, of course, should actually perform the promised tasks.

INCREMENTAL PROBLEM

The problem here is the same as in the earlier chapter. The programming logic employed is similar to that used in the earlier program. The main difference between this depicted program and that in the earlier chapter is the use of pointers. After learning pointers, the reader gets a firsthand idea on how a pointer can be used in a problem like this.

Problem statement

Compute the lengths of three sides of a triangle formed by three points whose co-ordinates are given. Check whether the triangle can be formed or not. Then compute the area of a triangle. Next take a point as input from the user and check whether it is inside or outside the triangle.

Solution

The program logic is similar to that applied in the earlier chapter. Functions used with the program are similar to those used earlier. The only change is in the representation of the vertices of the triangle as pointers, which has been learnt in this chapter. The program for solving the problem with pointers is given as follows:

Program

```c
#include <stdio.h>
#include <math.h>
#include <stdlib.h>
void createTriangle(int **,int **);
double getLength(int,int,int,int);
double getArea(double,double, double);
int insideOrOutside(int *,int *,int, int);
int main(void)
{
    int *x,*y;
    int i,xx,yy;
    double a,b,c, area;
    createTriangle(&x,&y);

    a=getLength(x[0],y[0],x[1],y[1]);
    b=getLength(x[1],y[1],x[2],y[2]);
    c=getLength(x[0],y[0],x[2],y[2]);
    if(a+b>c && b+c>a && c+a>b)
    {
        printf("Triangle can be drawn");
        area=getArea(a,b,c);
        printf("\n Area of the triangle is %lf\
            sq. units", area);
        printf("\n Enter the coordinates of the\
            point:");
        printf("\n x cordinate: ");
        scanf("%d",&xx);
        printf("\n y cordinate: ");
        scanf("%d",&yy);
        if(insideOrOutside(x,y,xx,yy))
        printf("\n Inside the triangle");
        else
        printf("\n Outside the triangle");
    }
    else
        printf("Triangle cannot be drawn");
    free(x);
    free(y);
    x=y=NULL;
```

```
        return 0;                                    n=(yOne-yTwo)*(yOne-yTwo);
}                                                    return sqrt((double)(m+n));
void createTriangle(int **a, int **b)            }
{                                                double getArea(double sA,double sB, double sC)
    int i;                                       {
    *a=(int *)malloc(3*sizeof(int));                 double s;
    if(*a==NULL)                                     s=(sA+sB+sC)/2.0;
    {                                                return sqrt(s*(s-sA)*(s-sB)*(s-sC));
        printf("\n Memory Allocation Error \n");  }
        return;                                  int insideOrOutside(int *a,int *b,int xx, int yy)
    }                                            {
    *b=(int *)malloc(3*sizeof(int));                 int i,k;
    if(*b==NULL)                                     double d[3], area, sumArea=0.0,aa,bb;
    {                                                for(i=0;i<3;++i)
        printf("\n Memory Allocation Error \n");      {
        return;                                          d[i]=getLength(*(a+i),*(b+i),*(a+(i+1)%3),
    }                                                        *(b+(i+1)%3));
        printf("\n Enter the coordinates of the\      }
            vertices of a triangle");                area=getArea(d[0],d[1],d[2]);
        for(i=0;i<3;++i)                             for(i=0;i<3;++i)
    {                                                {
        printf("\n Enter x[%d]:",i);                   aa=getLength(xx,yy,*(a+i),*(b+i));
        scanf("%d",(*a+i));                            bb=getLength(xx,yy,*(a+(i+1)%3),*(b+(i+1)%3));
        printf("\n Enter y[%d]:",i);                   sumArea+=getArea(d[i],aa,bb);
        scanf("%d",(*b+i));                          }
    }                                                if(fabs(area-sumArea)<0.00001)
}                                                        return 1;
double getLength(int xOne, int yOne, int xTwo,int yTwo)   else
{                                                        return 0;
    int m, n;                                    }
    m=(xOne-xTwo)*(xOne-xTwo);
```

CASE STUDY

Problem Statement

The Chief Operating Officer (CEO) signs vouchers , cheques, and documents where the amount is given in digits as well as in words. Every time before signing these, the CEO checks up whether the amount written in words matches with that of the digits. To do this swiftly the CEO needs a program in the computer that would accept the value written on vouchers, cheques, and documents and display the amount in words. The amount in any case should not exceed Rs 99 crores. A program has to be written to perform this task.

Analysis

The idea here is to express the amount in rupees in words. It must be noted that the largest amount that will be dealt with should never exceed Rs 999999999 and that this will always be a whole number. Whenever a value is inputted, it is divided with 10000000 to obtain a quotient that represents the crore part of the amount. Next, when the value is divided by 100000, the quotient represents lakh part inclusive of the crore part. This quotient when divided 100, a remainder is obtained that represents the only the lakh part of the amount. Now, when the value is divided by 1000 a quotient is obtained the division of which by 100 gives a remainder that represents the thousands part of the amount. The last operation is to divide the value by 10 and find the remainder which represents the amount less than ten rupee. Arrays of pointers have been used to store the corresponding words equivalent to the numbers. Hence after every division operation mentioned above, the corresponding word equivalent to the number is picked up from the respective array and displayed after the amount computed in appropriate order.

Design

The algorithm for the main program is given as follows:

1. START
2. STORE WORD EQUIVALENT FOR VALUES 0 TO 19 IN ARRAY NAMED ONE
3. STORE WORD EQUIVALENT FOR VALUES 0, LESS THAN 10, 20 TO 90 IN ARRAY NAMED TEN
4. FLAG = 0
5. WHILE(FLAG !=1)
6. BEGIN
7. PRINT "ENTER ANY NINE DIGIT VALUE"
8. INPUT N
9. IF N < 0
   THEN PRINT "ENTER VALUE GREATER THAN 0"
   ELSE
   1. PRINT " THE GIVEN AMOUNT IN WORDS IS RS."
   2. CALL NUM_TO_WORD((K = N/10000000), "CRORE")
   3. CALL NUM_TO_WORD((K = (N/100000)%100), "LAKH")
   4. CALL NUM_TO_WORD(((K = N/1000)%100), "THOUSAND")
   5. CALL NUM_TO_WORD(((K = N/100)%10), "HUNDRED")
   6. CALL NUM_TO_WORD((K = N%100), " ")
   7. PRINT "ONLY"
10. PRINT " DO YOU WANT TO CONVERT ONCE MORE : Y OR N"
11. INPUT OPTION
12. IF OPTION != Y
        THEN FLAG = 1
    ELSE
        FLAG = 0
13. END
14. STOP

The algorithm for the function CALL NUM_TO_WORD(VALUE, WORD) is given below:
1. START
2. RECEIVE VALUE K AND WORD
3. IF N > 19
       THEN PRINT " TEN[N/10] AND ONE[N%10]"
   ELSE
       PRINT " ONE[N]"
4. IF N != 0 THEN PRINT "WORD"
5. RETURN

C Implementation

```c
#include<stdio.h>
void num2word(long,char[]);
char *one[]={" ", "one", "two", "three", "four",
            "five", "six", "seven", "eight", "Nine",
            "ten", "eleven", "twelve", "thirteen",
            "fourteen", "fifteen", "sixteen",
            "seventeen", "eighteen", "nineteen"};
char *ten[]={" "," ", "twenty", "thirty", "forty",
            "fifty", "sixty", "seventy", "eighty",
            "ninety"};
int main()
{
 long n;
 int flag = 0;
 char ch;
 while(flag!=1)
 {
 printf("\n Enter any 9 digit value: ");
 scanf("%9ld",&n);
 if(n<=0)
     printf("\n Enter values greater than 0");
 else
 {
 printf("\n The given amount expressed in words\
         is:\n Rs");
 num2word((n/10000000),"crore");
 num2word(((n/100000)%100),"lakh");
 num2word(((n/1000)%100),"thousand");
 num2word(((n/100)%10),"hundred");
 num2word((n%100)," ");
 printf("only");
 }

 printf("\n\n Do you want to convert once more: y\
     or n \n");
 fflush(stdin);
 scanf("%c",&ch);
 if(ch!='y')
    flag=1;
 else
    flag=0;
 }

 return 0;
}

void num2word(long n,char ch[])
{
    (n>19)?printf("%s %s",ten[n/10],one[n%10]):
            printf("%s",one[n]);
```

```
 if(n)
printf("%s", ch);


}
```

Sample run result:
```
Enter any 9 digit no: 546789123
The given amount expressed in words is:
Rs fifty four crore sixty seven lakh eighty Nine
thousand one hundred t
wenty three only
```

```
Do you want to convert once more: y or n
y
Enter any 9 digit no: 123456789
The given amount expressed in words is:
Rs twelve crore thirty four lakh fifty six thousand
seven hundred eighty
Nine only
Do you want to convert once more: y or n
n
Press Enter to return to Quincy...
```

Chapter 9

User-defined Data Types and Variables

Learning Objectives

After reading this chapter, the readers will be able to

- learn about the user-defined data type called structure and its tag, members, and variables
- access, initialize, and copy structures and their members
- understand nesting of structures
- make and initialize arrays of structures
- comprehend pointer to structures
- use structures as function arguments and return values
- learn about union data types
- understand enumeration data types
- get acquainted with bitfields

9.1 INTRODUCTION

So far, fundamental data types have been used in the programs illustrated. However, C provides facilities to construct user-defined data types from the fundamental data types.

A user-defined data type may also be called a derived data type. The array type is a derived data type that contains only one kind of fundamental data types defined in C. This means that the array elements, represented by a single name, contain homogeneous data.

But what happens if the different elements in this cluster, known as array, are to be of different data types. Such non-homogeneous data cannot be grouped to form an array. To tackle this problem suitably, C provides features to pack heterogeneous data in one group, bearing a user-defined data type name, and forming a conglomerate data type. So, C provides facilities for the user to create a new data type called the 'structure' that is capable of holding data of existing type.

9.2 STRUCTURES

The array is an example of a data structure. It takes basic data types such as `int`, `char`, or `double` and organizes them into a linear array of elements of the same data type. The array serves most but not all of the needs of the typical C program. The restriction is that an array is composed of the same type of elements.

At first this seems perfectly reasonable. After all, why would one want an array to be composed of twenty Characters and two `integers`? Well, this sort of mixture of data types working together is one of the most familiar of data structures. Consider for a moment a record card which stores name, age, and salary. The name would have to be stored as a string, i.e., an array of characters terminated with an ASCII null character, and the age and salary would be integers. Hence, the only way one can work with this collection of data is as separate variables. This is not as convenient as a *single data structure* using a single name. Therefore, C provides a keyword `struct`, which is used to form a user-defined data type that can hold a collection of elements of different fundamental data types. This conglomerate, user-defined data type, is called a structure. At first it is easier to think of this as a record, although it is a little more versatile than what it appears to be.

A structure is a collection of variables under a single name. These variables can be of different types, and each has a name which is used to select it from the structure. Therefore, a structure is a convenient way of grouping together several pieces of related information.

Thus, a structure can be defined as a new named type, thus extending the number of available data types. It can use other structures, arrays, or pointers as some of its members, though this can get complicated unless one is careful.

A structure provides a means of grouping variables under a single name for easier handling and identification. Complex hierarchies can be created by nesting structures.

Structures may be copied to and assigned. They are also useful in passing groups of logically related data into functions.

9.2.1 Declaring Structures and Structure Variables

A structure is declared by using the keyword `struct` followed by an optional structure tag followed by the body of the structure. The *variables* or *members* of the structure are declared within the body.

The general format of declaring a simple structure is given as follows.

```
struct <structure_tag_name >{          Keyword
<data_type member_name1>;              Basic
<data_type member_name2>;              data type
    :
} <structure_variable1>,<structure_variable2>,...;
```

The `structure_tag_name` is the name of the structure. The `structure_variables` are the list of variable names separated by commas. Each of these `structure_variable` names is a structure of type `structure_tag_name`. The `structure_variable` is also known as an instance variable of the structure. Each `member_name` declared within the braces is called a `member` or `structure element`.

Like all data types, structures must be declared and defined. There are three different ways to declare and/or define a structure. These are

- Variable structure
- Tagged structure
- Type-defined structure

A variable structure may be defined as follows.

```
struct
{
member_list
}variable_identifier;
```

As an example the following statement is a definition of a variable structure:

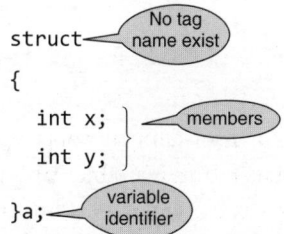

```
struct          No tag
                name exist
{
  int x;              members
  int y;
}a;             variable
                identifier
```

It does not offer any advantage over other declaration formats. A tagged structure has been described earlier. It has the following format:

```
struct tag_name
{
  member_list
}variable_identifier;
```

The preceding structure declaration may be expressed as a tagged structure as follows:

```
struct coordinate        tag name
{
   int x;
   int y;
}a;
```

This creates a structure variable named 'a' and has a separate instance of all members (x and y) in the structure coordinate. If one concludes the structure with a semicolon after the closing brace, no variable is defined. In this case, the structure is simply a type template with no associate storage. Once one has declared a tagged structure type, then the structure variable can be defined by specifying the following statement.

```
struct tag_name variable1, variable2, …;
```

Type-defined structures have been discussed later on (see Section 9.2.5).

The proper place for structure declarations is in the global area of the program before main(). This puts them within the scope of the entire program and is mandatory if the structure is to be shared by functions. If a declaration is placed inside a function, then its tag can be used only inside that function.

Here is an example of a structure that would be useful in representing the Cartesian coordinates of a point on a computer screen, that is, the pixel position.

```
struct point
{
   int x;
   int y;
};
```

The struct declaration is a user-defined data type. Here, the name of the structure is point. Variables of type point may be declared in the way variables of a built-in type are declared. For example,

```
struct point
{
   int x;
   int y;
} upper_right;
```

As mentioned earlier, the structure tag name provides a shorthand for declaring structures. This is shown as follows.

```
struct point
{
   int x;
   int y;
};
struct point upper_left,lower_right;
struct point origin;
```

Here, upper_left, lower_right, and origin are the names of three structures of type point. The following are some examples of declaration of structures and structure variables.

Example

```
1. struct personal_data
   {
      char name[100];
      char address[200];
      int year_of_birth;
      int month_of_birth;
      int day_of_birth;
   };
   struct personal_data monish, venkat, naresh;
```

The above statement is for defining a type of variable that holds a string of 100 characters called name, a string of 200 characters called address, and three integers called year_of_birth, month_of_birth, and day_of_birth. Any variable declared to be of type struct personal_data will contain these components, which are called members.

Different structures, even different types of structures, can have members with the same name, but the values of members of different structures are independent of one another. The same name for a member as for an ordinary variable in that program can also be used, but the computer will recognize them as different entities, with different values. This is similar to the naming convention for humans, where two different men may share the name 'Jogi Sharma', but are recognized as being different people.

See Fig. 9.1. The three structure variables declared are monish, venkat, and naresh. Each one of it contains the member fields declared within the structure personal_data.

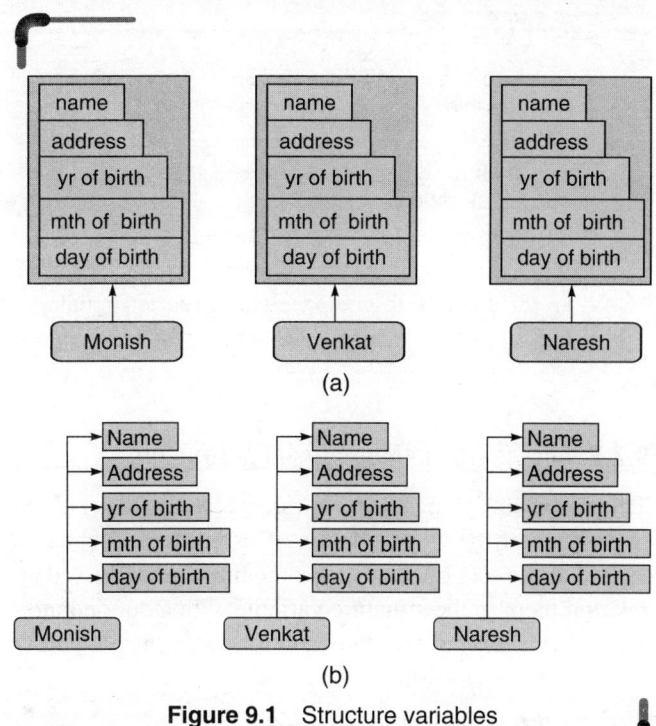

Figure 9.1 Structure variables

2. struct country

```
{
    char name[30];
    int population;
    char language[15];
}Country;
```

Here, a structure variable `Country` has been declared to be of structure type `country`. This structure variable holds a string called `name` having 30 characters, an integer variable `population` and a string called `language` with 15 characters.

3. struct country

```
{
    char name[30];
    int population;
    char language[15];
}India, Japan, Indonesia;
```

This structure named `country` has three structure variables `India`, `Japan`, `Indonesia`. All three structure variables hold the same kind of member elements, though with different values.

4. struct date   /* the tag */

```
{                  /* start of struct date template */
    int day;                        /* a member */
    int month;                      /* a member */
    int year;                       /* a member */
    float sensex;                   /* a member */
}dates, today, next;        /* instances */
```

This declaration has three structure variables `dates`, `today`, and `next`. These are also called *instances* and hold similar kind and number of variables, which may contain different values.

It has been seen that instances of structures can be declared at the same time the structure is defined. For example,

```
struct myStruct {
    int a;
    int b;
    int c;
} s1, s2;
```

would generate two instances of `myStruct`. `s1` would cover the first 12 bytes of the file (four bytes for each of the three integers) and `s2` would cover the next 12 bytes of the file, considering a 32-bit machine. So, from the declaration of members, the compiler can determine the memory space needed and identify the different members in the structure.

Observe that the structure declaration construct is a template that conveys to the C compiler how the structure is laid out in memory and gives details of the member names. A (tagged) template does not reserve any instances of the structure; it only conveys to the compiler what it means. This is explained with the help of the following example.

```
struct  date {
    int month;
    int day;
    int year;
};
```

This declares a new data type called `date`. The `date` structure consists of three basic data elements, all of type integer. It does not create any storage space and cannot be used as a variable. In essence, it is a new data type keyword, like int and char, and can now be used to create variables. Other data structures may be defined as consisting of the same composition as the date structure.

Structure type and variable declarations can be either local or global, depending on their placement in the code, just as any other declaration can be. Structures may be assigned, used as formal function parameters, and returned as functional values. Such operations cause the compiler to generate sequences of load and store instructions that might pose efficiency problems. C programmers particularly concerned about program speed will avoid such things and work exclusively with pointers to functions.

There are few actual operations that can be performed on structures as distinct from their members. The only operators that can be rightly associated with structures are '=' (simple assignment) and '&' (take the address). It is not possible to compare structures for equality using '==', nor is it possible to perform arithmetic on structures. Such operations need to be explicitly coded in terms of operations on the members of the structure.

Structure member declarations conform to the same syntax as ordinary variable declarations. Structure member names should conform to the same syntax as ordinary variable names and structure tags but again belong to a different 'universe', i.e., the same name could be used for a structure tag, an instance of the structure, and a member of the structure. Each structure defines a separate space as far as naming structure members is concerned.

The following rather bizarre and confusing codes are perfectly valid.

```
(a) struct a          (b) struct b
    {                     {
      int a;                char b;
      int b;                char a;
    } b;                  }a;
```

Structure members can be any valid data type, including other structures, aggregates, and pointers including pointers to structures and pointers to functions. A structure may not, for obvious reasons, contain instances of itself but may contain pointers to instances of itself.

9.2.2 Accessing the Members of a Structure

The members of a structure can be accessed in three ways. One of the ways consists of using the '.', which is known as the 'dot operator'. The members are accessed by relating them to the structure variable with a dot operator. The general form of the statement for accessing a member of a structure is as follows.

```
< structure_variable >.< member_name > ;
```

The . (dot) operator selects a particular member from a structure. It has the same precedence as () and [], which is higher than that of any unary or binary operator. Like () and [], it associates from left to right. For example, in

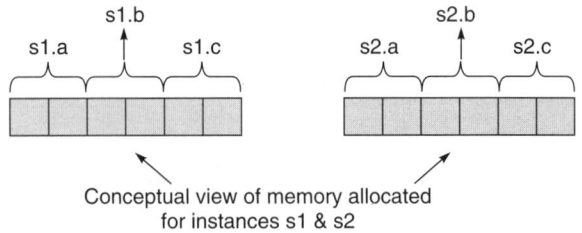

Conceptual view of memory allocated
for instances s1 & s2

```
struct myStruct
{
  int a;
  int b;
  int c;
} s1, s2;
```

the first member can be accessed by the construct

```
s1.a
```

For any other member of the structure, the construct for accessing it will be similar. Therefore, for assigning a value of 12, say, to the member b of the structure identified by the variable s2, the following statement is written

```
s2.b = 12;
```

To print this value assigned to the member on the screen, the following code is written.

```
printf("%d", s2.b);
```

Similarly, in the preceding example, member `b` of structure `s2` will behave just like a normal variable of type `int`. However, it is referred to as

```
s2.b
```

Now, consider the structure given as follows.

```
struct personal_data
  {
    char name[100];
    char address[200];
    int year_of_birth;
    int month_of_birth;
    int day_of_birth;
  };
```

and the declaration statement for the structure variables `monish`, `venkat`, and `naresh` is given by

```
struct personal_data monish, venkat, naresh;
```

To input the address of `monish`, the following code can be used.

```
scanf("%s", monish.address);
```

The member `address` of structure `personal_data` will behave just like a normal array of `char`. However, it is referred to as `monish.address`.

In the following example, the year `1982` is assigned to the `year_of_birth` member of the structure variable `monish`, of type `struct personal_data`. Similarly, the month `5` is assigned to the `month_of_birth` member, and day `4` is assigned to the `day_of_birth` member. The following statements show the assignment of the values to the member variables belonging to the structure variable `monish`.

```
monish.year_of_birth = 1982;
monish.month_of_birth = 5;
monish.day_of_birth = 4;
```

Hence, each member of a structure can be used just like a normal variable, but its name will be a bit longer. Therefore, the 'dot' is an operator that selects a member from a structure. This is just one of the ways of accessing any member in a structure. The other two ways will be described in the ensuing sections.

9.2.3 Initialization of Structures

A structure can be initialized in much the same way as any other data type. This consists of assigning some constants to the members of the structure. Structures that are not explicitly initialized by the programmer are, by default, initialized by the system. For integer and float data type members, the default value is zero. For char and string type members the default value is '\0'.

The general construct for initializing a structure can be any of the two forms given as follows.

```
struct <structure_tag_name>
{
  <data_type member_name1>;
  <data_type member_name2>;
}<structure_variable1> = {constant1,constant2, . .};
```

or

```
struct <structure_tag_name> <structure_variable>
        = {constant1,constant2,..};
```

The following are some examples using both the forms for initialization.

Example

5. Initialization of structure using the first construct.

```
#include <stdio.h>
struct tablets        ⟵ tag name
{
  int count;
  float average_weight;
  int m_date, m_month, m_year;       ⟩ members
  int ex_date, ex_month, ex_year;
}batch1={2000,25.3,07,11,2004};
       ⤷ structure      ⤷ initialization
          variable          constants
int main()
{
  printf("\n  count=%d,  av_wt=%f",batch1.count,
      batch1.average_weight);
  printf("\n mfg-date=%d/%d/%d", batch1.m_date,
      batch1.m_month batch1.m_year);
```

```
  printf("\n exp-date=%d/%d/%d", batch1.ex_date,
      batch1.ex_month, batch1.ex_year);
  return 0;
}
```

Output:

```
count=2000, av_wt=25.299999
mfg-date=7/11/2004
exp-date= 0/0/0
```

In the preceding example, observe that after the '=' operator, the number of constants within the braces, that is, { and }, are not equal to the total number of members within the structure *tablets*. There are eight members in this structure whereas there are five initializing constants. Hence, the first five members are assigned the constants given and the remaining members are assigned the default value of zero. This is a case of *partial initialization* where, always, the first few members are initialized and the remaining uninitialized members are assigned default values. Therefore, it is obvious that the *partial initialization* feature is supported in C.

It may, therefore, be stated that the initialization of all members in a structure is possible if the number of initializing constants located within the braces is equal to the number of members. Otherwise, partial initialization will be done and the rule of assigning the default values to the rest of the members will be followed.

Example

6. Initialization of structure using the second construct.

```
#include <stdio.h>
struct tablets
{
  int count;
  float average_weight;
  int m_date, m_month, m_year;
  int ex_date, ex_month, ex_year;
};
struct tablets batch1={2000,25.3,07,11,2004,06,
    10,2007};
int main()
{
  printf("\n  count=%d,  av_wt=%f  mg.",batch1.
    count, batch1.average_weight);
```

```
  printf("\n mfg-date= %d/%d/%d",batch1.m_date,
      batch1.m_month, batch1.m_year);
  printf("\n exp-date= %d/%d/%d",batch1.ex_date,
      batch1.ex_month, batch1.ex_year);
  return 0;
}
```

Output:

```
count=2000, av_wt=25.299999 mg.
mfg-date= 7/11/2004
exp-date= 6/10/2007
```

It must be noted that within the structure construct no member is permitted to be initialized individually, which means the following initialization construct is wrong.

```
struct games_ticket
{
  int value = 500;
      /* wrong procedure of initialization */
  int seat_num = 52;
      /* wrong procedure of initialization */
  int date, month, year;
}fan1;
```

The initialization statements

```
  int value = 500;
```

and `int seat_num = 52;`

placed within the `struct` construct are not permitted in C. The structure tag (here `games_ticket`) is not a variable name. It is just a name given to the template of a structure. Thus, the statement `games_ticket.value=500;` will cause the compiler to generate an error. `games_ticket` is a just a data type like `int` and not a variable. Just as `int=10` is invalid, `games_ticket.value=500;` is also invalid. The correct code allowed by C will be

```
struct games_ticket  /* structure tag */
{
  int value;                      /* member */
  int seat_num;                   /* member */
  int date, month, year;          /* members */
} fan1={500, 52};      /* structure variable and */
                       /* initializing values */
```

Here, the members `value` and `seat_num` are initialized with the values 500 and 52 respectively.

The rules described upto this point, for the initialization of structures, is valid for the old C compilers that do no comply with C99 standards. The compilers that follow C99 standard allow the initialization of individual members of a `structure`. This method of initialization was forbidden in old compilers that are not C99 compliant. To demonstrate this kind of named initialization of a structure look at the following examples.

7.
```
struct {
  float p, q,
  int r;
} k = { .p = 3.0, .q = 7.9, .r = 5};
```

The instance "k" of the above defined structure is initialized by assigning value to individual named members. Here a "dot" is used with the member's name for assigning a value.

8.
```
struct employee
{
  int emp_num;
  char designation[40];
  char kind_of_leave_applied[30];
  int number_of _days;
  int begin_date;
};
struct employee mangal_singh = {.kind_of_leave_
        applied = "Medical leave", .begin_date =
        230910, .emp_num = 0691};
```

The "`struct employee`" defines a template of a structure with tagname "`employee`". An instance of the structure is created by the statement "`struct employee mangal_singh`". This instance is initialized. But it may be noted that only some of the members are initialized. In the C compilers not complying to C99, such initialization is not allowed. For such compilers, while initializing an instance of a structure, the members of the structure have to be assigned a value or a character, whichever is appropriate, in the order of their definition and members not assigned are given default value of 0 or \0, which has been mentioned earlier. But, C99 allows the members of a structure to be initialized by name, which is shown in the above example.

Further note that the order of the initialization is different from that of the definition of the members in the structure. The member "`kind_of_leave_applied`" is placed first, the member

"`begin_date`" is placed second and the member "`emp_num`" is placed third, while the other remaining members are not assigned anything. Members uninitialized are filled up with the default value of 0. It may be observed that this not only decouples the order of the definition from the order of the initialization, but it's more readable. This means the programmer only need to fill out the portions of the structure that are presently relevant and is able to initialize the elements of the structure using the set notation without feeling the need to remember the order of the elements of the structure. Also, if new elements to the structure are added in later versions, they get initialized to a known value.

Some examples using named initialization in structures are given below for getting more familiar with its applications.

9. Demonstration of named initialization in a structure.
```
#include<stdio.h>
struct
{
  float x, y, z;
} s = { .y = 0.6, .x = 2.7, .z = 14.6};
int main()
{
  float p,q,r;
  p= s.x + s.y + s.z;
  q= s.z*s.x;
  r= s.z/s.x;
  printf("\n p = %5.2f",p);
  printf("\n q = %5.2f",q);
  printf("\n r = %5.2f",r);
  return 0;
}
```

Output:
```
p = 17.90
q = 39.42
r = 5.41
```

10. Another demonstration of named initialization in a structure.
```
#include<stdio.h>
struct test
{
  float x, y, z;
}s;
int main()
{
  float p,q,r;
```

```c
struct test s= { .y = 1.24, .x = 3.8, .z = 11.7};
p= s.x + s.y + s.z;
q= s.z*s.x;
r= s.z/s.x;
printf("\n p = %5.2f",p);
printf("\n q = %5.2f",q);
printf("\n r = %5.2f",r);
return 0;
}
```

Output:

```
p = 16.74
q = 44.46
r = 3.08
```

11. One more demonstration of named initialization in a structure.

```c
#include<stdio.h>
struct test
{
 float x, y, z;
 }s;
int main()
{
    float p,q,r;
    struct test s;
    s.y= 5.94;
    s.z= 19.45;
    s.x= 23.17;
    p= s.x + s.y + s.z;
    q= s.z*s.x;
    r= s.z/s.x;
    printf("\n p = %7.2f",p);
    printf("\n q = %7.2f",q);
    printf("\n r = %7.2f",r);
    return 0;
}
```

Output:

```
p = 48.56
q = 450.66
r = 0
```

12. A railway ticket generation program that uses named initialization in a structure.

```c
#include<stdio.h>
struct traveler
{
  int class;
  char train_num[40];
  char coach_num[6];
  int seat_num;
  char from[30];
  char to[30];
  char gender[10];
  int age;
  int dep_date[10];
  char name[80];
};
struct traveler passenger8 =
{
  .name = "JIT SINHA",
  .to = "Jaipur",
  .from = "Raigarh",
  .train_num = "superfast 154",
  .dep_date[0] = 30,
  .dep_date[1] = 8,
  .dep_date[2] = 2010,
  .gender = "M",
  .age = 28,
  .class = 1
};
int main()
{
  printf("\n enter coach number:");
  scanf("%s",passenger8.coach_num);
  printf("\n enter seat number:");
  scanf("%d", &passenger8.seat_num);
  printf("\nxxxxxxxxx Ticket xxxxxxxxx");
  printf("\n\n\n Name of Ticket holder : %s",
        passenger8.name);
  printf("\n\n Train : %s:",passenger8.train_num);
  printf("\n\n From : %s Date of Departure:",
        passenger8.from);
```

```
for(int i=0;i<3;i++)
printf(": %d :",passenger8.dep_date[i]);
printf("\n\n To: %s", passenger8.to);
printf("\n\n    Coach    No.:    %s    Seat
    No.:%d",passenger8.coach_num,passenger8.
    seat_num);
printf("\n\n\nxxxxxxxxxxxxxxxxxxxxxxxxxxxxxxxxx");
return 0;
}
```

Output:

```
enter coach number: S6

enter seat number: 41

xxxxxxxxxxxxxxxxxxx Ticket xxxxxxxxxxxxxxxxxxx
Name of Ticket holder : JIT SINHA

Train : Superfast 154:

From : Raigarh Date of Departure : : 30 :: 8 :: 2010 :
To: Jaipur

Coach No.: S6   Seat No.: 41
```

9.2.4 Copying and Comparing Structures

A structure can be assigned to another structure of the same type. Here is an example of assigning one structure to another.

Example

13. Copying one structure to another of the same type.

```c
#include <stdio.h>
struct employee
{
  char grade;
  int basic;
  float allowance;
};
int main()
{
  struct employee ramesh={'b', 6500, 812.5};
                    /* member of employee */
  struct employee vivek;
                    /* member of employee */
  vivek = ramesh;  /* copy respective members of
                        ramesh to vivek */
```

```c
  printf("\n vivek's grade is %c, basic is Rs %d,
      allowance is Rs %f", vivek.grade,vivek.
      basic, vivek.allowance);
  return 0;
}
```

Output:

```
vivek's grade is b, basic is Rs 6500, allowance
    is Rs 812.500000
```

The preceding example has illustrated that it is possible to copy the corresponding members of one *structure variable* to those of another *structure variable* provided they belong to the same structure type. It was mentioned earlier that the operator '=' can only be used on structure variables, as demonstrated in this example. The operator '&' can also be used on the structure variable. No other operators, arithmetic, logical, or relational, can be used with the structure variables.

Comparing one structure variable with another is not allowed in C. The components of a structure are laid out in memory in the order they are declared. The first component has the same address as the entire structure. Padding is introduced between components to satisfy the alignment requirements of individual components. This can be explained in terms of *slack bytes*. Sometimes hardware requires that certain data such as integers and floating point members, be aligned on a word boundary in memory. When data in a structure are grouped, the arrangement of the data may require that *slack bytes* be inserted to maintain these boundary requirements. For example, consider the following structure.

```c
struct test
{
  char c[25];
  long int l;
  char ch;
  int I;
};
```

On a byte-addressed machine, short of size two might be placed at even addresses and long int of size four at addresses that are multiples of four. In this structure, it is assumed that a long int is stored in a word that requires four bytes and must be on an address evenly divisible by four such as 20, 24, 28, or 32. It is also assumed that integers are stored in a two-byte word that requires an address evenly divisible by four. The 25 bytes string at the beginning of the structure forces slack bytes between the string and the long (see Fig. 9.2). Then the character after the long forces slack byte to align with the integer at the end of the structure.

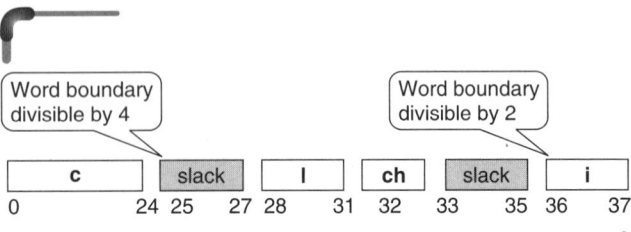

Figure 9.2 Slack bytes in a structure

Since these extra bytes are beyond the control of the program, one cannot guarantee what their values will be. The gce compiler aligns the structure fields on 4-byte boundaries. Considering the above structure, sizeof(test) will print 40 (25 bytes for char + 3 bytes padding + 4 bytes for long + 1 byte for char + 3 bytes padding + 4 bytes for int. Therefore, if two structures are compared and their first components are equal, the inserted slack bytes could cause an erroneous result. C prevents this problem by not allowing selection statements with structures. Generally, it is good to group structure fields of the same type together to minimize the extra padding. Of course, when comparing two structures, one should compare the individual fields in the structure. To determine byte offset of a member within a structure, ANSI C defines offsetof macro in stdef.h. This can also be implemented as follows.

```
#define offsetof (type, mem) ((size_t) ((char *)
        &((type *)0)->mem -\(char *) (type *)0))
```

To avoid wastage of space and to minimize the effects of padding, the members of a structure should be placed according to their sizes from the largest to the smallest. However, members of one structure can be compared with members of another on an individual basis. In fact, the members involved in the comparison will behave like any other variable. An example illustrating this feature follows.

Points to Note

1. Any member in a structure can be accessed by relating them to the structure variable with a dot operator.

2. Structures that are not explicitly initialized by the programmer are, by default, initialized by the system. In most of the C compilers, for integer and float data type members, the default value is zero and for char and string type members, the default value is '\0'.

3. Comparing one structure variable with another is not allowed in C. However, when comparing two structures, one should compare the individual fields in the structure.

Example

14. Comparison of individual members of structures.

```
#include <stdio.h>
struct employee
{
    char grade;
    int basic;
    float allowance;
};
int main()
{
  struct employee ramesh = {'b', 5750, 818.75};
  struct employee vivek = {'b', 6500, 812.5};
  if(ramesh.grade!= vivek.grade)
    printf("Ramesh and Vivek are employed on
        different grades");
  else if((ramesh.basic+ramesh.allowance)>(vivek.
        basic+vivek.allowance))
    printf("Ramesh is senior and his total
        remuneration is Rs%f",
        (ramesh.basic+ramesh. allowance));
  else if((ramesh.basic+ramesh.allowance)==(vivek.
        basic+vivek.allowance))
  printf("Ramesh and Vivek get the same total
        remuneration of Rs%f",
        (ramesh.basic+ramesh.allowance));
  else
    printf("Vivek is senior and his total
        remuneration is Rs%f",
            (vivek.basic+vivek.allowance));
  return 0;
}
```

Output:

```
Vivek is senior and his total remuneration is
    Rs 7312.500000
```

9.2.5_Typedef and Its Use in Structure Declarations

The typedef keyword allows the programmer to create a new data type name for an existing data type. No new data type is produced but an alternate name is given to a known data type. The general form of the declaration statement using the typedef keyword is given as follows.

```
typedef <existing data type> <new data type ,….>;
```

The typedef statement does not occupy storage; it simply defines a new type. typedef statements can be placed anywhere in a C program as long as they come prior to their first use in the code.

The following examples show the use of typedef.

```
typedef int id_number;
typedef float weight;
typedef char lower_case;
```

In the preceding example, id_number is the new data type name given to data type int, while weight is the new data type name given to data type float and lower_case is the new data type name given to data type char. Therefore, the following statements

```
id_number vinay, komal, jaspal;
weight apples, pears, mangoes;
lower_case a,b,c;
```

mean that vinay, komal, and jaspal are variable names that are declared to hold int data type. The new data type, id_number, suggests that the data content of the variable names vinay, komal, and jaspal are integers and that it gives their identification number. The two other examples shown also carry similar meanings. Therefore, by the typedef keyword mechanism, the suggested use of the type names can be understood easily. This is one of the benefits of using the typedef keyword. Moreover, typedef makes the code more portable.

Complex data type like structure can use the typedef keyword. For example,

```
typedef struct point
  {
    int x;
    int y;
  } Dot;
Dot left,right;
```

shows that left and right are the structure variables of structure type point.

When typedef is used to name a structure, the structure tag name is not necessary. Such an example follows.

```
typedef struct     /* no structure tag name used */
  {
    float real;
    float imaginary;
  } complex;           /* means complex number */
complex u,v;
```

The preceding example declares u and v as complex numbers having a real part and an imaginary part. The following are some examples involving structures and typedef.

Examples

15. A program that prints the weight of various sizes of fruits.

```
#include <stdio.h>
typedef struct fruits
{
  float big;
  float medium;
  float small;
  }weight;
int main()
{
  weight apples={200.75,145.5,100.25};
  weight pears={150.50,125,50};
  weight mangoes={1000, 567.25, 360.25};
  printf("\n\n  apples:  big  %7.2fkg,  medium
        %7.2fkg,         small    %7.2fkg",apples.
        big,apples.medium, apples.small);
  printf("\n\n pears: big %7.2fkg, medium %7.2fkg,
        small %7.2fkg",pears.big,pears.medium,
        pears.small);
  printf("\n\n mangoes: big %7.2fkg, medium %7.2fkg,
        small %7.2fkg", mangoes.big, mangoes.
        medium, mangoes.small);
  return 0;
}
```

Output:

```
apples: big 200.75kg, medium 145.50kg, small 100.25kg
pears: big 150.50kg, medium 125.00kg, small 50.00kg
mangoes: big 1000kg, medium 567.25kg, small 360.25kg
```

16. A program that prints the x – y coordinates of the two ends of a line.

```c
#include <stdio.h>
typedef struct               /* no tag */
{
  int x;
  int y;
}Dot;                        /* a new type name */
Dot left,right;
                /* declaring structures "left"
                              and "right" */
int main()
{
printf("\n Enter x & y coordinates of left and
      right:");
  scanf("%d %d %d %d",&left.x,&left.y,&right.x,
      &right.y);
  printf("\n left: x=%d, y=%d, right: x=%d,
      y=%d", left.x, left.y, right.x,right.y);
  return 0;
}
```

Output:
```
Enter x & y coordinates of left and right:4 20 30 20
left: x=4, y=20, right: x=30, y=20
```

9.2.6 Nesting of Structures

A structure can be placed within another structure. In other words, structures can contain other structures as members. A structure within a structure means nesting of structures. In such cases, the dot operator in conjunction with the structure variables are used to access the members of the innermost as well as the outermost structures.

Example

17. A program to demonstrate nesting of structures and accessing structure members.
```c
#include <stdio.h>
struct outer   /* declaration of outer structure */
{
  int out1;      /* member of outer structure */
  float out2;    /* member of outer structure */
  struct inner /* declaration of inner structure */
  {
  int in1;        /* member of inner structure */
```

```c
  float in2;     /* member of inner structure */
  }invar;
      /* structure_variable of inner structure*/
};
int main()
{
  struct outer outvar;
     /* declaring structure_variable of outer */
  outvar.out1= 2;  /* assigning values to members */
  outvar.out2= 10.57;
            /* assigning values to members */
outvar.invar.in1= 2* outvar.out1;
outvar.invar.in2= outvar.out2 + 3.65;
printf(" out1=%d, out2=%6.2f, in1=%d, in2=%6.2f",
      outvar.out1, outvar.out2,outvar.invar.in1,
      outvar.invar.in2);
  return 0;
}
```

Output:
```
out1=2, out2= 10.57, in1=4, in2= 14.22
```

It must be noted that an innermost member in a nested structure can be accessed by chaining all the concerned structure variables, from outermost to innermost, with the member using the dot operator. This technique has been used in the previous example, when the inner-most members in1 and in2, belonging to the structure inner, are assigned values.

What happens when the first structure type is declared outside and before the second structure type and is incorporated as a member of the second structure type? The following example depicts what happens in such a case. The structure members are accessed in the same way as was done in the earlier example.

Example

18. Write a program to demonstrate nesting of structures, accessing structure members, and using structure type declaration different from that in the previous example.
```c
#include <stdio.h>
struct first   /* declaration of first structure */
{
  int in1;                   /* member of first */
  float in2;                 /* member of first */
};
```

```
struct second   /* declaration of second structure */
{
   int out1;                /* member of second */
   float out2;              /* member of second */
   struct first inf;  /* structure_variable of first
                                        structure */
};
int main()
{
   struct second outs;   /* structure_variable of
                                 second structure */
   outs.out1= 2;              /* assigning values to
                                           members */
   outs.out2= 10.57;          /* assigning values to
                                           members */
   outs.inf.in1= 2* outs.out1;
   outs.inf.in2= outs.out2 + 3.65;
   printf(" out1=%d, out2=%6.2f, in1=%d, in2=%6.2f",
            outs.out1,  outs.out2,  outs.inf.in1,
            outs.inf.in2);
   return 0;
}
```

Output:

```
out1=2, out2= 10.57, in1=4, in2= 14.22
```

It must be understood that, in principle, structures can be nested indefinitely. Statements like the following are syntactically acceptable, but are bad style.

```
Outer_struct_variable.member1.member2.member3.
       member4.member5 = 3;
```

However, one may be curious to know what happens if a structure contains an instance of its own type. The following example may be examined in this context.

```
struct compute
{
   int int_member;
   struct compute self_member;
};
```

For the computer to compile a statement of this type, it would theoretically need an infinite amount of memory. In practice, however, the programmer will simply receive an error message along the following lines.

```
In function 'main':
field self_member has incomplete type
```

The compiler conveys to the programmer that 'self_member' has been declared before its data type 'compute' has been fully declared. Since the programmer is declaring 'self_member' in the middle of declaring its own data type, this is quite natural.

9.2.7 Arrays of Structures

Just as there can be arrays of basic types such as integers and floats, so also can there be *arrays of structures*. This means that the structure variable would be an array of objects, each of which contains the member elements declared within the structure construct. The general construct for declaration of an array structure is given as follows.

```
struct <structure_tag_name >
{
   <data_type member_name1>;
   <data_type member_name2>;
        ⋮
}<structure_variable>[index];
```

Or

```
struct <structure_tag_name> <structure_variable>[index];
```

Figure 9.3 depicts the arrays formed for the array objects declared to be of type structure_tag_name having structure_variable as its name. Here, the term 'index' specifies the number of array objects. In the figure, this has been shown to be from 1 to N.

Example

19. Write a program to illustrate the use of array of structures.

```
#include <stdio.h>
struct test1
{
   char a;
   int i;
   float u;
}m[3];
int main()
{
   int n;
   for(n=0;n<=2;++n)
   {
      printf("\n Enter ch, in, fl:");
```

```
fflush(stdin);        /* clear stdin stream */
                      /* input the values of array
                                    of structures */
scanf("%c %d %f",&(m[n].a),&(m[n].i),&(m[n].u));
fflush(stdout);       /* clear stdout stream */
                      /* output the values of array
                                    of structures */
printf("\n a=%c, i=%d, u=%f", m[n].a, m[n].i, m[n].u);
  }
  return 0;
}
```

Output:

```
Enter ch, in, fl:g 45 678.1956
a=g, i=45, u=678.195618
Enter ch, in, fl:j 76 345.5674
a=j, i=76, u=345.567413
Enter ch, in, fl:k 69 123.333547
a=k, i=69, u=123.333549
```

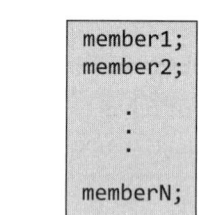

```
member1;
member2;
      .
      .
      .
memberN;
```

<structure_variable>[0]

```
member1;      member1;
member2;      member2;
   .    ...      .
   .             .
   .             .
memberN;      memberN;
```

<structure_variable>[1] <structure_variable>[N]

Figure 9.3 Array of structures

9.2.8 Initializing Arrays of Structures

Initializing arrays of structures is carried out in much the same way as arrays of standard data types. A typical construct for initialization of an array of structures would appear as follows.

```
struct <structure_tag_name >
                      /* structure declaration */
  {
    <data_type member_name_1>;
    <data_type member_name_2>;
          .
          .
    <data_type member_name_n>;
  };
/* declaration of structure array and initialization */
struct<structure_tag_name><structure_variable>[N]=
  {
    {constant01,constant02,...................constant0n},
    {constant11,constant12,...................constant1n},
          .

          .
    {constantN1,constantN2,...constantNn}};
```

The following example shows how the initialization technique referred to above is implemented.

Example

20. Write a program to print the tickets of the boarders of a boat using array of structures with initialization in the program.

```
#include <stdio.h>
struct boat      /** declaration of structure **/
{
  char name[20];
  int seatnum;
  float fare;
};
int main()
{
  int n;
  struct boat ticket[4]= {{"Vikram", 1,15.50},
      {"Krishna", 2,15.50}, {"Ramu", 3,25.50},
      {"Gouri", 4,25.50}};
                      /** initialization **/
  printf("\n Boarder Ticket num. Fare");
  for(n=0;n<=3;n++)
  printf("\n %s %d %f",ticket[n].name,ticket[n].
      seatnum,ticket[n].fare);
  return 0;
}
```

Output:

```
Boarder Ticket num. Fare
Vikram 1 15.500000
Krishna 2 15.500000
Ramu 3 25.500000
Gouri 4 25.500000
```

9.2.9 Arrays within the Structure

There can be arrays within a structure. In other words, any member within a structure can be an array. When arrays are used in a structure, they are accessed and initialized in a way similar to that illustrated in Example 20. In this example, name[20] is an array within the structure boat. Initialization of the structure means initialization of members: name[20], seatnum, and fare. The printf() statement within the for loop uses the dot operator to access the member name[20], an array, within the structure boat. Therefore, this example demonstrates how an array is used within a structure and also shows the way to initialize it.

Points to Note

1. By using typedef, no new data type is produced but an alternate name is given to a known data type.

2. typedef statements can be placed anywhere in a C program as long as they come prior to their first use in the code.

3. An innermost member in a nested structure can be accessed by chaining all the concerned structure variables, from outermost to innermost, with the member using the dot operator.

9.2.10 Structures and Pointers

At times it is useful to assign pointers to structures. A pointer to a structure is not itself a structure, but merely a variable that holds the address of a structure. This pointer variable takes four bytes of memory just like any other pointer in a 32-bit machine. Declaring pointers to structures is basically the same as declaring a normal pointer. A typical construct for declaring a pointer to a structure will appear as follows.

```
struct <structure_tag_name >
                    /* structure declaration */
  {
   <data_type member_name_1>;
   <data_type member_name_2>;
       .
       .
   <data_type member_name_n>;
  }*ptr;
```

or

```
struct <structure_tag_name>
  {
   <data_type member_name_1>;
   <data_type member_name_2>;
       .
       .
   <data_type member_name_n>;
  };
struct <structure_tag_name> *ptr;
```

This pointer, *ptr, can be assigned to any other pointer of the same type, and can be used to access the members of its structure. To access the members within the structure, the dot operator is used with the pointer variable. For example, to enable the pointer variable to access the member member_name_1, the following construct is used.

```
(*ptr).member_name_1
```

The bracket is needed to avoid confusion about the '*' and '.' operators. If the bracket around *ptr is done away with, the code will not compile because the '.' operator has a higher precedence than the '*' operator. It gets tedious to type so many brackets when working with pointers to structures. Hence C includes a shorthand notation that does exactly the same thing.

```
ptr-> member_name_1
```

This is less confusing and a better way to access a member in a structure through its pointer. The -> operator, an arrow made out of a minus sign and a greater than symbol, enables the programmer to access the members of a structure directly via its pointer. This statement means the same as the last line of the previous code example, but is considerably clearer. The -> operator will come in very handy when manipulating complex data structures.

For initializing the structure members through a pointer to the structure, any one of the following constructs is used.

```
(*ptr).member_name_x = constant;
```
or
```
ptr-> member_name_x = constant;
```

where x is 1 to N, and N is the total number of members in the structure. The following are examples using pointer to structure.

21. Write a program using a pointer to structure illustrating the initialization of the members in the structure.

```c
#include <stdio.h>
#include <conio.h>
struct test1
        /** declaration of structure "test" */
{
  char a;
  int i;
  float f;
};
int main()
{
    struct test1 pt; /* declaring pointer to the
                                    structure */
    clrscr();
    pt->a='K';          /* initializing char a */
    pt->i=15;           /* initializing int i */
    pt->f=27.89;        /* initializing float f */
    printf("\n a=%c, i=%d, f=%f",pt->a,pt->i,pt->f);
    printf("\n Enter new char, int, float:");
    scanf("%c %d %f",&pt->a,&pt->i,&pt->f);
                            /* input for members */
    printf("\n a=%c, i=%d, f=%f",pt->a,pt->i,pt->f);
    return 0;
}
                        /* function to link-in floating
                                point emulator */
void linkfloat()
{
  float a,*x;
  x=&a;
  a=*x;
}
```

Output:

```
a=k, i=15, f=27.889999
Enter new char, int, float: d 45 67.53
a=d, i=45, f=67.529999
```

The function `linkfloat()` needs to be explained. If this function is not included, the following error is generated.

```
scanf: floating point format not linked
Abnormal program termination
```

A similar message saying "floating point not loaded" is printed by the Microsoft C runtime system when the software needs a numeric coprocessor but the computer does not have one installed. One may fix it by returning the program using the floating-point emulation library.

A floating-point emulator is used to manipulate floating point numbers in runtime library functions such as `scanf()` and `atof()`. When compiling the source program if the compiler encounters a reference to the address of a float, it sets a flag to have the linker link in the floating-point emulator. In some cases in which reference to float seems to guess wrongly when the program uses floating point formats in `scanf()` but does not call any other floating point routines. The function `linkfloat()` forces linking of the floating point emulator into an application. There is no need to call this function. Just include it anywhere in the program. This provides a solid clue to the Borland PC linker that the floating-point library is need.

Another workaround is to define a function in a module that will be included in the link. The function is as follows:

```c
static void forcefloat (float *p)
{
  float f=*p;
  forcefloat(&f);
}
```

The problem can also be solved by including the following code in the program instead of the functions such as `linkfloat()` or `forcefloat()`.

```c
#include <math.h>
double dummy = sin(0.0);
```

This code forces the compiler to load the floating-point version of `scanf()`.

Examples

22. Write a program using a pointer to structure illustrating the initialization of the members in the structure using a different technique to avoid the floating point error problem.

```c
#include <stdio.h>
struct test1
{
  char a;
  int i;
  float f;
};
int main()
{
  float x;
  struct test1 *q,p;
  clrscr();
  printf("\n Enter char, int, float:");
  scanf("%c %d",&p.a,&p.i);
  scanf("%f",&x);
  p.f=x;
  q=&p;
  printf("\n a=%c, i=%d, f=%f",q->a,q->i,q->f);
  q=NULL;
  return 0;
}
```

Output:

```
Enter char, int, float:g 32 87.64
a=g, i=32, f=87.639999
```

23. Write a program using a pointer to structure illustrating the initialization of the members in the structure using `malloc()`.

```c
#include <stdio.h>
struct A
{
char ch;
int in;
float f;
};
int main()
{
  struct A *sp;
  int n,i;
  printf("\n How many members:");
```

```c
scanf("%d",&n);
sp=(struct A *)malloc(n*sizeof(struct A));
if(sp==NULL)
{
  printf("\n Memory allocation unsuccessful");
  exit(0);
}
for(i=0;i<n;++i)
{
printf("\n Enter ch, in and f:");
fflush(stdin);
scanf("%c %d %f",&sp[i].ch,&sp[i].in,&sp[i].f);
}
for(i=0;i<n;++i)
  printf("\n    ch=%c   in=%d   f=%f",sp[i].ch,
      sp[i].in, sp[i].f);
  return 0;
}
void linkfloat()
{
float a=0.0,*x;
x=&a;
a=*x;
}
```

Output:

```
How many members:2
Enter ch, in and f: g 31 76.56
Enter ch, in and f: k 32 78.34
ch=g in=31 f=76.559998
ch=k in=32 f=78.339996
```

There are many reasons for using a pointer to a struct. One of them is to make a two-way communication possible within functions. This aspect is explained with examples in the following section.

9.2.11 Structures and Functions

An entire structure can be passed as a function argument just like any other variable. When a structure is passed as an argument, each member of the structure is copied. In fact, each member is passed by value. In case the member is an array, a copy of this array is also passed. This can prove to be inefficient where structures are large or functions are called frequently. Passing and working with pointers to large structures may be more efficient in such cases. The general construct for passing a structure to a function and returning a structure is

```
struct structure_tag function_name(struct
          structure_tag structure_variable);
```

Several variations in this construct are made while using this construct. In some cases, the function may receive a structure but may return a void or some other data type. In another implementation, no parameters may be passed to a function but it may return a structure. Another option may be to pass a pointer to a structure and return any data type, including a user-defined structure. Hence, the preceding construct is formed based on the requirement. It must be noted that in any case the structure declaration and the definition of the structure variable should precede the function call construct stated above. The following are some examples involving structures with functions.

Examples

24. Write a program where a structure is passed to a function while it returns nothing.

```
#include <stdio.h>
struct A
{
  char ch;
  int in;
  float f;
};
void show(struct A);
int main()
{
  struct A a;
  printf("\n Enter ch, in and f:");
  fflush(stdin);
  scanf("%c %d %f",&a.ch,&a.in,&a.f);
  show(a);
  return 0;
}
/*** function show() ***/
void show(struct A b)
{
  printf("\n ch=%c, in=%d, f=%f",b.ch,b.in,b.f);
}
/*** function linkfloat() ***/
```

```
void linkfloat()
{
  float a=0.0,*x;
  x=&a;
  a=*x;
}
```

Output:

```
Enter ch, in and f:v 34 78.95
Ch=v, in=34, f=78.949997
```

25. Write a program that passes a pointer to a structure and returns nothing.

```
#include <stdio.h>
struct A
{
  char ch;
  int in;
  float f;
};
void read(struct A *);
 /* function prototype with pointer to structure
          as a parameter and void as return */
void show(struct A);
         /* function prototype with structure as
            a parameter and void as return */
int main()
{
  struct A a;
      /* declaring "a" as structure variable */
  read(&a);        /* call to function read() */
  show(a);
              /* call to function show() */
  return 0;
}
/*** function read() ***/
void read(struct A *p)
{
  printf("\n Enter ch, in and f:");
          /* request for values to members */
  fflush(stdin);        /* clear input stream */
  scanf("%c %d %f",&p->ch,&p->in,&p->f);
              /* input values to members */
}
/*** function show() ***/
```

```
void show(struct A b)
{
  printf("\n ch=%c in=%d f=%f",b.ch,b.in,b.f);
}
/*** function linkfloat() ***/
void linkfloat()
{
  float a=0.0,*x;
  x=&a;
  a=*x;
}
```

Output:

```
Enter ch, in and f:m 31 89.75
ch=m, in=31, f=89.75
```

26. Write a program using a function that does not require any parameter to be passed and returns a structure.

```
#include <stdio.h>
struct A
{
  char ch;
  int in;
  float f;
};
struct A read(void);
void show(struct A);
int main()
{
  struct A a;
  a=read();
  show(a);
  return 0;
}
struct A read(void)
{
  struct A p;
  printf("\n Enter ch, in and f:");
  fflush(stdin);
  scanf("%c %d %f",&p.ch,&p.in,&p.f);
  return p;
}
```

```
/*** function show() ***/
void show(struct A b)
{
  printf("\n ch=%c, in=%d, f=%f",b.ch,b.in,b.f);
}
/*** function linkfloat() ***/
void linkfloat()
{
  float a=0.0,*x;
  x=&a;
  a=*x;
}
```

Output:

```
Enter ch, in and f:g 30 92.55
ch=g, in=30, f=92.550003
```

From the preceding examples, it is evident that to modify the value of the members of the structure by a function, the programmer must pass a pointer to that structure to the function. This is just like passing a pointer to an int type argument whose value is to be changed.

If the programmer is only interested in one member of a structure, it is probably simpler to just pass that member to the function. This will make for a simpler function, which is easier to reuse. But, of course, if the value of that member has to be changed, a pointer to it should be passed to the function.

However, when a structure is passed as an argument to a function, each member of the structure is copied. This can prove expensive where structures are large or functions are called frequently. Passing and working with pointers to large structures may be more efficient in such cases.

Points to Note

1. A pointer to a structure is not itself a structure, but merely a variable that holds the address of a structure.
2. Passing and working with pointers to large structures may be more efficient while passing structures to a function and working within it.

9.3 UNION

A union is a structure all of whose members share the same storage. The amount of storage allocated to a union is sufficient to hold its largest member. At any given time, only one member of the union may actually reside in that storage. The way in which a union's storage is accessed depends, then, on the member name that is employed during the access. It is the programmer's responsibility to keep track of which member currently resides in a union.

A union is identified in C through the use of the keyword union in place of the keyword struct. Virtually all other methods for declaring and accessing unions are identical to those for structures.

9.3.1 Declaring a Union and its Members

The general construct for declaring a union is given as follows.

```
union tag_name
  {
    member1;
    member2;
        .
        .
    memberN;
    }variable1,variable2,variable3,…,variableX;
```

Similar to structure, the union also has a tag name, members, and variable names. In the preceding declaration construct, the variable names, variable1, variable2, variable3,…,variableX, are optional and therefore these may not be mentioned.

The general construct of declaring the individual union variables is

```
union tag_name variable1,variable2,…,variableX;
```

As an example, consider the following declarations for a union that has a tag named mixed.

```
union mixed
  {
    char letter;
    float radian;
    int  number;
    };
union mixed all;
```

The first declaration consists of a union of type *mixed*, which consists of a char, float, or int variable as a member. At a time only one member belonging to any one of the data types, that is char, int, or float, can exist. This is due to the provision of a single memory address that is used to store the largest variable, unlike the arrangement used for structures. Figure 9.4 depicts the way the three members letter, radian, and number are stored in memory, for a 16-bit machine.

Therefore, the variable all can only be a character, a float, or an integer at any one time. C keeps track of what all actually is at any given moment but does not provide a check to prevent the programmer accessing it incorrectly.

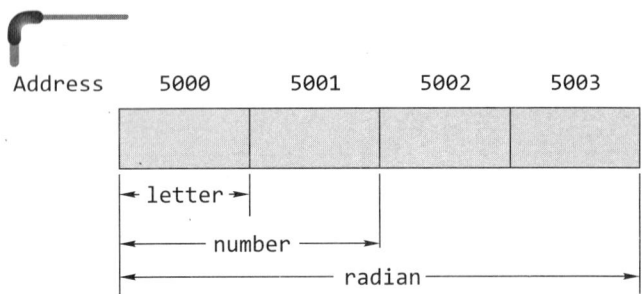

Figure 9.4 Three members of a union sharing a memory location for a 16-bit machine

It is evident from the previous example that a union is similar to a structure except that all the members in it are stored at the same address in memory. Therefore, only one member can exist in a union at any one time. The union data type was created to prevent the computer from breaking its memory up into several inefficiently sized pieces, which is called *memory fragmentation*.

The union data type avoids fragmentation by creating a standard size for certain data. When the computer allocates memory for a program, it usually does so in one large block of bytes. Every variable allocated when the program runs, occupies a segment of that block. When a variable is freed, it leaves a 'hole' in the block allocated for the program. If this hole is of an unusual size, the computer may have difficulty allocating another variable to 'fill' the hole, thus leading to inefficient memory usage. However, since unions have a standard data size, any 'hole' left in memory by freeing a union can be filled by another instance of the same type of union. A union works because the space allocated for it is the space taken by its largest member; thus, the small-scale tmemory inefficiency of allocating space for the worst case leads to memory efficiency on a larger scale.

Unions can also be a member of a structure. The following is an example showing such a structure.

```
struct conditions
  {
    float temp;
    union feels_like {
      float wind_chill;
      float heat_index;
      }
  } today;
```

As is known, `wind_chill` is only calculated when it is 'cold' and `heat_index` when it is 'hot'. There is no need for both at the same time. So when the `today` is specified, `feels_like` has only one value, either a float for `wind_chill` or a float for `heat_index`.

Within a `union`, data types can be of any kind; in fact it may even be of `struct` type.

9.3.2 Accessing and Initializing the Members of a Union

Consider, the general declaration construct of a union.

```
union tag_name
{
  member1;
  member2;
    ⋮
  memberN;
  }variable1,variable2,variable3,…,variableX;
```

For accessing members of, say, `variable1` to `N` of the union `tag_name`, the following constructs are used.

```
variable1.member1
variable2.member2
    ⋮
variableX.memberN
```

Only a member that exists at the particular instance in storage should be accessed. The general construct for individual initialization of a union member is

```
variableX.memberN = constant;
```

where `X` is any value `1` to `X` and `N` is any value `1` to `N`.

27. Write a program that illustrates the initialization of a member in a union.

```
#include <stdio.h>
#include <conio.h>
union test                /* declaration of union */
{
int i;                    /* integer member */
char c;                   /* character member */
}var;                     /* variable */
int main()
{
  var.i=65;     /* initializing integer member */
  printf("\n var.i=%d", var.i);
                          /* output integer member */
  printf("\n var.c=%c", var.c);
                          /* output character member */
  return 0;
}
```

Output:
```
var.i=65
var.c=A
```

Note See Fig. 9.5 for the storage location of union `test`.

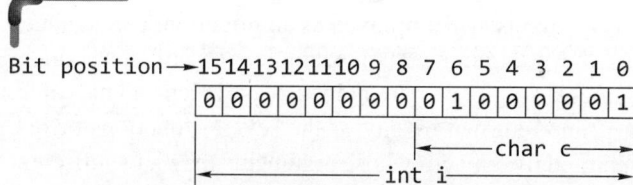

Bit position→15 14 13 12 11 10 9 8 7 6 5 4 3 2 1 0

| 0 | 0 | 0 | 0 | 0 | 0 | 0 | 0 | 0 | 1 | 0 | 0 | 0 | 0 | 0 | 1 |

char c
int i

Figure 9.5   The storage location of union `test`, for a 16-bit machine

Figure 9.5 shows the storage location of union `test`. The location has two bytes because the largest member in the union `test` is an integer named 'i'. The other member, 'c', being a character, occupies eight bits from bit 0 to bit 7. The integer member 'i' is assigned the value '65'. Hence, this value in binary form is stored in bits 0 to 15 as seen in the figure. So when `printf()` is executed, the value 65 for 'i' is printed on the screen. But the member 'c' has not been assigned any value. Therefore, the existing value of 65 in the referred storage location is taken when the `printf()` for the member 'char c' is executed. Referring to the ASCII table, the equivalent symbol for the decimal value 65 is 'A'. Thus when the second `printf()` is executed, the output is 'A'.

It must be remembered that while accessing member variables, the user should make sure that they can access the member whose value is currently in storage. For example, considering the union in Example 21, the following statements

```
var.i = 145;
var.c = 273.85;
printf("%d", var.i);
```

would produce an erroneous output. This results because the value assigned to var.c overlays the value assigned to var.i.

The initialization of only the first member of the union can be carried out during the declaration of the union variable. The initialization value must be of the same data type as the member. Again referring to Example 27, a declaration statement with initialization will appear as follows.

```
union test var={65};
```

Here, the value used to initialize the member 'i' is of the same data type as that of 'i'. But in this example, if the initialization value is a float data type, then the initialization will not be valid because the member 'i' is an integer data type. Therefore, the following construct will be wrong and invalid with reference to Example 27.

```
union test var={45.62};
```

A union is also employed as an important convenience for the programmer. For example, it is often useful to name a single cell to hold a type-independent value, say, one returned by any of the several functions or one returned by a macro whose arguments may have different types.

9.3.3 Structure versus Union

Memory allocation   The amount of memory required to store a structure is the sum of the size of all the members in addition to the slack bytes or padding bytes that may be provided by the compiler. On the other hand, in case of a union, the amount of the memory required is same as that of the largest member. This can be proved by the following program.

```
#include <stdio.h>
#include <stdlib.h>
#include <string.h>
struct S
{
  int i;
  char ch;
  double d;
};
union U
{
  int i;
  char ch;
  double d;
};
```

```
int main()
{
printf("\n Size of the structure is %d", sizeof
        (struct S));
printf("\n Size of the union is %d", sizeof(union U));
return 0;
}
```

Output:

```
Size of the structure is 16
Size of the union is 8
```

Member access   While all structure members can be accessed at any point of time, only one member of a union can be accessed at any given time. Because at a particular moment of time, only one union member will have a meaningful value. The other members have garbage values. It is the responsibility of the programmer to keep track of the active member. Consider the following program.

```
#include <stdio.h>
#include <stdlib.h>
#include <string.h>
struct S
{
  int i;
  char ch;
  double d;
};
union U
{
  int i;
  char ch;
  double d;
};
int main()
{
  struct S a={10,'A',3.1415};
  union U b={10,'A',3.1415};
  printf("\n a.i=%d a.ch=%c a.d=%lf",a.i,a.ch,a.d);
  printf("\n b.i=%d b.ch=%c b.d=%lf",b.i,b.ch,b.d);
  b.ch='B';
  printf("\n b.i=%d b.ch=%c b.d=%lf",b.i,b.ch,b.d);
  b.f=5.12345;
  printf("\n b.i=%d b.ch=%c b.d=%lf",b.i,b.ch,b.d);
  return 0;
}
```

Output:

```
a.i=10 a.ch=A a.d=3.141500
b.i=10 b.ch=
b.d=0.000000
b.i=66 b.ch=B b.d=0.000000
b.i=-1388133430 b.ch=Ê b.d=5.123450
```

Careful study reveals the aforesaid point.

Identifying active members There is no way to find which of the members is active at any moment of time. The program must keep track of active members explicitly.

Do's and don'ts for unions

Note It is important to remember which union member is being used. If the user fills in a member of one type and then tries to use a different type, the results can be unpredictable. The following operations on union variables are valid.

- A union variable can be assigned to another union variable.
- A union variable can be passed to a function as a parameter.
- The address of a union variable can be extracted by using & operator.
- A function can accept and return a union or a pointer to a union.
- *Don't* try to initialize more than the first union member.
- *Don't* forget that the size of a union is equal to its largest member.
- *Don't* perform arithmetical or logical operations on union variables.

Points to Note

1. At any given time, only one member of the union may actually reside in the storage.
2. In a union, the amount of memory required is same as that of the largest member.
3. It is important to remember which union member is being used. If the user fills in a member of one type and then tries to use a different type, the results can be unpredictable.
4. The following operations on union variables are valid:
   - A union variable can be assigned to another union variable.
   - A union variable can be passed to a function as a parameter.
   - The address of a union variable can be extracted by using & operator.
   - A function can accept and return a union or a pointer to a union.
5. No attempt should be made to initialize more than one union member.
6. Performing arithmetical or logical operations on union variables is not allowed.

9.4 ENUMERATION TYPES

Enumeration data types are data items whose values may be any member of a symbolically declared set of values. The symbolically declared members are integer constants. The keyword enum is used to declare an enumeration type. The general construct used to declare an enumeration type is

```
enum   tag_name{member1,   member2,…,   memberN}
           variable1,...,variableX;
```

In this declaration, either tag_name or variable may be omitted or both may be present. But at least one of them must exist in this declaration construct.

The enum tag_name specifies the user-defined type. The members are integer constants. By default, the first member, that is, member1, is given the value 0. The second member, member2, is given the value 1. Members within the braces may be initialized, in which case, the next member is given a value one more than the preceding member. So, each member is given the value of the previous member plus 1.

The general form of the construct for declaring variables of enum type separately is

```
enum tag_name variable1,...,variableX;
```

The variables can take on as values only the members in the member list. Therefore,

```
variable1 = member2;
```

assigns the value represented by member2 to variable1. A typical declaration would be

```
enum days {Mon, Tues, Wed, Thurs, Fri, Sat, Sun};
```

The above declaration means that the values 'Mon,...,Sun' may be assigned to a variable of type enum days. The actual values are 0,...,6 in this example and it is these values that must be associated with any input or output operations. The following example illustrates these features.

Example

28. Write a program to illustrate the assignment of default values to the members of data type enum.

```c
#include <stdio.h>
enum days{Mon, Tues, Wed, Thurs, Fri, Sat, Sun };
int main()
{
  enum days start, end;
  start= Tues;              /* means start=1 */
  end= Sat;                 /* means end=5  */
  printf("\n start = %d, end = %d", start,end);
```

```
    start= 64;
    printf("\n start now is equal to %d", start);
    return 0;
}
```

Output:

```
    start = 1, end = 5
    start now is equal to 64
```

It will be noticed that it is possible to assign a normal integer to an enum data type and no verification is carried out to find that an integer assigned to an enum data type is within range.

It is possible to associate numbers other than the sequence starting at zero with the names in the enum data type by including a specific initialization in the variable name list. This also affects the values associated with all the following variable names. For example, consider the following declaration construct.

```
enum coins{ p1=1, p2, p5=5, p10=10, p20=20, p50=50 };
```

Here, all the variables except p2 are initialized. Since p2 is next to p1, it will be assigned a value 2. Similar examples showing how the members in a enum data type are initialized are given below.

Example

29. Illustrations of initialization of members in enum data type

    (a) enum fruit {mango=10, orange, apple=6, pear}fru;

      Here, since mango is initialized to 10, orange has a value of 11. For the same reasons, because apple is assigned a value of 6, pear has a value of 7. It may be observed that multiple values initialization are allowed, but the member names must themselves be unique.

    (b) enum veg{tomato=15, beans=15, onions=15} veget1,veget2;

      Here, all the members are initialized with a value.

    (c) enum {teak,pine}tree;

      In this case, since no tag name has been specified, no other variable of type enum {teak,pine} can be declared.

    (d) enum veg{tomato,beans,onions}veg;

      The above example shows that a tag name can be reused as a variable name or as an enumerator. This is because the tag names have their own name space. Such usage, though valid, is not good programming practice.

      Few programmers use enum data types. The same effects can be achieved by use of #define although the scoping rules are different. The enum data types are rarely used in practice.

9.5 BITFIELDS

There are two ways to manipulate bits in C. One of the ways consists of using bitwise operators. The other way consists of using bitfields in which the definition and the access method are based on structure. The general format for declaring bitfields using a structure is given as follows.

```
struct bitfield_tag
  {
    unsigned int member1: bit_width1;
    unsigned int member2: bit_width2;
        ⋮
    unsigned int memberN: bit_widthN;
  };
```

In this construct, the declaration of variable name is optional. The construct for individually declaring the variables to this structure is given by

```
struct bitfield_tag variable_name;
```

Each bitfield, for example, 'unsigned int member1: bit_width1', is an integer that has a specified bit width. By this technique the exact number of bits required by the bitfield is specified. This way a whole word is not required to hold a field. This helps in packing a number of bitfields in one word. The savings made possible by using bits within a word rather than whole words can be considerable. This idea directly motivates the concept of packed fields of bits and operations on individual bits. Consider the following example.

```
struct test
{
  unsigned tx : 2;
  unsigned rx: 2;
  unsigned chk_sum : 3;
  unsigned p : 1;
} status_byte;
```

This construct declares a structure that has a variable name, status_byte, containing four unsigned bitfields. The number following the colon is the field width. Field variables may be assigned values. However, the value assigned to a field must not be greater than its maximum storable value. Individual fields are referenced as though they are structure members. The assignment

```
chk_sum = 6;
```

sets the bits in the field chk_sum as 110. The signed or unsigned specification makes for portability; this is important because bitfields are extremely implementation-dependent. For example, C does not specify whether fields must be stored left to right within a word, or vice versa. Some compilers may not allow fields to cross a word boundary. Unnamed fields may be used as fillers. In declaring the following structure, a two-bit gap is forced between the fields tx and rx.

```
struct
{
  unsigned tx : 2;
       : 2;
  unsigned rx : 4;
  }status;
```

The unnamed field of width 2 will cause the next field to begin in the following word instead of at the boundary of the last field. It should be noted that a field in a word has no address. Therefore, it is wrong to try and use the operator '&' with bitfields.

The use of bitfields may save some memory as against storing variables whose values are only going to be 1or 0 in characters, but it should be remembered that extra instructions will be required to perform the necessary packing and unpacking. Bitfields are very rarely used in practice.

Here is an example of assigning a byte to memory and then examining each bit. The bit fields are used in a structure, and the structure is used in a union.

```
#include <stdio.h>
#include <stdlib.h>
struct cbits {
  unsigned b1 : 1;
  unsigned b2 : 1;
  unsigned b3 : 1;
  unsigned b4 : 1;
  unsigned b5 : 1;
  unsigned b6 : 1;
  unsigned b7 : 1;
  unsigned b8 : 1;
};
union U {
  char c;
  struct cbits cb;
};
int main()
{
  union U look;
```

```
  /* Assign a character to memory */
  look.c = 'A';
  /* Look at each bit */
  printf( "\nBIT 1 = %d\n", look.cb.b1 );
  printf( "BIT 2 = %d\n", look.cb.b2 );
  printf( "BIT 3 = %d\n", look.cb.b3 );
  printf( "BIT 4 = %d\n", look.cb.b4 );
  printf( "BIT 5 = %d\n", look.cb.b5 );
  printf( "BIT 6 = %d\n", look.cb.b6 );
  printf( "BIT 7 = %d\n", look.cb.b7 );
  printf( "BIT 8 = %d\n\n", look.cb.b8 );
  return 0;
}
```

This program returns the bits (in terms of unsigned ints 0 or 1) for the character A stored in memory at the address of character variable named c. The output looks like this...

```
BIT 1 = 0
BIT 2 = 1
BIT 3 = 0
BIT 4 = 0
BIT 5 = 0
BIT 6 = 0
BIT 7 = 0
BIT 8 = 1
```

The output makes sense because 01000001 (binary) = 65 (decimal) = 101 (octal) = 41 (hexadecimal) which maps to an A in the ASCII character set. If one wants to do this with an integer, the size using the function sizeof(int) has to be first determined, then a structure is created with eight bit fields for each byte counted by sizeof(int).

Points to Note

1. The members in an enumerator are integer constants.
2. By default, the first member of a union is given the value 0.
3. With reference to bitfields, it should be noted that a field in a word has no address.

SUMMARY

A structure is a collection of variables under a single name. These variables can be of different types, and each has a name that is used to select it from the structure. There can be structures within structures, which is known as nesting of structures. Arrays of structures can be formed and initialized as required. Pointers may also be used with structures. Structures may be passed as function arguments and they may also be returned by functions.

A union is a structure, all of whose members share the same storage. The amount of storage allocated to a union is sufficient to hold its largest member. Enumeration data types are data items whose values may be any member of a symbolically declared set of values. Bitfields are identifiers whose bit-width can be specified and used to form packed words containing different fields.

KEY-TERMS

Accessing a structure member   The act of handling any member of a structure for the purpose of assigning a value or using the member in any expression.

Arrays of structures   It refers to the "structure variable" when it is an array of objects, each of which contains the member elements declared within the structure construct.

Initialization of structure   Assigning values to members of an instance variable.

Instance variable   One of the named pieces of data that make up a structure.

Non-homogeneous data   Data of different types such as integer, float, character, etc.

Structure   A collection of data grouped together and treated as a single object.

Type template   A document or file having a preset format, used as a starting point for a particular application so that the format does not have to be recreated each time it is used.

FREQUENTLY ASKED QUESTIONS

1. What is the difference between structure and union?

Memory allocation   The amount of memory required to store a structure is greater or equal to the sum of the size of all the members in addition to the slack bytes or padding bytes that may be provided by the compiler. On the other hand, in case of a union, the amount of the memory required is same as that of the largest member.

Member access   While all structure members can be accessed at any point of time, only one member of a union can be accessed at any given time. Because at a particular moment of time, only one union member will have a meaningful value. The other members have garbage values.

Identifying active members   There is no way to find which of the members is active at any moment of time. The program must keep track of active members explicitly.

2. Why can't structures be compared?

There can be unused padding bytes with structures as needed by alignment requirements for a platform and how they are filled is not defined by the standard. That's why a byte by byte comparison will also fail. This is because the comparison might fonder on random bits present in unused "holes" in the structure as padding used to keep the alignment of the later fields correct. So a memcmp() of the two structure will almost never work.

3. How can two structures be compared?

One way to compare two structures is comparing the individual fields in the structure.

4. Why do structures get padded?

Almost all modern processors support byte addressing, i.e. an address is the address of a byte. However there is often a constraint that larger data items (integers and floating-point numbers) should start at locations whose address is a multiple of the size of the data item. This constraint called, an alignment constraint, much simplifies the handling of such data items. Structure padding occurs because the members of the structure must appear at the correct byte boundary. This enables the CPU to access the members faster. If they are not aligned to word boundaries, then accessing them might take up more time. So the padding results in faster access.

Additionally the size of the structure must be such that in an array of the structures all the structures are correctly aligned in memory so there may be padding bytes (also known as slack bytes) at the end of the structure too.

5. How can the effect of padding be minimized?

Structure padding definitely introduces unused holes. There is no standard method to control the padding of structure. One way may be suggested that the order of the members of the structure be arranged from largest to smallest according to their respective sizes.

6. I get the following error message "Floating point formats not linked". What is wrong with the program?

When parsing the source file, if the compiler encounters, a reference to the address of a float, it sets a flag to have the linker link in the floating point emulator. A floating point emulator is used to manipulate floating point numbers in runtime of library functions like scanf() and atof() etc.

There are some cases in which the reference to the float does not necessitate the compiler to involve the emulator. The most common case is the one which uses scanf() to read a float in an array of structures and does not call any other functions related with floating point manipulation. In such cases the runtime error might be caused by giving the message " Floating point formats not linked ".

The solution of this problem is that the emulator will be used in such a fashion that the compiler can accurately determine when to link in the emulator. To force the floating point emulator to be linked into an application, just include the following functions in your program.

```
void FloatLink()
{
  float a = 0 , *b = &a;
  a = *b;
}
```

OR

```
static void forcefloat (float *p)
{
  float f=*p;
  forcefloat(&f);
}
```

There is no need to call these functions; just it is needed to include it anywhere in the program.

Another solution is to include the following statements at the top-level.

```
#include <math.h>

double dummy = sin(0.0);
```

This code forces the compiler to load the floating-point version of scanf().

EXERCISE

1. What is the difference between a structure and a union?

2. What is a member?

3. How is a structure different from an array?

4. What are member, tag, and variable name in a structure and what purpose do they serve?

5. What keyword is used in C to create a structure?

6. What is the difference between a structure tag and a structure instance?

7. What does the following code fragment do?

```
struct address {
    char name[31];
    char add1[31];
    char add2[31];
    char city[11];
    char state[3];
    char zip[11];
} myaddress = { "Barun Dasgupta",
        "Q_Software",
        "P.O. Box 1213",
        "Kolkata", "WB", "700 015"};
```

8. Assume you have declared an array of structures and that ptr is a pointer to the first array element (that is, the first structure in the array). How would you change ptr to point to the second array element?

9. Write a code that defines a structure named time, which contains three int members.

10. Write a code that performs two tasks: defines a structure named data that contains one type int member and two type float members, and declares an instance of type data named info.

11. Continuing with Exercise 10, how would you assign the value 100 to the integer member of the structure info?

12. Write a code that declares and initializes a pointer to info.

13. Continuing with Exercise 12, show two ways of using pointer notation to assign the value 5.5 to the first float member of info.

14. Define a structure type named data that can hold a single string of up to 20 characters.

15. Create a structure containing five strings: address1, address2, city, state, and zip. Create a typedef called RECORD that can be used to create instances of this structure.

16. Using the typedef from Exercise 15, allocate and initialize an element called myaddress.

17. What is wrong with the following code?

```
struct {
    char zodiac_sign[21];
    int month;
} sign = "Leo", 8;
```

18. What is wrong with the following code?

```
/* setting up a union */
```

```
union data{
    char a_word[4];
    long a_number;
}generic_variable = {"WOW", 1000};
```

19. What will be the output of the following program?

```
struct {
    int i;
    float f;
    }var;
int main()
{
    var.i=5;
    var.f=9.76723;
    printf("%d %.2f",var.i,var.f);
    return(0);
}
```

(a) Compile-time error

(b) 5 9.76723

(c) 5 9.76

(d) 5 9.77

20. What will be the output of the following program?

```
struct {
    int i;
    float f;
};
int main()
{
    int i=5;
    float f=9.76723;
    printf("%d %.2f",i,f);
    return(0);
}
```

(a) Compile-time error

(b) 5 9.76723

(c) 5 9.76

(d) 5 9.77

21. What will be the output of the following program?

```
struct values {
    int i;
    float f;
};
```

```
int main()
{
    struct values var={555,67.05501};
    printf("%2d %.2f",var.i,var.f);
    return(0);
}
```

(a) Compile-time error

(b) 55 67.05

(c) 555 67.06

(d) 555 67.05

22. What will be the output of the following program?

```
typedef struct {
    int i;
    float f;
    }values;
int main()
{
    static values var={555,67.05501};
    printf("%2d %.2f",var.i,var.f);
    return(0);
}
```

(a) Compile-time error

(b) 55 67.05

(c) 555 67.06

(d) 555 67.05

23. What will be the output of the following program?

```
struct my_struct {
    int i=7;
    float f=999.99;
    }var;
int main()
{
    var.i=5;
    printf("%d %.2f",var.i,var.f);
    return(0);
}
```

(a) Compile-time error

(b) 7 999.99

(c) 5 999.99

(d) None of these

24. What will be the output of the following program?
```
struct first {
  int a;
  float b;
  }s1={32760,12345.12345};
typedef struct {
  char a;
  int b;
  }second;
struct my_struct {
  float a;
  unsigned int b;
  };
typedef struct my_struct third;
int main()
{
  static second s2={'A',--4};
  third s3;
  s3.a=~(s1.a-32760);
  s3.b=-++s2.b;
  printf("%d%.2f\n%c%d\n%.
    2f %u",(s1.a)--,
    s1.b+0.005,s2.a+32,s2.b,
      ++(s3.a),--s3.b);
  return(0);
}
```
(a) Compile-time error
(b) 32760 12345.12
    A 4
    1 -5
(c) 32760 12345.13
    a -5
    0.00 65531
(d) 32760 12345.13
    a 5
    0.00 65530

25. What will be the output of the following program?
```
struct {
  int i,val[25];
```
```
  }var={1,2,3,4,5,6,7,8,9},
        *vptr=&var;
int main()
{
  printf("%d %d %d\n",var.i,,
          (vptr->i,(*vptr).i);
  printf("%d %d %d %d %d %d",
    var.val[4],*(var.val+4),vptr->val[4],
      *(vptr->val+4),(*vptr).val[4],
        *((*vptr).val+4));
  return(0);
}
```
(a) Compile-time error
(b) 1 1 1
    6 6 6 6 6 6
(c) 1 1 1
    5 5 5 5 5 5
(d) None of these

26. What will be the output of the following program?
```
typedef struct {
  int i;
  float f;
  }temp;
void alter(temp *ptr,int x,float y)
{
  ptr->i=x;
  ptr->f=y;
}
int main()
{
  temp a={111,777.007};
  printf("%d %.2f\n",a.i,a.f);
  alter(&a,222,666.006);
  printf("%d %.2f",a.i,a.f);
  return(0);
}
```
(a) Compile-time error
(b) 111 777.007
    222 666.006

(c) 111 777.01

222 666.01

(d) None of these

27. What will be the output of the following program?

```
union A {
    char ch;
    int i;
    float f;
}tempA;
int main()
{
    tempA.ch='A';
    tempA.i=777;
    tempA.f=12345.12345;
    printf("%d",tempA.i);
    return(0);
}
```

(a) Compile-time error

(b) 12345

(c) Erroneous output

(d) 777

28. Write a program using enumerated types which when given today's date will print out tomorrow's date in the form 31st January.

29. Write a simple database program that will store a person's details such as age, date of birth, and address.

Project Questions

1. Write a menu-based program in C that uses a set of functions to perform the following operations:
   (a) reading a complex number
   (b) writing a complex number
   (c) addition of two complex numbers
   (d) subtraction of two complex numbers
   (e) multiplication of two complex numbers
   Represent the complex number using a structure.

2. Declare a structure to store the following information of an employee-
   • Employee code
   • Employee name
   • Salary
   • Department number
   • Date of join(it is itself a structure consisting of day, month and year)

   Write a C program to store the data of 'n' employees where n is given by the user (Use dynamic memory allocation). Include a menu that will allow user to select any of the following features:
   (a) Use a function to display the employee information getting the maximum and minimum salary.
   (b) Use a function to display the employee records in ascending order according to their salary.
   (c) Use a function to display the employee records in ascending order according to their date of join.
   (d) Use a function to display the department wise employee records.

INCREMENTAL PROBLEM

The nature of the program for solving this problem has been changing with the use of different topics learnt in that particular chapter. Hence, the use of the "a user defined data type" in solving the incremental problem is being demonstrated here. Other than that similar functions and logic has been implemented as in the earlier chapter.

Problem statement

Check whether a triangle can be formed by determining the length of each side from the three given vertices and using the condition that in a triangle, the sum of any two sides is greater than the third side. Calculate the area of the triangle if it can be formed with the given vertices. Next, verify whether a given point is within or outside the triangle.

Solution

A two-dimensional point can be represented best by the following structure:

```
typedef struct
{
    int x;
    int y;
}Point;
```

Therefore, instead of a simple array, the vertices of the triangle are represented by an array of structure. The functions used perform the same tasks as in earlier chapters with some amendments in the parameters passed to them. The rest of the logic for determining whether the given point is within or outside the triangle is similar to that discussed in Chapter 7.

Program

The C Program for the problem using the derived data types, learnt in this chapter, is given as follows:

```c
#include <stdio.h>
#include <math.h>
typedef struct
{
    int x;
    int y;
}Point;
double getLength(Point,Point);
double getArea(double,double, double);
int insideOrOutside(Point [],Point);
int main(void)
{
    Point p[3],pt;
    int i,xx,yy;
    double a,b,c, area;
    printf("\n Enter the coordinates of the verti-
                ces of a triangle");
    for(i=0;i<3;++i)
    {
        printf("\n Enter x[%d]:",i);
        scanf("%d",&p[i].x);
        printf("\n Enter y[%d]:",i);
        scanf("%d",&p[i].y);
    }
    a=getLength(p[0],p[1]);
    b=getLength(p[1],p[2]);
    c=getLength(p[0],p[2]);
    if(a+b>c && b+c>a && c+a>b)
    {
        printf("Triangle can be drawn");
        area=getArea(a,b,c);
        printf("\n Area of triangle is %lf sq. units",
                area);
        printf("\n Enter the coordinates of the point:");
        printf("\n x cordinate:");
        scanf("%d",&pt.x);
        printf("\n y cordinate:");
        scanf("%d",&pt.y);
        if(insideOrOutside(p, pt))
            printf("\n Inside the triangle");
        else
            printf("\n Outside the triangle");
    }
    else
        printf("Triangle cannot be drawn");
    return 0;
}
double getLength(Point One, Point Two)
{
    int m, n;
    m=(One.x-Two.x)*(One.x-Two.x);
    n=(One.y-Two.y)*(One.y-Two.y);
    return sqrt((double)(m+n));
}
double getArea(double sA,double sB, double sC)
{
    double s;
    s=(sA+sB+sC)/2.0;
    return sqrt(s*(s-sA)*(s-sB)*(s-sC));
}
int insideOrOutside(Point p[],Point pt)
{
    int i,k;
    double d[3], area, sumArea=0.0,aa,bb;
    for(i=0;i<3;++i)
    {
        d[i]=getLength(p[i],p[(i+1)%3]);
    }
    area=getArea(d[0],d[1],d[2]);
    for(i=0;i<3;++i)
    {
        aa=getLength(pt,p[i]);
        bb=getLength(pt,p[(i+1)%3]);
        sumArea+=getArea(d[i],aa,bb);
    }
    if(fabs(area-sumArea)<0.00001)
    return 1;
    else
    return 0;
}
```

CASE STUDY

Problem Statement

A program has to be written that takes in student data and displays the same in the order of entry. It should provide the user the option to choose to the display of a particular student given the name or the roll number. Provision for displaying all the student records in ascending order of name or ascending order of grade should also be provided as options.

Analysis and Design

The primary feature of the program is to keep track of student records. Here a structure named `student` is declared with members `roll`, `name`, and `grade`. The number of records to be kept is given by the user and an array of structure is dynamically created. The following operations are performed using different functions.

- Displaying all student records
- Searching a student record
- Sorting the student records by name and grade

The algorithm of the main program is given as follows:

1. START
2. PRINT "ENTER THE NUMBER OF STUDENTS"
3. INPUT NUMBER_OF_STUDENT
4. ALLOCATE MEMORY SPACE S[NUMBER_OF_STUDENT] WHERE S IS A RECORD WITH FIELDS NAME, ROLL_ NUMBER AND GRADE
5. IF ALLOCATION OF MEMORY SPACE IS UNSUCCESSFUL GOTO 26
6. PRINT "ENTER STUDENT DATA"
7. CALL READ_DATA(S, NUMBER_OF_STUDENT)
8. PRINT "RECORDS OF ALL STUDENT"
9. CALL DISPLAY_ALL(S, NUMBER_OF_STUDENT)
10. PRINT "ENTER OPTIONS:
    1 FOR SEARCH
    2 FOR STUDENT RECORDS IN ALPHABETICAL ORDER
        OF THEIR NAME
    3 FOR STUDENT RECORDS IN DESCENDING ORDER OF
    THEIR GRADE
    4 EXIT "
11. INPUT OPTION
12. IF OPTION = 1 THEN GOTO 13
    ELSE IF OPTION = 2 THEN GOTO 16
    ELSE IF OPTION = 3 THEN GOTO 20
    ELSE IF OPTION = 4 THEN GOTO 27
    ELSE IF OPTION != 1 OR OPTION != 2 OR
    OPTION != 3 THEN GOTO 24
13. PRINT "SEARCH A STUDENT RECORD"
14. CALL SEARCH(S,NUMBER_OF_STUDENT)
15. GOTO 10
16. PRINT "RECORDS OF ALL STUDENT IN ASCENDING
    ORDER OF THEIR NAME"
17. CALL SORT_BY_NAME(S, NUMBER_OF_STUDENT)
18. CALL DISPLAY_ALL(S, NUMBER_OF_STUDENT)
19. GOTO 10
20. PRINT "RECORDS OF ALL STUDENT IN ASCENDING
    ORDER OF THEIR GRADE"
21. CALL SORT_BY_GRADE(S, NUMBER_OF_STUDENT)
22. CALL DISPLAY_ALL(S, NUMBER_OF_STUDENT)
23. GOTO 10
24. PRINT "ERROR IN CHOOSING OPTIONS"
25. GOTO 10
26. PRINT "ALLOCATION OF MEMORY SPACE UNSUCCESSFUL"
27. STOP

The algorithm of READ_DATA(S, NUMBER_OF_STUDENT) function is given as follows:

1. START
2. I ← 0
3. PRINT "ENTER NAME, ROLLNUMBER AND GRADE"
4. INPUT S[I].NAME, S[I].ROLL _NUMBER , S[I].GRADE
5. I ← I + 1
6. IF I < NUMBER_OF_STUDENT GOTO 3
7. RETURN

The algorithm of DISPLAY_ALL(S, NUMBER_OF_STUDENT) function is given as follows:

1. START
2. I ← 0
3. PRINT S[I].NAME, S[I].ROLL_NUMBER , S[I].GRADE
4. I ← I + 1
5. IF I < NUMBER_OF_STUDENT GOTO 3
6. RETURN

The algorithm of SEARCH(S, NUMBER_OF_STUDENT) function is given as follows:

1. START
2. PRINT "ENTER OPTIONS:
    FOR SEARCH BY ROLL NUMBER
    FOR SEARCH BY NAME
    FOR EXIT"
3. INPUT OPTION
4. IF OPTION = 1 THEN GOTO 8
5. ELSE IF OPTION = 2 THEN GOTO 10
6. ELSE IF OPTION = 3 THEN GOTO 14
7. ELSE IF OPTION != 1 OR OPTION != 2 OR
   OPTION!= 3 GOTO 12
8. CALL SEARCH_BY_ROLL(S, NUMBER_OF_STUDENT)
9. GOTO 15
10. CALL SEARCH_BY_ NAME(S, NUMBER_OF_STUDENT)
11. GOTO 15
12. PRINT "ERROR IN CHOOSING OPTIONS"
13. GOTO 2
14. RETURN

The algorithm of SEARCH_BY_ROLL(S, N) function is given as follows:

```
1.  START
2.  FOUND ← 0
3.  PRINT "ENTER STUDENT ROLL NUMBER TO SEARCH"
4.  INPUT R
5.  I ← 0
6.  IF R = S[I].ROLL_NUMBER THEN FOUND ← 1 :GOTO 11
7.  I ← I + 1
8.  IF I < N GOTO 6
9.  IF FOUND = 0 THEN PRINT "RECORD DOES NOT EXIST"
10. GOTO 12
11. PRINT S[I].ROLL_NUMBER, S[I].NAME AND S[I].
    GRADE
12. RETURN
```

The algorithm of SEARCH_BY_NAME (S, N) function is given as follows:

```
1.  START
2.  FOUND ← 0
3.  PRINT "ENTER STUDENT NAME TO SEARCH"
4.  INPUT TNAME
5.  I ← 0
6.  IF TNAME = S[I].NAME THEN FOUND ← 1 : GOTO 11
7.  ELSE I ← I + 1
8.  IF I < N GOTO 6
9.  IF FOUND = 0 THEN PRINT "RECORD DOES NOT EXIST"
10. GOTO 12
11. PRINT S[I].ROLL_NUMBER, S[I].NAME, S[I].GRADE
12. RETURN
```

The algorithm of SORT_BY_NAME (S, N) function is given as follows:

```
1.  START
2.  I ← 0
3.  J ← 0
4.  IF S[J].NAME >S[J+1].NAME THEN TEMP ← S[J] :
    S[J] ← S[J + 1]: S[J + 1] ← TEMP
5.  J ← J + 1
6.  IF J < N - I - 1 THEN GO TO 4
7.  I ← I + 1
8.  IF I < N - 1 THEN GOTO 3
9.  RETURN
```

The algorithm of SORT_BY_GRADE (S, N) function is given as follows:

```
1.  START
2.  I ← 0
3.  J ← 0
4.  IF S[J].GRADE <S[J+1].GRADE THEN TEMP ← S[J]
    : S[J] ← S[J + 1] : S[J + 1] ← TEMP
5.  J ← J + 1
```

```
6.  IF J < N - I - 1 THEN GO TO 4
7.  I ← I + 1
8.  IF I < N - 1 THEN GOTO 3
9.  RETURN
```

The program for the problem is given below:

```c
#include <stdio.h>
#include <stdlib.h>
#include <string.h>

struct student
{
  int roll;
  char name[50];
  float grade;
};

void readdata(struct student *, int);
void displayall(struct student *, int);
void sortbyname(struct student *, int);
void sortbygrade(struct student *, int);
void search(struct student *, int);

int main()
{

  struct student *s;
  int n;
  char flag;

  printf("\n\n ENTER THE NUMBER OF STUDENTS... ");
  scanf("%d", &n);
  s=(struct student *)malloc(n*sizeof(struct student));
  if(s==NULL)
  {
    printf("\nMEMORY ALLOCATION UNSUCCESSFUL\n");
    exit(0);
  }

  printf("\n\n ENTER THE STUDENT RECORDS....\n");
  readdata(s,n);     /* enter data of all student */
  printf("\n\n RECORDS OF ALL STUDENTS...... \n");
  displayall(s,n);     /* print data of students in
                            the order of entry */

  while(1)
  {
    printf("\n\n CHOOSE OPTIONS: \n 1 for SEARCH \n 2
            for STUDENT RECORD IN ORDER\ OF NAME \n 3
            for STUDENT RECORD IN ORDER OF GRADE \n 4
            EXIT \n");

    fflush(stdin);
scanf("%c",&flag);
```

```
switch(flag)
{

  case '1':
    printf("\n\n SEARCH A STUDENT RECORD.... \n");
    search(s,n);    /* find the data of the specified
                       student and print the same*/
    break;

  case '2':
    printf("\n\n RECORDS OF ALL STUDENTS ");
    printf("(in ascending order of their name) \n");
    sortbyname(s,n);
    displayall(s,n); /* print data of all students
                        in ascending order */
    break;

  case '3':
    printf("\n\n RECORDS OF ALL STUDENTS ");
    printf("(in ascending order of their GRADE) \n");
    sortbygrade(s,n);
    displayall(s,n); /* print data of all students
               in ascending order of their grade*/
    break;

  case '4':
    printf("\n\n Exit");
    exit(0);

  default:
    printf("error choosing options");
    break;
  }
}

  free(s);      /* free the allocated space */
  s=NULL;
  return 0;
  }
void readdata(struct student *s, int n)
 {
  int i;
  for(i=0; i<n; ++i)
  {
   printf("\n ROLL NUMBER ?:");
   scanf("%d",&s[i].roll);
   printf("\n NAME     ?:");
   fflush(stdin);
   scanf("%[^\n]",s[i].name);
   printf("\n GRADE     ?:");
   scanf("%f",&s[i].grade);
  }
 }
```

```
void displayall(struct student *s, int n)
{
 int i;
 for(i=0; i<n; ++i)
 {
  printf("\n %d \t %s \t %.2f",s[i].roll, s[i].
      name, s[i].grade);

 }
 }

void search(struct student *s, int n)
{
 int ch;
 void searchbyroll(struct student *, int);
 void searchbyname(struct student *, int);

 while(1)
 {
  printf("\n 1. SEARCH BY ROLL NUMBER ");
  printf("\n 2. SEARCH BY NAME ");
  printf("\n 3. EXIT ");
  printf("\n ENTER YOUR CHOICE... ");
  scanf("%d", &ch);
  switch(ch)
  {
    case 1:searchbyroll(s,n); break;
    case 2:searchbyname(s,n); break;
    case 3:return;
    default: printf("\n WRONG CHOICE\n");
  }
 }
 }

void searchbyroll(struct student *s, int n)
{
 int i,r,found=0;
 printf("\n ENTER ROLL TO SEARCH....");
 scanf("%d",&r);
 for(i=0; i<n; ++i)
 {
   if(s[i].roll==r)
   {
      printf("\n %d \t %s \t %.2f",s[i].roll,
         s[i].name, s[i].grade);
      found=1;
      break;
   }
  }

 if(found==0)
  printf("\n\a RECORD DOES NOT EXIST.");
 }
```

```c
void searchbyname(struct student *s, int n)
{
 int i,found=0;
 char name[50];
 printf("\n ENTER NAME TO SEARCH....");
 fflush(stdin);
 scanf("%[^\n]",&name);
  for(i=0; i<n; ++i)
   {
    if(strcmpi(s[i].name,name)==0)
     {
      printf("\n %d \t %s \t %.2f",s[i].roll,
          s[i].name, s[i].grade);
      found=1;
     }
   }
  if(found==0)
     printf("\n\aRECORD DOES NOT EXIST.");
}

void sortbyname(struct student *s, int n)
{
 int i,j;
 struct student t;
 for(i=0;i<n-1;++i)
     for(j=0; j<n-i-1; ++j)
         if(strcmpi(s[j].name, s[j+1].name)>0)
   {
     t=s[j];
     s[j]=s[j+1];
     s[j+1]=t;
   }
}

void sortbygrade(struct student *s, int n)
{
 int i,j;
 struct student t;
 for(i=0;i<n-1;++i)
    for(j=0; j<n-i-1; ++j)
        if(s[j].grade<s[j+1].grade)
   {
    t=s[j];
    s[j]=s[j+1];
    s[j+1]=t;
   }
}
```

The following program keeps track of student records. Here a structure named student is declared with members roll, name, and grade. The number of records to be kept is given by the user and an array of structure is dynamically created. The following operations are performed using different functions.

- Displaying all student records
- Searching a student record
- Sorting the student records by name and grade

```c
#include <stdio.h>
#include <stdlib.h>
#include <string.h>

struct student
{
    int roll;
    char name[50];
    float grade;
};

void readdata(struct student *, int);
void displayall(struct student *, int);
void sortbyname(struct student *, int);
void sortbygrade(struct student *, int);
void search(struct student *, int);

int main()
{
    struct student *s;
    int n;
    printf("\n\n ENTER THE NUMBER OF STUDENTS...");
    scanf("%d", &n);
    s=(struct student *)malloc(n*sizeof(struct
        student));
    if(s==NULL)
    {
        printf("\nMEMORY ALLOCATION
        UNSUCCESSFUL\n");
        exit(0);
    }

    printf("\n\n ENTER THE STUDENT RECORDS....\n");
    readdata(s,n);

    printf("\n\n RECORDS OF ALL STUDENTS...... \n");
    displayall(s,n);
    printf("\n\n SEARCH A STUDENT RECORD...... \n");
    search(s,n);

    printf("\n\n RECORDS OF ALL STUDENTS ");
    printf("(in ascending order of their name) \n");
    sortbyname(s,n);
    displayall(s,n);
    printf("\n\n RECORDS OF ALL STUDENTS ");
    printf("(in ascending order of their roll
        number) \n");
```

```
    sortbygrade(s,n);
    displayall(s,n);
    free(s);
    s=NULL;
    return 0;
}

void readdata(struct student *s, int n)
{
    int i;
    for(i=0; i<n; ++i)
    {
        printf("\n ROLL NUMBER ?:");
        scanf("%d",&s[i].roll);
        printf("\n NAME     ?:");
        fflush(stdin);
        scanf("%[^\n]",s[i].name);
        printf("\n GRADE    ?:");
        scanf("%f",&s[i].grade);
    }
}

void displayall(struct student *s, int n)
{
    int i;
    for(i=0; i<n; ++i)
    {
        printf("\n %d \t %s \t %.2f",s[i].roll,
            s[i].name, s[i].grade);
    }
}

void search(struct student *s, int n)
{
    int ch;
    void searchbyroll(struct student *, int);
    void searchbyname(struct student *, int);
    while(1)
    {
        printf("\n 1. SEARCH BY ROLL NUMBER");
        printf("\n 2. SEARCH BY NAME");
        printf("\n 3. EXIT");
        printf("\n ENTER YOUR CHOICE...");
        scanf("%d", &ch);
        switch(ch)
        {
            case 1:searchbyroll(s,n); break;
            case 2:searchbyname(s,n); break;
            case 3:return;
            default: printf("\n WRONG
CHOICE\n");
        }
    }
}

void searchbyroll(struct student *s, int n)
{
    int i,r,found=0;
    printf("\n ENTER ROLL TO SEARCH....");
    scanf("%d",&r);
    for(i=0; i<n; ++i)
    {
        if(s[i].roll==r)
        {
            printf("\n %d \t %s \t %.2f",s[i].roll,
                s[i].name, s[i].grade);
            found=1;
            break;
        }
    }
    if(found==0)
    printf("\n\a RECORD DOES NOT EXIST.");
}
void searchbyname(struct student *s, int n)
{
    int i,found=0;
    char name[50];
    printf("\n ENTER NAME TO SEARCH....");
    fflush(stdin);
    scanf("%[^\n]",&name);
    for(i=0; i<n; ++i)
    {
        if(strcmpi(s[i].name,name)==0)
        {
            printf("\n %d \t %s \t %.2f",s[i].roll,
                s[i].name, s[i].grade);
            found=1;
        }
    }
    if(found==0)
    printf("\n\aRECORD DOES NOT EXIST.");
}
void sortbyname(struct student *s, int n)
{
    int i,j;
```

```
    struct student t;                           {
    for(i=0;i<n-1;++i)                              int i,j;
    for(j=0; j<n-i-1; ++j)                          struct student t;
    if(strcmpi(s[j].name, s[j+1].name)>0)           for(i=0;i<n-1;++i)
    {                                               for(j=0; j<n-i-1; ++j)
        t=s[j];                                     if(s[j].grade>s[j+1].grade)
        s[j]=s[j+1];                                {
        s[j+1]=t;                                       t=s[j];
    }                                                   s[j]=s[j+1];
}                                                       s[j+1]=t;
                                                    }
void sortbygrade(struct student *s, int n)      }
```

C

Chapter 10

Files in C

Learning Objectives

After reading this chapter, the readers will be able to

- understand the concept of streams used in the C file system
- know about text and binary files
- comprehend how to process text files as well as binary files using standard library functions
- know about the sequential and random access of data stored in a disk file using proper standard library functions
- have an overview of advanced file management system and low-level input and output

10.1 INTRODUCTION

A file is a repository of data that is stored in a permanent storage media, mainly in secondary memory. So far, data was entered into the programs through the computer's keyboard. This is somewhat laborious if there is a lot of data to process. The solution is to combine all the input data into a file and let the C program read the information from the file when it is required. Frequently files are used for storing information that can be processed by the programs. Files are not only used for storing data,

programs are also stored in files. The editor, which is used to write or edit programs and save, simply manipulates files for the programmer. The Unix commands cat, cp, and cmp are all programs which process the files.

In order to use files one has to learn about *file I/O*, i.e., how to write information to a file, and how to read information from a file. It will be seen that file I/O is almost identical to the terminal I/O that has been used so far. The primary difference between manipulating files and terminal I/O is that the programs must specify which files are to be used because there are many files on the disk. Specifying the file to use is referred to as *opening* the file. When one opens a file, what is to be done with the file must also be mentioned, i.e., read from the file, write to the file, or both.

A very important concept in C is the *stream*. The stream is a common, logical interface to the various devices that comprise the computer. In its most common form, a stream is a logical interface to a file. As defined by C, the term 'file' can refer to a disk file, the screen, the keyboard, a port, a file on tape, and so on. Although files differ in form and capabilities, all streams are the same. The stream provides a consistent interface to the programmer. Stream I/O uses some temporary storage area, called buffer, for reading from or writing data to a file. This is illustrated in Fig. 10.1.

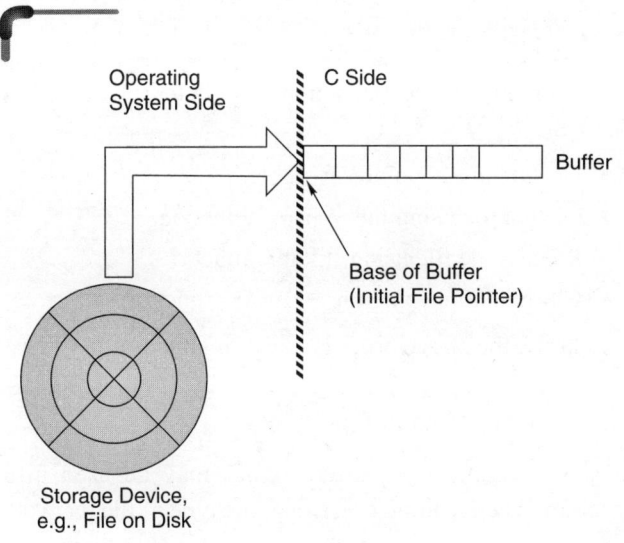

Figure 10.1   Stream I/O model

The figure models an efficient I/O. When a stream linked to a disk file is created, a buffer is automatically created and associated with the stream. A buffer is a block of memory used for temporary storage of data being written to and read from the file. Buffers are needed because disk drives are block-oriented devices. This means that they operate most efficiently when data is read and written in blocks of a certain size. The size of the ideal block differs, depending on the specific hardware in use. It is typically of the order of a few hundred to a thousand bytes. However, it is not necessary to be concerned about the exact block size.

The buffer associated with a file stream serves as an interface between the stream (which is character-oriented) and the disk hardware (which is block-oriented). As the program writes data to the stream, the data is saved in the buffer until it is full, and then the entire contents of the buffer are written, as a block, to the disk. A similar process takes place when reading data from a disk file. The creation and operation of the buffer are handled by the operating system and are entirely automatic; the programmer does not have to be concerned with them. C does offer some functions for buffer manipulation. In practical terms, this buffer operation means that during program execution, data that the program wrote to the disk might still be in the buffer, and not on the disk. If the program hangs up, because of a power failure, or in case of some other problem, the data that is still in the buffer might be lost, and the user will not know what is contained in the disk file. That is, data resides in the buffer until the buffer is flushed or written out into file. Any abnormal exit of code may cause problems.

A stream is linked to a file while using an open operation. A stream is disassociated from a file while using a close operation. The current location, also referred to as the current position, is the location in a file where the next file access will occur.

There are two types of streams: *text* and *binary*. A text file can be thought of as a stream of characters that can be processed sequentially. It can only be processed (logically) in the forward direction. For this reason a text file is usually opened for only one kind of operation, that is reading or writing or appending, at any given time. Similarly, since text files only process characters, they can only read or write one character at a time. Functions are provided that deal with lines of text, but these still essentially process one character at a time.

As text streams are associated with text files, they may contain a sequence of lines. Each line contains zero or more characters and ends with one or more characters that specify the end of the line. The maximum number of characters in each line is limited to 255 characters. It is important to remember that a 'line' is not a C string; there is no terminating NUL character ('\0'). When a text-mode stream is used, translation occurs between C's new-line character (\n) and whatever character(s) the operating system uses to mark end-of-line on disk files. On DOS systems, it is a carriage-return linefeed (CR-LF) combination. When data is written to a text-mode file, each '\n' is translated to a CR-LF; when data is read from a disk file, each CR-LF is translated to a '\n'. On Unix systems, no translation is done; new-line characters remain unchanged.

When text data files are used, there are two representations of data—*internal* and *external*. For example, a value of type int will usually be represented internally as two- or four-bytes (16- or 32-bit) of memory. Externally, though, that integer will be represented as a string of characters representing its decimal or hexadecimal value. Conversion between the internal and external representations is very easy. To convert from the internal representation to the external, printf or fprintf is used in almost all cases. For example, to convert an int %d or %i format might be used. To convert from the external representation to the internal, scanf or fscanf can be used, or the characters are read and then functions such as atoi, strtol, or sscanf are used.

Binary file is a collection of bytes. In C, a byte and a character are equivalent. Hence, a binary file is also referred to as a character stream, but there are two essential differences.

Firstly, the data that is written into and read from remain unchanged, with no separation between lines and no use of end-of-line characters. The NULL and end-of-line characters have no special significance and are treated like any other byte of data.

Secondly, the interpretation of the file is left to the programmer. C places no construct on the file, and it may be read from, or written to, in any manner chosen by the programmer.

In C, processing a file using random access techniques involves moving the current file position to an appropriate place in the file before reading or writing data. This indicates a second characteristic of binary files—they are generally processed using read and write operations simultaneously. For example, a database file will be created and processed as a binary file. A record update operation will involve locating the appropriate record, reading the record into memory, modifying it in some way, and finally writing the record back to disk at its appropriate location in the file. These kind of operations are common to many binary files, but are rarely found in applications that process text files.

Some file input/output functions are restricted to one file mode, whereas other functions can use either mode.

Points to Note

- When one opens a file, the operation that has to be carried on the file must also be specified, i.e., read from the file, write to the file, or both.
- C treats a disk file like a stream which can be opened either in text or in binary mode.
- The maximum number of characters in each line is limited to 255 characters.
- A 'line' of a text stream is not a C string; thus there is no terminating NULL character ('\0').
- In a binary file, the NULL and end-of-line characters have no special significance and are treated like any other byte of data.
- C places no construct on the binary file, and it may be read from, or written to, in any manner chosen by the programmer.

10.2 USING FILES IN C

To use a file four essential actions should to be carried out. These are

- Declare a file pointer variable.
- Open a file using the fopen() function.
- Process the file using suitable functions.
- Close the file using the fclose() function.

For clarity, the above order is not maintained.

10.2.1 Declaration of File Pointer

Because a number of different files may be used in a program, when reading or writing, the type of file that is to be used must be specified. This is accomplished by using a variable called a file pointer, a pointer variable that points to a structure FILE. FILE is a structure declared in stdio.h. The members of the FILE structure are used by the program in various file access operations, but programmers do not need to be concerned about them. However, for each file that is to be opened, a pointer to type FILE must be declared.

When the function fopen() is called, that function creates an instance of the FILE structure and returns a pointer to that structure. This pointer is used in all subsequent operations on the file. The syntax for declaring file pointers is as follows.

```
FILE *file_pointer_name,…;
```

For example,

```
FILE *ifp;
FILE *ofp;
```

declares ifp and ofp to be FILE pointers. Or, the two FILE pointers can be declared in just one declaration statement as shown below.

```
FILE *ifp, *ofp;
```

The * must be repeated for each variable.

10.2.2 Opening a File

To open a file and associate it with a stream, the fopen() function is used. Its prototype is as follows.

```
FILE *fopen(const char *fname, const char *mode);
```

File-handling functions are prototyped in <stdio.h>, which also includes other needed declarations. Naturally, this header must be included in all the programs that work with files. The name of the file to be opened is pointed to by fname , which must be a valid name. The string pointed at for mode determines how the file may be accessed.

Every disk file must have a name, and filenames must be used when dealing with disk files. The rules for acceptable filenames differ from one operating system to another. In DOS, a complete filename consists of a name that has one to eight characters, optionally followed by a period and an extension that has from one to three characters. In contrast, the Windows operating systems as well as most Unix systems permit filenames with up to 256 characters.

Readers must be aware of the filename rules of the operating system they are using. In Windows, for example, characters such as the following are not permitted: /, \, :, *, ?, ", <, >, and |.

A filename in a C program can also contain path information. The *path* specifies the drive and/or directory (or folder) where the file is located. If a filename is specified without a path, it will be assumed that the file is located wherever the operating system currently designates as the default. It is good programming practice to always specify path information as part of the filename. On PCs, the backslash character (\ ) is used to separate directory names in a path. For example, in DOS and Windows, the name

```
c:\examdata\marks.txt
```

refers to a file named marks.txt in the directory \examdata on drive C. It is to be remembered that the backslash character has a special meaning to C with respect to escape sequence when it is in a string. To represent the backslash character itself, one must precede it with another backslash. Thus, in a C program, the filename would be represented as follows.

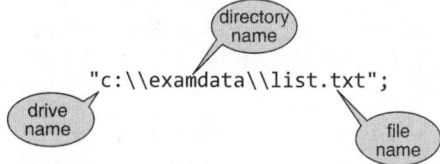

However, if the filename is entered by the user through the keyboard, a single backslash has to be entered. Not all systems use the backslash as the directory separator. For example,

```
Unix uses the forward slash (/).
```

File Modes—What Sort of Open

Before a file can be used for reading or writing, it must be opened. This is done through the fopen() function. fopen() takes two string arguments. The first of these is the filename; the second is an option that conveys to C what processing is to be done with the file: read it, write to it, append to it, etc. Table 10.1 lists the options available with fopen().

Table 10.1 File opening modes

Mode	Meaning
r	Open a text file for reading
w	Create a text file for writing
a	Append to a text file
rb	Open a binary file for reading
wb	Open a binary file for writing
ab	Append to a binary file
r+	Open a text file for read/write
w+	Create a text file for read/write
a+	Append or create a text file for read/write
r+b	Open a binary file for read/write
w+b	Create a binary file for read/write
a+b	Append a binary file for read/write

The following statements are used to create a text file with the name data.dat under current directory. It is opened in w mode as data are to be written into the file data.dat.

```
FILE *fp;
fp = fopen("data.dat","w");
```

fopen() requires two parameters—both are character strings. Either parameter could be a string variable. Following is an example where a file pointer " fp" is declared, the file name, which is declared to contain a maximum of 80 characters, is obtained from the keyboard and then the file is opened in the "write" mode.

```
char filename[80];
FILE *fp;
printf("Enter the filename to be opened");
gets(filename);
fp = fopen(filename,"w");
```

Checking the Result of Fopen()

The fopen() function returns a FILE *, which is a pointer to structure FILE, that can then be used to access the file. When the file cannot be opened due to reasons described below, fopen() will return NULL. The reasons include the following.

- Use of an invalid filename
- Attempt to open a file on a disk that is not ready; for example, the drive door is not closed or the disk is not formatted.
- Attempt to open a file in a non-existent directory or on a non-existent disk drive
- Attempt to open a non-existent file in mode r

One may check to see whether fopen() succeeds or fails by writing the following set of statements.

```
fp = fopen("data.dat","r");

if(fp == NULL)
{
   printf("Can not open data.dat\n");
   exit(1);
}
```

attempts to open the file named "data.dat" in read mode

Alternatively, the above segment of code can be written as follows.

```
FILE *fp;
if((fp = fopen("data.dat", "r")) ==NULL)
{
   printf("Can not open data.dat\n");
   exit(1);
}
```

Whenever fopen() is used in a program, it is recommended to test for the result of an fopen() and check whether it is NULL or not. There is no way to find exactly which error has occurred, but one can display an error message to the user and try to open the file again, or end the program.

10.2.3 Closing and Flushing Files

After completing the processing on the file, the file must be closed using the fclose()function. Its prototype is

```
int fclose(FILE *fp);
```

The argument fp is the FILE pointer associated with the stream; fclose() returns 0 on success or -1 on error. When a program terminates (either by reaching the end of main() or by executing the exit() function), all streams are automatically flushed and closed. Actually, in a simple program, it is not necessary to close the file because the system closes all open files before returning to the operating system. It would be a good programming practice to get into the habit of closing all files explicitly.

When a file is closed, the file's buffer is flushed or written to the file. All open streams except the standard ones (stdin, stdout, stdprn, stderr, and stdaux) can also be closed by using the fcloseall() function. Its prototype is int fcloseall(void);

The above function also flushes any stream buffers and returns the number of streams closed. A stream's buffers can be flushed without closing it by using the fflush() or flushall() library functions. Use fflush() when a file's buffer is to be written to disk while still using the file. Use flushall() to flush the buffers of all open streams. The prototypes of these two functions are

```
int fflush(FILE *fp);
int flushall(void);
```

The argument fp is the FILE pointer returned by fopen() when the file was opened. If a file was opened for writing, fflush() writes its buffer to disk. If the file was opened for reading, the buffer is cleared. The function fflush() returns 0 on success or EOF if an error occurred. The function flushall() returns the number of open streams.

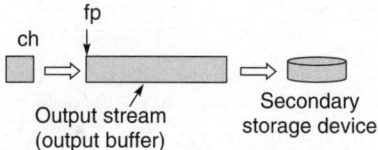

Output stream
(output buffer)

Secondary
storage device

10.3 WORKING WITH TEXT FILES

C provides four functions that can be used to read text files from the disk. These are

- fscanf()
- fgets()
- fgetc()
- fread()

C provides four functions that can be used to write text files into the disk. These are

- fprintf()
- fputs()
- fputc()
- fwrite()

10.3.1 Character Input and Output

When used with disk files, the term *character I/O* refers to single characters as well as lines of characters since a line is nothing but a sequence of zero or more characters terminated by the new-line character. Character I/O is used with text-mode files. The following sections describe character input/output functions for files with suitable examples.

putc() Function

The library function putc() writes a single character to a specified stream. Its prototype in stdio.h appears as follows

```
int putc(int ch, FILE *fp);
```

The argument ch is the character to be outputted. As with other character functions, it is formally considered to be of type int, but only the lower-order byte is used. The argument fp is the pointer associated with the file, which is the pointer returned by fopen() when the file is opened. The function putc() returns the character just written if successful or EOF if an error occurs. The symbolic constant EOF is defined in stdio.h, and it has the value –1.

Because no 'real' character has that numeric value, EOF can be used as an error indicator with text-mode files only.

The following program illustrates how to write a single character at a time into a text file.

```c
#include <stdio.h>
int main()                    declaring
                              pointer to
{                             FILE
  FILE *fp;
  char text[80];              file name
  int i, c;
  fp = fopen("abc.txt", "w");
  printf("\n ENTER TEXT");    write mode
  scanf("%[^\n]", text);
  for(c = 1; c <= 10; c++)
  {
    for(i = 0; text[i]; i++)
    putc(text[i], fp);
    putc('\n', fp);
  }
  fclose(fp);
  return 0;
}
```

To append more lines to the file abc.txt, the statement in bold font has to be replaced with the statement fp = fopen("abc.txt", "a");

fputs() Function

To write a line of characters to a stream, the library function `fputs()` is used. This function works just like the string library function `puts()`. The only difference is that with `fputs()` one can specify the output stream. Also, `fputs()` does not add a new line to the end of the string; to include '\n', it must be explicitly specified. Its prototype in `stdio.h` is

```
char fputs(char *str, FILE *fp);
```

The argument `str` is a pointer to the null-terminated string to be written, and `fp` is the pointer to type `FILE` returned by `fopen()` when the file was opened. The string pointed to by `str` is written to the file, ignoring its terminating `\0`. The function `fputs()` returns a non-negative value if successful or `EOF` on error.

Points to Note

- With disk files, the term *character I/O* refers to single characters as well as lines of characters.
- The function `putc()` returns the character just written if successful or `EOF` if an error occurs.
- The symbolic constant `EOF` is defined in `stdio.h`, and it has the value –1.
- `fputs()` does not add a "new line" to the end of the string written on to a file.
- The function `fputs()` returns a non-negative value if successful or EOF on error.

10.3.2 End of File (EOF)

When reading from a file, how can the program detect that it has reached the end of the file? One way is to have a special marker at the end of the file. For instance

- A # character on its own could be the last line.
- DOS uses **Ctrl-z** as the special character that ends a file. (It also knows how many characters there are in the file.) The use of **Ctrl-z** is historical and most people would want to do away with it.
- In Unix, **Ctrl-d** is used as the end-of-file character. Using a special character is not satisfactory. It means that a file that contains these characters as real text behaves abnormally.

Detecting the end of a file

Sometimes it is not known exactly how long a file is but it is still possible to read data from the file, starting at the beginning and proceeding to the end. There are two ways to detect end-of-file.

When reading from a text-mode file character by character, one can look for the end-of-file character. The symbolic constant `EOF` is defined in `stdio.h` as -1, a value never used by a 'real' character. When a character input function reads `EOF` from a text-mode stream, it ensures that it has reached the end of the file. For example, one could write the following.

```
while((c = fgetc(fp)) != EOF)
```

The variable returned from the `getc()` function is a character, so we can use a `char` variable for this purpose. However, there is a problem that could develop here if an `unsigned char` is used because C returns a `-1` for an `EOF` which an `unsigned char` type variable is not capable of containing. An `unsigned char` type variable can only have the values of `0` to `255`, so it will return a `255` for a minus one. The program can never find the `EOF` and will therefore never terminate the loop. This is easy to prevent. Always use a `char` type variable in returning an `EOF`.

There are three character input functions: `getc()` and `fgetc()` for single characters, and `fgets()` for lines.

getc() and fgetc() functions

The functions `getc()` and `fgetc()` are identical and can be used interchangeably. They input a single character from the specified stream. The following is the prototype of `getc()` in `stdio.h`.

```
int getc(FILE *fp);
```

The argument `fp` is the pointer returned by `fopen()` when the file is opened. The function returns the character that was input or it returns `EOF` on error.

If `getc()` and `fgetc()` return a single character, why are they prototyped to return a type `int`? The reason is that when reading files, one needs to be able to read in the end-of-file marker, which on some systems is not a type `char` but a type `int`.

fgets() Function

fgets() is a *line*-oriented function. The ANSI prototype is

```c
char *fgets(char *str, int n, FILE *fp);
```

The function reads from the stream pointed to by fp and places the output into the character array pointed to by str. It will stop reading when any of the following conditions are true.

- It has read n - 1 bytes (one character is reserved for the null-terminator).
- It encounters a new-line character (a line-feed in the compiler is placed here).
- It reaches the end of file.
- A read error occurs.

fgets() automatically appends a null-terminator to the data read. fgetc() gives the user more control than fgets(), but reading a file byte-by-byte from disk is rather inefficient. These functions are illustrated in the following programs. The following program displays the contents of a file on screen.

Examples

1.
```c
#include <stdio.h>
int main()
{
  FILE *fopen(), *fp;
  int ch;
  fp = fopen("a.txt", "r");
  if(fp == NULL)
  {
    printf("Cannot open the file a.txt \n");
    exit(1)
  }
  ch = getc(fp);
  while(ch != EOF)
  {
    putchar(ch);
    ch = getc(fp);
  }
  fclose(fp);
  return 0;
}
```

Alternatively, one could prompt the user to enter the filename again, and try to open it again.

2.
```c
#include <stdio.h>
#include <string.h>
int main()
{
  FILE *fopen(), *fp;
  int ch;
  char fname[30];
  printf("\n Enter the filename \n");
  fflush(stdin);       // clears the input stream
  scanf("%[^\n]",fname);
  fp = fopen(fname, "r");
  while(fp ==NULL || strcmp(fname, " ")!= 0)
  {
    printf("Cannot open the file %s for reading \n", fname);
    printf("\n Enter the filename \n");
    fflush(stdin);
    scanf("%[^\n]",fname);
    fp = fopen(fname, "r");
  }
  ch = getc(fp);
  while(ch != EOF)
  {
    putchar(ch);
    ch = getc(fp);
  }
  fclose(fp);
  return 0;
}
```

In this Example, filenames are taken from the user until a valid existing filename is entered or the space bar followed by the <Enter> key is pressed. The following program illustrates that reading a line at a time from a file can be performed using fgets().

3.
```c
#include <stdio.h>
int main()
{
  FILE *fp;
  char word[60];
  char *c;
  fp = fopen("abc.txt","r");
  do {
    c = fgets(word, 60,fp);
```

```c
    if(c != NULL)
    printf("%s", word);
    }
  while(c != NULL);
  fclose(fp);
  return 0;
  }
```

4. Write a C program that counts the number of characters and number of lines in a file.

```c
#include <stdio.h>
int main()
{
  FILE *fopen(), *fp;
  int ch, nc, nlines;
  char fname[30];
  nlines = 0;
  nc = 0;
  printf("Enter filename:");
  fflush(stdin);
  scanf("%s", fname);
  fp = fopen(fname, "r");
  if(fp == NULL)
  {
    printf("Cannot open the file %s for reading
        \n", fname);
    exit(0);
  }
  ch = getc(fp);
  while(ch != EOF)
  {
    if(ch  ==  '\n')
      nlines++;
    nc++;
    ch = getc(fp);
  }
  fclose(fp);
  if(nc != 0)
  {
    printf("There are %d characters in %s \n", nc,
        filename);
```

```c
    printf("There are %d lines \n", nlines);
  }
  else
    printf("File: %s is empty \n", filename);
  return 0;
}
```

5. Write a program to display the contents of a file, 10 lines at a time.

```c
#include <stdio.h>
int main()
{
  FILE *fopen(), *fp;
  int ch,  nline;
  char fname[40], ans[40];
  printf("Enter filename:");
  scanf("%s", fname);
  fp = fopen(fname, "r");
                         /* open for reading */
  if(fp == NULL)
           /* check whether file exists or not */
  {
    printf("Cannot open the file %s  \n", fname);
    exit(0);
  }
  nline = 1;
  ans[0] = '\0';
  ch = getc(fp);
             /* Read 1st character if any */
  while(ch != EOF &&  (ans[0] != 'Q' || ans[0] != 'q'))
  {
    putchar(ch);            /* Display character */
    if(ch  ==  '\n')
      nline++;
    if(nline == 10)
    {
      nline = 1;
      printf("[Press Return to continue, q to quit]");
      fflush(stdin);
      scanf("%s", ans);
    }
```

```
      ch = getc(fp);
   }
   fclose(fp);
   return 0;
}
```

The above program pauses after displaying 10 lines until the user presses either Q or q to quit or return to display the next 10 lines. The above program does the same as the Unix command 'more'.

6. Write a program to compare two files specified by the user, displaying a message indicating whether the files are identical or different.

```
#include <stdio.h>
int main()
{
   FILE *fp1, *fp2;
   int ca, cb;
   char fname1[40], fname2[40];
   printf("Enter first filename:");
   fflush(stdin);
   gets(fname1);
   printf("Enter second filename:");
   fflush(stdin);
   gets(fname2);
   fp1 = fopen(fname1,  "r");
                /* open first file for reading */
   fp2 = fopen(fname2,  "r");
                /* open second file for reading */
   if(fp1 == NULL)    /* check does file exist */
   {
     printf("Cannot open the file %s for reading
        \n", fname1);
     exit(1);            /* terminate program */
   }
   else if(fp2 == NULL)
   {
     printf("Cannot open %s for reading \n", fname2);
     exit(1);            /* terminate program */
   }
   else     /* both files opened successfully  */
   {
     ca = getc(fp1);
     cb = getc(fp2);
```

```
     while(ca != EOF  &&  cb != EOF  &&  ca == cb)
     {
       ca = getc(fp1);
       cb = getc(fp2);
     }
     if(ca == cb)
       printf("Files are identical \n");
     else if(ca !=  cb)
       printf("Files differ \n");
     fclose(fp1);
     fclose(fp2);
   }
   return 0;
}
```

7. Write a file copy program in C that copies a file into another.

```
#include <stdio.h>
int main()
{
   FILE *fp1, *fp2;
   int ch;
   char fname1[30], fname2[30];
   printf("Enter source file:");
   fflush(stdin);
   scanf("%s", fname1);
   printf("Enter destination file:");
   fflush(stdin);
   scanf("%s", fname2);
   fp1 = fopen(fname1, "r");
                        /* open for reading */
   fp2 = fopen(fname2, "w");
                        /* open for writing */
   if(fp1 == NULL)
           /* check whether file exists or not */
   {
     printf("Cannot open the file %s for reading
        \n", fname1);
     exit(1);            /* terminate program */
   }
   else if(fp2 == NULL)
   {
```

```
    printf("Cannot open the file %s for writing
        \n", fname2);
    exit(1);                /* terminate program */
    }
    else    /* both files has been opened successfully */
    {
      ch = getc(fp1);       /* read from source */
      while(ch != EOF)
      {
        putc(ch, fp2);      /* copy to destination */
        ch = getc(fp1);
      }
      fclose(fp1);          /* Now close the files */
      fclose(fp2);
      printf("Files successfully copied \n");
    }
    return 0;
}
```

8. Write a C program that accepts the names of two files. It should copy the first file into the second line by line. Use the `fgets()` and `fputs()` functions.

```
#include <stdio.h>
#include <stdlib.h>
int main()
{
    FILE *fp1, *fp2;
    char fname1[30], fname2[30], t[60];
    printf("Enter source file:");
    fflush(stdin);
    gets(fname1);
    printf("Enter destination file:");
    fflush(stdin);
    gets(fname2);
    if((fp1 = fopen(fname1, "r")) == NULL)
    printf("Unable to open %s for reading \n", fname1);
    else if((file_2 = fopen(fname2, "w")) == NULL)
    printf("Unable to open %s for writing \n", fname2);
    else
    {
      while((fgets(t, sizeof(t), fp1)) ! = NULL)
```

```
        fputs(t, fp2);
      fclose(fp1);
      fclose(fp2);
    }
    return 0;
}
```

The other two file-handling functions to be covered are `fprintf()` and `fscanf()`. These functions operate exactly like `printf()` and `scanf()` except that they work with files. Their prototypes are

```
int fprintf(FILE *fp, const char *control-string,
        ...);
int fscanf(FILE *fp, const char *control-string
        ...);
```

Instead of directing their I/O operations to the console, these functions operate on the file specified by `fp`. Otherwise their operations are the same as their console-based relatives. The advantage of `fprintf()` and `fscanf()` is that they make it very easy to write a wide variety of data to a file using a text format. The components of the control string are the same as for `scanf()`. Finally, the ellipses (...) indicate one or more additional arguments such as the addresses of the variables where inputs are to be assigned. The following program illustrates how the function `fscanf()` can be used to write into a text file.

```
9. #include <stdio.h>
   int main()
     {
       FILE *fp;
       if((fp = fopen("afile.txt", "w")) != NULL)
         {
           fprintf(fp, "%s", "Introduction\n");
           fprintf(fp, "%s", "To\n");
           fprintf(fp, "%s", "Computing\n");
           fclose(fp);
         }
       else
         printf("Unable to open the file for writing");
         return 0;
     }
```

A file named 'afile.txt' is created in the current directory, the content of which is as follows.

Introduction

To

Computing

The next program reads five integer values from the keyboard and stores them in the data file num.dat. In this program the user-defined character is used, as end-of-file marker instead of standard EOF.

10.
```c
#include <stdio.h>
int main()
{
  FILE *fp;
  int n[5],i;
  if((fp = fopen("num.dat", "w")) != NULL)
    {
      printf("Enter 5 numbers, to be stored in
        num.dat...");
      for(i = 0; i < 5; i++)
        {
          scanf("%d", &n[i]);
          fprintf(fp, "%d\n", n[i]);
        }
      fprintf(fp,"%d",9999);
      fclose(ptr);
    }
  else
    printf("Unable to open num.dat ...\n");
    return 0;
}
```

Output:

```
Enter 5 numbers, to be stored in num.dat ... 1 2
    3 4 5
```

The file num.dat now contains the numbers arranged in the following format.

```
1
2
3
4
5
9999
```

Here 9999 is used as end-of-file marker. It is not a member of the data set. While reading data from 'num.dat', the data is read until 9999 is found. The following program describes the usage where the numbers stored in the file 'num.dat' are summed up and displayed. Here fscanf() has to be used to read data from the file.

11.
```c
#include <stdio.h>
int main()
{
  FILE *fp;
  int n,s=0;
  if((fp = fopen("num.dat", "r")) != NULL)
  {
  fscanf(fp, "%d\n", &n);
  while(n!=9999)
  {
  s+=n;
  fscanf(fp, "%d\n", &n);
  }
  printf("Sum is %d",s);
  fclose(fp);
  }
  else
    printf("Unable to open num.dat ... \n");
    return 0;
}
```

Output:

```
Sum is 15
```

fscanf() is a *field*-oriented function and is *inappropriate* for use in a robust, general-purpose text file reader. It has two major drawbacks.

- The programmer must know the exact data layout of the input file in advance and rewrite the function call for every different layout.

- It is difficult to read text strings that contain spaces because fscanf() sees space characters as field delimiters.

Now one might think that calls to fprinf() and fscanf() differ significantly from calls to printf() and scanf(), and that these latter functions do not seem to require file pointers. As a matter of fact they do. The file pointer associated with printf() is a constant pointer named stdout defined in <stdio.h>. Similarly scanf() has an associated constant pointer named stdin. scanf() reads from stdin and printf() writes to stdout. This can be verified by executing the following program.

Example

```
12.  #include < stdio.h>
     int main()
     {
       int a, b;
       fprintf(stdout, "Enter two numbers separated
          by a space:");
       fscanf(stdin, "%d %d", &a, &b);
       fprintf(stdout, "Their sum is: %d.\n", a + b);
       return 0;

     }
```

There is a third constant file pointer defined as stderr. This is associated with the standard error file. stderr has the following use: in some systems such as MS-DOS and Unix, the output of the programs can be redirected to files by using the redirection operator. In DOS, for example, if abc.exe is an executable file that writes to the monitor, then its output can be redirected to a disk file abc.out by the command

```
abc>abc.out<CR>
```

Output that would normally appear on the monitor can thus be sent to the file abc.out. On the other hand, while redirecting output, one would not want any error messages such as 'Unable to open abc.dat for writing' to be redirected; one wants them to appear on the screen. Writing error messages to stderr

```
fprintf(stderr, "Unable to open newfile.dat for
          writing");
```

ensures that normal output will be redirected, but error messages will still appear on the screen.

All three are, in fact, objects of type *pointer to FILE*, and they may be used in any file-handling function in just the same way as a pointer returned by fopen(). In fact the macro putchar(c) is really nothing more than

```
putc(c,stdout)
```

It is sometimes useful to initialize a pointer to FILE to point to one of the standard items, to provide a 'standard input as default' type of operation.

```
FILE *ifp = stdin;
```

is a typical definition.

10.3.3 Detecting the End of a File Using the feof() Function

To detect end-of-file, there is library function feof(), which can be used for both binary- and text-mode files.

```
int feof(FILE *fp);
```

The argument fp is the FILE pointer returned by fopen() when the file was opened. The function feof() returns 0 if the end-of-file has not been reached, or a non-zero value if end-of-file has been reached. The following program demonstrates the use of feof(). The program reads the file one line at a time, displaying each line on stdout, until feof() detects end-of-file.

Example

```
13.  #include <stdlib.h>
     #include <stdio.h>
     #define SIZE 100
     int main()
     {
       char temp[SIZE];
       char fname[60];
       FILE *fp;
       printf("Enter name of filename:");
       fflush(stdin);
       scanf("%s", fname);
       if((fp = fopen(fname, "r")) == NULL)
       {
         fprintf(stderr, "Error in opening file");
         exit(1);
       }
       while(!feof(fp))
       {
         fgets(temp, SIZE, fp);
         printf("%s",temp);
       }
       fclose(fp);
       return 0;

     }
```

Output:

```
Enter name of filename:
first.c
#include <stdio.h>
int main()
{
  printf("C is Sea");
  return 0;
```

```
}
```

- DOS uses Ctrl-z as the special character that ends a file.
- In Unix, Ctrl-d is used as the end-of-file character.
- `fgets()` automatically appends a null-terminator to the data read.
- `fgetc()` gives more control than `fgets()`, but reading a file byte-by-byte from disk is rather inefficient.
- `fscanf()` is a field-oriented function and is inappropriate for use in a robust, general-purpose text file reader.

10.4 WORKING WITH BINARY FILES

The operations performed on binary files are similar to text files since both types of files can essentially be considered as streams of bytes. In fact, the same functions are used to access files in C. When a file is opened, it must be designated as text or binary and usually this is the only indication of the type of file being processed. To illustrate a binary file, consider the following program containing a function, `filecopy()`, that is passed the names of the source and destination files and then performs the copy operation just as the outlined steps. If there is an error in opening either file, the function does not attempt the copy operation and returns -1 to the calling program. When the copy operation is complete, the program closes both files and returns 0. The steps for copying a binary file into another are as follows.

1. Open the source file for reading in binary mode.
2. Open the destination file for writing in binary mode.
3. Read a character from the source file. Remember, when a file is first opened, the pointer is at the start of the file, so there is no need to position the file pointer explicitly.
4. If the function `feof()` indicates that the end of the source file has been reached, then close both files and return to the calling program.
5. If end-of-file has not been reached, write the character to the destination file, and then go to step 3.

Example

```
14. #include <stdio.h>
    int filecopy(char *, char *);
    int main()
```

```
{
  char source[80], destination[80];
  printf("\nEnter source file:");
  fflush(stdin);
  gets(source);
  printf("\nEnter destination file:");
  fflush(stdin);
  gets(destination);
  if(filecopy(source, destination) == 0)
    puts("\n Successfully copied");
  else
    fprintf(stderr, "Error in copying...");
return 0;
}
int filecopy(char *s, char *d)
{
  FILE *ofp, *nfp;
  int ch;
            /* Open the source file for reading
                            in binary mode. */
  if((ofp = fopen(s, "rb")) == NULL)
    return -1;
                  /* Open the destination file for
                      writing in binary mode. */
  if((nfp = fopen(d, "wb")) == NULL)
  {
    fclose(ofp);
    return -1;
  }
  while(1)
  {
    ch = fgetc(ofp);
    if(!feof(ofp))
      fputc(ch, nfp);
    else
      break;
  }
  fclose(nfp);
  fclose(ofp);
  return 0;
}
```

Output:

```
Enter source file: a.txt
```

```
Enter destination file: b.txt
Successfully copied
```

Points to Note

- At the time of file opening, it must be designated as text or binary for indicating the type of file being processed.
- The operations performed on binary files are similar to text files.

10.5 DIRECT FILE INPUT AND OUTPUT

Direct I/O is used only with binary-mode files. With direct output, blocks of data are written from memory to disk. Direct input reverses the process. A block of data is read from a disk file into memory. For example, a single direct-output function call can write an entire array of type double to disk, and a single direct-input function call can read the entire array from disk back into memory. The C file system includes two important functions for direct I/O: fread() and fwrite(). These functions can read and write any type of data, using any kind of representation. Their prototypes are

```
size_t fread(void *buffer, size_t size, size_t
    num,FILE *fp);
size_t fwrite(void *buffer, size_t size, size_t
    num, FILE *fp);
```

The fread() function reads from the file associated with fp, num number of objects, each object size in bytes, into buffer pointed to by buffer. It returns the number of objects actually read. If this value is 0, no objects have been read, and either end-of-file has been encountered or an error has occurred. One can use feof() or ferror() to find out whether end of file has been detected or an error has occurred. Their prototypes are

```
int feof(FILE *fp);
int ferror(FILE *fp);
```

The feof() function returns non-zero if the file associated with fp has reached the end of file, otherwise it returns 0. This function works for both binary files and text files. The ferror() function returns non-zero if the file associated with fp has experienced an error, otherwise it returns 0.

The fwrite() function is the opposite of fread(). It writes to file associated with fp, num number of objects, each object size in bytes, from the buffer pointed to by buffer. It returns the number of objects written. This value will be less than num only if an output error has occurred. To check for errors, fwrite() is usually programmed as follows.

```
if((fwrite(buffer, size, num, fp)) != num)
    fprintf(stderr, "Error writing to file.");
```

The following program describes the use of fread() and fwrite() functions. The program initializes an array. Then the fwrite() function is used to save the array to disk. After that, the fread() function is used to read the data into a different array. Finally, it displays both the arrays on-screen to show that they now hold the same data.

Example

```
15. #include <stdlib.h>
    #include <stdio.h>
    #define SIZE 10
    int main()
    {
      int i, a[SIZE], b[SIZE];
      FILE *fp;
      for(i = 0; i < SIZE; i++)
        a[i] = 2 * i;
      if((fp = fopen("dfile.txt", "wb")) == NULL)
      {
        fprintf(stderr, "Error opening file.");
        exit(1);
      }
      if(fwrite(a, sizeof(int), SIZE, fp) != SIZE)
      {
        fprintf(stderr, "Error writing to file.");
        exit(1);
      }
      fclose(fp);
      if((fp = fopen("dfile.txt", "rb")) == NULL)
      {
        fprintf(stderr, "Error in opening file.");
        exit(1);
      }
      if(fread(b, sizeof(int), SIZE, fp) != SIZE)
      {
```

```
      fprintf(stderr, "Error in reading file.");
      exit(1);
   }
   fclose(fp);
   for(i = 0; i < SIZE; i++)
      printf("%d\t%d\n", a[i], b[i]);
      return 0;
   }
```

Output:

```
0    0
2    2
4    4
6    6
8    8
10   10
12   12
14   14
16   16
18   18
```

10.5.1 Sequential Versus Random File Access

Every open file has an associated file position indicator, which describes where read and write operations take place in the file. The position is always specified in bytes from the beginning of the file. When a new file is opened, the position indicator is always at the beginning of the file, i.e., at position 0. Because the file is new and has a length of 0, there is no other location to indicate. When an existing file is opened, the position indicator is at the end of the file if the file was opened in the append mode, or at the beginning of the file if the file was opened in any other mode.

The file input/output functions covered earlier in this chapter make use of the position indicator, although the manipulations go on behind the scenes. Writing and reading operations occur at the location of the position indicator and update the position indicator as well. Thus, if one wishes to read all the data in a file sequentially or write data to a file sequentially, it is not necessary to be concerned about the position indicator because the stream I/O functions take care of it automatically.

When more control is required, the C library functions that help determine and change the value of the file position indicator, have to be used. By controlling the position indicator, random access of a file can be made possible. Here, random means that data can be read from, or written

to, any position in a file without reading or writing all the preceding data. This will be covered in the later sections of the chapter.

> **Points to Note**
> - Direct I/O is used only with binary-mode files.
> - `fread()` and `fwrite()` functions can read and write any type of data, using any kind of representation.
> - There are two type of file accessing method : sequential and random.
> - Every open file has an associated file position indicator. The position is always specified in bytes from the beginning of the file.

10.6 FILES OF RECORDS

Most C program files may be binary files, which can logically be divided into fixed-length records. Each record will consist of data that conforms to a previously defined structure. In C, this structure can be formed using a *struct* data type. The records are written into disk sequentially. This happens because as each record is written to disk, the file position indicator is moved to the byte immediately after the last byte in the record just written. Binary files can be written sequentially to the disk or in a random access manner.

10.6.1 Working with Files of Records

Using fscanf() and fprintf() The following structure records the code, name, and price of an item. Using this structure a file of records can be processed. Here 0 is used as end-of-file marker (logically) to indicate there are no records in the file.

> **Example**

```
16.  #include <stdio.h>
     struct item
     {
       int itemcode;
       char name[30];
       double price;
     };
     void append();
     void modify();
     void dispall();
     void dele();
```

```c
int main()
{
  int ch;
  struct item it;
  FILE *fp;
  fp=fopen("item.dat","w");
  if(fp==NULL)
  {
    printf("\n ERROR IN OPENING FILE...");
    exit(0);
  }
  printf("\n ENTER ITEM CODE:");
  scanf("%d",&it.itemcode);
  printf("\n ENTER ITEM NAME:");
  fflush(stdin);
  scanf("%[^\n]",it.name);
  printf("\n ENTER PRICE:");
  scanf("%lf",&it.price);
  fprintf(fp,"%d \t%s\t%lf\n",it.itemcode,
      it.name,it.price);
  fprintf(fp,"%d",0);
  fclose(fp);
  while(1)
  {
    printf("\n \t 1.APPEND RECORD");
    printf("\n \t 2.DISPLAY ALL RECORD");
    printf("\n \t 3.EDIT RECORD");
    printf("\n \t 4.DELETE RECORD");
    printf("\n \t 5.EXIT");
    printf("\n \t ENTER UR CHOICE:");
    scanf("%d",&ch);
    switch(ch)
    {
        case 1:append(); break;
        case 2:dispall();break;
        case 3:modify(); break;
        case 4:dele();   break;
        case 5:exit(0);
    }
  }
  return 0;
}
```

```c
void append()
{
  FILE *fp;
  struct item it;
  fp=fopen("item.dat","a");
  if(fp==NULL)
  {
    printf("\n ERROR IN OPENING FILE...");
    exit(0);
  }
  printf("\n ENTER ITEM CODE:");
  scanf("%d",&it.itemcode);
  printf("\n ENTER ITEM NAME:");
  fflush(stdin);
  scanf("%[^\n]",it.name);
  printf("\n ENTER PRICE:");
  scanf("%lf",&it.price);
  fprintf(fp,"%d \t%s\t%lf\n",it.itemcode,
      it.name,it.price);
  fprintf(fp,"%d",0);
  fclose(fp);
}
void dispall()
{
  FILE *fp;
  struct item it;
  fp=fopen("item.dat","r");
  if(fp==NULL)
  {
    printf("\n ERROR IN OPENING FILE...");
    exit(0);
  }
  while(1)
  {
    fscanf(fp, "%d",&it.itemcode);
    if(it.itemcode==0)
      break;
    fscanf(fp,"%s",it.name);
    fscanf(fp,"%lf",&it.price);
    printf("\n \t %d\t%s\t%lf",it.itemcode,
        it.name,it.price);
```

```
    }
  fclose(fp);
}
void modify()
{
  FILE *fp,*fptr;
  struct item it;
  int icd,found=0;
  fp=fopen("item.dat","r");
  if(fp==NULL)
  {
    printf("\n ERROR IN OPENING FILE...");
    exit(0);
  }
  fptr=fopen("temp.dat","w");
  if(fptr==NULL)
  {
    printf("\n ERROR IN OPENING FILE...");
    exit(0);
  }
  printf("\n ENTER THE ITEM CODE TO EDIT");
  scanf("%d",&icd);
  while(1)
  {
    fscanf(fp,"%d",&it.itemcode);
    if(it.itemcode==0)
     break;
    if(it.itemcode==icd)
    {
      found=1;
      fscanf(fp,"%s",it.name);
      fscanf(fp,"%lf",&it.price);
      printf("\n EXISTING RECORD IS...\n");
      printf("\n \t %d\t%s\t%lf",it.itemcode,
        it.name,it.price);
      printf("\n ENTER NEW ITEM NAME:");
      fflush(stdin);
      scanf("%[^\n]",it.name);
      printf("\n ENTER NEW PRICE:");
      scanf("%lf",&it.price);
      fprintf(fptr,"%d \t%s\t%lf\n",
        it.itemcode,it.name,it.price);
    }
```

```
    else
    {
      fscanf(fp,"%s",it.name);
      fscanf(fp,"%lf",&it.price);
      fprintf(fptr,"%d \t%s\t%lf\n",
        it.itemcode,it.name,it.price);
    }
  }
  fprintf(fptr,"%d",0);
  fclose(fptr);
  fclose(fp);
  if(found==0)
    printf("\nRECORD NOT FOUND...");
  else
  {
    fp=fopen("item.dat","w");
    if(fp==NULL)
    {
      printf("\n ERROR IN OPENING FILE...");
      exit(0);
    }
    fptr=fopen("temp.dat","r");
    if(fptr==NULL)
    {
      printf("\n ERROR IN OPENING FILE...");
      exit(0);
    }
  while(1)
  {
    fscanf(fptr,"%d",&it.itemcode);
    if(it.itemcode==0)
    break;
    fscanf(fptr,"%s",it.name);
    fscanf(fptr,"%lf",&it.price);
    fprintf(fp,"%d \t%s\t%lf\n",it.itemcode,
      it.name,it.price);
  }
  fprintf(fp,"%d",0);
  fclose(fptr);
  fclose(fp);
  }
}
```

```
void dele()
{
  FILE *fp,*fptr;
  struct item it;
  int icd,found=0;
  fp=fopen("item.dat","r");
  if(fp==NULL)
  {
    printf("\n ERROR IN OPENING FILE...");
    exit(0);
  }
  fptr=fopen("temp.dat","w");
  if(fptr==NULL)
  {
    printf("\n ERROR IN OPENING FILE...");
    exit(0);
  }
  printf("\n ENTER THE ITEM CODE TO DELETE");
  scanf("%d",&icd);
  while(1)
  {
    fscanf(fp,"%d",&it.itemcode);
    if(it.itemcode==0)
      break;
    if(it.itemcode==icd)
    {
      found=1;
      fscanf(fp,"%s",it.name);
      fscanf(fp,"%lf",&it.price);
    }
    else
    {
      fscanf(fp,"%s",it.name);
      fscanf(fp,"%lf",&it.price);
      fprintf(fptr,"%d \t%s\t%lf\n",
        it.itemcode,it.name,it.price);
    }
  }
  fprintf(fptr,"%d",0);
  fclose(fptr);
  fclose(fp);
```

```
  if(found==0)
    printf("\n RECORD NOT FOUND...");
  else
  {
    fp=fopen("item.dat","w");
    if(fp==NULL)
    {
      printf("\n ERROR IN OPENING FILE...");
      exit(0);
    }
    fptr=fopen("temp.dat","r");
    if(fptr==NULL)
    {
      printf("\n ERROR IN OPENING FILE...");
      exit(0);
    }
    while(1)
    {
      fscanf(fptr,"%d",&it.itemcode);
      if(it.itemcode==0)
        break;
      fscanf(fptr,"%s",it.name);
      fscanf(fptr,"%lf",&it.price);
      fprintf(fp, "%d \t%s\t%lf\n",it.itemcode,
        it.name,it.price);
    }
    fprintf(fp,"%d",0);
    fclose(fptr);
    fclose(fp);
  }
}
```

Using fread() and fscanf() The following program demonstrates how the records stored in a binary file can be read sequentially from the disk. This program will only work if the structure of the record is identical to the record used in the previous example. Here the file is opened using the fopen() function, with the file opening mode set to 'rb'. The file is read sequentially because after each read operation the file position is moved to point to the first byte of the very next record. It must be remembered that the feof() function does not indicate that the end of the file has been reached until after an attempt has been made to read past the end-of-file marker.

17.
```c
include <stdio.h>
struct item
{
  int itemcode;
  char name[30];
  double price;
};
void append();
void modify();
void dispall();
void dele();
int main()
{
  int ch;
  struct item it;
  FILE *fp;
  fp=fopen("item.dat","wb");
  if(fp==NULL)
  {
    printf("\n ERROR IN OPENING FILE...");
    exit(0);
  }
  printf("\n ENTER ITEM CODE:");
  scanf("%d",&it.itemcode);
  printf("\n ENTER ITEM NAME:");
  fflush(stdin);
  scanf("%[^\n]",it.name);
  printf("\n ENTER PRICE:");
  scanf("%lf",&it.price);
  fwrite(&it,sizeof(it),1,fp);
  fclose(fp);
  dispall();
  while(1)
  {
    printf("\n \t 1.APPEND RECORD");
    printf("\n \t 2.DISPLAY ALL RECORD");
    printf("\n \t 3.EDIT RECORD");
    printf("\n \t 4.EXIT");
    printf("\n \t ENTER UR CHOICE:");
    scanf("%d",&ch);
    switch(ch)
    {
      case 1:append(); break;
      case 2:dispall();break;
      case 3:modify();break;
      case 4:exit(0);
    }
  }
  return 0;
}
void append()
{
  FILE *fp;
  struct item it;
  fp=fopen("item.dat","ab");
  if(fp==NULL)
  {
    printf("\n ERROR IN OPENING FILE...");
    exit(0);
  }
  printf("\n ENTER ITEM CODE:");
  scanf("%d",&it.itemcode);
  printf("\n ENTER ITEM NAME:");
  fflush(stdin);
  scanf("%[^\n]",it.name);
  printf("\n ENTER PRICE:");
  scanf("%lf",&it.price);
  fwrite(&it,sizeof(it),1,fp);
  fclose(fp);
}
void dispall()
{
  FILE *fp;
  struct item it;
  fp=fopen("item.dat","rb");
  if(fp==NULL)
  {
    printf("\n ERROR IN OPENING FILE...");
```

```
    exit(0);
  }
  while(1)
  {
    fread(&it,sizeof(it),1,fp);
    if(feof(fp))
    break;
    printf("\n %d \t %s \t %lf",it.itemcode,it.
        name,it.price);
  }
  fclose(fp);
}
void modify()
{
  FILE *fp,*fptr;
  struct item it;
  int icd,found=0;
  fp=fopen("item.dat","rb");
  if(fp==NULL)
  {
    printf("\n ERROR IN OPENING FILE...");
    exit(0);
  }
  fptr=fopen("temp.dat","wb");
  if(fptr==NULL)
  {
    printf("\n ERROR IN OPENING FILE...");
    exit(0);
  }
  printf("\n ENTER THE ITEM CODE TO EDIT");
  scanf("%d",&icd);
  while(1)
  {
    fread(&it,sizeof(it),1,fp);
    if(feof(fp))
      break;
    if(it.itemcode==icd)
    {
      found=1;
      printf("\n EXISTING RECORD IS...\n");
```

```
      printf("\n \t %d\t%s\t%lf",it.itemcode,
        it.name,it.price);
      printf("\n ENTER NEW ITEM NAME:");
      fflush(stdin);
      scanf("%[^\n]",it.name);
      printf("\n ENTER NEW PRICE:");
      scanf("%lf",&it.price);
      fwrite(&it,sizeof(it),1,fptr);
    }
    else
    {
      fwrite(&it,sizeof(it),1,fptr);
    }
  }
  fclose(fptr);
  fclose(fp);
  if(found==0)
    printf("\nRECORD NOT FOUND...");
  else
  {
    fp=fopen("item.dat","wb");
    if(fp==NULL)
    {
      printf("\n ERROR IN OPENING FILE...");
      exit(0);
    }
    fptr=fopen("temp.dat","rb");
    if(fptr==NULL)
    {
      printf("\n ERROR IN OPENING FILE...");
      exit(0);
    }
    while(1)
    {
      fread(&it,sizeof(it),1,fptr);
      if(feof(fptr))
        break;
      fwrite(&it,sizeof(it),1,fp);
    }
    fclose(fptr);
    fclose(fp);
```

```
    }
  }
```

Using fgets() and fputc() It is not that only fread()
and fwrite() or fscanf() and fprintf() are used for
processing of files of records. fgets() and fputc() can
also be used. The following program illustrates this. The
program keeps the records of an item in a file stock.dat,
uses a structure item and processes the file, and prints out
all items where the quantity on hand is less than or equal
to the reorder level.

Example

```
18. #include <stdio.h>
    #include <stdlib.h>
    #include <ctype.h>
    #include <string.h>
    /* definition of a record of type item */
    struct item {
      char  name[20];
      float price;
      int   qty;
      int   reorder;
    };
    void show(struct item);
    int getrecord(struct item *);
    FILE *fp;               /* input file pointer */
    void show(struct item rec)
    {
      printf("\nitem name\t%s\n", rec.name);
      printf("item price\t%.2f\n", rec.price);
      printf("item quantity\t%d\n", rec.qty);
      printf("item reorder level\t%d\n", rec.reorder);
    }
    int getrecord(struct item *p)
    {
      int i = 0, ch;
      char temp[40];
      ch = fgetc(fp);
      while((ch == '\n') || (ch == ' ') && (ch != EOF))
        ch = fgetc(fp);
      if(ch == EOF)
        return 0;
                            /* read item name */
      while((ch != '\n') && (ch != EOF)) {
```

```
      temp[i++] = ch;
      ch = fgetc(fp);
    }
    temp[i] = '\0';
    strcpy(p->name, temp);
    if(ch == EOF) return 0;
              /* skip to start of next field */
    while((ch == '\n') || (ch == ' ') && (ch != EOF))
      ch = fgetc(fp);
    if(ch == EOF) return 0; /* read item price */
    i = 0;
    while((ch != '\n') && (ch != EOF))
    {
      temp[i++] = ch;
      ch = fgetc(fp);
    }
    temp[i] = '\0';
    p->price = atof(temp);
    if(ch == EOF) return 0;
              /* skip to start of next field */
    while((ch == '\n') || (ch == ' ') && (ch != EOF))
      ch = fgetc(fp);
    if(ch == EOF) return 0;
                    /* read item quantity */
    i = 0;
    while((ch != '\n') && (ch != EOF))
    {
      temp[i++] = ch;
      ch = fgetc(fp);
    }
    temp[i] = '\0';
    p->qty = atoi(temp);
    if(ch == EOF) return 0;
              /* skip to start of next field */
    while((ch == '\n') || (ch == ' ') && (ch != EOF))
      ch = fgetc(fp);
    if(ch == EOF) return 0;
                    /* read item reorder level */
    i = 0;
    while((ch != '\n') && (ch != EOF)) {
      temp[i++] = ch;
      ch = fgetc(fp);
    }
    temp[i] = '\0';
    p->reorder = atoi(temp);
    if(ch == EOF) return 0;
    return 1;
```

```
                          /* signify record has been
                            read successfully */
}
int main()
{
  struct item rec;
  fp = fopen("stock.dat", "r");
  if(fp == NULL) {
    printf("Unable to open the file %s\n", filename);
    if(fp != NULL)
    fclose(fp);
    exit(1);
  }

    while(! feof(fp)) {
    if(getrecord(&rec) == 1) {
      if(rec.qty <= rec.reorder)
        show(rec);
    }
    else
    {
    if(fp != NULL)
      fclose(fp);
    exit(1);
    }
  }
  if(fp != NULL)
    fclose(fp);
  exit(0);
  return 0;
}
```

Points to Note

- Most C program files may be binary files, which can logically be divided into fixed-length records.
- The records in a file are written sequentially onto the disk.
- Binary files can be written sequentially to the disk or in a random access manner.
- With fread() and fscanf(), the file is read sequentially and after each read operation, the file position indicator is moved to the first byte of the next record.
- The feof() function does not indicate that the end of the file has been reached until after an attempt has been made to read past the end-of-file marker.

10.7 RANDOM ACCESS TO FILES OF RECORDS

For random access to files of records, the following functions are used.

- fseek()
- ftell()
- rewind()

By using fseek(), one can set the position indicator anywhere in the file. The function prototype in stdio.h is

```
int fseek(FILE *fp, long offset, int origin);
```

The argument fp is the FILE pointer associated with the file. The distance that the position indicator is to be moved is given by offset in bytes. It is the number of bytes to move the file pointer. This is obtained from the formula: *the desired record number × the size of one record*. The argument origin specifies the position indicator's relative starting point. There can be three values for origin, with symbolic constants defined in stdio.h, as shown in Table 10.2.

Table 10.2 Possible origin values for fseek()

Constant	Value	Description
SEEK_SET	0	Moves the indicator offset bytes from the beginning of the file
SEEK_CUR	1	Moves the indicator offset bytes from its current position
SEEK_END	2	Moves the indicator offset bytes from the end of the file

The function fseek() returns 0 if the indicator is moved successfully or non-zero in case of an error. The following program uses fseek() for random file access. The program uses the previously created file item.dat and the structure item. It is assumed that there are four records in the file item.dat.

Examples

```
19. #include <stdio.h>
    #include <string.h>
    struct item{
      int itemcode;
      char name[30];
      double  price;
      };
    typedef struct item product;
    FILE *fp;
    int main()
    {
```

```
    product it;
    int rec, result;
    fp = fopen("item.dat", "r+b");
    printf("Which record do you want [0-3]? Press\
        -1 to exit...");
    scanf("%d", &rec);
    while(rec >= 0)
    {
      fseek(fp, rec*sizeof(it), SEEK_SET);
      result = fread(&it, sizeof(it), 1, fp);
      if(result==1)
      {
        printf("\nRECORD %d\n", rec);
        printf("Item code........: %d\n",
          it.itemcode);
        printf("Item name.......: %s\n", it.name);
        printf("Price...: %8.2f\n\n", it.price);
      }
      else
      printf("\nRecord %d not found!\n\n", rec);
      printf("Which record do you want [0-3]? Press
          -1 to exit...");
      scanf("%d", &rec);
    }
    fclose(fp);
    return 0;
}
```

The following program will further clear the concept of fseek().

```
20. #include <stdio.h>
    /* random record description—could be anything */
    struct rec
    {
      int x,y,z;
    };
    /* writes and then reads 10 arbitrary records from
            the file "junk". */
    int main()
    {
      int i,j;
      FILE *f;
      struct rec r;
      /* create the file of 10 records */
      f=fopen("junk","w");
      if(!f)
      {
```

```
        printf("File opening error for writing");
        exit(1);}
    for(i=1;i<=10; i++)
    {
      r.x=i;
      r.y=i*2;
      r.z=i*3;
      fwrite(&r,sizeof(struct rec),1,f);
    }
    fclose(f);
    /* read the 10 records */
    f=fopen("junk","r");
    if(!f) {
      printf("\n File opening error for reading");
      exit(1);}
    for(i=1;i<=10; i++)
    {
      fread(&r,sizeof(struct rec),1,f);
      printf("\n%d\t %d \t %d",r.x,r.y,r.z);
    }
    fclose(f);
    printf("\n");
                    /* use fseek to read the first 5
                        records in reverse order */
    f=fopen("junk","r");
    if(!f)
      {
      printf("\n File opening error for reading");
      exit(1);
      }
    for(i=4; i>=0; i--)
    {
      fseek(f,sizeof(struct rec)*i,SEEK_SET);
      fread(&r,sizeof(struct rec),1,f);
      printf("\n%d\t %d \t %d",r.x,r.y,r.z);
    }
    fclose(f);
    printf("\n");
    /* use fseek to read every other record */
    f=fopen("junk","r");
    if(!f)
      {
      printf("File opening error for reading");
```

```
      exit(1);
    }
  fseek(f,0,SEEK_SET);
  for(i=0;i<5; i++)
  {
    fread(&r,sizeof(struct rec),1,f);
    printf("\n%d\t %d \t %d",r.x,r.y,r.z);
    fseek(f,sizeof(struct rec),SEEK_CUR);
  }
  fclose(f);
  printf("\n");
  /* use fseek to read 4th record,
     change it, and write it back */
  f=fopen("junk","r+");
  if(!f)
    {
    printf("File opening error for reading and\
        writing");
     exit(1);}
  fseek(f,sizeof(struct rec)*3,SEEK_SET);
  fread(&r,sizeof(struct rec),1,f);
  r.x=9;
  r.y=99;
  r.z=999;
  fseek(f,sizeof(struct rec)*3,SEEK_SET);
  fwrite(&r,sizeof(struct rec),1,f);
  fclose(f);
  printf("\n");
                  /* read the 10 records to ensure
                       4th record was changed */
  f=fopen("junk","r");
  if(!f)
    {
    printf("File opening error for reading and\
        writing");
    exit(1);
    }
  for(i=1;i<=10; i++)
  {
    fread(&r,sizeof(struct rec),1,f);
    printf("\n%d\t %d \t %d",r.x,r.y,r.z);
  }
```

```
  fclose(f);
  return 0;
}
```

Output:

1	2	3
2	4	6
3	6	9
4	8	12
5	10	15
6	12	18
7	14	21
8	16	24
9	18	27
10	20	30
5	10	15
4	8	12
3	6	9
2	4	6
1	2	3
1	2	3
3	6	9
5	10	15
7	14	21
9	18	27
1	2	3
2	4	6
3	6	9
9	99	999
5	10	15
6	12	18
7	14	21
8	16	24
9	18	27
10	20	30

To set the position indicator to the beginning of the file, use the library function rewind(). Its prototype in stdio.h is

```
    void rewind(FILE *fp);
```

The argument fp is the FILE pointer associated with the stream. After rewind() is called, the file's position indicator is set to the beginning of the file (byte 0). Use rewind() to read some data from a file and to start reading from the beginning of the file again without closing and reopening the file.

To determine the value of a file's position indicator, use

ftell(). The prototype of this function, located in stdio.h, reads

```
long ftell(FILE *fp);
```

The argument fp is the FILE pointer returned by fopen() when the file is opened. The function ftell() returns a type long that gives the current file position in bytes from the start of the file (the first byte is at position 0). In case of an error, ftell() returns -1L (a type long −1).

There are a number of interesting points here.

- The direct access functions always work with long integers and traditionally, associated variables are declared as being of type long int.

- The record numbering starts at zero and the file examination part of the program is terminated by a negative input. Strictly the final parameter of fseek() ought to have been SEEK_SET, not zero.

- The value returned by ftell() is the byte position of the byte about to be read from the file. Therefore when a new line is encountered, it is the start address of the next record.

The functions fsetpos() and fgetpos() do the same things as fseek() and ftell(), only they use parameters of type fpos_t rather than long int. This, potentially, allows for larger files to be handled. The use of these functions must be preferred.

Points to Note

- By using fseek(), one can set the position indicator anywhere in the file.
- The function fseek() returns 0 if the indicator is moved successfully or non-zero in case of an error.
- To determine the value of a file's position indicator, use ftell().
- The record numbering starts at zero and the file examination part of the program is terminated by a negative input.

10.8 OTHER FILE MANAGEMENT FUNCTIONS

The copy and delete operations are also associated with file management. Though one could write programs for them, the C standard library contains functions for deleting and renaming files.

10.8.1 Deleting a File

The library function remove() is used to delete a file. Its prototype in stdio.h is

```
int remove(const char *filename);
```

The variable *filename is a pointer to the name of the file to be deleted. The only precondition is that the specified file must not be open. If the file exists, it will be deleted and remove() returns 0. If the file does not exist or if it is read-only, if the programmer does not have sufficient access rights (for Unix system), or in case of some other error, remove() returns -1.

The following program describes the use of the remove() function.

Example

```
21.#include <stdio.h>
   int main(void)
   {
     char file[80];
     /* prompt for filename to delete */
     printf("File to delete: ");
     gets(file);
     /* delete the file */
     if(remove(file) == 0)
       printf("Removed %s.\n",file);
     else
       perror("remove");
       return 0;
   }
```

In this program, a function perror() is used, the prototype for which is

```
void perror(const char *message);
```

perror() produces a message on standard error output, describing the last error encountered. The argument string message is printed first, then a colon and a blank, followed by the message and a new line. If the message is a NULL pointer or if it points to a null string, the colon is not printed.

10.8.2 Renaming a File

The rename() function changes the name of an existing disk file. The function prototype in stdio.h is as follows.

```
int rename(const char *oldname, const char *newname);
```

The filenames pointed to by oldname and newname follow the rules given earlier in this chapter. The only restriction is that both names must refer to the same disk drive; a file cannot be renamed on a different disk drive. The function rename() returns 0 on success, or -1 if an error occurs. Errors can be caused by the following conditions (among others).

- The file `oldname` does not exist.
- A file with the name `newname` already exists.
- One tries to rename on another disk.

Consider the following program.

Example

```
22.#include <stdio.h>

   int main(void)
   {
      char oldname[80], newname[80];
          /* prompt for file to rename and new name */
      printf("File to rename:");
      gets(oldname);
      printf("New name:");
      gets(newname);
                              /* Rename the file */
      if(rename(oldname, newname) == 0)
        printf("Renamed %s to %s.\n", oldname, newname);
      else
        perror("rename");
        return 0;
   }
```

Points to Note

- The copy and delete operations are also associated with file management.
- In case of `remove()` function the only precondition is that the specified file must not be open.
- The only restriction in `rename()` function is that both names must refer to the same disk drive; a file cannot be renamed on a different disk drive.

10.9 LOW-LEVEL I/O

This form of I/O is unbuffered. That is, each read or write request results in accessing the disk (or device) directly to fetch/put a specific number of bytes. There are no formatting facilities. Instead of file pointers, we use *low-level* file handles or file descriptors, which give a unique integer number to identify each file.

To open a file the following function is used.

```
int open(char *filename, int flag, int perms);
```

The above function returns a file descriptor or -1 for a failure. The flag controls the file access and has the following predefined in `fcntl.h`: O_APPEND, O_CREAT, O_EXCL, O_RDONLY, O_RDWR, O_WRONLY and others. `perms` is best set to 0 for most of our applications.

The function

```
creat(char *filename, int perms);
```

can also be used to create a file.

```
int close(int handle);
```

can be used to close a file.

The following functions are used to read/write a specific number of bytes from/to a file stored or to be put in the memory location specified by buffer.

```
int read(int handle, char *buffer,unsigned length);
int write(int handle, char *buffer, unsigned length);
```

The `sizeof()` function is commonly used to specify the length. The `read()` and `write()` functions return the number of bytes read/written or -1 if they fail.

Points to Note

- Low-level I/O has no formatting facilities.
- Instead of file pointers, low-level file handles or file descriptors, which give a unique integer number to identify each file, are used.

SUMMARY

Data can also be stored in disk files. C treats a disk file like a stream (a sequence of characters), just like the predefined streams `stdin`, `stdout`, and `stderr`. A stream associated with a disk file must be opened using the `fopen()` library function before it can be used, and it must be closed after use through the `fclose()` function. A disk file stream can be opened either in text or in binary mode.

After a disk file has been opened, data can be read from the file, written into the file, or both. Data can be accessed either in a sequential manner or in a random manner. Each open disk file has an associated file position indicator. This indicator specifies the position in the file, measured as the number of bytes from the start of the file, where subsequent read and write operations occur. With some cases, the position indicator is updated automatically by the system, and programmers do not have to be bothered with it. For random file access, the C standard library provides functions such as `fseek()`, `ftell()`, and `rewind()` for manipulating the position indicator.

Finally, C provides some rudimentary file management functions, allowing deletion and renaming of disk files. Low-level file handling functions, that do not use formatting and file position indicators, are also available.

KEY-TERMS

Binary file   Binary file is a collection of bytes or a character stream. The data that is written into and read from binary file remain unchanged, with no separation between lines and no use of end-of-line characters and the interpretation of the file is left to the programmer.

Buffer   A buffer is a block of memory used for temporary storage of data being written to and read from the file. It serves as an interface between the stream (which is character-oriented) and the disk hardware (which is block-oriented).

File management   It basically means all operations related to creating, renaming, deleting, merging, reading, writing, etc. of any type of files.

Path   The path specifies the drive and/or directory (or folder) where the file is located. On PCs, the backslash character is used to separate directory names in a path. Some systems like Unix use the forward slash (/) as the directory separator.

Random file access   Random access means reading from or writing to any position in a file without reading or writing all the preceding data by controlling the position indicator.

Record   A record consist of a collection of data fields that conforms to a previously defined structure that can be stored on or retrieved from a file.

Sequential file access   In case of sequential file access, data is read from or written to a file in a sequential manner while the position indicator automatically gets adjusted by the stream I/O functions.

Stream   The stream is a common, logical interface to the various devices that comprise the computer and is a logical interface to a file. Although files differ in form and capabilities, all streams are the same.

Text file   A text file is a stream of characters that can be processed sequentially and logically in the forward direction. The maximum number of characters in each line is limited to 255 characters.

FREQUENTLY ASKED QUESTIONS

1. What is file?

A file is a collection of bytes stored on a secondary storage device, which is generally a disk of some kind. It is identified by a name, which is given at the time of its creation. It may be amended, moved from one storage device to another or removed completely when desired.

2. What is a stream?

In C, the stream is a common, logical interface to the various devices that form the computer. When the program executes, each stream is tied together to a specific device that is source or destination of data. The stream provides a consistent interface and to the programmer one hardware device will look much like another. In its most common form, a stream is a logical interface to a file. Stream I/O uses some temporary storage area, called buffer, for reading from or writing data to a file. A stream is linked to a file by using an open operation. A stream is disassociated from a file using a close operation.

The C language provides three "standard" streams that are always available to a C program. These are-

Name	Description	Example
stdin	Standard Input	Keyboard
stdout	Standard Output	Screen
stderr	Standard Error	Screen

3. What is buffer? What's its purpose?

Buffer is a temporary storage area that holds data while they are being transferred to and from memory. Buffering is a scheme that prevents excessive access to a physical I/O device like a disk or a terminal. Its purpose is to synchronize the physical devices that the program needs.

The buffer collects output data until there are enough to write efficiently. The buffering activities are taken care of by software called device drivers or access methods provided by the operating system.

4. Why have buffers?

It speeds up input/output which can be a major bottleneck in execution times. That is, it is less time-consuming to transmit several characters as a block than to send them one by one.

5. What is FILE?

FILE is a structure declared in stdio.h. The members of the FILE structure are used by the program in the various file access operations. For each file that is to be opened, a pointer to type FILE must be declared. When the function fopen() is called, that function creates an instance of the FILE structure and returns a pointer to that structure. This pointer is used in all subsequent operations on the file. But programmers don't need to be concerned about the members of the structure FILE.

Because one may use a number of different files in the program, he or she must specify when reading or writing which file one wishes to use. This is accomplished by using a variable called a *file pointer*, a pointer variable that points to a structure FILE.

6. How many files can I open at once?

The number of files that can be opened at once will be determined by the value of the constant FOPEN_MAX that is defined in <stdio.h>. FOPEN_MAX is an integer that specifies the maximum number of streams that can be open at one time. The C language standard requires that the value of FOPEN_MAX be at least 8, including the standard streams stdin, stdout and stderr. Thus, as a minimum, it's possible to work with up to 5 files simultaneously.

7. What happens if anyone doesn't close a file?

By default, the file should be closed when the program exits; however, one should never depend on this. A file must be closed as soon as the programmer has finished the processing with it. This defends data loss which could occur if an error in another part of the program caused the execution to be stopped in an abnormal fashion. As a consequence, the contents of the output buffer might be lost, as the file wouldn't be closed properly. It should be noted that one must also close a file before attempting to rename it or remove it.

8. What is the difference between `fgets()` and `gets()` ?

gets()	fgets()
The function `gets()` is normally used to read a line of string from the keyboard.	The function `fgets()` is used to read a line of string from a file or keyboard.
It automatically replaces the `'\n'` by `'\0'`.	It does not automatically delete the trailing `'\n'`
It takes one argument.	It takes three arguments.
It does not prevent overflow.	It prevents overflow.

EXERCISE

1. What are the primary advantages of using a data file?

2. What is `FILE`?

3. What is the purpose of the `fopen()` function?

4. What is the purpose of the `fclose()` function? Is it mandatory to use this in a program that processes a data file?

5. What is the difference between a text-mode stream and a binary-mode stream?

6. Describe different file opening modes used with the `fopen()` function.

7. What is stream? Describe two different methods of creating a stream-oriented data file.

8. What are the three general methods of file access?

9. What is `EOF`? When is `EOF` used?

10. Describe the different methods for reading from and writing into a data file.

11. What is the difference between a binary file and a text file in C?

12. Compare `fscanf()` and `fread()` functions?

13. What is the purpose of the `feof()` function?

14. How do you detect the end of a file in text and binary modes? Write code to close all file streams.

15. Indicate two different ways to reset the file position pointer to the beginning of the file.

16. Is anything wrong with the following?

```
FILE *fp;
int c;
if((fp= fopen(oldname, "rb"))==NULL)
   return -1;
```

```
while((c = fgetc(fp)) != EOF)
    fprintf(stdout, "%c", c);
fclose(fp);
```

17. Write a program to copy one existing file into another named file.

18. Write a complete C program that can be used as a simple line-oriented text editor. The program must have the following capabilities.

   (i)   Enter several lines of text and store them in a data file

   (ii) List the data file

   (iii) Retrieve and display a particular line

   (iv) Insert *n* lines

   (v)   Delete *n* lines

   (vi) Save the new text and exit

   Carry out these tasks using different functions.

19. Write a program that opens a file and counts the number of characters. The program should print the number of characters when finished.

20. Write a program to compare two files and print out the lines where they differ.

21. Write an interactive C program that will maintain a list roll, name, and total marks of students. Consider the information associated with each roll to be a separate record. Represent each record as a structure. Include a menu that will allow the user to select any of the following.

   (i)   Add a new record

   (ii) Delete a record

(iii) Modify a record

(iv) Retrieve and display an entire record for a given roll or name

(v) Display all records

(vi) End of computation

22. Write a program that opens an existing text file and copies it to a new text file with all lowercase letters changed to capital letters and all other characters unchanged.

23. Write a function that opens a new temporary file with a specified mode. All temporary files created by this function should automatically be closed and deleted when the program terminates.

24. Write a C code that will read a line of characters (terminated by a \n) from a text file into a character array called buffer. NULL terminates the buffer upon reading a \n.

Project Questions

1. Write a C program that takes the name of a file as a command-line argument, opens the file, reads through it to determine the number of words in each sentence, displays the total number of words and sentences, and computes the average number of words per sentence. The results should be printed in a table (at standard output), such as shown below:

```
This program counts the words and sentences in
file "comp.text".
```

```
            Sentence:  1    Words: 29
            Sentence:  2    Words: 41
            Sentence:  3    Words: 16
            Sentence:  4    Words: 22
            Sentence:  5    Words: 44
            Sentence:  6    Words: 14
            Sentence:  7    Words: 32
```

```
File "comp.text" contains 198 words words in
7 sentences for an average of 28.3 words per
sentence.
```

In this program, you should count a word as any contiguous sequence of letters, and apostrophes should be ignored. Thus, "O'Henry", "government's", and "friend's" should each be considered as one word.

Also in the program, you should think of a sentence as any sequence of words that ends with a period, exclamation point, or question mark. A period after a single capital letter (e.g., an initial) or embedded within digits (e.g., a real number) should not be counted as being the end of a sentence. White space, digits, and other punctuation should be ignored.

2. Write a C program that removes all comment lines from a C source code.

INCREMENTAL PROBLEM

The additional feature that has been added in this program is creating a file and storing data and retrieving it from the file. Other than that, similar functions and logic has been implemented as in the earlier chapter.

Problem statement

Within a file, store the co-ordinates of the given sets of vertices with which triangles can be formed. Read the co-ordinates of each set of vertices and compute the areas of the triangles formed by them. Next find the set of vertices that forms the triangle with the largest area among the set of triangles.

Solution

The functions and programming logic used is the same as in the earlier chapter. The only addition is the use of a file to store the co-ordinates of the set of vertices with which triangles can be formed. The area of triangles formed by these set of vertices are determined using the function getArea(). Next, the co-ordinates of the set of vertices, with which the triangle with the largest area can be formed, is found by using the function findLargestArea().

Program

```c
#include <stdio.h>
#include <math.h>
#include <stdlib.h>
typedef struct
{
    int x;
    int y;
}Point;
double getLength(Point,Point);
double getArea(double, double, double);
void findLargestArea(void);
int main(void)
{
    Point p[3];
    int i;
    double a,b,c;
    char ans='y';
```

```c
    FILE *fp;
    fp=fopen("point.dat","a");
    if(fp==NULL)
    {
        printf("\n Cannot open file..\n");
        exit(1);
    }
    while(ans=='Y'||ans=='y')
    {
    printf("\n Enter the coordinates of the verti-
            ces of a triangle");
    for(i=0;i<3;++i)
        {
            printf("\n Enter x[%d]: ",i);
            scanf("%d",&p[i].x);
            printf("\n Enter y[%d]: ",i);
            scanf("%d",&p[i].y);
        }
        a=getLength(p[0],p[1]);
        b=getLength(p[1],p[2]);
        c=getLength(p[0],p[2]);
        if(a+b>c && b+c>a && c+a>b)
        {
            printf("Triangle can be drawn");
            fprintf(fp,"%d %d %d %d %d %d\n",p[0].x,
                p[0].y,p[1].x,p[1].y,p[2].x,p[2].y);
        }
        else
        printf("Triangle cannot be drawn");
        printf("\n Do you add more(y/n)?");
        fflush(stdin);
        scanf("%c",&ans);
    }
    fclose(fp);
    findLargestArea();
    return 0;
}
double getLength(Point One, Point Two)
{
    int m, n;
    m=(One.x-Two.x)*(One.x-Two.x);
    n=(One.y-Two.y)*(One.y-Two.y);
    return sqrt((double)(m+n));
}
double getArea(double sA,double sB, double sC)
{
    double s;
    s=(sA+sB+sC)/2.0;
    return sqrt(s*(s-sA)*(s-sB)*(s-sC));
}
void findLargestArea(void)
{
    FILE *fp;
    Point p[3], r[3];
    int i;
    double a,b,c, maxArea, area;
    fp=fopen("point.dat","r");
    if(fp==NULL)
    {
        printf("\n Cannot open file..\n");
        exit(1);
    }
    fscanf(fp,"%d %d %d %d %d %d", &p[0].x, &p[0].y,
            &p[1].x, &p[1].y, &p[2].x, &p[2].y);
    for(i=0;i<3;++i)
        r[i]=p[i];
    a=getLength(p[0],p[1]);
    b=getLength(p[1],p[2]);
    c=getLength(p[0],p[2]);
    maxArea=getArea(a,b,c);
    while(!feof(fp))
    {
        fscanf(fp,"%d%d%d%d%d%d",&p[0].x, &p[0].y,
                &p[1].x, &p[1].y,&p[2].x,&p[2].y);
        a=getLength(p[0],p[1]);
        b=getLength(p[1],p[2]);
        c=getLength(p[0],p[2]);
        area=getArea(a,b,c);
        printf("\n Area is = %lf", area);
        if(area>maxArea)
        {
            maxArea=area;
            for(i=0;i<3;++i)
                r[i]=p[i];
        }
    }
    printf("\n Triangle with largest area whose
            points are:");
    for(i=0;i<3;++i)
    printf("(%d,%d)", r[i].x, r[i].y);
    printf("\n and Area is = %lf", maxArea);
    fclose(fp);
}
```

Problem Statement

A computer Phone Book containing name of persons, their home, office and mobile phone numbers has to be prepared. This book should have the necessary provision for adding, editing and deleting phone numbers and display the phone number of any person from the Phone Book as and when required.

Analysis and Design

The following program keeps a track of the telephone numbers of different persons. It works like a telephone index. Through the program, telephone numbers of a person can be added, edited, and deleted. Three telephone numbers (home, office, and mobile) are maintained along with the name of the person. All the records can be displayed page wise. The searching of a record can also be performed by inputting the name of the person. Here a binary file is used to store the records. The access method is chosen as random. Careful study of the program will clarify the following:

- the use of fread(), fwrite(), rewind()
- the concept of binary files with random access
- sorting of records stored in a file

The algorithm of the main program is given as follows:

```
1.  START
2.  OPEN  FILE  PBOOK.DAT IN BINARY MODE
3.  IF FILE OPEN  OPERATION IS UNSUCCESSFUL  THEN
    GOTO 9
4.  PRINT "1. ADD  2. MODIFY 3. DELETE 4. SEARCH
    5. DISPLAY 6. EXIT"
5.  PRINT "ENTER CHOICE"
6.  INPUT CHOICE
7.  IF CHOICE = 1 THEN CALL  ADD()
    ELSE  IF
        CHOICE = 2 THEN CALL  MODIFY()
    ELSE  IF
        CHOICE = 3 THEN CALL  DELET()
    ELSE  IF
        CHOICE =  4 THEN CALL  SEARCH()
    ELSE  IF
        CHOICE = 5 THEN CALL  DISPLAY()
        ELSE GOTO 10
8.  GOTO 4
9.  PRINT " ERROR OPENING PHONE BOOK".
10. CLOSE "PBOOK.DAT" FILE
11. STOP
```

The algorithm of ADD() function is given as follows:

```
1.  START
2.  PRINT "ENTER NAME"
3.  INPUT NAME
4.  PRINT "ENTER HOME PHONE NUMBER"
5.  INPUT HOME_PHONE_NUMBER
6.  PRINT "ENTER OFFICE PHONE NUMBER"
```

```
7.  INPUT OFFICE_PHONE_NUMBER
8.  PRINT "ENTER MOBILE PHONE NUMBER"
9.  INPUT MOBILE_PHONE_NUMBER
10. WRITE  NAME, HOME_PHONE_NUMBER, OFFICE_PHONE
    NUMBER AND MOBILE_PHONE_NUMBER IN THE  FILE
11. SORT THE RECORDS ACCORDING TO ALPHABETICAL
    ORDER OF NAMES
12. RETURN
```

The algorithm of MODIFY() function is given as follows:

```
1.  START
2.  PRINT "ENTER NAME"
3.  INPUT  T
4.  NAME
5.  FLAG ← 0
6.  READ A RECORD FROM THE FILE "PBOOK.DAT"
7.  IF END OF FILE IS REACHED  THEN GOTO 9
8.  IF NAME=TNAME   THEN  FLAG   ← 1
9.  IF FLAG=0 THEN GOTO 5
10. IF FLAG=0 THEN PRINT "NAME DOES NOT EXIST IN
    RECORD" : GOTO 23
11. POSITION THE RECORD POINTER AT THE BEGINNING
12. READ A RECORD FROM THE FILE "PBOOK.DAT"
13. IF NAME!=TNAME   THEN GOTO 11
14. PRINT "ENTER NAME"
15. INPUT NAME
16. PRINT  "ENTER HOME PHONE NUMBER"
17. INPUT   HOME_PHONE_NUMBER
18. PRINT "ENTER OFFICE PHONE NUMBER"
19. INPUT OFFICE_PHONE_NUMBER
20. PRINT "ENTER MOBILE PHONE NUMBER"
21. INPUT MOBILE_PHONE_NUMBER
22. POSITION THE RECORD POINTER AT THE CORRECT
    LOCATION
23. WRITE  NAME, HOME_PHONE_NUMBER, OFFICE_PHONE
    NUMBER AND MOBILE_PHONE_NUMBER IN THE  FILE .
24. RETURN
```

The algorithm of DELET() function is given as follows:

```
1.  START
2.  PRINT "NAME TO DELETE:"
3.  INPUT TNAME
4.  FLAG ← 0
5.  READ A RECORD FROM THE FILE "PBOOK.DAT"
6.  IF END OF FILE IS REACHED  THEN GOTO 9
7.  IF NAME=TNAME   THEN  FLAG   ← 1
8.  IF FLAG=0 THEN GOTO 5
9.  IF FLAG=0 THEN PRINT "NAME DOES NOT EXIST IN
    RECORD" : GOTO 20
10. OPEN A FILE "TEMP.DAT" IN BINARY MODE
11. POSITION THE RECORD POINTER OF THE FILE
    "PBOOK.DAT" AT THE BEGINNING
```

```
12.  READ A RECORD FROM THE FILE "PBOOK.DAT"
13.  IF END OF FILE IS REACHED  THEN GOTO 16
14.  IF NAME!=TNAME  THEN
     WRITE  NAME, HOME_PHONE_NUMBER, OFFICE_PHONE_
     NUMBER AND MOBILE_PHONE_NUMBER IN "TEMP.DAT"
15.  GOTO 12
16.  CLOSE THE FILES "PBOOK.DAT" AND "TEMP.DAT"
17.  REMOVE THE FILE "PBOOK.DAT"
18.  RENAME "TEMP.DAT" TO "PBOOK.DAT"
19.  IF FLAG=1 THEN PRINT  "RECORD DELETED"
20.  RETURN
```

The algorithm of SEARCH() function is given as follows:

```
1.  START
2.  PRINT "ENTER NAME TO SEARCH"
3.  INPUT NAME
4.  FLAG ← 0
5.  READ A RECORD FROM THE FILE "PBOOK.DAT"
6.  IF END OF FILE IS REACHED  THEN GOTO 9
7.  IF NAME=TNAME  THEN FLAG ← 1: PRINT  NAME,
    HOME_PHONE_NUMBER, OFFICE_PHONE_NUMBER AND
    MOBILE_PHONE_NUMBER
8.  GOTO 5
9.  IF FLAG=0 THEN PRINT "NAME DOES NOT EXIST"
10. RETURN
```

The algorithm of DISPLAY() function is given as follows:

```
1.  START
2.  READ A RECORD FROM THE FILE "PBOOK.DAT"
3.  IF END OF FILE IS REACHED  THEN GOTO 6
4.  PRINT NAME, HOME_PHONE_NUMBER, OFFICE_PHONE
    _NUMBER AND MOBILE_PHONE_NUMBER
5.  GOTO 2
6.  RETURN
```

The program is given as follows:

```c
#include <stdio.h>
#include <conio.h>
#include <string.h>
#include <process.h>

struct student
{
  char name[75];
  double home_ph,off_ph,mob_ph;
}s,arr[100],temp;

long int recsize;
FILE *fp,*ft;
void add(void);
void display(void);
void end(void);
void search(void);
void modify(void);
```

```c
void delet(void);
int i,c,k;
int main(void)
{
    int ch,i,c,k,flag,dis,no;
    clrscr();
    recsize=sizeof(s);
    fp=fopen("pbook.dat","rb+");
    if(fp==NULL)
    {
        fp=fopen("pbook.dat","wb+");
        if(fp == NULL)
        {
            printf("\n\n\tFile Opening error!");
            getch();
            exit(0);
        }
    }
    while(1)
    {
        printf("\n\t 1 : ADD");
        printf("\n\t 2 : MODIFY");
        printf("\n\t 3 : DELETE");
        printf("\n\t 4 : SEARCH");
        printf("\n\t 5 : DISPLAY ALL");
        printf("\n\t 6 : EXIT");
        printf("\n\t Enter your choice(1-6)?");
        fflush(stdin);
        scanf("%d",&ch);
        switch(ch)
        {
            case 1:add();     break;
            case 2:modify();  break;
            case 3:delet();   break;
            case 4:search();  break;
            case 5:display(); break;
            case 6:end();     break;
        }
    }
    return 0;
}

void add(void)
{
    fseek(fp,0,2);
    clrscr();
    printf("\n\n\tEnter Name :");
    scanf("%[^\n]",s.name);
    fflush(stdin);
    printf("\tEnter Phone Numbers(0 if a phone\
        number does not exist)\n");
    printf("\t\tHome Phone :");
    scanf("%lf",&s.home_ph);
    fflush(stdin);
    printf("\t\tOffice Phone :");
    scanf("%lf",&s.off_ph);
```

```
    fflush(stdin);
    printf("\t\tMobile Number :");
    scanf("%lf",&s.mob_ph);
    fflush(stdin);
    fwrite(&s,recsize,1,fp);
    i=0;
    rewind(fp);
    while(fread(&s,recsize,1,fp)==1)
    {
        arr[i]=s;
        i++;
    }
    for(c=0;c<i-1;c++)
    {
        for(k=0;k<i-1;k++)
        {
            if(strcmp(arr[k].name,arr[k+1].name)> 0)
            {
                temp=arr[k];
                arr[k]=arr[k+1];
                arr[k+1]=temp;
            }
        }
    }
    rewind(fp);
    for(k=0;k<i;k++)
    fwrite(&arr[k],recsize,1,fp);
    clrscr();
}

void end(void)
{
    fclose(fp);
    clrscr();
    getch();
    exit(0);
}

void display(void)
{
    int no,dis;
    rewind(fp);
    no=1;
    dis=0;
    clrscr();
    printf("\n_____\n");
    printf (" _ _ N A M E _ _ _ _ _ _ _ _ | _ _ _ \
HOME____|___WORK____|___MOBILE___|\n");
    while(fread(&s,recsize,1,fp)==1)
    {
        printf("\n");
        printf("%2d)%-13s\t\t|",no,s.name);no++;
        printf("%-12.0lf|",s.home_ph);
        printf("%-12.0lf|",s.off_ph);
        printf("%-12.0lf|\n",s.mob_ph);
        dis++;
```

```
        if(dis==15)
        {
            dis=0;
            printf("\n\t\t\t Press ENTER to continue");
            getch();
            printf("\n\n_____\n");
            printf("__NAME_____|____\
HOME____|___WORK____|___MOBILE___|\n");
        }
    }
}

void search(void)
{
    int flag=0;
    char nm[75];
    rewind(fp);
    clrscr();
    printf("\n\n\tEnter the name to be searched :");
    printf("\n\t\tEnter Name :");
    scanf("%[^\n]",nm);
    fflush(stdin);
    while(fread(&s,recsize,1,fp)==1)
    {
        if(strcmp(s.name,nm)==0)
        {
            flag=1;
            printf("\n\t————Record found——— \n");
            printf("\n\tName : %-15s \n",s.name);
            printf("\tHome Phone : %-12.0lf",s.home_ph);
            printf("\n\tOffice Phone : %-12.0lf",s.
                off_ph);
            printf("\n\tMobile Number : %6c \n",s.
                mob_ph);
        }
    }
    if(flag==0)
    printf("\n\n\t— RECORD DOES NOT EXIST —\n\n");
}

void modify(void)
{
    int flag;
    char nm[75];
    rewind(fp);
    clrscr();
    printf("\n\n\tEnter the name of the record to be
        edited :");
    printf("\n\t\tEnter Name :");
    scanf("%[^\n]",nm);
    fflush(stdin);
    flag=0;
    while(fread(&s,recsize,1,fp)==1)
    if(strcmp(s.name,nm)==0)
    flag=1;
```

```
    if(flag==0)
    {
        printf("\n\n\t— RECORD DOES NOT EXIST —\n\n");
        return;
    }
    rewind(fp);
    while(fread(&s,recsize,1,fp) == 1)
    {
        if(strcmp(s.name,nm) == 0)
        {
            printf("\n\nEnter new data :");
            printf("\n\n\tEnter Name :");
            scanf("%[^\n]",s.name);
            fflush(stdin);
            printf("\tEnter Phone Numbers(0 if a
                phone number does not exist)\n");
            printf("\t\tHome Phone :");
            scanf("%lf",&s.home_ph);fflush(stdin);
            printf("\t\tOffice Phone :");
            scanf("%lf",&s.off_ph);fflush(stdin);
            printf("\t\tMobile Number :");
            scanf("%lf",&s.mob_ph);fflush(stdin);
            fseek(fp,-recsize,1);
            fwrite(&s,recsize,1,fp);
            break;
        }
    }
    i=0;
    rewind(fp);
    while(fread(&s,recsize,1,fp)==1)
    {
        arr[i]=s;
        i++;
    }
    for(c=0;c<i-1;c++)
    {
        for(k=0;k<i-1;k++)
        {
            if(strcmp(arr[k].name,arr[k+1].name)> 0)
            {
                temp=arr[k];
                arr[k]=arr[k+1];
                arr[k+1]=temp;
            }
        }
    }
    rewind(fp);
    for(k=0;k<i;k++)
    fwrite(&arr[k],recsize,1,fp);
    clrscr();
}

void delet(void)
{
    int flag;
    char nm[75];
```

```
    rewind(fp);
    ft=fopen("temp.dat","wb+");
    clrscr();
    printf("\n\n\tEnter the name to be deleted :");
    printf("\n\t\tEnter Name :");
    scanf("%[^\n]",nm);fflush(stdin);
    flag=0;
    while(fread(&s,recsize,1,fp)==1)
    if(strcmp(s.name,nm)==0)
    flag=1;
    if(flag==0)
    {
        printf("\n\n\t—RECORD DOES NOT EXIST —\n\n");
        return;
    }
    rewind(fp);
    while(fread(&s,recsize,1,fp) == 1)
    {
        if(strcmp(s.name,nm) != 0)
        fwrite(&s,recsize,1,ft);
    }
    if(flag == 1)
    printf("\n\n\t——— RECORD DELETED ———");
    getch();
    fclose(fp);
    fclose(ft);
    remove("pbook.dat");
    rename("temp.dat","pbook.dat");
    fp=fopen("pbook.dat","rb++");
    i=0;
    rewind(fp);
    while(fread(&s,recsize,1,fp)==1)
    {
        arr[i]=s;
        i++;
    }
    for(c=0;c<i-1;c++)
    {
        for(k=0;k<i-1;k++)
        {
            if(strcmp(arr[k].name,arr[k+1].name)> 0)
            {
                temp=arr[k];
                arr[k]=arr[k+1];
                arr[k+1]=temp;
            }
        }
    }
    rewind(fp);
    for(k=0;k<i;k++)
    fwrite(&arr[k],recsize,1,fp);
    clrscr();
}
```

C

Linked Lists

Chapter 11

Learning Objectives

After reading this chapter, the readers will be able to

- understand linked lists
- learn about operations on linked lists
- know about the applications of linked lists
- get familiar with self-referential structures
- comprehend the advantages and disadvantages of linked lists

11.1 INTRODUCTION

List is a finite, ordered sequence of data items known as *elements*. "Ordered" in this definition means that each element has a position in the list. In other words, there is a first element in the list, a second element, and so on. Each list element also has a data type.

Formally, a general list is of the form $a_1, a_2, a_3, ..., a_n$. We say that the size of this list is n. We will call the special list of size 0 a *null list*.

Such a list can be implemented either by *sequential allocation* or by *linked allocation*. By sequential allocation a list is processed using array. Linked list is another data structure to implement a list of items using linked list.

Before discussing linked lists, there is a need to revisit arrays.

Arrays are probably the most common data structures used to store large numbers of homogeneous data elements. Arrays are easy to declare and the array elements can also be accessed by the index numbers easily by using the symbols [and]. Therefore, arrays are used in most languages including C. However, arrays have some disadvantages also and they are as follows.

- *Fixed size* The size of an array is fixed. With a little extra effort, by dynamically allocating an array in the heap, specifying the size of the array can be deferred until the array is created at runtime, but after that it remains fixed. Arrays can be dynamically resized with the function `realloc()`, but that requires some programming effort.

- *Wastages of space* If the number of elements in an array is less than the size of the array, which is fixed in advance, then it leads to wastage of space.
- *Sequential storage* An array allocates memory for all its elements chunked together as one block of memory. For arrays, contiguous space is required. If the program ever needs to process larger number of elements, the code will crash.
- *Possibility of overflow* If the program ever needs to process more than the size, there is a possibility of overflow and the code breaks.
- *Difficulty in insertion and deletion* Inserting new elements at the front cannot be efficiently done because existing elements need to be shifted to make room. Similar is the case for deletion also. Therefore, these operations require a lot of movement of data, thereby leading to an inefficient and time-consuming algorithm. In case of deletion, the space of the deleted element cannot be freed.

An appropriate solution to these problems is the *linked list*, which, at some cost in memory space, permits lists to be constructed and modified easily. A linked list is an ordered collection of elements, where each element has at least one *pointer* for pointing to the next element of the list and at least one *value*. Such an element is known as the *node* of a linked list. The singly linked list is the most basic of all the linked data structures.

Both the array and the linked list are alternative implementation options for a sequence which is a collection of items with a defined order. Table 11.1 shows a comparison between these two implementations.

There are several variants of linked lists. These are as follows:

- Singly linked lists
- Circular linked lists
- Doubly linked lists
- Doubly circular linked lists

The simplest kind of linked list is a *singly linked list*, which has one link per node. The link is nothing but a pointer. This link points to the next node in the list, or to a NULL value or empty list if it is the final node.

Table 11.1 Comparisons between linked lists and arrays

Feature	Linked lists	Arrays
Memory allocation	No overflow is possible. All memory offered for an application available. The links need additional space.	All memory must be allocated before use. The memory space allocated can be exhausted or left unused.
Accessing items	Only sequential search is possible.	Random access is possible, when the order number is known.
Expressing order of items	No order is maintained since nodes may not be stored at continuous memory locations.	The location in memory indicates the order number of item.
Efficiency of operation	Insertions and deletions are effective, regardless of the position they are inserted in.	Many data movements are needed in insertions and in deletions of items.
Programming	Needs a bit of expertise.	Very easy

A more advanced linked list is the *doubly linked list* or *two-way linked list*. Each node has two links: one points to the previous node, or points to a NULL value or empty list if it is the first node; and the other points to the next node, or points to a NULL value or empty list if it is the final node.

In a *singly circularly linked list*, each node has one link, similar to an ordinary singly linked list, except that the next link of the last node points back to the first node. It is usual to retain an external pointer pointing to the last element in a singly circularly linked list, as this allows quick insertion at the beginning, and also allows access to the first node through the last node's next pointer.

In a *doubly circularly linked list*, each node has two links, similar to a doubly linked list, except that the previous link of the first node points to the last node and the next link of the last node points to the first node. As in a doubly linked list, insertions and removals can be done at any point with access to any nearby node.

Linked lists have their strengths and weaknesses, but they happen to be strong where arrays are weak. All the features of arrays follow from the strategy of allocating the memory for all its elements in one block of memory. Linked lists use an entirely different strategy. As will be clear later, linked lists allocate memory for each element separately and only when necessary. In this book, we will study only about singly linked lists.

Arrays are mapped into a contiguous block of addresses in the physical memory. The contiguous nature of the array is mainly responsible for its drawbacks. An alternative is the linked list. In a linked list,

- The elements need not be stored contiguously. The logical order of the list may not be the same as its physical order.
- To maintain a logical ordering, each element has a link to the next item.
- The elements may be removed from the list by skipping over them in the link path.
- The elements may be added to the list by linking them in; that is, modifying a few of the links.
- Sequential traversal (in logical order) can be performed by following the link path.

11.2 SINGLY LINKED LISTS

A singly linked list is simply a sequence of dynamically allocated objects, each of which refers to its successor in the list. It allocates space for each element separately in its own block of memory called a *linked list element* or *node*. Each node contains two fields: a *data* field to store whatever data type the list holds and a *next* field, which is a pointer, used to hold the address of the next node. The next field is used to link one node to the next node. The beginning of the linked list is stored in a pointer termed as head which points to the first node. The first node contains a pointer to the second node. The second node contains a pointer to the third node, and so on. The last node in the list has its next field set to NULL to mark the end of the list. No matter how many nodes get added to the list, head will always be the first node in the linked list.

The empty list Initially the pointer head is initialized as NULL indicating the empty list, i.e., the list with no node. A linked list is represented pictorially as shown in Fig. 11.1.

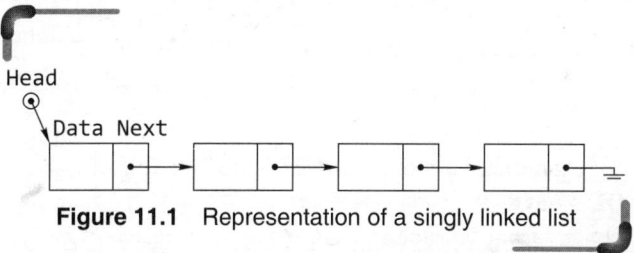

Figure 11.1   Representation of a singly linked list

Observe that the linked list is an ordered collection of elements called nodes each of which contains two items of information:

- a data element of the list and
- a link, i.e., a pointer that indicates the location of the successor of this list element which is a node.

In Fig. 11.1, arrows represent the links. The data part of each node consists of whatever data type the list holds and the next part contains the pointer to the next node. The grounded earth indicates NULL. Figure 11.2 shows several of the most commonly used singly linked list variants.

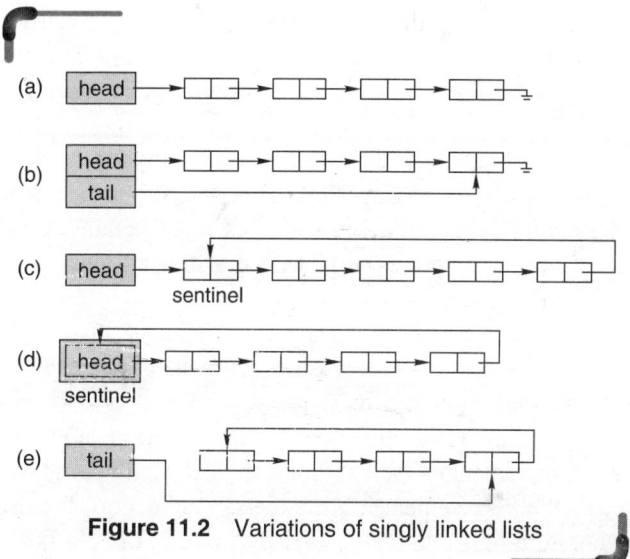

Figure 11.2   Variations of singly linked lists

The basic singly linked list is shown in Fig. 11.2(a). Each node of the list contains a pointer to its successor; the last node contains a null pointer. A pointer to the first node of the list, labeled head in the figure, is used to keep track of the list.

The basic singly linked list is inefficient in cases where nodes are required to be added at both ends of the list. While it is easy to add nodes at the head of the list, to add nodes at the other end, called the *tail*, one needs to locate the last element. If the basic singly linked list is used, the entire list needs to be traversed in order to find its tail.

Fig. 11.2(b) shows a way by which adding nodes to the tail of a list is more efficient. The solution is to keep a second pointer, tail, which points to the last element of the list. Of course, such efficiency comes at the cost of the additional space used to store the tail pointer.

The singly linked lists [see Fig. 11.2(c) and (d)] illustrate two common programming tricks. The list in Fig. 11.2(c) has an extra node at the head of the list called a ***sentinel***. This element is never used to store data but it should be present in the linked list to store the address of the first node. The principal advantage of using a sentinel is that it simplifies the programming of certain operations, e.g., since there is always a sentinel standing guard, we never need to modify the `head` pointer. Of course, the disadvantage of a sentinel, such as that shown in Fig. 11.2(c), is that extra space is required, and the sentinel needs to be created when the list is initialized.

The list in Fig. 11.2(c) is also a *circularly linked list*. Instead of using a NULL pointer to delimit the end of the list, the pointer in the last element points to the sentinel. The advantage of this programming trick is that insertion at the head of the list, insertion at the tail of the list, and insertion at an arbitrary position of the list are all identical operations.

Figure 11.2(d) shows a variation of a singly linked list using a sentinel in which instead of keeping a pointer to the sentinel, the sentinel itself serves as the handle for the list. This variant eliminates the need to allocate storage for the sentinel separately.

Of course, it is also possible to create a circular singly linked list that does not use a sentinel. Figure 11.2(e) shows a variation in which a single pointer is used to keep track of the list, but this time the pointer, `tail`, points to the last element of the list. Since the list is circular in this case, the first element follows the last element of the list. Therefore, it is relatively simple to insert at the head or at the tail of this list. This variation minimizes the storage required, at the expense of a little extra time for certain operations.

Figure 11.3 illustrates how the empty list (i.e., the list containing no list elements) is represented for each of the variations given in Fig. 11.2. Notice that the sentinel is always present in those list variants, which use it. On the other hand, in the list variants, which do not use a sentinel, null pointers are used to indicate the empty list.

Here in the implementation of a singly linked list only `head` is considered. A node of the singly linked list can be represented in C using the function `struct` as follows:

```
struct node
{
  int data;
  struct node *next;
};
```

The first field is an integer named `data` and the second is a pointer to the next node in the list as shown in Fig. 11.1. Such structures that contain a pointer that points to the same structure type are called *self-referential structures*. Therefore, a linked list is an ordered collection of structures connected by logical links that are stored as

a part of data in the structure itself. The link is in the form of a pointer to another structure of the same type. In this case, note that the data field is an integer but it could be any complex data type if required. In general, a node can be represented in the following manner:

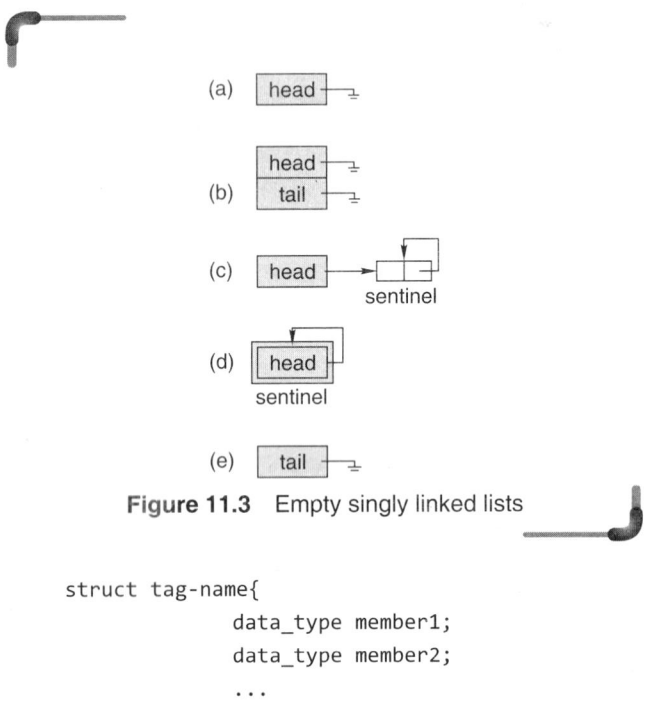

Figure 11.3 Empty singly linked lists

```
struct tag-name{
        data_type member1;
        data_type member2;
        . . .
        . . .
        struct tag-name *next;
    };
```

The structure may contain more than one item with different data types. However, one of the items must be a pointer to the `tag-name`.

Example:
```
#define NAMELEN 50
struct node
{
  char name[NAMELEN];      /* data: name */
  int year;                /* data: year */
  struct node *next;
                    /* pointer to the next node */
};
```

An example of a more complex node is as follows:
Data part:
```
typedef struct
{
  char code[8];            /* course code */
  char name[26];           /* course name */
  int credits;             /* course credits */
```

```
    int lectures;          /* no. of lecture hours */
    int labs;                /* no. of lab hours */
} course;
```

Node:
```
struct node
{
  course data;           /* course information */
  struct node *next;
                  /* pointer to the next node */
} ;
```

Singly linked list containing any of the nodes declared, as above, is known as a homogeneous linked list as it contains similar types of nodes. To represent non-homogeneous list (those which contain nodes of different types), a union may be used.

For instance, consider the following declaration of a node:

```
struct node
{
  int etype;
  union
    {
      int ival;
      float fval;
      char *sval;
    }
  struct node *next;
};
```

It declares a node whose elements may be either integer, or floating point number or string depending on the corresponding etype. Since a union is always large enough to hold its largest component, the sizeof and malloc() functions can be applied to allocate storage space for the node.

Here is a simple program, which uses pointer operations to build the singly linked list containing three nodes which have the values 1, 2, and 3 in the data field of the nodes respectively and displays it.

```
#include <stdio.h>
#include <stdlib.h>
struct node
{
  int data;
  struct node *next;
};
void makelist(struct node **);
void display(struct node *);
```

```
int main()
{
struct node *head;
head=NULL;
makelist(&head);
display(head);
return 0;
}
void makelist(struct node **h)
{
  struct node *first=NULL;
  struct node *second=NULL;
  struct node *third=NULL;
  /* allocate 3 nodes in the heap */
  first =(struct node *)malloc(sizeof(struct node));
  second=(struct node *)malloc(sizeof(struct node));
  third=(struct node *)malloc(sizeof(struct node));

  /* setup first node */
  first->data = 1;
  first->next = second;

  /* setup second node */
  second->data = 2;
  second->next = third;

  /* setup third node */
  third->data = 3;
  third->next = NULL;
  /* store the address of first node in head */
  *h=first;
}
void display(struct node *p)
{
  while(p!=NULL)
  {
    printf("%d ->",p->data);
    p=p->next;
  }
  printf("NULL");
}
```

Analysis of the above program To create the linked list, in the function makelist(), the following three steps are used.

1. Allocate the new node in the heap and set its data part to whatever needs to be stored.

2. Set the next pointer of the current node to point to the next node of the list. This is actually just a pointer assignment. Note that assigning one pointer to another pointer makes them point to the same thing.

3. Store the address of the first node in head.

In the function `display()`, a frequently used technique in linked list code is to iterate a pointer over all the nodes in a list. Traversing a linked list starts at the first node and each node in succession is examined until the last node has been processed. In the function `display()`, the pointer `head` is copied into a local variable p,which then iterates through the list. The end of the list is tested with `p!=NULL`. The statement `p=p->next` advances the local pointer p to the next node in the list. Alternately, some might prefer to write the loop using `for`, which makes the initialization, test, and pointer updating more optimized.

```
for(;p!=NULL;p=p->next) { ... }
```

Beginners are often confused about how the statement `p=p->next` makes p point to the next node in the linked list. Let us understand this with the help of an example. Suppose in a linked list containing four nodes p is pointing to the first node (see Fig. 11.4).

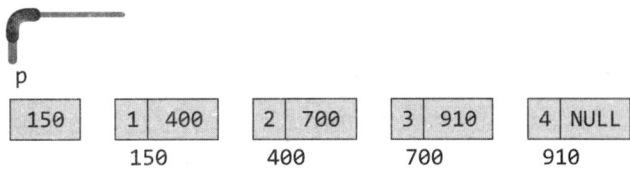

Figure 11.4   Actual representation of a singly linked list in memory

Instead of showing the links to the next node, Fig. 11.4 shows the address of the next node in the next part of each node. When the statement `p=p-> next` is executed, the right hand side of this expression yields 400. This address is now stored in p. As a result, p starts pointing to the node present at address 400. In effect, the statement has shifted p so that it has started pointing to the next node in the linked list. Figure 11.5 show a graphic representation of a linked list traversal.

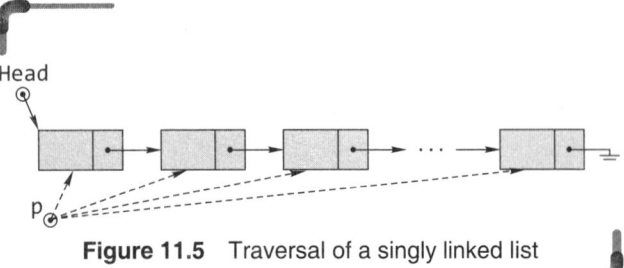

Figure 11.5   Traversal of a singly linked list

It is to be observed that in the function `makelist()`, the formal argument is a pointer to pointer of type `struct node` where &head is passed to this function. On the other hand,

in the function `display()`, only `head` is passed as parameter, so the formal argument is a pointer of type `struct node`. In C, changes to local parameters are never reflected back in the caller's memory. It is to be noted that the function `makelist()` is needed to change some variables of the caller's memory, namely the head variable. The traditional method to allow a function to change its caller's memory is to pass a pointer to the caller's memory instead of a copy.

So in C, to change an `int` in the caller, pass an `int *` instead. To change a `T`, pass a `T *`, where `T` is any data type. Therefore, if a value `struct node *` is to be changed, it is needed to passed as `struct node **` instead. The type of the head pointer is "pointer to a `struct node`". In order to change that pointer, we need to pass a pointer to it, which will be a "pointer to a pointer to a `struct node`".

Instead of defining `void makelist(struct node *)`, it is needed to define `void makelist(struct node **)`. The first form passes a copy of the `head` pointer. The second, correct form passes a pointer to the `head` pointer. In the code, &head is to be used as actual parameter in the calling function and `**` should be used in the parameter of the called function. Inside `makelist()`, the pointer to the head pointer is named `h`.

Figure 11.6 shows the memory diagram just before the first call to `makelist()` exits. The original value of the `head` pointer is in solid line. Notice how the `h` parameter inside `makelist()` points back to the real `head` pointer back in `makelist()`. `makelist()` uses `*h` to access and change the real `head` pointer.

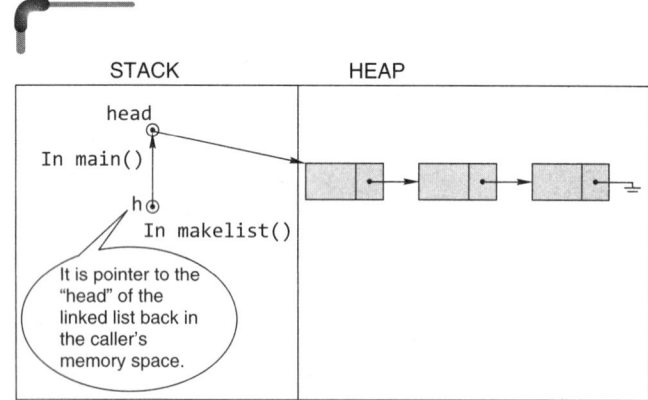

Figure 11.6   Memory diagram for pointer to a pointer to head

The general rule is that if there is a statement in the function that modifies the content of the pointer `head`, then the address of the pointer `head` must be passed to that function. This program is alright if the number of nodes is too few. It is not worthwhile to declare a pointer for each node. A better implementation is given below where the same pointer is used to create nodes. To make a list, the `append()` function may be called repeatedly.

```
void append(struct node **h)
{
  struct node *p,*tmp;
/* Creation of new node */
  p=(struct node *)malloc(sizeof(struct node));
  if(p==NULL)
  {
    printf("\n Memory allocation unsuccessful..");
    return;
  }
  printf("\n Enter data:…");
  scanf("%d",&p->data);
  p->next=NULL;
/* appending the newly created node in an empty
      linked list */
  if(*h==NULL)
  {
    *h=p;
    return;
  }
/* Traversal of list to find out the last node */
  tmp=*h;
  while(tmp->next!=NULL)
    tmp=tmp->next;
/* appending the newly created node after the
      last node */
  tmp->next=p;
}
```

The `append()` function has to deal with two situations:
First: Adding a node to an empty list.
Second: Adding the node to the end of the linked list.

If the linked list is empty then the pointer `head` will contain `NULL`. Hence space is allocated for the new node using `malloc()`. Then the `data` and the `next` field of this node are set up. Lastly, `head` is made to point to this node, since the first node has been added to the linked list and `head` must always point to the first node. Note that `*h` is nothing but equal to `head`.

If the list is not empty, then one has to traverse upto the last node and append the new node, address of which is stored in `p`, at the end of the last node. Traversal of a singly linked list has been discussed earlier. However, for the convenience of readers, it has been explained again. A pointer of type `struct node`, `tmp`, is made to point to the first node in the linked list through the statement

```
tmp=*h;
```

Then with `tmp`, the entire linked list is traversed using the statements:

```
while(tmp->next!=NULL)
  tmp=tmp->next;
```

Each time `tmp` points to the next node in the list through the `while` loop using the statement `tmp=tmp->next`. When `tmp` reaches the last node, the condition `tmp->next!= NULL` would fail. The position of the pointer after traversing the linked list is shown in Fig. 11.7.

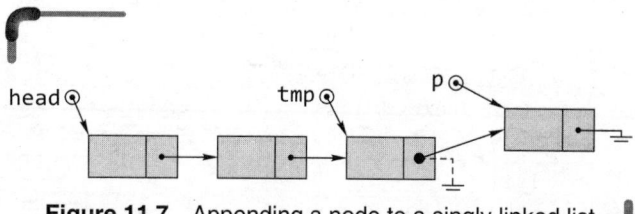

Figure 11.7 Appending a node to a singly linked list

Now the previous last node has to be connected to this new last node. `tmp` points to the previous node and `p` points to the new last node They are connected through the statement

```
tmp->next = p;
```

Compiling all the steps, the algorithm for appending a node to a singly linked list is as follows:

1. Whether the linked list is empty or not, one needs to create a new node and fill it with data.

2. If the address of the newly created node is stored in a pointer, say `p`, then set the `next` field of this node to `NULL`; because, the newly added node is always the last node.

3. If the linked list is empty, make `head` point to `p`. If the linked list is not empty, in that case, the current last node in the linked list (not `p`) is no longer the last one. So, the last node should be linked to `p` by assigning the `next` field of the last node to `p`.

In many cases, it will be more efficient if two pointers are used: one for first node (`head`), another for last node (`tail`). If an external pointer `tail` is used to point to the last node then traversing the list to the last node can be avoided. The linked list diagram looks like a train, doesn't it? It has a `head` and a `tail`. For best performance, both `head` and `tail` are required. For simplicity only `head` is considered here.

The recursive version of the `append()` function is as follows:

```
void append(struct node **h)
{
  if(*h==NULL)
  {
    *h=(struct node *)malloc(sizeof(struct node));
    if(*h==NULL)
    {
    printf("\n Memory allocation unsuccessfull..");
    return;
    }
    printf(" \n Enter data:");
    scanf("%d",&(*h)->data);
    (*h)->next=NULL;
  }
  else
    append(&(*h)->next);
}
```

The function `display()` has already been discussed. Following is a recursive version of this function.

```
void display(struct node *p)
{
  if(p==NULL)
  {
    printf("NULL");
    return;
  }
  else
  {
    printf("%d ->",p->data);
    display(p->next);
  }
}
```

The following main primitive operations can be performed on singly linked lists:

- Insert a node
  - After a particular node
  - After *n*th node
  - Before a particular node
- Search a particular node
- Remove a particular node
- Sort the nodes
- Destroy (delete all nodes)

These operations will be discussed in the following sections. In these sections, pointer pointing to the first node of the singly linked list is indicated by `head` in the figures but in the corresponding functions it is written as `*h`.

11.2.1 Inserting a Node in a Singly Linked List

General algorithm to insert a node may be described as follows:

1. Allocate memory for the new node and and fill it with data.
2. Determine the insertion point, i.e., the position within the list where the new node will be placed. To identify the position, the predecessor of the new node should be known.
3. Point the new node to its successor.
4. Point the predecessor to the new node.

The different ways of insertion of a node in a singly linked list are discussed in the following sub-sections.

Insertion of a Node after a Specified Node

Consider that the node, after which a new node is to be inserted, is specified by the value of the data field of that node, say it is stored in a variable `k`. Searching the node, after which the new node is to be placed, is carried out with the usual traversal pattern, using a local pointer variable say `tmp` to step through the nodes one at a time. As the loop executes, `tmp` points to the nodes of the list one after another. At each iteration, the content of the data field of the node currently being pointed by `tmp` is compared with the value being sought (stored in `k`) and if the two are equal then the loop is exited. Otherwise, `tmp` is updated to `tmp->next` so that the next node can be examined. It will continue until the last node has been visited in which case executing `tmp=tmp->next` causes `tmp` becoming `NULL`, which is used as an indication that the value contained in `k` is not in the list. The following loop performs this task:

```
for(tmp=head; tmp!=NULL && tmp->data!=k;
    tmp=tmp->next);
```

As a consequence of this loop, `tmp` is now pointing to the node after which a new node is to be inserted. Let a pointer `p` point to the new node to be inserted. Now follow the schematic diagram shown in Fig. 11.8.

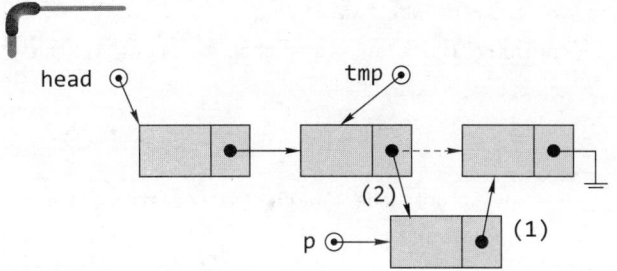

Figure 11.8 Insertion of a node after a particular node in a singly linked list

From Fig. 11.8, it is clear that the next field of p should point to what tmp was pointing to before insertion and then the next field of tmp should point to the node that is pointed to by p. This action consists of two statements:

```
p->next = tmp->next;          (1)
tmp->next=p;                  (2)
```

The order in which the two pointer assignments are made is important. If the order of the assignment statements is reversed, then the value of tmp->next would be lost before it is used and there would be no way to attach the new node (pointed by p) to the remainder of the list. This code can now be built into a function insaft() to insert a new node after a particular node in a singly linked list.

```
void insaft(struct node **h)
{
struct node *p,*tmp;
int k;
  if(*h==NULL)
  {
    printf("\n Linked List is EMPTY");
    return;
  }
printf("\n Enter the node after which new node\
      is to be inserted :");
scanf("%d",&k);
for(tmp=*h; tmp!=NULL && tmp->data!=k;
      tmp=tmp->next);
if(tmp==NULL)
  printf("\n NODE DOES NOT EXIST");
else
  {
    p=(struct node *)malloc(sizeof(struct node));
    if(p==NULL)
      {
        printf("\n Memory allocation unsuccessfull..");
        return;
      }
```

```
    printf(" \n Enter data:…");
    scanf("%d",&p->data);
    p->next=tmp->next;
    tmp->next=p;
  }
}
```

The recursive version of the preceding function is as follows. In this version, it is needed to pass a value to the data field of the node after which the new node has to be inserted.

```
void insaft(struct node **h, int k)
{
  struct node *p;
  if(*h==NULL)
  {
  printf("\n NODE DOES NOT EXIST or \
      Linked List is EMPTY..void INSERTION");
   return;
  }
  else if((*h)->data==k)
   {
   p=(struct node *)malloc(sizeof(struct node));
   if(p==NULL)
    {
      printf("\n Memory allocation unsuccessfull..");
      return;
    }
    printf(" \n Enter data:");
    scanf("%d",&p->data);
    p->next=(*h)->next;
    (*h)->next=p;
    return;
   }
   else
    insaft(&(*h)->next,k);
}
```

Note that in the function insaft(), there would be no change in head. Therefore, it is not required to pass &head as an actual parameter to the function. It is safe to replace all *h with h and the formal parameter would be struct node *h. This is illustrated in the next version of the insaft() function.

Consider that the node, after which the insertion of a new node is to be carried out, is specified by giving its position with the first node at position 1, second node at position 2, next node at position 3, and so on. Like done earlier, start by pointing the pointer variable h to the head of the singly linked list. A loop then moves h forward to the correct node as shown in the program. Therefore, h is now pointing to the node after which the new node has to be inserted. The rest is the same as before. Follow the definition of the function, which is given as follows:

```
void insaft_nth(struct node *h)
{
int position,i;
struct node *p;
if(h==NULL)
  {
    printf("\n Linked List is EMPTY");
    return;
  }
 printf("\n Enter the position after which new\
         node is to be inserted :");
 scanf("%d",&position);
 for(i=1;h!=NULL && i<position;++i)
   h=h->next;
 if(h==NULL)
   printf(" There are less than %d nodes \
     in the list",position);
 else
 {
   p=(struct node *)malloc(sizeof(struct node));
   if(p==NULL)
    {
     printf("\n Memory allocation unsuccessfull..");
     return;
    }
   printf(" \n Enter data: ");
   scanf("%d",&p->data);
   p->next=h->next;
   h->next=p;
  }
}
```

Its recursive version is as follows:

```
void insaft_nth(struct node *h,int position)
{
  static int i=1;
  struct node *p;
  if(h==NULL && i==1)
  {
    printf("\n Linked List is EMPTY");
    return;
  }
```

```
  else if(h==NULL && i>1)
  printf("There are less than %d nodes in the\
         list",position);
  else if(i==position)
    {
     p=(struct node *)malloc(sizeof(struct node));
     if(p==NULL)
     {
      printf("\n Memory allocation unsuccessfull..");
      return;
     }
    printf("\n Enter data: ");
    scanf("%d",&p->data);
     p->next=h->next;
     h->next=p;
    }
    else
    {
    i++;
    insaft_nth(h->next,position);
    }
}
```

Insertion of a Node Before a Specified Node

A function insbef() that inserts a new node can be defined as follows.

```
void insbef(struct node **h)
{
  struct node *p,*tmp,*prev;
  int k;
  if(*h==NULL)
  {
    printf("\n Linked List is EMPTY");
    return;
  }
printf("\n Enter the node before which new node\
       is to be inserted :");
scanf("%d",&k);
 /* Insertion at the beginning */
 if((*h)->data==k)
 {
   p=(struct node *)malloc(sizeof(struct node));
   if(p==NULL)
```

```
    {
       printf("\n Memory allocation unsuccessfull..");
       return;
    }
    printf(" \n Enter data: ");
    scanf("%d",&p->data);
    p->next=*h;
    *h=p;
  }
  tmp=(*h)->next;
              /* as the first node pointed by head
                 has been checked specially */
  prev=*h;
  while(tmp!=NULL)
  {
    if(tmp->data==k)
      break;
    else
    {
      prev=tmp;
      tmp=tmp->next;
    }
  }
  if(tmp==NULL)
    {
    printf("\n NODE DOES NOT EXIST");
    }
    else
    {
    p=(struct node *)malloc(sizeof(struct node));
    if(p==NULL)
    {
      printf("\n Memory allocation unsuccessfull..");
      return;
    }
    printf(" \n Enter data: ");
    scanf("%d",&p->data);
    p->next=tmp;
    prev->next=p;
  }
}
```

To insert a node before a particular node that holds a specific value in its data field, the node has to be located. Since the singly linked list is unidirectional, it is not possible to move backwards to find its predecessor so that the new node can be inserted. The predecessor of a particular node might be found if one traverses the list as long as the next field of a node becomes equal to that node. However, the best way is to use a pointer, prev which points to the preceding node that is pointed to by another pointer tmp. The pointer tmp is used to scan the list using

a loop. It is initialized to the node next to the first node (this is discussed in this section later on). It is advanced to the next node using the statement tmp=tmp->next. Before this assignment statement, tmp is assigned to prev so that at any moment of time the current node (pointed by tmp) and its predecessor (pointed by prev) can be accessed. If tmp->data is equal to the value of k (a variable used to specify the value of the node to be located), then the new node is inserted between the nodes pointed by prev and tmp respectively. The insertion scheme is depicted in Fig. 11.9.

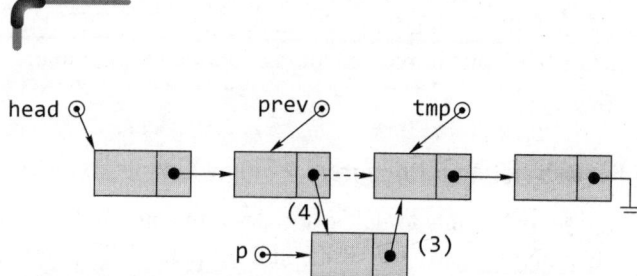

Figure 11.9 Insertion of a node before a particular node in a singly linked list

The pointer p is pointing to the newly created node that has to be inserted. Now, the next field of the node pointed to by p should point to the node pointed to by tmp, and the next field of the node pointed to by prev should point to the new node pointed by p. The following two program statements accomplish this.

$$p\text{->}next=tmp; \qquad (3)$$
$$prev\text{->}next=p; \qquad (4)$$

Insertion before the first node pointed to by head (in the function it is *h) of a singly linked list is treated specially because such insertion implies modification to the pointer head. Figure 11.10 shows this insertion scheme.

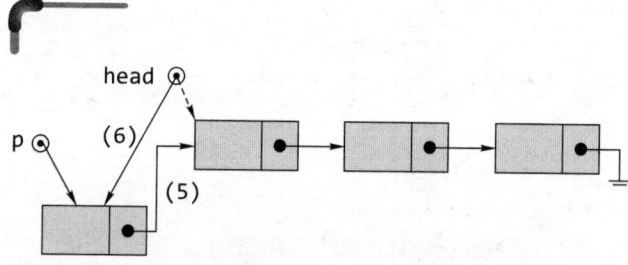

Figure 11.10 Insertion of a node at the beginning of a singly linked list

It is clear that the next part of the new node should point to the node that is pointed to by head (in the function it is *h) and this newly added node becomes the starting node of the list when head points to it. Therefore, the following two pointer assignments are required.

$$p->next=head; \qquad (5)$$
$$head=p; \qquad (6)$$

It is required to modify the content of the pointer head. The actual argument of the function insbef() would be &head and the formal parameter would be struct node **h.

If the node, before which a new node has to be inserted, is specified by giving its position, the insertion algorithm remains the same. Implementation of the same is left to the readers.

11.2.2 Deleting a Node from a Singly Linked List

Suppose, one wants to delete a node from a singly linked list that holds a particular value in its data field. The node has to be located first and then detached from the list by linking the predecessor of the node to its successor. Now the memory space for this node has to be disposed off by calling the function free(). As discussed earlier, a singly linked list is unidirectional. Two pointers tmp and prev are initialized in the loop so that they point to the current node being scanned and its predecessor respectively. At each iteration, the data field of the current node (pointed to by tmp) is investigated and then is advanced to the next node through the call tmp=tmp->next. Obviously, before advancing to the next node, tmp has to be assigned to prev. Removing the first node pointed to by head should be treated specially just like an insertion at the beginning. The rest of the scheme is outlined in Fig. 11.11.

The function for the deletion of a node from a singly linked list is as follows.

```c
void delnode(struct node **h)
{
  struct node *tmp,*prev;
  int k;
  if(*h==NULL)
  {
    printf("\n Linked List is EMPTY");
    return;
  }
  printf("\n Enter the node to be removed :");
  scanf("%d",&k);
  /* deletion at the beginning */
  if((*h)->data==k)
  {
    tmp=*h;
    *h=(*h)->next;
    free(tmp);
    return;
  }
  tmp=(*h)->next;
  prev=*h;
  while(tmp!=NULL)
  {
    if(tmp->data==k)
      break;
    else
    {
      prev=tmp;
      tmp=tmp->next;
    }
  }
  if(tmp==NULL)
    {
      printf("\n NODE DOES NOT EXIST");
```

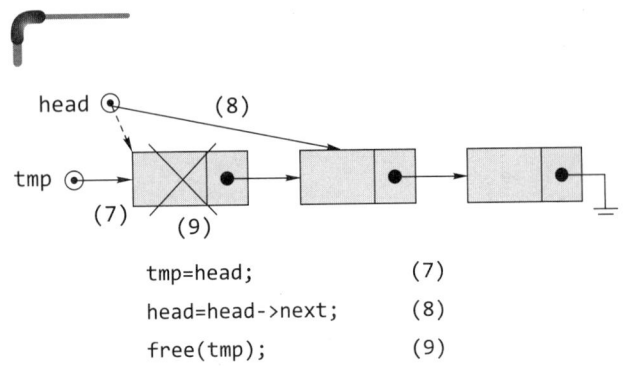

```
tmp=head;          (7)
head=head->next;   (8)
free(tmp);         (9)
```

(a) Deletion of the first node of a singly linked list

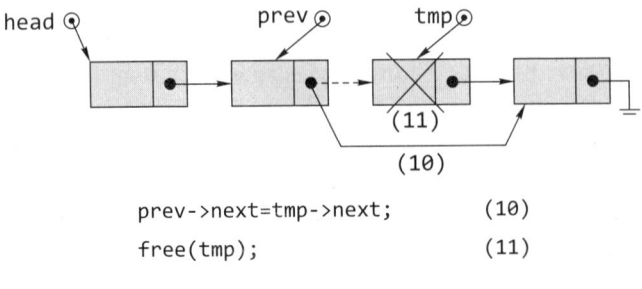

```
prev->next=tmp->next;    (10)
free(tmp);               (11)
```

(b) Deletion of an intermediate node of a singly linked list

Figure 11.11   Deletion of a node from a singly linked list

```
    }
    else
    {
        prev->next=tmp->next;
        free(tmp);
    }
}
```

The recursive version of this function needs an extra parameter k, which is the data value of the node to be deleted.

```
void delnode(struct node **h, int k)
{
    struct node *next_n;
    if(*h == NULL)
    {
        printf("\n Linked List is EMPTY or NODE does\
            not exist..void DELETION");
        return;
    }
    if((*h)->data == k)
    {
        next_n = (*h)->next;
        free(*h); /* if the nodes were malloc'ed */
        *h = next_n;
    }
    else
        delnode(&((*h)->next), k);
}
```

Readers are advised to create a program for the deletion of the *n*th node from a singly linked list as an exercise.

11.2.3 Sorting a Singly Linked List

The sorting of a singly linked list means arranging the nodes of the list in ascending values held in the data field. This can be accomplished in two ways: firstly arranging the nodes by physically disconnecting the links, and secondly, ordering the nodes by exchanging the values stored in the data fields of the nodes. The second method is considered here. The sorting method used here is bubble sort. In bubble sort, the loops used are as follows:

```
for(i=0;i<n-1;++i)
{
    for(j=0;j<n-i-1;j++)
    {
        ---------------------
    }
}
```

Here n is the number of nodes of the singly linked list, which can be computed using a function named count(). It uses the general traversal technique to obtain the number of nodes in a list. Two consecutive nodes are considered and if the value of the data field of the first is greater than that of the second, then the values are swapped. However, the problem is that every iteration associated with i in the outer loop needs to start from the first node of the singly linked list. So, before entering the j loop, the temporary pointer used for the traversal (in the function it is *p) must be set to point to the first node by the assignment statement p=head. In the inner loop, the statement j++ does not cause the pointer p to move to the next node so that the next two nodes of the list can be examined. So, in the inner loop, to advance to the next node, the statement p=p->next must be included. The definition of the function sort() that does the described operation is given here. In this function, a variable sorted is used to make the function more efficient by reducing the number of additional iterations, when the list has already been sorted.

```
void sort(struct node *h)
{
    struct node *p;
    int i,j,n=0,t,sorted;
    int *b;
    n=count(h);
    sorted=0;
    for(i=0;i<n-1 && !sorted;i++)
    {
        p=h;
        sorted=1;
        for(j=0;j<n-i-1;j++)
        {
            if(p->data>(p->next)->data)
            {
                t=p->data;
                p->data=(p->next)->data;
                (p->next)->data=t;
                sorted=0;
            }
            p=p->next;
        }
    }
}
```

Here is the definition of the function count(), which returns the number of nodes in a singly linked list.

Iterative version

```
int count(struct node *p)
{
  int i;
  for(i=0;p!=NULL;p=p->next)
    i++;
  return i;
}
```

Recursive function

```
int count(struct node *p)
{
  if(p==NULL)
    return 0;
  else
    return (1+count(p->next));
}
```

11.2.4 Destroying a Singly Linked List

Destroying a singly linked list means deleting all the nodes of a singly linked list. The function destroy() removes all the nodes from a singly linked list and returns them to the heap.

Iterative version

```
void destroy(struct node **h)
{
  struct node *q;
  if(*h==NULL)
  {
    printf("\n Linked list is empty");
    return;
  }
  while(*h!=NULL)
  {
    q=(*h)->next;
    free(*h);
    *h=q;
  }
}
```

Recursive function

```
void destroy(struct node **h)
{
  if(*h!=NULL)
  {
    destroy(&(*h)->next);
      free(*h);
      *h=NULL;441
  }
}
```

Point to Note

Be careful while coding to delete all the nodes of a linked list. The following version of the preceding function is incorrect.

```
void destroy(struct node *p)
{
while(p!=NULL)
{
  free(p);
  p=p->next;
}
}
```

The reason is that after freeing p contains an address that has already been de-allocated; therefore the statement p=p->next; has no fruitful meaning. As a result the code may crash.

To sum up a C program that can carry out any of the discussed operations on a singly linked list, with the help of all the C functions defined in this section, is given as follows.

```
#include <stdio.h>
#include <stdlib.h>
struct node
{
  int data;
  struct node *next;
};
void append(struct node **);
void dispall(struct node *);
void insaft(struct node *);
void insbef(struct node **);
void delnode(struct node **);
int count(struct node *);
void sort(struct node *);
void destroy(struct node **);
int main()
{
  struct node *head;
  int ch;
  head=NULL;
  while(1)
  {
    printf("\n 1.APPEND ");
    printf("\n 2.DISPLAY ALL ");
    printf("\n 3.INSERT AFTER A PARTICULAR NODE ");
```

```
  printf("\n 4.INSERT BEFORE A PARTICULAR NODE ");
  printf("\n 5.DELETE A NODE ");
  printf("\n 6.SORT ");
  printf("\n 7.DESTROY ");
  printf("\n 8.EXIT ");

  printf("\n ENTER UR CHOICE...");
  scanf("%d",&ch);
  switch(ch)
  {
    case 1:append(&head); break;
    case 2:dispall(head);break;
    case 3:insaft(head);break;
    case 4:insbef(&head);break;
    case 5:delnode(&head);break;
    case 6:sort(head);break;
    case 7:destroy(&head);break;
    case 8:exit(0);
    default:printf("WRONG CHOICE..");
  }
 }
 return 0;
}
```

11.2.5 More Complex Operations on Singly Linked Lists

Printing a Singly Linked List in Reverse Order

To print the nodes of a linked list in the reverse order (without using an additional singly linked list), two loops are used in a nested fashion. Two pointers tmp and last are used. tmp is used to traverse the list up to a point. First, the list is traversed up to the last node, and then up to the second last node and so on. The pointer last is used to point to the node where the traversal ends. That is, the list is scanned using tmp from the beginning of the list until it reaches the predecessor of the node that is pointed to by last. Then last is updated by the value of tmp. This process continues till last equals head (in the function it is h).

Iterative version

```
void dispall(struct node *p)
{
  struct node *tmp,*last;
  if(p==NULL)
    return;
  last=NULL;
  tmp=p;
```

```
  while(last!=p)
  {
    tmp=p;
     while(tmp->next!=last)
       tmp=tmp->next;
     printf("\t%d ",tmp->data);
     last=tmp;
  }
}
```

Recursive function

```
void dispall(struct node *p)
{
  if(p==NULL)
    return;
  else
  {
    dispall(p->next);
    printf("\t%d", p->data);
  }
}
```

Reversing a Singly Linked List

Using the previous function, the values of the data field of the nodes of a singly linked list can be printed in reverse order but the list remains as it is. To physically reverse a singly linked list (without using an additional singly linked list), i.e., the last node becomes the first node, the second last node becomes the second node, and so on. In order to reverse the entire list, reverse all of it other than the first node and then plug the first node at the end of the list. Now, there are two ways to reverse a linked list. The first version is an iterative (non-recursive) solution. Here is a function that takes head of a singly linked list as a parameter, reverses it, and returns a pointer to the beginning of the reversed list. As the returned address is assigned to head again, it is not required to pass the address of head to the function.

Function prototype declaration:

```
struct node *reverse_list(struct node *);
```

Function calling statement:

```
        head=reverse_list(head);
```

Function definition:

```
struct node *reverse_list(struct node *h)
{
  struct node *prev, *cur, *pNext;
```

```
  if (h == NULL)
    return NULL;
  prev = NULL;
  cur = h;
  do
  {
    pNext = cur->next;
    cur->next = prev;
    prev = cur;
    cur = pNext;
  } while (cur != NULL);
  return prev;
}
```

The special case, where the linked list is empty (NULL), is handled first; the reverse of a NULL list is a NULL list. If the list is not empty, the following three pointers are required:

- pointer to the current node (the one which needs its next field to be updated)
- pointer to the previous node (the one to which the current node should point to)
- pointer to the node next to the current node (to become the current after the current node gets its next field updated)

Start with the first node being the current one and the previous node being NULL (since the first node becomes the last and points nowhere). At each iteration of the do-while loop, the next field of the current node is updated and the pointers are updated. When the end of the list is reached and the loop stops; prev (which stores the previous value of cur) points to what used to be the last node and is now the first, so it is returned. Here is a recursive solution to the same problem:

```
struct node *reverse_list(struct node *h)
{
  struct node *tmp;
  if (h == NULL)
    return NULL;
  if (h->next == NULL)
    return h;
  tmp = reverse_list(h->next);
  (h->next)->next = h;
  h->next = NULL;
  return tmp;
}
```

The recursive function has two base cases. If the list is empty, it stays empty, and if the list is a single node, it remains the same. These two base cases could be combined into one, returning h if either condition is true. Otherwise, one can use it as the general case. reverse_list() is recursively called by passing the list starting with the second node, considering the current node to be the first. Since the next field of the current node has not changed, and it used to point to the first node of the remaining list, it now points to the last node of the remaining list. That node (the one pointed to by the current node) is updated to point to the current node, and the current node is updated to point nowhere (its next field becomes NULL).

Copying a Singly Linked List

A given singly linked list can be copied into another list by duplicating the values of each node. The following C program performs this task. Observe the function copy_list() that takes the target list and the source list as parameters and uses a new logic for creating a singly linked list.

```
#include <stdio.h>
#include <stdlib.h>
struct node
{
  int data;
  struct node *next;
};
void append(struct node **);
void dispall(struct node *);
void copy_list(struct node **, struct node *);
int main()
{
  struct node *head,*hd;
  int ch;
  char ans='y';
  head=hd=NULL;
  printf("\n CREATE THE FIRST LINKED LIST...\n");
  while(ans=='y' ||ans=='Y')
  {
    append(&head);
    printf("\n Do U add more node(y/n)?..");
    fflush(stdin);
    ans=getchar();
  }
  dispall(head);
  copy_list(&hd,head);
```

```
printf("\n THE LINKED LIST AFTER COPY...\n");
dispall(hd);
return 0;
}
void append(struct node **h)
{
  if(*h==NULL)
  {
    *h=(struct node *)malloc(sizeof(struct node));
    if(*h==NULL)
    {
    printf("\n Memory allocation unsuccessfull..");
    return;
    }
  printf(" \n Enter data:");
  scanf("%d",&(*h)->data);
  (*h)->next=NULL;
  }
  else
    append(&(*h)->next);
}
void dispall(struct node *p)
{
  if(p==NULL)
  {
    printf("NULL");
    return;
  }
  else
  {
  printf("%d ->",p->data);
  dispall(p->next);
  }
}
void copy_list(struct node **t, struct node *s)
{
struct node *tmp;
if(s==NULL)
  return;
while(s!=NULL)
{
if(*t==NULL)
{
  *t=(struct node *)malloc(sizeof(struct node));
  tmp=*t;
  }
```

```
else
{
  tmp->next =(struct node *)malloc
       (sizeof(struct node));
  tmp=tmp->next;
  }
tmp->data=s->data;
s=s->next;
}
  tmp->next=NULL;
}
```

The recursive version of the function copy_list() is as follows:

```
void copy_list(struct node **t, struct node *s)
{
  if(s!=NULL)
  {
   *t=(struct node *)malloc(sizeof(struct node));
   (*t)->data=s->data;
   (*t)->next=NULL;
   copy_list(&((*t)->next),s->next);
  }
}
```

Maintaining a Linked List in Ascending Order

Let us create a singly linked list where every new node added to the linked list gets inserted at such a place that the linked list is always maintained in ascending order. The following version of the append() function illustrates the same. The trick followed here is that while traversing the linked list, the data part of the node to be inserted is compared with that of the current node and that of its subsequent one and accordingly inserted.

```
void append(struct node **h)
{
    struct node *p, *tmp;
    p=(struct node *)malloc(sizeof(struct node));
    printf(" \n Enter data:");
    scanf("%d",&p->data);
    /* if list is empty or if new node is to be
                inserted before the first node */
if(*h==NULL)
{
  p->next=NULL;
  *h=p;
  return;
}
```

```
if((*h)->data>p->data)
{
p->next=*h;
*h=p;
return;
}
   /* traverse the entire linked list to search
          the position to insert the new node */
tmp=*h;
while(tmp!=NULL)
{
if(tmp->data<=p->data && (tmp->next==NULL ||
    (tmp->next)->data>p->data))
{
  p->next=tmp->next;
  tmp->next=p;
  return ;
}
tmp=tmp->next;    /* move to the next node */
}
}
```

11.3 APPLICATIONS OF LINKED LISTS

In computer programming, linked lists are extensively used in Database Management Systems, Process Management, Operating Systems, text editors, etc. An important application of linked lists is to represent polynomials and their manipulations. However, we will not go into the details of this representation in this book.

11.3.1 Dynamic Storage Management

In a multiprogramming computer environment, several programs reside in memory at the same time. Different programs may have different memory requirements. In order to satisfy their memory requirements, the operating system must be able to allocate a block of contiguous storage as required. At the same time, when the execution of a program is complete, the memory block allocated to it has to be freed and this freed block may now be allocated to another program.

To keep track of the allocated and free portions of memory, the memory manager of the operating system maintains a linked list of allocated and free blocks of storage.

A doubly linked list is used to maintain both the list of allocated blocks and the list of free blocks. Each node of this list contains a starting address, size, and status of the segment. This list is kept sorted by the starting address field to facilitate update of memory segments, because when a program terminates, the memory segment allocated to it becomes free, and so if any of the segments are freed, then they can be merged with the adjacent segment, if the adjacent segment is already free. This requires traversal of the list both ways to find out whether any of the adjacent segments are free. So this list is required to be maintained as a doubly linked list.

11.3.2 Garbage Collection and Compaction

During the program execution, blocks of storage that once were needed but which at some later time became unnecessary and unused are called *garbage*. *Garbage collection* is the process of collecting all unused blocks of memory and returning them to available space. This process is carried out in essentially two phases. In the first phase, known as the marking phase, all nodes in use are marked. In the second phase all unmarked nodes are returned to the available space list. This second phase is trivial when all nodes are of a fixed size. When variable size nodes are in use, it is desirable to compact memory so that all free nodes form a contiguous block of memory. In this case the second phase is referred to as *memory compaction*. Compaction works by actually moving blocks of memory from one location in the memory to another so as to collect all the free blocks into one single large block. Once this single block gets too small again, the compaction mechanism is called again to reclaim the unused storage. Here no storage releasing mechanism is used. Instead, the marking algorithm is used to mark blocks that are still in use. Then instead of freeing each unmarked block by calling a release mechanism to put it on the free list, the compactor simply collects all unmarked blocks into one large block at one end of the memory segment.

11.3.3 Representation of Polynomials

Representing polynomials using linked lists is advantageous because linked lists can accommodate a number of polynomials of growing sizes so that their combined size does not exceed the total memory available. The general form of a polynomial of degree n is

$$P(x) = a_0 + a_1x + a_2x^2 + a_3x^3 + \ldots + a_nx^n$$

Let us take $P(x) = 6x^4 + 3x^3 - 7x^2 + 4x - 5$. To represent each term of the polynomial using the nodes of a linked list, each node should consist of three elements, namely, coefficient, exponent, and a link to the next term.

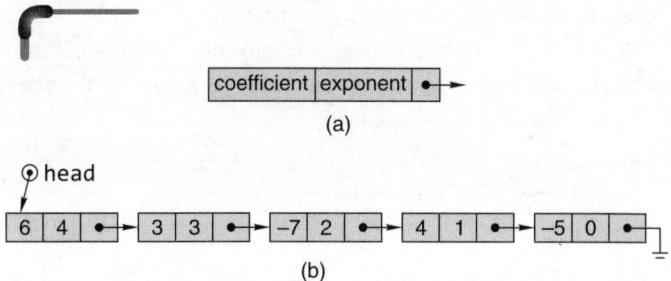

(a)

(b)

Figure 11.12   Representation of a polynomial using a linked list

While maintaining the polynomial, it is assumed that the exponent of each successive term is less than that of the previous term. If this is not the case, one can also use a function to build a list, which maintains this order. Once the linked list to represent the polynomial is ready then operations such as addition and multiplication can be performed. A term in the polynomial can be declared using the following structure definition.

```
struct node
{
  int coeff;
  int exp;
  struct node *next;
};
```

It is clear from this declaration that a singly linked list has been used to represent a term of the polynomial.

The functions to append the nodes for representing the polynomial and displaying it are similar to the functions `append()` and `display()`, respectively, for singly linked lists. Hence, the readers should be able to develop these on their own.

The function `addition()` is used to carry out the addition of the two polynomials. Two polynomials are pointed to by the pointers `first` and `second` which are passed to the function. In this function, the linked lists representing the two polynomials are traversed until the end of any one list is reached. While traversing, the polynomials are compared on term-by-term basis. If the exponents of the two terms being compared are equal, then their coefficients are added and the result is stored in a third polynomial. If the exponents are not equal, then the bigger exponent is added to the third polynomial. During the traversal if the end of one list is reached, the control breaks out of the while loop. Now the remaining terms of that polynomial are simply appended to the resulting polynomial. Lastly, the result is displayed using `display()`. The function to add two polynomials is as follows:

```
void addition(struct node *first, struct node
        *second, struct node **third)
{
  struct node *p;
  /* if both lists are empty */
  if(first == NULL && second == NULL)
    return;
  /* traverse till one node ends */
  while(first != NULL && second != NULL)
  {
  if (*third == NULL)
    {
    *third = (struct node *)malloc(sizeof(struct node));
    p = *third;
    }
  else
    {
    p->next = (struct node *)malloc(sizeof(struct
            node));
    p = p->next;
    }
  /* store a term of larger degree if polynomial */
  if(first->exp < second->exp)
    {
    p->coeff = second->coeff;
    p->exp = second->exp;
    second = second->next;
                /* move to the next node */
    }
  else if(first->exp > second->exp)
    {
    p->coeff = first->coeff;
    first->exp = first->exp;
    first = first->next;
                /* move to the next node */
    }
  else if(first->exp == second->exp)
    {
    p->coeff = first->coeff + second->coeff;
    first->exp = first->exp;
    first = first->next;
                /* move to the next node */
    second = second->next;
                /* move to the next node */
    }
  }
        /*assign remaining elements of the first
                polynomial to the result */
    while(first != NULL)
```

```
{
    if(*third == NULL)
    {
    *third = (struct node *)malloc(sizeof(struct
            node));
     p = *third;
    }
    else
    {
    p->next = (struct node *)malloc(sizeof(struct
            node));
    p = p->next;
    }
    p->coef = first->coef;
    p->exp = first->exp;
    first = first->next;
}

    /*assign remaining elements of the second
                polynomial to the result */
while(second != NULL)
{
    if(*third == NULL)
    {
    *third = (struct node *)malloc(sizeof(struct
            node));
     p = *third;
    }
    else
    {
    p->next = (struct node *)malloc(sizeof(struct
            node));
    p = p->next;
    }
    p->coef = second->coef;
    p->exp = second->exp;
    second = second->next;
}
p->next = NULL;
            /* at the end of list append NULL*/
}
```

In some critical applications, it may be required to manipulate very large integers, which cannot be stored in variables of type int or long in C. So a different representation scheme is required for large integers. Such a number can always be considered as a special type of polynomial. For instance, a number 1234 may be represented by the expression

$$1 \times 10^3 + 2 \times 10^2 + 3 \times 10^1 + 4 \times 10^0$$

Clearly, the expression is of the order $P(x) = x^3 + 2x^2 + 3x + 4$ where $x = 10$. To generalize, any decimal integer of n digits can be expressed as the value of a $(n - 1)$ degree polynomial.

$$P(x) = \sum_{i=0}^{n-1} a_i x^i \text{ for } x = 10$$

where $0 \leq a_i \leq 9$.

Addition of two large integers specified in this manner is very similar to addition of polynomials represented by linked lists. The only difference is that the coefficients must lie between 0 and 9. After addition, the coefficient may become more than 9. Let the sum of corresponding coefficients be S which is greater than 9 and the corresponding exponent be E, In that case, two nodes will result. One will contain the result of the expression S/10 as digit and E as the coefficient. The other node will contain the result of the expression S%10 as digit and E + 1 as exponent. The result of such addition is shown here.

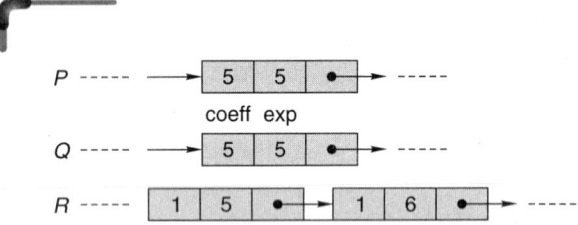

P = polynomial representing first integer

Q = polynomial representing second integer

R = resultant polynomial after addition

Figure 11.13 Addition of coefficients (digits) that result in a coefficient with value more than 9

11.4 DISADVANTAGES OF LINKED LISTS

Inspite of the several advantages of using linked lists, there are obviously some shortcomings too. One is pointer management. Pointers, if not dealt carefully, may lead to serious errors in execution. Linked lists also consume extra space than the space for actual data as the links among the nodes are maintained through the pointers. A major drawback of linked lists is that they are not suited for random access. To access a single node in linked storage, it is necessary to traverse a long path to reach the desired node, which takes a lot of time and space (because of using pointers).

11.5 ARRAY VERSUS LINKED LIST REVISITED

A list of items may be implemented using both array and linked list. An array uses sequential mapping in memory. In contrast a linked list uses non-sequential mapping in memory. Even if the array is dynamically allocated, an estimate of the maximum size of the list is required. Usually this requires a high over-estimate, which wastes considerable space. This could be a serious limitation, especially if there are many lists of unknown size.

Any element of an array can be randomly accessed through its index. The data in a linked list can be accessed in only linear fashion and cannot be accessed from an arbitrary location. For example to access the data in the third node, you have to start from the first, second and then only can reach third node. Unlike arrays, one cannot access the data of the third node directly.

Each of these implementations of the sequence of items has its advantages and disadvantages which are summarized below.

In terms of space

- In the linked-list implementation, one pointer must be stored for every element in the sequence, while the array stores only the elements themselves. Any element of an array can be randomly accessed through the array index.

- The space used for a linked list is always proportional to the number of elements in the list. This is not necessarily true for the array implementation. If a lot of items are added to a sequence and then removed, the size of the array can be arbitrarily greater than the number of items in the sequence.

In terms of time

- The array implementation requires O(n) worst-case time to add or remove an item with n items, because existing items need to be moved.

- In contrast, adding and removing items in a linked list can be implemented to require only O(1) time (if we maintain pointers to the last node in the list, and the node before the current one, as well as a pointer to the current node).

In terms of ease of implementation

The implementations of both the array and linked-list versions seem reasonably easy and straightforward. However, the methods for the linked-list version seem to be complex as for adding and removing elements in the linked-list requires pointer operations. Linked lists really test the understanding of pointers. Though the linked lists are pointer intensive, they have a natural visual structure for practicing this sort of thinking. It's easy to draw the state of a linked list and use that drawing to think through the code.

In terms of performance

Array-based implementation of a list can furnish slightly better performance than linked list implementation. A number of factors that contribute to slightly better performance of arrays are as discussed below.

Due to the scaling factor, the address of the next element in an array &a[i], where a is the array name, may be calculated from a current address and an element size - both held in registers:

```
&a[i]=a + i * sizeofa[i]
```

Both addresses may use a single register. Since no memory accesses are required, this is a single-cycle operation on a modern processor.

Again, for an array, contiguous memory is allocated. Using array, data is stored in consecutive memory locations allowing the next element to be fetched by accessing the current element of an array and using scaling factor. In contrast, with linked list implementations, there is additional overhead for pointers and the overhead normally introduced due to memory allocation through malloc(). There is no guarantee that successive elements in a linked list occupy successive memory locations. This leads to memory fetching to move to the next node from the current one.

SUMMARY

The array implementation of a list provides efficient access to individual data items by index. However, it has some shortcomings:

- The resize operation is inefficient (w.r.t. execution time)
- Wastage of space
- Addition at the beginning or middle of the list is tedious
- Deletion from the beginning or middle of the list is cumbersome

An array is stored in a contiguous block of memory and this contiguous nature of the array is also responsible for its drawbacks. A better alternative is the linked list. A linked list is a linear data structure in which each data item points to the next data item. This linking is accomplished by keeping an address variable (a pointer) together with each data item. This pointer is used to store the address of the next data item in the list.

There are different kinds of linked lists, namely, singly linked lists, circular singly linked lists, two-way or doubly linked lists, and circular doubly linked list. Normally, every linked list has a beginning and an end. In singly linked lists, one must never lose track of the beginning of the linked list or there is no way to find it, since links are pointing forward. To avoid this problem, there are two common variations of linked lists, namely, circular linked lists and doubly linked lists.

KEY-TERMS

Circular linked list   Circular linked list is a data structure in which each node has one link, similar to an ordinary singly linked list, except that the next link of the last node points back to the first node.

Compaction   Compaction is the process of moving blocks of memory from one location in the memory to another so as to collect all the free blocks into one single large block.

Doubly linked list   A doubly linked list is a data structure in which each item points to its successor and to its predecessor.

Garbage collection   Garbage collection is the process of collecting all unused blocks of memory and returning them to available space.

Linked list   Linked list is a data structure in which each data item points to the next data item. This "linking" is accomplished by keeping an address variable (a pointer) together with each data item.

Self-referential structure   A structure that contains a pointer that points to the same structure type is called a self-referential structure.

Singly linked list   A singly linked list is a data structure in which each item points to its successor.

FREQUENTLY ASKED QUESTIONS

1. Identify some specific advantages of link list over arrays.
Whenever it is required to insert and remove elements frequently, linked list presents a definite advantage over arrays.

2. Identify some advantages that arrays have over the linked list.
When the number of random accesses is many times more than the number of insertions and deletions, the array has a distinctive advantage over that of the linked list. This is due to the fact that elements in an array are arranged contiguously while storing in memory. This contiguous arrangement allows any element to be accessed in O (1) time by using its index. On the other hand, to access any element in linked list, a pointer has to be associated with the element. Getting a pointer to an element can be expensive if we do not know a great deal about the pattern in which the elements will be accessed. Arrays are also advantageous whenever the storage is at a premium because they do not require additional pointers to keep their elements "linked" together.

3. How would you detect a loop in a linked list? Write a C program to detect a loop in a linked list.

To detect a loop in a link list, choose two pointers to start of the linked list. Increment one pointer by 1 node and the other by 2 nodes. If there's a loop, the 2nd pointer will meet the 1st pointer somewhere. If it does, then you know there's one. A function for detecting a loop in a link list is given below:

```
int hasLoop(struct node *h)
{
  p=h;
  q=h->next;
  while(p!=NULL && q!=NULL)
  {
    if(p==q)
    return 0;
    p=p->next;
    q=(q->next)?(q->next->next):q->next;
  }
  return 1;
}
```

EXERCISE

1. Write down the advantages and disadvantages of linked lists, compared to arrays.

2. List the principal advantages of using a linked list for dynamical storage, rather than using the memory allocation functions `malloc()`, `calloc()`, and so on to create a dynamically sizable array.

3. Is it possible to create a linked list using only a head pointer? If so, how can this be accomplished?

4. What are the drawbacks of singly linked lists?

5. Write a C function to combine two singly linked lists in the following manner. Suppose, one list is L, expressed as $L = \{l_0, l_1, ..., l_m\}$ and the other list is M expressed as $M = \{m_0, m_1 ..., m_n\}$

where l_i and m_i represent nodes in their respective lists. After combination, the combined list should be l_0, m_0, l_1, m_1, ...

6. Write a C program to compute the following operations on polynomials represented as singly linked lists:

   (a) Evaluation of a polynomial

   (b) Multiplication of two polynomials

7. Write a C function to interchange the mth and nth nodes of a singly linked list.

8. How can a polynomial, involving two variables, be represented in a linked list? Write C functions to do the following:

   (a) Addition of two such polynomials

   (b) Multiplication of two such polynomials

9. Write a program to split a linked list into two linked lists.

10. Write a program to multiply two polynomials using singly linked lists.

11. Write a program to add two `long` integers. Each integer may contain 15 to 20 digits, which can be stored in nodes, a digit each or more depending on the user's choice. Add these long integers (from least significant digit backwards) and display the resultant list.

12. Write a program that reads information about cars (brand, year, color, kilometer, and price) from a text file and stores this information into a linked list. When the information is read, it should display the contents of the linked list and perform the following operations:

    (a) Add new car information to the end of the linked list

    (b) Add new car information to the beginning of the linked list

13. Write a program that reads car information (car number, brand, year, color, kilometer, and price) from a text file, stores these information into a linked list, and displays the contents of the linked list. It should also read car numbers (until zero is entered) and delete the nodes when car numbers are entered as an input for deletion of nodes. At the end it should again display the contents of the linked list.

Project Question

1. 2's compliment of a number is obtained by scanning it from right to left and complementing all the bits after the first appearance of a 1. Thus 2's complement of 11100 is 00100. Write a C program to find the 2's complement of a binary number. Also implement the subtraction of two integers using binary arithmetic.

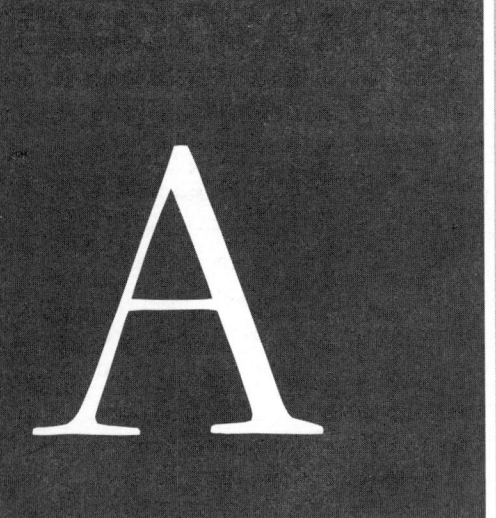

1. Write a program to convert a floating-point number into corresponding integer.

Solution

Algorithm in Step Form

1. START

2. FLOAT X <- 37.4

3. FLOAT Y <-6.3

4. INTEGER Q <-(INTEGER) X + (INTEGER) Y

5. PRINT Q

6. STOP

Algorithm in Flowchart Form

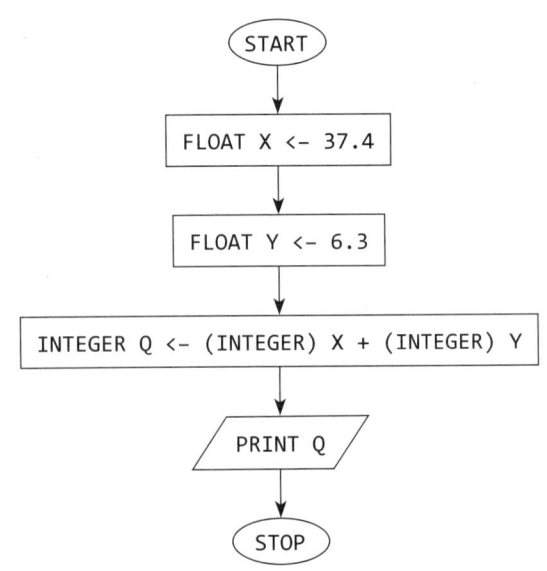

C Program

```c
#include <stdio.h>
int main(void)
{
    float x = 37.4, y = 6.3;
    int quotient = (int) x / (int) y;
    /*converting float to int */
    printf("Quotient = %d\n", quotient);    /*output*/
    return 0;
}
```

Output

```
Quotient = 6
```

2. Write a program to calculate the volume of a cylindrical tank whose radius and height are given in feet.

Solution

Algorithm in Step Form

1. START

2. PI <- 3.141

3. PRINT "ENTER RADIUS"

4. INPUT RADIUS

5. PRINT "ENTER HEIGHT"

6. INPUT HEIGHT

7. VOLUME <- PI*RADIUS*RADIUS*HEIGHT

8. PRINT VOLUME

9. STOP

Algorithm in Flowchart Form

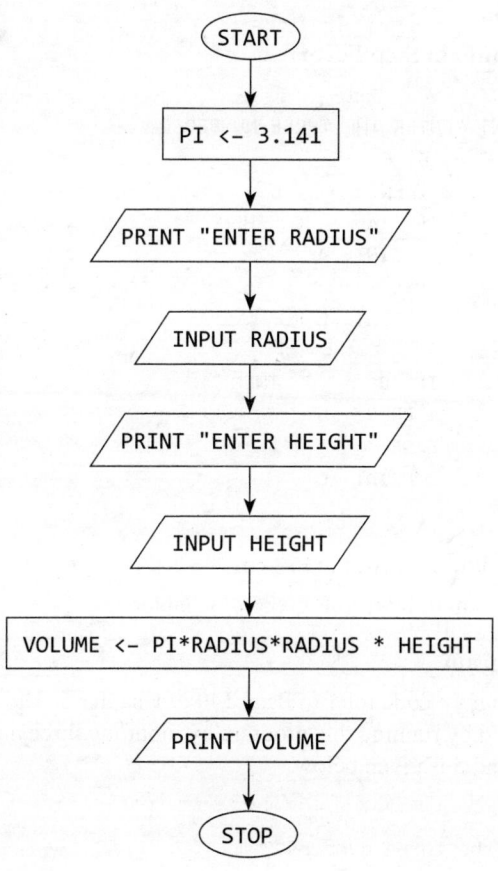

3. Write a program to find whether the given number is even or odd.

Solution

Algorithm in Step Form

Refer to Chapter 5, Example 5.

Algorithm in Flowchart Form

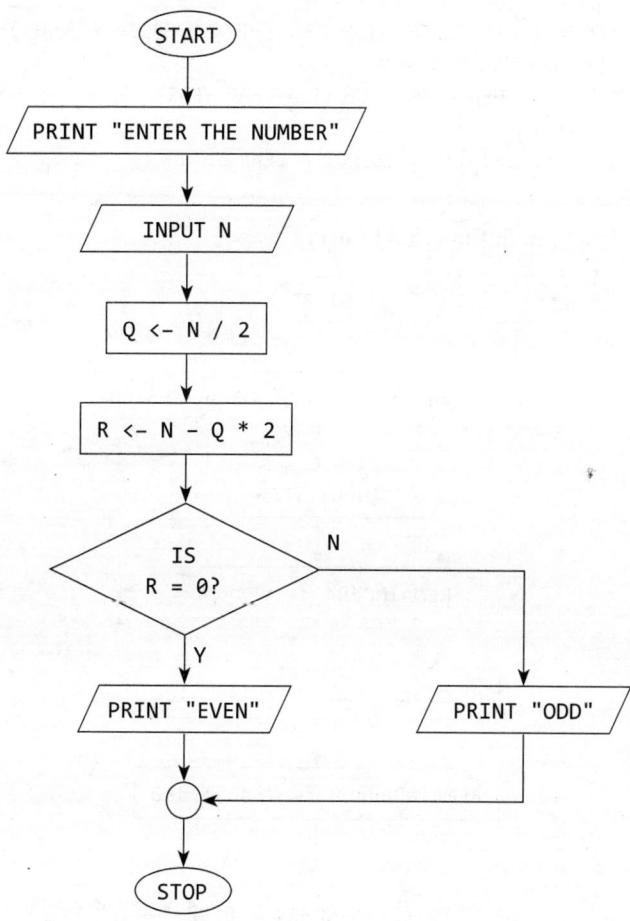

C Program

```c
#include <stdio.h>
#define pi 3.141
int main()
{
    float radius, height, volume;
    printf("\n Enter radius of tank in ft : ");
    scanf("%f", &radius);
    printf("\n Enter height of tank in ft : ");
    scanf("%f", &height);
    /* Volume of cylindrical Tank = pi x radius x
    radius x height */
    volume = pi*radius*radius*height;
    printf("Volume of Tank : %0.4f cu.ft.\n",
    volume);
    return 0;
}
```

Output

```
Enter radius of tank in ft: 3.5
Enter height of tank in ft: 5
Volume of Tank : 192.3862 cu.ft.
```

C Program

Refer to Chapter 5, Example 5. The output obtained by running this program by inputting two numbers 8 and 11 are given below.

Output

```
Enter the number8
EVEN
Enter the number11
ODD
```

4. Write a program that determines whether a given year is a leap year or not. Use logical operators && and ||.

Solution

Algorithm in Step Form

```
1. START
2. PRINT "ENTER THE YEAR TO BE TESTED"
3. INPUT YEAR
4. REMAINDER4 <-YEAR % 4
5. REMAINDER100 <-YEAR % 100
6. REMAINDER400 <-YEAR % 400
7. IF ( ( REMAINDER4 = 0  &&  REMAINDER100 ! = 0 )
   || REMAINDER400 = 0 )
          THEN PRINT "IT IS A LEAP YEAR"
     ELSE
          PRINT "IT IS NOT A LEAP YEAR"
8. STOP
```

Algorithm in Flowchart Form

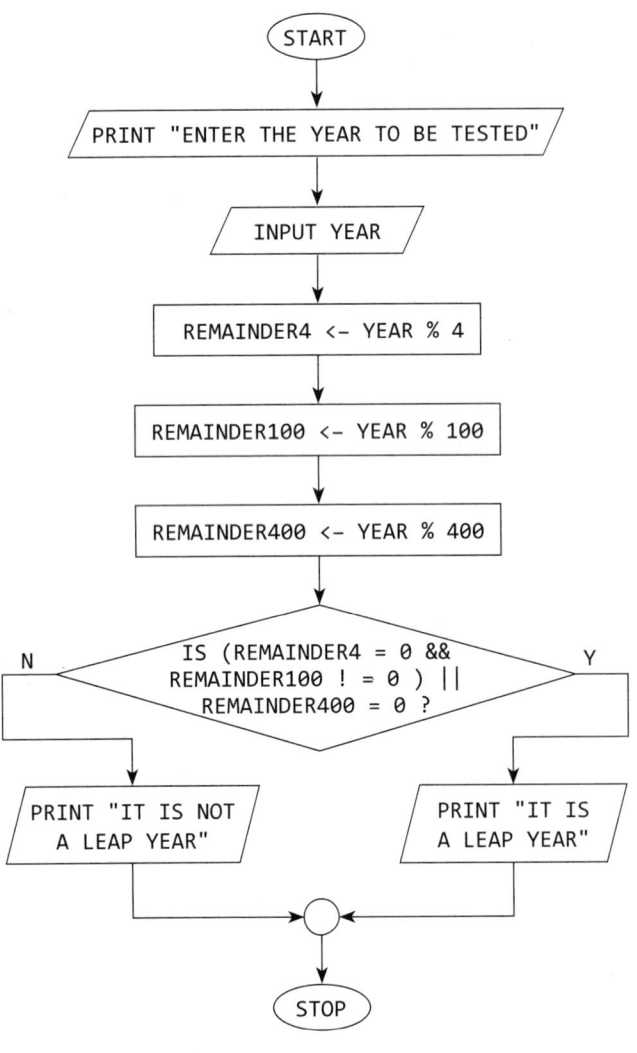

C Program

For program code and details of sample outputs after successful runs, refer to Chapter 5, Example 8.

5. Write a program to find the greatest of three numbers.

Solution

Algorithm in Step Form

```
1. START
2. PRINT "ENTER THE THREE NUMBERS"
3. INPUT A, B, C
4. IF A > B THEN
          IF  A  >  C  THEN
            PRINT  A
          ELSE
            PRINT  C
   ELSE
          IF  B  >  C  THEN
            PRINT  B
          ELSE
            PRINT  C
5. STOP
```

Algorithm in Flowchart Form

For flowchart, refer to Fig. 5.5 of Chapter 5.

C Program

For program code refer to Page 149 of Chapter 5. The output obtained by running this program by inputting three numbers 3, 11 and 5 is given below.

Output

```
Enter the three numbers 3

11

5

11
```

6. Write a program that checks whether a character entered by the user is a vowel or not.

Solution

Algorithm in Step Form

```
1. START
2. PRINT "ENTER A CHARACTER"
3. INPUT  C
4. IF C  = 'a'   OR  C = 'A'   THEN  GO TO  9
5. IF C  = 'e'   OR  C = 'E'   THEN  GO TO  9
6. IF C  = 'i'   OR  C = 'I'   THEN  GO TO  9
7. IF. C  = 'o'  OR  C = 'O'   THEN  GO TO  9
8. IF C  = 'u'   OR  C = 'U'   THEN  GO TO  9
   ELSE
        GO TO 10
9. PRINT "C IS ALWAYS A VOWEL"
     : GOTO  11
```

```
10. IF  C  =  'y'   OR  C  =  'Y'  THEN
        PRINT "C IS SOMETIMES VOWEL"
        : GO TO 11
    ELSE
        PRINT "C  IS  NOT A VOWEL"
11. STOP
```

Algorithm in Flowchart Form

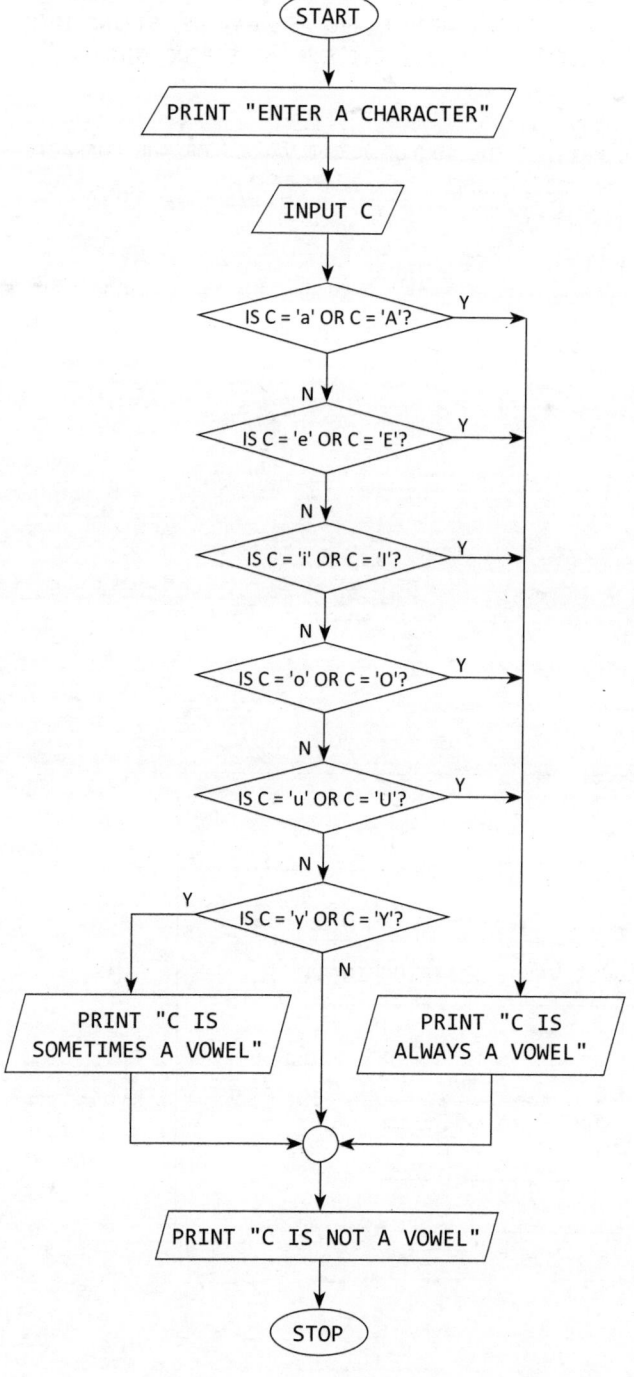

C Program

For program code, refer to Page 155 of Chapter 5. The output obtained by running this program by inputting three characters 'a', 'E' and 'z' is given below.

Output

```
Enter a character: a
a is always a vowel!
Enter a character: E
E is always a vowel!
Enter a character: z
z is not a vowel!
```

7. Write a program to calculate the average of integer numbers entered.

Solution

Algorithm in Step Form

For algorithm in step form, refer to Chapter 5, Example 21.

Algorithm in Flowchart Form

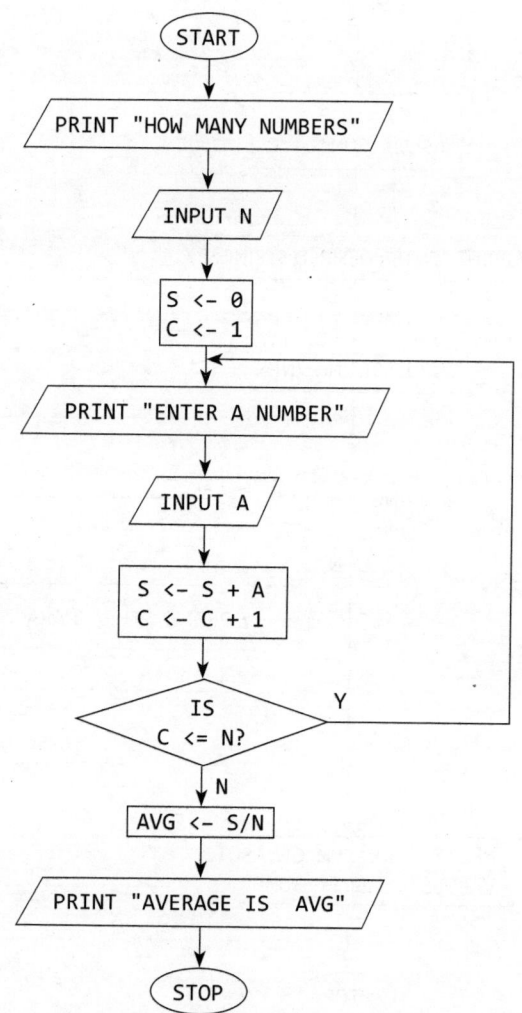

C Program

For program code, refer to Chapter 5, Example 21. The output obtained by running this program and inputting 5 numbers 5, 7, 8, 11 and 17 is given below.

Output

```
HOW MANY NUMBERS?5
Enter the number:5
Enter the number:7
Enter the number:8
Enter the number:11
Enter the number:17
AVERAGE IS 9.600000
```

8. Write a program that accepts any valid string and prints the ASCII value of each character in the string and compute the sum of all these ASCII values.

Algorithm in Flowchart Form

Solution

Algorithm in Step Form

```
1. START
2. K    <-   0
3. ASCII_SUM   <-   0
4. PRINT "ENTER VALID STRING CHARACTER"
5. INPUT STRING_IN(K)
6. WHILE STRING_IN(K)  != ' \0'
   BEGIN
   PRINT "THE CHARACTER HAS ASCII VALUE: STRING_IN(K)"
   ASCII_SUM  <-   ASCII_SUM  +  STRING_IN(K)
   K   <-   K + 1
   END
7. PRINT " THE SUM OF ASCII VALUES OF THE CHARACTERS
   :  ASCII_SUM"
8. STOP
```

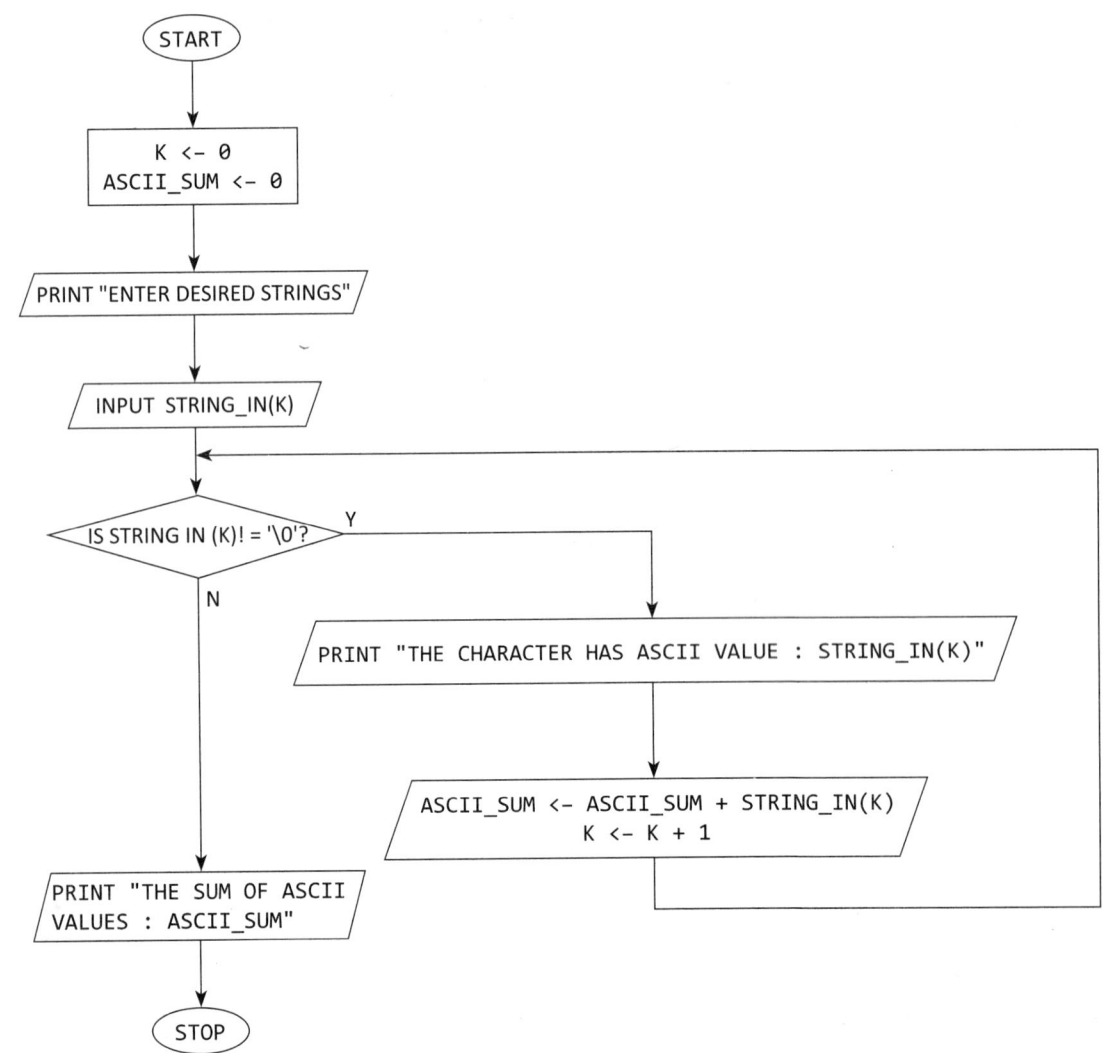

C Program

```c
#include <stdio.h>
#include <string.h>

int main()
{
  int k=0, ascii_sum = 0;
  char string_in[40];
  printf("\n Enter any desired string character\n");
  scanf("%s", string_in);
  while(string_in[k]!='\0')
  {
   printf("\nThe Character  %c   has the ASCII value
  %d\n", string_in[k], string_in[k]);
    ascii_sum = ascii_sum + string_in[k];
   k++;
  }
printf("\n The sum of ASCII values of all the string
characters : %d ", ascii_sum);
return 0;
}
```

Output

```
Enter any desired string character
manas
The Character  m has the ASCII value  109
The Character  a has the ASCII value  97
The Character  n has the ASCII value  110
The Character  a has the ASCII value  97
The Character  s has the ASCII value  115
The sum of ASCII values of all the string characters : 528
```

9. Write a program that computes the sum of the series

$$1 + x + \frac{x^2}{2!} + \frac{x^3}{3!} + \cdots \text{ upto 10 terms}$$

Solution

Algorithm in Step Form

1. START
2. PRINT "ENTER NUMBER OF TERMS"
3. INPUT N
4. PRINT "ENTER A NUMBER"
5. INPUT X
6. T   <-   1
7. S   <-   0
8. C   <-   1
9. S   <-   S + T
10. T   <-   T * X / C
11. C   <-   C + 1
12. IF C <= N THEN GO TO STEP 9
13. PRINT S
14. STOP

Algorithm in Flowchart Form

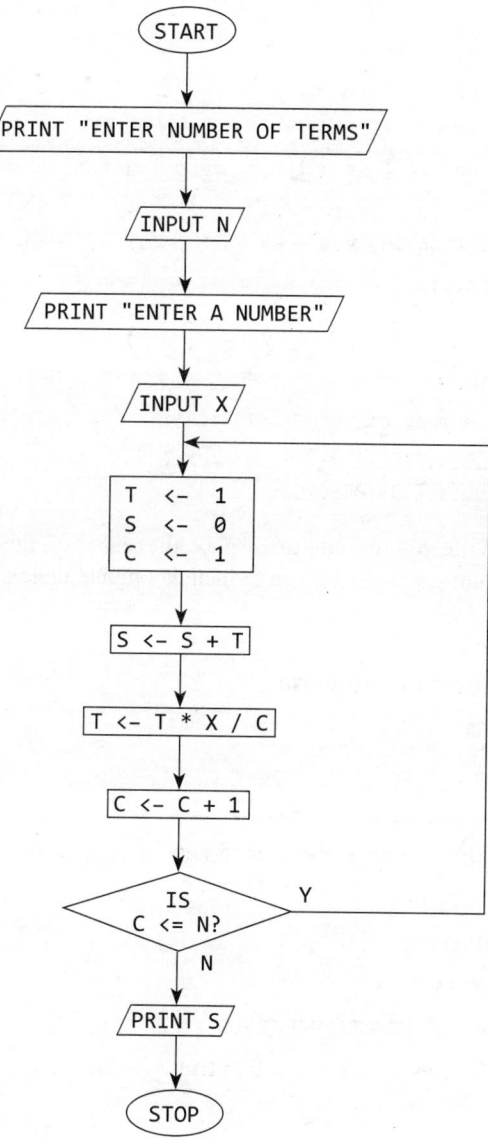

C Program

```c
#include<stdio.h>
int main()
{
```

```
double t = 1, s = 0,  x;
int c = 1,  n;
printf("\n Enter number of terms : ");
scanf("%d", &n);
printf("\n Enter a number :  ");
scanf("%lf", &x);

do
  {
       s = s + t;
       t = t * x / c;
       c = c + 1;
    } while( c <= n );

 printf("\n The sum s  =  %lf",  s);
 return 0;
}
```

Output

```
Enter number of terms : 10
Enter a number : 3.5
The sum s = 33.005676
```

10. Write a program to display the cube of the natural numbers up to a given term and compute their sum.

Solution

Algorithm in Step Form

1. START
2. SUM   <-   0
3. I   <-   1
4. PRINT "ENTER NUMBER OF TERMS"
5. INPUT N
6. WHILE   I <= N

   BEGIN

   PRINT " NUMBER AND CUBES : I, I*I*I "

   SUM   <-   SUM   + I*I*I

   I <-   I + 1

   END
7. STOP

Algorithm in Flowchart Form

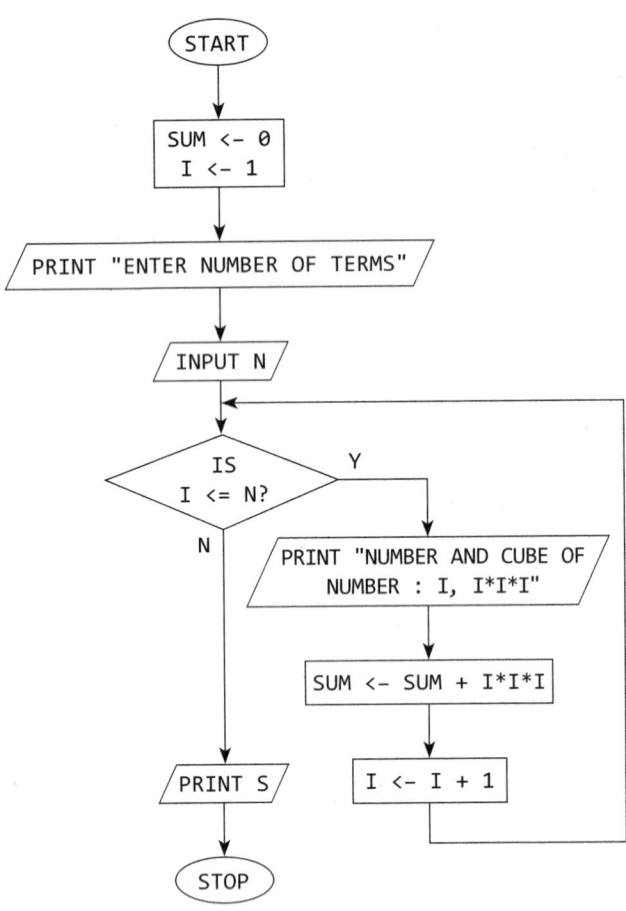

C Program

```c
#include <stdio.h>
int main()
 {
       int i,n, sum=0;
       printf("Enter number of terms : ");
       scanf("%d", &n);
       for(i=1;i<=n;i++)
       {
       printf("Number is : %d and cube of  %d is : %d
\n",i,i, (i*i*i));
       sum=sum+i*i*i;
       }
       printf("\n SUM = %d", sum);
       return 0;
 }
```

Output

```
Enter number of terms : 6
Number is : 1 and cube of  1 is : 1
Number is : 2 and cube of  2 is : 8
```

```
Number is : 3 and cube of  3 is : 27
Number is : 4 and cube of  4 is : 64
Number is : 5 and cube of  5 is : 125
Number is : 6 and cube of  6 is : 216
SUM = 441
```

11. Write a program that computes the sum of the digits of a given number.

Solution

Algorithm in Step Form

```
1. START
2. S  <-   0
3. PRINT "ENTER THE NUMBER"
4. INPUT  N
5. WHILE   N > 0
   BEGIN
   R   <-   N % 10
   S   <-   S + R
   N   <-   N / 10
   END
6. PRINT "SUM OF DIGITS : S"
7. STOP
```

Algorithm in Flowchart Form

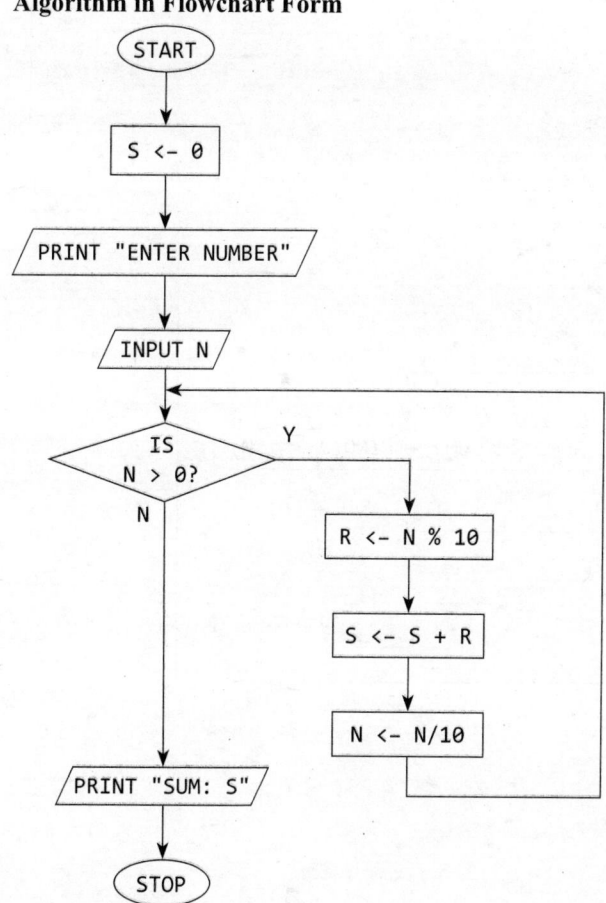

C Program

```c
#include <stdio.h>
int main()
{
    int n, s=0, r;
    printf("\n Enter the Number :");
    scanf("%d", &n);
      for( ; n > 0; n /= 10)
      {
         r = n % 10;
         s = s + r;
      }
    printf("\n Sum of digits %d", s);
    return 0;
}
```

Output

```
Enter the Number :498
Sum of digits 21
```

12. Write a program which uses Simpson's 1/3 rule to determine the integral of the polynomial function $f(x) = 0.2 + x^2$ from 0 to 2.

Solution

Algorithm in Step Form

```
 1. START
 2. SUM1   <-   0
 3. SUM2   <-   0
 4. PRINT "ENTER THE LOWER BOUND VALUE"
 5. INPUT  A
 6. PRINT "ENTER THE UPPER BOUND VALUE"
 7. INPUT  B
 8. PRINT "ENTER NUMBER OF SEGMENTS"
 9. INPUT  N
10. H  <-  ( B - A ) / N
11. I  <-  1
12. IF  N % 2 = 0  THEN
        WHILE  I  <=  ( N - 1 )
           BEGIN
           IF  I % 2  = 0  THEN
               SUM1 <-  SUM1 + FIND( A + I * H )
           ELSE
               SUM2 <-  SUM2 + FIND( A + I * H )
           I  <-   I + 1
           END
    ELSE
        PRINT "SINCE ODD SEGMENTS, SIMPSONS 1/3 RULE
        NOT APPLICABLE"
13. STOP

SUBROUTINE  FIND(X)
1. START
2. Y  <-  0.2 + X * X
3. RETURN Y
4. STOP
```

Algorithm in Flowchart Form

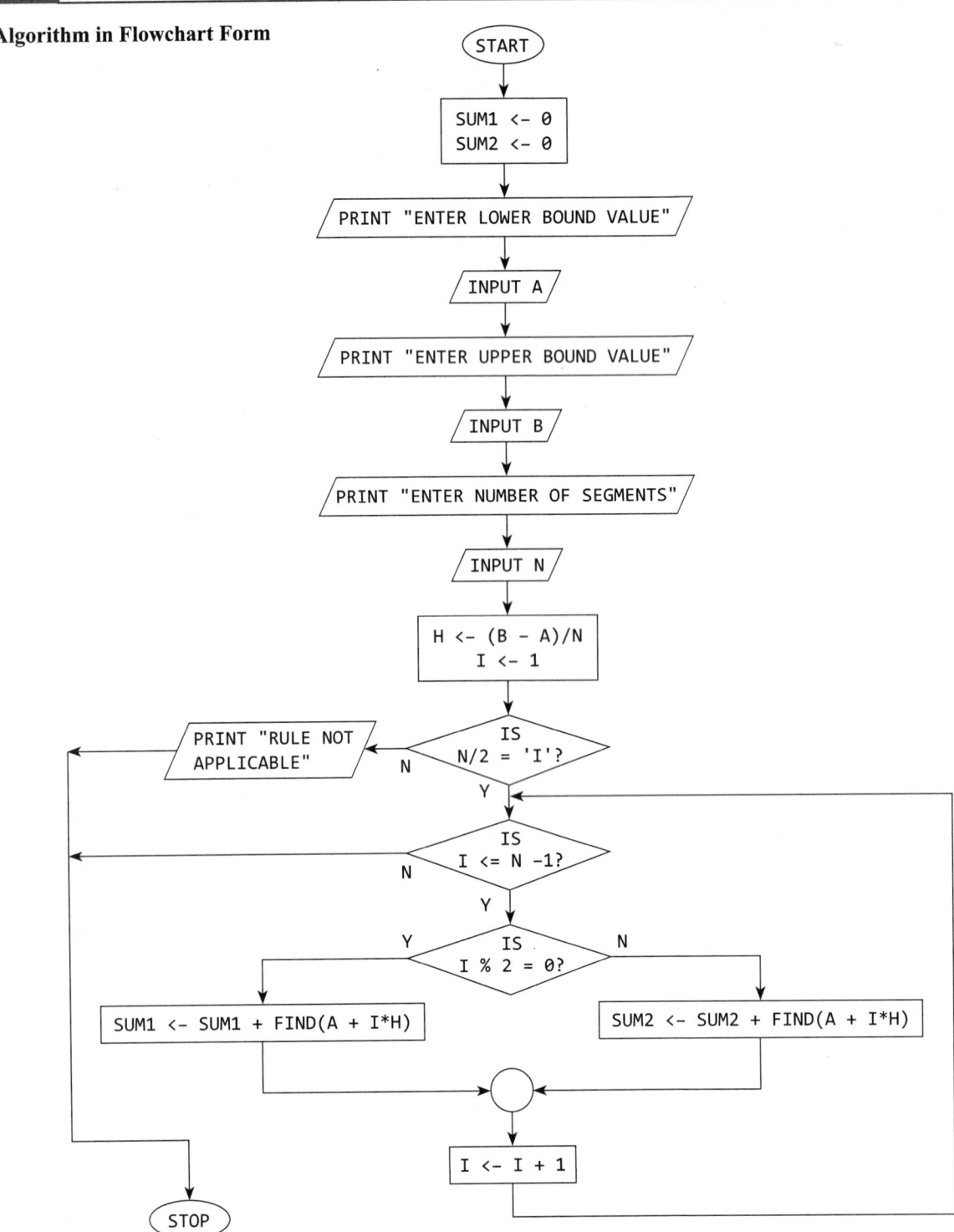

C Program

```c
#include<stdio.h>
#include<math.h>

float find(float x);
float find(float x)
{
   float y;
   y = 0.2 + x*x ;
   return y;
}


int main( )
{
 int n,  i;          /* n = number of segments */


/* a = lower bound,  b = upper bound */
float  sum1 = 0,  sum2 = 0,  total_sum,  a,  b,  h;

  printf("\nEnter the lower bound value = ");
  scanf("%f", &a);

  printf("\nEnter the upper bound value = ");
  scanf("%f", &b);

  printf("Enter the number of segments = ");
  scanf("%d",  &n);

  h = ( b - a ) / n;  /* width of each segment */
  if( n % 2 = = 0 )   /* Checking for even segment */
   {
     for( i = 1 ; i <= n-1 ; i++ )
      {
        if( i % 2 = = 0 )
         {
           sum1 =  sum1  +  find( a + i * h );
         }
        else
         {
           sum2 =  sum2  + find( a + i * h );
         }
      }

    total_sum = ( h / 3 ) * ( find(a)  +  find(b)  +
4 * sum2  + 2 * sum1 );
   printf( "The integration value is = %f", total_
sum);
   }
```

```c
else
{
  printf("Since number of segment is odd,Simpson's
  1/3 rule cannot be used");
   }
return 0;
}
```

Output

```
Enter the lower bound value = 0
Enter the upper bound value = 2
Enter the number of segments = 4
The integration value is = 3.066667
```

13. If the three sides of a triangle are entered through the keyboard, write a program to verify whether (i) the triangle is valid or not and (ii) if valid determine whether it is an "Equilateral" or an "Isosceles" or a "Scalene" triangle. Note that the triangle is valid if the sum of two sides is greater than the largest of the three sides.

Solution

Algorithm in Step Form

1. START
2. PRINT "ENTER THE LENGTHS OF THREE SIDES OF A TRIANGLE"
3. INPUT S1, S2, S3
4. ANS <- 'Y'
5. WHILE (ANS = 'Y') OR (ANS = 'y')
   BEGIN
   IF (S1 + S2) > S3 AND (S2 + S3) > S1 AND (S1 + S3) > S2   THEN
         PRINT " TRIANGLE CAN BE DRAWN"
         IF (S1 = S2 AND S2 = S3)   THEN
               PRINT " IT IS AN EQUILATERAL TRIANGLE"
         ELSE
         IF (S1 = S2) OR (S2 = S3) OR (S1 = S3) THEN
                  PRINT "IT IS AN ISOSCELES TRIANGLE"
         ELSE
                  PRINT "IT IS A SCALENE TRIANGLE"
   ELSE
         PRINT " TRIANGLE CANNOT BE DRAWN"
   PRINT "DO YOU WANT TO RE-ENTER THE LENGHTS AGAIN(Y/N)"
   INPUT ANS
   END
6. STOP

Algorithm in Flowchart Form

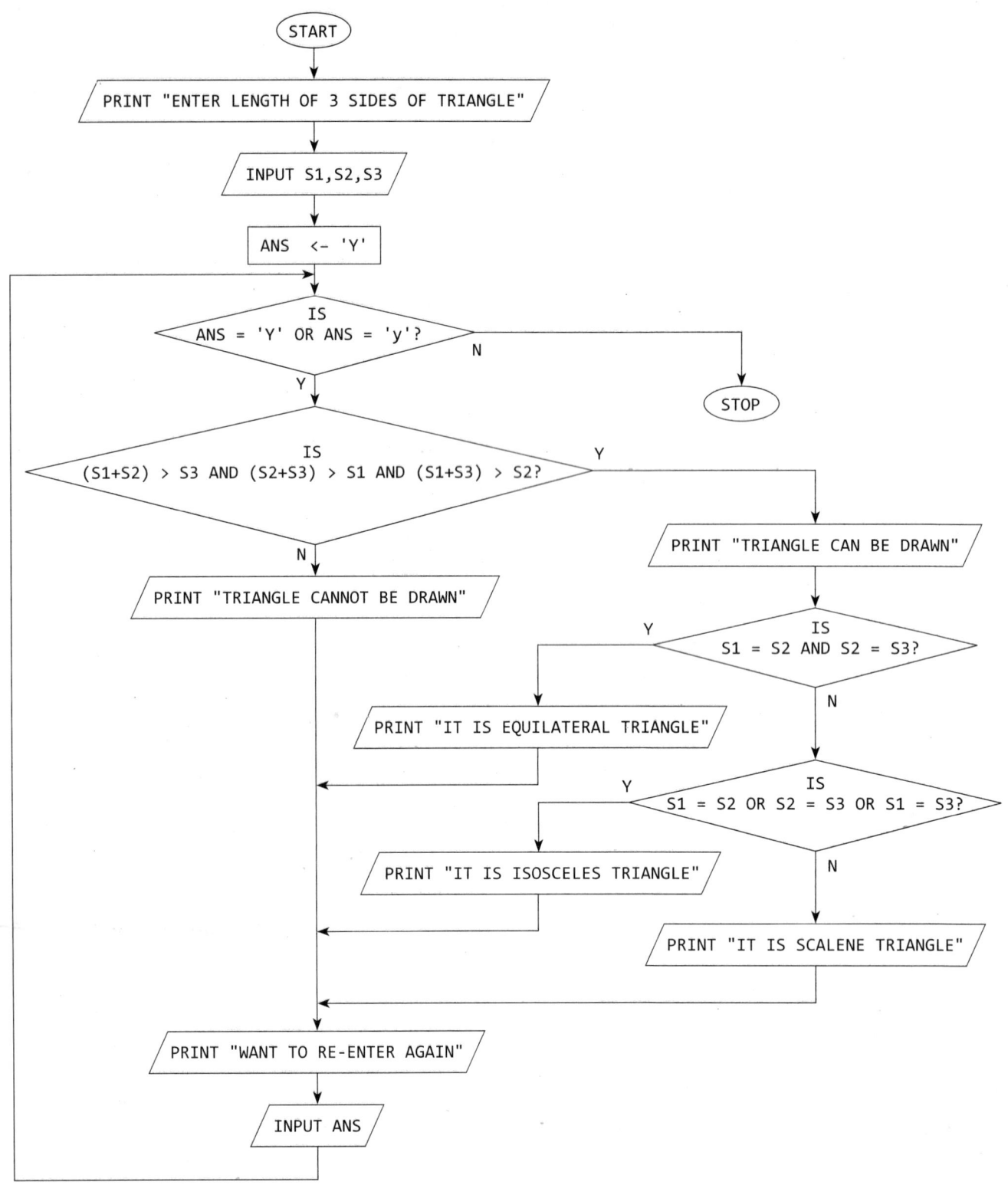

C Program

For program code, refer to Chapter 5, Page 185. The output obtained by running this program and inputting lengths of sides as 2, 3, and 4 is given below.

Output

```
Enter the lengths of three sides of a triangle:2
3
4
Triangle can be drawn
It is a scalene Triangle
```

14. Write a program that prints the sum of the following series up to n terms where n an x are given by the user :

$$x - x^3/3! + x^5/5! - \ldots \ldots$$

Solution

Algorithm in Step Form

```
 1. START
 2. PRINT "ENTER NUMBER OF TERMS (MUST BE GREATER
    THAN 0) "
 3. INPUT  N
 4. PRINT "ENTER A NUMBER"
 5. INPUT  X
 6. T   <-     X
 7. S   <-     0
 8. C   <-     1
 9. S   <-     S + T
10. D  <-  (2*C - 2)*(2*C - 1)
11. T   <-  T * ( - X * X) / D
12. C  <-   C + 1
13. IF  C  <=  N  THEN  GO TO STEP 9
14. PRINT  S
15. STOP
```

C Program

```c
#include <stdio.h>

int main()
{
    int i, n, d;
    double x, t, s;
    printf("\n HOW MANY TERMS(should be greater
    than 0)");
    scanf("%d",&n );
    printf( " \n ENTER THE VALUE OF x ") ;
    scanf("%lf",&x);
    s=t=x;
    for(c = 1 ; c <= n ; ++c)
    {
      d=(2*c-2)*(2*c-1);
      t = t * (-x * x) / (double)d ;
```

```c
      s += t;
    }
    printf( " \n sum is %lf " , s) ;
    return 0 ;
}
```

Algorithm in Flowchart Form

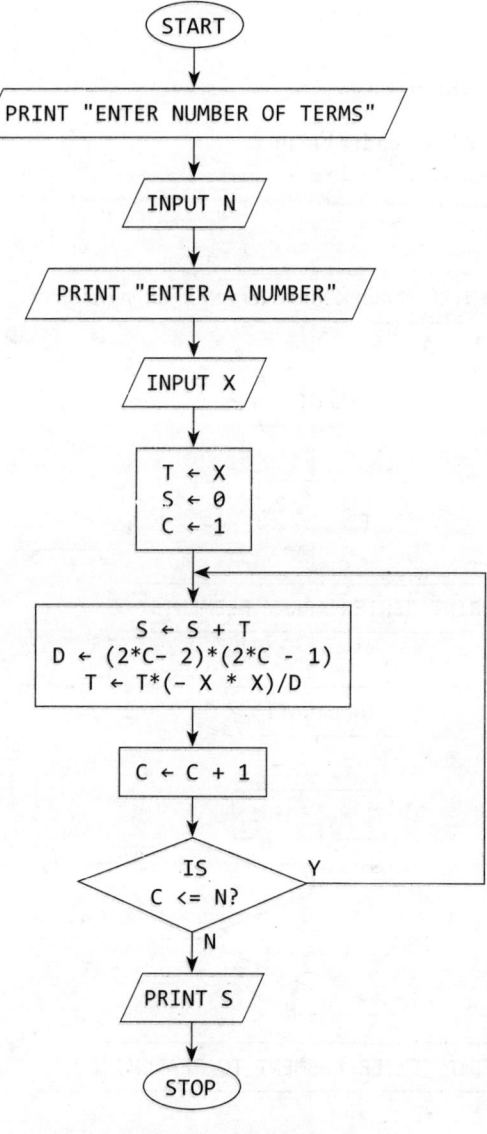

15. Write a program to sort the elements of an array in increasing order and find the position of the target element.

Solution

Algorithm in Step Form

```
1. START
2. PRINT "ENTER THE NO. OF ELEMENTS IN THE ARRAY"
3. INPUT N
```

4. I←0
5. PRINT "ENTER ARRAY ELEMENT"
6. INPUT LIST(I)
7. I←I+1
8. IF I<N THEN GOTO STEP 5
9. PRINT "ENTER THE ELEMENT TO SEARCH"
10. INPUT T
11. HIGH ← N - 1
12. LOW ← 0
13. FOUND ← 0
14. MID ← (HIGH + LOW)/ 2

15. IF T = LIST [MID]
       FOUND ← 1
    ELSE IF T < LIST[MID]
       HIGH ← MID-1
    ELSE
       LOW ← MID+1
16. IF (FOUND =0) and (HIGH > = LOW) THEN GOTO STEP 14
17. IF FOUND =0 THEN PRINT "NOT FOUND"
    ELSE PRINT "FOUND AT", MID.
18. STOP

Algorithm in Flowchart Form

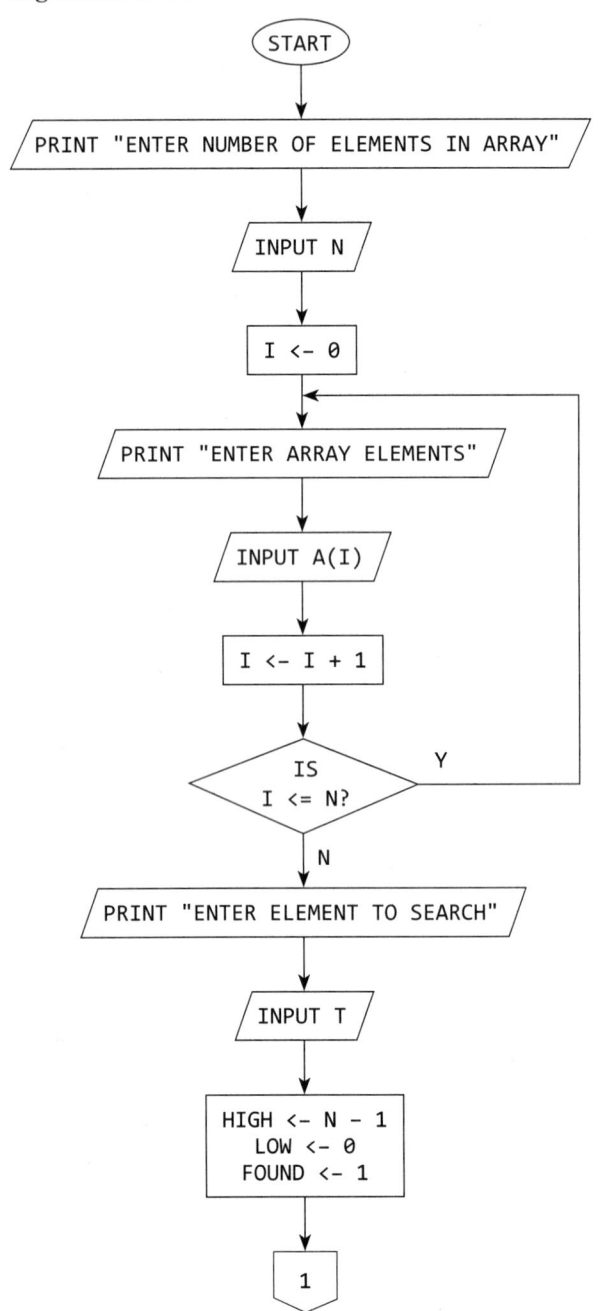

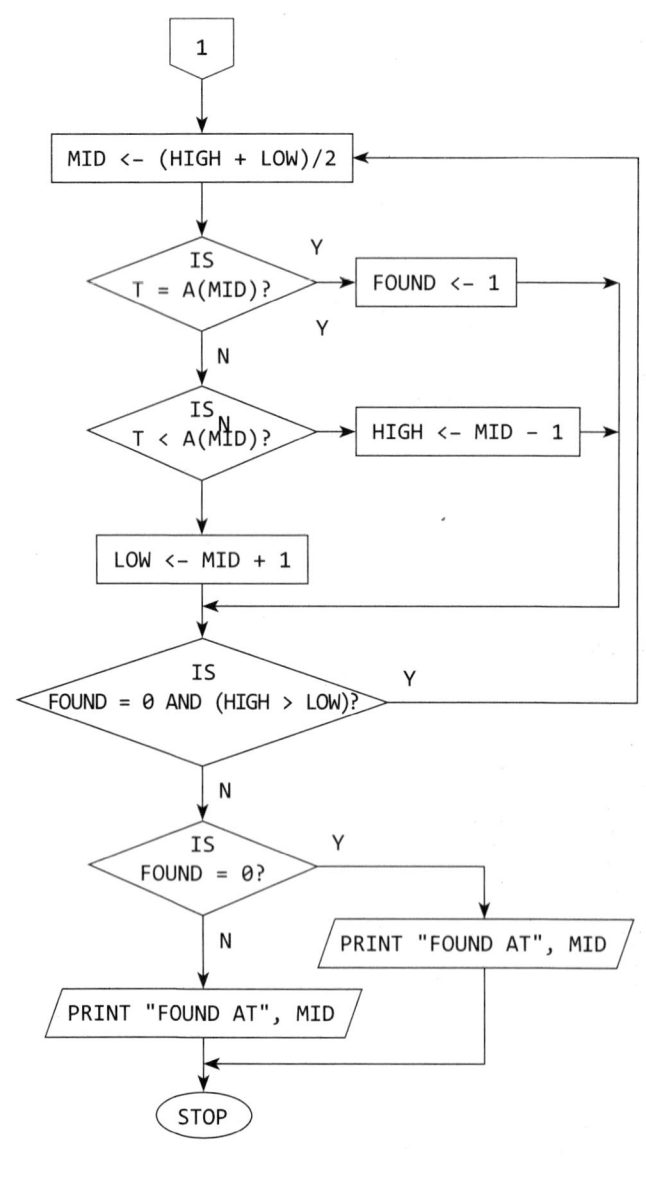

C Program

For program code, refer to Chapter 7, page 263, where outputs obtained after running this program are also given.

16. Write a program applying Bisection Method to find the root of $x^3 + 3x - 5 = 0$ between -1 and 2 within a tolerance of 0.01.

Solution

Comment: In the Step Form and Flowchart there may be some deviation from the conventional form but here it is unavoidable to include functions and macro in the algorithm.

Algorithm in Step Form

```
1. START
2. K  <-   0
3. C  <-   0
4. TOL  <-   0.01
5. PRINT "ENTER THE LOWER POINT VALUE"
6. INPUT A
7. PRINT "ENTER THE UPPER POINT VALUE"
8. INPUT B
9. PRINT "ENTER MAX NUMBER OF ITERATIONS"
10. INPUT N
11. C  <- ( A + B ) / 2
12. PRINT " TABLE HEADER K, A, B, C, FUNC(A), FUNC(B),
    FUNC(C)"
13. CALL DISPLAY SUB-ROUTINE FUNC_DISP(K, A, B, C)
14. IF  FUNC(C) = 0  THEN GO TO 13
15. WHILE  (( FUNC(C) >TOL) AND ( K < N ))
    BEGIN
       IF  FUNC(C) = SIGN FUNC(A)  THEN
               A  <-  C
       ELSE
               B  <-  C
    C  <-  (A + B)/2
    CALL DISP(K, A, B, C)
    K  <-   K + 1
    END
16. PRINT "ROOT FOUND AND NUMBER OF ITERATIONS REQUIRED"
17. PRINT " VALUE OF FUNC(C) "
18. STOP

SUBROUTINE  FUNC(X)
1. START
2. INPUT Y
3. Y   <-   X*X*X + 3*X - 5
4. RETURN Y
5. STOP
SUBROUTINE  FUNC_DISP(X)
1. START
2. PRINT "VALUE OF K, A, B, C"
3. PRINT "VALUE OF FUNC(A), FUNC(B), FUNC(C)"
4. RETURN 0
5. STOP
```

```
MACRO
SIGN(X) (X > 0) ?  1 : ( ( X < 0 ) ? - 1 : 0)
```

C Program

```c
#include<stdio.h>
#include<math.h>

/* Program applying Bisection Method for finding the
root of a non-linear equation */

/* sign function definition as a macro */
#define sign(x) (x > 0) ? 1 : ((x < 0) ? -1 : 0)
/* functions prototype */
float func(float x);
int func_disp (int k, float a, float b, float c);

int main(void)
{
    float a;            /* lower point */
    float b;            /* upper point */
    float tol = 1E-2;   /* tolerance value */
    float N;            /* maximum number of
                           iterations */
    float c = 0;        /* estimated root */
    int k = 0;          /* index */
    float diff;         /* average of difference
                           between a and b */

    /* Enter lower point, upper point and number of
    iterations */
    printf("\n Enter lower point value :");
    scanf("%f", &a);
    printf("\n Enter upper point value :");
    scanf("%f", &b);
    printf("\n Enter maximum number of iterations :");
    scanf("%f", &N);

    c = (a + b)/2;          /* midpoint */
    diff = (a - b)/2;

    /* Display the table header and initial data */
    printf("k\ta\t\tb\t\tc\t\tfunc(a)\t\tfunc(b)\t\tfunc(c)\n");
    func_disp(k, a, b, c);

    /* Evaluate the root by looping until the result is
    less than the tolerance and till the maximum number
    of iterations is not reached*/

    if (func(c) == 0)
    {
        /* If the first midpoint gives func(c) = 0, c is
the root */
```

```
    printf("Root is: %f \n", c);}
else
{
    while ((fabs( diff ) > tol ) && (k<N))
    {
        if (sign(func(c)) == sign(func(a)))
/* func(c) has same sign as func(a) */
        {
            a = c;
        }
        else   /* func(c) has same sign as func(b) */
        {
            b = c;
        }
        c = (a+b)/2;   /* midpoint updated */
        diff = (a - b)/2;
        func_disp(k+1, a, b, c); /* display current
                                        data */
        k++; /* incrementing index */
    }
}
/* Displaying the results */
```

```
    printf("\nRoot of the given equation is c=%.7f and
found after %d iterations\n", c, k);
    printf("The value of the function func(c) is:
%.10f\n", func(c));

return 0;
}
/* func function definition */
float func (float x)
{
 float y;
 y = x*x*x +3*x -5;              /* Given equation */
 return y;
}
/* display function definition */
int func_disp (int k, float a, float b, float c)
{
 printf("%d\t%.7f\t%.7f\t%.7f\t", k, a, b, c);
 printf("%.7f\t%.7f\t%.7f\n", func(a), func(b),
func(c));
 return 0;
}
```

Output

```
Enter lower point value :-1
Enter upper point value :2
Enter maximum number of iterations :10
```

k	a	b	c	func(a)	func(b)	func(c)
0	-1.0000000	2.0000000	0.5000000	-9.0000000	9.0000000	-3.3750000
1	0.5000000	2.0000000	1.2500000	-3.3750000	9.0000000	0.7031250
2	1.2500000	2.0000000	1.6250000	0.7031250	9.0000000	4.1660156
3	1.6250000	2.0000000	1.8125000	4.1660156	9.0000000	6.3918457
4	1.8125000	2.0000000	1.9062500	6.3918457	9.0000000	7.6456604
5	1.9062500	2.0000000	1.9531250	7.6456604	9.0000000	8.3099556
6	1.9531250	2.0000000	1.9765625	8.3099556	9.0000000	8.6517200
7	1.9765625	2.0000000	1.9882813	8.6517200	9.0000000	8.8250408
8	1.9882813	2.0000000	1.9941406	8.8250408	9.0000000	8.9123154

```
Root of the given equation is c=1.9941406 and found after 8 iterations
The value of the function func(c) is: 8.9123153687
```

Algorithm in Flowchart Form

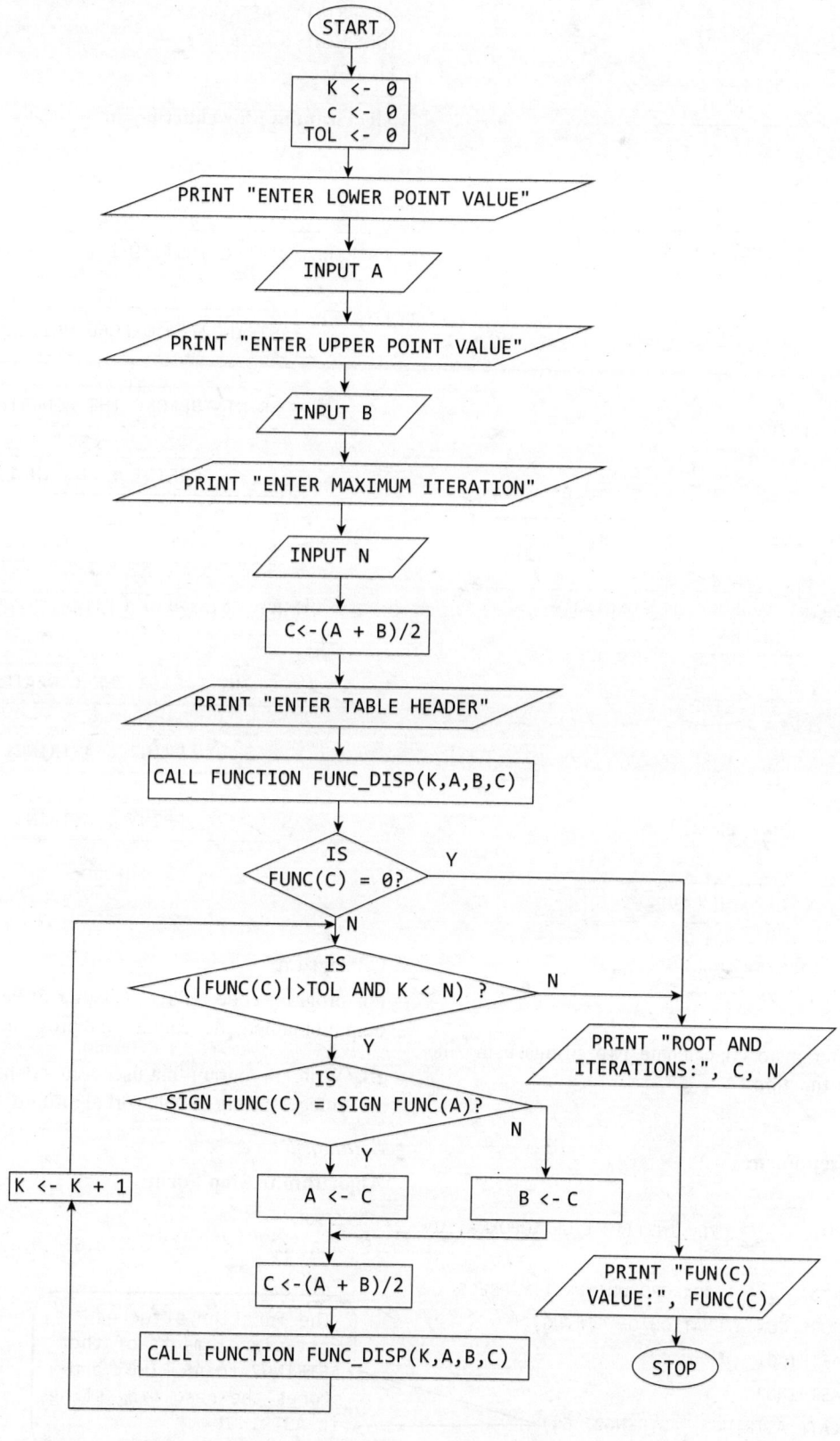

SUROUTINE FUNC(X)

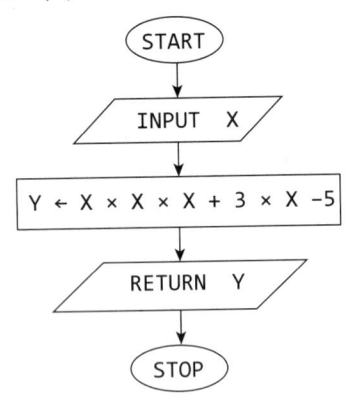

SUROUTINE FUNC_DISP(X)

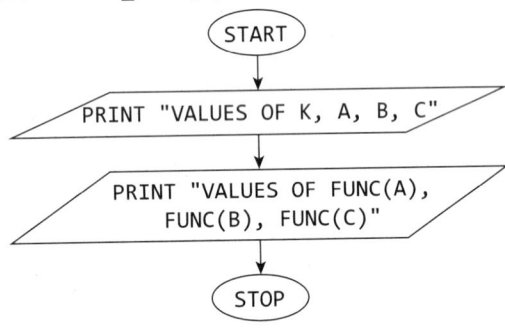

MACRO SIGN(X)

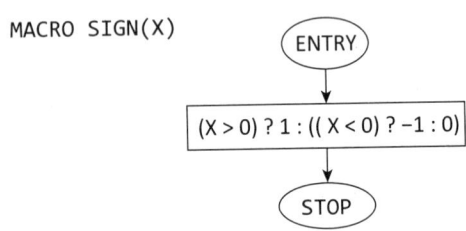

17. Write a program to concatenate two strings using the strncat( ) function.

Solution

Algorithm in Step Form

1. START
2. ASTRING1(80)   <-   "RCC INSTITUTE OF INFORMATION TECHNOLOGY"
3. ASTRING2(80)   <-   "OXFORD UNIVERSITY PRESS"
4. PRINT "BEFORE CONCATENATION OF STRINGS"
5. PRINT : ASTRING1
6. PRINT : ASTRING2
7. CALL STRNCAT(ASTRING1, ASTRING2, 6)

> The function attaches first six elements of the ASTRING2 to ASTRING1 and stores the resulting sting in ASTRING1

8. PRINT "AFTER CONCATENATION OF STRINGS"
9. PRINT : ASTRING1
10. PRINT : ASTRING2
11. STOP

Algorithm in Flowchart Form

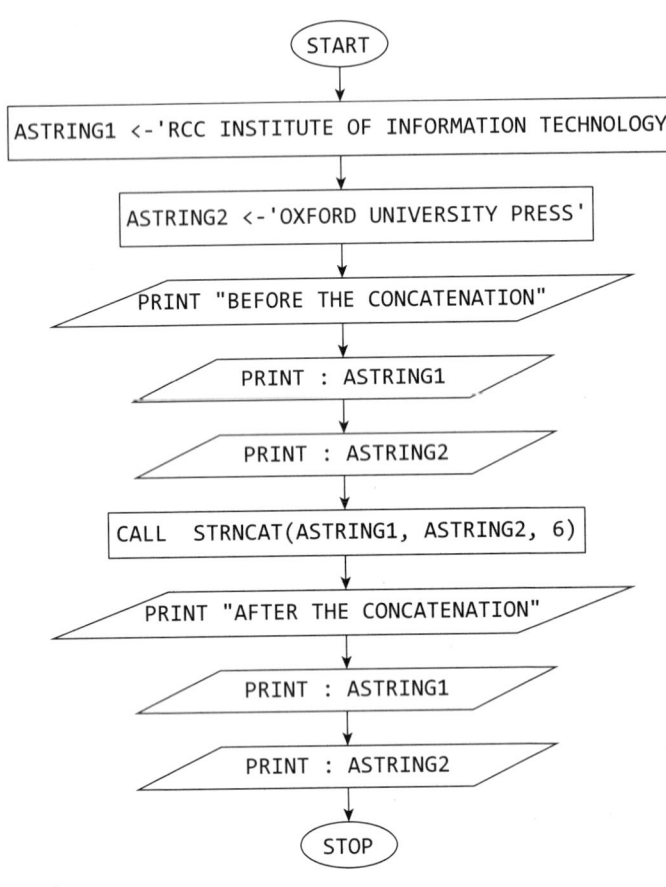

C Program

For program code refer to Chapter 6, Page 210, where the output obtained after running the program is also given.

18. Write a program that uses a function to sort an array of integers using bubble sort algorithm.

Solution

Algorithm in Step Form

1. START
2. ARR(10)   <-   (3,2,7,0,6,4,9,8,1,5)

```
3. PRINT "THE ARRAY BEFORE SORTING"
4. I <- 0
5. WHILE ( I < 10 )
    BEGIN
      PRINT : I, ARR(I)
      I <-  I +1
    END
6. CALL SORT(ARR, 10)
7. PRINT "THE ARRAY AFTER SORTING"
8. I <- 0
9. WHILE ( I < 10 )
    BEGIN
      PRINT : I, ARR(I)
      I <-  I + 1
    END
10. STOP

SUBROUTINE  SORT( A( ), N)
1. START
2. A( )  <-   ARR
```

```
3. N    <-   10
4. I  <-  0
5. WHILE ( I < N-1 )
    BEGIN
      J <- 0
      WHILE ( J < N - I - 1 )
        BEGIN
          IF ( A(J) > A(J + 1) )  THEN
            TEMP <-  A( J )
            A( J ) <-  A(J + 1)
            A(J + 1) <-  TEMP
      J <-  J + 1
      END
    I <-  I + 1
    END
6. STOP

SUBROUTINE SORT( A( ), n)
```

Algorithm in Flowchart Form

MAIN PROGRAM

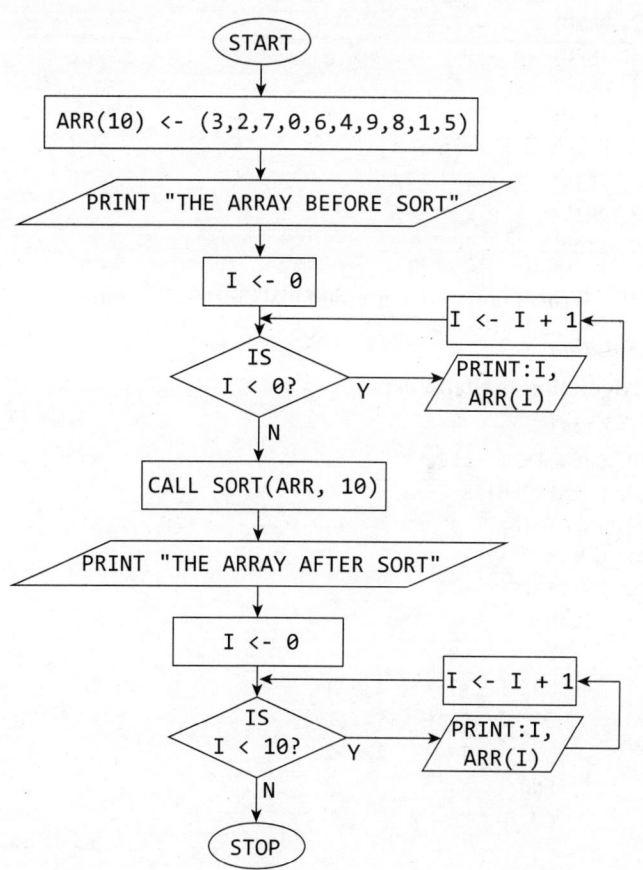

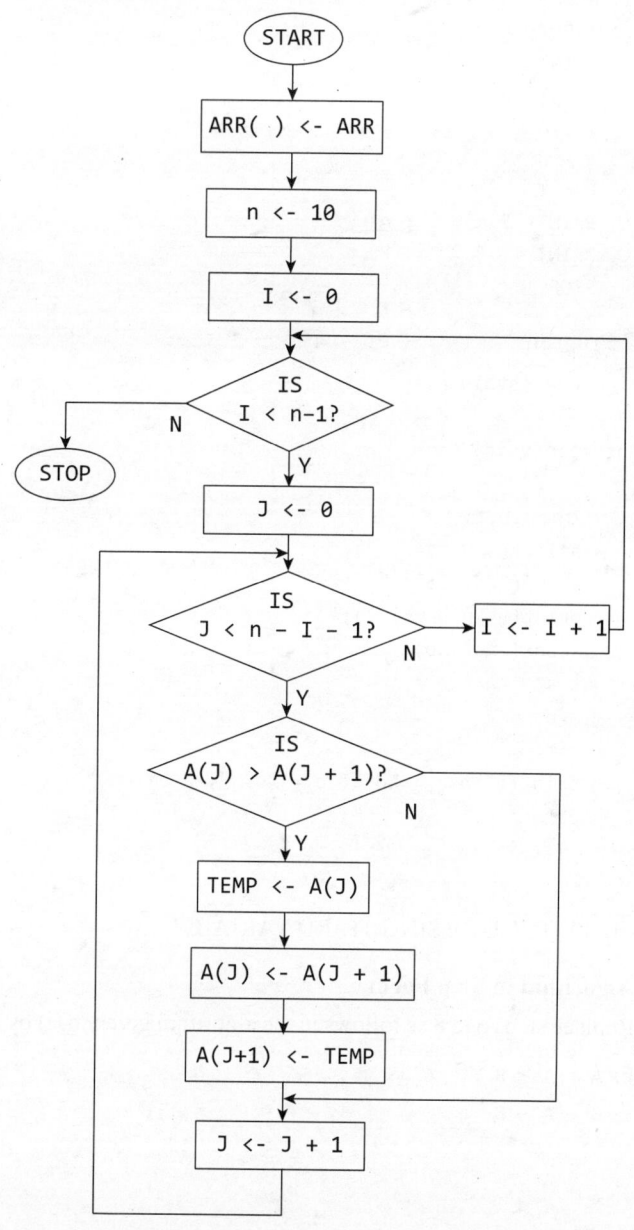

C Program

For program code, refer to example in Chapter 7, where the output obtained after running the program is also given.

19. (a) Write a program that swaps two integer variables (i) using a third variable and (ii) without using a third variable

   (b) Write the algorithm in step form for swapping two integer variables that uses a single statement without using methods used in (i) and (ii).

Solution

(a)

(i) USING THIRD VARIABLE

Algorithm in Step Form

```
1.  START
2.  PRINT " A = ? "
3.  INPUT  A
4.  PRINT "B = ?"
5.  INPUT  B
6.  T ← A
7.  A ← B
8.  B ← T
9.  PRINT   " A = " , A
10. PRINT   " B = " , B
11. STOP
```

C Program

```c
#include <stdio.h>

int main(void)
{
    int a,b,t;
    printf("\n a = ? ");
    scanf("%d",&a);
    printf("\n b = ? ");
    scanf("%d",&b);
    t=a;
    a=b;
    b=t;
    printf("\n a = %d \t b = %d? ", a,b);
    return 0;

}
```

(ii)   WITHOUT USING THIRD VARIABLE

Algorithm in Step Form

Replace steps 6 to 8 as follows in the algorithm given in (i) by

```
6. A ← A + B
7. B ← A - B
```

```
8. A ← A - B
```

C Program

```c
#include <stdio.h>

int main(void)
{
    int a,b;
    printf("\n a = ? ");
    scanf("%d",&a);
    printf("\n b = ? ");
    scanf("%d",&b);
    a=a+b;
    b=a-b;
    a=a-b;
    printf("\n a = %d \t b = %d? ", a,b);
    return 0;

}
```

(b)   USING   SINGLE   STATEMENT   WITHOUT   USING THIRD VARIABLE

Algorithm in Step Form

```
1. START
2. PRINT " A = ?"
3. INPUT  A
4. PRINT "B = ?"
5. INPUT  B
6. A ← A + B - (B ← A)
7. PRINT   " A = " , A
8. PRINT   " B = " , B
9. STOP
```

20. Write a program a program that creates a text file.

Solution

Algorithm in Step Form

```
1. START
2. OPEN TEXT FILE
3. PRINT "ENTER TEXT"
4. INPUT TEXT( )
5. C   <-   1
6. WHILE (C <= 10 )
   BEGIN
      I  <-   0
      WHILE ( TEXT( I ) )
          WRITE  TEXT(I)
          I  <-  I + 1
   END
   C   <-   C + 1
```

```
    END
7. CLOSE FILE
8. STOP
```

C Program

For program code, refer Chapter 10, Page 413.

21. Write a program which copies the data from one file to another file.

Solution

Algorithm in Step Form

```
1. START
2. PRINT "ENTER SOURCE"
3. INPUT FNAME1( )
4. FLUSH STDIN STREAM
5. PRINT "ENTER DESTINATION FILE"
6. FLUSH STDIN STREAM
7. INPUT FNAME2( )
8. FPTR1    <-   OPEN SOURCE FILE FNAME1 IN READ MODE
9. FPTR2    <-   OPEN DESTINATION FILE FNAME2 IN WRITE
   MODE
```

```
10. IF ( FPTR1 = NULL)  THEN
       PRINT "CANNOT OPEN FILE FOR READING" : FNAME1
       GO TO STOP
    ELSE
    IF  ( FPTR2 = NULL)  THEN
       PRINT "CANNOT OPEN FILE FOR READING" : FNAME1
       GO TO STOP
     ELSE
        CH   <-   FPTR1
        WHILE ( CH != END OF FILE )
          BEGIN
             WRITE  CH TO DESTINATION FILE FNAME2
             READ CH FROM SOURCE FILE FNAME1
          END
11. CLOSE FILE FNAME1
12. CLOSE FILE FNAME2
13. STOP
```

C Program

Refer to program code given in Chapter 10, Example 7.

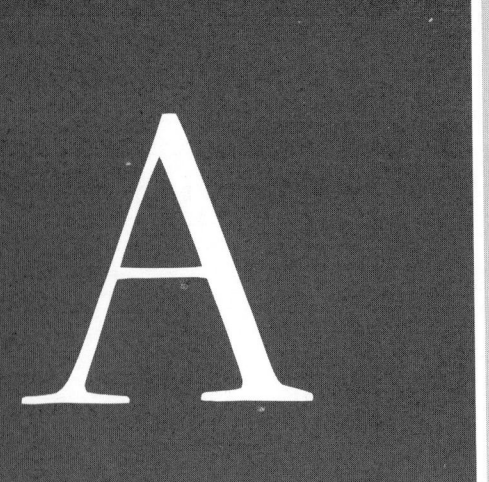

A

Appendix B

Library Functions

Function	Return Type	Description	Header File
abs(i)	int	Return the absolute value of i	stdlib.h
acos(d)	double	Return the arc cosine of d	math.h
asin(d)	double	Return the arc sine of d	math.h
atan(d)	double	Return the arc tangent of d	math.h
atan2 (d1,d2)	double	Return the arc tangent of d1/d2	math.h
atof(s)	double	Convert string s to a double-precision quantity	stdlib.h
atoi(s)	int	Convert string s to an integer	stdlib.h
atol(s)	long	Convert string s to a long integer	stdlib.h
calloc (u1,u2)	void*	Allocate memory for an array having u1 elements, each of length u2 bytes. Return a pointer to the beginning of the allocated space	malloc.h or stdlib.h
ceil(d)	double	Return a value rounded up to the next higher integer	math.h
cos(d)	double	Return the cosine of d	math.h
cosh(d)	double	Return the hyperbolic cosine of d	math.h
exit(u)	void	Close all files and buffers, and terminate the program, (Value of u is assigned by function, to indicate termination status)	stdlib.h
exp(d)	double	Raise e to the power d (e=2.7182818 … is the base of the natural (Naperian) system of logarithms	math.h
fabs(d)	double	Return the absolute value of d	math.h

Function	Return Type	Description	Header File
fclose(f)	int	Close file f. Return 0 if file is successfully closed	stdio.h
feof(f)	int	Determine if an end-of-file condition has been reached. If so, return a non-zero value; otherwise, return 0	stdio.h
fgetc(f)	int	Enter a single character form file f	stdio.h
fgets (s,i,f)	char*	Enter string s, containing i characters, from file f	stdio.h
floor(d)	double	Return a value rounded down to the next lower integer	math.h
fmod (d1,d2)	double	Return the remainder of d1/d2 (with same sign as d1)	math.h
fopen (s1,s2)	file*	Open a file named s1 of type s2. Return a pointer to the file	stdio.h
fprintf (f, ..)	int	Send data items to file f (remaining arguments are complicated—see Chapter 15)	stdio.h
fputc(c,f)	int	Send a single character to file f	stdio.h
fputs(s,f)	int	Send string s to file f	stdio.h
fread (s,i1,i2,f)	int	Enter i2 data items, each of size i1 bytes, from file f to string s	stdio.h
free(p)	void	Free a block of allocated memory whose beginning is indicated by p	malloc.h or stdio.h
fscanf (f, ..)	int	Enter data items from file f (remaining arguments are complicated—see Chapter 15)	stdio.h

contd

contd

Function	Return Type	Description	Header File
fseek (f,l,i)	int	Move the pointer for file f to a distance of 1 byte from location i (i may represent the beginning of the file, the current pointer position, or the end of the file)	stdlib.h
ftell(f)	long int	Return the current pointer position within file f.	stdio.h
fwrite (s,i1,i2,f)	int	Send i2 data items, each of size i1 bytes from string s to file f.	stdio.h
getc(f)	int	Enter a single character from file f.	stdio.h
getchar()	int	Enter a single character from the standard input device.	stdio.h
gets(s)	char*	Takes a string as input from the standard input device.	stdio.h
isalnum(c)	int	Determine if argument is alphanumeric. Return a non-zero value if true; 0 otherwise.	ctype.h
isalpha(c)	int	Determine if argument is alphabetic. Return a non-zero value if true; 0 otherwise.	ctype.h
isascii(c)	int	Determine if argument is ASCII character. Return a non-zero value if true; 0 otherwise.	ctype.h
iscntrl(c)	int	Determine if argument is ASCII control character. Return a non-zero value if true; 0 otherwise.	ctype.h
isdigit(c)	int	Determine if argument is decimal digit. Return	ctype.h
isgraph(c)	int	Determine if argument is graphic ASCII a non-zero value if true; 0 otherwise. character (hex 0x21-0x7e; octal 041-176). Return a non-zero value if true; 0 otherwise	ctype.h
islower(c)	int	Determine if argument is lowercase. Return a non-zero value if true; 0 otherwise	ctype.h
isodigit(c)	int	Determine if argument is an octal digit. Return a non-zero value if true; 0 otherwise	ctype.h
isprint(c)	int	Determine if argument is a printing ASCII character (hex 0x20-0x7e; octal 040-176). Return a non-zero value if true; 0 otherwise	ctype.h
ispunct(c)	int	Determine if argument is a punctuation character. Return a non-zero value if true; 0 otherwise	ctype.h

Function	Return Type	Description	Header File
isspace(c)	int	Determine if argument is a white space character. Return a non-zero value if true; 0 otherwise	ctype.h
isupper(c)	int	Determine if argument is uppercase. Return a non-zero value if true; 0 otherwise	ctype.h
isxdigit(c)	int	Determine if argument is a hexadecimal digit. Return a non-zero value if true; 0 otherwise	ctype.h
labs(l)	long int	Return the absolute value of l.	math.h
log(d)	double	Return the natural logarithm of d.	math.h
log10(d)	double	Return the logarithm (base 10) of d.	math.h
malloc(u)	void*	Allocate u bytes of memory. Return a pointer to the beginning of the allocated space.	malloc.h or stdlib.h
pow(d1,d2)	double	Return d1 raised to the d2 power	math.h
printf(...)	int	Send data items to the standard output device (arguments are complicated—see Appendix G)	stdio.h
putc(c,f)	int	Send a single character to file f	stdio.h
putchar(c)	int	Send a single character to the standard output device	stdio.h
puts(s)	int	Send string s to the standard output device	stdio.h
rand()	int	Return a random positive integer.	stdlib.h
rowind(f)	void	Move the pointer to the beginning of the file f.	stdio.h
scanf(...)	int	Enter data items from the standard input device (arguments are complicated—see Appendix G)	stdio.h
sin(d)	double	Return the sine of d.	math.h
sinh(d)	double	Return the hyperbolic sine of d.	math.h
sqrt(d)	double	Return the square root of d.	math.h
srand(u)	void	Initialize the random number generator.	stdlib.h
strcmp (s1,s2)	int	Compare two strings lexicographically. Return a negative value if s1 < s2; 0 if s1 and s2 are identical; and a positive value if s1 > s2	string.h

contd

contd

Function	Return Type	Description	Header File
strcmpi (s1,s2)	int	Compare two strings lexico-graphically, without regard to case. Return a negative value if s1 < s2; 0 if s1 and s2 are identical; and a positive value if s1 > s2	string.h
strcpy (s1,s2)	char*	Copy string s2 to string s1	string.h
strlen(s)	int	Return the number of characters in a string	string.h
strset (s,c)	char*	Set all characters within s to c (excluding the terminating null character \0).	string.h
system(s)	int	Pass command s to the operating system. Return 0 if the command is successfully executed, otherwise, return a non-zero value, typically –1.	stdlib.h
tan(d)	double	Return the tangent of d.	math.h
tanh(d)	double	Return the hyperbolic tangent of d.	math.h

Function	Return Type	Description	Header File
time(p)	long int	Return the number of seconds elapsed beyond a designated base time.	time.h
toascii(c)	int	Convert value of argument to ASCII.	ctype.h
tolower(c)	int	Convert letter to lowercase.	ctype.h or stdlib.h
toupper(c)	int	Convert letter to uppercase.	ctype.h or stdlib.h

Note Type refers to the data type of the quantity that is returned by the function. An asterisk (*) denotes a pointer.

c denotes a character-type argument.

d denotes a double-precision argument.

f denotes a file argument.

i denotes an integer argument.

l denotes a long integer argument.

p denotes a pointer argument.

s denotes a string argument.

u denotes an unsigned integer argument.